Leo Strauss'
Published but Uncollected English Writings
1937–1972

Edited by
Steven J. Lenzner
and
Svetozar Y. Minkov

ST. AUGUSTINE'S PRESS
South Bend, Indiana
2024

St. Augustine's Press, South Bend, Indiana 46680
Copyright © 2024 Jenny Strauss Clay
Copyright © 2024 Editors' Introduction by Steven J. Lenzner and Svetozar Y. Minkov
All rights reserved. No part of this book may be reproduced, stored in a retrieval system, or transmitted, in any form or by any means, electronic, mechanical, photocopying, recording, or otherwise, without the prior permission of St. Augustine's Press. For more information, contact:
St. Augustine's Press, P. O. Box 2285, South Bend, Indiana 46680.
Published in 2024
Manufactured in the United States of America

1 2 3 4 5 6   29 28 27 26 25 24

Library of Congress Cataloging-in-Publication Data
    Strauss, Leo, 1899–1973.
    Leo Strauss' published but uncollected English writings, 1937–1972 /
        Leo Strauss, Steven J. Lenzner and Svetozar Y. Minkov.
    Includes index.
    ISBN 978-158731-461-2 (paperback)
    ISBN 978-158731-462-9 (epub)
    Additional Cataloging-in-Publication Data is available from the
    Library of Congress.

    Library of Congress Control Number: 2024932652

∞ The paper used in this publication meets the minimum requirements of the American National Standard for Information Sciences Permanence of Paper for Printed Materials, ANSI Z39.48–1984.

The typeface used in this book is Monotype Ehrhardt.
Cover image: Leo Strauss (New York, 1939), modified; courtesy of Wikimedia Commons, https://creativecommons.org/licenses/by-sa/4.0/
Cover design by Winifred Gundeck
Book design by Susan P. Johnson

Published by
St. Augustine's Press
www.staugustine.net

Professor Leo Strauss Speaking with Unidentified Man
(Leo Strauss Collection AR 2205. Not dated. Print.)
Courtesy of the Leo Baeck Institute, New York City

Contents

	Editors' Introduction	xi
1	On Abravanel's Philosophical Tendency and Political Teaching (1937)	1
2	Review of Moses Hyamson's Edition of Maimonides (1939)	33
3	The Spirit of Sparta or the Taste of Xenophon (1939)	41
4	Review of James T. Shotwell, *The History of History* (1941)	73
5	Fārābī's *Plato* (1945)	75
6	Review of John O. Riedl's Edition of Giles of Rome, *Errores Philosophorum* (1946)	107
7	On a New Interpretation of Plato's Political Philosophy (1946)	109
8	On the Intention of Rousseau (1947)	145
9	On Husik's Work in Medieval Jewish Philosophy (1951/1952)	175
10	On Collingwood's Philosophy of History (1952)	187
11	On Walker's Machiavelli (1953)	211
12	The Mutual Influence of Theology and Philosophy (1954)	221
13	What Is Political Philosophy? (1955)	223

14	Social Science and Humanism (1956)	229
15	Letter to the *National Review* (1957)	241
16	Comment on W. S. Hudson, "The Weber Thesis Reexamined" (1961)	245
17	"Relativism" (1961)	249
18	Replies to Schaar and Wolin: II (1963)	269
19	Preface to *History of Political Philosophy* (1963)	275
20	Introduction to *History of Political Philosophy* (1963)	279
21	Plato, 427–347 B.C. (1963)	285
22	Preface to *The Guide of the Perplexed* (1963)	347
23	On the Plan of *The Guide of the Perplexed* (1965)	349
24	Review of Samuel I. Mintz, *The Hunting of Leviathan* (1965)	365
25	John Locke as "Authoritarian" (1967)	371
26	Liberal Education and Mass Democracy (1967)	375
27	A Note on Lucretius (1967)	397
28	Greek Historians (1968)	409
29	Philosophy as a Rigorous Science and Political Philosophy (1969)	419
30	Machiavelli and Classical Literature (1970)	421
31	A Giving of Accounts: Jacob Klein and Leo Strauss (1970)	437
32	Political Philosophy and the Crisis of Our Time (1972)	447
	Afterword by David Yanowski	477
	Acknowledgments	485
	Index	487
	About the Editors	491

Editors' Introduction

Rationale for the Volume

This book gathers in one volume everything Leo Strauss published in English that he did not include in any of his own books. We present these pieces in chronological order, rather than by topic, by venue, or in some other way. The chronological order thus connects the arrangement of essays to the author himself rather than to the editors' own interpretative categories.

Striving for completeness, we include: (a) essays published elsewhere in abridged form, such as "Relativism" and "Social Science and Humanism" (previously collected in *The Rebirth of Classical Political Rationalism*, edited by Thomas Pangle); (b) articles on Lucretius, Maimonides, and Plato that were published as wholes but were incorporated into more comprehensive essays;[1] and (c) Strauss-authorized amalgams of two pairs of essays: "The Crisis of Political Philosophy" and "The Crisis of Our Time"; and "What is Liberal Education?" and "Liberal Education and Responsibility."[2]

Leo Strauss's published but uncollected English writings constitute a remarkable body of work, both in philosophic and historical terms. The essays are comprehensive interpretations of either an author or an issue; the shorter reviews contain invaluable suggestions and observations. While the current collection would at any time be a contribution to political philosophy, we believe this is a particularly propitious time for its appearance. The welcome outpouring of interest in Strauss in recent years receives support through this publication from some of Strauss's most serious and artfully crafted pieces. Moreover, this volume helps counter some of the unhealthy byproducts of this long overdue recognition of Strauss's rank by drawing attention again to the primacy of Strauss's published writings. For though we have reason to be grateful for the publication in recent years of many of Strauss's unpublished lectures and essays and his correspondence with some of his leading contemporaries, these materials have tended to overshadow the serious study of those works upon which he sought to establish his reputation and legacy.

To be sure, Strauss's own books deserve pride of place for readers intent on establishing Strauss's considered views; yet, his other published writings deserve the attention of scholars and general readers, and they certainly stand much closer in rank to those books than do any materials he chose not to publish. Making generally available those published writings is simply giving the Strauss record its due. Moreover, given the fact that Strauss's later writings—i.e., those writings that postdate his complete rediscovery of exoteric writing in 1938—correspond almost exactly with his writings in English, this volume enables readers to have at their disposal all of Strauss's mature publications.[3]

One may very well ask why Strauss did not collect them himself. The simplest reason is that these pieces did not fit into the plans of his other books. Their inclusion would have transformed an ordered whole into a mere collection. In some cases, one can also speculate about other reasons. Strauss may have regarded "The Spirit of Sparta or the Taste of Xenophon" as too explicit in certain respects. The late Muhsin Mahdi more than once spoke of Strauss having said something to that effect about "Fārābī's *Plato*,"[4] which Strauss did include in the plan for a prospective book, "Philosophy and the Law," and made "free use of" for the introduction to *Persecution and the Art of Writing*.[5] However, Strauss did permit the essay to be republished late in his life,[6] even though the Rousseau subchapter in *Natural Right and History* (1953) makes use of the article.[7] And Strauss intended to omit "On Collingwood's Philosophy" from a planned volume on political philosophy and history because he considered it insufficiently generous to Collingwood."[8]

Highlights from the Major Essays Included in the Volume

Among the highlights of these works published between 1937 and 1972 are striking formulations not to be found in his books on the relationship between philosophy and society—perhaps the most prominent theme in Strauss's corpus taken as a whole; rare "personal" statements that shed light on his self-understanding as a philosopher; his first writing devoted solely

EDITORS' INTRODUCTION

to a classical thinker, "The Spirit of Sparta or the Taste of Xenophon"; his first writing devoted to Plato, "On a New Interpretation of Plato's Political Philosophy"; a searching engagement with Jean-Jacques Rousseau; his first writing treating the thought of Niccolò Machiavelli; a late treatment of Machiavelli's relation to classical writers; and a critical review of a book on Xenophon's *Hellenica* that brings to light the character of that work. These and the other pieces are a treasure trove for anyone interested in Strauss, political philosophy, or the history of political philosophy.

"On Abravanel's Philosophical Tendency and Political Teaching" (1937) is Strauss's first piece in English.[9] Strauss thought it "advisable to define the character of Abravanel's philosophical tendency by contrasting it with that of Maimonides."[10] Even though Abravanel "has to be characterized, to begin with, as a strict, even passionate adherent of the literal interpretation of the *Guide of the Perplexed*," his "unphilosophic, to some extent even anti–philosophic, traditionalism" accounts for the fact that political philosophy did not have for him "the central importance which it had for Maimonides."[11] It was then a "necessary consequence of Abravanel's anti–rationalist premises" that he had to exclude prophecy and the Messiah—"the two most exalted topics of Maimonides' political philosophy"—from "the field of political philosophy, properly speaking, altogether." Strauss essay culminates in the judgment that Abravanel's "soul was the soul of a priest."[12]

Strauss's first writing devoted solely to a classical thinker, "The Spirit of Sparta or the Taste of Xenophon" (1939), is also the first product of his rediscovery of the art of exoteric writing in its relation to "persecution," his introduction of the phrase "philosophic life," and his first sustained interpretation of a single text.[13] Strauss takes evident delight in showing that the little-regarded Xenophon was a literary master. Indeed, he almost adopts the premise of Xenophon's authorial mastery as his guiding principle of interpretation. Strauss opens the essay with a consideration of the penultimate chapter of the *Constitution of the Lacedemonians*, which seems to be a clumsily inserted critique of contemporary Sparta in the midst of a work expressly devoted to singing Sparta's praises. With a view to Xenophon's "great literary gifts," Strauss then declares that "if in a given case he apparently happens to do a bad job as a writer, or as a thinker, he actually does it deliberately and for very good reasons." Under these auspices, Strauss then proceeds to explore various enigmas and literary devices in Xenophon's text, notable among the silences, satire and the obscurity of the plan—or rather plans[14]—of the work. Strauss's essay itself has no clear plan; his first section is devoted to the first chapter of the work, which raises the expectation that he would supply a commentary proper. But this chapter-by-chapter discussion is not maintained in his six sections. Just as the most striking part of the *Constitution of the Lacedemonians* occurs near that work's end, the most striking passage of Strauss's occurs towards the end of his essay, when he turns from Xenophon to more general considerations of the philosophic pedagogy of classical writers. In Strauss's penultimate paragraph—the only paragraph in the essay that contains no proper names[15]—Strauss makes explicit the limited relation of "persecution" to the art of writing. Though philosophers did obscure their views for the sake of avoiding persecution, this act of prudent self-regard was only "the most obvious and the crudest reason"[16] for the art of exotericism. In the most memorable passage in "Spirit of Sparta," Strauss declares:

> By making the discovered truth almost as inaccessible as it was before it had been discovered, they [sc. the philosophers of the past—Eds.] prevented—to call a vulgar thing by a vulgar name—the cheap sale of the formulations of the truth: nobody should know even the formulations of the truth who had not rediscovered the truth by his own exertions, if aided by subtle suggestions from a superior teacher. It is in this way that the classical authors became the most efficient teachers of independent thinking. It should, however, not be overlooked that this exoteric literature, which provides the highest type of education, is found not only in classical times; it has reappeared in all epochs in which philosophy was understood in its full and challenging meaning, in all epochs, that is, in which wisdom was not separated from moderation. (70, below)

Strauss's concluding paragraph turns back to Xenophon and invokes for the first time in the essay a modern philosopher, namely, Rousseau, to whose unhealthy influence Strauss prescribes Xenophon as the "antidote." It is only appropriate that such an enigmatic essay should end so enigmatically.

Doubtless with a view to the well-being of future editors, Strauss provided a striking account of his intention in "Fārābī's *Plato*" in a letter to his brother-in-law, the great Arabist Paul Kraus.[17] Therein, Strauss writes:

> I decided to write an article on F´ Plato in order to show that according to F´ Plato, philosophy is so far being identical with political philosophy that it is simply identical with the subjects of the *Timaeus* = investigation of res naturales et divinae ['res divinae' in the sense of the *Timaeus*: the heavenly bodies —> Avicenna's esoteric philosophy as quoted by Averroes]: political-moral philosophy does not belong to philosophy proper. The apparent identification of philosophy with βασιλική or πολιτική serves

EDITORS' INTRODUCTION

the purpose of compensating, as it were, the distinction between perfectio humana and beatitudo. The situation is this: perfectio humana = beatitudo if perfectio and beatitudo were identified (they are <u>not</u> identified in §1, *pace* R.W.), F. would commit a grave heresy, of course; besides, he would deny beatitudo to be large majority of men: therefore he admits that if the philosophers are kings, their subjects who are not philosophers, will become happy. The identification of philosophy with πολιτική (in §18) serves to make clear that ruling and study, perfection and happiness are identical, that beatitudo = perfectio speculativa and <u>nothing else</u>. The <u>serious</u> meaning of "politics" is the <u>secret</u> kingship of the philosopher, viz. that the philosopher <u>by</u> <u>cautioning</u> [<u>qalīlan qalīlan</u>—§37], improving, and correcting, the received opinions by his <u>exoteric</u> teaching, is the <u>true</u> king. The philosopher is king, means that the philosopher exercises a humanizing and enlightening influence on the *jomhūr*—this is the only kind of government which is <u>absolutely</u> legitimate. (This is by the way also the teaching of Shakespeare's *Tempest*.)*

Let us here call attention to two obtrusive problems of "Fārābī's *Plato*." Strauss highlights—both in speech and action—the centrality of the political for Fārābī. He notes at the outset that "the most striking trait of Fārābī's philosophy" is his "presenting the whole of philosophy...within a political framework" (76). And Strauss devotes the two central sections of his essay—which comprise nearly three fourths of the work—to the topics "Philosophy and Politics" and "Philosophy and Morals." Such a procedure would seem to elevate the importance of the human and the political for philosophy. Yet in the fourth and final section of the essay—"The Subject Matter of Philosophy"—Strauss starkly[18] indicates that so far from being devoted to the study of the human things, philosophy is above all devoted to the investigation leading to the science of the beings—an investigation that does not appear to have any direct connection, or particular focus, on the human and political things. One must thus raise the question of what the status of political philosophy is for Strauss: does this essay elevate or subordinate it? Perhaps it does both at the same time, elevating it in form and manner of treatment and subordinating it in substance.

The second matter to which we wish to draw attention is Strauss's remarkable and repeated insistence on the unmistakable character of

---

* Translations are as follows: βασιλική, "kingly art"; πολιτική, "political art"; *qalīlan qalīlan*, "little by little, gradually"; and *jomhūr*, "the many, the multitude." N.B.: *qalīlan qalīlan* has been transliterated from the original Arabic as given by Strauss. On Strauss's treatment of section numbers in Fārābī, see 81n18 below. —Eds.

Fārābī's unbelief, his unqualified philosophic rejection of "the belief in the other life." To no point does Strauss recur more frequently and emphatically. At times he even takes on the character of a prosecutor fully intent on getting a conviction: Fārābī's "silence about the immortality of the soul in a treatise destined to present the philosophy of Plato from 'its beginning to its end' sets it beyond any reasonable doubt that statements asserting that immortality which occur in other writings of his, have to be dismissed as prudential accommodations to the accepted dogma" (90). Why did Strauss go to such great rhetorical lengths to try and to convict Fārābī and his Plato of not believing in the gods of the city? To be sure, Strauss had good reason for wishing to show Fārābī's heterodoxy: the dogmatic belief that philosophers of the past were believers in their societies' orthodoxies was an insuperable obstacle to understanding their thought. But why did Strauss make his case in such an insistent and apparently heavy-handed way? Given that the essay all but concludes with praise of the subtle and understated manner in which Fārābī communicated his "definite convictions concerning a number of important points," his procedure is all the more remarkable: "But what made him a philosopher, according to his own view of philosophy, were not those convictions, but the spirit in which they were acquired, in which they were maintained and in which they were intimated rather than preached from the house-tops" (106). Was Strauss's procedure at odds with his praise? Or is there another way to understand his rhetoric? If the matter of Fārābī's belief or unbelief was not a particularly "important point," then Strauss's rhetorical insistence on it may serve notice that he acted in accord with Fārābī's—and his own—"view of philosophy" by communicating in allusive manner such matters as he regarded of genuine import. By distracting us with the spectacular and (to his contemporaries) shocking whilst simultaneously indicating his distaste for shouting from the house-tops, Strauss invites his readers to seek out what he regarded as worthy of being intimated and induces them to discern the myriad ways in which he artfully communicated his thoughts about them.

"On a New Interpretation of Plato's Political Philosophy" (1946) is an analysis of John Wild's thought, or even his soul, revealing its strands as sediments of developments in the history of philosophy. Strauss uses Wild as a kind of symbol for several historical movements that have become petrified or dogmatized. Wild cannot turn to the Platonic dialogues with an honest willingness to learn since Wild already thinks he knows the answers to the questions of God, man, and world. Strauss shows modern science to have been launched in an effort to establish the intelligibility of the world. Together with this effort came a project aimed at establishing a prosperous and harmonious society here on earth, in order (among other matters) to show that the biblical solution to the problem of justice—and hence the biblical doubt about the permanent intelligibility of nature—is irrelevant. It appears that this twofold project has succeeded only partially and Wild is the perfect emblem of this partial success. He is still moved by the spirit of the Bible, but he is also attached to the offshoots of the modern project aimed at extinguishing the spirit of the Bible.[19]

"On the Intention of Rousseau" is Strauss's most searching engagement with Rousseau. It is also the essay that more than any other in Strauss's corpus sets forth common ground between the classics and a modern on the relationship between philosophy and society. Strauss seeks to discern Rousseau's intention by examining his *Discourse on the Science and the Arts*, a bold attack on the malign influence of science on morality written "in the heyday of the Enlightenment" (146). He suggests that Rousseau's apparent oscillation between the condemnation of the sciences and the praise of the great scientific benefactors was due not to inconsistency or confusion but to a self-conscious choice to speak "in two different characters" (152)—as a common man addressing the interests of the common man and as a philosopher addressing men of his own kind. Strauss nowhere states what Rousseau's intention is; it must be inferred, or discovered. But he does identify the thesis of the *Discourse*: "We may therefore express the thesis of the *Discourse* as follows: since the element of society is opinion, science, being the attempt to replace opinion by knowledge, essentially endangers society because it dissolves opinion" (161). Strauss elsewhere presents in his own name this "thesis" as the fundamental basis of the philosophic demand for exotericism,[20] but he thematically articulates its grounds most fully in this essay. So far from Rousseau's teaching being a perverse influence that must be stamped out to permit the restoration of "the sound approach"—as Strauss's unconventional concluding paragraph of "The Spirit of Sparta" posits—his Rousseau is here accorded the honor of setting forth a teaching that is at the core of both classical political philosophy and Strauss's rediscovery of the forgotten art of writing.

Strauss's treatment of R. G. Collingwood in "On Collingwood's Philosophy of History" bears a resemblance to his treatments of Wild and Abravanel insofar as it highlights tensions within his thought, not to say soul. Strauss even goes so far as to speak of Collingwood's remaining under a "spell" (203).[21] Strauss's articulation of tensions in Collingwood's thought goes hand in hand with the observation that "Collingwood moved consciously and with enthusiasm toward a goal which most of his contemporaries were approaching more or less unconsciously and haltingly" (190). But precisely because this conscious goal is "the fusion of philosophy and history," Collingwood "vacillated" between a rationalistic and non–rationalistic view of history (190). This vacillation reverberates in various dimensions of Collingwood's position, including Collingwood's simultaneous assertions that history is a theoretical pursuit and that the historian's entire personality must be involved in his work (191).

All but assuming the guise of a detective, Strauss identifies two beliefs whose existence provides Collingwood with protection against being "disturbed" by the alleged relativity of all historical knowledge (189–90): a lingering belief in progress, in "the superiority of the present to the past," and a belief in the equality of all ages (190). The beliefs that shield Collingwood from the disturbing implications of relativism reappear in another guise as the assumption that "present day historical thought is the right kind of historical thought" and, again, the belief in the equality of all ages. Strauss speaks of "two beliefs which contended for supremacy in Collingwood's thought" (200). But if "the belief in the equality of all ages is only a more subtle form of the belief in progress" (200), then there is no necessary contradiction within Collingwood's thought. Instead, the deficiencies of Collingwood's historiography can be traced his belief that "to know the human mind is to know its history." According to Strauss this belief contradicts the "tacit premise of all earlier thought": "the view that to know the human mind is something fundamentally different from knowing the history of the human mind"(201). Yet even if Strauss's critique compels us to conclude that Collingwood "lacked the incentive for re-enacting the thought of the past" or presupposed the possibility of historical objectivity while denying it (206–7, 200–1, 204–5), this need not mean that Collingwood's thought is not philosophic. The title of the essay, after all, refers to Collingwood's philosophy of history. And even apart from the absence of any reference to Collingwood's *Autobiography*, which Strauss says he belatedly read and appreciated (see n. 8 below), it remains for the reader to think through Strauss's analysis and form an independent judgment of Collingwood's thought and Strauss's alternative.[22]

Finally, the brief autobiographical comments Strauss gave towards the end of his life in "A Giving of Accounts" merit attention for at least three

EDITORS' INTRODUCTION

reasons: (1) they provide guidance on how to read the 1962 preface to *Spinoza's Critique of Religion,* the so-called "autobiographical preface";[23] (2) they highlight the debt Strauss owed to Lessing; and (3) they indicate Strauss's own understanding of the scope of his achievement.

Strauss opens the statement with an apology of sorts for speaking of himself. In the course of justifying this seeming breach of good taste, Strauss informs us that he is interested in his beginnings "only as a starting point of considerations, of [his] studies" and that examining the steps he took may help explain his "pitfalls." He further warns us that he "may commit errors of memory"—i.e., that his account may depart from strict historical truth.[24] In so doing, Strauss as it were provides a mirrored guide to how to read the preface to *Spinoza's Critique of Religion,* wherein Strauss provides an account of the steps that led him to the conclusion that "a farewell to reason" was not in order. If considerations of beginnings can help illumine steps ill-taken, they can no less shed light on steps well-taken to a most important insight, all the more if those steps are removed from the world of accident and contingency. In light of these remarks, one must consider whether the "autobiographical preface" is an intentionally forgetful, perhaps dramatized or idealized, account of the proper series of errors through which Strauss progressed—or should have progressed—to his determination that reason should not be bid adieu. That is to say, one needs to consider the possibility that the autobiographical preface is written as if Strauss's life proceeded in the accident-free manner of a Platonic dialogue.

"A Giving of Accounts" lets us see the scope of the liberties taken in the Spinoza preface in what he says about the debt he incurred to Lessing in the years covered by the Preface: "In this study [of Spinoza] I was greatly assisted by Lessing...Lessing was always at my elbow. This meant that I learned more from him than I knew at the time. As I came to see later Lessing had said everything I had found out about the distinction between exoteric and esoteric speech and its grounds" (442). In light of this acknowledgment, Strauss's almost complete neglect of Lessing in the Preface must be taken with a grain of salt.[25]

Whatever Strauss may have learned from Lessing about exoteric and esoteric speech (and philosophy), his self-conscious discovery—and presentation of that discovery—came in the form of his work on Maimonides, of whom Strauss says in "A Giving of Accounts":

> I got the first glimmer of light when I concentrated on his prophetology and, therefore, the prophetology of the Islamic philosophers who preceded

EDITORS' INTRODUCTION

him. One day when reading in a Latin translation of Avicenna's treatise, *On the Division of the Sciences*, I came across this sentence (I quote from memory): the standard work on prophecy and revelation is Plato's *Laws*. Then I began to begin to understand Maimonides's prophetology and eventually, as I believe, the whole *Guide of the Perplexed*. (443)

In saying that he "believed" he understood the whole of the *Guide*, Strauss indicates, in a becomingly subdued way, his own evaluation of his achievement: to understand the whole of the *Guide* is to be able to share as an equal Maimonides' thoughts *de Deo et mundo*.[26]

Note on the Texts

We have kept the orthography of the original publications, excepting common Latin abbreviations such as "i.e." and "e.g.," which are rendered in Roman rather than italic font and followed by a comma; also, the punctuation of quotations follows American rather than British convention. While parenthetical page numbers in this introduction refer to the present volume, the bracketed pagination throughout the text are the page numbers from the original publications. Footnotes are numbered continuously in each chapter, however, rather than recommencing on each page, as was sometimes the custom of the original publisher.

Steven J. Lenzner
Svetozar Y. Minkov
May 2023

---

1. We include here the Plato chapter from *History of Political Philosophy*, which adds treatments of Plato's *Laws* and *Statesman* to the study of the *Republic* that is largely adapted into *The City and Man*. Strauss wrote a commentary on the *Laws—The Argument and the Action of Plato's Laws* (Chicago: University of Chicago Press, 1975)— but not on the *Statesman*, even though he is reported to have said that his course on the *Statesman* was his most difficult course and that he believed that there is "an infinite number of most important revelations regarding the essence of philosophy in the *Statesman*." Leo Strauss to Seth Benardete, April 23, 1954, unpublished correspondence. The Strauss–Benardete correspondence, edited by Ronna Burger and Svetozar Minkov, is forthcoming from Mercer University Press. The Leo Strauss Archive contains a complete line-by-line commentary on the *Statesman*.

Editors' Introduction

2. We have included three pieces that have been co-signed by another author. The preface to *History of Political Philosophy*, which while it may have been written primarily by Joseph Cropsey, is consistent with Strauss's fundamental distinction between knowledge and hearsay. The Introduction to *History of Political Philosophy* is unsigned and presumptively could have been written by Leo Strauss and Joseph Cropsey, though it is likely Strauss's alone. The first paragraph of the translators' preface (signed by both Strauss and Shlomo Pines) to Maimonides' *Guide of the Perplexed* is clearly Strauss's. In the case of the introduction to Isaac Husik's essays, co-authored with Milton Nahm, we have been able to isolate Strauss's own contribution, which can be seen from reading the Hebrew translation of Strauss's portion. *Iyyun* 2 (1951): 215–23. One can also make a more substantive argument in recognizing Strauss's portion: see Jacob Taubes' review of *Philosophical Essays: Ancient, Medieval and Modern*, in *Philosophy and Phenomenological Research* 14, no. 2 (Dec. 1953): 269.

3. Some of the writings from the late thirties stand on the cusp of that rediscovery: they do not fall neatly into, to use the terms of Allan Bloom, either the works of "the pre-Straussian Strauss" or the mature Strauss, "Leo Strauss: September 20, 1899–October 18, 1973," *Political Theory* 2, no. 4 (Nov. 1974): 372–92.

4. He did so to one of the co-editors as well as to Heinrich Meier.

5. See *Jewish Philosophy and the Crisis of Modernity*, ed. Kenneth Hart Green (Albany: SUNY Press, 1995) and the preface to *Persecution and the Art of Writing*.

6. *Hobbes and Rousseau: A Collection of Critical Essays*, ed. Maurice Cranston and Richard S. Peters (Garden City, NY: Anchor Books, 1972): "Strauss's paper on the 'First Discourse' is reproduced in its original integral form" (3). In the first paragraph of section III of the original article, Strauss writes of Rousseau's success "in never revealing his principles coherently and hence fully," and follows that phrase with "nor in speaking through his publications merely to those whom he wanted to teach." This was corrected in an *erratum* notice in *Social Research* to "and thus in speaking through," while the 1972 Cranston-Peters version simply corrects "nor" to "or": "or in speaking through," suggesting that Strauss took the opportunity to revise the sentence. The 1972 version also has a typo corrected.—See also Masters' annotated bibliography: "57. Strauss, Leo. 'On the Intention of Rousseau,' *Social Research*, Careful and suggestive analysis, placing Rousseau's work in the context of the problems posed by classical philosophy. 58. Strauss, Leo. *Natural Right and History*. Chicago: University of Chicago Press, 1953. Chapter vi contains a subtle, highly compressed analysis of Rousseau's political philosophy in the context of the major issues presented by the doctrine of natural right. Underemphasizes the *Émile*." Roger Masters, *The Political Philosophy of Rousseau* (Princeton: Princeton University Press, 1968), 455; cf. Victor Gourevitch's "On Strauss on Rousseau," in *The Challenge of Rousseau*, ed. Eve Grace and Christopher Kelly (Cambridge: Cambridge University Press, 2013), 147–67.

7. Compare *Natural Right and History* (257–59) with "On the Intention of Rousseau" in the present volume (155–56, 161–63), especially the striking replacement of "one may even wonder whether" with "one is justified in saying that" regarding the concern with superiority, or pride, being the root of science (or even of philosophy) (*Natural Right and History*, 259; "On the Intention of Rousseau," 162).

EDITORS' INTRODUCTION

8   In a letter to Joseph Cropsey in late 1955, Strauss writes, "I am beginning to prepare my collection of essays to be entitled 'Political Philosophy and History.' I read my criticism of Collingwood after having read for the first time Collingwood's very impressive *Autobiography*. I still think that my critique is valid, but it is not generous enough. Above all, I am dissatisfied with what I say toward the end about 'interpretation–criticism.' So I decided to omit the Collingwood article, i.e., to regard it as non-existent and to write a new Introduction to the planned collection in which I shall try to make as clear as I can the co-operation of 'interpretation' and criticism." Leo Strauss to Joseph Cropsey, Dec. 29, 1955, uncatalogued collection, Leo Strauss Archive, Regenstein Library, University of Chicago. See also Nasser Behnegar's introduction to the winter 1956 course on Historicism and Modern Relativism, https://leostrausscenter.uchicago.edu/historicism–and–modern–relativism–winter–1956.

9   On Nov. 27, 1937, at the Cambridge University Jewish Society, Strauss gave a lecture on Abravanel entitled "Abravanel's Political Theories" in a series that became the basis of the book in which the essay first appeared, *Isaac Abravanel: Six Lectures*, edited by J. B. Trend and H. Loewe (Cambridge: Cambridge University Press, 1937). The occasion was the five-hundredth anniversary of the birth of Abravanel.

10 Isaac Husik, the subject of another essay included here, wrote to Strauss in early 1938 regarding his Abravanel article: "I am not quite sure that I subscribe to all that you say in the beginning. What you say on p. 97–8, the lower part of 97 and top of 98 [see at pp. 3–4 the section beginning with "Revelation was the determining factor" and ending with "they had to conceive, and they did conceive, of Moses or Mohammed as philosopher kings"—Eds.], is not peculiar to Judaism and Islam. Origen, too, and Abelard find it necessary to justify the study of Philosophy by citing the passage in Exodus where the Israelites were told to borrow from the Egyptians vessels of silver and vessels of gold—these symbolizing the wisdom of the philosophers." Isaac Husik to Leo Strauss, Jan. 22, 1938, Box 2, Folder 2, Leo Strauss Archive. See *Persecution and the Art of Writing* (New York: Free Press, 1952), 11. In another annotation to his copy of the Abravanel essay, Strauss notes Husik's point and the reference to Exodus 11:2.

11 In an annotation to his copy of the essay, Strauss writes "cf. Moreh [*Guide*] II 45 (282, 1–2): King = Messiah." See *Gesammelte Schriften*, ed. Heinrich Meier, 2:229.

12 Strauss notes first, "His descent was, as he believed, royal." Compare the reference to Xenophon's "truly royal soul" at the end of "The Spirit of Sparta or the Taste of Xenophon" (71).

13 Strauss never refers to his piece on Xenophon's *Constitution of the Lacedemonians*, not in his interpretation of Xenophon's Hiero in *On Tyranny*, or in his class session on the work in his 1963 course on Xenophon—or even in his private notes upon rereading the work in preparation for the course. Eventually, the piece had a great impact on the field, but already early on it was mentioned by two very prominent scholars: Hans Kohn, "The Totalitarian Philosophy of War," in *Proceedings of the American Philosophical Society* 82, no. 1 (Feb. 23, 1940): 57–72; and Helmut Kuhn (for the deed-speech antithesis), "The True Tragedy: On the Relationship between Greek Tragedy and Plato, II," *Harvard Studies in Classical Philology* 53 (1942): 37–88. For its subsequent impact on scholarship, see Christopher Nadon's "Leo Strauss's First Brush

Editors' Introduction

with Xenophon: 'The Spirit of Sparta or the Taste of Xenophon,'" *Review of Politics* 83, no. 1 (Winter 2021): 69–90.

14 Strauss discerns at least three: 58–59, 60–62, 68.

15 That paragraph—the 41st—is one of only two in the essay not to mention Xenophon; the other is the 35th, wherein Sparta, Athens and Socrates are mentioned.

16 *Persecution and the Art of Writing*, 17.

17 Dec. 10, 1943, private collection, Jenny Strauss Clay.

18 Strauss certainly does indicate this status of political philosophy in the two central sections, but the drift and the design of those sections serve to elevate its status and import.

19 An article by Nathan Tarcov has shown the review essay on John Wild to be also an anticipatory warning about the problems inherent in founding the school of Straussianism: "On a Certain Critique of 'Straussianism,'" *Review of Politics* 53, no. 1 (Winter 1991): 3–18.

20 See "A Giving of Accounts" (ch. 31) and "On a Forgotten Kind of Writing" in *What Is Political Philosophy?* (Glencoe, IL: Free Press, 1959), 221–32.

21 In early 1952, Paul Weiss, editor of the *Review of Metaphysics*, had written to Strauss suggesting that Strauss cut some material from the piece: "Thanks for a splendid paper. I am planning to get it in the next issue. Too bad that Collingwood is not alive to read it; he would like it for the criticism is at once sympathetic and just. I have a feeling that the paper could be strengthened by cutting out material in pp. 1–18, but I am not sure just what should be cut. I make this remark for you to reflect on; should you, on rereading, agree let me know before the 1st so that I can send a corrected mms. to the printer." Paul Weiss to Leo Strauss, Feb. 20, 1952, Box 3, Folder 16, Leo Strauss Archive. In a draft response, Strauss wrote, "I understand perfectly your feeling. [LS had crossed out "impression."—Eds.] But: on rereading the essay, I have seen again that the details are really necessary in order to bring out the character of C's position. I take it that C's work is the most philosophic book in English on the problem of history. While few people would subscribe to everything he says, the general characteristics of his work are typical in the dissatisfaction with Hegelianism (and Marxism) and on the other hand the unwillingness to break away from this kind of philosophy of history; the present concern with the thought of the past and the inadequacy of the historical method; and so on."

22 On Sept. 28, 1960, in a letter to Kendall, Strauss writes that Collingwood "is the only 20th century Anglo Saxon known to me who was a genuine philosopher," *Willmoore Kendall: Maverick of American Conservatives*, ed. John A. Murley and John E. Alvis (Lanham, MD: Lexington Books, 2002), 230. In an essay on "the Oxford political philosophers," Voegelin writes, "I do not enter into the theoretical problems of Collingwood's philosophy of history, because they have recently been submitted to a careful analysis in Leo Strauss's article 'On Collingwood's Philosophy of History'... I am in substantial agreement with Professor Strauss." Eric Voegelin, "The Oxford Political Philosophers," *Philosophical Quarterly* 3, no. 11 (April 1953), 111n16.

EDITORS' INTRODUCTION

23 Strauss wrote to Gershom Scholem on May 4, 1962: "The preface will come as close to an autobiography as is compatible with propriety" (*Gesammelte Schriften*, ed. Heinrich Meier, 3:746).

24 Strauss's memory may not be justly faulted for calling up Spinoza's *Theological Political Treatise* rather than the *Theologico-Political Treatise*. A more serious lapse may be Strauss's statement that he "ceased to take any interest in him [Heidegger] for about two decades" . . . "[a]fter that," meaning after Heidegger's "siding with the so-called Nazis in 1933" (see 441). Strauss's 1946 essay on John Wild shows this cessation of interest not to have been total (see 117n6; cf. 134). Finally, in referring to Avicenna, Strauss "quote[s] from memory": "the standard work on prophecy and revelation is Plato's *Laws*." Strauss does not seem to recall, or let on, that in the original, in the "On the Divisions of Practical Science" section of *On the Divisions of the Rational Sciences*, Avicenna writes "and the treatment of prophecy and the Law is contained in their [Plato's and Aristotle's] two books on the laws" (*Medieval Political Philosophy: A Sourcebook*, ed. Joshua Parens and Joseph C. Macfarland, 2nd ed. [Ithaca: Cornell University Press, 2011], 75). In the epigraph to *The Argument and the Action of Plato's Laws*, Strauss uses ellipses to omit Aristotle from the same sentence. The memory lapse and the ellipses may serve the same purpose: they point to Plato as the one who has treated prophecy and the Law.

25 Lessing is mentioned only once in the Preface to Strauss's work on Spinoza, seemingly in an aside. In a letter to Alexander Altmann dated May 28, 1971, Strauss writes that, because he was unable to fulfill his plan to write a book on Lessing, "Das Einzige, was ich tun konnte, war, meine besseren Schüler nachdrücklich auf Lessing hinzuweisen und bei passender Gelegenheit zu sagen, was ich Lessing verdanke" ("The only thing I could do was to point my better students emphatically to Lessing and to say on appropriate occasions what I owe to Lessing"); and indicates that he is sending "A Giving of Accounts" to Altmann under separate cover. Altmann quoted the letter in his own preface to *Moses Mendelssohn: Gesammelte Schriften Jubiläumsausgabe, Schriften zur Philosophie und Ästhetik*, 3(2), ed. Leo Strauss (Stuttgart-Bad Cannstatt, Friedrich Frommann Verlag [Günther Holzboog], 1974).

26 Strauss proceeded to say that Maimonides "used a kind of writing which is in the precise sense of the term, exoteric." In so doing, Strauss casts light on the common imprecision of the use of "esotericism" to denote the philosophic art of writing. Common usage notwithstanding, for Strauss, properly understood, "esotericism" is a nonsensical term. The "esoteric"—i.e., the genuine philosophic thoughts about the highest problems—can never become an "–ism." For an "–ism" is a doctrine—something set forth to be accepted—and, as such, is incompatible with independently grasping the phenomena as they are. For the same reason that it would never occur to one to speak of "philosophyism," one cannot properly employ "esotericism" to denote successful communication of philosophic thoughts.

1

On Abravanel's Philosophical Tendency and Political Teaching[1] (1937)

[95] Abravanel may be called the last of the Jewish philosophers of the Middle Ages. He belongs to the Middle Ages, as far as the framework and the main content of his doctrine are concerned. It is true that there are features of his thought which distinguish it from that of all or of most other Jewish medieval philosophers; but most of those features are probably of medieval Christian origin. Yet Abravanel is a son of the humanist age, and thus we shall not be surprised if he expresses in his writings opinions or tendencies which are, to say the least, not characteristic of the Middle Ages. Generally speaking, however, Abravanel is a medieval thinker, a Jewish medieval thinker.

The central figure in the history of Jewish medieval philosophy is Maimonides. Thus it will be advisable to define the character of Abravanel's philosophical tendency by contrasting it with that of Maimonides. One is all the more justified in proceeding thus, since there is scarcely any other philosopher whom Abravanel admired so much, or whom he followed as much, as he did Maimonides.

What was then the general tendency of Maimonides? The answer to this question seems to be obvious: Maimonides attempted to harmonize the teachings of Jewish tradition with the teachings of philosophical tradition, i.e., of the Aristotelian tradition. This answer is certainly not altogether wrong, but it is quite insufficient, since it fails to explain which ultimate assumptions enabled Maimonides to harmonize Judaism and Aristotle. Now

---

Originally published in *Isaac Abravanel: Six Lectures*, ed. J. B. Trend and H. Loewe (Cambridge: Cambridge University Press, 1937), 93–129. —Eds.

1. I wish to express my thanks to the Board of the Faculty of History for a grant enabling this essay to be written and to Mrs. M. C. Blackman for kindly revising the English.

CHAPTER 1

those truly decisive assumptions are neither of Jewish nor of Aristotelian origin: they are borrowed from Plato, from Plato's political philosophy.

At a first glance, the philosophical tradition from which [96] Maimonides starts seems to be identical with that which is the determining factor of Christian scholasticism. Indeed, to Maimonides as well as to Thomas Aquinas, Aristotle is *the* philosopher. There is, however, one striking and at the same time highly important difference between Maimonides and the Christian scholastic as regards the philosophical tradition on which they build. For Thomas Aquinas, Aristotle is the highest authority, not only in other branches of philosophy, but also in political philosophy. Maimonides, on the other hand, could not use Aristotle's *Politics*, since it had not been translated into Arabic or Hebrew; but he could start, and he did start, from Plato's political philosophy.[2] For the *Republic* and the *Laws*, which were inaccessible to the Latin Middle Ages,[3] had been translated into Arabic in the ninth century, and commentaries on them had been written by two of the most outstanding Islamic philosophers.[4] By considering these facts we gain, I believe, a clear impression of the philosophical difference which exists between the philosophy of Maimonides (and of his Islamic predecessors) on the one hand, and that of Christian scholasticism on the other: the place occupied in the latter by Aristotle's *Politics* is occupied in the former by Plato's *Republic* and *Laws*. I have read that in some Italian pictures Plato is represented holding in

---

2   For details I must refer the reader for the time being to my book *Philosophie und Gesetz* [*Philosophy and Law*, 1995—Eds.], Berlin (Schocken), 1935, and to my article "Quelques remarques sur la science politique de Maimonide et de Farabi," *Revue des Études Juives* (1936): 1–37. [Here Strauss omits the diacritics printed in the original French title, "Quelques remarques sur la science politique de Maïmonide et de Fārābī." A translation by Robert Bartlett was published as "Some Remarks on the Political Science of Maimonides and Farabi," *Interpretation* 18, no. 1 (1990): 3–30. —Eds.]

3   Cp. Ernest Barker, *Plato and his Predecessors*, 383: "For a thousand years the *Republic* has no history; for a thousand years it simply disappeared. From the days of Proclus, the Neo-Platonist of the fifth century, almost until the days of Marsilio Ficino and Pico della Mirandola, at the end of the fifteenth, the *Republic* was practically a lost book." The same holds true, as far as the Latin Middle Ages are concerned, of the *Laws*.

4   Fārābī's paraphrase of the *Laws* will be edited in the near future by Dr. Paul Kraus. The original of Averroes' paraphrase of the *Republic* seems to be lost; but this paraphrase is accessible in an often-printed Latin translation. The more reliable Hebrew translation is being edited by Dr. Erwin Rosenthal; see *Journ. Roy. Asiatic Soc.*, October 1934, 737 ff.

his hand the *Timaeus* and Aristotle his *Ethics*. If a pupil of Maimonides or of the Islamic philosophers[5] had found pleasure in representations [97] of this kind, he might have chosen rather the inverse order: Aristotle with his *Physics* or *Metaphysics* and Plato with his *Republic* or *Laws*.

For what is the meaning of the fact that Maimonides and the Islamic philosophers whom he followed start from Platonic political philosophy, and not from Aristotle's *Politics*? One cannot avoid raising this question, especially since the circumstance that the *Politics* was not translated into Arabic may well be, not a mere matter of chance, but the result of a deliberate choice, made in the beginning of this medieval development. Now, in order to answer that question, we must remind ourselves of the general character of the medieval world, and of the particular character of the Islamic philosophy adopted by Maimonides. The medieval world is distinguished both from the classical and from the modern world by the fact that its thought was fundamentally determined by the belief in Revelation. Revelation was the determining factor with the Islamic philosophers as well as with the Jewish and Christian philosophers. But, as was clearly recognized by such contemporary and competent observers as Ghazzāli, Maimonides and Thomas Aquinas, the Islamic philosophers did not believe in Revelation properly speaking. They were philosophers in the classical sense of the word: men who would hearken to reason, and to reason only. Consequently, they were compelled to give an account of the Revelation which they had to accept and which they did accept, in terms of human reason. Their task was facilitated by the fact that Revelation, as understood by Jews or Muslims, had the form of law. Revelation, thus understood, lent itself to being interpreted by loyal philosophers as a perfect, ideal law, as an ideal political order. Moreover, the Islamic philosophers were compelled, and so was Maimonides, to justify their pursuit of philosophy before the law to which they were subject; they had, therefore, to prove that the law did not only entitle them, but even oblige them, to devote themselves to philosophy. Consequently, they were driven to interpret Revelation more precisely as an ideal political order, the ideal character of which consists in [98] the very fact that it lays upon all men endowed with the necessary qualities the duty of devoting their lives to philosophy, that it awakens them to philosophy, that it holds out for their guidance at least the most important tenets of philosophy. For this purpose they had

---

5   When speaking of Islamic philosophers, I am limiting myself strictly to the *falāsifa*, the so-called Aristotelians.

Chapter 1

to assume that the founder of the ideal political order, the prophetic lawgiver, was not merely a statesman, but that he was, at the same time, a philosopher of the highest authority: they had to conceive, and they did conceive, of Moses or Mohammed as philosopher kings. Philosopher kings and a political community governed by philosopher kings were, however, the theme, not of Aristotelian but of Platonic political philosophy. Thus we may say: Maimonides and his Islamic predecessors start from Platonic political philosophy, because they had to conceive of the Revelation to which they were subject, as of an ideal political order, the specific purpose of which was guidance to philosophy. And we may add that their belief in the authority of Moses or Mohammed was perhaps not greatly different from what would have been the belief of a later Greek Platonist in the authority of Plato, if that Platonist had been the citizen of a commonwealth governed by Plato's *Laws*.

Judaism on the one hand, Aristotelianism on the other, certainly supplied the greatest part of the matter of Maimonides' teaching. But Platonic political philosophy provided at any rate the framework for the two achievements by which Maimonides made an epoch in the history of Judaism: for his codification of the Jewish law and for his philosophical defence of the Jewish law. It is open to question which of Plato's political works was the most important for Maimonides and the Islamic philosophers. But it is safe to say that the best clue to the understanding of their teaching is supplied by the *Laws*.[6] I cannot discuss here the true meaning of this most ironical of Plato's works, although I believe that only [99] the full understanding of its true meaning would enable us to understand adequately the medieval philosophy of which I am speaking. For our present purpose, it is sufficient to state that the *Laws* are certainly the primary source of the opinions which Maimonides and his teachers held concerning the relation between philosophy and Revelation, or, more exactly, between philosophy and law. Those opinions may be summarized in the following ways: (1) Law is based on certain fundamental beliefs or dogmas of a strictly philosophical character, and those beliefs are, as it were, the prelude to the whole law. The beliefs of this kind were called by Fārābī, who was, according to Maimonides,

---

[6] E. Barker, *loc. cit.* p. 351, says with regard to the Latin Middle Ages: "The end of the *Laws* is the beginning of the Middle Ages." This statement is all the more true of the Islamic and Jewish Middle Ages. Compare, for example, the quotations from Avicenna in *Philosophie und Gesetz*, p. 111, and from R. Sheshet in *Revue des Études Juives*, 1936, p. 2, n. 1.

the highest philosophical authority of his period, "opinions of the people of the excellent city." (2) Law contains, apart from those rational beliefs, a number of other beliefs which, while being not properly true, but representing the truth in a disguised way, are necessary or useful in the interest of the political community. The beliefs of this type may be called, as they were by Spinoza, who was, perhaps, the latest exponent of that medieval tradition, *pia dogmata*, in contradistinction to the *vera dogmata* of the first group.[7] (3) Necessary beliefs, i.e., the beliefs which are not common to philosophy and law, but peculiar to law as such, are to be defended (either by themselves or together with the whole law) by probable, persuasive, rhetorical arguments, not recognizable as such to the vulgar; a special science is to be devoted to that "defence of the law" or "assistance to the law."

We are now in a position to define more precisely the character of Maimonides' attempt to harmonize the Jewish tradition with the philosophical tradition. He effects the harmony between those two traditions by starting from the conception of a perfect law, perfect in the sense of Plato's *Laws*, i.e., of a law leading to the study of philosophy and based on philosophical truth, and by thus proving that Judaism is a law of this character. To prove this, he shows that the fundamental beliefs of Judaism are identical with the fundamental tenets of philosophy, i.e., with those tenets [100] on which an ideal law ought to be based. By showing this, he shows, at the same time, that those Jewish beliefs which are of an unphilosophical nature are meant by the Jewish legislator himself, by *the* philosopher legislator, to be necessary beliefs, i.e., beliefs necessary for political reasons. The assumption underlying this proof of the ideal character of the Jewish law is the opinion that the law has two different meanings: an exterior, literal meaning, addressed to the vulgar, which expresses both the philosophical and the necessary beliefs, and a secret meaning of a purely philosophical nature. Now this property of law had to be imitated by Maimonides in his philosophic interpretation of the law. For if he had distinguished explicitly between true and necessary beliefs, he would have endangered the acceptance of the necessary beliefs on which the authority of the law with the vulgar, i.e., with the great majority, rests. Consequently, he could make this essential distinction only in a disguised way, partly by allusions, partly by the composition of his whole work, but mainly by the rhetorical character, recognizable only to philosophers, of the arguments by which he defends the necessary beliefs. As a consequence, Maimonides' philosophical

---

7 *Tractatus theologico-politicus*, ch. 14 (§20, Bruder).

CHAPTER 1

work, the *Guide of the Perplexed*, is a most ingenious combination of "opinions of the people of the excellent city," i.e., of a strictly demonstrative discussion of the beliefs which are common to philosophy and law, with "defence of the law," i.e., with a rhetorical discussion of the unphilosophical beliefs peculiar to the law. Thus not only the law itself, but also Maimonides' philosophical interpretation of the law, has two different meanings: a literal meaning, addressed to the more unphilosophic reader of philosophic education, which is very near to the traditional Jewish beliefs, and a secret meaning, addressed to true philosophers, which is purely philosophical. This amounts to saying that Maimonides' philosophical work was liable to, and was intended to be liable to, two fundamentally different interpretations: to a "radical" interpretation which did honour to the consistency of his thought, and to a "moderate" interpretation which did honour rather to the fervour of his belief.

[101] The ambiguous nature of Maimonides' philosophical work must be recognized if one wants to judge properly of the general tendency of Abravanel. For Abravanel has to be characterized, to begin with, as a strict, even passionate adherent of the literal interpretation of the *Guide of the Perplexed*. The more philosophic interpretation of this work had appealed to some earlier commentators. Those commentators, who were under the spell of Islamic philosophy rather than of Christian scholasticism, are vehemently attacked by Abravanel,[8] who finds words of the highest praise for the Christian scholastics.[9] But Abravanel accepts the literal teaching of the *Guide* not only as the true expression of Maimonides' thought: that literal teaching is at the same time, if not identical with, at least the framework of, Abravanel's own philosophy.

The beliefs peculiar to the law are founded upon and, as it were, derived from one fundamental conviction: the belief in *creatio ex nihilo*.[10] That belief had been defended by Maimonides in his *Guide* with great care and vigour. The discussion of the creation of the world, or, in other words, the criticism of the contention of the philosophers that the visible world is eternal, forms literally the central part of the *Guide*. It is the central part of this work also

---

8   Cp. his judgements on Ibn Kaspi and others, quoted by Jacob Guttmann, *Die religionsphilosophischen Lehren des Isaak Abravanel*, Breslau, 1916, pp. 34–6 and 71.

9   See his commentary on Josh. X, 12 (f. 21, col. 2). I have used Abravanel's commentary on Joshua, Judges, Samuel and Kings in the Frankfort edition of 1736.

10 Cp. Abravanel, *Rosh'Amanah*, ch. 22, with Maimonides' *Guide*, Pt. II, ch. 25 in the beginning, and Pt. III, ch. 25 in the end.

because of the fact that the interpretation of the whole work depends on the interpretation of this very part. Indeed, this is the crucial question for the interpretation of Maimonides' philosophical work: whether the discussion of the question of creation expresses Maimonides' own opinion in a direct way, or whether it is in the service of the "defence of the law." However one may answer this question, the very question itself implies the recognition of the fact that the literal teaching of the *Guide* is most decidedly in favour of the belief in creation. Now [102] while Maimonides carefully maintains this belief, on which all other beliefs peculiar to the law depend, he takes a rather hesitating, if not self-contradictory position, as regards those other beliefs, i.e., as regards belief in the miracles, in Revelation, in the immortality of the soul, in individual providence, in resurrection. If he actually believed in *creatio ex nihilo*, he was as little under a stringent necessity to depreciate those beliefs, or to restrict their bearing, as were the Christian scholastics, who also had combined Aristotelianism with the belief in creation, and who accepted the Christian dogma as a whole. Abravanel accepted Maimonides' explicit doctrine of the creation as true—he defended it in a special treatise (*Shamayim Hadashim*), and he knew Christian scholasticism. It was, therefore, only natural that he should have defended, and that he did defend, on the very basis of Maimonides' doctrine of creation and against his authority, all the other beliefs which are dependent on the belief in creation and which Maimonides had endangered. Thus, his criticism of Maimonides' dangerous doctrines is, in principle, not more than an immanent criticism of the literal teaching of the *Guide*; it is not more than a subsequent correction of that teaching in the sense of the Jewish traditional beliefs. It would not be much of an exaggeration to say that Abravanel's philosophical exertions as a whole are a defence of the Jewish creed, as drawn up by Maimonides in his commentary to the Mishnah, against the implications, dangerous to this creed, of the teaching of the *Guide*.

The creed compiled by Maimonides was defended expressly by Abravanel in a special treatise (*Rosh'Amanah*). This treatise, by itself perhaps the most striking evidence of the admiration which Abravanel felt for Maimonides, gives us a clear idea both of Abravanel's own tendency and of his interpretation of Maimonides. Maimonides' arrangement of the Jewish beliefs, the so-called "Thirteen Articles of Faith," had been attacked by some later Jewish writers for philosophical as well as for religious reasons. Abravanel defends Maimonides against those critics by showing that Jewish orthodoxy is perfectly defined by the recognition of just those [103] thirteen articles which Maimonides had selected, and that the order of those articles

Chapter 1

is completely lucid. As regards the latter point, Abravanel asserts that the former part of those articles indicates the beliefs common to philosophy and law, while the latter part is concerned with those beliefs which either are not accepted, or which are even contested by the philosophers.[11] It is not necessary for our purpose to dwell on the detail of Abravanel's arguments. One point only must be stressed. After having devoted twenty-two chapters to defending Maimonides' compilation, Abravanel rather abruptly explains, in the two concluding chapters of his treatise, that a creed as such is incompatible with the character of Judaism as a divinely given law. For since any and every proposition of the law, any and every story, belief, or command contained in the law, immediately proceeds from Revelation, all those propositions are of equal value, and none of them ought to be thought of as more fundamental than any other. Abravanel does not think that by holding this opinion he is in conflict with the teaching of Maimonides; strangely enough, he asserts that that opinion was shared by Maimonides himself. According to Abravanel, Maimonides selected the thirteen more general articles of belief for the use of the vulgar only, who are unable to grasp the whole doctrine of faith. To prove this statement, he contends that Maimonides mentioned those articles only in his commentary to the Mishnah, i.e., in an elementary work which he wrote in his youth, but not in the *Guide*, in which he treats the philosophy of the Jewish law in a scientific way. Now this contention is not only wrong, but it is contradicted by Abravanel himself. He asserts, in the same treatise,[12] that the articles of belief—the first eleven out of the thirteen explicitly, the last two implicitly—occur as such in the philosophical first part of Maimonides' codification of the Jewish law (in the *Hilkhoth Yeṣodhe hat-Torah*); and in another writing of his,[13] he explains the decisive influence exercised by the articles of belief on the whole composition of the *Guide*. But however this may be, it is certain that Abravanel, by [104] denying the possibility of distinguishing between fundamental and non-fundamental beliefs, actually undermines the whole structure of the philosophy of the Jewish law which was built up by Maimonides.[14] Abravanel has sometimes been blamed for the inconsistency

---

11 *Rosh'Amanah*, ch. 10.

12 Ch. 19.

13 *Ma'amar Qāṣēr b^e Bhi'ur Ṣōdh ham-Moreh*.

14 Cp. in this connection, Abravanel's criticism of Maimonides' explanation of the Mosaic laws; see his commentary on I Kings III, 14 (f. 210, col. 2) and his commentary on Deut. XII, 28 (f. 286, col. 4). (I have used Abravanel's commentary on the Penta-

of his thought. I cannot praise him as a very consistent thinker. But a certain consistency ought not to be denied him. Accepting the literal teaching of Maimonides' *Guide* and trying to correct that teaching in the sense of the traditional Jewish beliefs, he was consistent enough to draw the final conclusion from his premises: he contested, if only occasionally, the foundation on which every philosophy of the law divine ultimately rests. However deeply he may have been influenced by the philosophical tradition in general and by the philosophical teaching of Maimonides in particular, his thought was decisively determined, not by philosophy, but by Judaism as a tradition based on a verbally inspired revelation.

The unphilosophic, to some extent even anti-philosophic, traditionalism of Abravanel accounts for the fact that for him political philosophy loses the central importance which it had for Maimonides. From what has been said about Maimonides' philosophy of Judaism, it will have appeared that the significance which he actually attaches to political philosophy is in exact proportion to his rationalism: identifying the fundamental beliefs of Judaism with the fundamental tenets of philosophy means at the same time interpreting the beliefs peculiar to Judaism in terms of political philosophy; and it means, in principle, interpreting Judaism as a whole as a perfect law in the Platonic sense. Accordingly, a follower of Maimonides, who rejected the thoroughgoing rationalism of the latter, as did Abravanel, deprived by this very fact political philosophy of all its dignity. One cannot raise the objection against this assertion that the Christian scholastics, [105] while far from being radical rationalists, did indeed cultivate political philosophy. For the case of those scholastics who were citizens of existing states was obviously quite different from the case of the Jewish medieval thinkers. For a medieval Jew, political philosophy could have no other field of application than the Jewish law. Consequently, the value which political philosophy could have for him was entirely dependent on how far he would accept philosophy in general and political philosophy in particular as a clue to the understanding of the Jewish law. Now according to Maimonides, the prophet, who brought the law, is a philosopher statesman, and at least the greater part of the Mosaic law is concerned with the "government of the city."[15] Abravanel, on the other hand, denies that philosophy in general is of the essence of prophecy. As re-

---

teuch in the Hanau edition of 1710.) Cp. also his criticism of Gersonides' method of drawing maxims out of the biblical narratives in the introduction to the commentary on Joshua (f. 5, col. 2).

15 *Guide*, Pt. III, ch. 27–28.

Chapter 1

gards political philosophy in particular, he declares that the prophet does not stoop to such "low" things as politics and economics. He stresses in this connection the fact that the originator of the biblical organization of jurisdiction was not Moses, but Jethro.[16] In making these statements, Abravanel does not contest that Moses, as well as the other prophets, exercised a kind of government. As we shall see later, he even asserts this expressly. But he obviously does not accept the view, presupposed by Maimonides, that prophetic government is a legitimate subject of political philosophy. Political philosophy, as he understands it, has a much more restricted field than it had for Maimonides; it is much more of the Aristotelian than of the Platonic type.[17] Abravanel's depreciation of political philosophy, which is a consequence of his critical attitude towards Maimonides' rationalism, thus implies a decisive limitation of the content of political philosophy.

Political philosophy, as outlined by Maimonides, had dealt with three main topics: the prophet, the king and the [106] Messiah. According to Maimonides, the prophet as such is a philosopher statesman, and the highest prophet, Moses, was that philosopher statesman who was able to give the perfect, and consequently eternal, unchangeable law.[18] As regards kingship, Maimonides teaches that the institution of a king is indispensable, and expressly commanded by the Mosaic law. The king is subordinate to the lawgiver; his function is to force men to obedience to the law, to establish justice and to be the military leader. He himself is bound by the law and, therefore, subject both to punishment in case of transgression of the law and to instruction by the supreme court, the guardians of the law. The king has extraordinary powers in case of urgent necessity, and his claims both to honour and to glory are acknowledged by the law.[19] The Messiah, as Maimonides conceives of him, is, in the first instance, a king, obedient to the law, and a successful military leader, who will rescue Israel from servitude, restore the kingdom of David in the country of Israel, establish universal peace, and

---

16 Commentary on I Kings III, 14 (f. 211, col. 1). Cp. however the commentary on Exod. XVIII, 13–27 (f. 134, col. 2–3).

17 As regards Abravanel's knowledge of Aristotle's *Politics*, see J. F. Baer, "Don Jizchaq Abravanel," *Tarbiz*, VIII, p. 241f., 245 n. 11 and 248. See also below, p. 113, n. 2 [p. 17, n. 47 in this edition—Eds.]. In his commentary on Gen. X, 1 ff. (f. 40, col. 1) Abravanel seems occasionally to adopt the Aristotelian doctrine of natural masters and servants.

18 Cp. *Guide*, Pt. I, ch. 54 with Pt. II, ch. 39–40.

19 See *Guide*, Pt. II, ch. 40; Pt. III, ch. 41 (Munk, p. 91*a*) and ch. 45 (Munk, p. 98*b*) as well as *Hilkhoth Melakhim*, ch. 1, §§3 and 8; ch. 3 *passim*; ch. 4, §10 and ch. 5, §2.

thus create, for the first time in history, the ideal earthly condition for a life devoted to knowledge. But the Messiah is not only a king; he is, at the same time, a prophet of a rank not much inferior to that of the lawgiver Moses: the Messiah, too, is a philosopher king. Even according to the literal teaching of Maimonides, the Messiah does not work miracles, and the Messianic age in general does not witness any alteration of the ordinary course of nature. It goes almost without saying that that age is not the prelude to the end of the visible world: the present world will remain in existence for ever.[20] Thus we may define the distinctive features of Maimonides' Messianology by saying that Messianism, as he accepts it, is a rational hope rather than a superrational belief.[21] Maimonides' rationalism accounts in [107] particular for the fact that he stresses so strongly the character of the Messiah as a successful military leader—he does this most definitely by inserting his thematic treatment of Messianology within that section of his great legal work which deals with "the kings and their wars." For military ability or deficiency seems to be the decisive natural reason for the rise or decline of states. Maimonides, at any rate, thinks that the reason for the destruction of the Jewish state in the past was the neglect of the arts of war and conquest.[22] Accordingly, he expects that military virtue and military ability will play a decisive part in the future restoration of the Jewish state.[23]

It is a necessary consequence of Abravanel's anti-rationalist premises that he must exclude the two most exalted topics of Maimonides' political philosophy from the field of political philosophy, properly speaking, altogether. As regards the prophets, the prophetic lawgiver and the law divine, he takes away their treatment from political philosophy by contesting the assertions of Maimonides that prophecy is a natural phenomenon,[24] and that philosophy belongs to the essence of prophecy.[25] For, by denying this,

---

20 *Hilkhoth Melakhim*, ch. 11–12; *Hilkhoth Teshubah*, ch. 9; *Guide*, Pt. II, ch. 29.

21 Notice the distinction between "belief" and "hope" in *Hilkhoth Melakhim*, ch. 11, §1.

22 See his letter to the community at Marseilles.

23 I am not competent to judge whether Maimonides' legal treatment of kings and wars is influenced by the Islamic conception of the Holy War. But it is certain that his stressing the importance of military virtue in his philosophic prophetology was influenced by the prophetology of the Islamic philosophers, who attach a much higher value to war and to the virtue of courage than Plato and Aristotle had done. Cp. *Revue des Études Juives*, 1936, pp. 19 f. and 35 f.

24 See Abravanel's commentary on *Guide*, Pt. II, ch. 32.

25 See, for example, commentary on I Kings III, 14 (f. 210, col. 4).

Chapter 1

he destroys the foundation of Maimonides' conception of the prophet as a philosopher statesman. The leadership of the prophet, as Abravanel sees it, is, just as prophecy itself is, of an essentially supernatural, and thus of an essentially superpolitical character. As regards the Messiah, Abravanel devoted to this theme a much more detailed and a much more passionate treatment than Maimonides had done.[26] Indeed, as we are informed by a [108] most competent historian, Abravanel stressed in his writings the Messianic hopes more than any other Jewish medieval author, and he was the first to give the Messianic beliefs of Israel a systematic form.[27] This increase of the interest in eschatological speculation is explained by the fact that Abravanel was a contemporary of the greatest revolutions in the history of the Jewish diaspora, and of that great revolution of European civilization which is called the end of the Middle Ages and the beginning of the modern period. Abravanel expected the coming of the Messiah in the near future. He saw signs of its imminence in all the characteristic features of his time, from the increase of heresies and unbelief down to the appearance of the "French disease."[28] Reflections of this kind show that his Messianistic view was not, as was, at least to some extent, that of Maimonides, of an evolutionist, but of a catastrophic character. It is hardly necessary to add that the Messianic age is for Abravanel a period rich in miracles, the most impressive of them being the resurrection of the dead. That age, which is the age of universal peace, even among the animals, as predicted by Isaiah, lasts only for a limited time; it is followed by the end of the present world.[29] It is preceded by a most terrible war, the final war. That war is, however, not so much a war of liberation, fought and won by Israel as Maimonides had taught; it is rather an event like the capture of Jericho, as told in the book of Joshua: Israel is a looker-on at the victory rather than the victor.[30]

---

26 In this connection, the fact has to be mentioned that some prophecies which, according to Maimonides, were fulfilled in the past, i.e., at a time comparatively near to their announcement, are interpreted by Abravanel as Messianic prophecies. Cp. the interpretation given in *Guide*, Pt. II, ch. 29, of Isa. XXIV, 17 ff. and Joel III, 3–5, with Abravanel's explanations of those passages in his commentary on the later prophets.

27 Baer, *loc. cit.* pp. 257–9.

28 That disease is, according to Abravanel, probably meant in Zech. XIV, 12 (see his commentary on that passage).

29 See G. Scholem's remark in *Encyc. Judaica*, IX, col. 688.

30 The "realistic" element of Abravanel's conception of the final war, i.e., his identification of the final war with the war which he thought to be imminent between the Chris-

Accordingly, in Abravanel's description of the Messiah,[31] the military abilities and virtues are, to say the least, not predominant.[32] To him, the Messiah is certainly much more a [109] worker of miracles than a military leader: the Messiah, not less than the prophets, belongs to the sphere of miracles, not of politics. Abravanel's Messianology as well as his prophetology are essentially unpolitical doctrines.[33]

Now these unpolitical doctrines belong, as it were, to the framework of what Abravanel himself would have called his political teaching, i.e., of his discussion of the best form of human government as distinguished from divine government. Since the unpolitical framework was to Abravanel doubtless incomparably more important than its political content, and since, besides, the understanding of the former is indispensable for the right appreciation of the latter, it will be proper for us to describe the background of his political teaching somewhat more exactly than we have done up to now. That background is not only of an unpolitical, but even of an antipolitical character. As has been shown recently by Professor Baer,[34]

---

tian nations of Europe and the Turks for Palestine, does not change the character of his conception as a whole.

31 See his commentary on Isa. XI.

32 Those qualities, I venture to suggest, are ascribed by Abravanel not so much to *the* Messiah (i.e., the Messiah ben David) as to the Messiah ben Joseph, a Midrashic figure, not mentioned by Maimonides.

33 Restating the genuine teaching of the Bible against Maimonides' rationalistic and therefore political teaching, Abravanel goes sometimes farther in the opposite direction than does the Bible itself. The most striking example of this which occurs to me is his interpretation of Judges I, 19: Judah "could not drive out the inhabitants of the valley, because they had chariots of iron." Abravanel explains this passage in the following way: "Judah could not drive out the inhabitants of the valley, *not* because they had chariots of iron."

As regards the difference between Maimonides' political teaching and Abravanel's unpolitical teaching, I have to emphasize the following example. According to Maimonides, the main reason for the fact (told in Exod. XIII, 17f.) that God did not lead Israel on the direct way, through Philistia, to Palestine, was His intention of educating them in courage (*Guide*, Pt. III, ch. 24, p. 53*a* and ch. 32, pp. 70*b*–71*a*); according to Abravanel, on the other hand, the main reason was His intention to divide the sea for Israel and to drown the Egyptians (and there was no sea on the way through Philistia); see commentary on the passage (f. 125, cols. 1–2).

34 *Loc. cit.* pp. 248–53. I have to make only some slight additions to the ample evidence adduced by Baer. (*a*) Abravanel's description of the innocent life in the first period as a life "in the field" (Baer, p. 252) is literally taken over from Seneca, ep. 90 (§42, *agreste*

Chapter 1

Abravanel takes over from Seneca's 90th letter the criticism there developed of human civilization in general (of the [110] "artificial" and "superfluous" things) and of the city in particular. Following Josephus and the Christian Fathers, he combines that Hellenistic teaching with the teaching, in important respects similar, of the first chapters of Genesis. He conceives of urban life and of coercive government, as well as of private property, as productions of human rebellion against the natural order instituted by God: the only life in accordance with nature is a state of liberty and equality of all men, and the possession in common of the natural goods, or, as he seems to suggest at another place,[35] the life "in the field," of independent families. This criticism of all political, "artificial" life does not mean that Abravanel intends to replace the conception of the city as of something "artificial" by the conception of the nation as of something "natural"; for, according to Abravanel, the existence of nations, i.e., the disruption of the one human race into a plurality of nations, is not less "artificial," not less a result of sin, than is the existence of cities.[36] Thus, his criticism of political organization is truly all-comprehensive. And the ultimate reason of this anti-political view is Abravanel's anti-rationalism, the predominance in his thought of the belief in miracles. It is true he accepts the classical teaching of man's "natural" way of life in the beginning, in the Golden Age. But that "natural" state is understood by Abravanel to be of an essentially miraculous character.[37] It is highly significant that he finds an

---

domicilium). (*b*) Abravanel uses in his commentary on Gen. XI, 1 ff. (f. 42, col. 2) the doctrine of Poseidonios, discussed by Seneca, of the government of the best and wisest men in the Golden Age, in a modified form; he says that in the first period of the world, Divine Providence extended itself without any intermediary over mankind, and that, therefore, there were then always wise men, versed in theology. Cp. also Seneca, ep. 90, 44. (*c*) The criticism of Cain as the first founder of the city (Baer, 251) is to be found also in Josephus, *Ant.* 1, §62. (*d*) Abravanel uses the general criticism of civilization [110] most properly in his interpretation of Exod. XX, 25 (f. 143, col. 1). (*e*) The distinction between the three ways of life (the bestial, the political, and the theoretical life) (Baer, 251) is obviously taken from Aristotle, *Eth. Nic.* 1095*b*, 17 ff. That distinction had been applied to the three sons of Adam, in the same way as it is by Abravanel, by Maimonides; see *Guide*, Pt. II, ch. 30 and Ephodi's commentary.

35 Commentary on Gen. XI, 1 ff. (f. 41, cols. 1–2).

36 *Ibid.* (f. 42, cols. 1–2). According to Abravanel's usage, "nation" often has the meaning of "religious community"; he speaks, for example, of the "Christian nation" (see, e.g., *Ma'yene hay–Yeshu'ah*, XI, 8, and commentary on I Kings XV, 6, f. 250, col. 3).

37 Cp. p. 109, n. 2*b* above [p. 14, n. 34*b* —Eds.], with commentary on Josh. X, 12 (f. 21, col. 3).

analogy of man's "natural" state in the life led by Israel in the desert,[38] where Israel had to rely entirely for everything [111] on miraculous providence. Abravanel, as it were, interprets the "life in the fields," praised by Seneca and the Bucolics, in the spirit of Jeremiah's words (II, 2): "I remember for thee the kindness of thy youth, the love of thine espousals; how thou wentest after me in the wilderness, in a land that was not sown." The "natural" state of mankind is in principle not less miraculous than the Messianic age in which that natural state is to be restored. Maimonides, who held, to say the least, a rather hesitating attitude towards miracles, had adopted, without making any reservation apart from those made by Aristotle himself, the Aristotelian principle that man is naturally a political being; Abravanel, on the other hand, who unhesitatingly accepts all the miracles of the past and of the future, judges of man's political existence as being sinful in its origin, and not instituted, but only, as it were, reluctantly conceded to man, by God.[39] And, he goes on to say, it is with the political and urban life as with the king.[40] That is to say, Abravanel's political teaching, his discussion of the value of monarchy, or, more generally, of the best form of human government, to which I am turning now, is only an application, if the most interesting application, of his fundamental conception, which is strictly anti-political.

Abravanel deals with the question of the best form of human government in his commentaries both on Deut. XVII, 14 f., i.e., on the law which seems to command to Israel the institution of a king, and to I Sam. VIII, 6 f., i.e., on the narration that God and the prophet Samuel were offended by the fact that Israel did ask Samuel for a king.[41] The question is for Abravanel

---

38   Commentary on Gen. XI, 1 ff. (f. 41, col. 3). Cp. also commentary on Exod. XVIII, 13–27 (f. 134, col. 2) on the connection between the absence of slavery among the Israelites while they were wandering through the desert (i.e., between their being then in a state of "natural" equality) and their miraculous maintenance by the manna.

39   Bound by Gen. II, 18, however, he occasionally adopts that Aristotelian proposition. See Baer, *loc. cit.* pp. 249 f.

40   Commentary on Gen. XI, 1 ff. (f. 41, col. 3).

41   The treatment of the question is in both versions (in the earlier version in the commentary on I Sam. VIII, 6 f. (f. 91, col. 2 – f. 93, col. 4), and in the later version in the commentary on Deut. XVII, 14 f. (f. 295, col. 2 – f. 296, col. 2) identical as regards the tendency, and even, to a large extent, literally identical. The earlier version is the more important as regards the details of the criticism of kingship; but only the later version provides us with an insight into Abravanel's conception of the ideal government as a whole: his explanation of Deut. XVII, 14 f. is only the continuation of his statements

CHAPTER 1

thus primarily an exegetical one: how are the two apparently opposed passages of the Bible to be reconciled? Proceeding [112] in the scholastic way, Abravanel begins with surveying and criticizing the earlier attempts, made by Jews and Christians,[42] to solve that exegetical problem. He shows that all those attempts, in spite of their divergencies, and apart from the individual deficiencies of each of them, are based on one and the same decisive assumption. All the earlier commentators mentioned by Abravanel assumed that Israel's asking for a king was a sin, not as such, but only because of the manner or circumstances of their demand. In other words, those commentators presupposed that Deut. XVII, 14f. expresses a Divine command to institute a king. This, however, includes the further presupposition that monarchy is a good, nay, that it is the best form of human government; for God would not have given His nation any political constitution but the best. Consequently, Abravanel has to discuss first whether monarchy is indeed the best form of human government, and secondly, whether the meaning of Deut. XVII, 14f. is that Israel is commanded to institute a king.

The first discussion is a criticism, based on reason only, of the monarchist teaching of *the* philosophers, i.e., of Aristotle[43] and his medieval followers. That discussion is, unfortunately, far from being of scholastic orderliness and precision.[44] But the main argument is quite clear. The philosophers who are criticized by Abravanel asserted the necessity of monarchic government by comparing the relation of the king to the political community with the relation of the heart to the human body, and with the relation of the First Cause to the universe.[45] Against such kinds

---

concerning the government of the Jewish nation in general, which are to be found [112] in his interpretation of Deut. XVI, 18ff. These statements have not been taken into account by Baer, nor by Ephraim E. Urbach, "Die Staatsauffassung des Don Isaak Abrabanel," *Monatsschrift für Geschichte und Wissenschaft des Judentums*, 1937, pp. 257–70, who come, therefore, to conclusions more or less different from those set forth in the present article.

42 The three opinions of Christian commentators, which are dealt with in the earlier version, are not, however, discussed in the later version.

43 See commentary on I Sam. VIII, 6f. (f. 92, col. 1).

44 It has been made somewhat more lucid in the later version.

45 Those comparisons were known to Abravanel not only from Christian sources, but also and primarily from Jewish and Islamic ones. In his commentary on Exod. XVIII, 13–27 (f. 134, col. 2) he expressly refers to Fārābī's *Principles of the beings* (i.e., to the Hebrew translation of *k. al-siyyāsāt al-madaniyya*) [113] as proving the necessity of hierarchy leading up to one chief, and in the sentence immediately following that

On Abravanel's Philosophical Tendency and Political Teaching

of proof Abravanel objects that [113] they are based on a μετάβασις εἰς ἄλλο γένος, on a μετάβασις from things natural and necessary to things merely possible and subject to the human will. Those philosophers tried, further, to prove the necessity of monarchic government by contending that the three indispensable conditions of well-ordered government are fulfilled only in a monarchy. Those conditions are: unity, continuity, and absolute power. As regards unity, Abravanel states that it may well be achieved by the consent of many governors.[46] As regards continuity, he doubts whether the annual change of governors, who have to answer for their conduct of public affairs after the expiration of their office, and who are, therefore, restrained by "fear of flesh and blood" (*Mora' Basar wa-Dham*) and by their being ashamed of their crimes becoming publicly denounced and punished, is not much to be preferred to the irresponsible, though continuous, government of one. As regards absolute power, Abravanel denies altogether that it is indispensable or desirable: the power of the governors ought to be limited by the laws. He adduces, further, in favour of the government of many, the principle of majority, as accepted by the Jewish law in matters of the interpretation of the law, and the statement made by Aristotle "in the beginning of the *Metaphysics*" that the truth is more easily reached by the collaboration of many than by the exertions of one.[47] After having thus disposed of the philosophic arguments in favour of monarchy, Abravanel turns to the teaching of experience; for, as Aristotle "has taught us," "experience prevails over the syllogism." Now the experience [114] of the present shows that such states as Venice, Florence,[48] Genoa, Lucca, Siena, Bologna and others, which are governed,

---

reference, he mentions the examples of the hierarchy in the human body, and of the universal hierarchy which leads up to the First Cause. (Cp. Fārābī, *loc. cit.* ed. Hyderabad, 1346, H., p. 54, and *Musterstaat*, ed. Dieterici, pp. 54 ff. See also Maimonides, *Guide*, Pt. I, ch. 72.) In the passage mentioned, Abravanel accepts those examples and the monarchist consequence derived from them, while he rejects them in his commentary on Deut. XVII, 14 f. and on I Sam. VIII, 6 f.

46 Cp. Marsilius of Padua, *Defensor pacis*, lib. I, cap. 15, §2.

47 The passage which Abravanel has in mind is the beginning of Α ἔλ. (993*a*, 30 ff.). I wonder why he did not quote such more suitable passages as *Politics*, III, 16 (1287*b*), and VII, 14 (1332*b*–1333*a*). It may be that he knew the *Politics* only from quotations.

48 Cp. Lionardo Bruni's *Oratio in funere Nannis Strozae* (in Baluzius, *Miscellanea*, III, pp. 230 ff.): "Forma reipublicae gubernandae utimur ad libertatem paritatemque civium maxime omnium directa: quae quia aequalissima in omnibus est, popularis nuncupatur. Neminem unum quasi dominum horremus, non paucorum potentiae in-

Chapter 1

not by monarchs, but by "judges" elected for limited periods of office, are much superior to the monarchies, as regards both administration of justice and military achievements. And the experience of the past teaches that Rome, when governed by Consuls, conquered the world, while it declined under the emperors. In eloquent sentences which betray a deep hatred of kings and their ways, Abravanel contrasts the admirable character of classical or modern republics with the horrors of monarchies. He arrives at the conclusion that the existence of a king is not only not necessary for a political community, but that it is even an enormous danger and a great harm to it, and that the origin of kingdoms is not the free election of the king by the people, but force and violence.[49]

In spite of his strong indictment of monarchic government, [115] Abravanel no less strongly contends that, if in a country a monarchy exists, the subjects are bound to strict obedience to the king. He informs us that he has not seen in the writings of Jews a discussion of the question whether the people has the right to rebel against the king, or to depose him in case the king becomes a tyrant, and that the Christian scholars who did discuss that question, decided that the people had such a right, according to the classical precedent of the defection of the ten tribes from

---

servimus.... Monarchiae laus veluti ficta quaedam et umbratilis (est), non autem expressa et solida.... Nec multum secus accidit in dominatu paucorum. Ita popularis una relinquitur legitima reipublicae gubernandae forma, in qua libertas vera sit, in qua aequitas juris cunctis partier civibus, in qua virtutum studia vigere absque suspicione possint.... Ingeniis vero ac intelligentia sic valent cives nostri ut in ea quidem laude pares non multi, qui vero anteponendi sint, nulli reperiantur. Acritas quidem inest atque industria, et in rebus agendis celeritas et agilitas, animique magnitudo rebus sufficiens. Nec in moderanda republica solum nec in domestica tantum disciplina... valemus, sed etiam bellica gloria insignes sumus. Nam majores quidem nostri ...finitimos omnes populos virtute bellica superarunt.... Nostra semper civitas... scientissimos rei militaris duces procreavit."

49 Cp. John of Salisbury, *Policraticus*, lib. IV, cap. 11: "Regum scrutare historiam, ad hoc petitum regem a Deo invenies, ut praecederet faciem populi.... Qui tamen non fuerat necessarius, nisi et Israel praevaricatus esset in similitudinem gentium, ut Deo rege sibi non videretur esse contentus.... Hospitem meum Placentinum dixisse recolo... hoc in civitatibus Italiae usu frequenti celeberrimum esse, quod dum pacem diligunt, et iustitiam colunt, et periuriis abstinent, tantae libertatis et pacis gaudio perfruuntur, quod nihil est omnino, quod vel in minimo quietem eorum concutiat.... Adiiciebat etiam quod merita populi omnem evacuant principatum, aut eum faciunt esse mitissimum...." *Ibid.* lib. VIII, cap. 17: "Nisi enim iniquitas, et iniustitia... tyrannidem procurasset, omnino regna non essent, quae... iniquitas aut per se praesumpsit, aut extorsit a domino."

Rehoboam. Abravanel, who had spoken about this subject "before kings with their wise men," judges that the people has no right to rebellion or deposition, even if the king commits every crime. For the people has, when crowning the king, made a covenant with him by which it promised to him obedience; "and that covenant and oath was not conditional, but absolute; and, therefore, he who rebels against the king is guilty of death, whether the king is righteous or wicked; for it is not the people that inquires into the king's righteousness or wickedness." Besides, the king represents God; he is an image of God as regards both absolute power (the extra-legal actions of the king correspond to the miracles) and unity (the king is unique in his kingdom, as God is unique in His universe). The king is, therefore, entitled to a kind of honour which has something in common with the honour owed by man to God. Consequently, any attempt on the side of the people to depose or to punish their king, is in a sense sacrilegious.[50] It is obvious that the second argument is contradictory to the assertions made by Abravanel two or three pages earlier, in his discussion of the value of monarchy. It would, however, be unfair perhaps to so prolific a writer as Abravanel, to attach too much stress to his inconsistencies; and in particular to the present inconsistency.[51] For if the second argument used [116] by him in support of his thesis, that the people has no right to depose or punish a tyrannous king, is inconsistent with his denial of the value of monarchy, the thesis itself is perfectly consistent with his main contention, that monarchy, as such, is an enormous danger and a great evil.

Was, then, the political ideal of Abravanel the republic? He does not use a word which could be translated by "republic"; the kind of government which he praises is called by him government of "many." This is very vague indeed. The statements occurring in his criticism of monarchy might convey the impression that his ideal was democracy. But, as we shall see later, he accepted the doctrine of the necessity of a "mixed" constitution. Thus, his ideal cannot have been a "pure" constitution of any kind. I believe we

---

50 Commentary on Deut. XVII, 16–20 (f. 296, col. 4; f. 297, col. 1). Abravanel further adduces a third argument which, however, applies to Jewish kings only. Cp. also his commentaries on Judges IV, 9 (f. 46, col. 1); on I Kings II, 37 (f. 202, col. 3); on I Kings XIII, 2 (f. 246, col. 1); and on I Kings XII *passim*.

51 Cp. also above, p. 112, n. 45. Another example of this kind of inconsistency may be mentioned in passing. In his commentary on I Sam. VIII, 7 (f. 93, col. 4), [116] i.e., only two or three pages after he had finished the proof that the existence of a king is not necessary in any nation, Abravanel says: "the king is necessary for the other nations" (for all nations except Israel).

Chapter 1

would not be wide of the mark if we defined his political ideal by saying that it was, like that of Calvin[52] one or two generations later, an "aristocracy near to democracy."[53] But in order to avoid any hypothesis, we shall do best to confine ourselves to the statement that Abravanel's political ideal was the republic. For "republic" is a term of a polemic and negative character; it does not say more than "not monarchy," without defining whether that non-monarchical government desired is democratic, aristocratic, oligarchic, and so on.[54] And what Abravanel says of the best form of human government is hardly more than just this: that it is unmonarchical.

But was the political ideal of Abravanel really the republican city-state? That this was the case is most unlikely from the outset. If it were the case, it would betray not only inconsistency—inconsistent Abravanel admittedly was—but even an almost insane looseness of thought. Indeed, it is [117] inconceivable that the very man who, in accordance with his deepest theological convictions, judged the city to be the work of human wickedness, should have been at the same time a genuine and unreserved admirer of the worldly greatness of Rome and Venice. One cannot explain the contradiction by supposing that Abravanel was merely a humanist orator who was able to devote eloquent sentences to any subject. For, eloquent though he could be, he certainly was no sophist: he had a strong and sincere belief in the one truth. The only possible explanation is that Abravanel's admiration for the classical and modern city-states was not more than a tribute which he paid to the fashion of his time; that it was a sidetrack into which he was guided occasionally, if on more than one occasion, by the influence of humanism, but primarily by his disgust at kings and their worldly splendour, which had a deeper root than the humanist influence.

Before beginning to define the true character of Abravanel's political ideal, let us emphasize the fact that the exaltation of the republican city-state belongs to the discussion, based on reason only, of the best form of human government, i.e., to a mere prelude to the central discussion of it, which is based on the Scripture only. After what has been said about Abravanel's philosophical tendency, there is no need for a further proof of the

---

52 *Institutio*, lib. IV, cap. 20, §8 (with regard to the Jewish commonwealth).

53 The aristocratic element in the ideal constitution, as conceived by Abravanel, i.e., of the Jewish constitution, is the *Synhedrion* of 70. Cp. also commentary on Exod. XVIII, 13–27 (f. 134, col. 3). Abravanel's ideal is characterized as *"status aristocratus"* by Menasseh ben Israel, *Conciliator*, qu. 6, ad Deut. (Frankfort, 1633, p. 227).

54 Cp. Montesquieu's definition in *De l'esprit des lois*, livre II, ch. 1.

On Abravanel's Philosophical Tendency and Political Teaching

assertion that only his interpretation of the teaching of the Scripture can provide us with his authentic conception of the ideal form of human government. What, then, does the Scripture teach concerning the human government of Israel?

This question is answered by Abravanel both precisely and lucidly. He begins by stating his thesis, which runs as follows: Even if he granted that the king is useful and necessary in all other nations for the ordering of the political community and for its protection—which, however, he does not grant, but even vigorously denies—even in that case the king would certainly not be necessary for the Jewish nation. For their king is God, and, therefore, they need, even incomparably less than the other nations, a king of flesh and blood. A king could be necessary for three purposes: for military leadership, for legislation, and for extraordinary power to punish [118] the wicked. All those purposes are achieved in Israel in the most perfect way by God, who vouchsafes His particular providence to His elected nation. Thus, a king is not necessary in Israel. He is even most dangerous in Israel. Experience has shown that all the kings of Israel and most of the kings of Judah led Israel and Judah into idolatry, while the judges and the prophets were, all of them, godfearing men. This proves that the leadership of "judges" is good, while that of kings is bad. The result, at which the discussion based on reason only had arrived, is confirmed by the scrutiny of the Scripture, and particularly of the biblical narratives. More exactly, that result has undergone, as a consequence of the scrutiny of the Bible, an important precision, which is, at the same time, an important correction: the ideal form of human government is not the republic as such, but a "republican" government, instituted and guided by God.[55]

Arrived at this point, Abravanel has yet to overcome the greatest difficulty. The earlier Jewish commentators, whose views he had criticized to begin with, were no less familiar with the innumerable passages of the Bible which attribute the kingship to God, than he himself was. They also remembered, no less well than he did, the evil which Israel and Judah had experienced under their wicked kings. But they remembered also the deeds and words of such godfearing kings as David, the author of many Psalms, as Solomon, the author of the Song of Songs, and as Jotham, Hezekiah, and Josiah, who were "saints of the Highest."[56] And, even more

---

55 See also Urbach, *loc. cit.* pp. 263f.
56 Cp. Abravanel's Introduction to his commentary on the Books of the Kings (f. 188, col. 3).

important than this, the Messiah for whose speedy coming they prayed, was conceived of by them as a king. Now, as regards the last point, Abravanel was consistent enough to deny that the Messiah is a king properly speaking: the Messiah, too, is, according to him, not a king, but a prophet and a judge.[57] But this conception of the leadership of the Messiah is already based on the truly decisive assumption [119] that the institution of a king in Israel was not expressly commanded by God. The earlier commentators were convinced that Deut. XVII, 14f. did express such a command. As long as the difficulty offered by that passage was not overcome, all other passages of the Bible which Abravanel might adduce in support of his thesis were of little weight. For none of those other passages contained a definite law concerning the institution of kingship in Israel.

Abravanel denies that Deut. XVII, 14f. expresses a command to institute a king in Israel. According to him, that passage merely gives permission to do this. We need not examine whether his interpretation is right or not. What matters for us is, that the interpretation rejected by Abravanel was accepted as legally binding by Jewish tradition, which was, as a rule, decidedly in favour of monarchy. The traditional interpretation had been accepted in particular by Maimonides, who had embodied it in his great legal work as well as in his *Sepher ham-Miṣvoth*.[58] According to the inter-

---

57   See Baer, *loc. cit.* p. 259.

58   It was accepted also, for example, by Naḥmanides, Moses of Coucy, Gersonides, and Bachya ben Asher. (This is not to deny that Gersonides' and Bachya's statements in their commentaries on Deut. XVII, 14f. are almost as much anti-monarchistic as those of Abravanel—there are a number of important literal concords between the statements of Abravanel and those of both Gersonides and Bachya—but still, both of them interpret the passage in question as conveying a command to institute a king.) As far as I know, the only Jewish medieval commentator who, in his commentary on Deut. XVII, 14ff., expressly understands that passage as conveying a permission is Ibn Ezra. The exceptional character of Abravanel's interpretation is implicitly recognized by Moses Hayyim Alshekh (*Mar'oth haṣ-Ṣobe'oth*, on I Sam. VIII, 6f.) who vigorously rejects that interpretation by referring himself to the Jewish tradition, and expressly by Menasseh ben Israel (*Conciliator*, ed. cit. p. 228), who says: "*Haec opinio (sc. Abravanelis) quamvis satis congrua verbis S. Scripturae, a multis tamen accepta non est, quia adversatur sententiae ac traditioni antiquorum.*" Abravanel's interpretation was tacitly accepted by Moses Mendelssohn (*Jerusalem*, Berlin, 1783, II, pp. 117ff.), and rejected by S. R. Hirsch and by Buber-Rosenzweig. Cp. also Isaak Heinemann, *Philos. griechische und jüdische Bildung*, Breslau, 1932, pp. 185f., and Urbach, *loc. cit.* p. 269. (The essay of Heinrich Heinemann in the *Jahrbuch der Jüdisch-literarischen Gesellschaft*, 1916, was not accessible to me.)

pretation accepted by the Jewish tradition, Deut. XVII, 14 f. would have to be translated as follows:

> When thou art come unto the land which the Lord thy God giveth thee, and shalt possess it, and shalt dwell therein; and shalt [120] say (or:[59] *then thou shalt say*), I will set a king over me, like as all the nations that are round about me; *Thou shalt in any wise set a king over thee.* Thou shalt set him king over thee, whom the Lord Thy God shall choose: one from among thy brethren shalt thou set over thee: thou mayest not put a foreigner over thee, which is not thy brother.

According to Abravanel's interpretation, the passage in question would read as follows:

> When thou art come unto the land which the Lord Thy God giveth thee, and shalt possess it, and shalt dwell therein; and shalt say, I will set a king over me, like as all the nations that are round about me; *then thou shalt set him king over thee whom the Lord Thy God shall choose:* one from among thy brethren shalt thou set king over thee: thou mayest not put a foreigner over thee, which is not thy brother.

According to the traditional interpretation, the purport of the law, contained in the passage, is that Israel is commanded to institute a king. According to Abravanel's interpretation, its purport is that, *if* Israel wishes to institute a king—and to do this, Israel is by the law implicitly permitted, but permitted only—then Israel may do it only in such and such a manner. Now Abravanel's interpretation, which is directly opposed to that of the Jewish tradition, is in substance identical with that implied in the Vulgate.[60] Abravanel is, of course, much more explicit than the Vulgate can be.[61]

---

59 According to Naḥmanides.

60 "Cum ingressus fueris terram, quam Dominus Deus tuus dabit tibi, et possederis eam, habitaverisque in illa, et dixeris: Constituam super me regem, sicut habent omnes per circuitum nationes; *eum constitues, quem Dominus tuus elegerit de numero fratrum tuorum....*" Cp. also the English translation: "...Thou shalt in any wise set *him* king over thee, whom the Lord thy God shall choose...."

61 It will be proper to give a more complete (if partially free) rendering of Abravanel's interpretation by putting his explanatory remarks on the biblical words into brackets. He explains: "When thou art come unto the land which the Lord Thy God giveth thee, and shalt possess it, and shalt dwell therein [i.e., it will be foolish that in the time of the wars, during the conquest of the land, you will not ask for a king; for this would be the most proper time for the need for a king; but after you will possess the land, and you will have divided it, and you will dwell in it in safety, and this will have hap-

CHAPTER 1

And, apart from this, he goes much further than the Latin transla-[121]tion does. He says, explaining the passage in question more precisely:

> (When thou shalt wish to do this), in spite of its not being proper, (thou mayest not do it but in such and such a manner). This is similar to the section of the law which runs as follows: When thou goest forth to battle against thine enemies, and the Lord thy God deliverest them into thine hands... and seest among the captives a beautiful woman, and thou hast a desire unto her... For there the precept is not that he shall desire her, and not that he shall take her to him to wife..., since this is permitted only, and an effect of the wicked inclination. But the precept is that, after the first cohabitation, thou shalt bring her home into thine house... Israel was not commanded in the Torah to ask for a king..., and the king was not necessary and indispensable for the government of their gatherings..., for God was their king truly... Therefore, when Israel asked for a king..., the anger of the Lord was kindled against them, and He said: they have not rejected thee, but they have rejected me, that I should not be king over them; and Samuel said: ye said unto me, Nay, but a king shall reign over us; when the Lord your God was your king. This shows that the sin consisted in their "kicking" at God's kingship and their choosing a human kingship. For this reason, neither Joshua nor the other Judges instituted a king."

The final expression of Abravanel's interpretation is that Deut. XVII, 14 f. contains a permission given "with regard to the wicked inclination" (*Yeṣer ha-Ra'*). Now this more precise expression, too, is in substance borrowed from a Christian source. That source is the *Postilla* of Nicolas of Lyra.[62]

---

pened by the providence of God, without there being then a king—then, without any necessity and need whatsoever] thou shalt say, I will set a king over me [namely] like as all the nations that are round about me [i.e., for no other necessity and purpose (but [121] to assimilate yourselves to the nations of the world); when this will happen], thou shalt [not] set [him] king over thee [whom you wish, but him] whom the Lord thy God shall choose...." Commentary on I Sam. VIII, 6 f. (f. 93, cols. 1–2).

62 Nicolas says on Deut. XVII, 14 f.: "non est praeceptum, nec simplex concessio, quia sic non peccasset populus Israel petendo regem, cujus contrarium dicitur I Reg. XII: sed est permissio quae est de malo. Bonum enim populi consistebat in hoc, quod solus Deus regnaret super eum, eo quod erat populus peculiaris Dei; veruntamen si importune regem habere vellent, permittebatur eis, sub conditionibus tamen...." This is explained more fully in the *Postilla* on I Reg. VIII: "illud quod dicitur Deut. 17 de constitutione regis... non fuit concessio proprie dicta, sed magis permissio, sicut repudium uxoris fuit permissum ad duritiam cordis eorum...." The comparison shows that Abravanel has merely replaced Nicolas' example by the example of the

"beautiful woman." But the point of view of Abravanel is identical with that of Nicolas. There is one important difference between the Jewish and the Christian commentator: while Abravanel thinks that monarchy is intrinsically bad, Nicolas is of the [122] opinion that monarchy is in principle the best form of government. Nicolas only contests that that which holds true of all other nations, holds equally true of Israel, the nation governed by God. Only this part of Nicolas' argument has been taken over by Abravanel. (Cp. the beginning of Abravanel's discussion concerning monarchy in Israel: "Even if we grant, that the king is most necessary in the nation for the ordering of the political community... he is not necessary in the nation of Israel....") Nicolas says on I Reg. VIII: "Ad maiorem praedictorum evidentiam quaeritur, utrum filii Israel peccaverint petendo super se regem. Et arguitur quod non, quia petere illud quod est bonum simpliciter, et de dictamine rationis rectae, non est peccatum; gubernatio autem populi per regem est optima, ut dicit Philosophus 3. Politicorum. et per consequens est de dictamine rationis rectae.... Item illud quod conceditur lege divina licitum est, quia nullum peccatum concedit, sed Deut. 17. c. concedit lex divina filiis Israel constitutionem regis.... [Notice that even in this "monarchist" objection Deut. XVII, 14 f. is understood to contain a *concessio* only.] Contra infra 12. c. dicitur: Scietis et videbitis.... Ad hoc dicendum quod, cum regnum sit optima politia, caeterae gentes a filiis Israel petendo vel constituendo super se regem non peccaverunt, sed magis bonum egerunt. Filii autem Israel hoc faciendo peccaverunt.... Cuius ratio est, quia Deus populum Israel elegit sibi specialem et peculiarem prae caeteris populis... et idem voluit esse rex immediatus illius populi... propter quod voluit homines gubernatores illius populi ab ipso immediate institui, tanquam eius vicarii essent, et non reges vel domini: ut patet in Moyse et Josue, et de iudicibus sequentibus...." (That Abravanel knew the *Postilla*, is shown by his express quotations from it—see Guttmann, *loc. cit.* p.46. But, apart from that, that interpretation given by earlier commentators of Deut. XVII, 14f. (or I Sam. VIII, 6f.) which he esteems most highly and which he discusses most fully, is the interpretation given by Paulus of Burgos, and this interpretation is to be found in Paulus' *Additiones* to the *Postilla*.) Cp. further Thomas Aquinas, *Summa theologiae*, II, 1, qu. 105, art. 1: "regnum est optimum regimen populi, si non corrumpatur. Sed... de facili regnum degenerat in tyrannidem... ideo *Dominus a principio* (Judaeis) *regem non instituit* cum plena potestate, sed judicem et gubernatorem in eorum custodiam; sed postea regem ad petitionem populi *quasi indignatus concessit*, ut patet per hoc quod dixit ad Samuel I Reg. 8, 7.... Instituit tamen a principio [123] circa regem instituendum, primo quidem modum eligendi.... Secundo ordinavit circa reges institutos...." The fact that the kings had absolute power, while the power of the judges was more limited, is stressed by Abravanel in the introduction to his commentary on Judges (f.40, col.1). Cp. also John of Salisbury, *Policraticus*, lib. VIII, cap. 18: "... primi patres et patriarchae vivendi ducem optimum naturam secuti sunt. Successerunt duces a Moyse sequentes legem, et iudices qui legis auctoritate regebant populum; et eosdem fuisse legimus sacerdotes. Tandem in furore Domini dati sunt reges, alii quidem boni, alii vero mali... populus... a Deo, quem contempserat, sibi regem extorsit... (Saul) tamen christus Domini dictus est, et tirannidem exercens regium non amisit honorem...." With this passage, the whole of Abravanel's political

CHAPTER 1

Thus [122] we are entitled to say that Abravanel's interpretation of Deut. XVII, 14 f., i.e., of the chief biblical passage, or, in other words, that his opinion concerning the incompatibility of monarchy with the constitution of Israel, goes immediately back to Christian, not to Jewish sources.

Generally speaking, both the Jewish and the Christian tradition, and in particular both the Jewish and the Christian Middle Ages, were in favour of monarchy. Anti-monarchist statements are, in both traditions, exceptional up to the humanist age. Thus one is at a loss to state which of the two traditions shows a comparatively stronger monarchist (or anti-monarchist) trend than the other. One could, however, dare to make such a statement if it were based on a com-[123]parison of comparable magnitudes, i.e., of a Jewish source which is at the same time authoritative and popular, with the corresponding Christian source. Now if we compare the manner in which the Jewish Bible on the one hand (i.e., the Targum Onḳelos, the Targum Jonathan, and the commentaries of Rashi, Ibn Ezra and Naḥmanides), and the Christian (Latin) Bible on the other (i.e., the *Glossa interlinearis*, the *Glossa ordinaria*, the *Postilla* of Nicolas of Lyra, and the *Additiones* of Paulus Burgensis) deal with the chief passage, i.e., with the law concerning the institution of a king, we find that the Jewish Bible shows not the slightest sign of an anti-monarchist tendency,[63] while the Christian Bible exhibits a definite anti-monarchist trend, based on theocratic assumptions.[64] The only exception to this rule in the Christian Bible

---

teaching should be compared. As regards the later development, I would refer the reader particularly to Milton, *Pro populo Anglicano defensio contra Salmasii Defensionem Regiam*, cap. 2. It is interesting in our connection to observe that, while Salmasius (*Defensio Regia*, cap. 2) makes ample use of the rabbinic interpretations of Deut. XVII, 14 f. (and of I Sam. VIII) for the proof of his royalist thesis, Milton much prefers Josephus to the "tenebrionibus Rabbinis" (cp. on Josephus below, p. 127 [pp. 30–31—Eds.]).

63 The Targum Onḳelos renders the passage literally. The Targum Jonathan renders the words "Thou shalt in any wise set a king over thee, whom the Lord thy God shall choose: one from among thy brethren shalt thou set king over thee," in the following way: "You shall inquire for instruction before the Lord, and afterwards appoint the king over you." Rashi does not say anything on the passage. Ibn Ezra simply says that the passage expresses a permission, Naḥmanides conceives of it as containing a command to ask for a king and to institute a king.

64 The *Glossa interlinearis* remarks on "et dixeris": "Tu non ego," and on "Constituam super me regem": "Non Deum sed hominem." The *Glossa ordinaria* (Augustinus, qu. 26) says: "Quaeri potest cur displicuit populus Deo, cum regem desideravit, cum hic inveniatur esse permissus? Sed intelligendum est merito non fuisse secundum volutatem Dei, quia hoc fieri non praecepit sed desiderantibus permisit." As regards the

On Abravanel's Philosophical Tendency and Political Teaching

[124] is the explanation of the passage in question given by Paulus of Burgos, i.e., by a baptized Jew. The result of this comparison confirms our impression that the immediate origin of Abravanel's anti-monarchist conclusions from his theocratic premises has to be sought for, not in Jewish, but in Christian sources.

Of Christian origin is, above all, Abravanel's general conception of the government of the Jewish nation. According to him, that government consists of two kinds of governments, of a government human and of a government spiritual or divine. This distinction is simply the Christian distinction between the authority spiritual and the authority temporal. Abravanel further divides each of these two governments into three degrees. As regards the government human, the lowest degree is the "little *Beth-Din*," i.e., the court of justice of every town. The members of those courts are elected by the people. The second degree of the government human is the "great *Beth-Din*," i.e., the *Synhedrion* in Jerusalem. The members of the *Synhedrion* are not elected by the people, but nominated either by the king, or, if there is no king, by the president of the *Synhedrion*, after consultation with the other members; the president himself is chosen by the members of the *Synhedrion*. This body, being an image of the seventy elders led by Moses, consists of seventy-one persons. The highest place in human government is occupied by the king. The king is chosen by God, not by the people, who have, therefore, no right whatsoever to rebel against the king or to depose him. The office of the king is not the administration of justice, but, in the first instance, military leadership, and then the extrajudicial punishment of the wicked in cases of urgency. His claim to obedience and honour is stressed by Abravanel scarcely less than it is by Maimonides; in this respect both alike are simply following Jewish tradition.[65] If one takes into [125] account Abravanel's criticism

---

Postilla, see above. Paulus Burgensis says "Praeceptum istud de constitutione regis non est permissive [124] intelligendum... sed est simplex concessio cum conditionibus in litera scriptis. Nec sequitur quod si sit concessio simplex, tunc non peccaset populus Israel petendo regem. Nam pertierunt regem aliter quam fuit sibi concessum."

65 Commentary on Deut. XVI, 18–XVII, 1, and on XVII, 8–15 (f. 293, cols. 1–2; f. 294, col. 1; f. 296, cols. 2–3). Cp. commentary on I Kings I (f. 196, col. 4) and Introduction to commentary on Judges (f. 39, col. 3, f. 40, col. 1). In the [125] commentary on Deut. XVI, 18–XVII, 13 (f. 293, col. 2 and f. 294, col. 2) Abravanel says, however, that the extraordinary power of jurisdiction belongs, not to the king, but to the *Synhedrion*. Following the ruling of the Jewish tradition, he points out that all appointments in Israel are for life, and, in principle, hereditary (*loc. cit.* f. 293, col. 2). In his "rational"

Chapter 1

of monarchy in general and of monarchy in Israel in particular, one has to define his view concerning the highest degree of human government in the Jewish nation more exactly by saying that the chief of that government is, according to the original intention of the legislator, not a king properly speaking, but a leader of the kind that Moses and the Judges were. As a matter of fact, Abravanel expressly states that "the first king who reigned over Israel" was Moses.[66] At any rate, the human government of the Jewish nation, as Abravanel sees it, consists of a monarchic element (Moses and his successors), of an aristocratic element (the Sanhedrin), and of a democratic element (the local judges elected by the people). It is a "mixed" government, in full accordance with the classical doctrine. The immediate source of this view of Abravanel is again a Christian one: Thomas Aquinas' description of the Jewish constitution in the *Summa theologiae*,[67] which has been altered by Abravanel only in detail. So much about Abravanel's conception of the government human. As regards the government spiritual, he again distinguishes three degrees: the prophet, who is the chief; the priests; and, in the lowest category, the Levites.[68] This distinction implies that the [126] hierarchy spiritual, not less than the hierarchy human, leads up to a monarchical head. In this, again, Abravanel is following the teaching of the Christian Middle Ages, according to which the government of the whole church must be monarchical: he merely replaces Petrus (or his successors) by the prophet.[69] The government spir-

---

discussion of the best form of human government, he showed a definite preference for short periods of office.

66 Commentary on I Kings I (f. 196, col. 4). See also commentary on Exod. XVIII, 13–27 (f. 134, col. 1).

67 II, 1, qu. 105, art. 1. Thomas defines the character of the government instituted by the *lex vetus* by calling that government a "politia bene commixta ex regno, inquantum unus praeest, ex aristocratia, inquantum multi principantur secundum virtutem, et ex democratia, id est, potestate populi, inquantum ex popularibus possunt eligi principes, et ad populum pertinet electio principum. Et hoc fuit institutum secundum legem divinam; nam Moyses et ejus successores (*sc.* Josua, Judices, et reges) gubernabant populum, quasi singulariter omnibus principantes, quod est *quaedam species regni*. Eligebantur autem septuaginta duo seniores secundum virtutem... et hoc erat aristocraticum. Sed democraticum erat quod isti de omni populo eligebantur...." Cp. also the passage from the same article quoted above, p. 121, n. 1 [p. 25, n. 62 —Eds.].

68 Commentary on Deut. XVI, 18–XVII, 1 (f. 293, col. 1), and on XVIII, 1–8 (f. 297, cols. 1–2).

69 Cp. Thomas Aquinas, *Summa contra Gentiles*, lib. IV, cap. 76.

itual, as conceived by Abravanel, is, of course, not purely monarchical; it contains also an aristocratic and, perhaps, a democratic element. This view of the spiritual hierarchy is also borrowed from Christians.[70] And it is for Abravanel no less a matter of course than it is for the papalist writers among the Christians, that human government, and, in particular, government by kings, which was not instituted by, but extorted from God, is much inferior in dignity to the government spiritual. And, besides, the aristocratic element of the human government of the Jewish nation, the *Synhedrion*, consists, as Abravanel points out, mainly of priests and Levites.[71] The ideal commonwealth, as understood by Abravanel, is governed mainly by prophets and priests; and the ideal leader is for him not, as for Maimonides, a philosopher king, but a priest king.[72] His political ideal is of a strictly hierocratic character. He was, as far as I know, the first Jew who became deeply influenced by Christian political thought. It deserves to be stressed that he adopted the views of the extreme papalists. He had preferred Christian scholasticism to the philosophy of the Jewish rationalists, and he arrived at a political ideal which was nearer to the ideal of Gregory VII[73] and Innocent III than to that of Maimonides. He had undermined Maimonides' political philosophy of the law by contesting its ultimate [127] assumption that the city is "natural," and by conceiving of the city as a product of human sin, i.e., he had started from unpolitical, and even antipolitical premises, and he arrived at the political creed of clericalism.

But however great the influence of Christian medieval thought on Abravanel's political teaching may have been, that influence scarcely accounts for his so-called republicanism. This part of his political creed is not of Christian medieval, but of humanist origin. Humanism means going back from the tradition to the sources of the tradition. *The* sources, however, are for Abravanel, not so much the historians, poets and orators

---

70 Bellarmin, *De Romano Pontifice*, lib. I, cap. 5: "Jam vero doctores catholici conveniunt omnes, ut regimen ecclesiasticum hominibus a Deo commissum, sit illud quidem monarchicum, sed temperatum ... ex aristocratia et dimocratia."

71 Commentary on Deut. XVII, 8–13 (f. 294, col. 2–3).

72 Commentary on I Kings I (f. 196, col. 4) and on Exod. XVIII, 13–27 (f. 134, cols. 1–2). Cp. John of Salisbury, *Policraticus*, lib. VIII, cap. 18 (quoted above, p. 121, n. 1 [pp. 25–26, n. 62 —Eds.]) and Augustinus Triumphus, *Summa de potestate ecclesiastica*, Pt. I, qu. 1, art. 7–8.

73 Cp. with Abravanel's statements those of Gregory VII and others, quoted by Carlyle, *A History of Mediaeval Political Theory in the West*, III (2nd ed.), pp. 94 and 99.

Chapter 1

of classical antiquity, but the literal sense of the Bible—and Josephus.[74] Josephus understood Deut. XVII, 14 f. as permitting only, not commanding, the institution of a king. And he unequivocally states that the government instituted by Moses was an aristocracy as opposed to a monarchy.[75] Above all, the ἄριστοι, who govern the Jewish state, are identified by him with the priests, whose chief is the high priest.[76] Thus we conclude that Abravanel's view of the Jewish government as a whole is taken over from Josephus. And by taking into account the result of our previous analysis, we shall sum up by saying that Abravanel restates the aristocratic and antimonarchist view of Josephus in terms of the Christian distinction between the authority spiritual and the authority temporal.

When speaking of the influence of humanism on Abravanel's political teaching, we have, then, to think not primarily of his "republicanism"— of his admiration for the greatness of republican Rome and for the patriotism of its citizens—which is rather on the surface of his thought. His humanism has indeed hardly anything in common with the "heathenish" humanism of men like Lionardo Bruni. Abravanel is a humanist of the kind represented by Coluccio Salutati, who [128] might be said to have served as his model.[77] That is to say, he is a humanist who uses his classical learning to confirm his thoroughly medieval conceptions rather than to free himself from them. He is distinguished from the medieval writers rather by the method which he uses than by the views which he expresses. This method may be called historical.[78] Abravanel tends to pay more attention to the sources of the tradition than to the tradition itself. He often urges the difference between the literal sense of the Bible and the Midrashic interpretations; in doing this, he is guided, not as a medieval rationalist might have been, by an opposition to the "mythical" or "mystical" tendencies of the Midrash—for these tendencies are in full accordance with his own deepest inclinations—but by an interest in establishing the pure, undistorted meaning of the divinely inspired text, by an interest not so much in proving that

---

74 As regards Abravanel's knowledge of Josephus, see Baer, *loc. cit.* p. 246.

75 *Ant.* lib. IV, §223, and lib. VI, §35.

76 See in particular *Contra Apion.*, lib. II, §§185–8 and 193–4, but also *Ant.* lib. IV, §§218 ("high priest, prophet, and *Synhedrion*") and 224.

77 Cp. Alfred von Martin, *Mittelalterliche Welt- und Lebensanschauung im Spiegel der Schriften Coluccio Salutatis*, Munich und Berlin, 1913, pp. 22, 61 ff., 82 ff., and 97 ff., and the same author's *Coluccio Salutati's Traktat Vom Tyrannen*, Berlin und Leipzig, 1913, pp. 75 ff.

78 With due caution.

a certain favoured doctrine is revealed, and therefore true, but to know exactly what Revelation teaches, in order to be able to adopt that teaching, whatever it may be. By preferring in this spirit the sources of the tradition to the tradition itself, he can scarcely avoid the danger of coming into conflict with the teaching of tradition. An important example of that criticism of traditional views, which is based on the return to the sources (both the literal sense of the Bible and Josephus), has attracted our attention in the foregoing pages. To the same connection belongs Abravanel's criticism of certain traditional opinions concerning the authorship of some biblical books, a criticism by which he paved the way for the much more thoroughgoing biblical criticism of Spinoza.[79] When considering these and similar facts, we may be inclined to complete our earlier statement that Abravanel's thought was fundamentally determined by the Jewish tradition by adding that his teaching tends to be more of a biblicist than of a traditionalist character. But after having granted this, we must stress all the more that [129] the assumptions of the pre-medieval world to which Abravanel turns back, sometimes by criticizing medieval opinions, are not fundamentally different from the medieval assumptions from which he started. He goes back, it is true, from the monarchist ideal of the Middle Ages to the aristocratic ideal of antiquity. But, as matters stand, this does not mean more than that he goes back from the moderate hierocratic ideal of the Middle Ages to the much more intransigent hierocratic ideal of the period of the Second Temple, as expounded by Josephus. He is distinguished from the Jewish medieval writers by the fact that he is much more clerical than they are.

His descent was, as he believed, royal. His soul was the soul of a priest —of a priest who had not forgotten that the Temple, built by King Solomon in the holy city, was "infinitely inferior in sanctity" to the tabernacle erected by Moses in the desert.[80] Whatever he may have had to learn from the Cynics or from the Bucolics of antiquity as regards the dubious merits of human arts and city life, his knowledge of the sinful origin of cities, and of towers, and of kingdoms, and of the punishment following the eating of the fruit of the tree of knowledge was not borrowed from any foreign source: it was the inheritance of his own race which was commanded to be a kingdom of priests.

---

79 Cp. L. Strauss, *Die Religionskritik Spinozas*, Berlin, 1930, pp. 280 f. [*Spinoza's Critique of Religion*, 1965, pp. 333 f. —Eds.]

80 Commentary on I Kings VI, 1 (f. 217, col. 3).

2

Review of Moses Hyamson's Edition of Maimonides (1939)

The Mishneh Torah. By Maimonides. Book I. Edited according to the Bodleian Codex with Introduction, Biblical and Talmudical References, Notes and English Translation by Moses Hyamson. New York: Bloch Publishing Company, Inc., 1937. XIII pp. + 93 + 93 folios. $5.00.

[448] Professor Hyamson has made a very important contribution to our knowledge of Maimonides, by making accessible to the public for the first time the most authentic version which has come down to us of the *Sepher ha-madda*, i.e., the first "book" of the *Mishneh Torah*. "The text in this edition closely follows, line by line, a unique manuscript in the Bodleian Library of the Oxford University"; that "manuscript has the unique distinction that it contains Maimonides' autograph at the end of Book II," i.e., practically at the end of the MS.; and the subscription in Maimonides' hand is "a certification by Maimonides that the manuscript had been revised and corrected by comparison with the author's original copy." How necessary is the work, the first half of which has now been achieved by Professor Hyamson, was eloquently pointed out by Professor A. Marx some years ago (see *JQR*, N.S., xxv, pp. 371 f.). The best way of appreciating the editor's achievement is to make a survey (which cannot but be somewhat arbitrary) of some of the most striking differences between the text of the new edition and that of the current editions.

It is hardly necessary to point out that the text of the new edition is much superior in grammatical correctness to the text of the current editions. It is no more surprising, if somewhat more interesting, to observe,

---

Originally published in *The Mishneh Torah*, Book 1, *Review of Religion* 3, no. 4 (May 1939): 448–56.—Eds.

CHAPTER 2

by comparing the two texts, how much the original has been adulterated under the direct or indirect influence of Christian censorship. I shall briefly indicate, by putting the readings of the current editions into angular brackets, the typical adulterations caused by that factor. [449]

גוים [עכ״ום]. הכומרים [כוהניהם]. כומרי אדום [כוהני עכ״ום]. מין [אפיקורוס]. נכרי [עכ״ום or גוי]. עבודה זרה [עכ״ום]. מלכיות הרשעה [מלכות עכ״ום or מלכיות]. שמד [גזרה]. משומד [מומר]. תלמוד [גמרא].

To the same connection belongs the omission in the current editions of the name of Jesus, which occurs in 'Aboda zara X, I, in Teshubah III, 10 (end), and IV, 2 (4). The most important group of the variants, for which we are indebted to Professor Hyamson's edition, consists of such readings as have, or may have, some bearing on the understanding of Maimonides' thought. For the convenience of the reader, I shall indicate some examples of those variants by arranging them according to subject matter.

I. *The character of the Mishneh Torah and its plan.* The *M.T.* begins with the motto (omitted in the current editions) "In the name of the Lord, the everlasting God" (Gen 21:33), i.e., with the same motto with which each part of the *Guide of the Perplexed* opens. That motto is explained in the *M.T.* ('Aboda zara I, 3) in the same way as it is in the *Guide* (II, Ch. 13 and Ch. 30; III, Ch. 29), namely as indicating, first, God's existence, and then, His governing the sphere as well as His creating the world. In Teshubah IV, 5, we now read "we have compiled in the H. Deot...," instead of the usual reading "we have explained in the H. Deot...." It is important to note that, when quoting in the *Sepher ha-madda* (and, indeed, the entire *M.T.*) an earlier chapter, Maimonides usually says "we have explained (in that or that chapter)" (see Teshubah V, 5, VIII, 3, and X, 6); on the other hand, the *M.T.* as such is called by him a "compilation" (of traditional materials). By occasionally using the expression "we have compiled" (instead of "we have explained") when expressly quoting the H. Deot (the laws concerning morals and hygiene), Maimonides possibly alludes to the peculiar character of that section of the *Sepher ha-madda*, as indicated in the *Guide*, III, Ch. 35 (394, 5–6 Joel) and Ch. 38, if not to the peculiar character of all parts of the M.T. other than its first four chapters. At the beginning of Yesode ha-torah III, we now read "And the spheres" ["The spheres"]. The new reading makes clear the inseparability of physics (= Yes. III–IV) from metaphysics (= Yes. I–II), and *vice versa*; it is explained in the *Guide*, I, Introd. (5, 6), where Maimonides says: "Physics are contiguous to metaphysics." Our insisting on apparently slight variations of expression [450] is justified by another variant, which, indeed, was already known from other sources. In Yes. IV, 8, Maimonides says: "Therefore, one must be careful as regards names (terms) [as regards their names (sc., the terms mentioned immediately before which designate soul or spirit)], in order that you (singular number!) will not err [in order that nobody will err with regard to them] and each individual term has to be understood (*sc.*, in each individual case) from its context." (The statement quoted refers not only to Biblical terms, but likewise to terms as used by Maimonides himself; this is shown by the parallel to Yes. IV, 8 in Tesh. VIII, 3; cf. also *Guide*, I, Introd. [9, 26 ff.]). The new reading conveys a much more general warning (a warning with regard to an unlimited number of words, and not only with regard to the two words mentioned immediately before), and it conveys at the same time a much more specified warning: it is addressed, not to all men, but to one man only. For the secret teaching which is transmitted, especially by words of manifold meanings, is addressed to "one man" only.

II. *Theology.* "One says [He says (*sc.*, the Scripture says)] 'By the life of Pharaoh' and 'By the life of thy soul,' and one does not say [and he does not say] 'By the life of the Eternal,' but 'The Eternal lives.'" (Yes. II, 10). The authentic reading is confirmed by the parallel passage in the *Guide* (I, Ch. 68 [112, 18]). In the enumeration of the names of God in Yes. VI, 2, we now read *Ehyé* instead of *Elohai.* Cf. *Keseph Mishneh* on the passage and *Guide*, I, Ch. 62 (105, 4) and Ch. 63 (106, 14 ff.). Speaking of man's imitation of God's moral attributes, Maimonides in one case says "to assimilate himself [to assimilate himself to Him]" (Deot I, 6). The omission of the object is perfectly understandable on the basis of the *Guide*, I, Ch. 54. "If the divinities were many [If there were many divinities]" (Yes. I, 7) "The worship of him whose name is Molech [The worship (*sc.*, the idol) the name of which is Molech]" 'Ab. zara VI, 3. The scriptural proof of God's incorporeality is introduced by the words "It is clearly set forth in the Pentateuch and in the prophet [prophets]" (Yes. I, 8). As a matter of fact, Maimonides mentions in that context one prophet only. "If He were living by life and knowing by knowledge, there would be many divinities: He, His life, and His knowledge." (Yes. II, 10). The current editions read "and knowing by knowledge external to Himself." One line before, Dr. Hyamson's text, as well as [451] the text of the current editions, reads "He does not know by a knowledge which is external to Himself." But, there, *de'ah* (knowledge) means intelligence, strictly speaking, whereas, one line further on, that term is used in a sense similar to that in which it occurs in

CHAPTER 2

the heading H. Deot (laws concerning moral qualities). The passage "We do not find that God ever revoked anything good (which he had promised) except at the destruction of the First Temple, when He had promised to the just that they would not die together with the wicked, and He revoked His words; this is clearly set forth in the talmudic treatise Shabbat" (Yes. X, 4), does not occur in the text of the new edition.

III. *Angelology*. Maimonides indicates the problem of the relation between the Biblical angelology and the philosophic doctrine of separate intelligences by the following irregular expression "the rank of those forms [that form] which is called *Hayot*" (Yes. II, 7). Compare one line further on the statement "the rank of the form which is called *Ishim*, and they are the angels who speak with the prophets."

IV. *Ethics*. "Man ought to direct all his actions [his heart and all his actions] to the knowledge of God alone" (Deot III, 2). "Their hearts (*sc.*, the hearts of men) are left to them (*sc.*, to their discretion)." The current editions read: "All is left to them" (Tesh. V. 3). "So also what he (David) said, 'Let a noble spirit uphold me,' that is to say, 'Suffer my spirit to accomplish its desire [Thy desires]'" (Tesh. VI, 4). The question of the limits of human liberty is the secret topic of Tesh. V, as is indicated by the beginning of that chapter: "The freedom of every man is given to him [Freedom is given to every man]." (Cf. *Migdal Oz* on the passage, and Tesh. V, 2 and VII, 1). For the interpretation of the passage, compare *Guide*, III, Ch. 17 (cf. 337, 24–28 and 338, 21–30 with 340, 10 ff.) and Ch. 19 (345, 10). In the enumeration of (faulty) extremes in Deot I, we observe the following two interesting variants: "extremely [particularly] humble," and "particularly pure as regards his body (*sc.*, his bodily appetites)," instead of "of a very pure heart" (I, 1). The second variant is illustrated by another variant which occurs somewhat later on (I, 4): "that he will be perfect [as regards his body *add.*]." (Cf. *Shinnuyé nushaot ad loc.*). "Every man whose moral dispositions are all of them in the middle (*sc.*, between the two faulty extremes), is called wise" (Deot I, 4). "All of them" has been omitted by the current editions, perhaps in order to avoid the apparent contradiction to Deot II, 3, where Mai-[452]monides shows that the extremes of humility and meekness were recommended by Jewish tradition. "It is impossible to understand or to know [something belonging to the knowledge of the Creator *add.*], while one is sick" (Deot IV, 1).

V. *The Law*. Rabbi Juda the Saint "compiled from all (those materials) the Mishnah which was taught in public [to the wise *add.*]." (Introd., 2b10 Hyamson). "These were the great ones [the greatest of the wise] . . . and together with them were thousands and tens of thousands [and tens of thousands *om.*] of other wise (men)." (*Ibid.*, 2b19 f.). "The great Bet-Din of seventy [seventy-one]" (*Ibid.*, 3b25). "Forty men [Forty generations]" (*Ibid.*, 3a8. Cf. also 4a12f.). "...Elijah at Mount Carmel, who offered up burnt offerings outside (the Temple), and Jerusalem was chosen [had been chosen for that purpose], and anyone who offered them up outside, incurred the penalty of excision" (Yes. IX, 3).

VI. *Eschatology*. To the statement "he who commits idolatry under compulsion, does not incur the penalty of excision and, needless to say, the judicial penalty of death," the current editions add the following remark, which does not occur in Dr. Hyamson's edition: "But if he is able to save himself and to escape from the power of the wicked king and does not do so, he is like a dog that returns to its vomit, and he is called a wilful idolater, and he is excluded from the world to come, and he descends to the lowest rank of *Gehinnom*" (Yes. V, 4). Cf. *Shinnuyé nushaot ad loc.* To the expression "the intelligences that are devoid of matter" (Yes. IV, 8) the current editions add the explanation "such as the angels that are form without matter." The addition creates the impression, contradictory to what had been indicated in Yes. II, 3, that there are immaterial creatures apart from the angels. In Yes. IV, 4, the current editions substitute the unambiguous term *niphsad* (perishable) for the ambiguous term niphrad, which may mean "separate, *sc.*, from matter," as well as "susceptible of disintegration." (For the first meaning, see Tesh. VIII, 3, and for the second meaning see Yes. IV, 3. The term occurs in yet another meaning in Yes. I, 10 and II, 3). Compare for this and the preceding variant *Shinnuyé nushaot ad loc.*

VII. *Words of particular significance*. In Deot II, 3, the current editions substitute in one case *middah* for *de'ah*. Maimonides prefers the latter because of its specific ambiguity. "In discussing Torah and discussing wisdom, the words of the wise [the words of a man] should [453] be few, and their meanings (or contents) should be many" (Deot. II, 4). In Deot IV, 21, the current editions substitute in one case *hanhagot* for *minhagot*. Maimonides seems to wish to avoid, in this context, the word *hanhagah*, which, according to him, is the "translation" of *merkabah*, i.e., of the term designating the most secret topic. He prefers *minhag* (custom), which he sometimes uses as a synonym of *nature*. In 'Ab. zara I, 3 and II, 1, we now read in a number of cases "people" or "peoples" instead of "world."

There is one point of no small importance with regard to which Dr. Hyamson's edition seems not to be quite satisfactory. One cannot see from

CHAPTER 2

his edition to what extent the division of chapters into numbered paragraphs is based on the MS., and to what extent that division is due to the editor's discretion. The indication which he gives in his Introduction (p. iv) is difficult to reconcile with his note at the bottom of page 34 a.

As regards the English translation, it is in most cases correct, and in many cases even excellent. It certainly will be most helpful to the general reader. Its most obvious shortcoming is that very often it is based, not on the MS. text, together with which it is printed, but on the text of the current editions. But, apart from this, the question may be raised whether a translation meeting all the conditions which excellent translations of most philosophic or halakic books have to fulfill, would be an adequate translation of a work of Maimonides. The answer to that question naturally depends on which view we hold of the character of Maimonides' writings. As far as the *Sepher ha-madda* is concerned, we could learn from the author's own statements what kind of a book it is. Being a part of the M.T., it is addressed to "all men" (*Guide*, II, Ch. 35 *in princ.*; cf. I, Introd. [3, 7] with Yes. IV, 13), i.e., it is not addressed to philosophers in particular; it is, therefore, less scientific and more exoteric than the *Guide*. The most striking proof of this is the fact that Maimonides, as it were, hesitates to use within the *M.T.* the word *nature*: he speaks, to begin with, not of the *nature* of the elements, but of their *custom* or their *way*. (Yes. III, 11 and IV, 2. Professor Hyamson wrongly renders the two words in question by "governing principle" and "nature.") Now, an exoteric book, if it is the work of an unexoteric or initiated mind, is, by its very nature, more difficult to decipher than is an esoteric book. For in an exoteric book, the author can explain his views only in a rather hap-[454]hazard and vague way. (Compare *Guide*, I, Introd. [6, 8–9], and Ch. 71 [125, 24]). One may venture to say that an exoteric work such as the *Sepher ha-madda* (or the *M.T.* as a whole) is much more esoteric than are most esoteric works. Or, to avoid that paradox, we shall simply say that the *Sepher ha-madda* is a book full of mystery. To see this, one only has to consider what secret teaching, according to Maimonides' principles, means. It means teaching the truth to those who are able to understand by themselves, while at the same time hiding it from the vulgar. The most important method, used by him, of thus teaching the truth, is to make contradictory statements about those exalted subjects with regard to which the truth shall flash up for one moment and then disappear again. Now, it is obvious to anyone who reads the *Sepher ha-madda* with a reasonable degree of care, that Maimonides uses the method of "contradictions" in that work not less than he does in the *Guide*. The most famous examples are the contradictory statements about piety which occur in the first two chapters of the H. Deot. From the translator's point of view, however, contradictions are of minor importance, as they do not, by themselves, present a serious difficulty of translation. But it is of decisive importance for the translator of the *Sepher ha-madda* to be aware of the fact that Maimonides, in a number of instances, reveals what he considers to be the truth by the use of ambiguous, as well as unambiguous words of secret meanings, and that he does this in the *Sepher ha-madda* not less than in the *Guide*. This being the case, a translation of the *Sepher ha-madda* ought to be as literal as possible: the same Hebrew word has, if possible, always to be rendered by the same English word, if the allusions intended by Maimonides are to be noticed by the reader who cannot understand the original. In a translation of a work of Maimonides, the principle of literalness has to overrule all other considerations, to the same, or even to a greater extent, than in the medieval translations of the works of Aristotle and Averroes.

In Yes. I, 6, Professor Hyamson translates *bᵉné adam* by "majority of mankind," one line further on by "men." At the beginning of 'Aboda zara, he translates the same expression by "the people." Towards the end of Yes. III, he translates it more literally by "children of men." It might be worth considering whether one ought not to translate it in all cases by "sons of man," since the translation "men" [455] would not remind us of the fact that the expression in question sometimes does not designate mankind as such, but only the great majority of mankind. Besides, the translation suggested would bring out the connection of that expression with the expressions, "sons of the prophets," and "sons of the wise." (As regards the ambiguity of "son," see *Guide*, I, Ch. 7). One might even raise the question whether in some cases Hebrew proper names ought not to be accompanied by a translation, e.g., in the case of Enosh ('Ab. zara *in princ.*), where an adequate translation might solve the difficulty presented by Maimonides' statement about that person. In Yes. II, 3, Professor Hyamson translates two Hebrew words of very different meanings by the same English words "such are," and thus renders unrecognizable an important hint given by Maimonides. In Yes. IV, 2, he translates both *'aphar* (dust) and *'ereṣ* (earth) by "earth." He translates *ḥaḥamim* by "sages," "our sages," "wise," "wise men," and "Chachamim." The translator is not to blame for his failure to find a single English rendering for that most important word *de'ah*. He translates it by "intelligence," "knowledge," "moral disposition," "moral principle," "mind," "passion," "sentiment," and "ide-

Chapter 2

alistic being." It may very well be that there is not a single English word which could be used for designating separate intelligences as well as knowledge, moral qualities, and mind. But it can safely be said that, until such an English word has been found, or coined, the reader of even the best English translation of the *Sepher ha-madda* will miss important points of Maimonides' teaching. For Maimonides did not use the ambiguous word in question without good reason.

The biblical and talmudical references given by Professor Hyamson are doubtless very useful, although they are less complete than they could easily have been made. But, by omitting to add references to the non-Jewish sources of the *Sepher ha-madda*, the editor unintentionally creates a somewhat misleading impression of that work. It would have been interesting, and even important for some readers, to know that the titles, both of the whole work, and of its first section, are practically identical with the titles of the first two books of Ghazzālī's *Ihyā*, not to mention other parallels which are perhaps less obvious. (Cf. Boaz Cohen, *JQR*, N.S., xxv, pp. 529 ff.). The editor has also omitted to give cross references to other passages of the *M.T.* or to the other [456] works of Maimonides. Such cross references are indispensable in order to enable the great majority of readers to notice the contradictions which both hide and reveal Maimonides' secret teaching.

3

The Spirit of Sparta or the Taste of Xenophon (1939)

> Xenophon non excidit mihi, sed
> inter philosophos reddendus est.
>
> —Quintilian

[502] Xenophon's treatise *Constitution of the Lacedemonians* appears to be devoted to praise of the Spartan constitution, or, which amounts to the same thing,[1] of the Spartan mode of life. A superficial reading gives the impression that his admiration of Sparta is unreserved. One is therefore all the more surprised to find him declaring quite abruptly, toward the end of the treatise, that contemporary Sparta suffers from very grave defects. Yet in all but the fourteenth of the fifteen chapters he praises contemporary Sparta about as much as the Sparta of old, and he seems to speak quite indiscriminately of what the Spartan legislator Lycurgus had enacted in the remote past and of what the Spartans were actually doing in his time. That is to say the treatise as a whole hides the censure, inserted toward the end, of contemporary Sparta. In order to hide that censure still more Xenophon uses a strange device: he does not put it right at the end, which would be its proper place[2] but where it would strike the eyes, but sandwiches it in somewhere in the last section of the treatise.

But why does he hide his censure of contemporary Sparta so ineptly? Could he not have concealed it much more effectively by simply omitting it? This of course is true; but the mere omission would have had a great disadvantage: nobody could then see that Xenophon was not blind to the

---

Originally published in *Social Research* 6, no. 4 (Nov. 1939): 502–36. —Eds.

1   *Cf.* Aristotle, *Politics*, 1295 b 1.
2   *Cf.* the "epilogue" of Xenophon's *Cyropaedia*.

Chapter 3

serious defects of the Sparta of his time; and any sensible reader who had those defects before him would have considered the author a biased fool or partisan or a [503] weakling corrupted by gifts, and he would not have taken at all seriously the author's praise of Lycurgus' legislation. Xenophon was therefore compelled to pronounce his censure of contemporary Sparta in order not to compromise his praise of the old Sparta. Now if he had put that censure at the end of the treatise he would have spoiled the total effect of a work which is devoted not to blaming, but to praising.[3]

This fails, however, to dispose of the objection that the way in which Xenophon half hides his censure of contemporary Sparta is very clumsy, and that, considering his great literary gifts, any hypothesis is preferable to the assumption that he used a literary device awkwardly. To that objection, which is sound as far as it is based on observation of Xenophon's exceptional talents, we answer that if in a given case he apparently happens to do a bad job as a writer, or as a thinker, he actually does it deliberately and for very good reasons. As far as the objection alludes to certain devices of higher criticism, we reply that methods of that kind should not be applied before the author's intentions have been truly understood. This is to say first that, by hiding his censure of contemporary Sparta clumsily, Xenophon gives us to understand that he hides certain much more important views of his in an extremely able manner; and second, that the duty of the interpreter is not to attempt to be wiser than Xenophon, but to exert all his powers of understanding and imagination in order to make some progress toward wisdom by taking Xenophon as his guide.

I

The first chapter of the treatise appears to be devoted to praise of Lycurgus' laws concerning procreation of children. Xenophon points out two important differences between the way in which the other Greeks bring up their future mothers and Lycurgus' provisions; but whereas he explains the second of these differences with perfect clarity, he only touches upon the first. All he says regarding it is: "The others feed the girls who are destined to bear [504] children, and who are supposed to be well educated, on both the most moderate quantity of vegetable food which is practicable, and on the smallest quantity of meat which is possible; as regards wine, they either keep the girls from it altogether or let them consume it only if it is diluted

---

3 See G. Prinz, *De Xenophontis Cyri institutione* (Göttingen 1911) p. 74.

The Spirit of Sparta or the Taste of Xenophon

with water."[4] He omits, then, any mention of what Lycurgus had enacted concerning the food and drink of girls; or rather he does not tell us by an explicit statement, but gives us all the information necessary between the lines, i.e., by the way in which he arranges the whole argument. For the statement quoted belongs to a context which is destined to set forth the differences between, and opposition of, the practices of other Greek cities and the practices established by Lycurgus;[5] it is, therefore, simply an introduction to a much more important statement, suppressed by Xenophon, that the eating and drinking habits of Spartan girls were different from and opposed to those of other Greek girls. Thus Xenophon gives us to understand that Lycurgus allowed the Spartan girls ample food and undiluted wine. Allowing them ample food appears to be a measure most conducive to the procreation of strong offspring, the purpose of his legislation which Xenophon is discussing in the context under consideration. Why then does he not state explicitly what Lycurgus had enacted with regard to the food of girls? The riddle is solved by the fact that "ample food" is closely connected in Xenophon's argument with "undiluted wine." For although there is good reason for giving young women ample food, allowing them undiluted Greek wine may be dangerous. We know from easily accessible sources that Spartan girls and women were famous for their laxity of manners in general, and especially in matters of sex;[6] and we know the close connection between Venus and Bacchus. Because of the famous licentiousness of Spartan women Xenophon says nothing of the quantity and quality of food and drink which Spartan girls con-[505]sumed, a wise omission in a treatise devoted to the praise of Sparta. But would it not have been wiser still if he had not even mentioned the opposed practices of other Greek cities? If we are not to assume that he was a fool who was unable to realize an obvious implication of his own statements, or that he was a worse writer than the most hurried reporter could possibly be, we must believe that he did it as a faint indication of the laxity of Spartan women.

This conclusion is confirmed by the whole argument of the first chapter and, indeed, of the whole treatise. Immediately after alluding to the diet of the Spartan girls Xenophon mentions their physical exercises. In

---

4 *Constitution of the Lacedemonians*, I, 3.

5 I, 3–4. *Cf.* I, 2, 5 and 10.

6 Plato, *Laws*, 637c1–2 (*cf.* e1–3) and 780d9 ff. *Cf.* also *Republic*, 548a–b, 549c–e and 550d12; Aristotle, *Politics*, 1269b9–12 and 1270a7–9; Euripides, *Andromache*, vv. 595–601.

CHAPTER 3

that context he pointedly speaks of the Spartan "females."[7] By using that expression he refers, I assume, to the fact that Spartan women were left to their animal natures much more than were Spartan men, because they were much less disciplined. Only education[8] could have made Spartan women continent and thus have acted as an antidote against "ample food and undiluted wine." Yet in the whole treatise Xenophon does not say a single explicit word about education, other than physical, of Spartan women,[9] whereas he emphasizes the fact that Spartan education made the Spartan men continent, and the related fact that as a con-[506]sequence of Lycurgus' legislation "it has become manifest that the male tribe is stronger than those of female nature even as regards modesty."[10] Xenophon says nothing of the women's moral education or of their sense of shame for the same reason that he says nothing of their diet.

For it was not modesty of women, but only modesty of men which was fostered by Lycurgus' legislation. This is brought out by Xenophon at the beginning of his account of the Spartan marriage laws, the third and last topic of the first chapter. There he explains Lycurgus' provisions for train-

---

7   He does this by speaking first of "the male and female tribe" and by then contrasting "the men" with "the females" (I, 4).

8   *Cf.* III, 2.

9   Notice the mention of education of girls other than Spartan in I, 3. Xenophon seems to speak of the education of Spartan girls in the second chapter, which is devoted to the education of children. There he uses only once the unambiguous word "sons"— at the beginning of the chapter, where he is not yet speaking of Spartan education but of education as practiced in other Greek cities. He immediately afterwards replaces "sons" by the ambiguous word "children," and uses it throughout the chapter. In II, 5, he speaks of the extremely frugal food of Spartan "male" children; this remark shows again that the food of Spartan "female" children was not frugal. In II, 11, (I am following the readings of the MSS) he informs us that if no older man were available to supervise the children the smartest of the "males" had to take command; this implies that Spartan boys and girls had their physical exercises together. (The bad consequences of the Spartan type of coeducation for the chastity of women were emphasized by Euripides, *loc. cit.*) This conclusion is not contradicted but rather confirmed by I, 4, where Xenophon speaks of rival contests among women as distinguished from contests among men; for rival contests of adults are one thing, and physical exercises of children are another. Compare J. S. Watson's translation of Xenophon's *Minor Works* (London 1891) p. 206, note 3.

10 II, 14 and III, 4. The irony of the second statement is still more clear if one compares such passages as Plato, *Laws*, 802e8–10, and Aristotle, *Politics*, 1260a22 ff. and 1277b20 ff. *Cf.* Xenophon, *Agesilaus*, 6, 7.

ing the Spartans in continence with regard to sexual intercourse. The husband was commanded to be ashamed if he were seen when entering or leaving his wife's room. Obedience to that command had, and was intended to have, a twofold effect: it increased the feeling of shame, and at the same time it increased desire. The increase in desire was common to husband and wife, whereas the increase in bashfulness was in the husband only.[11] The other marriage laws gave the husband a surprisingly large freedom to indulge in adultery himself and to permit his wife to indulge. As a matter of fact that freedom appears to have been practically limitless; for after having explained two laws of the kind which by themselves were liberal enough, Xenophon adds that Lycurgus "made *many* concessions of that sort." Although he lets us only guess at the effect which these concessions were bound to have on the chastity of women, who furthermore were not subject to any dietary restrictions, he clearly states that the women had reasons of their own to be satisfied with these laws: "for the women [in Sparta] desire to control two households."[12]

We conclude then that the first chapter of the *Constitution of the Lacedemonians*, apparently in praise of the Spartan legislation concerning procreation of children, is actually a disguised satire on Spartan women. Now Xenophon makes no distinction other than [507] verbal between the actual behavior of Spartan women, present or past, and the behavior decreed by Lycurgus' legislation. We must, therefore, say that the satire on Spartan women is also a satire on Sparta in general and on Lycurgus' legislation.

II

To show the excellence of Spartan education, Xenophon contrasts the public education of Sparta, which leads to virtue, with private education as practiced in other Greek cities, which leads to effeminacy. Here he uses the same device which he used before in discussing the Spartan laws on procreation of children: he indicates two major differences between, say, Athenian practice and Spartan practice, and although he clearly explains the second difference, he says nothing about a salient feature of the first and more important difference. Concerning this he says that Spartan education was public, while education in other Greek cities was private. Yet he mentions also that the other Greeks "send their children as soon as they understand what is spoken... immediately to teachers to learn letters,

---

11 *Cf.* I, 5.

12 I, 6–9. With regard to Spartan gynaecocracy, see Aristotle, *Politics*, 1269b24–34.

Chapter 3

and music, and the exercises of the palaestra."[13] And he says no word in either the immediate context or any other passage of the treatise about what Lycurgus had enacted or what the Spartans were actually doing regarding education in "letters and music." This omission is as little a matter of chance as was the preceding and almost exactly corresponding omission of the Spartan dietary laws for girls: Xenophon informs us between the lines that in Sparta there was no education worth mentioning in letters and music.[14]

What was in its stead? Physical education, of course. Yet Spartan education had some specific features which Xenophon is very anxious for us to realize. He emphasizes the fact that Spartan children were instructed in stealing as well as in robbing and deceiv-[508]ing; and he defends especially the Spartan practice of punishing severely the children who were caught when attempting to steal, by the following remark: "Some one might say, why, then, if he [Lycurgus] judged stealing to be good, did he inflict many stripes on him who was caught? Because, I answer, in all other things, too, which men teach, they punish him who does not execute the instruction properly. Accordingly, the Spartans punish those who are caught because of their stealing badly."[15] His praise of the Spartan education in "stealing well" is in obvious contradiction of his censure of that practice in the *Cyropaedia*, and of a reference to it in the *Anabasis* which is, I believe, generally recognized as ironic.[16] A consideration of these parallels led a recent editor of the *Constitution of the Lacedemonians* to doubt the sincerity of Xenophon's praise of this type of education.[17] The doubt is fully justified, but insincerity is too vague a term for what is more precisely to be called irony. Or was Xenophon, who not only spoke ironically of the Spartan education in stealing in the *Anabasis* but who was, after all, a pupil of Socrates, incapable of irony? Can it not be seen that his justification of the Spartan custom of punishing those who "steal badly" is based on the ironic premise that "stealing is good," an art comparable to grammar or music or perhaps even to economics? Another feature characteristic of Spartan education

---

13   II, 1. *Cf. Apologia Socratis*, 16.
14   The mention of "teachers" of children other than Spartan in III, 1 serves the same purpose, as appears from a comparison of that paragraph with the rest of the chapter.
15   II, 6–9.
16   *Cyropaedia*, I, 6, 31–32. *Anabasis*, IV, 6, 14–15.
17   F. Ollier, *La république des Lacédémoniens* (Lyon 1934) p. xxxiii.

and of Spartan life in general was arbitrary commands, with severe punishment, especially heavy whippings, for one caught disobeying the commands.[18] Xenophon's praise of that method of education is contradicted by what he says elsewhere about the superiority of education by persuasion and speech over education by compulsion.[19] We conclude then that the argument of the second chapter of the *Constitution of the Lacedemonians* is designed to let us glimpse the [509] fact that in Sparta instruction in letters and music was replaced by instruction in stealing and by severe whipping.[20]

This conclusion is open to an objection which at first glance seems irrefutable. The most obvious parallel to Xenophon's description of Spartan education is his description of Persian education near the beginning of the *Cyropaedia*. A comparison of the two descriptions shows that he considered Persian education definitely superior to Spartan, not to say that he considered the former to be absolutely perfect. Now in his description of Persian education he again mentions the education in letters which was the custom of people other than the Persians, and fails to mention any Persian education of that kind. We seem therefore to be forced to conclude that Xenophon thus hints at the barbaric character of Persian education as well. Although I do not think that this is not borne out by the whole *Cyropaedia*, and by what many educated Greeks have thought of Persian education, I limit myself here to pointing out one important difference between Persian and Spartan education as described by Xenophon. If the Persians lacked schools of music and letters they certainly had schools of justice, an educational institution of high standing which was totally absent from Sparta.[21] In these schools, the Persian boys were taught to give and take account of their doings, which naturally developed the power of speech. It developed in Cyrus, for instance, not only a charming talkativeness,[22] but

---

18 II, 2 and 8–10. *Cf.* IV, 6; VI, 2; IX, 5; X, 4–7.

19 *Memorabilia*, I, 2, 10. *Hiero*, 9, 2. *De re equestri*, 11, 6. *Cyropaedia*, I, 2, 2–3. *Oeconomicus*, 14, 7. The two last mentioned passages are direct parallels to *Respublica Lacedaemoniorum*, X, 4–7.

20 It is important to notice that Xenophon devotes only one chapter to the account of Spartan education (see the emphatic conclusion of the second chapter). This means that Lycurgus' regulations for adolescents and young men, which are discussed in the third and fourth chapters, cannot possibly be brought under the heading "education"— at least not by a man who knows what education really is. The reason that Xenophon could speak of Spartan "education" of boys, is indicated below [at n. 29 —Eds.].

21 *Cf.* II, 1 ff. with *Cyropaedia*, I, 2, 6.

Chapter 3

likewise a remarkable ability to harangue his soldiers as well as an almost Socratic habit of discovering the profitable truth, and of guiding men by having dialogues with them in both jest and earnest. But was Xenophon not a soldier who as such attached importance to deeds rather than words? How-[510]ever this may be, it is precisely with regard to military matters that he stresses the decisive importance of speech for commanding human beings, as distinguished from speechless animals.[23] Now Spartan children and adolescents were not trained in speech but in utter taciturnity: Lycurgus commanded the adolescents "to walk along in silence," and "you would hear no more sound of a voice from them than from stone statues."[24] Thus the Persians had no education in letters and music, but did have education in speech; while both letters and speech were ignored in Sparta.

Our contention has been that Xenophon, by mentioning education in letters and music in speaking of other Greeks and not mentioning it in speaking of the Spartans, wants us to give some thought to the absence of letters and music from Sparta. We might not have noticed the hint if we had not seen before the similar device used in discussing the upbringing of future mothers in Sparta and elsewhere. That was, however, much more obvious. He gave two complete sentences exclusively to an account of the diet of other Greek girls, thus compelling us to expect a corresponding statement dealing exclusively, or at least chiefly, with the Spartans, and the total disappointment of our expectation led us to realize that something is wrong with his whole discourse. But concerning education in letters and music, he merely mentions the topic in a single sentence which seems to declare, not that education in letters and music was to be found in other Greek cities, but that education in other Greek cities was private and at least partly entrusted to slaves. And that sentence finds its natural supplement in a later one which shows that education in Sparta was public and entrusted to citizens of high standing.[25] Therefore the curiosity raised by the first sentence is almost completely satisfied, and we are not compelled to remain vigilant to the same extent as we were in the case of his account of the girls or women. The difference in the use of the same device is hardly surprising once one has seen that music and [511] letters, and speech, are much more

---

22 *Cyropaedia*, I, 4, 3.
23 *Memorabilia*, III, 3, 11. *De re equestri*, 8, 13.
24 III, 4–5. [Cf. n. 13, above—Eds.]
25 II, 1–2.

directly connected with the hidden truth than is continence, which is only a rather remote, if indispensable, means for the true end of human life.

Xenophon concludes his account of Spartan education by praise of the continence of the Spartans in love between men and boys. He points out that "some people" will not believe his laudatory statements, and he gives us to understand why they are bound to be exaggerated. All that he says about the actual Spartan practice amounts to this, that in Sparta lovers refrain from sexual intercourse with boys no less than parents refrain from intercourse with their children, or brothers with brothers and sisters.[26] Now incest cannot possibly be avoided in a city where adultery is as common as it is in Sparta according to Xenophon's description, i.e., where it is very difficult, if not impossible, to know exactly who one's nearest relatives are.[27] Xenophon alludes to the obscurity of Spartan family relations by tracing the lax marriage laws back to the desire of the Spartans "to add brothers to their children," and by occasionally stating that "these [other men] are the fathers of the children whom he himself [the individual Spartan] rules."[28] Moreover, he concludes his description of how Spartan youths behave at the common meals by the remark, "And of the beloved boys he [Lycurgus] took care in the manner described."[29] Above all, he almost explicitly retracts his praise of Spartan bashfulness in matters of love between men and boys by declaring that when observing the Spartan youths going to the public mess rooms "you would believe them to be more bashful than the very virgins in the bridal chambers."[30] [512]

III

The two most striking features so far discussed of Spartan legislation or of Spartan life as described by Xenophon are the lax marriage laws and

---

26 II, 13.

27 *Cf.* Aristotle, *Politics*, 1262a32 ff.

28 I, 9 and VI, 2. Compare *Hellenica*, III, 3, 1–2, with *Agesilaus*, 1, 5.

29 III, 5 (according to the reading of the MSS). It is hardly unintentional that Xenophon uses in this context four words which allude in one way or another to matters of love. Nor ought we to overlook his playing on the relations between Spartan education (*paideia*) and love of boys (*paidikoi erotes*) in II, 12–14.

30 III, 5 (according to the reading of the MSS). The editors reject the MSS readings in this as well as in a number of similar cases in favor either of variants supplied by the indirect tradition or of conjectural readings, for no other reason than that they do not take into consideration the Aristophanean inclinations of Xenophon.

Chapter 3

the principle underlying Spartan education that "stealing is good." He justifies these two sets of rules by showing the good influence which they exercised on Spartan virtue: the lax marriage laws were conducive to the procreation of strong and healthy offspring, and the instruction in stealing was conducive to military efficiency.[31] We have therefore to take up the question of the place which Xenophon assigned to physical excellence and military efficiency within the framework of human excellence or virtue.

Xenophon clearly states his standard for judging the quality of human abilities and habits: the superiority of the soul over the body.[32] Therefore, the many things which he says in praise of the physical excellence of the Spartans cannot be more than a mere introduction to the much more important praise of the excellence of their souls. Hence we shall have to consider, rather more carefully than usual, the meaning of his emphatic statement that Lycurgus "compelled all [the Spartans] to practice all virtues publicly."[33]

We naturally expect to meet in his description the whole choir of the virtues, but we are disappointed just as we were before. Although Lycurgus was "very wise in the extreme [extremes],"[34] neither wisdom nor education in wisdom is mentioned in the whole treatise. There is no word of justice or schools of justice although punishment, and severe punishment, is mentioned on almost every page, and although the procedure concerning lawsuits is briefly [513] indicated.[35] The other Greek cities punished anyone who did an injustice in anything to another, but Lycurgus "inflicted no lesser penalties on him who appeared to neglect to be excellent. For he believed, as it seems, that from those who kidnap some people, or rob something, or steal, the damaged ones only suffer injustice, but that by the bad and unmanly ones whole cities are betrayed. So that he seems

---

31 I, 5–10 and II, 7.

32 X, 3. Xenophon illustrates the Spartan conception of "soul" in such passages as VII, 3–4 and X, 2–3. *Cf.* VIII, 1 (MSS).

33 X, 4.

34 I, 2. The expression used by Xenophon is ambiguous: it may mean that Lycurgus was exceedingly wise, but then it is redundant; or it may mean that he was very wise with regard to the extremes, and then it is not redundant but most appropriate: Xenophon leaves it undetermined whether the extremes with regard to which Lycurgus was very wise were good or bad. Arts are mentioned, as far as Sparta is concerned, almost exclusively in connection with war (I, 3; VII, 1; XI, 2; XIII, 5 and 7).

35 XIII, 11. Injustice is mentioned also in VII, 5 and XIV, 6.

to me to have fittingly inflicted on the latter the heaviest penalties." Xenophon then again omits something: he does not tell us what Lycurgus had believed or enacted concerning injustice. Or rather he expects us to remember his earlier finding that Lycurgus "believed stealing to be good."[36] Considering the facts that wisdom was not met with in Sparta, and that Socrates did not separate wisdom and moderation,[37] we are not surprised to observe that Xenophon fails to ascribe moderation to the Spartans except in the ambiguous sentence that in Sparta "the male tribe is stronger than those of female nature even as regards being moderate."[38] If, then, wisdom and justice and moderation are virtues alien to the Spartans, we must qualify Xenophon's statement that Lycurgus "compelled all [the Spartans] to practice all virtues publicly" with the limitation that he compelled them to practice all virtues with the exception of wisdom, justice and moderation. As a matter of fact, that limitation, implied in "publicly," is made by Xenophon himself when he repeats his emphatic statement later on in a somewhat modified form: Lycurgus "imposed even an irresistible necessity to practice the whole political virtue."[39] An irresistible necessity to practice wisdom, for instance, can hardly be imagined. One may sum up Xenophon's view of Spartan virtue by saying that there is [514] no greater difference between the virtue of Sparta and the virtue of other cities as cities than that between the virtue of "practicing" laymen and of negligent laymen. For if virtue is wisdom, and since wisdom is found in only a very few individuals, the difference between the so-called virtue of all citizens and true virtue must be even greater than the difference between the skill of a quack and the skill of a physician.[40]

The conclusion which we have reached thus far might be criticized as being based on an argument from silence. Although this objection is not quite valid, for it mistakes speech interspersed with silence for silence pure

---

36 X, 5–6 and II, 7–9.

37 *Memorabilia*, III, 9, 4.

38 III, 4. Xenophon states, it is true, that at the common meals of the Spartans "in the least degree insolence (i.e., the opposite of moderation)... occurs" (V, 6). But one immediately sees how reserved this praise is when one remembers that even at the doors of the Persian kings "one might observe much moderation" (*Anabasis*, I, 9, 3). With regard to *sophronizein* as used in XIII, 5, compare *Cyropaedia*, III, 1, 16 ff.

39 X, 7. For the meaning of "political virtue," compare Plato, *Phaedo*, 82a10–b8, and *Republic*, 430c3–5, and Aristotle, *Ethica Nicomachea*, 1116a15 ff.

40 *Cf.* X, 4 with *Memorabilia*, III, 9, 5.

Chapter 3

and simple, and although the principle that arguments from silence are not permissible must undergo important modifications before it can be applied to the writings of Xenophon, it will be wise to limit our further discussion of Xenophon's descriptions of Spartan virtue as strictly as possible to his explicit statements. We shall then say that the individual virtues which he explicitly mentions with regard to the Spartans are, not wisdom and moderation and justice, but continence and bashfulness and obedience.[41]

There is a certain affinity between continence (*enkrateia*) and moderation (*sophrosynē*), an affinity which permits identification of them for almost every practical purpose, and the use of the two terms in many cases synonymously. Yet the two qualities are far from being identical.[42] Moderation, which cannot be separated from wisdom, is of greater dignity than continence, which is merely the "basement" of virtue.[43] Continence is concerned with the pleasures of the body as well as with the pleasures deriving from property.[44] Not to repeat what we quoted before in discussing Xenophon's remarks about marriage laws and education,[45] we shall [515] merely point out that even the Spartan men do not seem to have been subject to very severe regulations concerning the quantity of food and drink which they could consume. Concerning drinking in particular, Lycurgus "gave permission that everyone should drink when he was thirsty, believing that the drink would thus be most innoxious as well as most pleasant." That is to say, Lycurgus made thirst, or the throat and the stomach, the measure of potation.[46] Much more significant were his laws concerning property. Xenophon tells us that Lycurgus prohibited the free from having anything to do with acquisitive occupations of any kind, and that he commanded them to devote themselves entirely to those activities which secure freedom to cities. He explains, moreover, how the whole set-up of the Spartan community prevented the Spartans from being eager to acquire wealth. Finally, he emphasizes the fact that the heavy weight of the Spartan money made secrecy in acquiring wealth utterly impossible. In the present case, the

---

41 *Cf.* II, 14 with 2.
42 *Cyropaedia*, I, 2, 8 and VIII, 1, 30–32; *Agesilaus*, 10, 2; *Apologia Socratis*, 19. It may be remarked in passing that Xenophon's view of the relation of the two qualities differs from Aristotle's not only in details but in fundamentals.
43 *Memorabilia*, I, 5, 4 and III, 9, 4.
44 *Memorabilia*, I, 5, 6.
45 See in particular I, 5.
46 V, 3–4. *Cf.* II, 1 end.

method which he chooses for letting us see the truth is that of proving too much. For whereas he states to begin with that acquisition of wealth as such is forbidden in Sparta, somewhat later on he states that acquisition of wealth by unjust means is prevented by the heavy weight of the Spartan money, which could be concealed only with great difficulty. The question naturally arises as to whether the Spartans could not procure for themselves gold or silver, which is more easily hidden. The answer must be in the affirmative, else it would not have been necessary to institute searches for gold and silver.[47] Furthermore, whereas his original statement implies that the set-up of Spartan life ruled out any interest in wealth, we soon learn from him that punitive measures were required to prevent the Spartans from acquiring money.[48] In addition, he draws our attention to the fact that, although wealth cannot be earnestly sought by the Spartans, wealth, and the difference between rich and poor citizens, does exist in the ideal Sparta.[49] [516] Was Spartan wealth, then, due exclusively to windfalls? Was the belief of the legislator that "stealing is good" and his failure to punish those who kidnap or rob or steal, of no account in this respect? Particularly interesting is Xenophon's remark that the Spartans desire "to add such brothers to their children who participate in descent and power, but have no claim to the property." That desire certainly implies some serious interest in wealth.[50] And what becomes of the noble poverty of the Spartans and their frugality if the king must be given "so much choice land in *many* subject cities that he will be neither in want of moderate means nor outstanding as regards wealth"?[51] Finally, we ought not overlook any longer that Xenophon states quite openly what he thinks of the continence in money matters of the ideal Spartans of the past; for he says "in former times, I know, they were afraid of being seen in the possession of gold."[52]

This quotation forms a natural transition from Spartan continence to the Spartan sense of shame, a quality which Xenophon stresses more than any other of their peacetime virtues.[53] Sense of shame or bashfulness, too,

---

47 VII, 2 and 5–6.

48 VII, 3–6. See F. Habben, *De Xenophontis libello*...(Münster 1909) p. 27.

49 V, 3; VI, 5; X, 7; XIII, 11.

50 I, 9. *Cf.* Habben, *op. cit.*, p. 15.

51 XV, 3.

52 XIV, 3. This remark is foreshadowed by the abrupt transition from VII to VIII.

53 I, 5; II, 2, 10, and 14; III, 4 and 5; V, 5.

Chapter 3

has something in common with that true virtue called moderation, which he does not attribute to the Spartans. And yet it is still more inferior to moderation than is continence. It was no less a person than Cyrus, the founder of the Persian empire, who according to Xenophon distinguished between moderation and sense of shame in approximately this way: the shamed avoid shameful things in the light of day, whereas the moderate avoid them even in secret.[54] Sense of shame, then, is certainly not a genuine virtue: it is concerned simply with external goodness, or with the appearance of goodness. Now it is easy to see that Lycurgus was interested in visible goodness only. It is for this reason that he inflicted so many penalties on him who was seen or caught when acting improperly; prescribed decent behavior for [517] adolescents walking on the roads; and dragged the Spartans out of their private houses into the public mess rooms.[55] Accordingly, what he brought to light was not the Spartans, but the public mess rooms; for his view that by creating that institution he would render impossible the transgression of his laws was merely a belief.[56] By educating the Spartans in bashfulness only, while withholding from them true education—education in letters and speech, education in wisdom and moderation and justice—in other words, by frightening them into submissiveness with the menace of severe and dishonoring punishments, he compelled them to do forbidden things in utter secrecy. He even educated his citizens from their very childhood in the art of concealment by teaching them to avoid being caught. The only relief found by the Spartans was spying on each other.[57] The famous Spartan sense of shame is then simply hypocrisy, and the so-called decline of the Spartans' virtue was merely a decline of their dissimulation: the present Spartans were distinguished from their forefathers merely by the fact that they visibly and openly disobeyed Lycurgus' laws.[58] Now since sense of shame is concerned with visible goodness or with public goodness only, it is, in a sense, identical with virtue practiced in public, or with political virtue.[59] To reduce

---

54 *Cyropaedia*, VIII, 1, 31.
55 I, 5; II, 10 f. and 13; III, 4; VII, 6 (see XIV, 3); X, 5. *Cf.* these passages with II, 8.
56 V, 2.
57 "He who designs to get something [i.e., especially the 'noble things,' or the honors of the city], must employ spies." *Cf.* II, 7 with IV, 4.
58 *Cf.* XIV, 3 and 7.
59 *Cf. Memorabilia*, III, 7, 5 with *Cyropaedia*, VIII, 1, 31.

The Spirit of Sparta or the Taste of Xenophon

the fallacy underlying the Spartan ideal to its principle we need merely repeat Xenophon's emphatic statement that Lycurgus compelled all the Spartans to practice all virtues publicly: that is, he did not (and he could not) compel them to practice virtue in private.[60]

The third and last of the Spartan peacetime virtues is obedience. Obedience is submission to the laws and to the rulers. Its value, therefore, depends on the wisdom of the laws or of the rulers in question: obedience to the foolish or unjust enactments of a tyrant [518] or a mob or of any other individual or group is certainly no virtue. Now we have seen what Xenophon thinks of the dignity of Lycurgus' laws which, while containing many concessions concerning adultery, do not contain the slightest provision for genuine education.[61] Seeing, moreover, that the root of the Spartans' obedience is the same as the root of their sense of shame, i.e., fear of severe whipping,[62] we should be permitted to go on to another topic but for one fact: Xenophon's Socrates is known to have taught that justice is

---

60 Notice the connection between "private pedagogues" (II, 2) and "letters and music" (II, 1). *Cf.* Plato, *Laws*, 666e.

61 Xenophon's judgment on the reasonableness, or lack of reasonableness of Lycurgus' legislation is indicated first by his allusions to the arbitrary character of the noble things (*kala*) recognized as such by the Spartans (II, 9 and 10; IV, 4; VI, 2). It is shown most clearly by his use, in speaking of Lycurgus, of the word *nomizein* in its two meanings: "enacting" and "believing" (see especially II, 4 and I, 6f.). For what Lycurgus "believed" is distinguished with some care from what he "saw" and what he "observed": in some cases, what he "believed" and "enacted" is opposed to what he "saw" and "observed," i.e., opposed to the nature of things, or more precisely to human nature (see in particular I, 5 and 7). As a consequence, his legislation is opposed to the views of the other Greeks, or of most men, or even of all men (see especially I, 7, II, 13, and III, 4). For the laws which are acknowledged by all men are the unwritten or natural laws (*Memorabilia*, IV, 4, 19 ff.). Since he opposes the views of all men or of all Greeks, Lycurgus deserves to be "wondered at" (*cf.* I, 2 with 1). Another way of expressing the same judgment is to say that Lycurgus' laws are "very old," and yet "very new" to the other Greek cities (X, 8); for the laws of the other Greeks are less old and therefore less barbaric (*cf.* Thucydides, I, 6, 6). Xenophon's statement that the Spartan laws are opposed to the laws of most or all men reads like an adaptation of a similar statement by Herodotus about the Egyptian laws (II, 35). The relation between Sparta and Egypt is a major theme of Plato's *Laws*, and it is discussed by Plato in the same spirit in which Xenophon points out the oldness of Lycurgus' laws. See also Herodotus, VI, 60, and Isocrates, *Busiris*, 17.

62 II, 2 and 10. (Not to mention the fact that the Greek word in question—*peitho*—is ambiguous.) *Cf.* also the scarcely disguised identification of obedience with fear in VIII, 3.

Chapter 3

identical with obedience to the laws, to any laws, and to have praised in the same context Lycurgus' educating the Spartans in such obedience.[63]

To understand the meaning of this passage in the *Memorabilia* we must briefly consider the character of the work of which it forms so outstanding a part. The intention of the *Memorabilia* is to show what Socrates did and what he said, not what he thought. More precisely, the intention of that work is not to show explicitly what [519] his private views were. In the main it openly states his public views, i.e., the opinions which he uttered in public and in private conversation with people who were merely members of the public. Their not quite serious nature is indicated between the lines, i.e., by occasional remarks which are in flagrant contradiction to his public views and which, therefore, are apt to be deleted by modern editors, as well as by the well known and so to speak famous deficiencies of the plan of both the whole work and a number of individual chapters.[64] It is, therefore, impossible to find what Xenophon's Socrates really thought by merely looking up or even by reading often an individual chapter or the whole work; in order to discover Xenophon's and Socrates' private views one must do some private thinking, and especially one must in each case deduct from Socrates' statements that deliberate distortion of the truth which was caused by his compliance with, and adaptation to, the specific imbecility of the interlocutor to whom he happened to talk. Or, to express the same thing somewhat differently, we cannot take at face value any individual statement of Xenophon's Socrates which is contradicted by the principle governing the plan of the whole work. That plan is based on the assumption that "speech" is superior to "deed."[65] On the other hand, the speech in which Socrates "proves" that justice is identical with obedience to the laws of the city starts from the assumption, suggested by Socrates and adopted without consideration by his interlocutor, that "deed" is more relevant than "speech."[66] Moreover, the

---

63 *Memorabilia*, IV, 4, 15. *Cf. Cyropaedia*, III, 3, 8, among many other passages.

64 With regard to the plan of the *Memorabilia*, compare Emma Edelstein, *Xenophontisches und Platonisches Bild des Sokrates* (Berlin 1935) pp. 78-137.

65 The positive part of the *Memorabilia* (I, 3 to the end) consists of 37 chapters of which only the first or, perhaps, the first three are devoted to "deed," whereas almost all the rest is devoted to "speech." *Cf.* also III, 3, 11 with Plato, *Gorgias*, 450c-d. For the meaning of the "deed-speech" antithesis, which is an ironical expression of the antithesis between practical or political life and theoretical life, compare Plato, *Apology*, 32a4–5 with *Crito*, 52d5.

66 *Memorabilia*, IV, 4, 10. *Cf.* also the beginning of that chapter.

argument which the interlocutor advances against Socrates' assertion that justice is identical with obedience to the laws misses the point, as is shown by a parallel argumentation used by a more intelligent or a franker man which [520] occurs in the same work,[67] and therefore Socrates' refutation of the interlocutor's denial is a mere *argumentatio ad hominem*. Besides, the talk opens with a statement by Socrates which refutes in advance his later thesis, i.e., that it is extremely difficult to find a teacher of the just things; for if just were the same as legal, every legal expert, nay, every member of the popular assembly would be a teacher of justice. And finally, after having "proved" his point, Socrates suddenly turns from the laws of the city to the unwritten (or natural) laws, and he thus, and only thus, indicates the crucial question, the question of the possible divergence and opposition of the laws of the city and the natural laws. We conclude, then, that neither Xenophon nor Socrates accepted seriously the view that justice is identical with obedience to the laws of the city, regardless of the justice of the laws. Therefore, the insertion of praise of Lycurgus' legislation into the "dialectic" proof of that view, far from refuting our interpretation of the *Constitution of the Lacedemonians*, actually is a strong argument in favor of it.[68]

Then what remains of Spartan virtue? Manliness, of course. It should be mentioned, however, that the ordinary term designating that virtue occurs only once in the whole treatise, and then in a passage where its meaning is exceedingly ambiguous.[69] True, a synonymous term does occur once in a passage where its meaning is entirely clear,[70] and in all the passages where Xenophon speaks of the Spartans' virtue, or *kalokagathia*, he is, of course, thinking mainly if not exclusively of their manliness.[71] Thus we are confronted with the question of how Xenophon judged of manliness [521] taken alone, a manliness not accompanied by wisdom, moderation

---

67 *Memorabilia*, I, 2, 41 ff.

68 It is hardly necessary to say that Xenophon, *Apologia Socratis*, 15, cannot be adduced as an argument to the contrary. For whoever bases an objection on that passage commits the mistake warned against by Socrates himself in that very context of believing without consideration the Delphian god (or his priestess, or the men who heard him or her say...), if not the still more serious mistake (indicated by the words "not even this") of believing a statement of the Delphian god which implies an impossibility. *Cf.* the parallel of a similar meaning in Plato's *Apology*, 20e–21a.

69 IX, 5 (according to the good MSS). "Unmanly people" are mentioned in X, 6.

70 IV, 2.

71 Compare, however, IX, 1 with the beginning of the treatise.

CHAPTER 3

or justice. It is in his eulogy of the Spartan king Agesilaus, the work of his which is in every respect nearest akin to the *Constitution of the Lacedemonians*, that he indicates his view that manliness taken alone is hardly distinguishable from madness.[72] Now manliness is primarily the virtue of war,[73] and thus the answer to the question of the dignity of manliness as compared with that of the other virtues implies the answer to the question of the dignity of war as such as compared with that of peace as such.

IV

We have started from the tacit assumption that the literary technique of those non-rhetorical Greek prose writers before Aristotle whose writings have come down to us is essentially different from the technique of the large majority of later writers: the former, being teachers of moderation, teach the truth according to the rule of moderation, i.e., they teach the truth exclusively between the lines. Accordingly, we have refrained from considering the conjecture which is an outcome of higher criticism—that Xenophon composed the censure of contemporary Sparta which he inserted toward the end of the treatise after the composition of the other fourteen chapters. This conjecture is based on the observation of the contradictions between that censure and the bulk of the treatise. But these contradictions are not the only ones which occur in the treatise. The conjecture in question is based, moreover, on observation of the most irregular way in which the censure of contemporary Sparta is inserted. But irregularities occur within every chapter and within many individual sentences of the treatise; and the difficulties offered by these cannot be called less than that presented by the most striking irregularity—provided one does not understand by a great difficulty one which is very easily noticed by even the most superficial reader. Considering the fact, for it is a [522] fact, that the use of irregularities of composition as well as of contradictions is characteristic of the technique employed by that small group of writers to which Xenophon belongs, we may take for granted (as we are entitled to do in the absence of any external evidence to the contrary) that Xenophon conceived all chapters of the treatise in one coherent movement of his mind.[74]

---

72 *Agesilaus*, 2, 12 and 7.

73 Notice the mention of "noble death" at the beginning of IX, the chapter devoted to manliness. *Cf.* Aristotle, *Ethica Nicomachea*, 1115a32–33.

74 The most striking difficulty which the treatise offers is that in the bulk of it Xenophon seems to speak quite indiscriminately of what Lycurgus had enacted in the past and

The Spirit of Sparta or the Taste of Xenophon

He sandwiches in his censure of contemporary Sparta exactly in the middle of the last section. That section is given to the Spartan kingdom and consists of two chapters: the first (Chapter 13) is devoted to the power and honor which the Spartan king enjoys when he is with the army, and the second (Chapter 15) treats of the honors which he enjoys at home.[75] By slipping between these [523] two a chapter which is devoted to the censure of contemporary Sparta, and in which not even the word "king" occurs, Xenophon seems to deprive his whole treatise of the great virtue of a lucid and unambiguous order. Or did he prefer an ambiguous order?

In building up his treatise, the author of the *Cyropaedia* and the *Hiero* and the *Agesilaus* naturally was guided by his high opinion of the institution of monarchy, or of the question of monarchy. Accordingly he was compelled to present the Spartan kingdom as the peak of Spartan institutions. Now "the vale best discovers the hill." Therefore he had to put

---

of what the Spartans were actually doing in his own time, whereas in his censure of contemporary Sparta he draws a sharp line of demarcation between the perfect Sparta of the past and the defective Sparta of the present. Yet he states at the very beginning of the treatise that he is going to discuss a phenomenon belonging to the past: "After having once perceived that Sparta, one of the most thinly populated cities, had come into sight as the most powerful as well as the most celebrated city in Greece, I fell to wondering how in the world this had happened. But after I had considered the institutions of the Spartiates, I no longer wondered" (I, 1). This introduction is almost exactly parallel to that of the *Memorabilia:* "I often fell to wondering by what speeches in the world the accusers of Socrates had convinced the Athenians that he deserved death at the hands of the city." In the case of Sparta as well as in that of Socrates, Xenophon refers to a definite event in the past which set him thinking about its causes; in neither case does he refer to a phenomenon which still existed. The event to which he refers at the beginning of the *Constitution of the Lacedemonians* is very probably the victory of the Spartans in the Peloponnesian war. In accordance with the beginning quoted he speaks in the first chapter mostly of what Lycurgus had enacted in the past, and only toward the end does he go over to the present. In II and III the past still outweighs the present. In IV–X, the passages devoted to the past are almost equal in number to those devoted to the present. In XI and XII, the present outweighs the past, and in XIII, i.e., in the chapter immediately preceding the censure of contemporary Sparta, Xenophon praises contemporary Sparta almost exclusively: so openly does he contradict himself, and so carefully did he prepare that flagrant contradiction. Needless to add, the subtle distinctions between "Lycurgus' enactments" and "the Spartans' actual practice" should be considered carefully. It is certainly not a matter of chance that in the chapters devoted to military matters the actual practice of the Spartans is so much in the foreground, whereas in the chapter devoted to continence concerning money, for example, Xenophon prefers to speak of Lycurgus' enactments.

75 XIII, 1 and XV, 8.

Chapter 3

the account of Spartan monarchy at the end of his praise of the Spartan constitution, and he had to arrange the several topics of his treatise in such a way that their sequence represented an ascent in a straight line from the lowest topic to the highest, which is monarchy.[76] He did this by choosing as his first topic the laws concerning procreation of children; for these laws are concerned with that side of man's nature which he has in common with the animals. From procreation of children (I), Xenophon gradually ascends by way of education (II), adolescents (III), adult men (IV), continence as regards pleasures of the body (V–VI), continence as regards wealth (VI–VII), obedience (VIII), manliness (IX), the whole political virtue (X), war (XI–XIII), to the heroic kingdom of Sparta (XIII and XV). This plan implies the view that the way from peace to war is an ascent: for war is the last topic before kingdom, which is the highest; it implies the view that peace is but the preparation for war and the means to it.[77] Now it is exactly this lucid and unambiguous plan which Xenophon completely spoils by inserting the fourteenth chapter, the censure of contemporary Sparta, for in so doing he destroys the coherence of the section devoted to monarchy (XIII and XV). And what he thus spoils is not merely the lucidity of his plan, but, which is much more important, the solemnity of his praise of the kingdom of Sparta. At the same time, however, he gives us to understand that [524] the end of the thirteenth chapter is the actual end of the praise of Lycurgus' legislation: he thus dismisses especially the solemn end of the treatise as something which is merely poetic and unserious. As a consequence he compels us to reconsider the plan of the first thirteen chapters taken alone. These are clearly divided into two main sections: the first (I–X) dealing with institutions related to peace and war alike, the second (XI–XIII) with institutions related to war exclusively.[78] The insertion of the fourteenth chapter ruins, then, the plan based on the view that the way from procreation of children to the heroic kingdom is an ascent; but far from ruining, it rather enhances the plan based on the view that the distinction between peace and war is of paramount importance for the judgment of any constitution. By inserting his censure of contemporary Sparta in the "wrong" place, Xenophon suggests that the praise of Spartan monarchy, which is in the foreground, must be reconsidered in the light

---

76 Note the solemn and poetic ending of the treatise.

77 It goes without saying that a plan implying that view is most appropriate to a praise of Sparta.

78 XI, 1. *Cf.* XII, 1 and XIII, 1.

The Spirit of Sparta or the Taste of Xenophon

of the distinction, which is rather in the background, between peace and war, and of all that is implied in that distinction; he gives us to understand that the belief underlying the first plan, that war is superior to peace, must be subjected to reflection.[79]

The result to which the examination of that belief leads is indicated in all that Xenophon says and leaves unsaid about Spartan virtue. It is indicated besides in his emphatic praise of the fact that Lycurgus' legislation fostered among the citizens of Sparta the spirit of dissension and rivalry as well as spying on each other.[80] For, according to the view of the classical thinkers, one cannot assert that war against other cities is the aim of the life of the city without being driven to assert that war of individual against in-[525]dividual is the aim of the life of the individual.[81] Moreover, Xenophon concludes the first section of the treatise—the section which is devoted to institutions related to peace and war alike—in such a way that that passage appears to be the end of the whole account of Spartan legislation; he thus indicates that institutions related to war exclusively do not deserve very serious attention.[82] Accordingly, he excuses himself for the prolixity of his very brief account of Spartan camp-life.[83] And, finally, by devoting the last chapter of the treatise to matters of peace rather than to matters of war, he shows, if in a distortion most appropriate to his subject, that the end ought to be peace, and not war.[84]

---

79   The "first plan" is more visible than the "second plan" if one disregards the fourteenth chapter. For the impressive ending of the treatise is warranted by the "first plan" only, and the most impressive things are the most visible ones. The "second plan" is obscured not only by that impressive ending, but by the fifteenth chapter as a whole, for that chapter deals again with matters of peace rather than of war, and the section devoted to matters of peace had been concluded at the end of the tenth chapter.

80   IV.

81   *Cf.* Plato, *Laws*, 626c–630d, and Aristotle, *Politics*, 1324a5–1325a15.

82   X, 8. (*Cf.* also XI, 1). The Spartan military institutions may not deserve discussion for yet another reason. "Xénophon vante beaucoup dans cet ouvrage les formations de l'armée spartiate; mais lui-même, pendant la retraite des Dix Mille, avait fait adopter par tous les corps des formations athéniennes, et, lorsqu'il décrira la bataille de Thymbrée, c'est des formations et de la tactique athéniennes qu'il dotera l'armée de Cyrus." Ollier, *op. cit.* p. xxxiii. The judgment on Spartan military organization, which is implied in the discrepancies pointed out by M. Ollier, is clearly indicated in XI, 7. Other shortcomings of the Spartan army are indicated in XII, 2–4, as can be seen from a comparison of that passage with *Cyropaedia*, IV, 2, 1–8, and *Agesilaus*, 2, 24.

83   XII, 7.

CHAPTER 3

V

The title indicates that the subject of the treatise is the constitution of the Lacedemonians, and the apparent plan all but compels us to assume that that constitution is monarchic.[85] By spoiling his plan, however, Xenophon shows that that assumption is wrong.[86] If we exclude therefore all he says about the Spartan kings, we find that his treatment of the constitution proper is [526] very scanty: not a single chapter of the *Constitution of the Lacedemonians* is explicitly devoted to that topic. Thus the title seems to be inadequate. Now inadequate titles appear to have had a peculiar attraction for Xenophon: the titles of the *Anabasis* and of the *Education of Cyrus* are no less inadequate than that of the *Constitution of the Lacedemonians*. Now the title of the *Education of Cyrus* was certainly chosen in order to draw our attention away from Cyrus' brilliant achievements toward his modest education; or, more precisely, in order to induce us to pay the greatest attention to his rather obscure education.[87] In a similar way, the title *Constitution of the Lacedemonians* was chosen to induce us to observe the somewhat obscure constitution of Sparta.

Xenophon conceals the true nature of that constitution by not even mentioning the apparently very powerful "Little Assembly," of which he speaks elsewhere.[88] He also hides rather carefully the fact that Sparta had not one but two kings.[89] Moreover, he speaks most clearly of the government of Sparta in a chapter which is explicitly devoted, not to Spartan govern-

---

84 For Xenophon's view of peace and war, see especially *Memorabilia*, II, 6, 21 f. *De vectigalibus*, 5; *Hiero*, 2, 7; *Oeconomicus*, 1, 23; and *Cyropaedia*, VIII, 4, 7–8. *Cf.* also *Symposium*, 1, 10 with *Respublica Lacedaemoniorum*, XI, 3.

85 *Cf.* XV, 1.

86 Xenophon shows that the power of the Spartan kings is limited to the functions of priests and of leaders of the army: whereas the king has "power and honor" in time of war, he enjoys only "honors" in time of peace (*cf.* XIII, 1 and 10 f. with XV, 8). The Spartan king is thus induced by the very constitution to prefer war to peace. (*Cf.* Thucydides, VIII, 5, 3, and Isocrates, *Nicocles*, 24.) By letting us see this, Xenophon indicates his judgment of the wisdom of that provision.

87 A full account, entitled *Ghengis Khan's Education*, of the whole life and work of that conqueror and empire-builder would afford a tolerably adequate parallel to Xenophon's *Education of Cyrus*.

88 *Hellenica*, III, 3, 8.

89 In the whole thirteenth chapter, no single mention of the two kings occurs. At the beginning of the fifteenth chapter, Xenophon speaks again exclusively of "the king." In XV, 3 he leaves it undetermined whether Sparta was ruled by one or two kings, thus

The Spirit of Sparta or the Taste of Xenophon

ment, but to a certain Spartan virtue. Yet the virtue in question is obedience; and since he does not even mention the kings when speaking of Spartan obedience, but does emphasize the power of the ephors in that context, he leaves no serious doubt that the actual rulers of Sparta were the ephors. The ephors, he says, rule like tyrants.[90] But tyrants do not rule in accordance with laws.[91] Are the ephors then [527] not subject to the laws of the city, i.e., to the laws of Lycurgus?[92] Or was Lycurgus himself not a lawgiver, subject to none but the Delphian god? Of one thing Xenophon appears to be convinced: the fact that Lycurgus did "not even attempt" to establish the Spartan order of life until he had made "like-minded" the most powerful men in the city. Whereas he makes it perfectly clear that these powerful men accompanied Lycurgus when he went to Delphi to ask the god for confirmation of the laws "which he himself had given," he says merely that they "helped in establishing the power of the office of the ephors."[93] It is perhaps not out of place to question the identity of the man or men with whom the most powerful Spartiates collaborated in establishing the power of the ephors. Did they collaborate simply with each other? In other words, how far can Lycurgus be distinguished from the most powerful Spartiates or from the ephors? "Lycurgus is said to have lived in the days of the descendants of Heracles."[94] But all Spartan kings were, or claimed to be, descendants of Heracles. Is Lycurgus then a man who never dies?[95] However superstitious we may suppose Xenophon to have been, he certainly did not believe that such a man does or could exist *in rerum natura*. We are then led to the conclusion that, according to Xenophon, Lycurgus did not exist at all, or that "Lycurgus" was a mere name covering something much less solemn than an almost divine lawgiver belonging to a remote and venerable

---

preparing us for the disclosure, in the following paragraph, that the Spartan kingdom was no monarchy. But after this paragraph he does not mention the second king again.

90   VIII, 4. *Cf.* Plato, *Laws*, 712d4–5, and Aristotle, *Politics*, 1270b14–15. The fact that "constitution" is as such irreconcilable with "tyranny" shows that the very title of the treatise is ironic; *cf. Hellenica*, VI, 3, 8.

91   *Memorabilia*, IV, 6, 12.

92   *Cf.* Aristotle, *Politics*, 1270b30.

93   VIII, 1, 3 and 5.

94   This sentence is ambiguous: it also alludes to the extinction of the true race of Heracles in the remote past. *Cf.* below, pp. 532–3.

95   X, 8. *Cf. Agesilaus*, 1, 2. In accordance with this, Xenophon uses the past and the present indiscriminately in speaking of the Spartan legislation.

CHAPTER 3

past. This conclusion is borne out by the following statement regarding the time and place proper for pitching camp: "the Lycurgus with regard to this is the king."[96] "Lycurgus" is, then, a name designating authority or the men in authority. The statement quoted implies besides that the Lycurgus concerning the most important affairs of the city (in [528] other words the actual rulers subject to nothing but Delphian confirmation of their measures, or the tyrannic rulers of Sparta) is the ephors—if not those most powerful Spartiates who are able to sway the ephors. It is left to our discretion to decide whether the most powerful men in Sparta are different from, or identical with, those most wealthy Spartiates whose existence is alluded to by Xenophon on more than one occasion.

VI

The Constitution of the Lacedemonians, far from being an encomium of Sparta, is actually a most trenchant, if disguised, satire on that city and its spirit. To justify this contention fully we have to indicate the reasons which induced Xenophon first to satirize Sparta, and then to conceal the satire.

He himself clearly indicates the reason for his writing a satire on Sparta. At the end of the tenth chapter, which reads as if it were the end of the whole treatise and which is in fact the esoteric end, he tells us that "all praise" the Spartan institutions. And the beginning of the treatise is the words "But I."[97] Praising and admiring Sparta was a fashion in his time. Fashions of that kind are bound to be more or less unreasonable and therefore an inducement to a discerning man, who judges the unreasonable to be ridiculous, to satirize them. Xenophon was such a man. To the "all" who praise the Spartan institutions, he answers by a treatise which opens with the words, "But I ... fell wondering [and] I investigated these institutions."

One of the most famous admirers of Sparta was Critias, who was a poet and an enemy of Socrates and an oligarch. Critias was the author of two works, one in prose but one in verse, both entitled *Constitution of the Lacedemonians*. These were used by Xenophon and may be said to have

---

96 XIII, 10 (according to the good MSS). A parallel to this use of a proper name for designating a function is supplied by *Cyropaedia*, I, 4, 6 (*Sakas*).

97 Compare also the emphatic transition from "all of us" to "I" in VIII, 1. Xenophon uses in all other cases the first person singular; and whereas elsewhere he says "I shall explain," "I believe," "I wonder," etc., he constantly speaks of what "I know" in the chapter devoted to the outspoken censure of contemporary Sparta. *Cf.* Plato, *Republic*, 544c2–3, and 7th Letter, 324c2–3.

been the model of his treatise on [529] the Spartan constitution.[98] As in all cases of the kind, what matters is not so much the agreements as the differences between the imitation and the model. Critias, who praises the Spartans, does not hesitate to attribute to them the virtue of moderation; Xenophon, who investigated their mode of life, and who knew better what moderation is, answers him by silence, i.e., by being silent on Spartan moderation. The hasty Critias does not hesitate to assert that the Spartan mode of life produces men fit for both thought and toil;[99] the slow Xenophon answers him by speech interspersed with silence, i.e., by emphasizing repeatedly how much the Spartans toiled and by being silent on their thinking.[100] We shall then say that the relation of Xenophon's treatise to the two writings of Critias is fundamentally that of the long speech of Protagoras in Plato's work of that name to actual speeches, now forgotten, of that personality.

But why does Xenophon conceal his satire on Sparta, or on Athenian laconism, so carefully, whereas it is a matter of common knowledge that Plato's *Protagoras* is a comedy? The *Constitution of the Lacedemonians* is sometimes censured for its exceeding scarcity of factual information on Sparta. But briefness of expression, brachylogy, was one of the most famous characteristics of the Spartans. Considering that briefness of expression is one of the most ordinary devices for not disclosing the truth, we may assume that the famous brachylogy of the Spartans had something to do with their desire to conceal the shortcomings of their mode of life. Such a desire may be called bashfulness. By expressing himself most briefly when discussing the Spartan vices, and by thus writing a disguised satire on Sparta, Xenophon adapts himself to the peculiar character of his subject and thus achieves a feat in [530] the art of writing which is surpassed only by Plato's *Laws*. For whereas Xenophon and Plato in their other works, as well as Herodotus and Thucydides and perhaps other writers before them, teach the truth according to the rule of moderation, the *Constitution of the Lacedemonians* as well as the *Laws* deviates somewhat from this established principle by teaching the truth according to the rule

---

98   *Cf.* Habben, *op. cit.*, p. 52 ff. Notice also the poetic ending of the treatise.
99   Fr. 6 (Diels).
100 See II, 5; III, 7; IV, 7; X, 7; and especially V, 8. (In V, 4, which corresponds to Critias, fr. 6, l. 10 ff., he replaces *nūs* by *gnōmai*. *Cf. Symposium*, 2, 26.) It may be remarked in passing that the difference between, and opposition of, "toil" and "thought," which escaped Critias' notice, explains why Xenophon so likes the word *rhadiurgia*; the life of contemplation is definitely not a life of toil. *Cf.* III, 2 and IX, 1 with *Symposium*, 4, 13.

CHAPTER 3

of bashfulness: both works are most bashful speeches about the most bashful of men.[101]

A censure of Sparta, moreover, was liable to be misunderstood by uncritical readers as a praise of Athens; for at the time when Xenophon wrote the uncritical reader scarcely saw an alternative to the choice between the Spartan and the Athenian spirit. And Xenophon did not wish to praise Athens. First of all, he had reasons of his own which forbade him to praise that city and that constitution which had condemned Socrates to death. And, besides, his taste did not allow him to praise Athens: he was an Athenian and for an Athenian to praise Athens was an easy thing, and the noble things are difficult.[102] By writing his censure of Sparta in such a way that the superficial and uncritical reader could not help taking it as praise of Sparta, Xenophon certainly prevented the uncritical admirer of Athens from being confirmed in his prejudices.

Finally, if one satirizes something one considers the thing in question ridiculous. One considers ridiculous those shortcomings of other people which do not hurt one. Educated people consider ridiculous only those shortcomings which betray lack of education. But being educated and therefore desiring not to offend others, they hide their laughter as well as they can from the uneducated. That is to say, an educated man will utter his ridicule of the lack of education, or barbarism of a given man or city or nation, only in the absence of the uneducated. In other words, a good satire on the barbarism of a given man or city or nation will be [531] inaccessible to the superficial reader. This at least was Xenophon's view as he indicated in that chapter of his *Education of Cyrus* which teaches us how educated people jest: they jest about the uneducated in the absence of the latter. At the beginning of that chapter, he describes such jesting conversation as "most graceful speeches which incite to what is good."[103] The *Constitution of the Lacedemonians* is a speech of that kind: by being a most ably disguised satire on Spartan lack of education, it is a most graceful recommendation of education.

The treatise of Xenophon is, then, a remarkable document of Attic taste: it represents a higher type of comic speech than does classical comedy. Yet, just as there is no jest without underlying seriousness, there is

---

101 Note especially the extremely bashful manner in which Xenophon speaks of the subjects of the Spartans in XII, 2–4 and VII, 2, as compared with *Cyropaedia*, IV, 2, 1 ff.

102 *Cf.* for a similar case of conscience, Plato, *Menexenus*, 235d.

103 *Cyropaedia*, II, 2.

The Spirit of Sparta or the Taste of Xenophon

no good taste which is not something more than taste. The true name of that taste which permeates Xenophon's writings is, not education, but philosophy.

Philosophic life was considered by the classical thinkers as fundamentally different from political life. And as far as political life raised a universal claim, i.e., as far as the city left no room for a private life which was more than economic, philosophic life, which of necessity is private, of necessity became opposed to political life. The incarnation of the political spirit was Sparta: Sparta and philosophy are incompatible.[104] Thus Sparta became, on the one hand, the natural starting point for any ruthless idealization of political life, or for any true utopia; and, on the other hand, it became the natural subject of any ruthless attack on political life, or of any philosophic satire. By satirizing Sparta, the philosophers then did not so much mean Sparta, the actual Sparta of the present or of the past, as the spirit of Sparta, or the conviction that man belongs, or ought to belong, entirely to the city. For it would be an overstatement to say that philosophy was compatible with Athens: Socrates was executed for not believing in the gods of Athens, in the gods of the city. By considering and [532] reconsidering this fact, we grasp the ultimate reason why political life and philosophic life, even if compatible for almost all practical purposes, are incompatible in the last analysis: political life, if taken seriously, meant belief in the gods of the city, and philosophy is the denial of the gods of the city.

Socrates did not believe in the gods of the city, nor did his pupil Xenophon. But both master and pupil took every imaginable care to hide from the public their unbelief, so much so that even at the present time, when nobody believes any longer in the gods of Greek cities, one steps on slippery ground in dealing with Socrates' or Xenophon's belief or unbelief. Since they uttered their unbelief only in such a manner that the large majority might in no circumstances become aware of it, proofs of their unbelief necessarily are of such a character that they will not convince the majority of readers. But the only alternative to accepting as valid such proofs as the nature of the matter allows is higher criticism in the nineteenth-century style, i.e., deleting important passages of Xenophon's writings, making a large number of superfluous textual emendations and assuming that Xenophon was not familiar with, or not able to live up to, the most elementary rules of lucid composition.

---

104 It is a joke of Socrates to speak of "Spartan [and Cretan] philosophy"; see Plato, *Protagoras*, 342a–b.

CHAPTER 3

Belief in the gods of the city was apt to be connected with the belief that a god had given the laws of the city. The Spartans for instance believed that the Delphian god had given them their laws. Xenophon did not share that belief. He held the view that "Lycurgus" had finished the elaboration of his laws before he went to Delphi to ask Apollo for confirmation. Accordingly he distinguishes between the Spartans' obedience to Lycurgus' laws and their obedience to the god.[105]

Belief in the gods of the city was bound up with the belief in the existence of demigods or heroes, and therefore in particular with the belief in the possibility of sexual intercourse between immortal gods and mortal men. The Spartans for instance believed that their kings were descendants of Heracles, and that [533] Heracles was the son of Zeus and a mortal mother.[106] The obvious plan of Xenophon's treatise is based on compliance with that belief: the treatise ascends from a fact which is common to men and animals, to the Spartan kings, who are assumed by the laws of Lycurgus to be not human beings but heroes. Xenophon did not accept that assumption, for he clearly realized that belief in the divine or heroic descent of the Spartan kings presupposes belief in the marital fidelity of all Spartan queens, and he had no high opinion of the chastity of Spartan women in general and of Spartan queens in particular.[107] Accordingly, he spoiled that plan of his treatise which corresponded to the Spartan claim in question. But he went further: he clearly realized that the unjustified and unjustifiable claim of the Spartan kings was merely one consequence among many of the erroneous views which the Spartans and others held of the deity. He indicated this by speaking at the beginning of the treatise of how people feed their children, and by stating at the beginning of the last section that Sparta "feeds the king and those with him," and shortly thereafter, that the Spartan king, in his turn, "offers sacrifices to Zeus and to those with him." To indicate his view still more clearly, he soon goes over from the plurality of the gods ("Zeus and those with him") to a duality ("Zeus and Athena") and finally to the singular ("The god").[108]

---

105 *Cf.* VIII, 5 and XIV, 7 with Plato, *Laws*, 624a1–6 and 634e1–2.
106 *Cf.* XV, 9 and 2 with *Agesilaus*, 1, 2, and *Cynegeticus*, 1, 9.
107 *Cf.* I, 4–9 with *Agesilaus*, 1, 5 and *Hellenica*, III, 3, 1–3 and VII, 1, 31.
108 I, 3 and XIII, 1–3. *Cf. Apologia Socratis*, 24. A censure of the moral side of the Spartan view of the gods is implied in the last sentence of XIII, 3, as appears from a comparison of that passage with II, 7.

The Spirit of Sparta or the Taste of Xenophon

The *Constitution of the Lacedemonians* appears to be praise of an admirable constitution. Since Xenophon was an adherent of aristocracy, the point of reference with regard to which he judges constitutions is the quality of the education which corresponds to the constitution in question. It is, therefore, noteworthy that he does not mention piety at all when he speaks of Spartan education. Thus he lets us see that piety is no essential part of the highest type of education. Or are we to judge his failure to mention piety in the same way we judged his failure to mention moderation and [534] wisdom? This would hardly be correct; for, whereas he does not mention moderation and wisdom at all when praising the Spartans, he has many things to say of their piety, i.e., of their sacrifices and oracles and hymns.[109] He deals most fully with Spartan piety when recounting how they start their military expeditions. He concludes that account, which is almost completely devoted to the various sacrifices offered up by the king at the beginning of a campaign, by saying: "When you see these things, you would believe that the others are bunglers in military matters and that the Lacedemonians alone are truly experts in warlike matters."[110] Worship of the gods, which plays no role in education, is an essential part of the art of war. In Xenophon's view of the dignity of war as compared with the dignity of peace and leisure and education, his judgment on piety is implied.

In the time of Xenophon, impiety constituted a criminal offence. Thus philosophy, which is essentially incompatible with acceptance of the gods of the city, was as such subject to persecution.[111] Philosophers had therefore to conceal if not the fact that they were philosophers, at least the fact that they were unbelievers. On the other hand, they desired to communicate their views to a small number of people who were able and willing to accept these views; and since they could not possibly talk to the larger part of that small number because the larger part was not yet born, they had no choice but to write books and publish them. The difficulty implied in the contradiction between the necessarily secret character of the philosophic teaching and the necessarily public character of publications was overcome by a literary technique which made it possible to reveal the truth to a small, if competent, minority, while hiding it from the large majority. That technique was the outcome of a very simple discovery. If a man tells

---

109 For Xenophon's view of piety, see especially *Memorabilia*, IV, 6, 4, and *Agesilaus*, 11, 1–2.
110 XIII, 5. *Cf.* also IV, 5–6 and XIII end.
111 *Cf. Memorabilia*, I, 2, 31 with Plato, *Apology*, 23d4–7.

Chapter 3

a charming story, most people will enjoy the story—the imitated characters, the imitated actions or events, the imitated landscape, the [535] imitated speeches of the characters, and even the imitation itself—but only a minority of readers will recover from the charm, reflect upon the story and discover the teaching which it silently conveys. Silent or secret teaching is then certainly possible. That it is an actual fact of the past is shown, above all, by the stories and histories of Herodotus, Thucydides and Xenophon, as well as by the Socratic writings of Xenophon and Plato. One may add that this kind of literature disappeared only at a rather recent date: its disappearance was simultaneous with the disappearance of persecution, just as its reappearance is simultaneous with the reappearance of persecution.

It would, however, betray too low a view of the philosophic writers of the past if one assumed that they concealed their thoughts merely for fear of persecution or of violent death. They concealed the truth from the vulgar also because they considered the vulgar to be unfit to digest the truth: the large majority of men, the philosophers of the past thought, would be deprived of the very basis of their morality if they were to lose their beliefs. They considered it then not only a matter of fear and safety, but also a matter of duty to hide the truth from the majority of mankind. By making the discovered truth almost as inaccessible as it was before it had been discovered, they prevented—to call a vulgar thing by a vulgar name—the cheap sale of the formulations of the truth: nobody should know even the formulations of the truth who had not rediscovered the truth by his own exertions, if aided by subtle suggestions from a superior teacher. It is in this way that the classical authors became the most efficient teachers of independent thinking. It should, however, not be overlooked that this exoteric literature, which provides the highest type of education, is found not only in classical times; it has reappeared in all epochs in which philosophy was understood in its full and challenging meaning, in all epochs, that is, in which wisdom was not separated from moderation. Its disappearance almost coincides with the victory of higher criticism and of systems of philosophy which claimed to be sincere but which certainly lacked moderation.

[536] One cannot study Xenophon, who seems to have been one of the greatest classical admirers of Sparta, without being constantly reminded of that greatest of all modern admirers of Sparta, Jean Jacques Rousseau. If it is true, as is sometimes asserted, that the restitution of a sound approach is bound up with the elimination of Rousseau's influence, then the thesis of the present article can be summed up by saying that the teaching

The Spirit of Sparta or the Taste of Xenophon

of men like Xenophon is precisely the antidote which we need. It goes without saying that it is not the intention of the present article to refute, or to prove, such a far-reaching thesis. It will, however, not have been written in vain if it induces some readers to reconsider the traditional and current view of Xenophon, which, while being understandable and even to a certain extent justifiable, is almost an insult to this truly royal soul. For such a man was he that he preferred to go through the centuries in the disguise of a beggar rather than to sell the precious secrets of Socrates' quiet and sober wisdom to a multitude which let him escape to immortality only after he had intoxicated it by his artful stories of the swift and dazzling actions of an Agesilaus or a Cyrus, or a Xenophon.

4

Review of James T. Shotwell, *The History of History* (1941)

SHOTWELL, JAMES T. *The History of History*, Volume 1. [Revised edition of *An Introduction to the History of History.*] New York: Columbia University Press. 1939. 407 pp. $3.75.

There are two ways in which one may attempt to elucidate the meaning of history. One may engage in a quest for the causes of historical phenomena as such, that is, in a philosophy of history. Or one may raise the more elementary question of how it came to pass that a certain type of phenomena is looked upon as "historical," in other words, is designated by a term which originally designated not phenomena but a human attitude toward them, a certain type of inquiry. The title of Professor Shotwell's book suggests that he has recognized the urgency of the elementary and therefore truly philosophic question. And the book itself bears out this impression to a considerable extent.

The present volume is devoted to the development of history from prehistoric times up to Augustine's *City of God*. The point of view from which the author discusses this development is that of nineteenth and twentieth century scientific history. "This scientific history" of our time, he says, "impartial, almost unhuman in its cold impartiality," serves no other purpose than "to fulfill the imperative demand of the scientific spirit—to find the truth and set it forth" (p. 11). The main thesis of the volume is that history in the proper sense of the word began with the Greeks (p. 8); for them history "was but another name for... science, critical analysis" (p. 20), and among them emerged what Voltaire called *l'esprit de discussion et de critique*, whereas the outlook of the Babylonians, Assyrians, Egyptians, Jews and

---

Originally published in *Social Research* 8, no. 1 (Feb. 1941): 126–27. —Eds.

Chapter 4

Christians was determined by forces which block the path of scientific inquiry. The author's tendency expresses itself most clearly in his remark (which, as matters stand, sounds like a prayer rather than a statement of fact) that Lucretius' *On the Nature of Things* "is a poem for the twentieth century" (p. 266).

Whether or not one share [*sic*—Eds.] Professor Shotwell's views and sympathies, one cannot accuse him of being blind to what he must consider the shortcomings of the classical historians. No useful purpose would be served by a summary of his critical remarks which, be it said, are never irrelevant to the main issue as stated by him from the outset. Only one question must be raised. He judges the classical historians with reference to the demand of the modern scientific spirit "to find the truth and set it forth." There can be no doubt that the writers concerned were interested in finding the truth. But to what extent were they interested in telling it, or able to tell it, without reserve? If I am not greatly mistaken, it is only by answering that question, which up to now has never, to my knowledge, been publicly discussed, that we shall be able to understand the relation, repeatedly emphasized by Shotwell, between classical history and classical poetry and rhetoric.

5

Fārābī's *Plato*[1]
(1945)

> Eben derselbe Gedanke kann,
> an einem andern Orte, einen
> ganz andern Wert haben.*
>
> —Lessing,
> *Leibniz, von den ewigen Strafen.*

[357] It is generally admitted that one cannot understand the teaching of Maimonides' *Guide for the Perplexed* before one has understood the teaching of "the philosophers"; for the former presents itself as a Jewish correction of the latter. To begin with, one can identify "the philosophers" with the Islamic Aristotelians, and one may describe their teaching as a blend of genuine Aristotelianism with Neo-platonism and, of course, Islamic tenets. If, however, one wants to grasp the principle transforming that mixture of heterogeneous elements into a consistent, or intelligible, whole, one does well to follow the signpost erected by Maimonides himself.

In his letter to Samuel ibn Tibbon, he makes it abundantly clear that he considered the greatest authority in philosophy, apart from Aristotle himself, not Avicenna or Averroes, nor even Avempace, but Fārābī. Of Fārābī's works, he mentions in that context only one by its title, and he recommends it to ibn Tibbon in the strongest terms. Thus we may assume to begin with that he considered it Fārābī's most important book. He calls that book *The principles of the beings*. Its original title is *The political governments*.

Originally published in the *Louis Ginzberg Jubilee Volume* (New York: American Academy for Jewish Research, 1945), 357–93. N.B.: "Fārābī" is often given as "Fārābi" throughout the text. In the chapter title, the entire word is in uppercase with no diacritics. —Eds.

* "The same thought can have a completely different meaning in another place." Lessing, *Leibniz: On Eternal Punishment.* —Eds.

1 I wish to express my thanks to Professor A. H. Halkin for kindly checking my translations from the Arabic.

CHAPTER 5

There can then be no doubt as to the proper beginning, i.e., the only beginning which is not arbitrary, of the understanding of Maimonides' philosophic background: one has to start from [358] an analysis of Fārābī's *Political governments*. It would be unwise to attempt such an analysis now. In the first place, we lack a satisfactory edition.[2] Above all, the full understanding of the book presupposes the study of two parallel works of Fārābī's, *The principles of the opinions of the people of the virtuous city*[3] and *The virtuous religious community*, the second of which has not yet been edited at all. Maimonides presumably preferred *The political governments* to these parallel presentations. To discover the reason for that preference, or, at any rate, to understand *The political governments* fully, one has to compare the doctrines contained in that book with the doctrines contained in the parallel works, and thus to lay bare the teaching characteristic of *The political governments*. For that teaching consists, to some extent, of the silent rejection of certain tenets which are adhered to in the two other works.

We limit ourselves here to stressing one feature of *The political governments* (and, *mutatis mutandis*, of the two parallel works) which by itself clearly indicates the most striking trait of Fārābī's philosophy. As is shown already by the difference between its authentic and its customary title, the book treats the whole of philosophy proper (i.e., with the omission of logic and mathematic) within a political framework. In this respect, Fārābī takes as his model, not any of the Aristotelian writings known to him or to us, but Plato' [*sic*—Eds.] *Republic* and, to a lesser extent, Plato's *Laws* which also present the whole of philosophy within a political framework. To account

---

2 The original was edited in Hyderabad in 1346 H. Ibn Tibbon's Hebrew translation was edited by Filipowski in the האסיף ס', Leipzig 1849, 1–64. Cf. also F. Dieterici's German translation (*Die Staatsleitung von Alfārābī*), Leiden 1904. The text underlying the Hyderabad edition as well as the German translation is less complete than the one underlying the Hebrew translation; the passage from p. 62, line 21 in Filipowski's edition till the end is missing in both the Hyberabad and the German translation; it can partly be traced in Fārābī's *Musterstaat* (ed. Dieterici, 71f.). A comparison of the Hebrew translation of *The political governments* with the parallel in the *Musterstaat* shows that the text of the former is also incomplete: the whole concluding part of *The political governments* (roughly corresponding to *Musterstaat* 72–end) is at present lost. [See Leo Strauss, "A Lost Writing of Fārābī's," trans. Gabriel Bartlett and Martin D. Yaffe, Appendix D in *Reorientation: Leo Strauss in the 1930s*, ed. Martin D. Yaffe and Richard S. Ruderman (New York: Palgrave Macmillan, 2014).—Eds.]

3 Edited by Dieterici under the title *Der Musterstaat*, Leiden 1895.

Fārābī's Plato

for this Platonizing procedure, [359] it is not necessary to look out for any particular Platonist tradition: the *Republic* and the *Laws* were accessible to Fārābī in Arabic translations.

Fārābī followed Plato not merely as regards the manner in which he presented the philosophic teaching in his most important books. He held the view that Plato's philosophy was the true philosophy. To reconcile his Platonism with his adherence to Aristotle, he could take three more or less different ways. First, he could try to show that the explicit teachings of both philosophers can be reconciled with each other. He devoted to this attempt his *Concordance of the opinions of Plato and Aristotle*. The argument of that work is partly based on the so-called *Theology of Aristotle*: by accepting this piece of neo-platonic origin as a genuine work of Aristotle, he could easily succeed in proving the substantial agreement of the explicit teachings of both philosophers concerning the crucial subjects. It is however very doubtful whether Fārābī considered his *Concordance* as more than an exoteric treatise, and thus whether it would be wise of us to attach great importance to its explicit argument.[4] Secondly, he could show that the esoteric teachings of both philosophers are identical. Thirdly, he could show that "the aim" of both philosophers is identical. The third approach is used by him in his tripartite work *The aims of the philosophy of Plato and of Aristotle*, or, as Averroes quotes it, *The two philosophies*. The second part of that work is devoted exclusively to Plato's philosophy. By studying that central part which alone is at present accessible in a critical edition,[5] one is enabled to [360] grasp fully the character of Fārābī's Platonism and therewith of Fārābī's own philosophy, and thus to take the first step toward the understanding of the philosophic background of Maimonides.

---

4   Cf. Paul Kraus, "Plotin chez les Arabes," *Bulletin de l'Institut d'Égypte*, v. 23, 1940–41, 269. —Note the use of the term "opinion" in the title of the *Concordance*. Cf. note 69 below.

5   *Plato Arabus*, v. II. *Alfarabius: De Platonis philosophia*, edd. F. Rosenthal and R. Walzer, London (Warburg Institute) 1943. The edition is accompanied by a Latin translation and by notes. It will be quoted in the following notes "Fārābī, *Plato*"; figures in parentheses after §§ will indicate pages and line of the text. — The first part of Fārābī's *Two philosophies* was edited under the title *k. taḥṣīl al-sa'āda* in Hyderabad in 1345 H.; the third part (dealing with the philosophy of Aristotle) is not yet edited. The whole is accessible in the incomplete Hebrew translation by Falkera (*Reshit hokma*, ed. by David, 61–92).

CHAPTER 5

I. FIRST IMPRESSIONS

Fārābī's exposition of Plato's philosophy claims to be a complete survey of its main topics:[6] Platonic topics which are not mentioned in it, are considered by him either unimportant or merely exoteric. The procedure which he chooses, may be called genetic: he does not present the final Platonic "dogmata" by following the scheme supplied by the division of philosophy into logic, physics and ethics or any other scheme; nor does he adopt the procedure of Theo of Smyrna by describing the sequence in which the Platonic dialogues should be read; on the other hand, he does not engage in a historical study of the "development" of Plato's thought;[7] he simply describes what he considers the inner and necessary sequence of the investigations of the mature Plato. He tries to assign to each step of Plato's investigations one Platonic dialogue; one way or the other, he succeeds in thus accounting for most, if not for almost all, of the dialogues belonging to the traditional *Corpus Platonicum*. What he says about the individual dialogues, sounds in some cases fairly fanciful. He certainly had no access to all of them, and we do not know to what extent the indirect knowledge which he owed to Aristotle, Galen, Theo, Proclus, or others has been distorted on the more or less circuitous way in which it reached him. But it is unimportant what he believed or guessed about the purport of [361] this or that dialogue which he never read. What matters is what he thought about the philosophy of Plato as a whole which he certainly knew from the *Republic*, the *Timaeus* and the *Laws*.

According to Fārābī, Plato was guided by the question of the perfection of man, or of happiness. After having realized that man's perfection or his happiness is identical with, or at least inseparable from, "a certain science ($ἐπιστήμη$) and a certain way of life ($βίος$)," he tries to discover both the science and the way of life in question. The successive examination of all sciences and ways of life which are generally accepted ($ἔνδοξοι$), leads him

---

6 Its title is: "The philosophy of Plato, its parts, and the grades of dignity of its parts, from its beginning to its end." Cf. also the end of the *Taḥṣīl* (quoted in Fārābī, *Plato*, IX).

7 How little Fārābī was concerned with history, is shown most clearly by the fact that he presents Plato's investigations as entirely independent of the investigations of any predecessors, although he knew of course (from the *Metaphysics*, e.g.) that Plato was a disciple of Socrates as well as of other philosophers. It is only when describing one of the last steps of Plato's, that he mentions "the way of Socrates" which a historian would have explained at the beginning of his exposition. — Cf. p. 376 f., below.

Fārābī's Plato

to the result that none of them meets his demands.[8] Compelled to discover the desired science and way of life by himself,[9] he finds first that the former is supplied by philosophy and that the latter is supplied by the royal or political art, and then that "philosopher" and "king" are identical. This identity implies that virtue is, if not identical with, at least inseparable from, philosophy. Since this contradicts the popular notions of the virtues, he investigated first the various virtues;[10] he found that the genuine virtues are different from the virtues "which are famous in the cities" (from the ἀρεταὶ πολιτικαί or δημώδεις).[11] But the central question concerns, on the basis of the result mentioned, the precise meaning of "philosopher." This subject to whose discussion the *Phaedrus* is devoted,[12] divides itself into four parts: 1) the φύσις of the future philosopher (the philosophic ἔρως); 2) the ways of philosophic investigation (diairesis and synthesis); 3) the ways of teaching (rhetoric [362] and dialectic); 4) the ways of transmitting the teaching (oral or in writing). After the question of what human perfection is, has thus received a full answer, Plato had to turn his attention to the conflict between happiness fully understood and the generally accepted opinions about happiness, or, in other words, to the conflict classically represented by the fate of Socrates, between the views and the way of life of the philosopher and the opinions and the way of life of his unphilosophic fellow-citizens. Rejecting both the assimilation of the philosopher to the vulgar and the withdrawal from political life, he had to seek a city different from the cities which existed in his time: the city completed in speech[13] in the *Republic* whose results are supplemented in various ways by the *Timaeus*, the *Laws*, the *Menexenus* and other dialogues. The final question which he raised, concerned the way in which the cities of his time could be gradually converted to the life of the perfect city.

---

8   The Platonic model of Fārābī's presentation of the successive examination of the generally received sciences and arts is to be found in the *Apology of Socrates* (21b9–22e5). Cf. also for the whole first part of the treatise *Euthydemus* 282a–d3 and 288d5–290d8.

9   Cf. note 7 above.

10 With the exception of justice; cf. the distinction between justice and the virtues in Fārābī's *Plato* §30 (22, 5).

11 *Phaedo* 68c5–69c3 and 82a11 ff.; *Republic* 430c3–5; 500d8; 518d9–e3; 619c6 ff.; *Laws* 710a5 and 968a2. Cf. *Eth. Nic.* 1116a17 ff.

12 At the beginning of his summary of the *Phaedrus* (§22), Fārābī uses *tafaḥḥaṣa* instead of the usual *faḥaṣa*, thus indicating the particular significance of that passage.

13 Cf. *Republic* 369c9, 472e1, 473e2, 501e4–5 and 592a11.

CHAPTER 5

It is evident at first sight—and closer investigation merely confirms the first impression[14]—that this view of Plato's philosophy cannot be traced to Neoplatonism. The apparent identification of philosophy with the royal art, the apparent subordination of the subject of the *Timaeus* to the political theme of the *Republic*, the implicit rejection of the "metaphysical" interpretation of the *Philebus*, the *Parmenides*, the *Phaedo* and the *Phaedrus* might lead one to suspect that, according to Fārābī, Plato's philosophy is essentially political. Since Fārābī considered the Platonic view of philosophy the true view, we would thus be driven to believe that Fārābī himself attributed to philosophy an essentially political meaning. This belief would be so paradoxical, it would be so much opposed to all opinions which we have inherited, that we cannot but feel very hesitant to accept it. What is then Fārābī's real view of the relation of philosophy and politics in Plato's philosophy? [363]

II. PHILOSOPHY AND POLITICS

The expression "Plato's philosophy" is ambiguous. When Fārābī uses it in the heading of his treatise and again in its concluding sentence, he refers to Plato's investigations as summarized in the treatise. "Plato's philosophy" thus understood is essentially concerned with happiness and in particular with the relation of philosophy to happiness; and since happiness is the subject of political science,[15] we are justified in saying that "Plato's philosophy" is essentially a political investigation. Within the context of this political philosophy, Fārābī's Plato discusses among other things the essential character of philosophy: in order to establish the relation of philosophy to happiness, he has to establish first what philosophy itself is. Now it would be rash, if not altogether foolish, to assume that the philosophy whose relation to happiness is the theme implying all Platonic subjects, exhausts itself in the investigation of its own relation to happiness. We are thus led to another meaning of "Plato's philosophy," *viz.*, what Fārābī's Plato himself understood by "philosophy." The second meaning ought to be authoritative, if for no other reason at least for this that Fārābī himself means to introduce his readers, not to his own view, but to Plato's view: Fārābī gradually leads his readers from what he presents as his view of philosophy to what he considers the genuinely Platonic view.[16]

---

14 Fārābī, *Plato*, 17 f., 20, 22–24.
15 Fārābī, *Iḥṣā al-'ulūm*, ch. 5. Cf. Maimonides, *Millot ha-higgayon*, ch. 14.

Fārābī's Plato

Philosophy would be essentially political, if the sole subject of philosophy were "the political things," and in particular "the noble things and the just things." Such a view is traditionally attributed to Socrates as distinguished from Plato.[17] Fārābī [364] alludes to this difference between the Platonic and the Socratic view when speaking of "the way of Socrates" which consisted of, or culminated in, "the scientific investigation concerning justice and the virtues": he does not identify that investigation, or "the way of Socrates" generally speaking, with philosophy. In fact, he distinguishes philosophy as unmistakably from "the way of Socrates" as he distinguishes it from "the way of Thrasymachus."[18] Philosophy could be identified with political philosophy, if "justice and the virtues" were the main subjects of philosophy, and this would be the case, if justice and the virtues were the highest subjects in general. A Platonist who would adopt such a view, might be expected to refer to the "ideas" of justice and the other virtues: Fārābī is completely silent about these as well as about any other "ideas."[19] His Plato is so far from narrowing down philosophy to the study of political things that he defines philosophy as the theoretical art which supplies "the science of the essence of each of all beings."[20] That is to say: he identifies philosophy with "the art of demonstration."[21] Accordingly, his Plato actually excludes the study of political and moral

---

16 Observe the distinction, made at the end of the *Taḥṣīl*, between "Plato's philosophy" and "the aim of Plato's philosophy," and also the reference to the different ranks of dignity of the different parts of Plato's philosophy in the title of the *Plato*.

17 Aristotle, *Metaphysics*, 987b1 ff. Cf. *Eth. Eud.* 1216b3ff.; Plato, *Gorgias* 521d6–8; *Phaedrus* 229e2–230a2; *Ap. Socr.* 38a1–6. (Cf. also Xenophon, *Memor.* I.1, 11–16).—That Fārābī knew of the differences between Plato and Socrates, appears from his *Concordance* (*Philosophische Abhandlungen*, ed. by Dieterici, 19 f.).

18 Fārābī, *Plato* §30 (22, 4–5). Cf. §28.—The opposite view is held by Rosenthal-Walzer (XII). [Strauss's parenthetical references to *The Philosophy of Plato* match the marginal numbers in bold and the line numbers in Muhsin Mahdi's edition—*Philosophy of Plato and Aristotle* (Ithaca, NY: Cornell University Press, 1969); the section numbers in Strauss's piece, however, do not match any numbers in Mahdi's edition.—Eds.]

19 *Ib.*, XVIII. Cf. *Republic* 504d4 ff.

20 *Ib.*, §§2 (4, 1–3) and 16 (12, 10–15). As regards the science of the essence of each of all beings, cf. *Republic* 480a11–13, 484d5–6, 485b5–8, 490b2–4; *Parmenides* 130b–c; *Phaedrus* 262b7–8 and 270a–d1.

21 Observe the absence of the art of demonstration from the list of the parts of logic in §§8–11; see in particular §11 (9, 8). As regards the use of "philosophy" in the sense of "art of demonstration," cf. Maimonides, *Millot ha-higgayon*, ch. 14.

Chapter 5

subjects from the domain of philosophy proper. His investigations are guided throughout by the fundamental distinction (constantly repeated in Fārābī's exposition) between "science" and "way of life," and in particular between that science and that way of life which are essential to happiness. The desired science is the science of the essence of each of all beings or, more generally expressed, the science [365] of the beings which is distinguished from the science of the ways of life.[22] The science of the beings is supplied by philosophy which is a theoretical art fundamentally distinguished from the practical arts, whereas the desired way of life is supplied by the highest practical art, i.e., the royal art. With a view to the fact that the theoretical art called "philosophy" (i.e., the art of demonstration) is the only way leading to the science of the beings, i.e., the theoretical science *par excellence*, the science of the beings too is called "philosophy."[23] Theoretical science (the science of Timaeus) is presented in the *Timaeus* whose subjects are "the divine and the natural beings," and practical or political science (the science of Socrates) is presented (in its final form) in the *Laws* whose subject is "the virtuous way of life."[24] Since philosophy is essentially theoretical and not practical or political, and since it is essentially related to theoretical science only, only the subjects of the *Timaeus*, and not moral or political subjects, can be called philosophic in the precise sense of the term.[25] This, it seems to me, is, according to Fārābī, "the aim" of Plato.

The precise meaning of "philosophy" can easily be reconciled with the broader meaning underlying Fārābī's expression "Plato's philosophy." For

---

22 Fārābī, *Plato*, §§6 (6, 15 f.), 8 (7, 13 f.; cf. 7, 16 f.) and 9 (8, 2 f.).

23 Cf. §§22 (15, 18 ff.) and 23 (16, 13–15) where "philosophy" evidently means, not the art by means of which the science of the beings is acquired, but, if not that science itself, at least the actual investigation of beings which leads to that science.

24 §§16 and 26–28. Cf. §16 with §18 *in princ.*; cf. also §12 (9, 11–17). The implied attribution of the teaching of the *Laws* to Socrates is not altogether surprising; cf. Aristotle, *Politics* 1265a11 ff.

25 This view can be traced (considering the etymology of "philosophy") to the Aristotelian distinction between φρόνησις and σοφία: it is φρόνησις, and not σοφία, which is concerned with moral or political subjects. Cf. also *Metaphysics* 993b19 ff.—The same view is underlying Maimonides' interpretation of the story of Adam's fall in the *Guide* (I.2): prior to the fall, Adam possessed the highest intellectual perfection: he knew all the νοητά (and, of course, also the αἰσθητά), but had no knowledge of "good and evil," i.e., of the καλά and αἰσχρά. Cf. also *Millot ha-higgayon* ch. 8 on the difference between demonstrative and moral knowledge.

the philosopher who, transcending the sphere of moral or political things, engages in the quest for the essence [366] of all beings, has to give an account of his doings by answering the question "why philosophy?" That question cannot be answered but with a view to the natural aim of man which is happiness, and in so far as man is by nature a political being, it cannot be answered but within a political framework. In other words, the question "why philosophy?" is only a special form of the general question "what is the right way of life?," i.e., of the question guiding all moral or political investigations. This question and the answer to it which are strictly speaking merely preliminary, can nevertheless be described as philosophic since only the philosopher is competent to elaborate that question and to answer it. One must go one step further and say, using the language of an ancient, that $\sigma o\varphi\iota\alpha$ and $\sigma\omega\varphi\rho o\sigma\upsilon\nu\eta$, or philosophy (as quest for the truth about the whole) and self-knowledge (as realization of the need of that truth as well as of the difficulties obstructing its discovery and its communication) cannot be separated from each other. This means, considering the relation of the questions "why philosophy?" and "what is the right way of life?" that one cannot become a philosopher without becoming engaged in "the scientific investigation concerning justice and the virtues." Yet it must be understood that philosophy proper on the one hand and the reflection on the human or political meaning of philosophy, or what is called moral and political philosophy, on the other, do not belong to the same level. If Fārābī's Plato had disregarded that difference of level, he would not have distinguished philosophy as the way leading to theoretical science from the practical or political arts or sciences, but would have accepted the usual view, adopted in the other writings of Fārābī, according to which philosophy consists of theoretical philosophy and practical philosophy.

Both that usual view and the view suggested in the *Plato* imply that philosophy is not essentially political. Both these views imply that philosophy is not identical with political philosophy or with the art to which political philosophy leads, the royal or political art. Yet, it may be objected, precisely in the *Plato* philosophy is explicitly identified with the royal art. Our first answer has to be that this is not the case. Even they who believe that Fārābī adopted the political interpretation of [367] Plato's philosophy, have to admit that his Plato identified, not philosophy with the royal art, but the "true" philosophy with the "true" royal art.[26] This is not very precise. What Fārābī says is, first

---

26 Fārābī, *Plato*, 25 and XI.

Chapter 5

of all, that, according to Plato, the *homo philosophus* and the *homo rex* are the same thing.[27] This by itself does not mean more than that a human being cannot acquire the specific art of the philosopher without at the same time acquiring the specific art of the king and *vice versa*: it does not necessarily mean that these two arts themselves are identical. Fārābī continues as follows: "[According to Plato,] each of the two (*sc.* the philosopher and the king) is rendered perfect by one function and one faculty." The philosopher reaches his perfection by the exercise of one specific function and by the training of one specific faculty, and the king reaches his perfection by the exercise of another specific function and by the training of another specific faculty. Fārābī: "[According to Plato,] each of the two (*sc.* the philosopher and the king) has one function which supplies the science desired from the outset and the way of life desired from the outset; each of the two (*sc.* functions) produces in those who take possession of it, and in all other human beings that happiness which is truly happiness." The function of the philosopher supplies by itself both the science of the beings and the right way of life and thus produces true happiness in both the philosophers and all other human beings; the function of the king supplies by itself both the science of the beings and the right way of life and thus produces true happiness in both the kings and all other human beings. One may say that in the last of his three statements on the subject Fārābī practically identifies philosophy with the royal art: philosophy proves to contain the royal art (since it supplies the right way of life which is the product of the royal art) and the [368] royal art proves to contain philosophy (since it supplies the science of the beings which is the product of philosophy). But one would be equally justified in saying that even the last statement does not do away with the fundamental distinction between philosophy and the royal art: while it is true that the specific function of the philosopher which is primarily directed toward the science of the beings, cannot be exercised fully without producing the right way of life, and that the specific function of the king which is primarily directed toward the right way of life, cannot be exercised fully without producing the science of the beings, it is no less true that philosophy is primarily and essentially the quest for the science of the beings, whereas the royal art is primarily and es-

---

27 *Ib.*, §18. As regards "homo" in the expression "homo philosophus," cf. *Eth. Nic.* 1178b5–7 with §16 (12, 10–13). (In the translation of §32 [22, 15] "vir perfectus" and "vir indagator" should be replaced by "homo perfectus" and "homo indagator." The translator must not presume to decide for the author the question as to whether perfection, or investigation, is a prerogative of the male sex.)—Cf. notes 35 and 54 below.

Fārābī's Plato

sentially concerned with the right way of life. Even the last statement does then not necessarily do away with the difference of level between philosophy proper and moral or political investigations. While Fārābī's third statement leaves no doubt as to this that philosophy and the royal art are coextensive, he certainly does not say with so many words that they are identical.[28]

It would be unfair however to insist too strongly on subtleties of this kind and thus to overlook the wood for the trees. We certainly cannot assume that the average reader will consider [369] Fārābī's second or central statement his last word on the subject. For all practical purposes, Fārābī identified philosophy with the royal art: why then did he hesitate to do so overtly?[29] How is that identification intelligible seeing that philosophy is a theoretical art and the royal art is a practical art? We must try to understand why, after having brought into prominence the essentially theoretical character of philosophy as distinguished from the royal art, Fārābī blurs that distinction by implying that philosophy supplies the right way of life, the product of the royal art, in the same way, and, as it were, in the same breath, in which it supplies the science of the beings. We must try to understand why, after having taught that philosophy must be supplemented by something else in order to produce happiness, he teaches that philosophy does not need to be supplemented by something

---

28 In a different context—§25 (20, 9)—he states that, according to Plato, the royal function exercised in the perfect city is "philosophy *simpliciter*" (not, as R.-W. translate, "philosophia ipsa"). But "philosophy *simpliciter*" which embraces the theoretical perfection as well as other perfections is not identical with "philosophy" which consists of the theoretical perfection alone (see *Taḥṣīl* 42, 12 ff. and 39, 11 ff.). Besides, the fact that the royal function exercised in the perfect city is philosophy, does not mean more than that in the perfect city philosophy and kingship are united: it does not mean that they are identical in the perfect city; still less does it mean that they are identical as such. Finally, the royal function exercised in the perfect city is not identical with the royal art: the royal art, or the perfect king, exist also in imperfect cities (§23).—It should also be noted that in the last remark occurring in the *Plato*, which explicitly bears on the subject, not the identity, but the union of theoretical and practical sciences is, not so much asserted, as demanded: §28.—Note also the silence about politics in the latter part of §22 (15, 18 ff.) as compared with the first part: while the φύσις of the philosopher is the same as that of the king or statesman, the specific work of the former is different from that of the latter.—Cf. note 57 below.

29 The very identification of "philosophy" and "king" requires an explanation considering that that identification occurs in what appears to be a summary of the *Politicus*. For the *Politicus* is based on the explicit thesis that philosopher and king are not identical. See *Sophist* 217a3–b2 and *Politicus in princ.* Cf. also *Phaedrus* 252e1–2 and 253b1–3.

CHAPTER 5

else in order to produce happiness.[30] If he understands by "philosophy" in both cases the same thing, he flatly contradicts himself. This would not be altogether surprising. For, as we ought to have learned from Maimonides who knew his Fārābī, contradictions are a normal pedagogic device of the genuine philosopher.[31] In that case it would be incumbent upon the reader to find out by his own reflection, if guided by the author's intimations, which of the two contradictory statements was considered by the author to be true. If he understands by "philosophy" in both cases different things, that ambiguity would be equally revealing: no careful writer would express himself ambiguously about an important and at the same time thematic subject without good reasons.

The question of the relation of philosophy to the royal art is inseparably connected, in Fārābī's argument, with the question of the relation of human perfection to happiness. To begin with, he teaches that, according to Plato, philosophy does supply [370] the science of the beings and therewith man's highest perfection, but has to be supplemented by something else in order to produce happiness. That supplement is the right way of life which is the product of the royal art.[32] By asserting that the philosopher is identical with the king, he seems to suggest that philosophy by itself is sufficient to produce happiness. But whereas he leaves in doubt the precise relation of philosophy to the royal art, he makes it perfectly

---

30 Cf. §18 with the passages mentioned in note 32.
31 *Guide* I.Introd. (9b–11b Munk).
32 Philosophy is the theoretical art which supplies the science of the beings, and that science is man's highest perfection: §§16 and 2. [Cf. also the allusion to the relation of "perfection" to "science" in §§14 (11, 4) and 23 (16, 4f.; see *app. crit.*) as compared with §12 (9, 12). Observe the distinction between "philosophy" and "perfection" in §§22 (15, 14) and 32 (22, 15). A divergent view is intimated in §§4 (5, 7) and 6 (6, 3–4).] Happiness requires the right way of life in addition to man's highest perfection: cf. §3 with §§2, 16 (12, 10–13) and 1 (3, 13f.). [Cf. the allusion to the relation of "happiness" to "way of life" as distinguished from "science" in §16 (12, 7–10) and of "happiness" to "practical art" as distinguished from "theoretical art" in §18 (13, 4–5) as compared with §16.] In §1 (3, 8) Fārābī does not say (as R.-W. make him say) "beatitudo quae summa hominis perfectio (est)," but "beatitudo quae est ultimum quo homo perficitur." Falkera translates the expression by "beatitudo ultima" thus certainly avoiding the identification of "happiness" with "perfection." —As regards the distinction between perfection and happiness, cf. Maimonides, *Guide* III.27 (60a Munk), where human perfection is described in the same way as by Fārābī's Plato and where the remark is added that perfection is the cause of the eternal life (see Ephodi *ad loc.*); this implies that happiness (the eternal life) is distinguished from perfection.

Fārābī's Plato

clear in his second statement that philosophy by itself is sufficient to produce happiness. And whereas it is difficult to understand why he should speak circumlocutorily about the relation of philosophy to the royal art, it is easy to understand why he should speak evasively, or even contradictorily, about the relation of philosophy to happiness. We contend that he uses the identification of philosophy with the royal art as a pedagogic device for leading the reader toward the view that theoretical philosophy by itself, and nothing else, produces true happiness in this life, i.e., the only happiness which is possible.

It is easy to see that the initiation in the doctrine that happi-[371]ness consists "in consideratione scientiarum speculativarum,"[33] required some preparation and adjustment. Aristotle was free to state that doctrine without much ado since he was under no compulsion to reconcile it with the belief in the immortality of the soul or with the requirements of faith, to disregard here political requirements proper. Medieval thinkers were in a different position. By studying how Fārābī proceeds concerning a relatively simple aspect of the matter, we may be enabled to grasp his intention concerning its more complex aspects.

At the beginning of the treatise with which he prefaces his exposition of the philosophies of Plato and of Aristotle, he employs the distinction between "the happiness of this world in this life" and "the ultimate happiness in the other life" as a matter of course.[34] In the *Plato*, which is the second and therefore the least exposed part of a tripartite work,[35] the distinction of the two *beatitudines* is completely dropped.[36] What that silence means, becomes unmistakably clear from the fact that in the whole *Plato* (which contains after all summaries of the *Phaedrus*, the *Phaedo* and the *Republic*) there is no mention whatsoever of the immortality of the soul: Fārābī's Plato silently rejects Plato's doctrine of immortality,[37] or rather

---

33 Thomas Aquinas, *Summa theologica*, 1.2, qu. 3, a. 6. Cf. *Eth. Nic.* 1177b17–26 with a25–27. Cf. also *Republic* 519c5–6 with *Politicus* 272a8–d4.

34 *Taḥṣīl*, 2. Cf. *Iḥṣā al-'ulūm*, ch. 5 (near the beginning).

35 Consider Cicero, *Orator* 50 and *De oratore* II.313 f.

36 In Falkera's translation we find one mention of "the happiness of this world" (*Reshit hokma* 72, 20) and one mention of "the ultimate happiness" (72, 12). (These readings are not noted in the *app. crit.* of the *Plato*).

37 Fārābī, *Plato* XVIII and 24. — Fārābī also substitutes a moral meaning of the Platonic doctrine of metempsychosis for its literal meaning: cf. §24 (18, 5–19, 3) with *Phaedo* 81e–82b. (In the Latin translation of the passage — p. 13, 17 f. — the "an defunctus

CHAPTER 5

he considers it an exoteric doctrine. Fārābī goes so far as to avoid [372] in his summaries of the *Phaedo* and of the *Republic* the very term "soul," and as to observe, throughout the *Plato*, a deep silence about the νοῦς,[38] to say nothing of the νοῖ.

He could go to such lengths in the *Plato*, not merely because that treatise is the second and by far the shortest part of a tripartite work, but also because it sets forth explicitly, not so much his own views, as the views of someone else. We have noted the difference of treatment which he accords to the two *beatitudines* in the *Plato* on the one hand, and in the *Taḥṣīl* on the other. Employing fundamentally the same method, he pronounces more or less orthodox views concerning the life after death in *The political governments* and *The virtuous religious community*, i.e., in works in which he expounds his own doctrine. More precisely, in *The virtuous religious community* he pronounces simply orthodox views, and in *The political governments* he pronounces heretical, if what one could consider still tolerable views. But in his commentary on the *Nicomachean Ethics* he declares that there is only the happiness of this life and that all divergent statements are based on "ravings and old women's tales."[39]

Considering the importance of the subject, we will be excused for adducing a third example. In his *Enumeration of the Sciences* in which he speaks in his own name, Fārābī presents the religious sciences (*fiqh* and *kalām*) as corollaries to political science. At first sight one might believe that by assigning to the religious sciences that particular status Fārābi merely wants to say that religion, i.e., revealed religion, i.e., the revealed law (the *sharī'a*)[40] comes first into the sight of the philosopher as a political

---

esset... atque transformatus" ought to be changed into "an putaret se mortuum esse et in illam bestiam atque eius figuram transformatum." Cf. with Fārābī's statement Cicero, *De officiis* III.20, 82: "Quid enim interest, utrum ex homine se convertat quis in beluam an hominis figura immanitatem gerat beluae?" —In §1 (3, 11f.) Fārābī intimates the necessity of external goods for happiness; cf. the passage with *Eth. Nic.* 1177a28ff., 1178a23ff. and b33ff. on the one hand, and Thomas Aquinas' *Summa theol.*, 1.2, qu.4. a.7 on the other.

38 Νοεῖν is mentioned in §27 (20, 16). In the summary of the *Phaedo*, Fārābī mentions once "corpus animatum": §24 (18, 16).

39 Ibn Tufail, *Hayy ibn Yaqdhān*, ed. by L. Gauthier, Beyrouth 1936, 14. Cf. also Averroes' account quoted by Steinschneider, *Al-Fārābī*, 94.—Cf. note 58 below.

40 In the *Plato*, there is no mention of *sharī'a* (nor of *milla*). The root verb of *sharī'a* (*shara'a*) occurs shortly before the statement, discussed in the text, concerning religion: §6 (6, 6).—"Belief" is mentioned in §§4 (5, 2f.) and 22 (15, 5).

fact: precisely as a philosopher, he suspends his judgment as to the [373] truth of the super-rational teaching of religion. In other words, one might believe that Fārābī's description of the religious sciences is merely a somewhat awkward way of making room for a possible revealed theology as distinguished from natural theology (metaphysics). Every ambiguity of this kind is avoided in the *Plato*. Through the mouth of Plato, Fārābī declares that religious speculation, and religious investigation of the beings, and the religious syllogistic art do not supply the science of the beings,[41] of which man's highest perfection consists, whereas philosophy does supply it. He goes so far as to present religious knowledge in general and "religious speculation" in particular[42] as the lowest [374] step of the ladder

41   Fārābī, *Plato* §6. It is significant that the final result of Plato's investigation concerning religion is stated with the greatest precision, not in §6 (the section dealing with religion) where one would first look for it, but at the beginning of §8. (Cf. the beginning of §8 with the beginnings of §§7 and 9–11.) Falkera who wrote for a somewhat different public, omits the conclusions reached by Plato concerning religion in both §6 and §8. Cf. Maimonides' exclusion of religious subjects from the *Guide*: III.8 *vers. fin.*— R.-W. make this comment on §6: "Certe deorum cultus a Platone non reicitur... Cum... Alfarabii opinionibus haec omnia bene quadrare videntur." (See also p. XIV). But divine worship is not rejected by Fārābī either who, explicitly following Plato, considers conformity with the laws and beliefs of the religious community in which one is brought up, a necessary qualification for the future philosopher (*Taḥṣīl* 45, 6 ff.). Above all, in §6 Fārābī speaks, not of religious worship, but of the cognitive value of religion. His view concerning that matter is in full agreement with Plato's view as appears from such passages as *Timaeus* 40d6 ff., *Seventh Letter* 330e, and *Ion* 533d ff. Compare also Socrates' failure to refute the charge that he denied the existence of the gods of the city of Athens in the *Apology of Socrates*, and the critique of the divine laws of Crete and Sparta in the first book of the *Laws*. Fārābi interpreted the thesis of the *Apology* (with special regard to 20d7ff.) in this way: Socrates says to the Athenians that he does not deny their divine wisdom, but that he does not comprehend it, and that his wisdom is human wisdom only. Cf. Simon Duran, *Magēn abot* (Livorno 1785), 2b. According to Averroes' interpretation of the Socratic saying as quoted, or interpreted, by Fārābī, that saying specifically refers to the divine wisdom based on, or transmitted by, prophecy. (Paraphrase of *De sensu et sensato*, Paris Bibliotheque Nationale, Ms. Hébreu 1009, fol. 172 d).

42   According to Fārābi, Plato examined the cognitive value of religious speculation, of the religious investigation of the beings, and of the religious syllogistic art. But whereas he states that Plato ascribed a limited value to the two latter disciplines, he is completely silent about the result of Plato's examination of "religious speculation." The religious syllogistic art is the *fiqh*, and the religious investigation of the beings is the *kalām* in so far as it is based on some sort of physics—cf. *Iḥṣā* ch. 5 on the study of sensible beings by the *mutakallimūn*—; "religious speculation" may well refer to

CHAPTER 5

of cognitive pursuits, as inferior even to grammar and to poetry. With grammar, or rather with language, religion has this in common that it is essentially the property of a particular community.

One might think to begin with that in order to get hold of Fārābī's views, one ought to consult primarily the works in which he sets forth his own doctrine, and not his expositions of the doctrines of other men, especially if those other men were pagans. For may one not expound, as a commentator, or as a historian, with the greatest care and without a muttering of dissent such views as he rejects as a man? May Fārābī not have been attracted as a pupil of philosophers by what he abhorred as a believer? I do not know whether there ever was a "philosopher" whose mind was so confused as to consist of two hermetically sealed compartments: Fārābī was a man of a different stamp. But let us assume that his mind was of the type conveniently attributed to the Latin Averroists. It almost suffices to state that assumption in order to realize its absurdity. The Latin Averroists limited themselves to giving a most literal interpretation of extremely heretical teachings. But Fārābī did just the reverse: he gave an extremely unliteral interpretation of a most tolerable teaching. Precisely as a mere commentator of Plato, he was almost compelled to embrace a tolerably orthodox doctrine concerning the life after death.[43] His refusal, amounting to a flagrant deviation from the letter of Plato's teaching, to succumb to Plato's charms, proves it more convincingly than any explicit statement of his could have done, [375] that he considered the belief in a happiness different from the happiness of this life, or the belief in the other life, utterly erroneous. His silence about the immortality of the soul in a treatise destined to present the philosophy of Plato "from its beginning to its end" sets it beyond any reasonable doubt that statements asserting that immortality which occur in other writings of his, have to be dismissed as prudential accommodations to the accepted dogma. The same consideration applies to what the commentator, or historian, Fārābī says about religion: it is not easy to see what Platonic passage could have

---

mystical knowledge of God Himself. (Cf. *E.I.*, *s. v. Nazar*).—As regards the religious syllogistic art, cf. Steinschneider, *Al-Fārābī*, 31, where a remark of Fārābī concerning "the religious (תורייס) syllogisms" is quoted; cf. also Maimonides, *Millot ha-higgayon*, ch. 7, *vers. fin.*

43 *The* commentator who after all was more than a mere commentator, directly attacks the teaching of the *Republic* concerning the life after death; see his *Paraphrasis in Platonis Rempubl.* (*Opera Aristotelis*, Venice 1550, III, 182c, 40–45 and 191d 11–39).

compelled, or even induced, a believing Muslim to criticize the value of "the syllogistic religious art," i.e., of the Islamic science of *fiqh*.

Fārābī avails himself then of the specific immunity of the commentator, or of the historian, in order to speak his mind concerning grave matters in his "historical" works rather than in the works setting forth what he presents as his own doctrine. This being the case, one has to lay down, and scrupulously to follow, this canon of interpretation: Apart from purely philologic and other preliminary considerations, one is not entitled to interpret the *Plato*, or any part or passage of it, by having recourse to Fārābī's other writings. One is not entitled to interpret the *Plato* in the light of doctrines, expounded by Fārābī elsewhere, which are not mentioned in the *Plato*. It goes without saying that in case the teaching of the *Plato* is in conflict with the teachings of the *Taḥṣīl*, *The political governments*, *The enumeration of the sciences* and so on, the presumption is in favor of the teaching of the *Plato*. Compared with the *Plato*, all these other writings are exoteric. And if it is true, as Fārābī intimates by reminding us of the teaching of the *Phaedrus* concerning the deficiencies of writing as such, that all writings as such are exoteric,[44] we have to say that the *Plato* is merely less exoteric than the other works indicated and therefore that every hint however subtle which occurs in the *Plato*, deserves to take precedence over the most emphatically and the most frequently stated doctrines of his more exoteric works. For [376] there is not necessarily, not in all cases, a connection between a writer's conviction of the truth, or untruth, of an assertion, and the frequency, or rarity, with which he makes it.[45]

Fārābī's silence about the ideas and about the immortality of the soul shows certainly that he does not hesitate to deviate from the letter of Plato's teaching if he considers that literal teaching erroneous. He may have believed that Plato himself considered the doctrines in question merely exoteric. But he may, or he may not have believed that the teaching which he ascribes to Plato by his silence as well as by his speech, was the Platonic teaching: he certainly considered it the true teaching. His *Plato* is then not a historical work. He presents Plato as a man who had to discover the very meaning of philosophy entirely by himself, thus implying that he had no philosophic predecessors whatsoever. Yet he knew of course, especially from the *Metaphysics*, that Plato was not the first philosopher.

---

44 Cf. *Phaedrus* 275c ff., *Timaeus* 28c4–5, *Seventh Letter* 341d4–e3. Cf. Maimonides, *Guide* I.Introd. (4a Munk).

45 Maimonides, *Treatise on Resurrection*, ed. by Finkel, 19, 17 ff.

Chapter 5

In accordance with this, he remarks that the subject of the *Menexenus* had been neglected by Plato's predecessors;[46] considering the extreme care with which the *Plato* is written, that remark is meaningful only if the subjects of all other Platonic dialogues had been treated by predecessors of Plato. He presents, not so much the historical Plato, as the typical philosopher who, as such, after having reached maturity of the mind, "comme un homme qui marche seul et dans les ténèbres,"[47] has to start afresh and to go his own way however much he may be assisted by the exertions of his teachers. His attitude to the historical Plato is comparable to the attitude of Plato himself to the historical Socrates, and to the attitude of the Platonic Socrates himself to, say, historical Egypt: "With what ease dost thou, o Fārābī, invent Platonic speeches."[48] By this very fact he reveals himself as a true Platonist. For Platonists are not concerned with the historical (accidental) truth, since they are exclusively interested [377] in the philosophic (essential) truth.[49] Only because public speech demands a mixture of seriousness and playfulness, can a true Platonist present the serious teaching, the philosophic teaching, in a historical, and hence playful, garb. The sovereign use which Fārābī makes of the historical materials, presupposes of course that such materials were at his disposal. For the historian, it is of utmost importance that the extent, and the character, of the information available to Fārābī, be established as exactly as possible. But even this cannot be done properly, if one does not bear in mind the non-historical purpose of the *Plato*: a number of apparently fanciful remarks on the purport of various dialogues may be due to Fārābī's desire to intimate an important philosophic truth rather than to misinformation. To consider the author of the *Plato* a mere epitomist of a lost Greek text, means to disregard, not only the admiration which men of the competence of Avicenna and Maimonides felt for Fārābī, but likewise the exceedingly careful working of the *Plato* itself. But even if Fārābī's interpretation of Plato's philosophy as a whole should eventually prove to be borrowed from a hitherto unknown source, we still would have to understand that interpretation by itself, and we still would have to digest the fact a that [recte: "that a"—Eds.] man of Fārābī's rank adopted it as a true account of the classic philosophy

---

46 Cf. §31 with §16. Cf. note 7 above.
47 Descartes, *Discours de la méthode*, II.
48 *Phaedrus*, 275b3–4.—It should be noted that Fārābī's rejection of poetry applies—just as Plato's rejection of poetry—to common poetry only: §8.
49 Cf. *Protagoras* 347c3–348a6 and *Charmides* 161c3–6.

Fārābī's Plato

and published it in his own name. It may be added that by transmitting the most precious knowledge, not in "systematic" works, but in the guise of a historical account, Fārābī indicates his view concerning "originality" and "individuality" in philosophy: what comes into sight as the "original" or "personal" "contribution" of a philosopher is infinitely less significant than his private, and truly original and individual, understanding of the necessarily anonymous truth.

But let us return to the point where we left off. For an obvious reason, Fārābī did not wish to break a silence which was eloquent for those only who could read the Platonic dialogues dealing with the immortality of the soul. There was a further, and in a sense, even more compelling reason for [378] concealing the philosophic doctrine concerning happiness. To identify happiness with the perfection which consists of the science of the beings, is tantamount to closing the very prospect of happiness to the large majority of men. For reasons of philanthropy,[50] if for no other reason, Fārābī was compelled to show a possibility of happiness to men other than philosophers. Therefore, he distinguishes between perfection and happiness: he asserts that philosophy, being a theoretical art, supplies indeed the science of the beings and thus man's highest perfection, but has to be supplemented by the right way of life in order to produce happiness. More generally expressed, he accepts to begin with the orthodox opinion that philosophy is insufficient to lead man to happiness. Yet, he makes clear, the supplement to philosophy which is required for the attaining of happiness, is supplied, not by religion, or revelation, but by politics. He substitutes politics for religion. He thus lays the foundation for the secular alliance between philosophers and enlightened princes. It is true, he immediately thereafter retracts his concession by stating that philosophy by itself supplies the right way of life and therewith by itself produces happiness, but he adds the clause that philosophy produces the happiness, not only of the philosophers, but of all other human beings as well. This extravagantly philanthropic remark would have to be dismissed as a sheer absurdity, or its text would have to be emended, if it were meant to be final; for how can the mere fact that a single philosopher is in existence somewhere in India have the slightest influence on the happiness, or misery, of people living in the remotest parts of Frankistan

---

50 Cf. *Eth. Nic.* 1094b9f. and 1099b18–20 with *Politics* 1325a8–11.—As regards the "philanthropic" appearance of the teaching of Plato's *Republic*, cf. Aristotle, *Politics* 1263b15 ff.

CHAPTER 5

who have nothing in common with him or philosophy? The statement that philosophy produces the happiness of all human beings merely serves the purpose of indicating the whole extent of the difficulty facing Fārābī; it thus paves the way for a provisional solution and therewith indirectly for the final solution. The provisional solution is that philosophy produces the happiness of the philosophers and of all those non-philosophers who are actually [379] guided by philosophers. In other words, the required supplement to philosophy is, not just the royal art, but the actual exercise of the royal art by philosophers within a definite political community. Fārābī goes still further. He declares that not only the happiness of the non-philosophers—of the citizens as citizens—, but the very perfection, and therewith the happiness, of the philosophers themselves is impossible except in the virtuous city whose most important part are the philosophers.[51] He calls the virtuous city emphatically "an other city":[52] he thus indicates that he means to replace, not simply religion in general by politics in general, but "the other world" or "the other life" by "the other city." "The other city" stands midway between "this world" and "the other world," in so far as it is an earthly city indeed, but a city existing, not actually, but only "in speech." Fārābī's Plato does not leave it at that: he raises the question of how the virtuous city could become actual, and he answers that this could only be achieved by "the legislator of this city." "Therefore he investigated thereafter what kind of man the legislator must be."[53] Fārābī does not reveal to the [380] readers the result

---

51 §25 (cf. in particular 20, 13f.). Cf. §24 *vers. fin.*—Cf. with §25 (20, 10) which R.-W. correctly render by "et philosophos in ea (civitate) partem maximam esse," Augustinus' *Civitas Dei* XI.9: "(sancti angeli) quae hujus (sc. sanctae) civitatis...magna pars est."

52 §25 (19, 12 and 20, 4). Cf. the use of "other" in §§1 (3, 11–13), 11 (9, 8) and 22 (16, 2). Cf. also §§14 (11, 6) and 24 (17, 7).—Fārābī speaks also of the "other nation" in particular and of nations in general, but he prefers to speak of the "other city" and of cities (he uses "city" three times as often as "nation"): "Where first were great and flourishing cities, there was first the study of philosophy." (Hobbes). In his account of the studies to be pursued in the perfect community, he uses exclusively "city" (§26). As regards the non-quantitative aspect of the difference between city and nation, one has to consider §7, where only "nation," and not "city," is mentioned: the nation is kept together by a common language. The bond of the city, on the other hand, is the law; cf. §32 (22, 18–23, 1).

53 §29.—Fārābī's technique of writing is illustrated by the fact that immediately thereafter (§30 *in princ.*), he uses فعل (fecit)—cf. §29 (21, 11) بالفعل (*actu*)—, and not, as he usually does, تبين له (*ei manifestum fuit*), or another term designating a purely mental activity.—The فعل near the beginning of §30 refers back, not only to §29, but to

Fārābī's Plato

of this Platonic investigation.[54] In the treatise which precedes the *Plato*, he asserts the identity of legislator and philosopher, but for the reasons mentioned before one is not entitled to assume that the teaching of Fārābī's Plato is identical with that set forth by Fārābī in his own name.[55] The silence of the *Plato* about the subject permits us then to imagine for a moment that the legislator is a prophet, the founder of a revealed religion. Since the legislator, as the founder of the virtuous city, creates the indispensable condition for the actualization of happiness, happiness would thus not be possible but on the basis of revelation. Fārābī's Plato does not close that loophole by identifying the prophet, or the legislator, with the philosopher. He intimates indeed that the function of the legislator is not the highest human perfection, [381] and he takes it for granted that there could be a plurality of virtuous cities,[56] thus excluding the belief in a single true, or final, revealed religion. But the real remedy employed in the *Plato* is far more radical: toward the end of the treatise,

---

§§26–29. In this connection it may be mentioned that R.-W.'s division of the *Plato* into sections is somewhat arbitrary. Fārābī's own division is clearly indicated by the use of فلما ["when"—Eds.] or ولما ["as soon as"—Eds.] at the beginning of a paragraph. Accordingly, section I consists of §§1–3, section II of §§4–5, section III of §§6–11, section IV of §§12–15, section V of §§16–22, section VI of §§23–25, section VII of §§26–29, and section VIII of §§30–32.

54 He is equally reticent as regards the result of Plato's investigations concerning religious speculation (§6), σωφροσύνη (§19), love and friendship (§21). Compare with the last example the different procedure as regards courage: §20. His typical procedure is to state first what Plato "investigated" and thereafter what he "made clear" or what "became clear to him." Every deviation from that scheme requires an explanation. One has then to pay special attention not only to the "investigations" not followed by mentions of what Plato "made clear" or of what "became clear to him," but likewise to the cases in which no investigation is mentioned. Probably the most important example of omissions of "investigation" is the statement concerning the identity of philosopher and king: §18 (13, 6–11). It is hardly necessary to add that the difference between what Plato made clear (*sc.* to others) and what become clear to him is not altogether negligible.—Cf. notes 12, 40, and 53 above.

55 For the interpretation of the statement on the legislator, one has to consider Fārābī's interpretation of Plato's *Laws*. He conceives of the *Laws*, not, as Plato himself had done, as a correction of the *Republic*, but as a supplement to the *Republic*: whereas according to Plato the *Republic* and the *Laws* deal with essentially different political orders (πολιτεῖαι), Fārābī's view is closely akin to that of Cicero (*Legg.*, I.5, 15; 6, 14; 10, 23; III.2, 4), according to whom the *Republic* deals with the best political order and the *Laws* deal with the best laws belonging to the very same best political order.

56 Cf. §29 with §2. Cf. §25 (20, 5 and 12) with *Musterstaat* 70, 9 and *Pol. gov.* 72 and 74.

Chapter 5

Fārābī makes it absolutely clear that there can be, not only philosophers, but even perfect human beings (i.e., philosophers who have reached the goal of philosophy) in imperfect cities.[57] Philosophy and the perfection of philosophy and hence happiness do not require—this is Fārābī's last word on the subject—the establishment of the perfect political community: they are possible, not only in this world, but even in these cities, the imperfect cities. But—and this is the essential implication—in the imperfect cities, i.e., in the world as it actually is and as it always will be, happiness is within the reach of the philosophers alone: the non-philosophers are eternally barred, by the nature of things, from happiness. Happiness consists "in consideratione scientiarum speculativarum" and of nothing else.[58] Philosophy is the necessary and sufficient condition of happiness.

[382] It would be a mistake however to consider Fārābī's emphatic statements about the political aspect of philosophy a mere stepping-stone destined to facilitate the ascent from the popular notions about the happiness of the other world to philosophy. For the philosopher necessarily lives in political society, and he thus cannot escape the situation created by the naturally difficult relations between the philosopher and the non-philosophic citizens, "the vulgar": the philosopher living in a society which is not ruled by philosophers, i.e., the philosopher living in any ac-

---

57 Cf. §32 *in princ.* with §§23, 24 *vers. fin.* and 25.—In the last three paragraphs, Fārābī indicates his real view of the relation of philosopher and king by the different manners in which he enumerates philosophers, kings, legislators, and the virtuous: §§30 (22, 6 f.), 31, and 32 (22, 15). That view can be states as follows: "king" is an ambiguous term which designates either the man who possesses the political art and who is necessarily subject to the legislator, or the philosopher who has reached his goal by having completed the philosophic investigation.

58 Cf. §§1–2 and the remark of Averroes (quoted by Steinschneider, *Al-Farabi*, 106): "In li. enim de Nicomachia videtur [Fārābī] negare continuationem esse cum intelligentiis abstractis: et dicit hanc esse opinionem Alexandri, et quod non est opinionandum quod finis humanus sit aliud quam perfectio speculativa." (Cf. Thomas Aquinas' commentary on *Eth. Nic.*, X, lect. 13 *vers. fin.*).—Our interpretation of the thesis of the *Plato* is confirmed, to a certain extent, by Falkera's remark (*Reshit hokma* 72, 22–25) that, according to Plato, true happiness consists of knowledge, *viz.* knowledge of God which is not possible without the knowledge of the creatures. Fārābī does not speak of God, but of all beings. As regards a similar change from the philosophic to a more theologic view, cf. the authentic text of Maimonides' *Mishna tora*, H. De'ot IV 1 (Hyamson 50, 19 f.) with the vulgate text. [This instance of *"Al-Farabi"* contains no macra.—Eds.]

96

Fārābī's Plato

tual society, is necessarily "in grave danger."[59] Fārābī intimates his solution by speaking of the twofold account which Plato gave of Socrates' life: he tells us that Plato repeated his account of Socrates' way and that he repeated his mention of the vulgar of the cities and nations which existed in his time.[60] As we might have learned from Maimonides, "repetition" is a normal pedagogic device which is destined to reveal the truth to those who are able to understand by themselves while hiding it from the vulgar: whereas the vulgar are blinded by the features common to the first statement and the "repetition," those who are able to understand will pay the utmost attention to the differences, however apparently negligible, between the two statements and in particular to the "addition," made in the "repetition," to the first statement.[61] According to Fārābī, Plato's first account of the way of Socrates deals with Socrates' attitude toward the opinions and habits of his fellow-citizens. The second account, on the other hand, deals with Plato's correction of the Socratic attitude, or with Plato's attitude.[62] Socrates' attitude was determined by the fact that he limited his investigations to moral and political [383] subjects,[63] i.e., that he neglected natural philosophy. Being merely a moral philosopher, he was a moralist. Hence, he did not look beyond this alternative: either to comply with the accepted rules of conduct and the accepted opinions or openly to challenge them and therewith to expose himself to persecution and violent death.[64] As a consequence of his uncompromising attitude, he fell victim to the rage of the multitude. The attitude of Plato was fundamentally different. As we have seen, he considered philosophy an essentially theoretical pursuit, and therefore he was not a moralist: his moral fervor was mitigated by his insight into the nature of beings; thus he could adjust himself to the requirements of political life, or to the ways and opinions of the vulgar. In his treatment of the subjects in question, he combined

---

59 §32 *in princ.* Cf. Plato, *Phaedo* 64b; *Republic* 494a4–10 and 520b2–3.

60 §§30 (22, 1) and 32 (22, 14).

61 *Guide*, III.3 *in princ.* and 23 (50a Munk).

62 Note the emphatic هو (which R.-W. left untranslated) in §32 (23, 2): Plato described in his *Letters* what *he* thought about the manner of dealing with his fellow-citizens. Compare this with the corresponding هو in §16 (12, 10): *he* (Plato) was compelled to present philosophy because he did not find it among the arts and sciences which were generally known.

63 Cf. §16 with §§28 and 30 (22, 4–5).

64 §24 (19, 3–11).

the way of Socrates with the way of—Thrasymachus.[65] While the intransigent way of Socrates is appropriate in the philosopher's dealings with the political élite only, the less exacting way of Thrasymachus is appropriate in his dealings with the vulgar and the young. By combining the two ways, Plato avoided the conflict with the vulgar and thus the fate of Socrates. Accordingly, the "revolutionary" quest for the other city ceased to be a necessity: Plato substituted for it a much more "conservative" way of action, *viz.* the gradual replacement of the accepted opinions by the truth or an approximation to the truth. The replacement, however gradual, of the accepted opinions is of course a destruction of the accepted opinions.[66] But being emphatically gradual, it is best described as an undermining of the accepted opinions. For it would not be gradual, if it were not combined with a provisional acceptance of the accepted opinions: as Fārābī elsewhere declares, conformity with the opinions of the religious community in which one is brought up, is a necessary qualification for the future [384] philosopher.[67] The goal of the gradual destruction of the accepted opinions is the truth, as far as the élite, the potential philosophers, is concerned, but only an approximation to the truth (or an imaginative representation of the truth)[68] as far as the general run of men is concerned.[69] We may say that Fārābī's Plato replaces Socrates' philosopher-king who rules openly in the perfect city by the secret kingship of the philosopher who lives privately as a member of an imperfect community. That kingship is exercised by means of an exoteric teaching which, while not too flagrantly contradicting the accepted opinions, undermines them

---

65 §30. Even if that paragraph should be meant to be a summary of the *Clitopho* only, we cannot disregard the fact that Fārābī knew the Thrasymachus of the *Republic*. His statement on the combination of the way of Socrates with that of Thrasymachus is based on *Republic* 498c9–d1.

66 §32.

67 Cf. note 41 above. Cf. the first two maxims of Descartes' "morale par provision" (*Discours de la méthode*, III). Cf. also Fontenelle, *Éloge de Mr. Lémery*: "Les choses fort établiés ne peuvent être attaquées que par degrés."—As regards the necessity of the gradual change of laws, cf. Plato, *Laws* 736d2–4 and Aristotle, *Politics* 1269a12 ff.

68 Cf. note 48 above.

69 Note Fārābī's replacing "the truth" (22, 17) first by "the virtuous way of life" or "the correct *nomoi*" (23, 3) and then by "opinions" (23, 6). Falkera appropriately translates اراء ("opinions") in this context by עצות ("plans" or "designs"). (In §22, he translates اراء equally appropriately in that context by אמונות). The meaning of עצות is explained by him in *Reshit hokma* 70, 6 ff. Cf. also Maimonides, *Guide*, I.34 (40b Munk).

Fārābī's Plato

in such a way as to guide the potential philosophers toward the truth.[70] Fārābī's remarks on Plato's own policy define the general character of all literary productions of "the philosophers."

In conclusion it may be remarked that the distinction between perfection and happiness is not altogether exoteric. When [385] Fārābī says that happiness is "ultimum quo homo perficitur," he thinks of the pleasure attending the actualization of man's highest perfection. For it is pleasure which "renders perfect" (τελειοῖ) the exercise of a faculty, and it is a specific pleasure together with the exercise of man's highest perfection which constitutes human happiness.[71] This being the case, happiness is not simply identical with human perfection or its exercise. Fārābī indicates the particular importance of pleasure by saying of the Platonic dialogue which praises true pleasure (what he says of no other Platonic dialogue) that it is "attributed" (i.e., merely attributed) to Socrates;[72] for Socrates was compelled by his moralism to stress the conflict between the noble and the pleasant rather than their harmony.

III. PHILOSOPHY AND MORALS

The relation of philosophy to morals is adumbrated in the third paragraph of the *Plato*. In the first paragraph, Fārābī had stated that a certain science and a certain way of life are essential to happiness. In the second paragraph, he answers the question as to what that science is. The third paragraph deals with the way of life in question, but it does not deal with it thematically: its thematic subject is, not the desired way of life, but happiness. Fārābī thus intimates that he is not going to disclose what the de-

---

70 The distinction made by Fārābī between the attitude of Socrates and that of Plato corresponds, to a certain extent, to the distinction made by Muhammad b. Zakariyyā al-Rāzī in his *k. al-sīrat al-falsafiyya*, between the attitude of the young Socrates and that of the mature Socrates. Rāzī's opponents had asserted that his model Socrates "n'a pas pratiqué la dissimulation, ni vis-à-vis du vulgaire ni vis-à-vis des autorités, mais il les a affrontées en leur disant ce qu'il considérait être vrai en des termes clairs et non-équivoques." Rāzī admits that this account is correct as far as the young Socrates is concerned: "les traits qu'ils rapportent de Socrate lui ont été propres au début de sa carrière jusqu'à une date assez avancée da sa vie, date à laquelle il en a abandonné la plupart." Paul Kraus, "Raziana" I, *Orientalia*, N.S., v. 4, 1935, 322f.— As regards the life of the philosopher in an imperfect community, cf. Plato's *Republic* 496d ff.

71 *Eth. Nic.* 1174b23, 1175a21, 1176a24–28. Cf. *Politics* 1339b18–20.

72 §15.

CHAPTER 5

sired way of life is. He says: "Deinde postea investigavit, quid esset beatitudo quae revera beatitudo esset et ex qua scientia oreretur et quis esset habitus et quae actio. Quam distinxit ab ea quae beatitudo putatur sed non est. Et aperuit vitam virtuosam [R.-W.: optimam] esse eam qua haec [R.-W.: illa] beatitudo obtineretur." The virtuous way of life leads to "*haec beatitudo*," i.e., to the apparent happiness which is distinguished from the true happiness; the virtuous way of life is fundamentally distinguished from the desired way of life which is essential to true happiness. Our interpretation is confirmed by Falkera's translation: "he made it known that the virtuous [386] way of life is the one by which the happiness *of this world* is obtained." The happiness of this world is naturally distinguished from, and inferior to, the happiness of the other world: the virtuous way of life does not lead to the happiness of the other world. In accordance with Fārābī's statement, Maimonides teaches that the moral virtues serve the well-being of the body or man's "first perfection" as distinguished from the well-being of the soul or man's "ultimate perfection" which consists of, or is produced by, knowledge or contemplation alone.[73]

Fārābī does not say then what the desired way of life is; he merely makes it known what it is not. Yet by denying that the desired way of life is the virtuous way of life, he tacitly asserts that the desired way of life is the contemplative way of life. He states later on that the desired way of life is supplied by the royal art and immediately thereafter he seems to suggest that the royal art is identical with philosophy. The identification of philosophy as the highest theoretical art with the royal art as the highest practical art can be literally valid only if the specific products of both arts, the science of the beings and the desired way of life, are identical, in other words, if contemplation itself is the highest form of action.[74]

The translators can justly be blamed for the unnecessarily unliteral character of their translation. On the other hand, they deserve praise for bringing out in their translation their understanding of the passage mentioned. For while that understanding amounts to a radical misunderstanding of Fārābī's ultimate intention, it does not proceed from an accidental error: Fārābī wanted to be understood by the majority of his readers in exactly the same way in which he has been understood by his modern

---

73 *Guide*, III 27. Accordingly, Maimonides treats medicine and morals in one and the same section of the *Mishne tora* (H. De'ot).

74 Aristotle, *Politics* 1325b16–22.

Fārābī's Plato

translators. He has built up the three first paragraphs as a whole[75] and the third paragraph in particular in such a way as to create the impression as if he were going to identify the [387] desired way of life with the virtuous way of life. For he makes his readers expect that the third paragraph will be devoted to the disclosure of what the desired way of life is; and the only way of life mentioned in the third paragraph is the virtuous way of life. He knew of course that he would be met half-way by the large majority of his readers. Not only will most readers not observe the difference between the expected subject of the paragraph (the desired way of life) and its actual subject (happiness), because their expectation will determine what they perceive; most readers will besides expect from the outset, i.e., independently of any suggestions of the author, that the author will identify the desired way of life with the virtuous way of life, because they themselves believe in their identity.[76]

The question of morals is taken up again by Fārābī in his discussion of the ordinary practical arts. Those arts, he says, do not supply the desired way of life, but only the useful things (τὰ συμφέροντα) which are necessary (ἀναγκαῖα) and the gainful things (τὰ κερδαλέα) which are not necessary, but practically identical with the virtuous (or noble) things (τὰ καλά).[77] That is to say: the desired way of life does not belong to the class of the noble things, and since the virtuous way of life is the noble thing *par excellence*, the desired way of life is fundamentally different from the virtuous way of life. By identifying, at least for all practical purposes, the noble with the gainful, Fārābī indicates that the virtues in particular are merely a means toward "the happiness of this world" or man's "first perfection."[78]

After having gone thus far, he distinguishes between the truly useful and the truly gainful or noble on the one hand, and what [388] the vulgar believes to be useful and gainful or noble on the other. He makes it clear that the (truly) gainful and the (truly) noble things are the desired science

---

75 The first three paragraphs, and not merely, as R.-W. assume, the first paragraph by itself, form the first section of the *Plato*. Cf. note 53 above.

76 Cf. the remarks of Montesquieu on this subject in *De l'Esprit des Lois*, "Avertissement de l'auteur" and XXV.2.

77 §12 (10, 1–10). Cf. Aristotle, *Politics* 1291a1 ff. Cf. Plato, *Republic* 558d11–e4.

78 Cf. §3 as interpreted above with §1 (3, 10 f.): the apparent happiness consists of health, riches, honours, and the like. Cf. the distinction between philosophy or the political art on the one hand, and the noble things on the other in §22 (14, 5; cf. 14, 18); and the distinction between the philosopher, the perfect human being and the virtuous in §§31 f.

Chapter 5

and the desired way of life, whereas philosophy which leads to the desired science and the desired way of life, is the truly useful.[79] He thus paves the way for the identification of the desired way of life essential to happiness with the truly virtuous way of life,[80] and for the distinction between genuine virtue, love and friendship on the one hand, and what the vulgar considers virtue, love and friendship on the other.[81]

If Fārābī's last word on the subject is then hardly discernible from what the most influential moral teachers of mankind have always insisted upon, why did he suggest in the first place a doctrine as shocking as the distinction between the way of life which is essential to happiness, and the virtuous way of life is bound to be? There can be only one answer: his first statement is indispensable for the proper understanding of his ultimate statement; his ultimate statement is as remote from the generally accepted doctrine as is his first statement. If he had identified from the outset the desired way of life with the truly virtuous way of life, he would have created the impression that the difference between the truly virtuous way of life and the virtuous way of life "which is famous in the cities," is identical with the difference between the highest morality and a lower morality. Actually however he holds the view that the only virtuous way of life in the ordinary sense of the term is moral strictly speaking. For the moral life consists of the submission to the demands of honour and duty without reasoning why; it consists of choosing, and doing, the just and noble for no reason other than because it is just and noble. The choice of the just and noble as such is the specifically moral purpose. The difference between moral choice and a choice which is not moral, is essentially a difference of purpose, and not a difference of knowledge. On the other hand, the difference between the truly virtuous way of life and [389] all other ways of life is based, not on a difference of purpose, of quality of the will, but on a difference of knowledge. In other words, there is a broad agreement between the conduct of moral man and that of the philosopher: that agreement permits one to apply one and the same term ("virtue") to both. But the same conduct is interpreted in a fundamentally different manner by moral man on the one hand, and by the philosopher on the other: that difference compels Fārābī to deny to begin with that the desired way of life is the virtuous way of life.

---

79 §§12 (10, 10–11, 3) and 17–18.
80 §§22 (15, 15–17); 23 (16, 12 and 17, 4); 24 (17, 15–20); 32 (22, 17).
81 §§19–21 and 25.

Fārābī's Plato

IV. THE SUBJECT MATTER OF PHILOSOPHY

"Philosophy" designates the theoretical art which supplies the science of the essence of each of all the beings as well as both the actual investigation of things which leads to that science and that science itself. The science of the essence of all beings is sometimes simply called "that (*sc.* that specific) science of all the beings" or "that (*sc.* that specific) science of all the beings."[82] "Being" is not identical with "thing"; all "beings" are "things," but not all "things" are "beings." There are "things" which are not the subjects of any science, and hence not the subjects of philosophy in particular.[83] Other "things" are adequately dealt with by other sciences, by grammar e.g., but do not concern the philosopher precisely because they are not "beings." The perfection of a "being" is a "thing," but being the perfection of the "being," it is not itself a "being."[84] A way of life is a "thing," but not a "being"; hence the science of the beings is fundamentally distinguished from the science of the ways of life.[85] The ἀναγκαῖα, κερδαλέα, συμφέροντα, καλά and so on are, as such, "things," but not "beings."[86] Since all "things" other than "beings" are essentially dependent on "beings," being their qualities, relations, actions, products, and so on, and since [390] therefore the full understanding of the essence of all these "things" ultimately presupposes the understanding of the essence of all "beings," philosophy can be called "the science of the essence of all the things."[87]

In one passage, Fārābī calls the science of the beings the "science of the natural beings."[88] By doing so, he certainly implies that the beings *par excellence* are the natural beings as distinguished from the artificial beings.[89] But what about the supernatural, the incorporeal beings? In another passage, he calls the science of the beings with special reference to the subject matter of the *Timaeus* the science of "the divine and the natural beings."[90] There are two ways of reconciling the two divergent statements.

---

82 §§4 (4, 13); 6 (6, 14); 8 (7, 12); 12 (9, 12 and 15); 16 (12, 11).
83 §10 (8, 14–16). Cf. §22 (16, 7 f.).
84 §1 *in princ.* Cf. *Iḥṣā al-'ulūm* ch. 4, section on metaphysics, *in princ.*
85 §§1 (3, 12–14); 6 (6, 15 f.); 8 (7, 13 f. and 16 f.); 9 (8, 2 f.).
86 Cf. §§12–13. [I.e., "the necessary, profitable, useful, noble [things]" —Eds.]
87 §7 (7, 4).
88 §8 (7, 13 f.).
89 Cf. *Metaphysics* 991b6 f. with the passages indicated in note 20 above.

CHAPTER 5

In the first place, one may say that in the first statement "natural" is used in a broad sense and designates all beings which do not owe their existence to human art: "ad philosophiam naturalem pertinet considerare ordinem rerum quem ratio humana considerat sed non facit, ita quod sub naturali philosophia comprehendamus et metaphysicam."[91] Since the explicit reference to "the divine beings" occurs in a summary of the *Timaeus*, the manner in which Plato uses the terms designating divine things in the *Timaeus* cannot be completely disregarded. In the *Timaeus*, Plato applies such terms to the maker of the universe, the gods who manifest themselves so far as they wish (Zeus, Hera, and so on), the visible universe, the heaven, the stars, the earth. Hence, one could also say that the divine beings referred to by Fārābī are simply the most outstanding group of natural beings in the sense of beings "which are bodies or in bodies," i.e., the heavens.[92] The identification of the heavenly bodies with God is said to have been the esoteric [391] teaching of Avicenna.[93] We observed already the deep silence of the Plato about the νοῖ, the *substantiae separatae*, as well as about the "ideas." We have to add that in his treatise on Aristotle's philosophy, which is the sequel to his *Plato*, Fārābī does not discuss Aristotle's metaphysics.[94] The second interpretation of the two passages under consideration is of course irreconcilable with the teaching which Fārābī sets forth when speaking in his own name.

But does he not explicitly mention, if only once, "spiritual things," thus admitting quite unequivocally the existence of *substantiae separatae*? Our first answer has to be that spiritual things are not spiritual beings. Yet, someone might retort, there cannot be spiritual things, if there are no spiritual beings, just as there cannot be a δαιμόνιον, if there are no δαίμονες.[95] However this may be, it suffices to state that Fārābī's only mention of spiritual things occurs in a summary of popular opinions, or at any rate of opinions of men other than Plato, about a certain subject. In the same context, he uses four times the term "divine things."[96] In three

---

90 §26 (20, 15 f.).

91 Thomas Aquinas' commentary on *Eth. Nic.*, I, lect. 1. Cf. *Summa theologica*, 2.2, qu. 48.

92 *Timaeus* 30a2; 34a7–b9; 40b5–c2 and d4; 69c2–4; 92c5–9. Cf. *Eth. Nic.* 1141b1–2.

93 Cf. Averroes, *Tahāfut al-tahāfut* X (ed. by M. Bouyges, Beyrouth 1930, 421).

94 Fārābī, *Plato* XVIII.

95 §22 (15, 2). Cf. Plato, *Apology of Socrates* 27b3–c3.

96 §22 (14, 16; 15, 6 and 12 and 13).

Fārābī's Plato

out of the four cases, he attributes the use of the term to people other than Plato. The only remark in which he mentions "divine things" while relating Plato's views, refers to the desire for divine things which is distinguished from bestial desire. He does not explain what these divine things are. I am inclined to believe that they are identical with the science of the beings and the right way of life. He mentions in the same context divine desires and divine love, evidently understanding by them passions or qualities of human beings; somewhat later, he calls these passions or qualities "praiseworthy and divine," thus indicating that "divine" does not necessarily refer to the superhuman origin of a passion e.g., but may simply designate its excellence.[97] At any rate, in the [392] whole passage under consideration "divine" is used as part of the dichotomy "divine-human" or "divine-bestial." Now, in what is best described as the "repetition" of that passage, Fārābī replaces that dichotomy by the dichotomy "human bestial":[98] what he called "divine" in the first statement, is finally called by him "human."[99]

---

97 *Ib.* (15, 3 f. and 7 f.). Cf. *Eth. Nic.* 1099b14–18, and Plato, *Laws* 631d4–6. (Cf. Lessing, *Von Adam Neusern* §14 *vers. fin.*)

98 §24. For the understanding of the "first statement"—§22 (14, 4–15, 12)—one has to consider the fact that Fārābī avoids there the expressions "he made clear" and "it became clear to him" while he speaks fairly frequently of what Plato "mentioned." Cf. notes 53–54 above. — As regards Fārābī's silence about God, cf. the following remark of Martin Grabmann ("Der lateinische Averroismus des 13. Jahrhunderts," *Sitzungsberichte der Bayerischen Akademie der Wissenschaften, Philos.-hist. Abtlg.*, 1931, Heft 2, 29): "Boetius von Dacien gebraucht ähnlich wie Siger von Brabant, Martinus von Dacien und überhaupt viele andere Professoren der Artistenfakultät für Gott die ausgesprochen metaphysische Bezeichnung ens primum—vielfach reden die Artisten nur vom primum—oder principium und überlässt den Theologen den Namen Deus." Cf. notes 41 and 58 above. ["Boethius of Dacia, much like Siger of Brabant, Martin of Dacia, and in general like many other professors of the faculty of arts, uses for God the expressly metaphysical designation ens primum ('first being') — often the scholars speak only of the primum ('first') — or principium ('principle'), and leaves the name Deus to the theologians."—Eds.]

99 The importance of the topic "homo" or "humanus" is indicated from the outset by the density of "homo" in §1. Almost equally important as the distinctions homo-Deus (§22) and homo-bestia (§24) are the distinctions homo-vir (cf. §14) and homo-civis or homo-vulgus. (It should be noted that the densities of "homo" on the one hand, and those of "civitas," "natio," "vulgus" and "lex" on the other are fairly clearly distinguished). — In the section dealing with the theoretical arts — §§6–11 (6, 10–9, 10) — "homo" is avoided in the passage dealing with religion, while it occurs most frequently in the passage dealing with poetry. It is true, "homo" is also avoided in the passage

Chapter 5

It would be rash to maintain that the foregoing observations suffice for establishing what Fārābī believed as regards any substantiae separatae. They do suffice however for justifying the assertion that his philosophy does not stand and fall with the acceptance of such substances. For him, philosophy is the attempt to know the essence of each of all beings: his concept of philosophy is not based on any preconceived opinion as to what allegedly real things are truly real things. He has infinitely more in common with a philosophic materialist than with any non-philosophic believer however well-intentioned. For him, philosophy is essentially and purely theoretical. It is the way leading to the science of the beings as distinguished from the [393] science of the ways of life. It is the way leading to that science rather than that science itself: the investigation rather than the result.[100] Philosophy thus understood is identical with the scientific spirit "in action," with σκέψις in the original sense of the term, i.e., with the actual quest for truth which is animated by the conviction that that quest alone makes life worth living, and which is fortified by the distrust of man's natural propensity to rest satisfied with satisfying, if unevident or unproven, convictions. A man such as Fārābī doubtless had definite convictions concerning a number of important points, although it is not as easy to say what those convictions were as the compilers of textbooks and of most monographs seem to think. But what made him a philosopher, according to his own view of philosophy, were not those convictions, but the spirit in which they were acquired, in which they were maintained and in which they were intimated rather than preached from the house-tops. Only by reading Maimonides' *Guide* against the background of philosophy thus understood, can we hope eventually to fathom its unexplored depths.

---

dealing with rhetoric; but there it is replaced by a repeated "nos." — Cf. notes 27, 41 and 48 above.

[100] Not without good reasons does he introduce philosophy as the art which supplies the science of the beings, and not as that science itself. — Consider also §26.

6

Review of John O. Riedl's Edition of Giles of Rome, *Errores Philosophorum* (1946)

Giles of Rome, *Errores Philosophorum*. By John O. Riedl, trans. Milwaukee, Wis.: Marquette University Press, 1944. lix, 67 pages. $3.00.

[62] This volume contains, above all, the first critical edition of Aegidius Romanus' *Errores philosophorum* (written around 1270). In his introduction the editor discusses extensively and most competently the available MSS., the authenticity and date of composition of the treatise, and the sources used by the author. In the footnotes to the text he indicates, and frequently quotes, passages on which Aegidius has drawn, or might have drawn, as well as parallels from the other works of the author and from the works of Thomas Aquinas.

    The *Errores* is a valuable document of the thirteenth century conflict between the Christian teaching and the teaching of "the philosophers," i.e., of Aristotle and the Islamic and Jewish Aristotelians. It consists chiefly of a compilation of the "erroneous" theses of Aristotle, Averroes, Avicenna, Ghazzālī, Alkindi, and Maimonides. As Koch points out, Aegidius took over Maimonides' diagnosis of the weakness of the philosophic position: the foundation of all errors of Aristotle is the view that nothing ever comes into being except through a preceding motion (pp. lii f.).

    Generally speaking, the *Errores* does not add much to what we know from Ghazzālī, Maimonides and Thomas Aquinas about the issues involved in the conflict between revelation and Aristotelian philosophy. It is characteristic of the intellectual situation in Christian Europe that Fārābī, the most outstanding Islamic philosopher and the originator of the attitude that is generally known as "Averroism," is not even mentioned in the *Errores*. [63]

Originally published in *Church History* 15, no. 1 (Mar. 1946): 62–63. —Eds.

Chapter 6

From the text as established by Koch it appears that Aegidius quotes Maimonides' *Guide for the Perplexed* as *Expositio Legis* (not *legum* as was hitherto believed) (p. xlvii). This otherwise unknown title, presumably the title of a practically unknown Latin translation, corresponds perfectly with what Maimonides himself says in his introduction about the intention of his work. It corroborates our suggestion that the *Guide* is primarily not a philosophic work, but an exegetic one.

The translation makes the impression of being very reliable. "*Disciplinales scientiae*" in ch. XII §8 (p. 62 f.) has to be rendered by "mathematical sciences" and not by "disciplined knowledge."

7

On a New Interpretation of Plato's Political Philosophy (1946)

I

[326] Professor Wild's recent book on Plato[1] is not simply a historical work. His presentation of Plato's doctrine of man is animated by the zeal of a reformer and is meant to bring about a radical reorientation of the "philosophy of culture." Thoroughly dissatisfied with modern philosophy in all its forms, and unwilling to take refuge in Thomism, Wild turns back to classical philosophy, to the teaching of Plato and Aristotle, as the true teaching. At present very few will be prepared to accept his basic premise. But it is safe to predict that the movement which his book may be said to launch in this country will become increasingly influential and weighty as the years go by. However one may have to judge of his thesis, or of his book, the question that underlies his book, and to which his thesis is an answer, goes farther to the roots of the problems of the social sciences than any other question of which I am aware that has been publicly raised in recent times.

That question concerns the legitimacy of the modern approach in all its forms, as distinguished from the classical approach. It revives, after more than a century of silence, the issue which is known as *la querelle des anciens et des modernes* and which is generally supposed to have been settled, if not by Newton and Rousseau, at any rate by Hegel. Wild's book shows certainly that this apparently obsolete issue has again become a question. Indeed, only those who rush in where sensible men would fear

---

Originally published in *Social Research* 13, no. 3 (Sept. 1946): 326–67.—Eds.

1 John Wild. *Plato's Theory of Man. An Introduction to the Realistic Philosophy of Culture.* Cambridge: Harvard University Press, 1946. x & 320 pp. $5.

Chapter 7

to tread will claim that it has already found, or could yet have found, a sufficient answer. We are barely beginning to realize the [327] bearing and the extent of its implications. In Wild's book this underlying question is what must command the most serious attention of every social scientist who does not wish to be, or to be called, an obscurantist.

The test of extreme severity which modern civilization is undergoing before our eyes on the plane of action is accompanied by an increasingly insistent attack of a theoretical character on the principles of modern civilization. This attack cannot be met by a mere defense. Defensibility is not truth. The world abounds with defensible positions that are irreconcilable with one another. To limit oneself to the defense of a position means to claim the advantages of prescription; but one cannot enjoy those advantages without exposing oneself to the reasonable suspicion that one is defending a vested interest of some kind or another which does not bear being looked into by an impartial third. To claim the advantages of prescription is particularly unbecoming for the adherents of the modern principles—principles that are inseparable from the demand for the liberation of one's mind from all prejudices. The very resolution to defend a position may be said to entail the loss of a most important freedom, a freedom the exercise of which was responsible for the success of the modern venture: defenders cannot afford radically to doubt. Adherents of the modern principles who lack the ability to take a critical distance from the modern principles, to look at those principles not from their habitual point of view but from the point of view of their opponents, have already admitted defeat: they show by their action that theirs is a dogmatic adherence to an established position.

Thus the only answer to the attack on the modern principles which is legitimate on the basis of those principles themselves is their free and impartial reexamination. The method of such a reexamination is predetermined by the nature of the modern principles. They were evolved in opposition to, and by way of transformation of, the principles of classical philosophy. Up to the present day no adherent of the modern principles has been [328] able to assert them with any degree of definiteness without explicitly and more or less passionately attacking the classical principles. Therefore a free examination of the modern principles is necessarily based on their conscientious confrontation with those of classical philosophy.

To confront them with the principles of mediaeval philosophy would not suffice. Generally speaking, mediaeval philosophy has in common with modern philosophy the fact that both are influenced, if in different ways, by the teaching of the Bible. That influence does not necessarily become a subject of critical investigation if modern philosophy is confronted with mediaeval philosophy, whereas it necessarily comes immediately to the center of attention if modern philosophy is confronted with classical philosophy. Besides, it was classical rather than mediaeval philosophy which was attacked by the founders of modern philosophy. At any rate, the founders of modern political philosophy conceived of their work as directed against classical philosophy in all its forms; in the passages of their writings where they state their intention most clearly they do not even mention mediaeval philosophy as a significant opponent.[2]

It would be a mistake to believe that the principles to be confronted with each other, especially those of classical philosophy, are readily accessible in the works of the historians of philosophy. The modern students of classical philosophy are modern men, and hence they almost inevitably approach classical philosophy from a modern point of view. Only if the study of classical philosophy were accompanied by constant and relentless reflection on the modern principles, and hence by liberation from the naive acceptance of those principles, could there be any prospect of an adequate understanding of classical philosophy by modern men. One may seriously doubt whether there is a single study which fully meets this indispensable requirement. A sign of this is the [329] fact that one rarely, if ever, comes across studies on classical philosophy which do not make ample use of modern terminology, and thus continually introduce non-classical thoughts into what claim to be exact presentations of classical philosophy.

Until a relatively short time ago most students of earlier philosophy started from the assumption that modern philosophy is decisively superior to classical philosophy. Accordingly they were compelled to try to understand classical philosophy better than it understood itself, that is, they were prevented from wholeheartedly complying with the demand of genuine historical understanding or of historical exactness according to which one has to try to understand the thinkers of the past exactly as they understood themselves. It is obvious that one's understanding of the thought of the past will tend to be the more adequate the more one is interested in the thought of the past; but one cannot be seriously interested in it, cannot

---

2   See Machiavelli, *The Prince*, chs. 14 and 15 (compare *Discorsi* I, Introd. and ch. 58); Bodin, *Six livres de la république*, preface; Hobbes, *De cive*, XII.3 (compare preface), and *Leviathan*, ch. 21 (p. 113 Everyman's Library edition).

Chapter 7

be driven to it by philosophic passion, if one knows beforehand that the thought of the present is decisively superior to that of the past.

This is confirmed by the generally accepted view that "the historical school," in the wide sense of the term, brought about a better historical understanding and a keener awareness of the demands of historical exactness than was available in the philosophy of the eighteenth century: these "romantics" did not believe in the *essential* superiority of their time to the past. The fusion of philosophic and historical interest which we can observe especially around the year 1800 in Germany, and out of which the modern study of classical philosophy grew, was animated by a "longing of the soul" for classical antiquity. Both the greatness and the failings of modern understanding of classical philosophy can be traced to those fateful years: one would only delude oneself by believing that the fundamental thoughts of such men as Friedrich Schlegel and Hegel have ceased to be the philosophic basis of our understanding of the classics merely because a large number of their individual assertions have been rejected by their followers or opponents. These thinkers, guided by Schiller's [330] distinction between naive and sentimental poetry, conceived of the thought of the classics as "naive," that is, as related to life directly, and for this reason lacking the "reflection" of the modern "self-consciousness." Therefore, however much their historical understanding may have surpassed that of the Enlightenment, their final judgment on the respective merits of modern and classical philosophy coincided with that of their predecessors, since at least from the point of view of philosophy the shortcomings of naivete are much more serious than its advantages. The view prevailed, and is still prevalent, in spite of or because of the discovery of "history," that classical philosophy did not raise the truly fundamental questions of a "reflexive" character which concern "subjectivity," and which were raised with increasing clarity in the course of the modern development.

The average historian of our time is a spiritual descendant not so much of Hegel himself as of nineteenth-century historicism. Historicism assumes that all periods are equally "immediate" to "the truth," and hence it refuses to judge the thought of the past with reference to "the truth" of our time. Its intention is to understand the thought, say, of Plato exactly as Plato understood it himself, or to interpret Plato's statements with a view to the center of reference not of modern thought but of his own thought. It is constitutionally unable, however, to live up to its intention. It assumes that, generally speaking and other things being equal, the thought of all epochs is equally "true," because every philosophy is essentially the expression of its time,[3] and it makes this assumption the basis of its interpretation of classical philosophy. But classical philosophy, which claimed to teach *the* truth, and not merely the truth of classical Greece, cannot be [331] understood on the basis of this assumption. By rejecting the claim of the classics as untenable, if not as simply absurd, historicism asserts just as much as did the Enlightenment and German idealism that the modern approach (for historicism is admittedly characteristically modern) is decisively superior to the classical approach. Historicism supplies as little as other modern schools a philosophic motive for the genuinely historical effort to understand classical philosophy in exactly the same way as it understood itself.

To understand classical philosophy one must be seriously interested in it, must take it as seriously as possible. But one cannot do this if one is not prepared to consider the possibility that its teachings are simply true, or that it is decisively superior to modern philosophy. No prejudice in favor of cherished modern convictions must deter the historian from giving the thinkers of old the full benefit of the doubt. When he engages in the study of classical philosophy he must cease to take his bearings by the modern signposts with which he has grown familiar since his early childhood; he must learn to take his bearings by the signposts that guided the classical philosophers. Those old signposts are not immediately visible; they are concealed by heaps of dust and rubble. The most obvious, although not by any means the most dangerous, impediments to genuine understanding of the classics are the superficial interpretations which are offered in textbooks and many monographs and which seem to unlock by one formula the mystery of classical philosophy. The signposts that guided the classics must be recovered before they can be used. Before the historian has succeeded in recovering them he cannot help being in a condition of utter bewilderment: he finds himself in a darkness that is illumined only by his knowledge that he knows, that is, understands, nothing. When he engages in the study of classical philosophy he must know that he embarks on a journey whose end is completely hidden from him. He is not likely to return to the shores of our time as exactly the same man who departed from them.

---

3   According to a view that is very popular today, the historicist thesis can be proved by historical evidence: historical evidence is said to prove that all philosophic teachings are "relative" to their "times." Even if this were so, nothing would follow from it, since the "relatedness" of a teaching to its "time" is essentially ambiguous and does not necessarily mean dependence of the teaching on its "time"; a particular time may have been particularly favorable to the discovery of *the* truth.

Chapter 7

[332] Our lack of an adequate interpretation of classical philosophy is due to the lack of a philosophic incentive to such an interpretation. This lack is now filled for the first time in a number of generations by insight into the necessity for a free reexamination of the modern principles, a reexamination that necessarily presupposes an adequate understanding of classical philosophy. What at first sight is merely the result of the demands of historical exactness is actually the result of the demand for a philosophic reexamination of our basic assumptions. This being the case, insistence on the fundamental difference between philosophy and history—a difference by which philosophy stands or falls—may very well, in the present situation, be misleading, not to say dangerous to philosophy itself.

II

On the basis of this discussion of the standard with reference to which present-day books on classical philosophy ought to be judged, we may turn now to Wild's book on Plato's doctrine of man. It is evident at once that for Wild himself, whatever doubts may be entertained by some of his readers, *la querelle des anciens et des modernes* no longer exists. He considers it definitely settled in favor of the classics. After having disposed of this fundamental question, which as such is a theoretical question, he can pursue a practical or political intention on the foundation of the classical teaching.

This leads to dangerous consequences. The teaching of the classics can have no immediate practical effect, because present-day society is not a *polis*. It does not suffice to say that man is always man and that there is no other difference between modern society and the society envisaged by the classics than that the former is more "complex" than the latter, or that the difference between them is only one of size; for even if this were true, the classics themselves regarded size as of crucial importance for determining the character of a society. To be somewhat more specific, it is true that what Plato teaches us about tyranny is [333] indispensable for the understanding of present-day "totalitarianism," but one would misunderstand that contemporary phenomenon by simply identifying it with the tyranny of old; it suffices here to remark that present-day "totalitarianism" is essentially based on "ideologies," and ultimately on popularized or distorted science, whereas ancient tyranny did not have such a basis. Since there are essential differences between modern society and the society envisaged by the classics, the classical teaching cannot be immediately applicable to modern society, but has to be *made* applicable to it, that is, must be modernized or distorted.

On a New Interpretation of Plato's Political Philosophy

Wild is not unaware of the danger to which he exposes himself. He opens his book with the following declaration: "This book is not an attempt to expound the whole of Plato's philosophy, nor even of a single part of his philosophy, as 'historic' exposition is often understood. Its aim is not so much to reveal the thought of Plato as to reveal the nature of human culture and its inversion, using Plato, the philosopher, as a guide. Though such a purpose may seem strange to a certain version of history as antiquarian research, I am sure that it would not seem strange to Plato." Certainly, Plato considered the philosophic question of the best political order infinitely more important than the historical question of what this or that individual thought of the best political order; hence he never wrote a book on other people's "theories of man." But it is equally certain that he would have preferred an adequate historical investigation to an inadequate philosophic investigation: "it is better to finish a little task well than a great one inadequately."

Wild would have come nearer to the spirit of Plato's unconcern with, or even contempt for, the merely historical truth if he had expounded his own "philosophy of culture" in his own name, or if, following the example of Sir Thomas More, he had written a free imitation of the *Republic*, that is, if he had taken the responsibility for a teaching which is actually his own teaching and not sought refuge behind the shield of Plato's dazzling authority. [334] Nothing would have prevented him from pointing out on every occasion how much he had learned from Plato.

By embarking on the un-Platonic venture of writing a book on Plato's "theory of man" he has forfeited every right to appeal to Plato's sovereign disregard for historical truth and must bow to the standards of historical exactness. His failure to submit to these standards, combined with his failure to write a non-historical book on the "theory of man" or "the realistic philosophy of culture," merely leads to the result that he is not compelled really to prove his most important assertions. It exposes him to the danger of substituting for proof of the historical contention that Plato held certain views some sort of philosophic reasoning showing that the views in question are sound, and of substituting for the demonstration of philosophic theses references to Platonic passages where those theses are asserted. For instance, he obviously believes in the necessity and possibility of a natural theology;[4] since he writes a book on Plato he can leave it at referring to Platonic passages in which it is presupposed, or demonstrated, that the

---

4   Wild, pp. 11, 30, 109, 220, 229, 290, 292.

CHAPTER 7

existence of God is knowable to unassisted theoretical reason, and he is not compelled squarely to set forth a demonstration of the existence of God.

Wild's refusal to expound the whole of Plato's "theory of man" is irreconcilable with his view that our disasters are due to rejection of the classical teaching; for if this view is sound, one has to recover the classical teaching as a whole before one can even think of selecting parts from it. Prior to such complete recovery every selection is arbitrary, having no other principle than modern predilections. If it is true that *la querelle des anciens et des modernes* is the paramount issue, one merely blurs that issue by substituting for a downright modern teaching a modernized Platonic teaching.

For the reasons indicated, Wild is compelled to assume that we can find in the classical teaching the solution to our modern problem. Our problem is caused by the insufficiency of modern philos-[335]ophy. Hence the classics must be presumed to supply us with an analysis, diagnosis and therapy of the modern disease. Wild opposes the "realism" of classical philosophy to the "idealism" of modern philosophy, and he asserts that "idealism" is identical with the phenomenon characterized by Plato as sophistry.[5]

The temptation to identify modern philosophy with sophistry is considerable, and Wild is not the first to succumb to it. But can that identification be maintained in cold blood? German idealism, against which Wild's attack is primarily directed, was always inclined to conceive of its relation to the philosophy of the Enlightenment as analogous to the relation of classical philosophy to the Greek sophists. As a matter of fact, one sometimes has the impression that Wild merely replaces the thesis "sophistry is to classical philosophy as Enlightenment is to German idealism" by the thesis "sophistry is to classical philosophy as German idealism is to Wild." The truth is, however, that whereas German idealism never lost sight of the fundamental difference between modern thought in all its forms and classical thought in all its forms, Wild rests satisfied with the unqualified identification of idealism *tout court*—and hence in particular modern idealism, German and non-German—with sophistry. If his contentions on this point were to be taken seriously he would have had to limit himself to asserting that sophistry is the remote, indirect and unintentional, if necessary, consequence of the fundamentally unsophistical and genuinely philosophic effort of modern philosophy, and he would have

---

5   Wild, pp. 4 ff., 12 ff., 21, 234, 249, 254, 271, 301, 304, 310 ff.

had to take the trouble of submitting some non-rhetorical and non-sophistical proof of this very far-reaching assertion.[6]

[336] The difficulties to which the identification of idealism with sophistry is exposed are sufficiently illustrated by Wild's own hesitations. On the one hand, he unqualifiedly identifies idealism with sophistry (311); on the other hand he asserts that idealism is the root of sophistry (271, 279 ff., 79), and hence that it is different from sophistry. He exonerates idealism still more by intimating that it is only one of the roots of sophistry. The root of sophistry is said to be "transcendental confusion," and certain "transcendental confusions" lead to errors different from idealism which also lead to sophistry (229 ff., 234, 297). But even "transcendental confusion" is not necessarily *the* root of sophistry, for while it is called on one occasion "the ultimate root of sophistry" (232), on another occasion it is said to "lie close to the root of sophistry" (238). We are thus gradually led to the view that "transcendental confusion" may lead to idealism as well as to other heresies, and that idealism as well as other errors may lead to sophistry—a view that is plausible, if not very enlightening, since even truth itself can be sophistically misused (273).

To this Wild might conceivably answer as follows: "transcendental confusion" is an "active tendency" which, following its own law, leads to an extreme beyond which "sophistry can go no further," in other words, to

---

6 Wild mentions the following characteristic traits of "idealism": the subordination of ontology to logic (p. 2); the denial of the intentionality of thought (280 n., 301); the view "that all things are constantly thinking, or that there are unconscious or non-thinking thoughts" (214); the confusion of material things with the forms, the objects of thought, and hence the denial of matter, motion and change (5, 234, 238, 290). His last word on the subject is the identification of idealism with "the confusion of man with the creator" (311), that is, with the view that all meaning, order and truth are originated by, or relative to, "consciousness," "reason," "the subject," "man" or *Existenz*. (Compare E. Husserl, *Ideen*, §§47, 49, 55, and M. Heidegger, *Sein und Zeit*, §44, as well as "Vom Wesen des Grundes" in *Festschrift für Edmund Husserl*, Halle 1929, pp. 98 ff. I refer to Husserl and Heidegger because they most clearly reveal that Wild's identification of idealism with the denial of intentionality or with the subordination of ontology to logic does not go to the root of the matter.)

Wild's position is at least as much opposed to English empiricism, for example, as it is to German idealism. Yet he has chosen to present German idealism as *the* villain. A man who claims to be a Platonist is under an obligation to stress the fact that German idealism attempted to restore important elements of Plato's and Aristotle's teaching in opposition to western (English and French) philosophy, if on the basis of a foundation laid by western philosophy.

Chapter 7

the position of Protagoras, "the original sophist par excellence" (239); and Protagoras' position is idealism (239, 254, 306). But—to say nothing of the fact that, according to what he says elsewhere, sophistry *can* go beyond Protagoras, that is, toward "unmitigated naturalism" (254)—it is [337] hard to understand how one can treat the "idealism" of Protagoras and the "idealism" of Kant, Hegel or Husserl as fundamentally identical. In other words, one definitely goes beyond the limits of legitimate polemical excitement by identifying modern philosophic idealism with sophistry and thus implying that men like Kant or Husserl were "subjective deceivers," that they were "submitting to the sensory bias of [their audience] ... and careless of the truth," and that, "with a little argumentative skill and persuasive capacity" they were making out "an original theory" to "look at least as good as the truth, if not a great deal better" (284, 310; the last quotations are taken from passages explicitly dealing with the essence of sophistry). To express the same criticism somewhat less harshly, Wild has considerable success in the rhetorical feat of rousing the reader's wrath against the scoundrels who are guilty of "transcendental confusion" or "transcendental carelessness" (297), but he does not completely convince one that ordinary confusion or ordinary carelessness is necessarily the outcome of too concentrated contemplation of "transcendental agencies" (298).

To see how Wild arrives at his surprising assertion one merely has to compare what he considers to be the essence of sophistry with the most characteristic trait of modern idealism. Sophistry, he asserts, is essentially the construction of "theories," "systems" or "ideal replicas" of reality, whereas philosophy "gives itself entirely to the task of hunting [reality] as it already is" (280, 308, 310). Modern idealism explicitly conceives of being as "constructed" or "constituted" by, or otherwise dependent on, the spontaneity of the "subject"; in its "classical" form, at any rate, it was based on the view that we can genuinely understand only what we "make" or "construct." But is there not all the difference in the world between constructing "subjective theories" because one denies that there is a fundamental difference between science and opinion or sense perception (sophistry), and constructing "ideal" "models" because one holds that only such construction makes possible science, as distinguished from opinion or [338] sense perception (modern idealism)? Modern idealism is so far from being identical with or even akin to sophistry, in Wild's sense of the term, that it stands or falls by the Platonic-Aristotelian distinction between science and opinion or sense perception.

On a New Interpretation of Plato's Political Philosophy

Wild's inability to do justice to modern philosophy[7] is due to his failure to give serious consideration to the question why modern philosophy revolted against the classical tradition, in other words, to the difficulties to which classical philosophy was and is still exposed. According to the classics, science presupposes that the world is intelligible, and this, Plato and Aristotle held, is impossible if intelligence does not "rule" the world. Classical science, one may say in order to simplify the discussion, ultimately depends on the possibility of natural theology as a science (compare Wild, 258). It was especially due to the influence of the Bible that the classical view became questionable, even for many of its adherents. Certainly the final form of classical science, that is, Aristotelian science (11, 17, 292), stands or falls by the doctrine of the eternity of the visible universe, a doctrine diametrically opposed to the Biblical doctrine of creation. One would have to have the courage to call Luther and Calvin sophists before one could dare to assert that only sophists can question the satisfactory character of the reconciliation attempted by Maimonides and Thomas Aquinas between the Biblical and the Aristotelian teachings. Wild, however, barely alludes to the Reformation when speaking of the origins of the modern break with classical philosophy. At any rate a case could be made for the view that it was reflection guided by the Biblical notion of creation which ultimately led to the doctrine that the world as created by God, or the "thing-in-itself," is inaccessible to human knowledge, or to the idealistic assertion that the world as far as we can under-[339]stand it, that is, the world as studied by human science, must be the "work" of the human mind.[8]

Be this as it may, in reading Wild's book one suddenly realizes the value of that textbook version of the primary motivation of modern philosophy which, if memory is a trustworthy guide, starts from the well-known fact that the difficulties to which classical philosophy is exposed find today their most massive expression in the success of modern natural science.

---

7   A further example: "This mysterious mistrust of universal knowledge is identified by Plato as the source of social corruption.... It is visible now in the sharp separation of 'the theoretical' from 'the practical' which stems from Kant" (122). The author obviously did not consider Kant's "Über den Gemeinspruch: Das mag in der Theorie richtig sein, taugt aber nicht für die Praxis." He must have mistaken Kant for Burke.

8   See Kant, *Kritik der reinen Vernunft*, ed. by Vorländer, p. 131, and *Kritik der Urteilskraft*, §§84 ff.; Hobbes, *De corpore*, XXV.1, *De homine*, X.4–5, and *Leviathan*, chs. 37 and 31; also Bacon, *Advancement of Learning*, pp. 88, 94 ff., 132 ff. (Everyman's Library edition), and Descartes, *Meditationes*, I.

CHAPTER 7

Wild seems to believe that he can reject modern philosophy while he does not dare to reject modern science. He certainly makes the most naive use of the fairly recent distinction between philosophy and science (78 ff. and 200 ff.) without considering that there is no place for this distinction in classical philosophy or science.[9] He thus tacitly assumes that modern "science" can be reconciled with, or integrated into, classical "philosophy." But he does not give one the slightest notion of how this could be achieved. Or does he believe that one can bridge the gulf between the "evolutionism" of modern biology and Aristotle's basic doctrine of the eternity of the species by triumphantly pronouncing that "classical philosophy [was] in Aristotle and Aquinas, and, indeed, universally before the decay of modern scholasticism...indubitably and incurably in its treatment of nature an evolutionary philosophy" (5)? Whatever may be the limitations of modern natural science, its obvious success has brought about a situation in which the possibility of natural theology has lost all the evidence it formerly possessed, and a much more serious reflection than Wild deems necessary would be required for checking "irresponsible, sophistic speculation" (79) about natural theology, to say nothing of what would be required for restoring it as a genuine science.

[340] In order to maintain the thesis that modern idealism is identical with sophistry Wild has not merely to disregard completely the fundamental issue involved in the conflict between modern and classical philosophy, and to misinterpret modern philosophy; he is also compelled to misinterpret the Platonic doctrine of sophistry. According to his interpretation of the *Sophist*, Plato saw the essence of sophistry (as distinguished from philosophy, which is the "reproduction" of the truth) in the "production" of "artificial constructions" and "novel theories and original speculations" or "systems," and in "productive" or "creative" thinking "about the most general and the most important things" (280 ff., 304 ff., 308). Plato does not, of course, say anything about "novel theories," "original speculations" or "systems." What he does say in the "vital discussion" (279) of the essence of sophistry[10] is that sophistry is the production in

---

9 In speaking of the Platonic distinction between mathematics and dialectics Wild identifies *dianoia* with "scientific insight" and *noesis* with "philosophic insight" (189, 197 ff.), thus contradicting what Plato clearly says in the *Republic* (533c–d; compare *Seventh Letter*, 342a–b).

10 In the "preliminary" discussion (*Sophist*, 221c5 to 231e) the Eleatic stranger mentions the fact that the sophist might "make" the doctrines he sells, but he makes it quite

speech of inexact imitations of all things, or the reproduction in spoken images of the apparent proportions of reality.

Wild himself virtually admits (281 ff.) that sophistry thus understood is as much and as little "productive" or "creative" as philosophy itself, which in the same context (*Sophist*, 235d1 to 236c7) is possibly hinted to be the production in speech of exact imitations of what is, or the reproduction in spoken images of the true proportions of reality. Even if it is granted that philosophy cannot be described in precise language as the production of exact imitations of reality, one would still not be entitled to say that according to Plato sophistry is essentially the production in speech of inexact imitations of the most important things; for, to say nothing of other considerations, the sophist shares this trait, according to Plato, not only with the popular orator but above [341] all with many simpleminded "men in the street"[11] and indeed (since mere diffidence in one's opinions about the whole does not liberate one from the spell of those opinions) with all non-philosophers as such.[12] Nor does one render Plato's thesis correctly by suggesting that the sophist is responsible for, or is the first originator of, the "fancies" of other men, since Plato makes it quite clear that the "fancies" which the sophist defends, elaborates or destroys originate with an entirely different type.[13]

If the construction of "theories" were sophistry every erring philosopher who as such substitutes a "theory" of his own for the truth would

---

clear that it is irrelevant whether the sophist "makes" his doctrines himself or has them supplied by others (224e2). It is the young Theaetetus, who has never seen a sophist (239e1; compare *Meno*, 92b7 ff.), who stresses the "productive" character of sophistry (231d9–11). Whatever this may mean, the Eleatic stranger states shortly afterward that this aspect of sophistry is certainly not the most characteristic one (232b3–6; compare 233c10–d2).

11 Compare *Sophist*, 268a–c, with *Apologia Socratis*, 22d7.

12 To avoid this difficulty Wild suggests that "just as all men are philosophers, and Socrates is the typical man, so are all men also sophists" (275). From this it would follow that Socrates, too, is a sophist, and not the opposite of the sophist, as suggested elsewhere (38, 306). Besides, the whole argument of the *Sophist*, and even of Wild's book, presupposes that the sophist is a specific human type distinguished not only from the philosopher but from the orator, the hunter, the tyrant, the lover, the statesman, the painter, the merchant and so on. This is not to deny that Plato sometimes uses "sophist" in a much wider sense; but this wider sense as such is not the precise sense. The common man is a "sophist" in almost the same sense in which the bricklayer or the shoemaker is a "scientist" (see *Statesman*, 258c6–e7, and *Theaetetus*, 146d1–2).

13 *Republic*, 493a6–9; *Statesman*, 303b8–c5.

Chapter 7

be a sophist. Wild is consistent enough to use "sophistry" and "false philosophy" as synonymous terms (64, 232, 234). But this is certainly not the Platonic view. In a passage of the *Theaetetus* (172c3 ff.) which is taken by Wild to deal with the opposition between philosophy and sophistry (254) Thales, who from Plato's point of view doubtless held a "false philosophy," is mentioned as a representative of the philosophic attitude. If Wild were right the designation of sophist would belong not only to the venerable Parmenides,[14] who identified the One with "a spatial whole" which he "imagined" (221 ff.) and who "committed acosmism," "absolutism" and "pantheism," but to Plato himself, whose "dynamic ontology" ("a brilliant and fertile suggestion") suffers from the "confusion of logic with ontology" (292, 296), and [342] even to Aristotle, who denied the creation of the world and hence the creator (311). Hardly anyone, except perhaps some theologians, would escape that fate.

According to the classical view sophistry is not false philosophy but a particular mode of the absence of philosophy, or, to speak somewhat more exactly, the use of philosophy for non-philosophic purposes by men who might be expected to know better, that is, who are somehow aware of the superiority of philosophy to all other pursuits. What characterizes the sophist is neither the construction of "original theories," of which all pre-Socratics and the author of the *Timaeus* were at least as guilty as the modern philosophers, nor, on the other hand, self-complacent scepticism, but the purpose for which he uses his "constructive" or "destructive" speeches.[15]

---

14 Wild's statements on pp. 128 ff. imply that Heraclitus, Parmenides and other great men were sophists.

15 Aristotle, *Rhetoric*, 1355b17–22, and *Metaphysics*, 1004b22–26. The view outlined above is confirmed by a comparison of Callicles (in the *Gorgias*) with the sophists. Callicles is not a sophist, as Wild implies (38, 306), but a despiser of sophistry, and he is this precisely because he is not in any way aware of the superiority of philosophy, or wisdom, to all other pursuits. While he is thus more opposed to Socrates than are Gorgias and Polos, he is on the other hand nearer to Socrates than are Gorgias and Polos, because he and Socrates are "lovers" (compare *Gorgias*, 481d1–5, with *Sophist*, 222d7 ff.). Socrates and Callicles are passionately given to the pursuit of what they consider best (to philosophy and politics, respectively), but the sophist's pursuit of philosophy is lukewarm, because he is passionately concerned with pleasures other than those deriving from understanding, or from understanding in common (true friendship), and especially with the pleasures deriving from "prestige." Wild's failure to distinguish between the "Callicles" type and the "sophist" type underlies also his interpretation of *Republic* 487b to 497a (121–31). He gratuitously assumes that passages refer to sophists which unmistakably refer to politicians. In the same context he also erro-

Since he believes that the sophist is the originator of the most fundamental errors (305, 118, 121) Wild is driven to assert that sophistry is *the* "inversion" of philosophy: "of all the modes of ignorance surely that of the sophist... is the most formidable" (278, 305). According to Plato there are at least two equally "formidable" vices, diametrically opposed to philosophy and to [343] each other: sophistry and the self-satisfied stupidity of the ignoramus, who mistakes his opinions for knowledge (*Sophist*, 267e10 ff. and 229c), as Wild himself on one occasion almost openly admits (128). The opposition of these two vices to each other permits the philosopher, and even compels him, to fight the one with the other: against the sophistic contempt for "commonsense" he appeals to the truth divined by "commonsense," and against the popular satisfaction with "commonsense" he allies himself with the sophistic doubt of it.[16] By insisting onesidedly on the opposition between the philosopher and the sophist one blurs the equally fundamental opposition between the philosopher and the "unsophisticated" non-philosopher, and thus is finally led to make the thoroughly un-Platonic assertion that "all men are philosophers" (275). While in one sense the sophist is *the* antagonist of the philosopher, in another sense the non-sophistic non-philosopher is *the* antagonist: the sophist, as distinguished from the vulgar, may be the "friend" of the philosopher.[17]

Sophistry (in the Platonic sense), far from being something like original sin, as Wild makes it out to be (305 ff., 311, 169), is, from the philosophic point of view, play or childish amusement; and the sophist, far from being the evil one or his emissary, is rather to be characterized as a man of mature age who has never grown up.[18] As Plato shows by the more trustworthy "deed" rather than by "speech"—by his *demonstratio ad oculos* of sophists,

---

neously identifies the sophist with the half-philosopher, or the man who, though lacking necessary natural gifts and destined by nature for the humbler arts, devotes himself to the study of philosophy (compare *Republic*, 495d7, with *Phaedrus*, 245a7).

16 See *Sophist*, 239e5 to 240a2; *Theaetetus*, 196e1 to 197a4; *Protagoras*, 352b2 to 353a; *Republic*, 538e5–6. Wild, who does not always say the same things about the same topics (*Gorgias*, 490e9–11), almost says on one occasion (99) what I said above in contradicting his predominant sentiment. See also his remark (167) that "the public tyrant," and hence not the sophist, "is the most inverted... of men."

17 *Republic*, 498c9–d1; *Apologia Socratis*, 23d4–7; *Phaedo*, 64b1–6; *Laws* 821a2 ff.; *Hippias maior*, 285b5–c2.

18 *Sophist*, 234a–b, 239d5, 259c1–d7. Compare *Parmenides*, 128d6–e2, and *Republic*, 539b2–d2.

CHAPTER 7

especially in the *Protagoras* and the *Euthydemus*—sophistry, from the philosophic point of view, is strictly speaking ridiculous, and what is ridiculous is a harmless deformity.[19] And if the objection is [344] made that Socrates warns the young Hippocrates against the dangers which might threaten him at the hands of Protagoras, the answer is obvious that Socrates also warns Protagoras against the dangers threatening him at the hands of that fool and son of a fool, Hippocrates, and his like, and that what is dangerous to the "Hippocrates" type is not necessarily dangerous to others.[20] The unintelligent indignation about sophists which Wild imputes to Socrates is characteristic not of Socrates but of the men who persecuted and killed him.[21]

It is in obvious contrast to a teaching to which Plato adhered to the last—that all vice and all wrongdoing are ultimately involuntary, because they proceed from ignorance (*Laws*, 731c2-7 and 860c7-d1)—that Wild traces sophistry, "the greatest evil," to something like wilful ignorance (306). The ultimate reason why he believes that sophistry is essentially "creative thought" or "false philosophy" or *the* "inversion" of philosophy, would seem to be that he reads Plato in the spirit not of Plato but of the Bible. He identifies the sophist with "the maker of an idol,"[22] and sophistry with the "vain philosophy" and "science falsely so called" of the Epistle to the Colossians and the First Epistle to Timothy. In his presentation sophistry takes on all the colors of idolatry, which is "the cause, the beginning and the end of all sin," and of infidelity, which has its root in pride.

Lest the foregoing remarks be misunderstood, it must be said that they apply only partly to any attempt to interpret Platonic philosophy in Biblical terms. While all such attempts are extremely questionable, there is no necessity whatever that they be made in the particular manner which

---

19 *Philebus*, 49b5–c5; Aristotle, *Poetics*, 1449a34–37.

20 *Protagoras*, 316c2–5 and 319b1–e1 (compare *ibid*., 310c3–4, with *Republic*, 549e3 to 550a1); *Theaetetus*, 151b2–6; *Republic*, 492a5–8; *Meno*, 91e2 to 92a2.

21 *Meno*, 91c1–5; compare *Republic*, 536c2–7.

22 Wild, 284 (also 81): "the maker of an idol (*eidolon*)." Unfortunately Plato, in the passage to which Wild refers as well as elsewhere in the *Sophist* (235b8 to 236c7, 264c4–5, 265b1, 266d7–8, 268c9–d1) uses *eidolon* to designate the genus which embraces both "replicas" (the products of the philosopher) and "fancies" (the products of the sophist, among others). See especially 266b2–c6, where Plato speaks of the "idols" made by God.

Wild has chosen, both [345] in his presentation of Plato's philosophy and in his criticism of modern philosophy. That particular manner has as little Biblical support as it has philosophic support.

III

The contention that we can find in classical teaching the solution to our problem is exposed to a further difficulty, caused by what one may well call "the fundamental opposition of Plato and Aristotle." To justify his enterprise Wild has to assert that there is a fundamental harmony between the two philosophies. He admits that there is a certain "contrast" between them: Plato "is always tending to regard things from a practical or moral point of view, while Aristotle is always tending to regard things from the detached theoretical point of view." But he holds that this "contrast" merely represents "two distinct though inseparable phases of one and the same philosophy."

According to Wild, Plato's answers are more elaborate or more satisfactory than Aristotle's in regard to practical philosophy, and the opposite is true in regard to theoretical philosophy (6, 11, 16 ff., 22, 42). In discussing Plato's theoretical philosophy he follows in the main the school of interpretation which asserts that Plato in his "later" dialogues abandoned the "separation" of ideas and sensible things, and thus adopted a "dynamic" view fundamentally different from the "static" view expounded in the "earlier" dialogues as well as in Aristotle's reports (215 ff., 233 ff., 289 ff.). Wild is unable to prove his contention because he states the crucial Platonic theses from the beginning in Aristotelian terms (if not in scholastic or modern terms), and thus understands Plato's answers as answers to the questions not of Plato but of Aristotle; that is to say, he begs the question.

It is reasonable to suspect that Plato does not supply his readers with explicit or final answers to his most important questions; but this does not entitle one to insert into Plato's argument Aristotle's explicit and final answers, as Wild constantly does (199, 223, 225, 245, 267 ff., 287, 290 ff.), before one has carefully con-[346]sidered, and excluded by sound reasoning, the possibility that Plato's tentative answers point in an entirely different direction from that chosen by Aristotle. Wild has failed to consider that possibility. If one cannot leave it at what Plato explicitly said, one has to consider first of all, and with the utmost care, Aristotle's reports about Plato's teaching, which go considerably beyond the evidence supplied by Plato's writings. Wild barely alludes to those reports.

CHAPTER 7

That Wild is seeking in a false direction for the answer to Plato's central question can perhaps most easily be seen from the following example. One of the few passages on which Wild bases his thesis regarding Plato's "dynamic ontology" is *Sophist*, 247e, where "being" is tentatively defined as "power," although he considers that definition "an undeveloped suggestion" or "a sort of stopgap" (291 ff.). In interpreting the context of that passage ("criticism of materialism and idealism") he asserts that the "materialists" and "idealists" really tried to define being, whereas the "pluralists" and the "monists," whose views are discussed by Plato immediately before, "merely took being for granted as obvious" (285, 288). But Plato makes it quite clear that he considers the "pluralists" and the "monists" more exact than the "materialists" and the "idealists" (*Sophist*, 245e6–8, 242c4–6), that is, that he believes the two former groups to take less for granted than the two latter ones. Wild had to disregard this crucial information in order to enhance the significance of the tentative definition of being as power. The reason for Plato's statement is that, in his opinion, one does not raise the question of being at all if one does not raise it in terms of the question "one and many."[23]

[347] It would seem that in order to prove a basic agreement between Plato and Aristotle the most important thing to do would be to show that both admitted either the supremacy of theory or that of practice or morality. Wild, however, believes that there cannot be an unqualified supremacy of either: "the practical is the richer and more inclusive order, whereas the theoretical is the higher and more determining order" (25). This is neither the Platonic nor the Aristotelian view. If it is assumed that according to Plato wisdom is essentially practical (*phronesis*) [*sic*—Eds.], or the idea of the good ("the highest object of learning") is essentially practical (30), it is necessary to say that according to Plato the practical order is the highest order. As concerns Aristotle, he leaves not the slightest doubt that theory,

---

23 Fundamentally the same misunderstanding underlies Wild's assertion, allegedly based on *Statesman* 284e to 285, that "in the lower arts which deal with physical things, ... measurement takes a quantitative form, as in building and stonecutting," whereas "in the higher arts, which deal with non-physical structures (as education for example), measurement is qualitative, and the work is measured by the 'mean,' the 'fit'. . . It is a great mistake to suppose that these latter arts are therefore less 'exact' than those subject to quantitative measurement" (47). Plato states explicitly that the art of weaving, nay, that all arts have to measure their work by the mean or the fit (*Statesman*, 284a5–b3 and d4–6), and that the art of building is more exact than music, the most important part of the art of education (*Philebus*, 56c4–6; *Republic*, 376e2–4).

to him, is absolutely superior in dignity to practice, or that he regards the practical or moral order (25 ff.) as very far from including the theoretical order.[24]

[348] Wild's "synthesis" of Platonism and Aristotelianism is based on a disregard of the real issue. Those scholars (Erich Frank for instance) who hold that there is a fundamental opposition between Plato and Aristotle assert that according to Aristotle not simply theory, but the theoretical or philosophic way of life, is fundamentally different from, and absolutely superior to, the practical way of life, whereas according to Plato the philosophic way of life is intrinsically practical or moral. Wild admits that they are right as regards Plato (39 ff.), and his more or less implicit attempt to disprove their contention regarding Aristotle has failed. The best one can say about his exposition is that it has left the controversy exactly as it was.

---

24 See *Nicomachean Ethics*, 1141a18 ff., 1177a17 ff., 1178b7 ff. Since Wild's assertion that "wisdom or philosophy" must be "both theoretical and practical" (17, 76) is based largely on Thomas' *Summa theologica*, one may also refer to the latter, 2,2 q. 45 a.3 and q. 19 a.7, where it is made clear that according to philosophy wisdom is purely theoretical, whereas according to theology wisdom is both theoretical and practical; and to 1,2 q. 58 a. 4–5, where it is made clear that moral virtue and wisdom (in the philosophic sense) are perfectly independent of each other.

Wild's assertion that the practical or moral order is more inclusive than the theoretical order would seem to be based on this syllogism: the practical order comprises all objects of action; but action consists of theory and of action proper; hence the practical order comprises all objects of theory and all objects of action proper (compare Wild, 23). Wild obviously mistakes theory as a way of life, which as such is an object of choice or action, for the objects of theory, which as such are not objects of choice or action. The same mistake underlies his assertion that according to Aristotle the theoretical order is higher than the practical order "since before we can devise adequate means to achieve an end, this end must be known" (17). The end meant in the Aristotelian passage to which Wild refers (*Nicomachean Ethics*, 1145a7 ff.) is wisdom or theory as the end of human endeavor, that is, as true happiness, which as such belongs not to the theoretical but to the practical order (compare Thomas' commentary on the *Ethics*, 1, lect. 19). One may also say that Wild gratuitously assumes that all good things or all ends belong as such to the practical or moral order (23 n. 57: see *Nicomachean Ethics*, at the beginning, *Metaphysics*, 993b20 ff., *De anima*, 433a27–30).

According to Wild the practical order is characterized by contrariety, whereas the theoretical order is beyond all contrariety (28, 31, 35). But theory as a habit has as much a contrary as any moral habit (28 n. 68), and not only "Plato's practical concepts," as Wild contends, but his theoretical ones as well (such as being and non-being, same and other, motion and rest, hard and soft, heavy and light) are divided into contraries.

Chapter 7

This is not to deny the validity of Wild's assertion that all the subjects treated thematically in Plato's writings are discussed from a practical point of view—in other words, that in discussing them Plato never loses sight of the elementary Socratic question of how one ought to live—whereas Aristotle's analyses have left that question far behind. He is equally right in describing Plato's practical procedure in such terms as "protreptic," "exoteric" or "maieutic," and by stressing the connection between Plato's practical approach and his use of images or myths.[25] But here again Wild's eagerness to arrive at "results" has prevented him from devoting sufficient attention to a most serious theoretical problem. He has not stopped to ponder the apparently overwhelming difficulty which is indicated most clearly by the term "exoteric." To put it simply, if the teaching of Plato's dialogues is exoteric, it is hard to see how one could ever get hold of Plato's esoteric or serious teaching. If one accepts the *Seventh Letter* as authentic, as Wild does (13), one has to go farther and say that Plato never wrote a book about the subjects with which he was seriously [349] concerned, and that according to his most emphatic declaration no one who understands anything at all about these subjects—"nature's highest and first things"—would ever write on them (*Seventh Letter*, 341b5 ff. and 344d4–5). Since the meaning of any Platonic teaching decisively depends on his teaching concerning "nature," we thus seem to be led to the conclusion that no serious Platonic teaching is really accessible to us.

No one could state the difficulty more forcefully, and at the same time indicate the solution more unintentionally, than Professor Cherniss did in a recent comment on the passage to which I have just referred. He says: "For myself, I do not believe that Plato wrote [the *Seventh*] *Epistle*; but if I did, I should recognize that he has himself borne witness beforehand against anything which I might write about the real purport of his thought, and I should account it the madness born of stubborn insolence to seek to describe or even to discover the serious doctrine of a man who has condemned all those who ever have made the attempt or ever will."[26]

Cherniss fails to consider that according to the *Seventh Letter*, as well as according to the *Phaedrus*, no writing composed by a serious man can

---

25 Wild, 6, 11, 16, 31 ff., 43, 74, 174, 205 ff., 291.

26 Harold Cherniss, *The Riddle of the Early Academy* (Berkeley 1945) p. 13. I am in full agreement with Cherniss' contention that the dialogues are the only solid basis for the understanding of Plato's teaching, and with his warning against "the easy error of mistaking general agreement [on the relative chronology of the three large groups into which all the dialogues can be distributed] for demonstration" (p. 4).

be quite serious,[27] and hence that the passage on which he bases his verdict must be understood with a grain of salt. The *Seventh Letter* does not condemn the attempt to discover the serious teaching, for since the latter is intended to be the true teaching, such condemnation would be tantamount to a condemnation of philosophy; the *Seventh Letter* merely denies that the serious teaching is communicable as other teachings are. Nor does it absolutely condemn the attempt to communicate the serious teaching in writing. The author of the *Seventh Letter* [350] goes on to say that if the serious teaching were useful for human beings, he would consider it the most noble action of his life to communicate it in writing to "the many"; but, he says, the attempt would not be salutary for human beings, "save for some few who are capable of discovering [the serious teaching] by themselves by means of slight indication."[28] According to the *Seventh Letter* nothing would have prevented Plato from writing about the highest subjects in such a way as to give subtle hints to those for whom those hints would suffice, and thus not to communicate anything at all about the highest subjects to the large majority of readers. There is sufficient evidence in the dialogues to show that this was precisely what Plato did,[29] and thus that the dialogues have the function not of communicating but of intimating the most important truths to "some," while they have at the same time the much more obvious function of producing a salutary (civilizing, humanizing and cathartic) effect on all.

But it is one thing to try to discover Plato's serious teaching, and an entirely different thing to present one's interpretation of that teaching in writing or in any other public "speech." Cherniss is right in stressing the fact that according to the *Seventh Letter* Plato disowned beforehand any writing that would claim to present "the real purport of his thought." The *Seventh Letter* suggests that no one who, following Plato's indications, has understood his teaching would ever think of expounding it in public, because it would fill most readers with an unjustified contempt or else with a "lofty and vain expectation that they have learned some impressive things." It suggests, in other words, that no irresponsible man, or no one who would treat lightly a Platonic admonition, would ever succeed in understanding anything of Plato's serious teaching.

---

27 *Seventh Letter*, 344c3–7; *Phaedrus*, 276d1–e3 and 277e5 ff.

28 *Seventh Letter*, 341d2–e3. Compare *Phaedrus*, 275d5–e3 and 276a5–7, as well as *Protagoras*, 329a, 343b5, 347e.

29 *Republic*, 506b8 to 507a5, 509c3–10, 517b5–8, 533a1–5; *Sophist*, 247e5 to 248a1, 254c5–8; *Philebus*, 23d9–c1; *Statesman*, 262c4–7, 263a, 284c7–d2; *Timaeus*, 28c3–5.

CHAPTER 7

One does not need the evidence of the *Seventh Letter* in order [351] to see that Plato "prohibited" written expositions of his teaching. Since Plato refrained from presenting his most important teaching "with all clarity," the prohibition against written expositions of his teaching is self-enforcing: everyone who presents such an exposition becomes, to use a favorite Platonic expression, "ridiculous," inasmuch as he can easily be refuted and confounded by passages in the dialogues which contradict his exposition.[30] No interpretation of Plato's teaching can be proved fully by historical evidence. For the crucial part of his interpretation the interpreter has to fall back on his own resources: Plato does not relieve him of the responsibility for discovering the decisive part of the argument by himself. The undying controversy about the meaning of the idea of the good is a sufficiently clear sign of this. Who can say that he understands what Plato means by the idea of the good if he has not discovered by himself, though guided by Plato's hints, the exact or scientific argument which establishes the necessity and the precise character of that "idea," that is, the argument which alone would have satisfied Plato and which he refused to present to us in the *Republic* or anywhere else?

Plato composed his writings in such a way as to prevent for all time their use as authoritative texts. His dialogues supply us not so much with an answer to the riddle of being as with a most articulate "imitation" of that riddle. His teaching can never become the subject of indoctrination. In the last analysis his writings cannot be used for any purpose other than for philosophizing. In particular, no social order and no party which ever existed or which ever will exist can rightfully claim Plato as its patron.

This does not mean that the interpretation of Plato is essentially arbitrary. It means, on the contrary, that the rules of exactness [352] governing the interpretation of Plato's books are much stricter than those governing the interpretation of most books. Careful consideration of what various passages in the dialogues say about the character of good writings will gradually teach one, if this Platonic information is applied to one's reading of the dialogues, to get hold of very specific hermeneutic rules. The principle of

---

30 Cherniss' interpretation, for example, culminates in the thesis that "no idea [is] ontologically prior or posterior to any other," and that Plato "could not in fact have thought of the world of ideas as such as a hierarchy at all" (53 ff.). This thesis manifestly contradicts the teaching of the *Republic*, according to which the idea of the good is the cause of all other ideas and rules over them (compare Cherniss' note on the idea of the good, on p. 98).

these rules may tentatively be stated as follows: for presenting his teaching Plato uses not merely the "content" of his works (the speeches of his various characters) but also their "form" (the dialogic form in general, the particular form of each dialogue and of each section of it, the action, characters, names, places, times, situations and the like); an adequate understanding of the dialogues understands the "content" in the light of the "form." In other words, a much more careful consideration of the narrower and the wider context of each statement is required for the understanding of Plato's books than for the understanding of most books. An adequate understanding of the dialogues would enable the reader to discover the decisive indications of Plato's serious teaching. It would not supply him with ready-made answers to Plato's ultimate and most important questions.

Wild is in a way aware of the undogmatic character of the Platonic dialogues. Plato, he says, "specifically warns us against taking his own thoughts, least of all his own words, with any seriousness except as possible guides or 'reminders' of the real things in us and around us" (1). If we assume for the sake of convenience that this is a correct rendering of what the *Phaedrus* says about the deficiencies of writings as such, we will still have considerable difficulty in seeing how one can use Plato's thoughts as guides for the understanding of reality if one does not know these thoughts, and how one who is not a prophet (*Laws*, 634e7 ff.) can know Plato's thoughts without listening to Plato's words. However this may be, Wild tends to take a statement about the deficiencies of writings as such—the statement of a man who has written his works with unsurpassed care—not as an indication of the fact that the dialogues are meant to remedy these deficiencies [353] as far as possible, and hence not as an admonition to read the dialogues with the utmost care, but as an encouragement to careless reading.

Thus Wild almost constantly divorces from their context the statements of Plato, or rather of Plato's characters, and integrates them into a whole that has no Platonic basis whatever.[31] He does not even take the quite ordinary precaution of refraining from ascribing to Plato views that are expressed not by Socrates or other "spokesmen" of Plato but by sophists like Protagoras (101 ff.). Very rarely if ever does he take the trouble of exhibiting to the reader the "ascent" from the popular views from which the discussion frequently starts to the less provisional views at which it

---

31 Apart from the examples mentioned elsewhere in this article, I would refer the reader to Wild's interpretation of *Philebus*, 34c ff. (153 ff.).

Chapter 7

arrives, and thus he is led to ascribe the same importance to statements which are of very different specific weights. Starting from the correct principle that we must interpret Plato's myths in terms of his philosophy, and not his philosophy in terms of his myths (180), but disregarding the relation between the "content" and the "form" of the dialogues, he is led to believe that we must interpret Plato's myths in terms of the non-mythical statements of Plato's characters. In other words, since he disregards what is implied by Plato's comparison of written or unwritten speeches with living beings (*Phaedrus*, 264b3–e2)—the principle that in a good writing every part, however small, is necessary and nothing is superfluous—he tends to believe that the images or myths occurring in the dialogues are fully explained in the dialogues.[32]

For instance, in explaining the image of the cave in the begin-[354]ning of the seventh book of the *Republic*, he assumes that the four sections of that image correspond exactly to the four sections of the divided line to which Plato had shortly before compared the four kinds of apprehension.[33] He is thus prevented from grasping clearly the extent to which the image of the cave goes beyond the other statements of the *Republic*. To mention only the most obvious point, in the other statements of the *Republic* the

---

32 See pp. 150, 188 ff. Wild has failed to set forth clearly what he considers the function of the myths to be. According to one set of statements (180, 205 ff.) the myths are meant to lead the reader to the "formal analysis" of the subject that is mythically represented. Elsewhere (31 ff., 155 ff., 174, 179) he says that the myths are meant to suggest "historicity," which cannot be apprehended by "formal analysis." In another set of passages (73 ff., 123) he says that the myths are meant to supply us with "grounded opinions" concerning "the nature of the supreme principle, and the ultimate destiny of the soul."

33 See pp. 181 ff. The four parts of the "divided line" are: conjecture, conviction, reasoning, and intellectual perception. The four parts of the image of the cave are: the unperturbed life in the cave (to 515c3), the momentary and ineffectual perturbation of that life (to 515e5), the escape from the cave (to 516e2), and the descent to the cave (to 517a7). Wild is compelled by his assumption to regard the second part of the cave image as the description of an "ascent" (183 ff., 196), that is, of an actual disenchantment, whereas according to Plato no disenchantment whatever can take place within the cave: there the suspicion of "nature" is suppressed (or completely distorted) by him who has that suspicion. The dramatic presentation of this stage is "Callicles" (see especially the use that he makes of "nature" in his "philosophic" exposition, *Gorgias*, 482c4 ff.). As regards the correspondence between "reasoning" and "escape from the cave," and its implication, it should be noted that in the image of the cave the highest stage is not the "seeing" of the sun (the intellectual perception of the idea of the good) but the "reasoning" about the sun (516b8 ff. and 517c1 ff.).

stress is laid on the difference between sensible and intelligible objects, but the image of the cave shifts the emphasis to the difference between artificial and natural things: the cave-dwellers, that is, the non-philosophers, do not have any notion of "nature" and hence they do not even know artificial things as what they are; the artificial things as they understand them (that is, the objects of their conventional opinions, "the shadows of artificial things") are taken by them for *the* truth.[34] Led by the power of Plato's suggestions, Wild sees somehow that life in the cave is characterized by "social subjectivism" and "artificiality" (191 ff.). But by not realizing that this crucial information is part of the extent by which the myth goes beyond the non-mythical statements he fails both to see that the cave represents the city,[35] and to appre-[355]ciate the specific weight of that information. The final result is lack of clarity about Plato's view of the relation between philosophy and politics.

IV

Modern writers who do not sufficiently reflect on the essential traits of modern thought are bound to modernize, and thus to distort, the thought of the classics. Accordingly, Wild understands Plato's political philosophy as a "realistic philosophy of culture." He quotes with approval the remark of a scholar that Thomas Aquinas "wrote no special treatise on the subject of culture," and that "he does not use the word at all in its modern connotation" (7). But he does not wonder whether exactly the same remark does not apply to Plato.

The "philosophy of culture" was an outgrowth of German idealism, and "culture" as a philosophic term implied a fundamental distinction between "culture" as the realm of freedom and "creativity," and "nature" as the realm of necessity; it implied the denial of natural norms of "cultural" activity. Plato, on the other hand, was primarily concerned with discovering "the natural order which must guide men's endeavors" (Wild, v).

---

34 This, I think, is the clue to the passage about the ideas of artificial things in the tenth book of the *Republic*.

35 See (apart from the "wall" in 514b4) the almost explicit statement in 539e2–5 (compare 479d3–5, 517d8 ff., 520c, 538c6–d4 and e5–6). Note too the "political" form of the image of the cave in the "political" part of the *Republic* (414d2 ff.). The political character of the cave is also indicated by the fact that the only natural beings whose shadows are seen by the cave-dwellers are human beings (515a5–8); for the interpretation compare *Theaetetus*, 174a8 ff. and 175b9 ff.

CHAPTER 7

The historical root of our concept of "culture" is the fundamental change in the meaning of "nature" which became visible in the seventeenth century, and particularly in Hobbes' concept of "the state of nature." According not only to Plato and Aristotle but to "the sophists" as well, the natural was what may loosely be called the ideal, but since the seventeenth century it has come to mean what one implies when speaking of the "control" or the "conquest" of nature, in other words, what man's rational efforts have to be directed against. Wild is so unaware of this fundamental difference that he can speak of "the Callicles-Hobbesian state of nature" (95).

[356] By understanding Plato's political teaching in terms of "culture" he is naturally led to impute to Plato the view that there is such a thing as "scientific control over nature" (253) and that the arts or crafts serve the purpose of achieving "rational control, so far as this is possible, over each phase of human and subhuman nature" (88, 46, 54).[36] Possibly feeling the inadequacy of the term "culture," but obviously not sufficiently concerned with clarity about the central subject of his book, he cannot make up his mind whether "culture" is identical with "the technical hierarchy," and is thus fundamentally different from "life," as he says in one set of passages (88, 135), or whether it is identical with the "great practical order" as a whole, and thus comprises all sound human activities, as he suggests in another set of passages (46, vi, 33 ff., 43 ff.).[37] In view of the connection that modern philosophy has gradually established between "culture" and "history," it is not surprising that Wild, moved by the spirit not of Plato but of Marx,[38] Heidegger and God knows whom, speaks of "systematic anticipation of the future," the "historic nature of [the] transcendental inversion" and so on (29, 119, 165, 174, 179).

---

36 For the Platonic view of the relation between nature and art see especially *Republic*, 341d7–e.

37 Accordingly, in the only passage in which he explains what he understands by "philosophy of culture," he says first that it is "a branch of political philosophy, a division of ethics," and immediately thereafter suggests that it is identical with the "complete practical philosophy" (6; compare 42).

38 See Wild (62): "As true technical control is gained over the human environment, these forcible makeshifts [the use of military force or secret power over men] will wither away." That this view is diametrically opposed to the Platonic view appears most clearly from *Theaetetus*, 176a5–b1. On the other hand, the Marxian "dogma that all war is of economic origin" is not so much opposed to Plato's view as Wild believes (97 n. 27); see *Phaedo*, 66c5–8, and *Republic*, 372d7 to 374a2.

On a New Interpretation of Plato's Political Philosophy

What is true of "culture" applies equally to the "realism," or more specifically the "hardheaded realism" (v), which Wild ascribes to Plato. If one wished to use a slogan that would indicate in not too misleading a fashion the intention of the greatest modern critics of classical political philosophy (such as Machiavelli, Hobbes, Spinoza, Locke, Rousseau, the *Federalist*) one [357] would have to say that they oppose to the "idealistic" doctrine of antiquity and the Middle Ages a "realistic" one. Divorced from any analysis as it is in Wild's presentation, the praise of political "realism" merely expresses the already "historical" fact that "idealism" has ceased to be the ruling fashion.

The political significance of the "realistic" political philosophy of the modern era, which refuses to take its bearings by "transcendent" standards, consists in the fact that it raises the status of man, that is, of every man, and thus for the first time supplies a philosophic basis for aspirations toward democracy, more precisely toward liberal democracy. This fact must be faced squarely by anyone who wishes to restore Plato's teaching in accordance with "the living aspirations of our time" (8).

In the spirit of his identification of modern thought with sophistry Wild identifies the social-contract doctrines of "social materialists... like Callicles and Glaucon" with "the famous social-contract theory which has played such an important role in modern political thought" (93 ff.). In doing so he overlooks the fact that the views of Callicles, as well as those of Plato and Aristotle, presuppose a natural inequality of men, whereas the famous "social-contract theorists" of modern times assume a natural equality of all men, or at least the irrelevance for natural right of men's natural inequality.

In fact, Wild is practically silent on the grave question of equality, about which Plato had so much to say. And yet, as he indicates in his preface, Wild turns to the classics because he believes that "our democratic way of life" is based on the classical view of human nature, whereas communism and national socialism are derived from German idealism. He turns to Plato in particular because he is afraid of the "reactionary drift of historic Aristotelianism" (vi, 7 ff.).

Plato, according to Wild's contention, recognized the superiority of the individual to society or the state, and "the recognition of this basic fact by Plato and by classical philosophy in general has been responsible for that respect which has been commonly [358] accorded to the human individual throughout the course of Western culture, at least until modern times." From Plato we can learn "what is the basis of individual rights," but modern philosophy is "anti-personal" and thus leads to "a contempt

Chapter 7

for the individual bearer of [the] rational faculty." The modern view, in other words, is said to lead to "a theory of the totalitarian state," "where, to quote Hegel, 'Staatsmacht, Religion und die Principien der Philosophie zusammenfallen'" (123 ff., 2, vi, 132–36, 158).

If one does not know it at once one merely has to take the trouble of reading the context from which Wild's quotation is taken, in order to see that Hegel merely rephrases Plato's statement according to which political misery will not cease until philosophy and political power coincide, and that the reason for his rephrasing it is his awareness of the absence from Plato's thought of the principle of "subjective freedom," that is, of the "Protestant conscience." Hegel is so far from being a "totalitarian" that he rejects Plato's political philosophy precisely because he considers it "totalitarian." Plato, he asserts, did not know the idea of freedom, an outgrowth of the Christian doctrine that "the individual *as such* has an infinite value"; according to Plato man is free only in so far as he is a philosopher.[39] Whatever may have to be said about Hegel's attempt to trace to Christianity the idea of the freedom of the individual, or of the rights of man, he saw with unsurpassed clarity that when Plato indicates the absolute superiority of "the individual" to society or the state, he does not mean every individual, but only the philosopher.

Wild's wish to make Plato out to be something like a political liberal leads him to assert that according to Plato "all men are [359] philosophers," or wisdom "is accessible to all" (275, 108), although Plato does not tire of saying that no one can become a philosopher who does not have specific natural gifts, and that philosophic natures are extremely rare.[40] The only text that Wild adduces to prove what is perhaps his most "original theory" is a passage in the *Protagoras* which he reads: "every living member of a living community, by his daily thoughts, is a practitioner of the art of philosophy" (101 ff.). Since that passage is part of a speech of the sophist Protagoras, Wild unwittingly characterizes as sophistic the view that he attributes to Plato, and thus possibly makes an approach to the Platonic view in a somewhat un-Platonic manner.[41]

---

39 *Encyclopädie*, §§552 and 482. Respect for every man as bearer of the rational faculty is, of course, Kantian rather than Platonic or Aristotelian. No one has a right to speak of the implicit "abolition" of slavery in the *Republic* (Wild, 107 n. 63) if he does not at the same time, and much more emphatically, speak of Plato's explicit abolition of the family (about which Wild is completely silent); the former is inseparable from the latter.

40 *Republic*, 428d11 to 429a4, 476b10–c1, 491a8–b5, 495a10–b2, 503b7–d12; *Timaeus*, 51e; *Seventh Letter*, 343e to 344a.

On a New Interpretation of Plato's Political Philosophy

If one accepts the Platonic theses that wisdom constitutes the only absolutely valid title to rule, or to participate in ruling (111), and that wisdom (which is virtue in the strict sense) requires certain very rare natural gifts, one is driven to admit that the natural inequality among men as regards intellectual gifts is politically decisive, that is, that democracy is against natural right. To reconcile his democratic convictions with his Platonism Wild is compelled to assert that the translation of *aristokratia* by "aristocracy" is "thoughtless," and that "Plato's *Republic* is a 'classless society'" in which "all phases or parts of the state are ruled by wisdom which belongs to no special individual or group."[42] Is it necessary to mention that in Plato's perfect city only the philosophers, an extremely small group, if not just one man, have the right to rule, a right absolutely independent of popular consent, to say nothing of popular control? As regards the "classless" character of Plato's perfect city, it suffices to remark that Plato calls its three parts, one of which is the philosophers, "races" (or [360] "classes") and "nations" (or "tribes"), and membership in the various different classes is explicitly said to be, as a rule, hereditary.[43]

Wild simply substitutes for Plato's rule of philosophers, that is, of a specific type of men, the "rule" of philosophy, that is, the "rule" of popularized philosophy or science over the minds of the whole citizen-body. Because of his failure to try to understand modern philosophy he is blind to the fundamental difference between the "aristocratic" concept of philosophy or science, which is characteristic of classical philosophy and is irreconcilable with the idea of popular enlightenment, and the "democratic" concept, which emerged first through the efforts of men like Bacon, Descartes and Hobbes[44] and is the philosophic basis of popular enlightenment or of the revolutionizing influence of philosophy on society as a whole.

---

41   Compare *Theaetetus*, 180c7–d7, with *Protagoras*, 316d3 to 317b6.

42   Wild, 107. In a footnote he adds: "Thus the *number* of guardians is a matter of indifference. They may be 'one or many.'" The word that Wild renders as "many" means in the context "more (than one)"; compare *Republic*, 487a, 503b7–d12.

43   *Republic*, 415a7–b1, 420b7, 428e7, 460c6, 466a5, 577a1 and b3; *Timaeus*, 17c7; *Critias*, 110c3. Note especially *Timaeus*, 24a–b and 25e, on the kinship between Plato's perfect order and the Egyptian caste system. For the interpretation of *Republic*, 415a7–b1, see *Cratylus*, 394a–d, and Aristotle, *Politics*, 1255a40 ff.

44   Bacon, *Novum Organum*, I.122; Descartes, *Discours de la méthode*, I, at the beginning; Hobbes, *Leviathan*, chs. 13 and 15, and *Elements of Law*, I ch. 10 §8; Kant, *Zum ewigen Frieden*, Zusatz 2 (compare Julius Ebbinghaus, *Zu Deutschlands Schicksalswende*, Frankfurt a.M. 1946, 27 ff.); Hegel, *Phänomenologie des Geistes*, Vorrede (ed. by Lasson, 2nd ed., p. 10), and *Rechtsphilosophie*, Vorrede (ed. by Gans, 3rd ed., p. 13).

CHAPTER 7

If all men are potential philosophers there can be no doubt as to the natural harmony between philosophy and politics which is [361] presupposed by the idea of popular enlightenment. Regardless of his attitude to popular enlightenment, Plato would have believed in such a harmony if he had held, as Wild thinks he did, that it is of the essence of the philosopher, who as such has left the "cave" of political life, again to descend to it.[45] But according to the *Republic*, in which Plato treated this subject more comprehensively than anywhere else, the philosopher's "descent" is due to compulsion or force, and this kind of compulsion is legitimate only in the perfect social order: in an imperfect society the philosopher is not likely to engage in political activity of any kind, but will rather lead a life of privacy.[46]

If the question whether there is a natural harmony between philosophy and politics is stated in Platonic terms, the answer is likely to depend, for all practical purposes, on whether one believes that the actualization of the perfect order is "normal" or an improbable possibility. Plato certainly accepted the second alternative, as Wild admits (108). The ultimate answer will depend on how one judges of the possibility of its actualization, regardless of considerations of probability. The end of the seventh book of the *Republic* leaves hardly any doubt as to Plato's denial of that possibility.

In regard to Hobbes' "paulatim eruditur vulgus" compare Luther's "der gemeine Mann wird verständig" (*Von weltlicher Oberkeit*). Wild's mistaking the philosopher for every man seems to be due to the apparent ambiguity of what Plato says about the relation between education and the political or legislative art (67): Plato "seems hardly to have made up his mind as to which really directs the other" (66). Wild solves the difficulty for Plato by asserting, on the one hand, that "statesmanship attends rationally to all the non-rational needs of the human flock" and "education attends rationally to the specifically rational needs of the rational animal" (68), and, on the other, that Plato's state is a theocracy which does not admit of a separation between church and state (109 ff., 117, 122) and hence obviously attends to "the rational needs of the rational animal." Plato has solved the difficulty in the *Republic*, whose subject is precisely the relation between education and politics, by distinguishing two kinds of education (522a2–b3), the education of all, and the education of potential philosophers.

45 Wild, 180, 273 ff., 123, 136. For a rather divergent statement see 160.
46 *Republic*, 519b7 to 520c3, 592a7–b6, 496c5–e2. According to Wild, *Republic* 518a–b5 teaches that ascent and descent are of the essence of the philosopher, as distinguished from the sophist, who "does not move at all." In that passage Plato attributes descent and ascent to two different types. Wild's statement that the sophist "does not move at all and suffers no real confusion" (274) is contradicted not only by Plato's presentations of sophists and by *Sophist* 254a4 (quoted by Wild in the same context), but by Wild's own repeated statements that the philosopher and the sophist "are *moving* in opposite directions" (305 ff., 240, 254, 294; the italics are Wild's).

However this may be, the question can be settled *ad hominem* as follows. According to Plato's repeated assertion, the perfect order cannot become actual if the ruling philosophers do not possess direct and adequate knowledge of the idea of the good, and Wild suggests that such knowledge is not possible.[47] Since [362] the philosopher's descent to the "cave" is supposed to take place after he has achieved direct and adequate knowledge of the idea of the good, it follows from Wild's suggestion that that descent can never take place: the philosopher will have to devote himself throughout his life to the unfinished and unfinishable task of philosophy. While Wild's suggestion is contradicted by numerous passages in the *Republic*, it would seem to be supported by the *Phaedo*, to which he refers.[48] One could explain the difference between the teachings of the two dialogues by the difference between their conversational settings, and a case could be made for the view that the setting of the *Phaedo* allows of a more "realistic" presentation of philosophy than does that of the *Republic*.[49]

One would grossly misunderstand Wild's intentions if one were to draw the conclusion that he is on the verge of transcending the "political" interpretation of Plato's philosophy. His admission that philosophy has an essentially fragmentary character is merely the prelude to a suggestion that philosophy must be subordinated to theology.[50] Only on the basis of

---

47 Wild, 175 ff., 188, 203, 30, 74, 143. See especially *Republic*, 505a4–b1 (compare 504c1–4) and 516b4–8, 532a7–b3.

48 Wild, 143, 188. Compare *Phaedo*, 99c8–e1, with *Republic*, 516b4–8. See *Laws*, 897d8–e1, and 898d9 ff.

49 The *Republic*, one could say, is deliberately "utopian," not merely regarding politics but likewise regarding philosophy: the citizens and rulers that it envisages are "gods or sons of gods" (*Laws*, 739d6). But whereas the political utopia cannot guide political action (except in the vague sense of "inspiring" it), the philosophic utopia can and must guide philosophic "action." In other words, whereas there are no examples of a genuine "political order" (compare *Statesman*, 293c5–7), there are a number of examples of genuine philosophers. The *Phaedo* also throws light on Wild's assertion regarding the reason why the philosopher must "descend." The philosopher, he says, "is bound by the ties of nature to his fellow prisoners in the Cave" (273 ff.). The *Phaedo*, however, shows how little Socrates was bound by any ties to his nearest relatives, to Xantippe and his children (60a). Note also the somewhat divergent remarks of the *Phaedo* and the *Republic* about war (see note 38 above).

50 This is the implication of the following statement: "Thus [that is, on the basis of a certain confusion] theology will be interpreted in terms of philosophy, philosophy in terms of science, and science will be operationally interpreted in terms of technical procedure" (200). See also 77.

CHAPTER 7

this suggestion can he maintain within the Platonic framework the natural harmony [363] between philosophy and politics and at the same time deny the possibility of direct and adequate knowledge of "the supreme principle"; for what cannot be achieved by philosophy left to itself may be achieved by philosophy illumined by theology. Divine revelation, and not philosophy, supplies that sufficient knowledge of the idea of the good which is indispensable for the actualization of the perfect social order.

It is by making this tacit assumption that Wild finds an example of Plato's perfect city in the early Apostolic church, in which "one and the same wisdom... demands... the subordination of all the vital activities of the general body to the general doctrinal plan, formulated and guarded by the great councils, maintained and enforced by the schools and administrative offices of the Church" (108). We need not dwell on Wild's notion of "the Platonic-Christian state," which he also calls the "rational or Platonic state" (116 ff.). It goes without saying that there is no place in Plato's teaching for a theology that "lays down certain specifications which determine the general form of philosophy" (77), and that Wild is somewhat nearer to Plato when he designates as mythology what in his own language would be theology (73 ff., 203). Not without good reason did Plato replace the Egyptian rule of priests by his rule of philosophers.

One may add that according to Wild the only example of a perfect social order was of rather short duration. He asserts a parallelism between the decline of Plato's aristocracy first into timocracy and then into oligarchy and the decline of the early church first into post-Constantinian Catholicism and then into modern life, with its fundamental principle of the separation of church and state. If Wild still believes in the natural harmony between philosophy and politics, this can be due only to his anticipation of an early transformation of our present "anarchy (democracy)" into "the Platonic-Christian state" (109 ff., 117). One is left wondering with what right he can oppose Maritain's assertion that "only religion can save man from totalitarianism" and quietly state that "this theory simply does not accord with [364] the facts" (9). The only explanation of which I can think is that he was for a moment dazzled, if not enlightened, by the flame of philosophy.

V

One can imagine a man writing a book on the political problem of our time in the guise of a book on Plato's political philosophy. While it would be a very bad book if regarded as an interpretation of Plato, it might be excellent as a guide amidst the perplexities of our age. Wild almost promises such a book by demanding that we "try to translate Plato's social vocabulary into living terms, and exemplify his discussion by familiar modern examples, subordinating literal, 'historical' accuracy to philosophical exactitude" (106 ff.).

We have seen that Wild claims to look at the crucial political issue of our time from the point of view of a "progressive" interpretation of the American "democratic way of life." By imputing, rightly or wrongly, his own antifascist views to Plato he obviously wishes to counteract the misuse of Plato's teaching by fascists, and thus to deprive fascism of one of its strongest "ideological" weapons. He holds that only so-called scholars could interpret "the *Republic* as an 'aristocracy,'" and that "this favorite fallacy of German nineteenth-century scholarship," which "has now become fashionable in America," underlies the interpretation of the *Republic* as the "original philosophical charter of Fascism" (116, 107). We shall have to consider briefly how a man who is obviously a real scholar, who has obviously acquired by signal achievements the moral right to call the great historians and philologists of nineteenth-century Germany so-called scholars, and who, in addition, has put on the armor of "philosophical exactitude"—how such a man saves democracy and crushes fascism.

He suggests that "the root conception of fascist political thought" is the denial of "the supremacy of the legislative branch over the executive," a denial prepared by the use of "the very words 'sovereign,' 'leader,' and even 'executive'" (100, 104). To [365] mention only one of a host of objections that must be obvious to everyone, Wild's suggestion is a very poor defense of democracy because, as every schoolboy knows. the legislative power may be vested in one or a few, as well as in all or the representatives of all. Wild says too little, that is, nothing that is not completely vague, about popular influence on the legislative branch, and he says too much, that is, contradictory things, about the relation between "the legislative process" and "wisdom" (103, 106). In a sense more serious is what follows from his suggestion regarding the relation between Plato and fascism. If the denial of the supremacy of the legislative branch is fascism, or comes dangerously close to fascism, certainly the author of the *Statesman*, who as a matter of principle denied the very necessity of laws, to say nothing of a legislative branch of government, would be one of the most outstanding forerunners of fascism. At any rate, neither Plato nor Aristotle could even dream of competing with John Locke as unambiguous and unreserved defenders of the supremacy of the legislative branch as such.

CHAPTER 7

Wild makes a distinction between "what we mean by 'democracy' today" and actual democracy (111–17): "What we mean by 'democracy' today is movement in the direction away from" fascism; actual democracy is something between oligarchy (rule by "those higher up in the productive hierarchy") and anarchy ("the conquest of individualistic consumption over productive order"). The only salvation is some form of socialism. But "socialism in actual practice must be transformed into some form of authoritarianism, Christian socialism or State socialism, or into some form of tyranny such as so-called national socialism" (113). "State socialism," which is apparently the same as "socialism proper," is rejected because it is "materialistic" and attempts "to make every man a drone" (113). Hence the final alternative is "some rational authoritarianism, either Christian socialism or Nazi socialism, either control by rational authority or control by irrational authority" (117). Thus national socialism, as distinguished from socialism proper, which apparently has to be classi-[366]fied as irrational authoritarianism, finally acquires the status of rational authoritarianism. The reason is stated by Wild with unusual clarity: "Anarchy (democracy) can proceed no farther.... Our great democracies must go one way or the other. *Order must be achieved*.... There is no longer any way of postponing the choice," which is the choice between Christian socialism and national socialism (117; italics mine). One cannot demand more emphatically that democracy be abandoned at once in favor of one of the two forms of "rational authoritarianism"—Christian socialism or national socialism.

This demand accords very well with the following diagnosis of fascism. In their fight against the "parasitic 'political bosses'" (presumably the union leaders) "those higher up in the productive hierarchy" (that "'orderly class'" to which "such traces of law and order as still remain belong"), or "the orderly rich," are "forced to band together for defense against the encroachments of 'democracy.' If they succeed, they will set up a Fascist regime of law and order, accentuating the traditional hierarchies of the state, and ruthlessly suppressing all 'democracy.' The only other possibility is that a political genius or stinging drone may 'protect' the people from such a class revolution and become an absolute dictator" (115).

I do not for a moment believe that Wild intends to preach fascism or national socialism. In the same breath in which he makes the statements quoted in the preceding paragraphs he says that "even the anarchy of pure 'democracy' is preferable" to fascism, and that "the tyrannical state" is "the lowest depth to which human life can sink" (116 ff.). In the language of the prophet in the tenth book of the *Republic*, Wild can rightly say to those who are tempted by his statements to choose national socialism in preference to democracy, or democracy in preference to national socialism: "the responsibility is with the chooser, Wild has no responsibility." I have not the slightest doubt that what he says about the issue of democracy versus fascism is the outcome of that same "philosophical exactitude" which characterizes his [367] whole work, or of that "insolent assertiveness of transitory conjecture" which he ascribes to "democratic man" (165).

A man who claims to be a Platonist, and who publishes in this country at this time a book on Plato's political philosophy, bears more than the ordinary responsibility that is borne by every writer. Wild has not merely grossly failed to give a not too grossly misleading picture of Plato's views, and especially of his political views; he has also supplied the numerous enemies of Plato and of Platonic studies with the strongest weapon for which they could wish. Someone had to write something like the present article in order that the question which underlies Wild's book, but which has never been a question for him, be prevented, as far as this is possible or necessary, from suffering the same fate that his book so richly deserves.

8

On the Intention of Rousseau (1947)

I

[455] The antiquarian controversy about the intention of Rousseau conceals a political controversy about the nature of democracy. Modern democracy might seem to stand or fall by the claim that "the method of democracy" and "the method of intelligence" are identical. To understand the implications of this claim one naturally turns to Rousseau, for Rousseau, who considered himself the first theoretician of democracy,[1] regarded the compatibility of democracy, or of free government in general, with science not as a fact which is manifest to everyone but rather as a serious problem.

An adequate understanding of Rousseau's thesis presupposes a detailed interpretation of the *Contrat social* and *Émile*. For reasons of space alone, to say nothing of others, we must limit ourselves here to a discussion of Rousseau's "first discourse" which is now conveniently accessible, thanks to Mr. George Havens, in a beautiful and well annotated edition.[2] Rousseau

---

Originally published in *Social Research* 14, no. 4 (Dec. 1947): 455–87. —Eds.

1 "La constitution démocratique a jusqu'à présent été mal examinée. *Tous* ceux qui en ont parlé, ou ne la connaissaient pas, ou y prenaient trop peu d'intérêt, ou avaient intérêt de la présenter sous un faux jour... La constitution démocratique est certainement le chef-d'œuvre de l'art politique; mais plus l'artifice en est admirable, moins il appartient à tous les yeux de le pénétrer" (*Lettres écrites de la Montagne*, VIII, p. 252, Garnier ed.; the italics are mine).

2 Jean-Jacques Rousseau. *Discours sur les sciences et les arts.* [Édition critique avec une introduction et un commentaire par George R. Havens.] New York: Modern Language Association of America. 1946. xiii & 278 pp. $3. This work will be cited in the following notes as "Havens"; Rousseau's first discourse will be referred to as *Discours* and the pages and lines cited will be those of the first edition which are indicated in Havens' edition.

CHAPTER 8

himself said that all his writings express the same principles. There are then no other Rousseauan principles than those underlying his short discourse on the sciences and arts, however imperfectly he may [456] have expressed them in that earliest of his important writings.[3]

The specific thesis of the *Discours* is slightly obscured by the immediate purpose for which it was written. It was composed as an answer to the question raised by the Academy of Dijon whether the restoration of the sciences and arts had contributed to moral betterment. Accordingly, what strikes the reader first is the fact that Rousseau had the courage, in the heyday of the Enlightenment, "to blame the sciences and to praise ignorance" in the interest of morality. Yet the denial of the harmony between civilization and morality is not the specific thesis of Rousseau. It was anticipated by the very question of the Academy of Dijon. It was anticipated above all by a tradition whose most famous representatives would seem to be Montaigne and Seneca and which can be traced, with some degree of justice, to Socrates.[4] As a matter of fact, what Rousseau calls Socrates' praise of ignorance occupies an important place in the *Discours*, which quotes *in extenso* a pertinent passage from Plato's *Apology of Socrates*. But one has merely to restore the quotation to its immediate context to realize the most obvious difference between the *Discours* and the tradition to which it is related. Rousseau quotes Socrates' censure of the poets and the "artists"; he fails to quote his censure of the politicians.[5] Far from being directed against the democratic or republican politicians or statesmen, as was Socrates' "praise of ignorance," Rousseau's "praise of ignorance" is even inspired by a republican or demo-[457]cratic impulse: he attacks the Enlightenment as a pillar of despotism or of absolute monarchy.[6]

---

3   "J'ai écrit sur divers sujets, mais toujours dans les mêmes principes" (*Lettre à Beaumont*, p. 437, Garnier ed.; compare *ibid.*, p. 457). See also Rousseau's letter to Malesherbes of January 12, 1762 (Havens, p. 5). Havens rightly says: "Le premier *Discours* [de Rousseau] est la pierre angulaire de toute son œuvre." As to Rousseau's own judgment on the *Discours*, see *Discours*, "Avertissement," and Havens, p. 169 note 24.

4   *Discours*, 1–2; 13, 8–14, 5; 30, 10–12; Havens, pp. 25, 64–71, and 167. Also compare *Discours*, 47, 9–15, with Xenophon's *Oeconomicus*, 4.2–3 and 6.5 ff., and *Discours*, 57, 16–19 (the idea of a comparison of agriculture and philosophy) with the subject of the *Oeconomicus* as a whole. Regarding the general thesis of the *Discours*, compare Xenophon's *Cyropaedia*, I 2.6, *Resp. Lac.*, 2, and *Memorabilia*, IV 7.

5   Compare *Discours*, 22, 12–24, 9, with *Apology of Socrates*, 21b ff. Socrates speaks not of artists but of artisans. The change from "artisans" to "artists" may also be due to Rousseau's democratic intention; it is at any rate in agreement with that intention.

146

On the Intention of Rousseau

Rousseau's view is not unintelligible. That enlightenment is a pillar of absolute monarchy was admitted by the two men who are still popularly considered the greatest defenders of despotism in modern times, Machiavelli and Hobbes. To see this, one has to take into account the fact that Rousseau regards the Enlightenment, which he attacks in the *Discours*, as essentially hostile to religion[7] and thus by considering the Enlightenment a pillar of despotism he implies that despotism, as distinguished from free government, can dispense with religion. Now, Machiavelli had intimated that whereas free commonwealths absolutely require religion as perhaps their strongest bond, the fear of God can be replaced by the fear of an able prince, and he had described, in the same context, the age of the good Roman emperors, and not the republican period of Rome, as the golden age when everyone could hold and defend any opinion he pleased.[8] As for Hobbes, whose political demands find their complete fulfilment only in absolute hereditary monarchy, he had taught that the civil order rests on fear of violent death as distinguished from fear of "Powers Invisible," that is, religion. Since the fear of invisible powers naturally endangers the effectiveness of the fear of violent death, the whole scheme suggested by Hobbes requires for its operation the weakening, if not the elimination, of the former kind of fear; it requires such a radical change of outlook as can be brought about only by the diffusion of scientific knowledge. The absolute monarchy favored by Hobbes beyond any other form of government is possible, strictly speaking, only as enlightened, and enlightening, monarchy.[9]

---

6 *Discours*, 6, 6–27; 16, 21 ff.; 21, 1; 28; 54, 18–21 (compare with *Contrat social*, 1 6<?>). See also some later statements by Rousseau on the purport of the *Discours* (Havens, pp. 5, 53, and 172) as well as Diderot's and d'Argenson's comments (Havens, pp. 31 and 33). That Rousseau's praise of Louis XIV in the *Discours* (55, 15–17) is of doubtful sincerity is apparent from a moment's consideration of an earlier passage (*ibid.*, 28, 11–22).

7 *Discours*, 36, 8–37, 4; 59, 6–60, 3; 11, 3–16.

8 *Discorsi*, I 10–11 (compare I 55). See also Spinoza, *Tractatus politicus*, VI 40 (separation of religion and state in monarchies) and VIII 46 (need for public religion in aristocracies and, by implication, in democracies).

9 *De cive*, X 18–19; *Leviathan*, chs. 12 (pp. 54–57, Everyman's Library ed.), 14 (p. 73), 29 (p. 175), 30 (pp. 180 and 183), and 31 (end). Compare Ferdinand Tönnies, *Thomas Hobbes*, 3rd ed. (Stuttgart 1925) pp. 53–54, 195, and 273–76. For a present-day discussion see Louis Marlo, "Le droit d'insurrection," in *Les doctrines politiques modernes*, ed. by Boris Mirkine-Guetzévitch (New York 1947) pp. 111–34. Marlo says: "...[le]

Chapter 8

The ground for Rousseau's attack on despotism was laid by Montesquieu's *De l'esprit des lois*, which appeared about a year before the *Discours* was conceived. Montesquieu contrasted fear as the principle of despotism with virtue as the principle of democracy. The virtue in question he characterized as political virtue—that is, patriotism or love of equality—and he explicitly distinguished it from moral virtue; he was compelled, however, implicitly to identify political virtue with moral virtue.[10] Montesquieu found the natural home, as it were, of virtue in classical antiquity, and he contrasted the "small souls" of the subjects of the modern monarchies with the human greatness of the citizens of the classical commonwealths.[11] He stressed the opposition between classical political science, which took its bearings by virtue, and modern political science, which was attempting to find a substitute for virtue in economics.[12] He dwelled on the inseparable connection between the principle of democracy, on the one hand, and the prohibitions against luxury and against the undue freedom and power of women, on the other.[13] He indicated that [459] the cultivation of superior talent is not a primary need, and perhaps no need at all, for democracies.[14] He questioned "the speculative sciences" and "the speculative life" with a view to the demands of a healthy and vigorous republic.[15]

---

progrès de la science... favorise le coup d'état et détruit matériellement et moralement les forces de résistance" (p. 124).

10 Compare *Esprit*, Avertissement de l'auteur and V 2, with III 3, III 5, and IV 5. The same ambiguity characterizes the thesis of the *Discours* (compare, for example, 20, 3 ff., with 44, 7 ff.). See Havens, pp. 183 note 72, and 200 note 137.

11 Compare *Esprit*, III 3, III 5, IV 4, and XI 13, with the following passages of the *Discours*: 6, 17–18; 20, 3 ff.; 26, 5 ff.; 29, 1 ff.; 47, 9–49, 3; 51 note.

12 "Les politiques grecs, qui vivaient dans le gouvernement populaire, ne reconnaissaient d'autre force qui pût les soutenir que celle de la vertu. Ceux d'aujourd'hui ne nous parlent que de manufactures, de commerce, de finances, de richesses et de luxe même" (*Esprit*, III 3). "Les anciens Politiques parloient sans cesse de mœurs et de vertu; les nôtres ne parlent que de commerce et d'argent" (*Discours*, 38, 12–15).

13 *Esprit*, VII. Compare *Discours*, 6 note, on the connection between luxury and monarchy (for the example of Alexander and the Ichthyophagi, compare *Esprit*, XXI 8), and 37, 12–45, 12.

14 Compare *Esprit*, V 3 (mediocrity of talents) with *Discours*, 53, 6 ff., and *Contrat social*, IV 3 (equality of talents).

15 *Esprit*, IV 8, XIV 5 and 7, XXIII 21. Compare also the censure of China in the *Discours* (16, 18–17, 18) with *Esprit*, VIII 21.

On the Intention of Rousseau

To arrive at the theses of the *Discours*, Rousseau merely had to isolate Montesquieu's analysis of democracy, or of republics in general, and to make explicit certain points that Montesquieu had left unstated. It is true, he could not do this without deviating for ["from"—Eds.] Montesquieu's teaching as a whole, or without criticizing him.[16] For in spite of all his admiration for the spirit of classical antiquity, Montesquieu oscillated, at least apparently, between the classical republic and the modern (limited) monarchy, or, what is perhaps more precise, between the type of republic represented by classical Rome and that represented by eighteenth-century England.[17] The apparent oscillation was due to his awareness of the problem inherent in "virtue" as a political principle. The demands of virtue are not identical with those of political liberty; in fact, they may be opposed to them. To demand that virtue should rule is likely to be tantamount to demanding a large measure of interference with the private life of the citizens; the demand in question may easily conflict with that indulgence of human whims and weaknesses which Montesquieu seems to have regarded as an integral part of humanity. Observations such as these led him to stipulate that the requirements of virtue be limited by considerations of "prudence" and hence to identify the virtue of the legislator with moderation, which he regarded as a virtue of a lower order. From the point of view of liberty [460] as distinguished from virtue he preferred the English order to that of the classical republics, and from the point of view of humanity as distinguished from virtue he preferred the commercial republics to the military republics. He was thus led, or led back, to the modern approach, which consisted in trying to find a substitute for virtue in the spirit fostered by trade or even in the feudal notion of honor.[18] Rousseau refused, at least at first, to follow Montesquieu in his return, or his adaptation, to the modern principle. While he thus remained faithful to the cause of virtue, he did not prove to be completely impervious to the critique of virtue that motivated Montesquieu's return to modernity.

---

16 "Le chevalier Petty a supposé, dans ses calculs, qu'un homme en Angleterre vaut ce qu'on le vendrait à Alger. Cela ne peut être bon que pour l'Angleterre: il y a des pays où un homme ne vaut rien; il y a en où il vaut moins que rien" (*Esprit*, XXIII 18 [*Esprit*, XXIII 17—Eds.]). "L'un vous dira qu'un homme vaut en telle contrée la somme qu'on le vendroit à Alger; un autre en suivant ce calcul trouvera des pays où un homme ne vaut rien, et d'autres où il vaut moins que rien" (*Discours*, 38, 15–26).

17 *Esprit*, II 4, V 19, XX 4 and 7; compare VI 3 with XI 6.

18 *Esprit*, III 5, XI 4, XIX 5, 9–11, 16, XX 1, XXIX 1 (compare III 4). For a discussion of this problem, see, for example, Burke's letter to Rivarol of June 1, 1791, in *Letters of Edmund Burke, A Selection*, ed. by H. J. Laski (Oxford World Classics) pp. 303–04.

CHAPTER 8

At any rate, it is not misleading to say that in the *Discours* Rousseau starts by drawing the most extreme conclusions that a republican could draw from Montesquieu's analysis of republics. He directs his explicit and passionate attack not merely against luxury and against the economic approach of modern politics but likewise against "the sciences and the arts," which, he contends, presuppose luxury and foster it. He attacks especially science or philosophy as incompatible in its origin, its exercise, and its effects with the health of society, patriotism, wisdom or virtue. He is consistent enough to praise the Spartans for not having tolerated in their midst arts and artists, as well as science and scholars, and he even praises the Caliph Omar for having ordered the burning of the books of the library of Alexandria.[19] While contending that science as such is immoral, he considers modern science even more dangerous than pagan science. He does not say whether the particular character of modern science is due to the particular character of its origin; he limits himself to indicating that whereas science is normally preceded by ignorance, modern science was preceded by something worse than [461] ignorance—namely, medieval scholasticism—and to tracing the liberation from scholasticism not to the Reformation but to "the stupid Moslem" (the conquest of Constantinople).[20] Realizing the difference between, and the possible opposition of, virtue in the strict sense and political virtue, he occasionally praises, in the spirit of his later attacks on civil society as such, the life of the savages.[21] The theses of the *Discours* are explicitly based on nothing but historical inductions and philosophical reasoning, that is, on considerations fully accessible to the "natural light." Although Rousseau's attack on the Enlightenment partly agrees with the views of the Biblical tradition and though he occasionally defers to these views, his argument is certainly not based on specifically Biblical beliefs.[22] One cannot even say that it is based

---

19 *Discours*, 13, 8–14, 5; 17, 2–7; 21, 3–5; 29, 6–11; 32, 7–21; 34, 12–35, 2; 37, 13 ff.; 49, 16–18; 51, 28; 54, 3–18; 60, 15 ff.

20 *Discours*, 4, 7–21; 7, 6–14; 25, 1–5; 37, 18–38, 15; 59, 6 ff. Compare Havens, p. 219 note 196.

21 *Discours*, 5, 14–6, 27; 19, 15–24; 44, 7 ff. Compare Havens, pp. 9, 49, 54, 181 note 62.

22 *Discours*, 3, 4–5; 31, 2–4; 32, 1–4; 44, 2–4; Havens, pp. 85, 173 note 33, and 177 note 48. See also the passages indicated in note 7 of this article. Compare the end of note i of the *Discours sur l'origine de l'inégalité*. That Rousseau never changed his mind in this respect is apparent, not only from the general statement quoted before (note 3 of this article) but above all from what one may call his last word on the subject. In his *Rêveries*

on natural theology. Rousseau introduces one of his most important authorities almost explicitly as a polytheist and he implies that the state of innocence is characterized by polytheism.[23] When he attacks science on the grounds of its detrimental effect on religion, he has in mind "civil religion," that is, religion considered merely as a social bond.

II

The contemporary critics of Rousseau's "praise of ignorance" were quite understandably under the impression that he had [462] denied all value to science or philosophy and that he had suggested the abolition of all learning. In his rejoinders, however, he declared that they had not understood him and that he considered preposterous the views that were generally attributed to him. Yet, since he had said the things which he practically denied having said, one seems forced to conclude that he had not meant them. According to the editor of the *Discours*, Rousseau had meant only that science must not be preferred to, or made independent of, morality. But, he adds, Rousseau was so carried away by his enthusiasm for virtue or by his rhetorical power as to exaggerate grossly, to maintain a "somewhat puerile thesis" and unconsciously to contradict himself.[24] This interpretation might seem to be borne out by the *Discours* itself. Especially toward its end, Rousseau explicitly admits the compatibility of science and virtue. He bestows high praise upon the learned societies whose members must combine learning and morality; he calls Bacon, Descartes, and Newton the teachers of the human race; he demands that scholars of the first rank should find honorable asylum at the courts of princes in order to enlighten the peoples from there and thus contribute to the peoples' happiness.[25]

---

d'un promeneur solitaire he says: "Dans le petit nombres [*sic*—Eds.] de livres que je lis quelquefois encore, Plutarque [that is, not the Bible] est celui qui m'attache et me profite le plus" (IV, at the beginning). Compare the statement with *Rêveries*, III.

23 Compare 44, 7 ff. with 26, 11 (the beginning of the prosopopoeia of Fabricius, that is, of the core of the whole *Discours*). Compare Archbishop Beaumont's *Mandement*, §7 beginning.

24 Havens, pp. 36, 38, 46, 52, 58, 59, 64, 80, 87, 88, 176 note 45, 179 note 54, 239 note 259, 248 note 298.

25 *Discours*, 55, 4–56, 22; 62, 15–16; 64, 3–65, 6; 24, 10–25, 2. Compare especially 66, 3–12, with the parallels in the "profession de foi du vicaire Savoyard." Compare Havens' notes on these passages, as well as Havens, pp. 32–33 and 173 note 35 on the favorable reception of the *Discours* by the *philosophes*. The apparent concessions to

CHAPTER 8

The view of Rousseau's intention that Havens adopts—a view that led, and leads, directly to Kant's assertion of the primacy of practical reason—is exposed to a difficulty that I consider insuperable. It is a view suggested by one of the men who attacked [463] the *Discours* shortly after its publication.[26] But Rousseau declared about ten years later that none of those who had attacked him had ever succeeded in understanding his crucial thesis.

It cannot be denied that Rousseau contradicts himself. The contradiction confronts us, as it were, on the title page. The title is followed by a motto from Ovid, whose name is added to the motto, and who is condemned in the text of the *Discours* as one of those "obscene authors whose very names alarm chastity."[27] To solve the difficulty in a manner that does not do injustice to Rousseau's intelligence or literary ability, one is tempted to suggest that he entrusted the two contradictory theses—the thesis favorable to the sciences and the thesis unfavorable to them—to two different characters, or that he speaks in the *Discours* in two different characters. This suggestion is not so fanciful as it might appear at first sight. In the concluding paragraphs Rousseau describes himself as a "simple soul" or a "common man" (*homme vulgaire*) who as such is not concerned with the immortality of literary fame; but in the preface he gives us clearly to understand that he intends to live, as a writer, beyond his century.[28] He draws a distinction between himself who knows nothing and, being neither a true scholar nor a *bel esprit*, is only a common man, and those who teach mankind salutary truths; yet he knows that as the author of the *Discours* (which teaches the salutary truth that the sciences are dangerous) he cannot help also belonging to the second type, that is, to the philosophers or the scientists.[29] Just as the *Discours* may be said to have

---

the common view seem to be retracted, at least partly, in the final paragraphs (65, 8 ff.). Yet these very paragraphs seem destined to explain why Rousseau had stressed throughout the *Discours* the incompatibility of science and virtue, for by limiting his final suggestion to "the present state of things," he seems to indicate that the general thesis of the *Discours* is valid only so long as society is not radically reformed: only in a corrupt society are science and virtue incompatible. See, however, note 40 below.

26 Havens, p. 239 note 259. See also Havens, pp. 40–41: Havens asserts, and Rousseau denies, that a certain critic of the *Discours* has "saisi l'état de la question."

27 *Discours*, 15, 13–15.

28 *Discours*, II, 14–16 and 65, 8 ff. It is hardly an accident that that section of the *Discours* which Rousseau wrote immediately after the conception of the work was a prosopopoeia.

29 *Discours*, I, 1–11; 1, 7–9; 56, 11–22; 64, 19; 65, 8 ff. Compare Havens, p. 201 note 142.

two different authors, it may be said to be addressed to two different audiences. In the concluding section Rousseau makes it clear that in his capacity as a common man he addresses common men. Yet in the preface he [464] states that he writes only for those who are not subjugated by the opinions of their century, of their country, or of their society, that is, only for true scholars; in other words, he states that the *Discours* is addressed not to "the people" or "the public" but only to "a few readers."[30] I suggest, then, that when Rousseau rejects science as superfluous or harmful, he speaks in the character of a common man addressing common men, and when speaking in that character he does not exaggerate at all by rejecting science absolutely. But far from being a common man, he is a philosopher who merely appears in the guise of a common man: as a philosopher addressing philosophers he naturally takes the side of science.

It can be proved that this is the correct interpretation of the *Discours* and therewith fundamentally of Rousseau's thought. In defending the *Discours* against the same critic who may have originated the accepted view of his intention, Rousseau explains the frontispiece of the *Discours* as follows: "The torch of Prometheus is the torch of the sciences which is made for the purpose of inspiring the great minds... the satyr who sees the fire for the first time, runs toward it and wishes to embrace it, represents the common men who, seduced by the lustre of the letters, give themselves indiscreetly to studies. The Prometheus who shouts and warns them of the danger is the citizen of Geneva. This allegory is just, beautiful and, I venture to believe, sublime. What shall one think of a writer who has pondered over it and has not succeeded in understanding it?"[31] Rousseau who warns the common men of the dangers of science is so far from considering himself a common man that he boldly compares himself to Prometheus who brings the light of science, or of the love of science, to the few for whom alone it is destined.

About ten years later Rousseau declares in his *Lettre à M. de Beaumont*: "the development of enlightenment and vice always takes place in the same ratio, not in the individuals, but in the peoples—a distinction which I have always carefully made and [465] which none of those who have attacked me has ever been able to understand."[32] Science is not compatible

---

30 Compare *Discours*, I, 14–II, 16, with 2, 1–5. See Havens, p. 56.
31 Compare Havens, pp. 227 note 224 and 247 note 297.
32 "...Ces réflexions me conduisirent à de nouvelles recherches sur l'esprit humain considéré dans l'état civil; et je trouvai qu'alors le développement des lumières et des

Chapter 8

with the virtue of "the peoples"; it is compatible with the virtue of certain individuals, that is, of "the great minds." Science is bad, not absolutely, but only for the people or for society; it is good, and even necessary, for the few among whom Rousseau counts himself. For, as he says in the *Discours*, the mind has its needs as well as the body; but whereas the needs of the body are the foundations of society, the needs of the mind lead to what is merely an ornament of society; the satisfaction of the needs of the mind is not the one thing needful for society and is for this very reason bad for society;[33] but what is not a necessity for, and hence a danger to, society is a necessity for certain individuals. Since the needs of the body are "the need" par excellence, Rousseau can also say that society is based on "need,"[34] whereas science is not, and he can therefore imply that science, being radically "free," is of higher dignity than society. As he put it when defending the *Discours* against its critics, "science is not made for man," "for us," "for man in general"; it is good only for certain individuals, for the small number of true scholars, for "heavenly intelligences." One cannot help being reminded of Aristotle's praise of the philosophic life which is the only free life and essentially transsocial and of which man is capable not qua mere man but qua partaking of the divine.[35] It is only to the few who are capable of a life devoted to science that Rousseau seriously wishes to address himself, not [466] only in the *Discours*, but in all his writings with the possible exception of the merely apologetic ones.[36]

---

vices se faisait toujours en même raison, non dans les individus, mais dans les peuples: distinction que j'ai toujours soigneusement faite, et qu'aucun de ceux qui m'ont attaqué n'a jamais pu concevoir" (*Lettre à Beaumont*, p. 471, Garnier ed.).

33 *Discours*, 5, 14–6, 6; 33, 3–9; 34, 15–35, 6. Compare *Lettre à d'Alembert*, p. 121, Fontaine ed.

34 *Discours*, 6, 6–8.

35 *Discours*, 62, 12–14 and 63, 3–10. See Havens, pp. 36, 37, 45, 52, 53, and 60. Compare Aristotle, *Nicomachean Ethics*, 1177a32 ff. and b26–31, and *Metaphysics*, 982 b25–983a11.

36 "Tout ceci est vrai, surtout des livres qui ne sont point écrits pour le peuple, tels qu'ont *toujours* été les miens...[Quant à *l'Émile*] il s'agit d'un nouveau système d'éducation, dont j'offre le plan à l'examen des sages, et non pas d'une méthode pour les pères et les mères, à laquelle je n'ai jamais songé. Si quelquefois, *par une figure assez commune*, je *parais* leur adresser la parole, c'est, ou pour me faire mieux entendre, ou *pour m'exprimer en moins de mots*" (*Lettres écrites de la Montagne*, V, p. 202, Garnier ed.). See on the other hand *ibid.*, IX, p. 283: "Si je parlais à vous seul, je pourrais user de cette méthode; mais le sujet de ces *Lettres* intéresse un peuple entier..." The *Let-*

The view set forth in the preceding paragraph is confirmed by the *Discours*, although rather by seemingly incidental remarks than by the guiding theses.[37] In fact, one of these theses appears to contradict our interpretation, for Rousseau seems to contend in the last section of the *Discours* that science is compatible with society. Actually, however, he does not go beyond saying that the study of science by the very few who are by nature destined for it may be permissible from the point of view of society and even salutary, provided they use their natural gifts for enlightening the people about its duties; and what he manifestly does in the *Discours* is not more than precisely this, namely, enlightening the people about its duties. He does not endorse, he even rejects, the suggestion that the philosopher should make accessible to the [467] people the philosophic or scientific knowledge itself: science is permissible or salutary only in so far as it is not, as such, a social factor. Its social effect is necessarily disastrous: enlightenment paves the way for despotism. Accordingly Rousseau repeatedly and most emphatically attacks popularized science or the diffusion of scientific knowledge.[38] There can be no doubt that in rejecting popularized

---

ters happen to be an apologetic work. See also *ibid.*, III, pp. 152–53, the distinction between the "hommes sages qui sont instruits et qui savent raisonner" and who alone can have "une foi solide et sûre," on the one hand, with "les gens bons et droits qui voient la vérité partout où ils voient la justice" and who are apt to be deceived by their zeal, as well as "le peuple" "en toute chose esclave de ses sens," on the other.

In the preface to his *Lettre à d'Alembert*, Rousseau makes the following remark which is important for the understanding of the *Discours* in particular: "il ne s'agit *plus* ici d'un vain babil de philosophie, mais d'une vérité de pratique importante à tout un peuple. Il ne s'agit *plus* de parler au petit nombre, mais au public; *ni de faire penser les autres, mais d'expliquer nettement mes pensées. Il a donc fallu changer de style:* pour me faire mieux entendre à tout le monde, j'ai dit moins de choses en plus de mots..." (Italics in quoted passages are mine.)

37 "The peoples" are explicitly addressed (29, 18); Rousseau expresses his respect for true scholars (2, 5) or for the small minority to whom it is appropriate to erect monuments in honor of the human mind (63, 8–10); he indicates that ignorance is despicable (4, 12–13); he speaks of the populace as unworthy to approach the sanctuary of the sciences (62, 1–4). Above all, he quotes Montaigne's "J'aime à contester et discourir, mais c'est avec peu d'hommes et pour moi" (12 note).

38 *Discours*, II, 6–14; 24, 19–21; 36, 10–37, 11; 59 note; 61, 12–63, 7. "Ne verra-t-on jamais renaître ces temps heureux où les peuples ne se mêlaient point de philosopher, mais où les Platon, les Thalès et les Pythagore, épris d'un ardent désir de savoir, entreprenaient les plus grands voyages *uniquement* pour s'instruire..." (*Discours sur l'origine de l'inégalité*, note j; the italics are mine). Compare *Rêveries d'un promeneur solitaire*, III, p. 18, and VII, p. 72, Garnier ed.

Chapter 8

science Rousseau did not exaggerate, but expressed directly and adequately what he seriously thought.

We must add an important qualification. When Rousseau asserts that there is a natural incompatibility between society and science, he understands "natural" in the Aristotelian sense,[39] and he means that genuine science is incompatible with a healthy society. In answering one of the critics of the *Discours* he warns the reader against the conclusion "that one should burn all libraries and destroy the universities and academies *today*" (italics mine). In a corrupt society, in a society ruled despotically, science is the only redeeming thing; in such a society, science and society *are* compatible; in such a society the diffusion of scientific knowledge, or, in other words, the open attack on all prejudices is legitimate because social morality cannot become worse than it already is. But Rousseau, who wished to live beyond his time and who foresaw a revolution, wrote with a view to the requirements of a healthy society which might be established after the revolution and which would have to take as its model Sparta rather than Athens. This prospect was bound to influence his own literary activity.[40]

[468] Everyone will admit that in the *Discours* Rousseau attacks the Enlightenment in the interest of society. What is commonly overlooked is the fact that he attacks the Enlightenment in the interest of philosophy or science as well. In fact, since he considers science superior in dignity to society, one must say that he attacks the Enlightenment chiefly in the interest of philosophy. When he attacks the belief that the diffusion of

---

39   See the motto of the *Discours sur l'origine de l'inégalité*.

40   "Il y a des préjugés qu'il faut respecter... Mais lorsque tel est l'état des choses que plus rien ne saurait changer qu'en mieux, les préjugés sont-ils si respectables qu'il faille leur sacrifier la raison, la vertu, la justice, et tout le bien que la vérité pourrait faire aux hommes?" (*Lettre à Beaumont*, pp. 471–72, Garnier ed.). For another application of the same principle, see *Lettre à d'Alembert*, pp. 188–90, Fontaine ed. Compare Havens, pp. 45, 46, 54, and 229 note 232. On Rousseau's anticipation of a revolution, see Havens, pp. 38, 46, and 50.

When Rousseau indicates toward the end of the *Discours* that "in the present state of things" he will not strive for literary fame or attempt to instruct the peoples in their duties he does not mean then that the incompatibility of science and society is due to "the present state of things," but rather that he considers the present situation so hopeless that he cannot perform the social duty of the philosopher beyond what he has been doing in the *Discours*. The statement in question may also reflect a crisis in his self-confidence (see Havens, p. 226 note 222). It was the success of the *Discours* that induced him to continue performing what he considered his social duty by writing the second *Discours*, the *Contrat social*, and *Émile*.

scientific knowledge has a salutary effect on society, he is chiefly concerned with the effect of that belief on science. He is shocked by the absurdity of philosophy having degenerated into a fashion or of the fight against prejudice having itself become a prejudice. If philosophy is identical with the liberation of one's mind from all prejudices, the degeneration of philosophy into a prejudice would destroy forever, humanly speaking, the possibility of intellectual freedom.[41]

III

Rousseau himself admitted that he did not reveal in the *Discours* the principles underlying that work.[42] Since the purpose of the work is to warn the people against any contact with the sciences, it would of course have been impossible to stress there the superior dignity of science; to do this would have been tantamount to inviting the people to learning. In other words, since philosophy can become known on the market place only as popu-[469]larized philosophy, a public attack on popularized philosophy inevitably becomes an attack on philosophy *tout court*. Rousseau then exaggerates in the *Discours* by attacking science as simply bad; he does this, however, not because he is carried away by irresponsible zeal or rhetoric, but because he is fully alive to the responsibilities that his principles impose upon him. In a public utterance on the incompatibility of science and society he had, according to his principles, to side flatly with society against science. This is not in contradiction with the fact that the *Discours* is ultimately addressed only to "the few," for every book is accessible, not merely to those to whom it is ultimately addressed, but to all who can read. Nor is our contention at variance with the circumstance that Rousseau revealed in his later writings certain points which he did not reveal in the *Discours*; for by failing to reveal in the later writings certain points which he had revealed in the *Discours*, he succeeded in never revealing his principles coherently and hence fully, nor in [and thus in] [or in] speaking through his publications merely to those whom he wanted to reach.* It is only by combining the information supplied by the *Discours* with that supplied by Rousseau's later writings that one can arrive at an understanding

---

41 Compare the passages indicated in note 38 above, especially the beautiful passage in the preface: "Tel fait aujourd'hui l'esprit fort et le philosophe, qui, par la même raison n'eût été qu'un fanatique du temps de la ligue."
42 Compare Havens, pp. 51 and 56. See also note 36 above.
* See Editors' Introduction, xxi, n. 6.—Eds.

of the principles underlying each and all of his writings. Whereas the *Discours* does not state clearly the precise qualification of his attack on science, it states more clearly than the later writings the decisive reason why science and society are incompatible.

The foregoing remarks do not agree with the fairly common opinion according to which Rousseau was absolutely frank—an opinion that derives apparently strong support from his protestations of his unbounded sincerity.[43] We have therefore to explain as clearly and as briefly as possible Rousseau's views regarding the duty of truthfulness.

Rousseau discusses this subject in the fourth "promenade" of the *Rêveries d'un promeneur solitaire*. The importance of the [470] discussion may easily escape the unwary reader. In the first place, his habits will be confirmed by the artful character of the whole book, which claims to be written in a situation and in a mood in which considerations of prudence have ceased to carry any weight; it claims to be more outspoken even than the *Confessions* since it is said to be written exclusively for the author, who has no longer any thought or hope of reaching his readers. Moreover, the matter to which Rousseau applies his rule of conscience by way of expounding it is of the utmost triviality; he discusses at great length and in the spirit of unusual scrupulousness the question whether an author may pretend that his work is the translation of a Greek manuscript,[44] and also a number of minor falsehoods which it had been Rousseau's misfortune to utter. As for the rule itself, which he claims to have followed throughout his adult life, it can be reduced to the proposition that the obligation to speak the truth is founded exclusively on the utility of truth. From this it follows that one may not only suppress or disguise truths devoid of all possible utility, but may even be positively deceitful about them by asserting their contraries, without thus committing the sin of lying. Rousseau takes the trouble to add that the few lies he had uttered throughout his adult life were due to timidity or weakness.[45] It is perhaps more important to note

---

43 For example, near the beginning of the *Rêveries* he describes himself as follows: "Sans adresse, sans art, sans dissimulation, sans prudence, franc, ouvert, impatient, emporté..."

44 This question is a substitute for the somewhat more relevant question whether Rousseau was entitled to ascribe a certain profession of faith to a Catholic priest. That profession happens to be the central subject of the preceding "promenade."

45 "...tant d'hommes et de philosophes, qui dans tous les temps ont médité sur ce sujet, ont tous unanimement rejeté la possibilité de la création [*sc.* de la matière], excepté

that he limits [471] himself to discussing only one kind of the truths that are devoid of all utility, namely, the merely useless truths: he does not say a word about the other kind which would have to be called dangerous truths. But we are entitled to infer from his general rule that he would have considered himself obliged to conceal dangerous truths and even to assert their contraries—assuming that there are such truths.

In the light of this conclusion, we can understand the specific contribution of the *Discours* to the exposition of Rousseau's principles. In the introduction he declares that he takes the side of truth. He does this by teaching the truth that science and society are incompatible. But this is a useful truth. The *Discours* is so far from siding with truth as such that it attacks science precisely because it is concerned with truth as such, regardless of its utility, and hence is not, by its intention, protected against the danger of leading to useless or even harmful truths. And Rousseau contends that all the secrets that nature hides from the people are so many evils against which she protects them; science accessible to the people would be like a dangerous weapon in the hands of a child.[46] The practical consequence that this assertion entails cannot be evaded by reference to Rousseau's contention that in times of extreme corruption no truth is any longer dangerous, for he wrote for posterity rather than for his own time. To say nothing of the fact that persecution was not precisely extinct in Rousseau's age.[47]

In accordance with the general character of the *Discours* Rousseau maintains the thesis that the scientific or philosophic truth (the truth about the whole) is simply inaccessible rather than that it is inaccessible

---

peut-être un très petit nombre qui paraissent avoir sincèrement soumis leur raison à l'autorité; sincérité que les motifs de leur intérêt, de leur sûreté, de leur repos, rendent fort suspecte, et dont il sera toujours impossible de s'assurer tant que l'on risquera quelque chose à parler vrai" (*Lettre à Beaumont*, p. 461, Garnier ed.). In the same work Rousseau expresses the principle explained in the *Rêveries* as follows: "Pour moi, j'ai promis de dire [la vérité] en toute chose *utile*, autant qu'il serait en moi" (p. 472; italics mine), and "Parler au public avec franchise, avec fermeté, est un droit commun à tous les hommes, et même un devoir en toute chose *utile*" (p. 495 note; italics mine). Compare also the statement on the art of changing public opinion in the *Lettre à d'Alembert*, pp. 192ff., Fontaine ed. Regarding the general question of Rousseau's "prudence," see Havens, pp. 165 note 8 and 177 note 48.

46 *Discours*, I, 9–11; 3, 2–5; 29, 11–30, 4; 33, 18–19; 34, 12–13; 36, 5–10; 55, 6–20; 56, 18–22. Compare *Lettre à d'Alembert*, p. 115 note, Fontaine ed.

47 See p. 470 and note 45 above.

CHAPTER 8

to the people. He asserts therefore the dangerous character of the quest for knowledge rather than that of knowledge acquired:[48] the quest for knowledge is dangerous because the truth [472] is inaccessible and therefore the quest for truth leads to dangerous errors or to dangerous skepticism.[49] Science presupposes and fosters doubt; it forbids assent in all cases in which the truth is not evidently known, and it is at least possible that the truth about the most important subjects is not evidently known. But society requires that its members be sure regarding certain fundamentals. These certainties, "our dogmas," are not only not the acquisitions of science, but are essentially endangered by science: they become exposed to doubt because their lack of evidence is brought to light as soon as they are scientifically investigated. They are the objects not of knowledge but of faith. They, or the ends which they serve, are sacred.[50] It is the faith in the sacred foundations of society, or in that which makes them sacred, that Rousseau has in mind when praising ignorance: he praises ignorance accompanied by reverent assent. It is fundamentally distinguished from the ignorance, also praised by him, which is accompanied by suspense of assent and which may be the ultimate result of the scientific effort. Following a lead given by Rousseau, we may distinguish the two kinds of ignorance as popular ignorance and Socratic ignorance; both kinds are opposed by him to the dogmatism of pseudoscience or of popularized science.[51]

Since Rousseau believed that genuine faith could only be the outcome of sound reasoning and would therefore be a privilege [473] of the

---

48 The central thesis of the *Discours* is not affected by this incongruity since both contentions lead to the conclusion that quest for knowledge is dangerous to society.

49 *Discours*, 11, 14–16; 29, 6–15; 33, 8–34; 60, 1–2.

50 If the foundations of society are identical with the civil religion, and if the civil religion is identical with the religion of the Gospels, it follows that the suppression of all books with the exception of the Gospels, or at any rate of all scientific books, might be legitimate. It is the problem implied in the second conditional clause of the preceding sentence that Rousseau indicates by praising the Caliph Omar for having ordered the burning of the books of the library of Alexandria: "... supposez Grégoire le Grand à la place d'Omar et l'Évangile à la place de l'Alcoran, la Bibliothèque auroit encore été brûlée, et ce seroit peut-être le plus beau trait de la vie de cet illustre Pontife" (*Discours*, 60, 23–27). Compare *Acts*, 19: 17–20, and Havens, p. 46.

51 *Discours*, 36, 20–37, 4; 1, 8–9; 23, 18–24; 14; 34, 6–8; 34, 18–24; 55, 18–20. It should be noted that the true doctrine—namely, that science and society are incompatible—the exposition of which is the purpose of the *Discours*, is based not on faith but on reasoning (see concluding paragraph of Section I of this article).

wise, it is preferable to say that according to him opinion rather than faith is the basis of society. In conformity with this position he indicates in the *Discours* that only genuine scholars are not subjugated by the opinions of their century, their country, or their society, whereas the majority of men necessarily are.[52] We may therefore express the thesis of the *Discours* as follows: since the element of society is opinion, science, being the attempt to replace opinion by knowledge, essentially endangers society because it dissolves opinion. It is fundamentally for this reason, it would seem, that Rousseau considered science and society incompatible. Now, the view that the element of society is opinion becomes dangerous only if quest for knowledge is a human possibility and especially if it is the highest human possibility. Rousseau asserts therefore in the *Discours* that science is bad as such rather than that it is merely bad for society. By expressing the useful truth that he wants to convey in an exaggerated manner, he expresses it in a most reserved manner.

It is advisable to illustrate the reasoning underlying the *Discours* by a few more specific considerations, which are at least intimated in the same work. According to Rousseau, civil society is essentially a particular, or more precisely a closed, society. A civil society, he holds, can be healthy only if it has a character of its own, and this requires that its individuality be produced or fostered by national and exclusive institutions. Those institutions must be animated by a national "philosophy," by a way of thinking that is not transferable to other societies: "the philosophy of each people is little apt for another people." On the other hand, science or philosophy is essentially universal: it is common to all wise men. The diffusion of philosophy or science necessarily weakens the [474] power of the national "philosophies" and therewith the attachment of the citizens to the particular way of life of their community. In other words, whereas science or philosophy is essentially cosmopolitan, society must be animated by the spirit of patriotism, a spirit which is by no means irreconcilable with national hatreds. Political society being essentially a society that has to defend itself against other states, it must foster the

---

52 *Lettres écrites de la Montagne*, III (see note 36 above). Compare note 30 above. See also the remark in the *Discours* (37, 6–7) that the popularizers of science are enemies of "l'opinion publique." While public opinion is the element and, in a sense, the standard of free society, it becomes questionable from a transpolitical point of view. Compare *Lettre à d'Alembert*, p. 192, Fontaine ed.: "opinion publique" is merely "opinion d'autrui." Compare *Discours*, 65, 18, and *Contrat social*, II 12 and IV 7.

Chapter 8

military virtues and it normally develops a warlike spirit. Philosophy, on the contrary, is destructive of the warlike spirit.[53]

Furthermore, free society presupposes that its members have abandoned their original or natural liberty in favor of conventional liberty, that is, in favor of obedience to the laws of the community or to uniform rules of conduct to the making of which everyone can have contributed. Civil society requires conformance, or the transformation of man as a natural being into the citizen; compared with man's natural independence, all society is therefore a form of bondage. But philosophy demands that the philosopher follow his "own genius" with absolute sincerity, or without any regard to the general will or the communal way of thinking; in philosophizing, man asserts his natural freedom. Philosophy and society therefore necessarily come into conflict as soon as philosophy becomes a social factor.[54]

Moreover, free society comes into being through the substitution of conventional equality for natural inequality. The pursuit of science, however, requires the cultivation of talents, that is, of natural inequality; its fostering of inequality is so characteristic that one may even wonder whether the concern with superiority, [475] that is, desire for glory or pride, is not the root of science. Whatever might have to be said about political glory, it is less conspicuous than the glory attending on intellectual achievement—Sparta was less brilliant than Athens—and, above all, society, as such, having its roots in need cannot possibly have its roots in pride.[55]

IV

To say that science and society are incompatible is one thing; to say that science and virtue are incompatible is another thing. The second thesis could be reduced to the first, if virtue were essentially political or social.

---

53 In the *Discours* Rousseau states the case chiefly from the point of view of society (11, 12–14; 27, 15–17; 45, 10–49, 15) and therefore accepts "the military ideal of the Romans" (Havens, p. 206). But one cannot say that he does this "without criticism" (*ibid.*, 206); in *Discours*, 33, 2–3, he condemns wars as unmistakably as he condemns tyranny. Compare *Discours sur l'origine de l'inégalité*, note j; *Gouvernement de Pologne*, chs. 2 and 3; *Lettres écrites de la Montagne*, I, pp. 131–33, Garnier ed.; *Contrat social*, II 8 (toward the end); and the first pages of *Émile*. See also Havens, p. 187 note 85.

54 *Discours*, 5, 17–6, 2; 63, 3–11. Compare *Gouvernement de Pologne*, ch. 2; *Contrat social*, I 1, 6 and 8; and the first pages of *Émile*.

55 *Discours*, 53, 6–12. Compare *ibid.*, II, 14–16; 19, 10–11; 21, 17–18; 29, 8; 30, 8–17; 32, 12–13; 41, 1–2; 41, 11–14; 65, 8–11; 66, 11–14; Havens, pp. 211 note 172, 223 note 215, 226 note 222; *Contrat social*, I 9 (end) and II 1.

On the Intention of Rousseau

There can be no doubt that Rousseau frequently identifies virtue with political virtue. Yet, the mere fact that he sometimes attacks civil society, as such, in the name of virtue by praising the virtue of primitive man shows that he makes a distinction between political virtue and another kind of virtue.[56] This does not mean that his attack on science in the name of virtue, as such, is simply an exaggeration, for it is at least possible that the distinction between two kinds of virtue is only provisional. In his later writings Rousseau explicitly distinguishes between "goodness" and "virtue": goodness belongs to man as a natural being, whereas virtue or morality belongs to man as a citizen, since it essentially presupposes the social contract or convention. The good man as distinguished from the virtuous man is only good for himself, because he is good only as long as he derives pleasure from being good or, more generally expressed, because he cannot do any-[476]thing which he does not do with pleasure. A being is good to the extent to which he is self-sufficient, "solitary," or not in need of others and hence absolutely happy. A man who is good and not virtuous is therefore unfit for society or for action. In the most important case he will be a *contemplatif solitaire* who finds in the joys and raptures of pure and disinterested contemplation—for example, the study of plants in the spirit of Theophrastus—perfect happiness and a godlike self-sufficiency. A man of this kind, that is, the philosopher, in so far as he is exclusively concerned with learning as distinguished from teaching, is a useless member of society because he is exclusively concerned with his own pleasures, and "every useless citizen may be regarded as a pernicious man."[57]

---

56 Compare notes 10 and 21 above. *Discours*, 14, 1–15; 21, 17–21; 26, 5–28, 10. Compare 49, 18, with 50, 2–3 and 51, 3 ff.; compare 8, 18–19 ("la vertu est la force et la vigueur de l'âme") with 47, 9–15 and *Gouvernement de Pologne*, ch. 4 ("à cette vigueur d'âme, à ce zèle patriotique..."). What Rousseau says about the incompatibility of science and political virtue must not be mistaken for, indeed it belongs to an entirely different level from, what he says about the incompatibility of the teaching of the Gospels, or of humanity in the sense of the Gospels, and patriotism. For the teaching of the Gospels is as much a teaching of duties as is the teaching of political society. The conflict between Christianity and political society is an intramoral conflict, whereas that between science and society is not.

57 *Discours*, 35, 4–6; *Rêveries*, V–VII; *Contrat social*, I 8 and III 4; *Émile*, IV, vol. 1, p. 286, and V, vol. 2, pp. 274–75, Garnier ed. Compare note 38 above, as well as Havens, pp. 183 note 74 and 172 note 32. "Wer wollte nicht dem im höchsten Sinne verehrten Johann Jakob Rousseau auf seinen einsamen Wanderungen folgen, wo er, mit dem Menschengeschlecht verfeindet, seine Aufmerksamkeit der Pflanzen- und Blumenwelt

CHAPTER 8

We note in passing that it is somewhat misleading to say that according to Rousseau virtue is an active quality, whereas goodness is merely passive. This description fits only one type of goodness, the goodness of the pre-social or primitive man who is "a stupid animal." It does not quite fit the goodness of the man who is good and at the same time wise. The latter's not being active or even his being "idle" means that he has withdrawn from the hustle of the active life and devotes himself to solitary contemplation. In other words, one misunderstands Rousseau's notion of natural goodness if one does not bear in mind the fact that it refers to two different types, who stand at the opposite poles of humanity (the primitive man and the wise) and who yet belong together as natural men, as self-sufficient beings, or "numerical units," in contradistinction to an intermediate type, the citizen or social man, that is, the man who is bound by duties or obligations and who is only [477] a "fractionary unit."[58] It is the function of Rousseau's autobiographical statements to present to the reader an example of, and an apology for, the natural or good man who is, or is becoming, wise without being virtuous.

To return to our argument, it is as a radically selfish pursuit of pleasure that Rousseau in his capacity as citizen of Geneva attacks philosophy or science at the beginning of his career, in the *Discours*.[59] At its end, in the *Rêveries*, he openly confesses that he himself has always been a useless member of society, that he has never been truly fit for civil society, and

---

zuwendet und in echter gradsinniger Geisteskraft sich mit den stillreizenden Naturkindern vertraut macht" (Goethe, "Der Verfasser teilt die Geschichte seiner botanischen Studien mit," in *Goethes morphologische Schriften*, selections by Troll, Jena 1926, p. 195). It does not seem that the importance of Rousseau's *Rêveries* for Goethe's work as a whole, and in particular for the *Faust*, is sufficiently appreciated.

58 *Rêveries*, VIII, p. 80, Garnier ed., and VII, pp. 64 and 71; *Émile*, I, vol. 1, p. 13, Garnier ed. Compare Havens, p. 184 note 74. The notion connecting "natural man" with "wise man" is "genius" (compare *Discours*, 10, 1; 61, 20; 62, 13–14 and 19; 63, 5–11; Havens, p. 227 note 224). Émile, who is called a natural man, is an "esprit commun" or "homme vulgaire" (see pp. 463–64 of this article) who as a child comes as near to a natural man as a future citizen could come; that is to say, he is only an approximation to a natural man. Compare *Émile*, I, vol. 1, pp. 16 and 32. Compare Montesquieu, *De l'esprit des lois*, IV 8: "les sciences de speculation... rendent [les hommes] sauvages."

59 A life devoted to science is irreconcilable with a life devoted to duty (33, 3–9); science as "agréable" is distinguished from what is "utile" or "salutaire" (54, 11–12; 56, 21–22; 53, 15–16; 5, 14–22; 36, 7–10); there is a necessary connection between science, on the one hand, idleness and luxury, on the other (37, 14–18; 34, 15–16; 36, 11–12). Compare *Lettre à d'Alembert*, pp. 120, 123, and 137, Fontaine ed.

that he has found perfect happiness in the pleasure of solitary contemplation. In tacit reference to what he had indicated in the *Discours* about the connection between society and the needs of the body, he says in the *Rêveries* that nothing related to the interest of his body could ever truly occupy his soul. But even there, or rather precisely there, he feels obliged to excuse his life before the tribunal of society by explaining how the way of life which was really his own, and hence his happiness, had been forced upon him by his misfortunes: cut off from society by the malice of men, from pleasant dreams by the decline of his imagination, from thinking by the fear of thinking of his sufferings, he devoted himself to the sweet and simple pleasures of the study of botany.[60] Since he now admits [478] that he himself, the citizen of Geneva, is, and always was, a useless citizen, he can no longer with propriety allow society to regard him as a pernicious man: whereas in the *Discours* he had said that "every useless citizen may be regarded as a pernicious man," he says in the *Rêveries* that his contemporaries have done wrong, not in removing him from society as a useless member, but in proscribing him from society as a pernicious member. His last word on his central theme would then seem to be that science and citizenship are indeed irreconcilable, but that society can afford to tolerate a few good-for-nothings at its fringes, provided that they are really idle, that is, do not disturb society by subversive teachings—in other words, provided society does not take cognizance of them or does not take them seriously.[61]

V

Having reached this point we have still to face the greatest difficulty to which our attempt at a consistent understanding of Rousseau's intention is exposed. How can the conclusion at which we have arrived be reconciled with Rousseau's admission that science and virtue are compatible in superior minds or that they are incompatible only in "the peoples"? How can his admission that he was always a useless member of society, and in fact unfit for society or for a life of virtue and duty, be reconciled with his public spirit and sense of duty as evidenced by his political writings and

---

60 *Rêveries*, V–VII. Compare especially the remarks on the idleness of the *contemplatif solitaire* Rousseau (pp. 46, 64, and 71, Garnier ed.) with *Émile*, III (vol. 1, p. 248, Garnier ed.) where we read: "tout citoyen oisif est un fripon." Compare *Rêveries*, VII, p. 68, with *Discours*, 5, 14 ff.

61 This view is already indicated in the *Discours* (36, 11–16). Compare *ibid.*, 35, 2–6, with *Rêveries*, VI (end).

CHAPTER 8

by his conviction that the understanding reader of the "Profession de foi du vicaire Savoyard" would "bless a hundred times the virtuous and firm man who had dared to instruct mankind in this manner?"[62] One may answer, indeed one must answer, that the natural antagonism between science and society, or between science and virtue, does not preclude the possibility that science and society may be brought into some kind of agreement by violence, that is, the possibility that the philosopher can be forced by society, or by [479] himself as a citizen, to put his talents to the service of society[63] by teaching the peoples their duties while refraining from teaching them philosophy or science. But this answer is clearly insufficient. Rousseau did not limit himself to teaching the peoples their duties; he rather taught them their rights. His political teaching is not a popular or civil teaching; it is indubitably a philosophic or scientific teaching. His political teaching is a part of the whole edifice of philosophy or science, presupposing natural science and crowning it.[64] If society and science are incompatible, if science must not in any circumstances become a social factor, social science, which is intended to be a practical teaching, would seem to be impossible. How then is Rousseau's own political philosophy possible on the basis of his view of the relation of science and society?

Rousseau admits that in a corrupt society (such as the one in which he lived) only science, and even general enlightenment, can provide man with a measure of relief. In a society where it is no longer necessary or desirable that any prejudices be respected, one may freely discuss the sacred foundations of society and freely seek not merely for remedies of the prevailing abuses, but for what would be simply the best solution to the political problem.[65] Under such conditions the direct and scientific presentation of that

---

62 *Lettres écrites de la Montagne*, I, p. 124, Garnier ed. Compare note 40 above.
63 Compare Plato's statement of the problem in the *Republic*, 519, c4–520 b4, with *Discours*, 56, 1–11 and 57, 1–6.
64 Regarding Rousseau's view of the place and the character of political philosophy, see *Discours*, 3, 10–4, 3 (compare Havens' notes) and the beginning of the preface to the *Discours sur l'origine de l'inégalité*.
65 Compare p. 467 of this article. Rousseau's thesis is a modification of the more common view according to which private men are not allowed to dispute what would be the best political order for the society to which they belong. Compare Calvin, *Institutio*, IV 20 §8 (vol. 2, p. 521, Tholuck ed.), and Hobbes, *Leviathan*, ch. 42 (p. 299, Everyman's Library ed.).

solution would at its worst be an innocent pastime; but assuming that there is a prospect of a revolution, the new political science might prepare public opinion not merely for the restoration of a healthy society, but for the establishment of a more perfect society than ever existed before.

[480] From Rousseau's point of view the problem of society cannot be clearly seen and hence truly solved except on the basis of that radical criticism of society or of that fundamental reflection on the relation between society and science with which we have been hitherto concerned. The fundamental reflection reveals society as essentially a kind of bondage; the antagonism between science and society is the most important example of the antagonism between natural liberty and man-made bondage. The natural independence of man over against society determines the general character of the best solution to the political problem: the best solution is a society in which man remains as free as possible.

To discover the precise solution, Rousseau proceeds as follows. Like Hobbes and Locke, he finds the sufficient natural basis of society in everyone's natural desire for self-preservation. As soon as man's faculties have developed beyond a certain point he is unable to preserve himself without the aid of others. The foundations of society are then really not more than the needs of the body, the selfish and most pressing needs of each individual. It is these needs that immediately motivate the concern with freedom: no superior can be presumed to have the same interest in the individual's self-preservation as the individual himself. To enjoy the advantages of society everyone must accept its burdens; everyone must submit his own will, which is directed toward his own good, to the general will, which is directed toward the common good. Freedom in society is possible only within these limits. Man is free in the political sense if he is subject only to the impersonal will of society, and not to the personal or private will of any other individual or group of individuals. To avoid any kind of personal dependence or any kind of "private government," everyone and everything must be subjected to the social will, which expresses itself only in the form of general laws to the establishment of which everyone must have been able to contribute by his vote. Rousseau knew very well that "the total alienation of each associate with all his rights to the whole community," or the complete submission of the private will to the general will, in order to be reasonable [481] or legitimate requires that a number of conditions be fulfilled which rarely are fulfilled. The real difficulty to which his doctrine of the general will is exposed, the difficulty to which it is exposed on the level of the question it is meant to answer, is

CHAPTER 8

expressed by these two questions: How can the general will which is always well intentioned since it is always directed toward the good of society, be presumed to be always enlightened about the good of society? And how can the transformation of natural man, who is guided exclusively by his private will, into the citizen, who unhesitatingly prefers the general will to his private will, be effected?[66]

Now, according to Rousseau, this problem can only be stated by political philosophy; it cannot be solved by it; or, more precisely, its solution is endangered by the very political philosophy that leads up to it. For its solution is the action of the legislator or of the "father" of a nation, that is, of a man of superior intelligence who by ascribing divine origin to a code which he has devised, or by honoring the gods with his own wisdom, induces the citizen body to submit freely to his code. This action of the legislator is necessarily endangered by philosophy, since the arguments by which the legislator has to convince the citizens of his divine mission, or of the divine sanction for his laws, are necessarily of doubtful solidity.[67] One might think that once the code were ratified, a "social spirit" developed, and the wise legislation accepted on account of its proved wisdom rather than its pretended origin, the belief in the divine origin of the code would no longer be required; but this suggestion overlooks the fact that the living respect for old laws, "the prejudice of antiquity," which is indispensable for the health of society, can only with difficulty survive the public "debunking" of the accounts regarding their origin. In other words, the transformation of natural man into the citizen is a problem coeval with society itself, and therefore society has a continuous [482] need for at least an equivalent for the mysterious and awe-inspiring action of the legislator. The legislator's action, as well as its later equivalents (traditions and sentiments), serve the purpose of "substituting a partial and moral existence for the physical and independent existence which we have received from nature." Only if the opinions or sentiments engendered by society overcome, and as it were annihilate, the natural sentiments, can there be a stable and healthy society.[68] That is to say: society has to do everything possible to make the

---

66 "Les particuliers voient le bien [*sc.* public] qu'ils rejettent; le public veut le bien qu'il ne voit pas...Voilà d'où naît la nécessité du législateur" (*Contrat social*, II 6).

67 Compare in this connection Rousseau's discussion of the problem of miracles in the *Lettres écrites de la Montagne*, II–III.

68 *Contrat social*, II 6 and 7; III 2 and 11. In the chapter on the legislator (II 7) Rousseau clearly refers only to Moses and Mohammed as examples of legislators; but he clarifies

citizens oblivious of the very facts that are brought to the center of their attention, as the foundations of society, by political philosophy. Society stands or falls by a specific obfuscation against which philosophy necessarily revolts. The problem posed by political philosophy must be forgotten, if the solution to which political philosophy leads shall work.

This intelligible, if uncomfortable, position could satisfy Rousseau who had the "well-contrived head for which doubt is a good cushion." The easiest way out of this predicament, the way that "the next generation" could not help choosing, was to accept his final and practical solution (his "rediscovery of the community," his notion of the general will, the primacy of conscience or of sentiment and tradition) and to throw overboard, or to forget, his theoretical premise ("the state of nature," the independent individual, the primacy of theoretical reason). The simplest solution of Rousseau's problem is the "romantic" solution. It may be said to be a genuine solution since it consists precisely in doing what Rousseau himself demanded for the era following the establishment, or restoration, of a true society—namely, in forgetting the "individualistic" premise and keeping all one's thoughts and wishes within the compass of man's social life. The price, which has to be [483] paid for it, is, directly or indirectly, the subordination of philosophy to society, or the integration of philosophy into "culture."

It is true of course that Rousseau's doctrine of the legislator is meant to clarify the fundamental problem of society rather than to suggest a practical solution for modern Europe, except in so far as that doctrine adumbrates Rousseau's own function. The precise reason why he had to go beyond the classical notion of the legislator was that that notion is apt to obscure the sovereignty of the people, that is, to lead, for all practical purposes, to the substitution of the supremacy of the law for the full sovereignty of the people. The classical notion of the legislator is irreconcilable with the demand, so strongly made by Rousseau, for periodic appeals from the whole legal and constitutional order to the sovereign will of the people, or from the will of past generations to the will of the living generation.[69]

---

his position sufficiently by quoting in one footnote a passage from Machiavelli's *Discorsi* and by praising in another footnote the theologian Calvin (the legislator of Geneva) as a statesman of the first order. Compare Plato, *Laws*, 634 d7–e4 (757 d–e and 875 a1–d5), and Aristotle, *Politics*, 1269 a15 ff. (also *Metaphysics*, 995 a3–6 and 1074 b1–14).

69 *Contrat social*, III 18. (For the interpretation consider Paine, *Rights of Man*, pp. 12 ff., Everyman's Library ed.). Compare *The Federalist*, ed. by E. M. Earle (Washington:

CHAPTER 8

Rousseau had, therefore, to find a substitute for the action of the legislator, a substitute that would be compatible with the highest possible degree of freedom of the people. According to his final suggestion, the most fundamental function originally entrusted to the legislator,[70] namely, the transformation of natural man into the citizen, has to be discharged by a civil religion of the kind described from somewhat different points of view in the *Contrat social*, on the one hand, and in *Émile*, on the other. We need not go into the question whether Rousseau himself believed in the religion he presented in the profession of [484] faith of the Savoyard vicar, a question that cannot be answered by reference to what he said when he was persecuted on account of that profession. What is decisive is the fact that according to his explicit view of the relation of knowledge, faith and "the people," the citizen body cannot have more than opinion regarding the truth of this or any other religion. One may even wonder whether any human being can have genuine knowledge in this respect since, according to Rousseau's last word on the subject, there are "insoluble objections" to the religion preached by the Savoyard vicar.[71] Therefore every civil religion would seem to have, in the last analysis, the same character as the legislator's account of the origin of his code, in so far as both are essentially endangered by the "dangerous pyrrhonism" fostered by the rigorous demands of philosophy or science: the "insoluble objections," to which even the best of all religions is exposed, are dangerous truths. Rousseau's personal horror, and impatience, of intolerance is primarily responsible for

---

National Home Library Foundation) no. 49, pp. 328–39: frequent appeals to the people prevent opinion, or the prejudices of the community, from acquiring the necessary strength.

70 Regarding the other problem that the legislator has to solve, namely, the enlightening of the general will about its objects, Rousseau seems to have believed that not its solution, but indeed a prerequisite for its solution in a complex society is supplied by a political system that favors the wealthy and the rural population over against *la canaille*. This political demand transforms the egalitarian implication of his doctrine of the general will into something comparable to the "sophisms" of classical politics. (Compare Aristotle, *Politics*, 1297 a14 ff., and Xenophon, *Cyropaedia*, I 2.15.) That Rousseau was aware of this can be seen from what he says in approving the constitutional changes effected by Servius Tullius (*Contrat social*, IV 4; compare *ibid.*, III 15).

71 *Rêveries*, III, pp. 23 and 27, Garnier ed.; *Lettre à Beaumont*, p. 479, Garnier ed.; *Lettres écrites de la Montagne*, I, pp. 121–36, Garnier ed., and IV, p. 180. Compare notes 36 and 45 above. For the question of "insoluble objections," compare Leibniz, *Théodicée*, Discours préliminaire, §§24–27.

the fact that he did not dwell in his writings subsequent to the *Discours* on the consequences that this view entails.

VI

Rousseau maintained then, to the last, the thesis that he had set forth most impressively at the beginning of his career. That thesis, to repeat, is to the effect that there is a fundamental disproportion between the requirements of society and those of philosophy or science. It is opposed to the thesis of the Enlightenment, according to which the diffusion of philosophic or scientific knowledge is unqualifiedly salutary to society, or more generally expressed, there is a natural harmony between the requirements of society and those of science. One can trace Rousseau's thesis directly to Descartes' distinction between the rules regarding the [485] reform of one's own thoughts and those regarding the reform of society.[72] But considering the facts that Descartes' relation to the Enlightenment is ambiguous as well as that Rousseau attacks modern politics in the name of classical politics, it is preferable to understand Rousseau's thesis as a restatement of the view underlying classical political philosophy, and his attack on the thesis of the Enlightenment as a part, although the most important part, of his attack on modern politics in the name of classical politics.[73] It may therefore be permissible to conclude our essay on Rousseau's intention with a cursory consideration of the relation of his political philosophy to classical political philosophy.

For the proper understanding of that relation, one must disregard the accidental difference, which is due to the difference in the social status of philosophy in the classical period, on the one hand, and in that of Rousseau, on the other. The classical statements about science and society, especially those of Plato, still had to serve the purpose of combating a common prejudice against philosophy, whereas Rousseau had to fight perhaps an even more dangerous prejudice in favor of philosophy: by his time, philosophy had become not merely a generally revered tradition, but a fashion. In order to grasp the essential difference, it is advisable to

---

72 *Discours de la méthode*, II–III. Descartes is mentioned in the *Discours* twice (34, 19 and 62, 15). Compare also *ibid.*, 63, 6 ("marcher seuls"), with *Discours de la méthode*, II (Adam–Tannéry 16, 30).

73 Regarding Rousseau's relation to classical politics, compare the passages indicated or quoted in notes 5, 11, 12, 20, 22, 35, 39, 63, and 68 above. Compare the explicit reference to Plato's *Republic* in *Discours*, 41 note, and to the *Laws*, *ibid.*, 19 note.

Chapter 8

start as follows. The basic premise of classical political philosophy may be said to be the view that the natural inequality of intellectual powers is, or ought to be, of decisive political importance. Hence the unlimited rule of the wise, in no way answerable to the subjects, appears to be the absolutely best solution to the political problem. This demand is obviously irreconcilable for all practical purposes with the character of the political community. The disproportion between the requirements of science and those [486] of society leads to the consequence that the true or natural order (the absolute rule of the wise over the unwise) must be replaced by its political counterpart or imitation, which is the rule, under law, of the gentlemen over those who are not gentlemen.

The difficulties to which this doctrine as a whole is exposed have tempted political thinkers from very early times to take the natural equality of all men as a starting point for their reflections. These attempts gained considerably in significance when the natural character of the inequality of intellectual capacities was explicitly questioned, and therewith the stronghold of the classical position was attacked as a consequence of the emergence of a heightened belief in the virtue of method as distinguished from natural gifts. It is this radical change that led to the Enlightenment attacked by Rousseau. In opposition to the Enlightenment he reasserts the crucial importance of the natural inequality of men with regard to intellectual gifts.[74] But he avoids the political consequences that the classics drew from this principle, by appealing to another classical principle, namely, the disproportion between the requirements of science and those of society: he denies that the conclusion from the fact of natural inequality to the demand for political inequality is valid. The disproportion between the requirements of science and those of society permits him to build a fundamentally egalitarian politics on the admission, and even the emphatic assertion, of the natural inequality of men in the most important respect. One is tempted to say that Rousseau was the first to meet Plato's and Aristotle's challenge to democracy on the level of Plato's and Aristotle's reflections, and that it is this fact that accounts for his unique position in the history of democratic doctrine.

It goes without saying that the relation between Rousseau and the classics is not exhausted by that part of the discussion which is carried on by Rousseau on the level of classical political philosophy. Rousseau makes a

---

74 Compare *Discours*, 61, 20; 62, 13–14 and 19; 63, 5–11; compare also the end of the *Discours sur l'origine de l'inégalité* as well as *Contrat social*, I 9 and II 1.

radical departure from classical political [487] philosophy by accepting the principle of Machiavelli's criticism of classical political philosophy and by building his doctrine on modern natural science. He is thus led to replace the classical definition of man as the rational animal by the definition of man as a free agent, or the idea of human perfection by that of human perfectibility, to exaggerate the distinction between political virtue and genuine virtue into the opposition between virtue and goodness, and, last but not least, to initiate the fateful combination of the lowering of the moral standards with the moral pathos of "sincerity." All the serious difficulties with which the understanding of Rousseau's teaching remains beset, even if the principle suggested in the present article is accepted, can be traced to the fact that he tried to preserve the classical idea of philosophy on the basis of modern science. Only in a few cases is there any need for recourse to his private idiosyncrasies to clear up apparent or real contradictions in his teaching. In particular, I do not wish to deny that on a few occasions his irritable *amour-propre* may have blurred his amazingly lucid vision.[75]

---

75 Compare *Discours*, 29, 1–5.

9

On Husik's Work in Medieval Jewish Philosophy (1951/1952)

Part 1: *"L. Strauss: On Husik's Work in Medieval Jewish Philosophy" (1951)*

[260] Husik's interest in the medieval Jewish philosophy grows out of the problematic character of modern Jewish thought. Therefore, his approach to the subject is not a philosophical but purely historical one. It was Husik's opinion that philosophy, being always free and non-dogmatic, cannot be subordinated to any religious content. Nor can Judaism, as the religion of the divine law, be subordinated to philosophy. Accordingly, [259] Husik thinks that medieval Jewish philosophy, in so far as it believed in the authority of the divine law, was either a very naive philosophy, whose naïveté is now lost, or no philosophy at all. For modern man, who forms his views on the basis of historical criticism, medieval Jewish philosophy seems to be an illusion even though a necessary and useful illusion in the struggle against superstition. Husik made no attempt to reconcile Judaism, i.e., "the spirit of Justice," with philosophic systems and opposed Hermann Cohen's views on Judaism which were founded on a philosophical idealisation of the Jewish religion. By maintaining his position, Husik found himself faced with three main difficulties: his concept of historical objectivity annihilates completely what he called "rationalist Jewish philosophy"; the extreme historistic position, taken by Husik, brings him into

---

Part 1—Originally published in "English Summaries," *Iyyun: Jerusalem Philosophical Quarterly* 2 (1951): 260–59. (Pages are numbered in dextrosinistral order.)

Part 2—Originally published as the introduction to I. Husik's *Philosophical Essays: Ancient, Mediaeval & Modern*, ed. Milton C. Nahm and Leo Strauss (Oxford: Basil Blackwell, 1952). We have included in this volume only that part authored by Strauss—and translated into the Hebrew at *Iyyun* 2 (1951): 223–15. —Eds.

CHAPTER 9

conflict with all attempts at a modern philosophical interpretation of Judaism and reconstitutes explicitly the traditional religious view; and finally, in defining the task of the modern Jewish philosophy as that of reconciling the Bible with philosophy, Husik returns to Cohen's position and to the basic doctrines of most medieval Jewish thinkers.

Part 2: *"Introduction to Husik's Philosophical Essays" (1952)*

[xxi] The direction which Husik's interest took might seem to find its sufficient explanation in the fact that he was both a Jew and a philosopher. It would be more accurate, however, to say that, while this fact would account for his interest in Jewish philosophy, it was his realisation of the problematic character of Jewish philosophy that [xxii] explains his interest in the history of Jewish philosophy and, therefore, especially in Jewish mediæval philosophy.

No one could insist more strongly than Husik did on the purely historical, nay, antiquarian character of all relevant modern studies on Jewish mediæval philosophy. He knew too well, however, that "History for History's sake" is an absurdity. His insistence on the merely antiquarian character of all relevant modern studies on Jewish mediæval philosophy was only the consequence, or the reverse side, of his conviction that in the modern world Jewish philosophy is not merely nonexistent but impossible. To establish this conviction, he had to explain why Jewish philosophy was possible in the past. And since he believed "that we cannot speak of a Jewish philosophy until the movement in the Middle Ages which culminated in the philosophy of Maimonides," it was only the study of Jewish mediæval philosophy that enabled him to discern the precise reason why in the modern world Jewish philosophy is impossible. It was because of his view that in the modern world Jewish philosophy is impossible that Jewish mediæval philosophy could be not of immediate, but of only historical interest to him. But the historical studies which established and elucidated this view served a function that was ultimately philosophic rather than historical.

To the superficial observer, Husik's attitude towards Jewish philosophy might appear to have been little more than an expression of his attitude towards the Jewish problem as a social problem. Husik had his roots in the Jewish tradition or, more specifically, in the closed Jewish community of Eastern Europe of the late nineteenth century. The young Husik had to liberate himself from what he then called "the spiritual bondage of the

On Husik's Work in Mediæval Jewish Philosophy

Ghetto," "the self-centered spirit" of traditional Judaism, "the narrow bigotry of racial and religious exclusiveness." He broke away from a manner of life which was "a life apart from the rest of the world." Thus he was naturally attracted by Jewish mediæval philosophy, which was the greatest monument remembered within the Ghetto-walls, of Jewish participation in the life of "the world." Yet most of the mediæval Jewish philosophers appeared to be Jews in the very act of their philosophising. They addressed their philosophic works to Jews and to Jews only. The emancipation of the Jews in the modern era, however, required that the Jew should contribute to civilisation "not as a Jew, but as a man." Desiring to participate without reserve in modern civilisation, the [xxiii] modern Jew could not take as his models the mediæval Jewish philosophers. Thus Husik had to show that the type of procedure characteristic of Jewish mediæval philosophy was no longer viable. Or, to stress another aspect of the same strand in Husik's thought, if self-respecting Jews were to participate in modern civilisation, they had frankly to admit to themselves and to others the limitations of the Jewish heritage. Those who are in the habit of calling this whole attitude "assimilationist" are free to follow their bent provided they do not forget that philosophy itself is a kind of assimilation, assimilation to God or the Truth.

In fact, in order to judge fairly Husik's attitude towards Jewish philosophy, one merely has to consider his notion of philosophy. Philosophy, he says, "cannot afford to be either Jewish or Christian. It must aim to be universal and objective." Philosophy is "independent reflection" or "free inquiry." It is incompatible with "any belief in authority as such." It cannot "be bound by the religion in which one is born." "Philosophy *quā* philosophy [cannot] have a given basis forced upon it. Philosophy will be of value so long, and only so long, as it keeps itself independent of any special religious or other dogmatic doctrines." Furthermore, philosophy strives for knowledge for its own sake and hence cannot as such be enlisted in the service of any other cause, not even in that of ethical monotheism. Finally, philosophy is the attempt to discover the all-important truth on the basis of premises at the disposal of man as man. It is therefore essentially the affair of man as man, not of the Jew as Jew. From this point of view, the idea of a Jewish philosophy is as self-contradictory as the idea of a Christian mathematics or of a German physics.

Husik reached the same conclusion by considering the idea of a Jewish philosophy from the point of view of Judaism. "Judaism is not a philosophy or science; it is a religion. It is a positive and historic faith." More

Chapter 9

specifically, Judaism is Law, divine, unchangeable, all-comprehensive law. Judaism means the Torah, and the correct translation of *torah* is law. Accordingly, "the most important monuments of post-Biblical Jewish literature are devoted to the legal aspects of the Bible," not in any way to philosophy. The attitude characteristic of Judaism is "naïve dogmatism," as distinguished from, and opposed to, the "rationalism" characteristic of philosophy. Philosophy is therefore not "indigenous to Judaism." The belief in [xxiv] an original Jewish philosophy is "unhistorical." "We can scarcely speak of philosophy in connection with the Bible" or with the Talmudic literature. "The impulse to philosophising came from the Greeks." "Philo can scarcely be called a philosopher." "The first Jew, so far as we know, to devote himself to philosophical and scientific discussions" was Isaac Israeli (*ca.* 855–955). "We have no Thomas Aquinas. Maimonides does not occupy that place, and no one dreams of giving him such a place." Considering the basic relation of Judaism and philosophy, it is not surprising to observe that in times of persecution "the philosophic and scientific devotees" among the Jews "were the first to yield, and many of them abandoned Judaism."

From these premises, Husik was led to the conclusion that "the attempt of the mediæval Jewish philosophers to establish Judaism on a philosophical basis could not, from the nature of the case, have been a success" or that the task which they set themselves was "hopeless." Husik's detailed argument can be reduced to three main assertions. In the first place, he questioned the genuinely philosophic character of Jewish mediæval philosophy. To the extent to which the mediæval thinkers admitted the authority of the divine law and conceived of the efforts of reason as necessarily subservient to that authority, they ceased to be philosophers. Naturally, they believed that they were accepting the authority of the divine law on the basis of stringent historical proof and that they were following in their philosophic reflections reason alone. This, however, was a delusion. Their philosophic activity "was the outcome of an intellectual naïveté which we have lost forever." In the second place, Husik denied that the efforts of Jewish mediæval philosophy led to a justification of the teaching of the Bible. In attempting to reconcile the Bible with philosophy, they read Greek philosophy "into the Bible by a method which we do not now regard as legitimate." The agreement between the Bible and reason was proved by "the fiction of interpretation," i.e., by the substitution of an allegoric meaning for the genuine meaning of the Biblical texts. Finally, in so far as Jewish mediæval philosophers did use arguments of a genuinely philosophic character to prove genuinely Biblical teachings, Husik denied that they were successful. In particular, he did not believe that the problem of divine knowledge and divine providence could be solved "on the basis of ordinary theism." It is possible that this [xxv] belief led him to take a sympathetic view of the frankly anti-theological philosophy of Spinoza.

Jewish philosophy was, then, possible in the Middle Ages and is impossible in the modern time because the mediæval thinkers had "an intellectual naïveté which we have lost for ever." Husik traced that naïveté to the absence in mediæval thought of historical and literary criticism and, indeed, of an adequate historical knowledge. Mediæval rationalism failed because rationalism can "not take the place of a knowledge of history." As regards historical criticism of the Biblical text in particular, it was dangerous in the Middle Ages to state in plain terms even the most modest suggestions pointing in that direction. The absence of a historical approach is the crucial negative condition for the employment of the allegoric method, as well as for the development of "a harmonistic attitude in the presence of conflicting authorities." The modern turn to history culminates in "the modern theory of evolution." This doctrine forces us to trace the Bible not to God, but to the genius of the Jewish people. It destroys therewith for ever the foundation, not only of the Jewish tradition in general, but of Jewish mediæval philosophy in particular. Above all, the study of both Greek philosophic and Jewish literature that is conducted in the spirit of historical objectivity leads to "a truer understanding... of the provinces of positive religion and of scientific and philosophical thought." It was with the rise of that truer understanding that "Jewish philosophy has ceased."

To hold the view that the idea of a Jewish philosophy is a delusion is perfectly compatible with the admission that this delusion was under certain conditions inevitable and even salutary. Husik did not stint his praise of the achievement of Maimonides and other Jewish mediæval philosophers. In the Middle Ages, only a philosophy that was emphatically Jewish could vindicate within Judaism the authority of reason or take up successfully the fight against superstition and obscurantism. It is true that the authority of reason was recognised by the classical philosophers. It is also true, however, that the classical philosophers were not confronted by the claims of Revelation. To have succeeded in vindicating the authority of reason in the presence of the claims of Revelation "is an achievement of absolute, not of relative value."

Chapter 9

This will, perhaps, suffice to clarify the reasons for Husik's conception that his mediæval studies were simply historical. They do [xxvi] explain in fact why there is no immediate connection between his philosophic and his historical studies. His chief philosophic interest was in the philosophy of law, and he insisted on the fact that "Judaism always meant law." He thought that "the most important question in law is justice" and, while "the spirit of science is still Greek in its origin," "the passion for justice is still Hebrew." He never attempted, however, to establish a connection between the philosophy of law and the philosophy of Judaism, unless his purely historical effort to show the Biblical as well as the classical influences on Grotius be judged an exception. He attached particular importance to the efforts of Stammler and Kelsen. He paid little attention, however, to the work of Hermann Cohen, from which the doctrines of Stammler and Kelsen derive, a fact which can only be explained by Husik's attitude towards Jewish philosophy. He admitted that "the philosophical greatness of Hermann Cohen is beyond question," but he was dissatisfied "with Cohen as a Jewish philosopher." Cohen "made his Judaism tell in his philosophy," with the result that he was forced into "doubtful interpretations" of Judaism and especially of Jewish mediæval philosophy. In interpreting the thought of the past, and especially Jewish thought, Cohen employed a method which he called "idealising" interpretation. This consisted, to use the famous Kantian expression, in understanding the great thinkers of the past better than they understood themselves. Husik rejected this approach as "subjectivistic." He may well have thought that only if "systematic" philosophy and history of philosophy are kept strictly separate can the requirements of historical objectivity be fulfilled.

Husik's achievement bears witness to the fact that most valuable work can be done on the basis of his philosophy. "Objectivity," as Husik understood it, means in the first place the insistence upon the difference between facts and hypotheses. That difference had become somewhat obscured by the temporary success of the "higher criticism" of the nineteenth century. One cannot but admire the courage and the learning with which Husik maintained against all other contemporary students the genuine character of the entire *Categories* of Aristotle. "Objectivity" means, furthermore, impartiality or the refusal to engage in special pleading. Animated by the unobtrusive and unshakeable pride that prevents a man from stooping to make unwarranted claims for the group to which he belongs, Husik never [xxvii] for a moment attached to Jewish philosophies a greater philosophic or historical importance than they in fact possessed. His freedom from any apologetic tendencies has rarely been rivalled by other students in his field. "Objectivity" means also the ability to withstand the temptation to interpret the thought of the past in terms of modern thought, to say nothing of modern fashions. In the case of the study of Jewish mediæval philosophy, that ability presupposes clarity, based on solid knowledge of the texts, concerning the fundamental difference between modern and mediæval philosophy. Historians who try to modernise Jewish mediæval philosophy cannot help but lay greater stress on its Platonic than upon its Aristotelian elements, since Plato is, or seems to be, nearer to modern thought than Aristotle. Husik's sober picture of Jewish mediæval philosophy brings out very forcefully the almost overwhelming influence of Aristotle. But this by itself would not be enough. History of philosophy is a modern discipline, a product of modern philosophy. And modern philosophy emerged by way of transformation of, if in opposition to, Latin or Christian scholasticism. Modern students are therefore tempted to interpret Jewish mediæval philosophy on analogy to Christian scholasticism or to conceive of Maimonides as the Jewish counterpart to Thomas Aquinas. A special effort is needed to realise the fundamental difference between Jewish mediæval philosophy and Christian scholasticism. Husik has made this special effort. In this he was doubtless assisted by his familiarity with that tradition of Jewish rationalism the main supports of which were the writings of Maimonides and which, as a tradition, was perhaps never completely interrupted.

The character of a thing sets it off from other things. It is its "limit." One cannot describe the work of a scholar which has a character without speaking of that work's limitations. Were we to conceal the difficulties with which his position is beset we should certainly not act in the spirit of the Husik who never ceased extolling and practising the duty of intellectual honesty. These difficulties may be reduced to three heads. They are related to the problems of objectivity, of historical evolution, and of the idea of a Jewish philosophy.

Husik especially opposed the "subjectivism" of Hermann Cohen. Yet, in reviewing a work of one of Cohen's disciples, he granted that "it is better frankly and deliberately to embrace subjectivity than to [xxviii] claim its opposite which cannot be realised, for pure objectivity does not exist." One cannot demand pure objectivity in such matters as are essentially controversial among honest and competent people. If it be true that all philosophic subjects are of this nature or that all philo-

Chapter 9

sophic controversies reveal "our helpless struggle... in the face of the unknown," there can be no objective history of philosophy, unless the history of philosophy can be made independent of any specifically philosophic assumptions. Now, the very first thing that the historian of philosophy has to do is to delimit his field of inquiry or to distinguish his subject matter clearly from the subject matter of the other branches of history. History of philosophy presupposes knowledge of what philosophy is. But what philosophy is, is as controversial as any other philosophic subject. History of philosophy will then necessarily be subjective because its very basis is necessarily subjective. To begin with, there is indeed no reason why one should not define philosophy as the attempt to replace opinions about God, world, and man by genuine knowledge of God, world, and man. It is controversial, nevertheless, whether there is direct experience of God—or, more specifically, mystical experience—which supplies genuine knowledge of God as the first cause of all beings and it is obvious that the manner in which this question is answered determines completely the precise meaning of philosophy. Husik summarily identified Jewish philosophy with Jewish rationalist philosophy and excluded Jewish mysticism and, in particular, the Kabbala from his history of that philosophy. We need not insist on the fact that he dealt in his work with the teaching of Yehuda Halevi, who, according to Husik's own presentation, is a mystic rather than a rationalist. What is decisive is the fact that Husik's definition of the subject matter of the history of Jewish philosophy would appear to be as subjective as that suggested by others whom he blamed for having unduly broadened the term "philosophy" by identifying Jewish philosophy with Jewish thought in general. It is true that all arbitrariness could be avoided if the historian would regard as philosophers only those competent thinkers who regarded themselves as philosophers. In fact, this would appear to be the only legitimate historical procedure or the only procedure compatible with the demands of objectivity, if the task of the historian of philosophy be indeed that of understanding the great thinkers of the past as they understood themselves. But this leads to a new and perhaps [xxix] still more serious difficulty in regard to Jewish mediæval philosophy. It would be easy to show that certainly the greatest of the Jewish mediæval thinkers, Maimonides, did not regard himself as a philosopher. The ultimate consequence of a strictly objective procedure would then resemble the evaporation of the subject matter of the history of Jewish mediæval philosophy.

On Husik's Work in Mediæval Jewish Philosophy

The specific philosophic assumption that underlies Husik's historical studies is revealed not so much by the definitions of philosophy which he suggested, as by what he indicated concerning the relation of truth and history. He considered the emergence of a historical approach as the decisive reason for the obsolescence of Jewish mediæval philosophy and, with it, of Jewish philosophy as such. "We are all the products of history," and this must be understood not only of our habits and prejudices but of our purest and freest thoughts as well. A man's thought will in the best case still be dependent on "the science of his day." Therefore, there cannot be final certainty. There cannot be certainty, that is, that the science of one's day is not fundamentally false. "It matters not whether the science is true or false. There have been many false sciences, and who knows whether a century later our science will not be upset in turn?" One cannot express the difficulty more tellingly than Husik himself does by speaking of "our helpless struggle in the face of the unknown." In his analysis of Jewish philosophy, Husik assumed that the foundations of Jewish orthodoxy had been destroyed "for ever" by historical criticism. The modern Jew cannot help but reject "the old theory" of Judaism, according to which the substance of Judaism is the Torah as the unchangeable divine law, in favour of "the modern theory of evolution," according to which the Torah is the historical product of the genius of the Jewish people. Hence, the modern Jew is entitled and even obliged to "differentiate between the essential and the unessential in the Jewish Weltanschauung." "As a result of this process of selection a great part of the material is simply thrown overboard as unessential and the result of historical accident. What remains is kept for the time being as the eternal root of Judaism. But since we are all the products of history, who can warrant that the future may not see things otherwise than we do, and either go back or forward in the process of selection?" It is impossible to accept this too sanguine prospect, which still takes it for granted that in spite of our uncertainty concerning the modes of "selection" which may prevail in the future, we can be certain that the principle of "selection" (as opposed to the principle of obedient acceptance of the whole) is established for ever. If human thought is radically historical, if the science of the day, and hence especially the historical science of the nineteenth and twentieth centuries which has destroyed "the old theory" of Judaism, may very well be upset in turn, one must admit, in fact one has already admitted, the possibility of a full restoration of "the old theory," i.e., of Jewish orthodoxy.

Chapter 9

Husik's studies on Jewish mediæval philosophy are animated by the spirit of historical objectivity. They are not animated by a distinctly Jewish spirit or conceived from a distinctly Jewish point of view. These studies could have been the work of a sufficiently equipped non-Jew or of a sufficiently equipped Jew for whom his being a Jew was merely an accident of birth. But Husik was deeply attached to Judaism. Being a philosopher, he was forced to clarify the meaning of that attachment and to bring it into harmony with his attachment to philosophy. His statements on this subject betray a certain vacillation which is not surprising, since "one scarcely knows what so-called modern Judaism stands for." He was not always sure whether the Judaism to which he was attached was primarily a spiritual force and not rather a racial entity. What keeps Judaism in existence "is the desire of the Jew to retain his identity. The philosophy which puts this desire in articulate terms may vary from age to age, the instinctive desire which prompts it is one and unchangeable. The blood of race is thicker than the water of metaphysics." Still, the view that seems to have prevailed with Husik was that "the genius of the Jewish people ... created certain ideas and institutions which have proved their value by being accepted by the greater part of civilised humanity," and that these ideas and institutions rather than mere race commanded his allegiance. "The unity of God and the idea of Ethics and Social Justice is all that is left of Judaism." This Jewish heritage, he felt, is as essential for civilisation as the Greek spirit of science and philosophy. From this conclusion, he was naturally led to demand that the Jewish heritage—"the passion for justice" or "the fear of the Lord"—be brought into some working relation with philosophy and science, or, more precisely, with modern philosophy and science. He was led, in other words, to subscribe to the demand for a modern [xxxi] philosophy of Judaism. "All will not be well in Judaism until the position of the Bible as a Jewish authority is dealt with in an adequate manner by Jewish scholars who are competent to do it ... the scholar who is going to undertake it ... must be a philosopher and thinker of eminent abilities. And he must have a love of his people and sympathy with its aspirations." That is to say, what is needed is a modern Jewish philosopher. This whole strand in Husik's thought is in full agreement with the principles of Hermann Cohen. It is therefore hard to see how Husik could with consistency have avoided agreeing with the principle of Cohen's approach to Jewish mediæval philosophy. For the fundamental problem for the modern Jewish philosopher—the relation of the spirit of science and of the spirit of the Bible—was also the fundamental problem for the mediæval Jewish philosopher. The modern Jewish philosopher will naturally try to learn as much as possible for his own task from his illustrious predecessors. Since he has achieved greater clarity at least about certain aspects of the fundamental issue than the mediæval thinkers had, he will not be exclusively concerned with what the mediæval thinkers explicitly or actually intended in elaborating their doctrines. He will be much more concerned with what these doctrines mean in the light of the fundamental issue regardless of whether the mediæval thinkers were aware of that meaning or not.

It would be wrong to belittle the strength of these objections. It might be more dangerous, especially in our time, to overestimate their force and to believe that they make doubtful the guiding intention of Husik the scholar. In spite of certain vacillations, he was convinced that a Jewish philosophy is impossible. This conviction was supported by the observation of the difficulties in which the greatest Jewish thinker of his time had become entangled. Owing to the historical character of all modern thought, Cohen was forced to accompany his philosophy of Judaism with interpretations of Jewish mediæval philosophy, and these interpretations were extremely objectionable from the point of view of historical exactness. The concern with the "idealising" interpretation proved to be ruinous to the concern with exact interpretation. A position that forces its holder to attach great importance to historical studies and at the same time prevents him from conducting these studies in an exact manner appears to be untenable. The demand for objectivity, for understanding the thought of the past as it really has been, without distorting it—this demand is not the powerless last gesture of the dying and deadening spirit of the nineteenth century, but the vivifying and invigorating call of that desire in man which prompts him to hate the lie in the soul more than anything else. This was the solid ground on which Husik stood. On this basis, the difficulties with which his position remains beset must be soluble. They cannot be solved without a far-reaching revision of his general views as well as of his interpretation of Jewish mediæval thought. But all these changes will have to be inspired by the intention that guided his scholarly work.

10

On Collingwood's Philosophy of History
(1952)

I

[559] R. G. Collingwood's *The Idea of History* (Clarendon Press, 1946) "is an essay in the philosophy of history." Philosophy of history, as Collingwood understood it, is of very recent origin. It emerged as a sequel to the rise of "scientific history" which took place in the latter part of the nineteenth century (254). If one assumes that "scientific history" is the highest or final form of man's concern with his past, the understanding of what the "scientific historian" does, or epistemology of history, may become of philosophic interest. And if the older or traditional branches of philosophy cannot make intelligible the "new historical technique" or solve the problems "created by the existence of organized and systematized historical research"; if, in other words, "the traditional philosophies carry with them the implication that historical knowledge is impossible" (5–6), epistemology of history becomes of necessity a philosophic concern or a philosophic discipline. But philosophy of history must be more than epistemology of history. In the first place, epistemology of history is likely to be of vital concern only to certain technicians, and not to men as men. Above all, thought about historical thought must be thought about the object of historical thought as well. Hence philosophy of history must be both epistemology of history and metaphysics of history (3, 184). Philosophy of history comes then first to sight as an addition to the traditional branches of philosophy. But philosophy hardly permits of mere additions. Certainly philosophy of history cannot be a mere addition: philosophy of history necessarily entails "a complete philosophy conceived from an historical

---

Originally published in *Review of Metaphysics* 5, no. 4 (June 1952): 559–86. —Eds.

CHAPTER 10

point of view" (7, 147). For the discovery on which philosophy of history is based concerns the character of all human thought; it leads therefore to an entirely new understanding of philosophy. In other words, it was always admitted that the central theme of philosophy is the question of what [560] man is, and that history is the knowledge of what men have done; but now it has been realized that man is what he can do, and "the only clue to what man can do" is what he has done (10); therefore, "the so-called science of human nature or of the human mind resolves itself into history" (220, 209). Philosophy of history is identical with philosophy as such, which has become radically historical: "philosophy as a separate discipline is liquidated by being converted into history" (x).

Collingwood was prevented by his death from elaborating his philosophy of history in the full sense of the term. He believed that he could do no more than to attempt "a philosophic inquiry into the nature of history regarded as a special type or form of knowledge with a special type of object" (7). Since philosophy of history in the narrower sense admittedly points to philosophy of history in the comprehensive sense, it might seem that Collingwood unjustifiably postponed the discussion of the fundamental issue. But it is perhaps fairer to say that philosophy of history in the comprehensive sense presupposes philosophy of history in the narrower sense, or that the fusion of philosophy and history presupposes the soundness or adequacy of "scientific history": if the historical understanding of the last four or five generations is not decisively superior to the historical understanding that was possible in the past, the conversion of philosophy into history loses its most convincing, or at least its most persuasive, justification.

Scientific history, being "now a thing within the compass of everyone" (320), is the cooperative effort of a very large number of contemporaries which is directed toward the acquisition of such knowledge as "ideally" forms part of "a universal history" or of knowledge of "the human past in its entirety" (27, 209). It is a theoretical pursuit; it is "actuated by a sheer desire for truth" and by no other concern (60–61). The attitude of the scientific historian, however, is not that of a spectator. Knowledge of what men have done is knowledge of what men have thought: "All history is the history of thought" (215, 304). Scientific history is thought about thought. Past thought cannot be known as such except by being re-thought, or re-enacted, or re-lived, or re-produced (97, 115, 218). For the scientific historian, the past is not something foreign, or dead, or outside his mind: the human past is living in his mind, [561] though living as past. This does not mean that the entire past can be re-enacted by every scientific historian; there must be a kind of sympathy between the historian's thought and his object; and in order to be truly alive, "the historian's thought must spring from the organic unity of his total experience, and be a function of his entire personality with its practical as well as its theoretical interests" (305). Since "all thinking is critical thinking" and not a mere surrender to the object of thought, re-thinking of earlier thought is identical with criticism of earlier thought (215–16, 300–01). The point of view from which the scientific historian criticizes the past is that of the present of his civilization. Scientific history is then the effort to see the human past in its entirety as it appears from the standpoint of the present of the historian's civilization (60, 108, 215). Yet history will not be self-knowledge if the historian sees the past in the light of the present of his civilization without making that present his primary theme. The scientific historian's task is therefore to show how the present of his civilization, or the mind of the present-day, or that "determinate human nature" which is his civilization, has come into existence (104, 169, 175, 181, 226). Since scientific history is a peculiarity of modern Western thought, it may be described as the effort of present-day Western man to understand his peculiar humanity and thus to preserve it or enrich it.

Since genuine knowledge of the past is necessarily criticism and evaluation of the past from the point of view of the present, it is necessarily "relative" to the present, i.e., to the present of a given country or civilization. The point of view of a given historian is "valid only for him and people situated like him" (60, 108). "Every new generation must rewrite history in its own way" (248). Objectivity in the sense of universal validity would then seem to be impossible. Collingwood was not disturbed by this danger to "scientific" history (cf. 265). There were two reasons for his confidence. In the first place, the belief in progress, and hence in the superiority of the present to the past, still lingered on in his thought. He could therefore believe that if historical knowledge is relative to the present, it is relative to the highest standpoint which has ever existed. To see that the belief in progress survived in [562] Collingwood's thought, it almost suffices to look at the Table of Contents of his book: he devoted more space to Croce, to say nothing of other present-day thinkers, than to Herodotus and Thucydides. He took it for granted that the historian can and must distinguish "between retrograde and progressive elements" in the phenomena which he is studying (135). More than half of his book is devoted to a comparison of the modern scientific conception of history with "the medieval conception of history with all its errors" (56) and the classical

CHAPTER 10

conception with its grave "defects" (41–42). The second reason why Collingwood was not disturbed by the "relativity" of all historical knowledge was his belief in the equality of all ages. "The present is always perfect in the sense that it always succeeds in being what it is trying to be," or the present has no standard higher than itself (109). There are no ages of decline or of decay (164). Augustine looked at Roman history from the point of view of an early Christian, and Gibbon did so from that of an enlightened eighteenth century Englishman: "there is no point in asking which was the right point of view. Each was the only possible for the man who adopted it" (xii). The historian who sees the past from the point of view of a present must not be worried by the prospect of a future progress of historical knowledge: "the historian's problem is a present problem, not a future one: it is to interpret the material now available, not to anticipate future discoveries" (180). Being thus protected against the surprises which the future may have in store, the scientific historian can be satisfied that the historical knowledge which is relative to the present, and is based on the material accessible at present, fulfills all the requirements of certainty or science. The fact that all historical knowledge is relative to the present means that it is relative to the only standpoint which is possible now, to a standpoint which is in no way inferior to any standpoint which was possible in the past or which will be possible in the future. Regardless of whether or not Collingwood found a way for reconciling the two different reasons indicated, each of them, if sound, would justify him in assuming that understanding of the past from the point of view of the present is unobjectionable, and in fact inevitable.

The procedure which we have just outlined is characteristic of *The Idea of History*. Collingwood moved consciously and [563] with enthusiasm toward a goal which most of his contemporaries were approaching more or less unconsciously and haltingly, that goal being the fusion of philosophy and history. But he was not very much concerned with examining the means by which he tried to reach his goal. He vacillated between two different views of history, the rationalistic view of Hegel and a non-rationalistic view. He never clearly realized that these two views are mutually incompatible. The historical reason for this failure was his lack of acquaintance with Nietzsche's epoch-making critique of "scientific history."

There is a tension between the idea of universal history and the view that in history "the mind of the present day apprehends the process by which this mind itself has come into existence through the mental development of the past" (169). If the modern Western historian studies Greek civilization, he may be said to re-enact the genesis of his own civilization, which has formed itself "by reconstructing within its own mind the mind of the Hellenic world" and thus to enter upon the possession of his inheritance (163, 226–27); he may be said to attempt to understand himself as modern Western man, or to mind his own business. But the case of the modern Western historian who studies Chinese or Inca civilization is obviously different. Collingwood did not reflect on this difference. He justly rejected Spengler's view that "there is no possible relation whatever between one culture and another." But he failed to consider the fact that there are cultures which have no actual relations with one another, and the implications of this fact: he dogmatically denied the possibility of "separate, discrete" cultures because it would destroy the dogmatically assumed "continuity of history" as universal history (161–64, 183). — According to one view held by Collingwood, the idea of scientific history, "the idea of an imaginary picture of the past [is], in Kantian language, *a priori*... it is an idea which every man possesses as part of the furniture of his mind, and discovers himself to possess in so far as he becomes conscious of what it is to have a mind" (248); scientific history is therefore the actualization of a potentiality of human nature. According to another view also held by Collingwood, one cannot speak of the furniture of the human mind, and not even of *the* human mind, which as such would be subject to [564] "permanent and unchanging laws"; the idea of scientific history is not, in principle, coeval with the human mind but is itself "historical"; it has been acquired by Western man on the basis of his unique experience (of the Christian experience in particular); it is rooted in modern Western thought and its needs; it is meaningful only for modern Western thought (xii, 12, 48–49, 82, 224, 226, 255). — Collingwood regarded history as a theoretical pursuit, but he also said that the historian's thought must be "a function of his entire personality with its practical as well as its theoretical interests." — All history, Collingwood repeatedly said, is the history of thought or of rational activity or of freedom (215, 304, 315, 318): one cannot abandon "Hegel's belief that history is rational" without abandoning history itself (122); by speaking of "the contingency of history," the historian "expresses [the] final collapse of his thought" (151). Accordingly, Collingwood held that understanding of the thought of the past is not only compatible with criticism of thought of the past from the point of view of the present, but inseparable from it. On the other hand, however, he tended to believe that the ultimate facts of history are free choices which are not justifiable by rational activity; or that the ultimate facts of history are mere beliefs;

CHAPTER 10

and hence that history is not rational or that it is radically contingent or that it is, so to speak, a sequel of different original sins. Accordingly, he tended to hold that the historian cannot criticize the thought of the past but must remain satisfied with understanding it (cf. 316–18).

Collingwood's failure to clarify his position sufficiently can be explained in part by the need which he felt "to engage in a running fight" with positivism or naturalism (i.e., "the confusion between historical process and natural process") (228, 181–82). His main preoccupation was with vindicating "the autonomy of history" against the claims of modern natural science. The view that historical knowledge is partly dependent on modern natural science was based on the fact that man's historical life is dependent on nature; and man's knowledge of nature is not identical with modern natural science. Collingwood was therefore driven to assert "the autonomy of history" without any qualification: "the historian is master in his own house; he owes nothing to the scientist or to anyone else," for [565] "ordinary history," rightly understood, "contains philosophy inside itself" (155, 201). History does not depend upon authority nor on memory (236–38). "...[I]n history, just as there are properly speaking no authorities, so there are properly speaking no data" (243).* "Freed from its dependence on fixed points supplied from without, the historian's picture of the past is thus in every detail an imaginary picture, and its necessity is at every point the necessity of the *a priori* imagination. Whatever goes into it, goes into it not because his imagination passively accepts it, but because it actively demands it" (245). It is because of its "autonomy" that history must be universal history (246): truth is totality. Collingwood should not have hesitated to call this view "idealistic" (cf. 159). It is indeed not a solipsistic view: historical thought is both autonomous and objective; the historian's house "is inhabited by all historians" (155). More precisely, it is inhabited by all present-day historians.† It is a house without windows: the mind of the present day is autonomous or master in its own house because it cannot understand the thought of the past without criticizing it, i.e., without transforming it into a modification of present day thought, or because it is not disturbed by problems which it cannot solve ("To ask questions you see no prospect of answering is the fundamental sin in science"—281) or because it is not disturbed by the possibilities of the future ("the only clue to what man can do is what man has done"—10, 180). A particularly noteworthy consequence

---

* Strauss begins the sentence, which is entirely a quotation, with a lowercase "i–." —Eds.

† Strauss sometimes hyphenates the adjectival "present-day," as here. —Eds.

of Collingwood's idealism is the banishment of biography from history: the limits of biography are "biological events, the birth and death of a human organism: its framework is thus a framework not of thought but of natural process" (304). This decision had the additional advantage of keeping the subjectivity of scientific history within limits which, for Collingwood, were reasonable. If the "biographical" is sub-historical, it will as little go into the making of the subject which acquires or possesses historical knowledge, as it will become an element of the object of historical knowledge. Historical knowledge will not become relative to the individual historian. It will retain its objectivity by being relative to "the mind of the present day." A difficulty is created by the circumstance that "the historian's thought must spring from the organic unity of his total experience," [566] which experience, being total, could be thought to include his "immediate experience with its flow of sensations and feelings" and those "human emotions [which] are bound up with the spectacle of [his] bodily life" (304): "total experience" would seem to include the most "personal" experiences.

To do justice to Collingwood's idea of history, one must examine his practice as a historian. The largest part of his book is devoted to a history of historical knowledge. That history is on the whole conventional. In studying earlier thinkers, Collingwood never considered the possibility that the point of view from which the present day reader approaches them, or the questions which he addresses to them, might be in need of a fundamental change. He set out to praise or blame the earlier thinkers according to whether they helped or hindered the emergence of scientific history. He did not attempt to look at scientific history, for once, from the point of view of the earlier thinkers. What is not quite conventional in Collingwood's history, are some of his judgments: he had the courage to wonder whether Thucydides and Tacitus deserve the title of historians (29, 38–39). Furthermore, his history of historical knowledge is somewhat obscured by an ambiguity which he did not consistently avoid. His discussion of "Human nature and human history" culminated in the assertion that historical knowledge is coeval with the historical process, because the historical process is a process in which man inherits the achievements of the past, and historical knowledge is the way in which man enters upon the possession of that inheritance (226–27; cf. 333–34). In this crucial context Collingwood thus identified historical knowledge with accepting a tradition or living in a tradition. As a rule, however, he assumed that historical knowledge is not coeval with historical life but is an "invention" made at a certain time in Greece (19) and developed later on by the heirs of the Greeks.

Chapter 10

The most revealing section of Collingwood's history of historical knowledge is his statement about the Greek conception of history. The Greeks created scientific history. This fact is paradoxical, for Greek thought was based "on a rigorously anti-historical metaphysics" (18–20). The "chief category" of that metaphysics "is the category of substance," and [567] "a substantialist metaphysics implies a theory of knowledge according to which only what is unchanging is knowable" (42). "Therefore history ought to be impossible," i.e., impossible as a science; history must be relegated to the realm of "opinion." Yet the very view that what is truly, or what is truly knowable, is the permanent, implied a fundamental distinction between the permanent and the changeable, and hence the insight that change is necessary: the Greeks' pursuit of the eternal presupposed "an unusually vivid sense of the temporal." In addition, they lived in a period of rapid and violent change: hence their "peculiar sensitiveness to history." For this reason however "their historical consciousness" was of a peculiar kind: it was "not a consciousness of age-long tradition molding the life of one generation after another into a uniform pattern; it was a consciousness of violent περιπέτειαι, catastrophic changes from one state of things to its opposite..." (22; cf. 26, 34). But since they believed that only the permanent is knowable or intelligible, they regarded "these catastrophic changes in the condition of human life" as unintelligible. They did not deny "that in the general pattern of these changes certain antecedents normally led to certain consequents," and that these sequences can be established by observation; but they could not tell why "certain antecedents normally led to certain consequents": "There is here no theory of causation." "This conception of history was the very opposite of deterministic": the sequences of antecedents and consequents are not necessary; they can be modified by the men who know of them; "thus the Greeks had a lively and indeed a naïve sense of the power of man to control his own destiny." Since the Greeks were compelled to consider history "as, at bottom, not a science, but a mere aggregate of perceptions," they had to identify "historical evidence with the reports of facts given by eye witnesses of these facts." They did not uncritically accept those reports. But their criticism could not go beyond making quite certain whether the eye witness really told what he had seen, and reaching a decision as to which of various conflicting reports deserved to be accepted. This conception of historical evidence limited history to the study of "events which have happened within living memory to people with [568] whom [the historian] can have personal contact"; it made impossible scientific history of the remote past: the historian cannot be more than "the autobiographer of his generation" (22–27).

Some critical remarks seem to be necessary. When asserting that thinking historically and thinking in terms of substance are incompatible, Collingwood presupposed that "it is metaphysically axiomatic that an agent, being a substance, can never come into being and can never undergo any change of nature" (43). Did the Greeks then not know that human beings, for example, come into being? Or is it necessary to refer to Aristotle's statement that coming into being simply is said only of substances? Why then should the Greeks have been unable to observe and to describe the coming into being of substances and their changes? Collingwood asserted that in "substantialist" classical historiography "all the agencies that appear on the stage of history have to be assumed ready-made before history begins" (45) and that the classics therefore regarded nations and cities as substances, "changeless and eternal" (44). He did not even attempt to prove that the classics conceived of cities and nations as substances. But even if they did, their almost daily experience would have convinced them that cities at any rate are not "changeless and eternal" substances, that they are founded and grow and decay and perish, to say nothing of other changes which they undergo. Why then should the Greeks have been unable to observe and describe the coming into being and the changes of cities? To say nothing of the fact that it is safe to infer what men could do from what they did. "...[T]he Greeks could not even contemplate the possibility of raising the problem which we should call the problem of the origin of the Hellenic people" (34).* But, to take the most obvious case, were there no Greek thinkers who taught that the human race had come into being, that in the beginning men roamed in forests, without social bonds of any kind and in particular without language, and hence without the Greek language? Certainly these thinkers did not merely contemplate the possibility of raising the problem of the origin of the Hellenic people, but they did raise it and, according to their lights, solved it. Collingwood did not see [569] that the reflections of the Greek philosophers on the nature and origin of language are equivalent to reflections on the nature and origin of nations. If they did not attempt to give historical accounts of the genesis of this or that nation, or of any nation, they had reasons like these: They did not have at their disposal historical evidence of events of this kind; they regarded the city as a higher

---

* Strauss left the "t–" at the beginning of the quotation as a lowercase letter. — Eds.

Chapter 10

form of society than the nation; and they thought that societies in their full vigor and maturity were more instructive regarding the highest possibilities of man than are societies newly coming into being. There may be a connection between these views and "substantialism." It suffices to note that Collingwood did not even try to reveal that connection. Prudence would have dictated to Collingwood to refrain from speaking of "substantialism" and to limit himself to saying that the classics were, for whatever reason, more concerned with the permanent and hence with the recurrent than with what is merely temporal and local, or that they believed that the unique can ultimately be understood only in the light of the permanent or recurrent. From this he could legitimately have concluded that from the point of view of the classics, history is inferior in dignity to philosophy or science. To prove his thesis, it would have been necessary for him to show, in addition, that the primacy of the concern with the permanent or recurrent precludes or endangers serious concern with what happens here and now or what happened there and then. He did not show this. To say nothing of other considerations, one may be chiefly concerned with the permanent or recurrent and yet hold that a given unique event (the Peloponnesian War, for example) supplies the only available basis for reliable observation which would enable one to form a correct judgment about certain recurrences of utmost importance. A man who held this view would of course study that unique event with utmost care, and, assuming that he was a superior man, he might have surpassed as a historian, i.e., as a man who understands actions of men, all the scientific historians of the nineteenth and twentieth centuries.

Collingwood held that the Greeks had a "historical consciousness" of a particular kind: it was "not a consciousness of age-long tradition molding the life of one generation after [570] another into a uniform pattern," but a consciousness of "catastrophic changes" (22). This statement is, to say the least, very misleading. "The Greeks" were perfectly conscious of the existence of "age-long traditions molding the life of one generation after another into a uniform pattern." But they believed, or at any rate Plato believed or suggested, that Greek life—in contradistinction especially to Egyptian life—was not dominated by such traditions: "you Greeks are always children...you are, all of you, young in soul; for you do not possess in your souls a single ancient opinion transmitted by old tradition nor a single piece of learning that is hoary with age." The Greeks were less dominated by age-long traditions than were other nations because there lived in their midst men who had the habit of questioning such traditions, i.e., philosophers. In other words, there was a greater awareness in Greece than elsewhere of the essential difference between the ancestral and the good. On the basis of this insight there existed in classical Greece "a historical consciousness," not merely of "catastrophic changes" but also of changes for the better, of progress, and this consciousness was a consciousness not merely of progress achieved but also of the possibility of future progress. Collingwood did not even allude to this element of "the Greek conception of history." He apparently never tried to understand "the historical consciousness" which expresses itself in the first book of Aristotle's *Metaphysics*, for example. Consideration of this book alone would have sufficed to make him hesitate to write that "the Greek historian was only the autobiographer of his generation" (27).

But let us concede that a man like Thucydides was primarily concerned with "catastrophic change" rather than with long periods in which practically no change, or only slow changes for the better, took place; and let us assume that Collingwood has given an account, based on Thucydides' work, of this preference, although Collingwood did not even attempt to do this. Was he entitled to say that the Greeks were forced to regard catastrophic changes as unintelligible, i.e., as in no way traceable to determinate causes? The mere fact that he could not help censoring Thucydides for being "the father of psychological history" which is "natural science of a [571] special kind" (29) would seem to prove that there was at least one Greek who regarded catastrophic change as intelligible. According to Collingwood, the Greeks regarded the change from a state of extreme wealth or power to a state of extreme poverty or weakness, as a mysterious rhythm; "the universal judgment that very rich men, as such, fall ... is, in Aristotle's view, only a partially scientific judgment, for no one can say why rich men should fall" (24). If Collingwood had considered the analysis of the characters of the rich and the powerful in the second book of the *Rhetoric*, or the analysis of tyranny and dynastic oligarchy in the *Politics*, he could have told us that Aristotle had a good explanation for the fall of rich and powerful men if they are not virtuous or lucky. Collingwood mistook for no theory of causation what is in effect a theory of causation that includes chance as a cause of historical events.

Only because Collingwood disregarded, among other things, what the classics have to say about the power of chance, could he confidently assert that "the Greeks had a lively and indeed a naïve sense of the power of man to control his own destiny" (24) or that for Hellenic thought "self-consciousness [was] a power to conquer the world" (36) or that classical

CHAPTER 10

thought implied "that whatever happens in history happens as a direct result of the human will" (41). It taxes the imagination to understand how the same man could have written these sentences a few pages after he had written "that these catastrophic changes in the condition of human life which were to the Greeks the proper theme of history, were unintelligible" (22).

As for Collingwood's remark that, for the Greeks, history was "at bottom... a mere aggregate of perceptions" (24), it suffices to say that one page later he noted that men like Herodotus and Thucydides succeeded in calling up a fairly "coherent" "historical picture" of the events which they studied. In his discussion of the Greek conception of historical evidence, he was silent about the basic distinction between seeing with one's own eyes and hearsay, and the use which the classical historians made of that distinction for evaluating traditions or reports. In particular, he did not consider that seeing with one's own eyes includes understanding of the [572] nature of man and of the nature of political things, an understanding which fulfills in Greek history approximately the same function which "historical imagination" fulfills in Collingwood's "scientific history."

Collingwood's account of the classical conception of history, which had to be "in every detail an imaginary picture" in order to conform with his standards of historical truth (cf. 245), indirectly reveals more about "the idea of history" than do all the subsequent sections of his book. The idea of history is more than the view that knowledge of what men have done or thought is possible or necessary. It is the view that such knowledge properly understood is identical with philosophy or must take the place of philosophy. The idea of history thus understood is indeed alien to classical thought. According to Collingwood, it could not emerge before classical "substantialism" was abandoned and classical "humanism" was profoundly modified. If history is the account, or the study, of what men have done, and philosophy is the study of something which is presupposed by all human doings, the idea of history requires in the first place that the apparent presuppositions of all human doings be resolved into products of human doings: this is what Collingwood meant by the need for abandoning "substantialism." The apparent presuppositions of all human doings are objects of human knowledge, as distinguished from the products or results of human action. The first step in the direction of the idea of history was therefore that the distinction between knowledge and action or between theory and practice be questioned. Knowledge had to be conceived as a kind of making or production. Collingwood referred in the usual manner to Vico's *verum et factum convertuntur* (64). But he failed to go back to Vico's source, i.e., to Hobbes, and hence he could rest satisfied with the conventional way of describing the genesis of the idea of history. Now, if the thinker or maker is man as man, or every individual regardless of time and place, philosophy remains "unhistorical." If there is to be an essential connection between thought, or the content of thought, and time and place, what we know or think must be such a making as is essentially dependent on the making of earlier men, or rather of earlier men who lived "here," and [573] yet it must be different from earlier thought. It cannot be different from earlier thought if it could have been anticipated, i.e., thought, by earlier men: it must be the unforeseen and unforeseeable outcome of earlier thought. It is this requirement which Collingwood had in mind when he demanded the abandonment or radical modification of Greek "humanism" which attributed "far too little to the force of a blind activity embarking on a course of action without foreseeing its end and being led to that end only through the necessary development of that course itself" (42), i.e., without being led to that end by the plan of a god or of nature (55, 57, 58, 81, 104). He described the requirement in question somewhat more accurately when he contrasted Greek thought with the determinism of seventeenth century natural science which laid the foundation for conceiving of thought as such, and of every "stage" of thought, as the necessary and unintended "product of a process" (23, 57, 58, 81, 87). For the reason indicated, he failed, however, to raise the question regarding the connection between the conception of thinking as making and the peculiar "determinism" of modern natural science. He thus failed to see that the basic stratum of "the idea of history" is a combination of the view that thinking is making, or "creative," with the need, engendered by that view, of giving a "deterministic" account of thinking, or such a "genetic" account as presupposes at no point anything except "motion" or "process." Collingwood's "idealism" prevented him from looking beyond the antagonism of "idealism" and "naturalism" or from seeing that "history" and "scientific materialism" are inseparable from each other. (Compare, however, the remark on p. 269 about the kinship between scientific history and Baconian natural science.)

II

Collingwood did not prove "by deed" the superiority of scientific history to the common-sense type of history which prevailed, on the most differ-

Chapter 10

ent levels, in the past. His most important statements are errors which competent men in earlier times would not have committed simply because they were [574] more careful readers than we have become. Scientific history is based on the assumption that present day historical thought is the right kind of historical thought. When it is confronted with the fact that earlier historical thought is different from present day historical thought, it naturally concludes that earlier historical thought is defective. And no one can be blamed if he does not study very carefully such doctrines or procedures as he knows in advance to be defective in the decisive respect. Collingwood wrote the history of history in almost the same way in which the eighteenth century historians, whom he censored so severely, are said to have written history in general. The latter condemned the thought of the past as deficient in full reasonableness; Collingwood condemned it as deficient in the true sense for history.

This is not to deny that Collingwood also believed in the equality of all ages and that he therefore tended to regard the historical thought of any one period as equally sound as that of any other period. One might think that to the extent to which he held that belief, he would have tried to understand the historical thought of each period of the past on its own terms, without measuring it by the standard of scientific history. Yet the belief in the equality of all ages leads to the consequence that our interpretation of the thought of the past, while not superior to the way in which the thought of the past interpreted itself, is as legitimate as the past's self-interpretation and, in addition, is the only way in which we today can interpret the thought of the past. Accordingly, there arises no necessity to take seriously the way in which the thought of the past understood itself. In other words, the belief in the equality of all ages is only a more subtle form of the belief in progress. The alleged insight into the equality of all ages which is said to make possible passionate interest in the thought of the different ages, necessarily conceives of itself as a progress beyond all earlier thought: every earlier age erroneously "absolutized" the standpoint from which it looked at things and therefore was incapable of taking very seriously the thought of other ages; hence earlier ages were incapable of scientific history. [575]

The two beliefs which contended for supremacy in Collingwood's thought implied that earlier thought is necessarily relative to earlier times. "The *Republic* of Plato is an account, not of the unchanging ideal of political life, but of the Greek ideal as Plato received it and reinterpreted it. The *Ethics* of Aristotle describes not an eternal morality but the morality of the Greek gentleman. Hobbes' *Leviathan* expounds the political ideas of seventeenth century absolutism in their English form. Kant's ethical theory expresses the moral convictions of German pietism..." (229). Collingwood understood then the thought of a time in the light of its time. He did not then re-enact that thought. For to re-enact the thought which expresses itself in Plato's *Republic*, for example, means to understand Plato's description of the simply good social order as a description of the true model of society with reference to which all societies of all ages and countries must be judged. Collingwood's attitude towards the thought of the past was in fact that of a spectator who sees from the outside the relation of an earlier thought to its time.

The deficiencies of Collingwood's historiography can be traced to a fundamental dilemma. The same belief which forced him to attempt to become a historian of thought, prevented him from becoming a historian of thought. He was forced to attempt to become a historian of thought because he believed that to know the human mind is to know its history, or that self-knowledge is historical understanding. But this belief contradicts the tacit premise of all earlier thought, that premise being the view that to know the human mind is something fundamentally different from knowing the history of the human mind. Collingwood therefore rejected the thought of the past as untrue in the decisive respect. Hence he could not take that thought seriously, for to take a thought seriously means to regard it as possible that the thought in question is true. He therefore lacked the incentive for re-enacting the thought of the past: he did not re-enact the thought of the past.

We draw the conclusion that in order to understand the thought of the past, one must doubt the view which is at the bottom of scientific history. One must doubt the principle which is characteristic of "the mind of the present day." One [576] must abandon the attempt to understand the past from the point of view of the present. One must take seriously the thought of the past, or one must be prepared to regard it as possible that the thought of the past is superior to the thought of the present day in the decisive respect. One must regard it as possible that we live in an age which is inferior to the past in the decisive respect, or that we live in an age of decline or decay. One must be swayed by a sincere longing for the past.

Collingwood had to face this necessity when he had to speak of Romanticism. According to him, Romanticism is in danger of developing into "a futile nostalgia for the past," but "that development was checked by the presence in Romanticism of...the conception of history as a progress" (87). This remark lacks precision. Its deficiency is partly due to

CHAPTER 10

Collingwood's insufficient familiarity with the German intellectual movement around the year 1800. For instance in his statement on Friedrich Schiller (104–105), he limited himself to a survey of Schiller's lecture on the value of universal history without taking any notice of Schiller's essay on naïve and sentimental poetry. Similarly he asserted that "Hegel wrote the first sketch of his philosophy of history in the Heidelberg *Encyclopædia*" (111). The romantic soul, we prefer to say, is characterized by longing, by "futile" longing, by a longing which is felt to be superior to any fulfillment that is possible "now," i.e., in post-revolutionary Europe. A perfect expression of Romanticism is *Madame Bovary*: the dead Emma, who, in spite of, or because of, the fact that she had an "esprit positif," had spent her life in a longing that led to nothing but failure and degradation, is more alive than the contemporary representatives of the ancient faith and the modern faith who, with the corpse of Emma between them, engage in a noisy disputation, i.e., share between themselves the rule over the nineteenth century. True Romanticism regards the highest possibility of the nineteenth or twentieth century, "futile" longing, as the highest possibility of man, in so far as it assumes that the noble fulfillments of the past were based on delusions which are now irrevocably dispelled. True Romanticism believes that while the past was superior to the present as regards "life" or "culture" or "art" or "religion" or the [577] nearness of God or gods, the present is superior to the past as regards the understanding of "life" or "culture," etc. It believes therefore that the present is superior to the past in regard to knowledge of the decisive truth, i.e., in the decisive respect. It therefore never submits its notions of "life" or "culture" or "art" or "religion" to a criticism which is enlightened by what the assumed models of "life" or "culture," etc., explicitly thought about these themes. Hence Romanticism perpetuates the belief in the superiority of modern thought to earlier thought, and Romantic history of thought is fundamentally as inadequate, or as "un-historical," as non-romantic, progressivist history of thought.

Collingwood believed that "in history as it actually happens there are no mere phenomena of decay: every decline is also a rise" (164). This sanguine statement cannot be reconciled with his remark that if we abandoned scientific history, "we should be exemplifying and hastening that downfall of civilization which some historians are, perhaps prematurely, proclaiming" (56). Here Collingwood admitted that a decline which is not "also a rise" is possible. Yet this momentary insight did not bear fruit in his understanding of earlier thought. He blamed Tacitus for representing history "as essentially a clash of characters, exaggeratedly good and exaggeratedly bad," and he blamed the philosophies of Tacitus' age as "defeatist philosophies which, starting from the assumption that the good man cannot conquer or control the wicked world, taught him how to preserve himself unspotted from its wickedness" (39–40). Since Collingwood dogmatically excluded the possibility of unqualified decay, he could not imagine that there might be ages in which virtuous political action is impossible, and "defeatist" withdrawal is the only sane course of action; he could not consider the possibility that such ages may allow of an excess in wickedness in tyrannical rulers, and of a heroic virtue in their victims, for which there are no parallels in happier epochs. His "historical consciousness" or historical imagination did not leave room for the possibility which Tacitus assumes to have been a fact. His historical consciousness could not be broadened by a study of Tacitus because scientific history recognizes no authority, but [578] is master in its own house: it is not guided by a presumption in favor of the judgments which the wise men of old passed on their own times.

Collingwood was forced to admit the possibility of decline when he discussed the conditions under which progress is possible. For to admit that progress is possible and not necessary means to admit the possibility of decline. But it is precisely his discussion of the conditions of progress which shows how largely he remained under the spell of the belief in necessary progress or how far he was from understanding the function of historical knowledge. Progress, he said, "happens only in one way: by the retention in the mind, at one phase, of what was achieved in the preceding phase" (333). The retention of earlier achievements is "historical knowledge" (326). It is therefore "only through historical knowledge that [progress] comes about at all" (333). Collingwood assumed that "what was achieved in the preceding phase" has merely to be retained; he did not consider the possibility that it may have to be recovered because it had been forgotten. Accordingly, he identified historical knowledge, not with the recovery of earlier achievements, but with their retention: he uses Aristotle's knowledge of Plato's philosophy, and Einstein's knowledge of Newtonian physics, as examples of historical knowledge (333–34). He further assumed that progress requires the integration of earlier achievements into a framework supplied by the later achievement. He did not consider the possibility that progress may consist in separating recent achievements from their present framework and integrating them into an earlier framework which must be recovered by historical knowledge proper. But whatever might be

Chapter 10

true of progress, certainly the awareness of progress requires that the thought of the past be known as it actually was, i.e., as it was actually thought by past thinkers. For, if to understand the thought of the past necessarily means to understand it differently from the way the thinkers of the past understood it, one will never be able to compare the thought of the present with the thought of the past: one would merely compare one's own thought with the reflection of one's own thought in ancient materials or with a hybrid begotten by the intercourse of one's own thought [579] with earlier thought. What we might be inclined to regard as decisive insights alien to the thought of the past may in fact be delusions produced by the oblivion of things known to the thinkers of the past. Awareness of progress presupposes the possibility of understanding the thought of the past "as it really has been." It presupposes the possibility of historical objectivity.

Collingwood implicitly denied the possibility of historical objectivity by asserting that criticism of the thought of the past from the point of view of the present is an integral element of understanding the thought of the past (215). The historian is forced to raise "such questions as: Was this or that policy a wise one? Was this or that economic system sound? Was this or that movement in science or art or religion an advance, and if so, why?" (132). Such questions cannot be answered except from the standpoint of the historian's time (60, 108). This conclusion depends in the first place on the premise that there are no unchangeable standards for judging human actions or thoughts. But it depends also on the further premise that the historian's primary task is to pass judgment on the past. Yet before one can pass judgment on the wisdom of, for example, a given policy, one must establish the character of that policy. "For example, to reconstruct the history of a political struggle like that between the Roman emperors of the first century and the senatorial opposition, what the historian has to do is to see how the two parties conceived the political situation as it stood, and how they proposed to develop that situation: he must grasp their political ideas both concerning their actual present and concerning their possible future" (115). The primary task of the political historian would then seem to consist in understanding a given situation and given ends as they were understood by those who acted in the situation. The contemporaries of a struggle that is similar to the contest between the Roman emperors and the senatorial opposition have an easier access to that historical phenomenon than have people who lack experience of this particular kind of politics. But this does not make the understanding of the phenomenon in question relative to different situations: the difference in regard to the length and the diffi-[580]culty of the way towards the goal does not affect the goal itself. In addition, "historical imagination" liberates the historian from the limitations caused by the experiences peculiar to his time.

It may be objected that the very selection of the theme implies the inescapable subjective element: the reason for the historian's interest in a given situation is different from the reason for the actors' interest in it. The reason for the historian's interest in a historical phenomenon expresses itself in the questions which he addresses to the phenomenon concerned and hence to his sources, and this question is in principle alien to his sources. "The scientific historian no doubt spends a great deal of time reading... Herodotus, Thucydides, Livy, Tacitus, and so forth..., but he reads them... with a question in his mind, having taken the initiative by deciding for himself what he wants to find out from them... the scientific historian puts them to the torture, twisting a passage ostensibly about something quite different into an answer to the question he has decided to ask" (269–70). There is no doubt that one may use the classical historians as a quarry or as ruins, to supply oneself with materials for erecting the edifice called the economic history of classical antiquity, for example. In doing this one makes the assumption that economic history is a worthwhile enterprise, and this assumption is indeed apparently relative to the preoccupations of the nineteenth and twentieth centuries, and alien to the classical historians. An intelligent or conscientious use of the classical historians for a purpose alien to them requires, however, a clear recognition of the fact that that purpose is alien to them and of the reason for that being so. It therefore requires that the classical historians first be understood on their own terms, i.e., as answering their own questions, and not the questions with which the modern historian tortures them. Collingwood admitted this necessity in his way: "The question [the scientific historian] asks himself is: 'What does this statement mean?' And this is not equivalent to the question 'What did the person who made it mean by it?' although that is doubtless a question that the historian must ask, and must be able to answer" (275). But this admission is much too weak. The answer to the question "What did the person who made the statement mean by it?" must [581] precede the answer to the question "What does this statement mean within the context of my question?" For "the statement" is the statement as meant by the author. Before one can use or criticize a statement, one must understand the statement, i.e., one must understand

CHAPTER 10

it as its author consciously meant it. Different historians may become interested in the same statement for different reasons: that statement does not alter its authentic meaning on account of those differences.

Collingwood severely criticized "the scissors-and-paste historian" who reads the classical historians "in a purely receptive spirit, to find out what they said" and "on the understanding that what they did not tell him in so many words he would never find out from them at all" (269). But he did not realize that both "the scissors-and-paste historian" and the scientific historian make the same mistake: they use the classical historians for a purpose alien to the latter before having done justice to the purpose of the classical historians. And both make this identical mistake for the same reason: they take "history" for granted. Whatever may be the standpoint or the direction of interest or the guiding question of the present day historian, he cannot use his sources properly if he does not, to begin with, rigorously subordinate his question to the question which the author of his sources meant to answer, or if he does not, to begin with, identify his question with the question consciously raised by the author whose work he intends to use. The guiding question of the historian who wants to use Herodotus, for example, must become, for some considerable time, the question as to what question was uppermost in Herodotus' mind, i.e., the question of what was the conscious intention of Herodotus, or the question regarding the perspective in which Herodotus looked at things. And the question regarding Herodotus' guiding intention, as well as the answer to it, is in no way affected by the diversity of questions with which modern historians approach Herodotus. In attempting to answer the question regarding Herodotus' intention, one must not even assume that Herodotus was a "historian." For in making this assumption one is likely to imply that he was not a "philosopher" and thus to exclude without examination the possibility that Herodotus' intention [582] cannot be understood without a complete revision of our "categories." Collingwood did not merely fail duly to appreciate the fact that the historian must provisionally subordinate his own question to the questions which the authors of his sources meant to answer. He likewise failed to consider the possibility that the historian may eventually have to retract his own question in favor of the questions raised by the authors of his sources.

Yet while the critical function of the historian may not become noticeable most of the time, or ever, the historian is, nevertheless, necessarily a critic. He selects a theme which he believes to be worthwhile: the critical judgment that the theme is worthwhile precedes the interpretation. He provisionally subordinates his question to the question guiding his author:

eventually the historian's own question re-asserts itself. Nor is the interpretation proper—the activity which follows the reasoned selection of the theme and which is coextensive with the subordination of the historian's question to the question guiding his author—separable from criticism. As Collingwood put it, it is a "self-contradictory task of discovering (for example) 'What Plato thought' without inquiring 'Whether it is true'" (300). One cannot understand a chain of reasoning without "re-enacting" it, and this means without examining whether or not it is valid. One cannot understand premises without understanding them as premises, i.e., without raising the question whether they are evident or intrinsically necessary. For if they are not evident, one must look for the supporting reasoning. The supporting reasoning, a crucial part of the teaching of the author as the author understood it, might easily pass unnoticed if one failed to look for it, and one is not likely to look for it unless one is prompted to do so by a realization of the inevident character of the premises concerned. Therefore the establishment of the fact (if it is a fact) that an author makes a dogmatic assumption may be said to be inseparable from the interpretation of the author in question.

But the fact that the historian is necessarily a critic does not mean, of course, that his criticism necessarily culminates in partial or total rejection; it may very well culminate in total acceptance of the criticized view. Still less does it mean that [583] the historian necessarily criticizes the thought of the past from the point of view of present day thought. By the very fact that he seriously attempts to understand the thought of the past, he leaves the present. He embarks on a journey whose end is hidden from him. He is not likely to return to the shores of his time as exactly the same man who departed from them. His criticism may very well amount to a criticism of present day thought from the point of view of the thought of the past.

The fact that interpretation and criticism are in one sense inseparable does not mean that they are identical. The meaning of the question "What did Plato think?" is different from the meaning of the question "Whether that thought is true." The former question must ultimately be answered by a reference to texts. The latter question cannot possibly be settled by reference to texts. Every criticism of a Platonic contention implies a distinction between the Platonic contention, which must be understood as such, and the criticism of that contention. But interpretation and criticism are not only distinguishable from each other. To a certain extent they are even separable from each other. Plato's thought claims to be an imitation of the whole; as such it is itself a whole which is distinguished from the

Chapter 10

whole simply. It is impossible to understand the imitation without looking at the original. But it is possible to look at the original in compliance, or without compliance, with the directives supplied by the imitation. To look at the original in compliance with the directives supplied by the imitation means to try to understand the whole as Plato understood it. To understand the whole as Plato understood it is the goal of the interpretation of Plato's work. This goal is the standard which we presuppose, and to which we ultimately refer, whenever we find someone's interpretation of Platonic doctrine defective: we cannot find an interpretation defective without having "seen" that goal. The attempt to understand Plato's thought as Plato understood it is inseparable from criticism, but that criticism is in the service of the striven-for understanding of Plato's thought. History as history, as quest for the understanding of the past, necessarily presupposes that our understanding of the past is incomplete. The criticism which is inseparable from interpretation is fundamentally dif-[584]ferent from the criticism which would coincide with the completed understanding. If we call "interpretation" that understanding or criticism which remains within the limits of Plato's own directives, and if we call "criticism" that understanding or criticism which disregards Plato's directives, we may say that interpretation necessarily precedes criticism because the quest for understanding necessarily precedes completed understanding and therewith the judgment which coincides with the completed understanding. The historian who has no illusions about the difference of rank between himself and Plato will be very skeptical in regard to the possibility of his ever reaching adequate understanding of Plato's thought. But what is impossible for most men is not therefore intrinsically impossible. If one denies the legitimacy of the goal which we called adequate understanding of Plato's thought, i.e., if one denies the possibility of historical objectivity, one merely substitutes a spurious right of subjectivity and of arbitrary assertions for the honest confession that we are ignorant of the most important facts of the human past.

It is then indeed a "self-contradictory task of discovering 'What Plato thought' without inquiring 'Whether it is true.'" It is indeed impossible to understand a line of Plato if one is not concerned with what Plato was concerned with, i.e., the truth about the highest things, and hence if one does not inquire whether what Plato thought about them is true. It is indeed impossible to understand what Plato thought without thinking, i.e., without articulating the subjects about which Plato thought. Thinking about Plato's subjects cannot be limited by what Plato said or thought. It must take into consideration everything relevant, regardless of whether

Plato seems to have considered it or not. That is to say, trying to understand Plato requires remaining loyal to Plato's guiding intention; and remaining loyal to Plato's intention means to forget about Plato and to be concerned exclusively with the highest things. But Collingwood assumed that we must not forget about Plato in spite, or rather because, of the fact that we must aim at no other end than the truth regarding the highest things. This assumption is legitimate and is not defeated by its consequences, if it means that we may have to learn something [585] from Plato about the highest things which we are not likely to learn without his guidance, i.e., that we must regard Plato as a possible authority. But to regard Plato as a possible authority means to regard him for the time being as an actual authority. We must, indeed, ourselves articulate the subjects about which Plato thought, but in doing this we must follow Plato's indications as to the manner in which these subjects should be articulated. If Plato took something for granted which we are in the habit of doubting or even of denying, or if he did not push the analysis of a given subject beyond a certain point, we must regard it as possible that he had good reasons for stopping where he stopped. If it is necessary to understand Plato's thought, it is necessary to understand it as Plato himself understood it, and therefore it is necessary to stop where he stopped and to look around: perhaps we shall gradually understand his reasons for stopping. As long as we have not understood Plato's thought, we are in no position to say "Whether it is true." The "historian of philosophy" is a man who knows that he has not yet understood Plato's thought and who is seriously concerned with understanding Plato's thought because he suspects that he may have to learn from Plato something of utmost importance. It is for this reason that Plato's thought cannot become an object, or a spectacle, for the historian. It is to be feared that Collingwood underestimated the difficulty of finding out "What Plato meant by his statements" or "Whether what he thought is true."

History, i.e., concern with the thought of the past as thought of the past, takes on philosophic significance if there are good reasons for believing that we can learn something of utmost importance from the thought of the past which we cannot learn from our contemporaries. History takes on philosophic significance for men living in an age of intellectual decline. Studying the thinkers of the past becomes essential for men living in an age of intellectual decline because it is the only practicable way in which they can recover a proper understanding of the fundamental problems. Given such conditions, history has the further task of explaining why the

Chapter 10

proper understanding of the fundamental problems has become lost in [586] such a manner that the loss presents itself at the outset as a progress. If it is true that loss of understanding of the fundamental problems culminates in the historicization of philosophy or in historicism, the second function of history consists in making intelligible the modern notion of "History" through the understanding of its genesis. Historicism sanctions the loss, or the oblivion, of the natural horizon of human thought by denying the permanence of the fundamental problems. It is the existence of that natural horizon which makes possible "objectivity" and therefore in particular "historical objectivity."

11

On Walker's Machiavelli (1953)

The Discourses of Niccolò Machiavelli, Translated from the Italian with an Introduction and Notes by Leslie J. Walker, S.J. Yale University Press, 1950. 2 vols. 585 & 390 pp. $15.00.

[437] Walker prefaces his translation of the *Discorsi* with a long introduction in which he sets forth his interpretation as well as his criticism of Machiavelli's views. He regards it as possible that Machiavelli was "the most influential of writers on politics that the world has thus far seen" (6). He is certain that Machiavelli's originality consists partly, if not primarily, in the discovery of a new method (80–82). The purpose of the new method is to discover "empirical laws" which express relations "between causes and effects, i.e., between human actions and their consequences, harmful and beneficial" (2, 63, 69). Accordingly, the new method leads up to "generalizations and maxims" which "are always teleological": ends are presupposed. This does not mean that Machiavelli presupposes, i.e., accepts, any ends: he advises politicians "what to do in order to realize their aims, be they what they may." "He advises all and sundry because he desires to convince his readers that his new method is universal in its applicability" (72–73, 69, 118). This amounts to saying that Machiavelli's new method is not merely a part of his epoch-making achievement but its core. The method which Machiavelli invented is "the inductive method." Machiavelli used it long before Bacon "philosophized" about it (92). That method as practiced by Machiavelli consists in proving a general proposition regarding causes and desirable or undesirable effects by reference to a judicious "collection of examples all bearing on the same point" (85, 82–83). "The standpoint

---

Originally published in *Review of Metaphysics* 6, no. 3 (Mar. 1953): 437–46. —Eds.

CHAPTER 11

which is basic to this method" is then "the standpoint of expediency" as distinguished from "the standpoint of morality" (8).

Walker feels that his contention regarding the novelty of Machiavelli's method is in need of proof. He asserts that "the practice of considering negative instances was far more [438] extensively used by St. Thomas Aquinas than it was by Machiavelli, who is but a tyro in this respect." "But neither St. Thomas nor any other mediaeval thinker...[proves his] theorems by citing similar instances taken from ancient and contemporary history," to say nothing of other differences between their procedure and that of Machiavelli (84). Walker admits that "there are...similarities in method, some of them quite striking," between Machiavelli and Aristotle. But "there are also marked differences." "Aristotle's *Politics* contains at least as many, if not more, precepts or maxims than the *Discourses* of Machiavelli, but rarely does Aristotle cite even a single historical example to show that in practice they would work, whereas Machiavelli invariably cites several..." Furthermore, Machiavelli's method, in contradistinction to Aristotle's, is "essentially historical." It was "to his reading of ancient historians," and apparently not to his study of Aristotle, that "Machia-velli's interest in history and his realization of its significance to the politician was undoubtedly due" (86–89). It would then seem that the new method emerged by virtue of a synthesis between Aristotle's political philosophy and "history," i.e., coherent records of past events.

Walker does not set forth very clearly what he understands by "the standpoint of expediency." When he speaks of Machiavelli's method, he gives the impression that, from the standpoint of expediency, one considers the suitability of means to any presupposed ends, without being able or willing to distinguish between good and bad ends. But in other places Walker admits that, at least in the *Discorsi*, Machiavelli does distinguish between good and bad ends (119). In accordance with this strand of his interpretation, Walker disagrees with those who hold that "what Machiavelli calls *virtù*... is technique pure and simple": *virtù* has normally the same meaning as *virtus* in Livy and connotes in particular "devotion to the common good." Yet "there are difficulties and also some exceptions." Severus, Cesare Borgia and Agathocles are described by Machiavelli as "virtuous," although in these cases "devotion to the common good is definitely excluded" or at least "not relevant" (100–102). The meaning of "expediency" would then seem to remain obscure. However this may be, it is perfectly clear that according to Machiavelli "in the sphere [439] of politics" certainly "a good end justifies what is morally wrong" (120–121, 103).

Especially interesting is what Walker has to say about Machiavelli's attitude towards religion. He admits that Machiavelli had a greater admiration for the religion of the Romans than for Christianity, nay, that he was "an out-and-out pagan" or that his "writings are thoroughly pagan from start to finish." Yet he also says in the same context that Machiavelli did not reject "any" Christian doctrine. He speaks of Machiavelli's "frank recognition in *Principe*, Ch. 11 ["Of ecclesiastical principalities"] that providence watches not merely over the Church but over the temporal estates of the Pope." Accordingly, he sees "no reason to suppose that his paganism ever led him to repudiate the Church in his heart of hearts" (117; cf. 3, 7). Walker attaches decisive importance to *Principe*, Ch. 11. It is in the light of this chapter that he understands the passages in which Machiavelli speaks about fortune and its "purposiveness": Fortuna is God. Machiavelli "has been frequently accused of being an atheist, but I find no evidence of atheism either in the *Discourses* or in *The Prince*." In support of his contention he quotes this statement of Burckhardt about the humanists: "They easily got the name of atheists if they showed themselves indifferent to religion and spoke freely against the Church; but not one of them ever professed, or *dared to profess*, a formal, philosophical atheism" (78–80; my italics). From all this one could easily derive the following suspicion: in order to know what Machiavelli thought about the truth of religion, one need only know whether the teaching of the *Principe* concerning ecclesiastical principalities was meant seriously or jocularly.

Walker is very far from approving all that Machiavelli says in the *Discorsi*. He begins "by stating plainly" that he rejects "the famous principle that the end justifies the means" "root and branch, and regards it, together with its corollaries, as most pernicious" (2). Yet he believes that it is only fair to criticize Machiavelli, not "from the standpoint of morality," but "from the standpoint of expediency" "because he himself appeals to expediency and it is the only criterion which his method allows him to use" (8). More than that: the novel [440] question which Machiavelli addresses to political things—the question regarding the consequences, as distinguished from the moral worth, of political conduct and political institutions, or the question regarding the political consequences of moral conduct—"is extremely interesting and of the utmost importance." The criticism of Machiavelli should therefore limit itself to an examination of his answer, that answer being that moral conduct sometimes leads to political ruin (84, 104). Accordingly Walker tries to prove that immoral conduct never leads to political advantage (104–114).

Chapter 11

Walker is not the first to contend that Machiavelli's achievement consists chiefly or exclusively in the discovery of a new method. In fact, it would appear that the view about Machiavelli which predominates today is a vague compromise between the view which Walker adopts and the historicist interpretation of Machiavelli's thought which Walker rejects. At any rate, these two interpretations—the interpretation of Machiavelli as a "scientist" and the historicist interpretation—constitute today the most massive obstacles to an understanding of his thought. Walker himself writes that "Machiavelli says expressly very little" about method (135). On the basis of the evidence adduced by Walker, it would be more accurate to say that Machiavelli says nothing about method. The only passage quoted by Walker which might be thought to refer to a new method is a statement in the Preface to Book I of the *Discorsi* which our translator renders as follows: "I have decided to enter upon a new way; as yet untrodden by anyone else," and which he interprets to mean "a new way and a new method" (82). But the "way" which Machiavelli has decided to take is as little a "method" as was the way on which Columbus embarked in search of unknown seas and lands. Machiavelli set out to discover, not "new ways and methods," as Walker translates, but *modi ed ordini nuovi*. *Modus et ordo* is the Latin translation of Aristotle's *taxis* (cf. Thomas on *Politics*, 1289a2–6, liber IV., lectio I). Machiavelli then sets out to discover, not a new method of studying political things, but new political "arrangements" in regard to both structures and policies. Walker will perhaps urge the irrelevancy of Machiavelli's saying nothing or next to nothing about his method, and the novelty of his method, on the [441] ground that Machiavelli was not a philosopher (93). I have no legitimate means of knowing what Walker understands by a philosopher. But he will certainly admit that Machiavelli was a man who must be assumed to have known what he was doing.

But is it not true that Machiavelli, in contradistinction to Aristotle in particular, invariably cites several examples in order to show the result of adopting or not adopting the institutions or policies which he recommends? The way, as yet untrodden by anyone else, upon which Machiavelli enters, leads to the discovery that the institutions and policies of classical antiquity can be and ought to be imitated by modern man: the purpose of the *Discorsi* as a whole is to liberate men from the error of believing that the institutions and policies of classical antiquity cannot be imitated and ought not to be imitated by modern man. Accordingly, Machiavelli is compelled to show in each case that a given institution or policy of the ancients was good (and therefore ought to be imitated), that its modern equivalent is bad, and that sometimes a modern state or individual did act as the ancients did (and therefore that the ancient practice can be imitated by modern man). Machiavelli does not prove these three points explicitly in every case by citing at least one example for each, one of the reasons being that he was not a pedant. At any rate, he is forced to "cite invariably several examples," not because he deviates from the ancients, and especially from Aristotle, but because he is forced to combat a prejudice which did not hamper the ancients. Furthermore, Machiavelli states explicitly that the discovery of new modes and orders (even if they are only relatively new) is "dangerous" (*Discorsi*, I, beginning). It is less dangerous to state novel teachings by telling stories—and citing examples means telling stories—which instruct silently, than by stating them in the form of "maxims or generalizations." One must therefore investigate whether the examples cited by Machiavelli do not convey something beyond the maxim which they are said to prove.

In *Discorsi* III, 18, Machiavelli discusses the difficulty of understanding the enemy's "present and near" actions. He cites four examples. All of them deal with cases where errors in recognizing the enemy's "present and near" actions [442] were committed. There is a strict parallelism of the examples:* twice an ancient example is followed by a modern example. The two last examples deal explicitly with "victories." The ancient "victory" had this character: there had been a drawn battle between the Romans and the Aequi; each army believed that its enemy had won, and each therefore marched home; by accident a Roman centurion learned from certain wounded Aequi that the Aequi had abandoned their camp; he therefore sacked the camp of the Aequi and returned to Rome as a victor. The modern "victory" had this character: an army of the Florentines and an army of the Venetians had been facing one another for several days, neither daring to attack the other; since both armies began to suffer from lack of necessities, each decided to retire; by accident the Florentine captains learned from a woman who, "secure on account of her age and her poverty," wished to see some of her relatives in the Florentine camp, that the Venetians had retired; they therefore changed their plans and wrote to Florence that they had repelled the enemy and won the war. In the ancient example we find a bloody battle, wounded enemy soldiers, and the plundering of the enemy camp. In the modern example, we find

---

*   Here the punctuation was a period in the original. —Eds.

CHAPTER 11

a phony battle, an old and poor woman, and a boastful letter. It might be true that, concerning the difference between ancients and moderns in respect of *virtù*, these examples teach little that is new. But it is of some importance for the understanding of the *Discorsi* to realize that the spirit of comedy, not to say of levity, is not altogether absent from this work whose subject matter would seem to allow of nothing but gravity.

In *Discorsi* III, 48, Machiavelli notes "that the general of an army ought not to rely on an obvious mistake which an enemy is seen to make, for it will *always* be a fraud, since it is not reasonable that men should so lack caution" (Walker's translation; my italics). Immediately after having noted this allegedly universal rule, he cites an example in which an enemy made an obvious mistake without any tincture of fraud. This example forces the reader to reformulate Machiavelli's explicit "generalization or maxim" and to wonder why Machiavelli, while speaking of manifest blunders, himself commits a manifest blunder. For if we must read "between the [443] lines" of Machiavelli's *History of Florence*, as Walker does not hesitate to say (17), it is barely possible that we may have to read "between the lines" of the *Discorsi* as well.

Walker does not give a single valid reason for doubting that Machiavelli's method is identical with the method of Aristotle. By observing that Machiavelli cites examples "invariably" and Aristotle only rarely, one does not prove that Aristotle did not reach his "generalizations and maxims" by starting from examples: the *Politics* all but opens with the expression "we see." Besides, "Machiavelli's interest in history and his realization of its significance to the politician" is in perfect accord with Aristotle's precept and example. When speaking of the ancient historians, Walker mentions Xenophon—rightly in that Xenophon is the author whom Machiavelli quotes more frequently in the *Discorsi* than any other (with the obvious exception of Livy); but wrongly in that Machiavelli quotes only the *Hiero* and the *Education of Cyrus*, i.e., writings which Machiavelli knew to be not historical (cf. *Discorsi* II, 13). It is also necessary to take issue with Walker's assertion that Machiavelli, in contradistinction to Thomas Aquinas, was "but a tyro" as regards "the practice of considering negative instances." *Discorsi* II, 12 proves sufficiently that Machiavelli had mastered perfectly the art of scholastic disputation and that he could have written the whole work in the form of *quaestiones disputatae* if he had desired to do so. This is not to deny that the chapter in question is a parody of scholastic disputations: the central "authority" for the superior view are "poetic fables."

As regards Machiavelli's view of morality and religion, I must confine myself here to two remarks. It is misleading to say, as Walker does, that *virtù* "has normally no ethical significance" (100), since "normally" is not clearly defined, and might very likely be understood to mean a statistical average. It is much better to say that Machiavelli sometimes understands by *virtù* what everyone understands by "virtue," i.e., moral virtue; that he sometimes understands by *virtù* merely political virtue, the virtue of the citizen, of the statesman or of the public-spirited founder; and that he sometimes understands by *virtù* merely manliness and shrewdness combined ("virtue" as Callicles understood it). In a word, *virtù* is for [444] Machiavelli a term of deliberate ambiguity: Machiavelli cannot criticize moral virtue (i.e., its inherent claim to be the norm of political life) except by reminding the reader of moral virtue. He first criticizes moral virtue in the name of political virtue, and thereafter he criticizes political virtue in the name of "Calliclean" virtue. Since political virtue is closer to the root, to "Calliclean" virtue, than is moral virtue, it has *verità effettuale*: "political virtue" designates the sum of habits which are required for maintaining a free and glorious society. Only if one has realized the precarious character of political virtue, i.e., the "unnatural" character of a free society, can one devise the proper means for establishing and preserving a free society and the virtue belonging to it. Therefore, one must first descend from political virtue to Calliclean virtue, which may be said to be the only virtue that is natural. Machiavelli replaces "the standpoint of morality" by what is very inadequately called "the standpoint of expediency," not because he is thrilled by the promises of a new method, but because he believes he has discovered that the generally accepted view of morality arises through the oblivion of the social function of morality: men falsely, but necessarily, understand as categorically and universally valid certain rules of conduct which are valid (i.e., reasonable) only conditionally and in most cases (cf. Marsilius, *Defensor Pacis* II c.12 sect. 7–8). Walker believes he has detected a contradiction in what Machiavelli says about religion. "In *Discorsi* I, 11 he cynically remarks that people, who were neither ignorant nor rude, were persuaded by Friar Girolamo Savonarola that he had conversed with God, though no one had ever seen him do anything out of the common. This on the principles laid down earlier in the chapter should be accounted a virtue, but in Savonarola it is apparently a fault" (18–19). The difficulty disappears immediately if one contrasts Savonarola's attitude toward divine guidance with the attitude of Papirius (*ibid.*, I, 14).

Chapter 11

Perhaps the least defensible part of Walker's Introduction is his attempt to refute Machiavelli's view from "the standpoint of expediency." I must limit myself to the discussion of one or two characteristic examples. Machiavelli "recommends that in a conquered province a ruler should emulate Philip II of Macedon and 'make everything new', i.e., be utterly [445] and unrestrainedly ruthless in eradicating opposition." To this Walker objects, "What of Machiavelli's basic and thoroughly sound principle that no government can be secure unless it has the good will of the governed?" I fear that Machiavelli would not regard this as a solid objection. He would probably make the following counter objections. A government does not have to fear the ill will of the dead. A ruler does not lose the goodwill of his subjects if he enriches them at the expense of foreigners and possibly by enslaving or eradicating those foreigners. Machiavelli holds the view that a government cannot be secure unless it has the good will of "the governed," i.e., of the many; but sometimes the many do not mind if the few are eradicated. Eventually Walker grants everything that Machiavelli maintains: "Philip's success was by no means *wholly* due to the brutality which he *sometimes* displayed." For Machiavelli never meant more than just this: that "a broad-minded statesmanship" which is the indispensable condition of success, can "sometimes" not dispense with "brutality" (124–125; my italics).

Machiavelli recommends "killing the sons of Brutus," i.e., "murdering anyone who constitutes a potential danger to a newly established regime." To this Walker objects that, according to Machiavelli himself, "it is impossible to establish a new regime by methods, however brutal, if the people are against it." Walker himself says "if": "the people" are not invariably opposed to brutal methods if those are applied to the few or to foreigners. "... the excessively harsh treatment of political opponents in Florence usually provoked a reaction in favor of the old regime."* Machiavelli does not suggest that one should use the strongest medicine "usually," but only on the rare occasions when it is likely to lead to success. "Hence for his examples Machiavelli has to rely on the remote past, yet even in the remote past the use of such methods was by no means always successful." Machiavelli does not claim that it was always successful. Walker "would almost think" that Machiavelli "has lost his sense of perspective and seems to prefer the methods of barbarism to those of his own more civilized age" (112). I wonder whether, by making a

---

*   Strauss begins the quotation with an ellipsis and initial lowercase "t–."—Eds.

distinction between barbarism and civilization, Walker does not abandon the standpoint of expediency.

[445] If Machiavelli, the originator of a "most pernicious" teaching, was perhaps "the most influential of writers on politics that the world has thus far seen," and if "the world" has not been merely the spectator of Machiavelli's influence, "the world" is susceptible to the influence of Machiavelli. "The world" can be corrupted by Machiavelli because it is, in a sense, "corrupt" or carries within itself the seeds of its corruption. If Machiavelli has been as influential as Walker says that he has been, "the world" would seem to be a good place for the judicious practice of wickedness, or for a way of life which "uses" virtue most of the time and has recourse to vice only in rare, if decisive, moments. And in fact, all moralists who are worth their salt have always felt that pure, intransigent justice is the road to the hemlock, the cross, and the stake, rather than to advantage in this world. "The oppressor's wrong, the proud man's contumely, the law's delay, the insolence of office, and the spurns that patient merit of the unworthy takes," which drove Hamlet to despair, do not appear to have occasioned much concern in Walker. Otherwise, I believe, he would not have entertained the notion that the road of "expediency" always leads to intransigent justice.

As for the translation, Walker has "endeavored to make it as literal as possible" (162). I regret to say that he has not been quite successful. His translation cannot be said to be superior to that of Detmold. The most valuable part of Walker's work are the references to Livy in the Notes, and the Index of the authors mentioned or quoted in the *Discorsi*.

12

The Mutual Influence of Theology and Philosophy (1954)

[126] Western civilization has two roots which are in conflict which each other, the biblical and the Greek-philosophic. No one can be both a philosopher and a theologian or a third which is beyond the conflict between philosophy and theology, or a synthesis of both. For a philosopher there can never be an absolute sacredness of a particular or contingent event, he [125] transcends the dimension of divine codes altogether and embarks on a free quest for principles through reasoning based on sense perception. Whereas the biblical attitude is that one particular code is accepted as truly divine and all other allegedly divine codes are simply denied; this implies a radical rejection of mythology. The biblical solution stands or falls with the belief in God's omnipotence which requires monotheism. The biblical God is known in a humanly relevant sense only by his revelations and the Bible is the account of what God has done and promised. The Greek books of philosophy are the work of definitive authors whereas the Bible is a compilation of sources.

The conflict between the Bible and Greek philosophy is based on the dualism of action and thought. This conflict is the secret of the vitality of the West. The Bible refuses to be integrated into a philosophical framework, just as philosophy refuses to be integrated into a biblical dogma. Philosophy purports to be the right way of life, the philosopher finds his [happiness] in acquiring the highest possible degree of clarity which he can acquire. He sees no necessity whatever to assent to something which

---

Originally published in "English Summaries," *Iyyun: Jerusalem Philosophical Quarterly* 5 (1954): 126–24. (Pages are numbered in dextrosinistral order.) The following corrections have been bracketed: "happiness" for the original "hapiness" (237) and "it" for "its" (238). —Eds.

CHAPTER 12

is not evident to him. It is the quest of knowledge regarding the whole; the right way of life forever remains questionable.

Today there is a disintegration of philosophy and on the other hand there is a negative proof of the inadequacy of any non-believing position. Classical philosophy is said to have been based on the unwarranted belief that the whole is intelligible, but this is a misinterpretation: according to the classical position man has merely an awareness of the whole. However a historical proof of the fact of revelation is impossible, miracles are not demonstrable and the fulfillment of the prophets is open to great difficulties.

The revealed law is supposed to be the best of all laws, it has an excess of reason since it is suprarational. Yet this element can also not be proved and unassisted human reason is ignorant of divine revelation. Nevertheless philosophy demands that revelation should establish its claim before the tribunal of human reason, whereas revelation as such refuses to acknowledge that tribunal. Philosophy is victorious as long as it limits itself to repelling the attack which theologians make on it. But philosophy in its turn suffers defeat as soon as [it] starts on an offensive of its own and tries to refute not the necessarily inadequate proofs of revelation but revelation itself. Modern science and historical criticism have not even refuted the most fundamentalistic orthodoxy. Their attack on revelation is based on [124] the dogmatic exclusion of the possibility of miracles and of verbal inspiration. However we have no sufficient knowledge of the nature of God to exclude miracles. The philosophic argument in natural theology is based on an analogy from human perfection, but God's perfection implies that he is incomprehensible. It is true that Spinoza denied the incomprehensibility of God and therefore held miracles to be impossible. However Spinoza's conception of adequate knowledge of the essence of God is arbitrary, and his account of the whole is not beyond reproach.

The historical refutation of revelation presupposes natural theology and this is not available. Nor has theology ever refuted philosophy. From the point of view of philosophy revelation is only a possibility. Man can live as a philosopher, that is to say, untragically and all alleged refutations of revelation presuppose unbelief in revelation in the same ways as all alleged refutations of philosophy presuppose already faith in revelation. There seems to be no ground common and therefore superior to both.

Philosophy should admit the possibility of revelation and in this case its choice is based on faith. The quest for evident knowledge rests itself on an unevident premise which in turn constitutes the value problem.

13

What Is Political Philosophy? (1955)

I

[124] Political philosophy is the attempt to replace opinions about the political fundamentals—the nature of political things and the right or good political order—by knowledge of them. Political philosophy is therefore to be distinguished from political thought in general. All political philosophy is political thought but not all political thought is political philosophy. Political thought is as such indifferent to the distinction between opinion and knowledge; but it is essential to political philosophy to be set in motion and to be kept in motion by the disquieting awareness of the fundamental difference between conviction or belief and knowledge. Political thought is as old as the human race; but political philosophy appeared at a knowable time in the recorded past. It is advisable to distinguish political philosophy also from political theory; for by political theory people understand today frequently comprehensive reflections on the political situation of the time which [led] up to the suggestion of a broad policy; in such reflections the question regarding the political fundamentals is not necessarily raised. Furthermore political philosophy is to be distinguished from political theology, i.e., political teachings which are based on divine revelation. As regards social philosophy, it has the same subject matter as political philosophy but it regards it from a different point of view. Political philosophy rests on the premise that the political association—one's country or

---

Originally published in "English Summaries," *Iyyun: Jerusalem Philosophical Quarterly* 6 (1955): 124–19. (Pages are numbered in dextrosinistral order.) The following corrections have been bracketed: "led" for the original "lead" (239); placement of semicolon outside of "the good" (242); and "haphazardly" for "haphazzardly" (243). —Eds.

CHAPTER 13

one's nation—is the most comprehensive or the most authoritative association, whereas social philosophy conceives of the political association as a part of a larger whole which it calls "society." The relation of political philosophy to political science is ambiguous because of the ambiguity of the term "political science." That term designates on the one hand such investigations of political things as are guided by the model of the natural [123] sciences, and on the other hand the work which is actually being done by the members of political science departments. "Scientific" political science is in fact incompatible with political philosophy; from the point of view of "scientific" political science, political philosophy represents a wholly discredited and decrepit tradition which issued in nothing except in vague and inane speculations. On the other hand the useful work done by members of political science departments is not only compatible with political philosophy but points to political philosophy as its necessary supplement. Political philosophy is necessarily preceded by knowledge of political things or by political knowledge. If not the highest, at any rate the most elaborate form of political knowledge is that which is pursued by members of political science departments. This form of political knowledge has become indispensable with the emergence of "dynamic mass societies," i.e., societies which are characterized by both immense complexity and rapid change. Political knowledge of every form and of every level rests on assumptions concerning the nature of political things. It is the function of political philosophy to subject these assumptions to critical and coherent analysis. Political philosophy as we have tried to circumscribe it, has been cultivated since its beginning almost without any interruption until a relatively short time ago. Today it is in a state of decay and perhaps of putrefaction. If we inquire into the reasons for this great change, we receive these answers: political philosophy is unscientific, or it is unhistorical. Science and History, these two great powers of the modern world, have eventually succeeded in making questionable the very possibility of political philosophy. The rejection of political philosophy as unscientific is characteristic of present day positivism. According to this positivism, only factual judgments as distinguished from value judgments are within the competence of reason. Social science positivism is exposed to the following objections: (1) It is impossible to study all important social phenomena without making value judgments. (2) It has never been proven, it has merely been asserted, that conflicts between different values or value systems are essentially insoluble for human reason. (3) It is not true that scientific knowledge is the only solid knowledge which men possess.

(4) Positivism necessarily transforms itself into historicism. Historicism rejects the question of *the* good society, i.e., the question with which political philosophy stands or falls, with a view to the essentially historical character of [122] society and of human thought. It is distinguished from positivism because it abandons the distinction between facts and values: every understanding implies specific evaluations. The crucial issue between political philosophy and historicism concerns the status of those permanent characters of humanity, such as the distinction between the noble and the base, which are in fact admitted by the intelligent historicist: can these permanencies be used as criteria for judging of the worth of different historical standards? Are they not superior in dignity to the differing historical standards?

II

The character of classical political philosophy appears with the greatest clarity from Plato's *Laws*, which is his political work par excellence. The dialogue opens with the contention that the Cretan and Spartan codes are the work of gods. It leads up in a number of well chosen steps to the view that neither the Dorian codes nor any other code can be the work of a god: the cause of any code must be human beings, the human legislator, the *politeia*, or the regime. Therefore the theme of political philosophy has to be the regime rather than the laws. Both the manner in which the ascent from divine codes to human regimes takes place and the explicit subject of the first sixth of the *Laws* draw our attention to the crucial importance of the virtue of moderation. Moderation is exercised to an eminent degree by the chief interlocutor, a philosopher. Moderation is not a virtue of thought; Plato likens philosophy to madness, the very opposite of sobriety or moderation. But moderation is the virtue controlling philosophic speech. Moderation establishes a harmony between the virtue of the perfect human being (knowledge) and the virtue of the perfect citizen (full loyalty to the established regime). A regime is the order or the form which gives society its character. A regime is therefore a specific manner of life. It is the form of life as living together, the manner of living of society and in society. This manner depends decisively on the predominance of human beings of a certain type, on the manifest domination of society by human beings of a certain type. A regime means that whole which we today are in the habit of viewing in a fragmentized form: regime means simultaneously the form of life of a society, its style, its moral taste, form of society, form of state, form of government, spirit of laws. We may try to

Chapter 13

articulate the simple and unitary thought that expresses itself in the term *Politeia* as [121] follows. Life is an activity which is directed toward some goal; social life is an activity which is directed toward such a goal as can be pursued only by society; but in order to pursue a specific goal as its comprehensive goal, society must be organized, ordered, constructed, constituted, in a manner which is in accordance with that goal; this however means that the authoritative part of society must be akin to that goal. There is a variety of regimes, and their claims necessarily conflict with each other. Thus the character of political life itself causes us to wonder which of the given conflicting regimes is better and ultimately, which regime is the best regime. The question of the best regime guides the reflections of the classical political philosophers. The practical meaning of this question appears most clearly when one considers the ambiguity of the term "good citizen" as used by Aristotle. According to one meaning, the good citizen is a man who serves his country well regardless of the difference of regimes; i.e., the good citizen is the patriot whose loyalty belongs first and last in all circumstances to his fatherland. According to another meaning, "good citizen" is essentially relative to the regime; the good citizen is identical with the good human being only in the case of the good citizen of the best regime. The root of this ambiguity is the fundamental difference between "one's own" and "the good"[;] this relation finds its political expression in the relation between the fatherland and the regime. Today classical political philosophy is frequently attacked on these two grounds: (1) it is said to be undemocratic; (2) it is said to be based on an obsolete cosmology. As regards the first ground, one has to consider the fact that modern democracy is fundamentally different from the democracy which Plato and Aristotle had in mind. Modern democracy is based on the emancipation of technology as well as on universal education. These presuppositions of modern democracy have led to well known difficulties which endanger modern democracy itself. They can be overcome only by a return to the classical notion of both technology and education. As regards the second ground, we observe that classical political philosophy was originated by Socrates, the teacher of the knowledge of ignorance.

III

In modern political philosophy one may distinguish three strata or three waves. Modern political philosophy was originated by Machiavelli who [120] opposed the "utopianism" of both traditional political philosophy and traditional political theology. He demanded that the high and lofty standard of politics—virtue—be abandoned in favor of those lower standards on which actual societies act; by lowering the standard one would almost guarantee the success of the scheme elaborated in accordance with the lower standards, or one would conquer chance. The scheme as developed by Machiavelli himself was modelled on the ancient Roman republic but was meant to be an improvement on its model: what the Romans had done [haphazardly] or instinctively, was to be done now, after Machiavelli had understood the reasons for Rome's success, consciously and deliberately. Machiavelli's two great political writings were meant to prepare the gradual emergence of a "realistic" republican life by means of enlightenment. Machiavelli is the first philosopher who consciously attempted to control the future by embarking on a campaign of propaganda. He achieved his greatest success through a transformation of his scheme—a transformation which was inspired by his own principle and which was effected in the first place by Hobbes and secondarily by Locke; not the promotion of virtue but the satisfaction of the elementary wants or the safeguarding of the elementary rights ought to be the purpose of civil society. Economism is Machiavellianism which has come of age. This serpentine wisdom, this degradation of man, called forth Rousseau's passionate protest. With Rousseau there begins the second wave of modernity, the wave which bore both German idealistic philosophy and romanticism. In this stage the attempt was made to restore the high level of classical political philosophy while one preserved what one still regarded as important achievements of the first wave of modernity. Hence the return to Platonic or Aristotelian notions was only the initial step of a movement which led to a much more radical form of modernity, to a form of modernity which was still more alien to classical thought than the thought of the Enlightenment had been. Virtue gave way eventually to Freedom and Individuality; and the attempt to conquer chance culminated in the emergence of philosophy of History: the same "realistic" tendency which had led to the lowering of standards in the first wave, led to Philosophy of History in the second wave. For Philosophy of History was meant to show the necessary coincidence of the Is and the Ought. The third wave of modernity begins with Nietzsche. Nietzsche retained what appeared to him to be the [119] insight acquired by the historical consciousness of the 19th century. But he denied the rational or reasonable character of the historical process. He taught then that all human thought ultimately rests on premises which are not evident and cannot become evident but are im-

Chapter 13

posed on it by a mysterious fate. He tried to articulate this conception through his doctrine of the Will to Power. The difficulty inherent in the philosophy of the Will to Power led after Nietzsche to the explicit renunciation of the very notion of eternity. Modern thought reaches its full self consciousness in explicitly condemning to oblivion the notion of eternity. For oblivion of eternity is the price which modern man had to pay, from the very beginning, for attempting to conquer chance.

14

Social Science and Humanism (1956)

Part 1: *"Leo Strauss: Social Science and Humanism"*

[128] In this paper, humanism is understood in contradistinction to science on the one hand and to civic art on the other. The social sciences especially dwell in the region where science, the civic art and humanism meet. But science and humanism are not always on friendly terms, because the scientific spirit is characterized by detachment and simplification, whereas the spirit of humanism is marked by attachment, breadth and common sense. It becomes thus clear that the spirit of science has severe limitations which can be overcome only by the humanistic approach.

Reconstruction of science requires that the whole be sufficiently grasped in advance, prior to the analysis of specialization. However, the whole, as primarily known, is an object of common sense which expresses itself in common language. In the same way, social science abstracts from essential elements of social reality, because the social scientist has to follow a system of relevances entirely different from that of the citizen. While the social scientist is concerned with regularities of behaviour, the citizen is concerned with good government. The social scientist draws a sharp line between values and facts and regards himself as unable to pass any value judgements. But in order to counteract the dangers inherent in specialization, a conscious return is needed to common sense thinking. We must identify the whole in reference to which we ought to select and

---

Part 1—Originally published in "English Summaries," *Iyyun: Jerusalem Philosophical Quarterly* 7 (1956): 128–27. (Pages are numbered in dextrosinistral order.)

Part 2—Originally published in *The State of the Social Sciences*, ed. Leonard D. White (Chicago: University of Chicago Press, 1956), 415–25. —Eds.

CHAPTER 14

integrate themes of research. The true matrix of social science is the civic art and social science will have to learn to speak the language of the citizen and of the statesman in order to fulfil its proper functions. In this age for instance, liberal democracy will have to be studied in constant regard to its potential alternatives, and especially to communism.

We see therefore that the only alternative to an ever more specialized and aimless social science lies in the pursuit traditionally known as ethics. Social science, being the pursuit of human knowledge, is always a kind [127] of self-knowledge. Humanism implies that the moral principles become more knowable to man as he transcends the horizon of sectionalism and becomes a citizen of the world. But this kind of humanism is not enough. Man, while being at least potentially a whole, can become so only by being a part of a larger whole. The macrocosmos is not human, and therefore man can only be understood in the light of the subhuman. The human meaning of science is that the higher values are understood in the light of the lower. Consequently mere humanism is powerless to withstand the onslaught of modern science.

The author goes then on to criticize the opposite view that the social sciences deal with phenomena which are inaccessible to detached observation. According to this opinion, understanding of social behaviour means the acceptance of the values of the societies or the individuals whom one studies. It follows that all position of this kind are equally true or untrue and cannot be criticized, but merely understood. The fact that we are opposed to cannibalism for instance, is thus due entirely to our historical situation which may and will change. But it remains true that we can nevertheless transcend our historical situation and enter into [an] entirely different perspective.* If we therefore commit ourselves to the values of civilization, our very commitment compels us to take a vigorous stand against the destruction of its values.

To understand genuinely the value system of a given society means being deeply moved by the values to which the society in question is committed. Universal sympathetic understanding is thus impossible, one cannot both enjoy the advantages of universal understanding and those of existentialism. So called sympathetic understanding necessarily ends when rational criticism reveals the untruth of the position which we are attempting to understand sympathetically. The possibility of such rational criticism is necessarily admitted by relativism when it claims to reject ab-

---

* It was necessary to make the bracketed addition. —Eds.

solutism on rational grounds. It appears that the field within which relativism can practise sympathetic understanding is restricted to the community of relativists which are united by identically the same rational insight into the truth of relativism. Relativism, if it were acted upon, would lead to complete chaos, because it appeals to reason in the very act of destroying reason.

Part 2: *"Social Science and Humanism"*

[415] We have been assigned the task of discussing humanism and the social sciences. As appears from our program, humanism is understood in contradistinction to science, on the one hand, and to the civic art, on the other. It is thus suggested to us that the social sciences are shaped by science, the civic art, and humanism, or that the social sciences dwell in the region where science, the civic art, and humanism meet and perhaps toward which they converge. Let us consider how this meeting might be understood.

Of the three elements mentioned, only science and humanism can be said to be at home in academic life. They certainly exhibit one characteristic of academic life. According to an old adage, man is a wolf to man, woman is more wolfish to woman, but a scholar in his relations to scholars is the most wolfish of all. Science and humanism are then not always on friendly terms. We all know the scientist who despises or ignores humanism, and the humanist who despises or ignores science. To understand this conflict, tension, or distinction between science and humanism, we do well to turn for a moment to the seventeenth century, to the age in which modern science constituted itself. At that time Pascal contrasted the spirit of geometry (i.e., the scientific spirit) with the spirit of finesse. We may circumscribe the meaning of the French term by referring to terms such as these: subtlety, refinement, tact, delicacy, perceptivity. The scientific spirit is characterized by detachment and by the forcefulness which stems from simplicity or simplification. The spirit of finesse is characterized by attachment or love and by breadth. The principles to which the scientific spirit defers are alien to common sense. The principles with which the spirit of finesse has to do are within common sense, yet they are barely visible; they are felt rather than seen. They are not available in such a way that we could make them the premises of our reasoning. The spirit of finesse is active [416] not in reasoning but rather in grasping in one view unanalyzed wholes in their distinctive characters. What is meant today by the contrast between science and humanism represents a more

Chapter 14

or less profound modification of Pascal's contrast between the spirit of geometry and the spirit of finesse. In both cases the contrast implies that, in regard to the understanding of human things, the spirit of science has severe limitations—limitations which are overcome by a decidedly non-scientific approach.

What are these limitations as we observe them today within the social sciences? Social science consists of a number of disciplines which are specialized and which are becoming ever more specialized. There is certainly no social science in existence which could claim that it studies society as a whole, social man as a whole, or such wholes as we have in mind when we speak, for example, of this country, the United States of America. De Tocqueville and Lord Bryce are not representative of present-day social science. From time to time one or the other special and specialized science (e.g., psychology or sociology) raises the claim to be comprehensive or fundamental; but these claims always meet strong and justified resistance. Co-operation of the various disciplines may enlarge the horizon of the co-operating individuals; it cannot unify the disciplines themselves; it cannot bring about a true, hierarchic order.

Specialization may be said to originate ultimately in this premise: In order to understand a whole, one must analyze or resolve it into its elements, one must study the elements by themselves, and then one must reconstruct the whole or recompose it by starting from the elements. Reconstruction requires that the whole be sufficiently grasped in advance, prior to the analysis. If the primary grasp lacks definiteness and breadth, both the analysis and the synthesis will be guided by a distorted view of the whole, by a figment of a poor imagination rather than by the thing in its fullness. And the elements at which the analysis arrives will at best be only some of the elements. The sovereign rule of specialization means that the reconstruction cannot even be attempted. The reason for the impossibility of reconstruction can be stated as follows: The whole as primarily known is an object of common sense; but it is of the essence of the scientific spirit, at least as this spirit shows itself within the social sciences, to be distrustful of common sense or even to discard it [417] altogether. The common-sense understanding expresses itself in common language; the scientific social scientist creates or fabricates a special scientific terminology. Thus scientific social science acquires a specific abstractness. There is nothing wrong with abstraction, but there is very much wrong with abstracting from essentials. Social science, to the extent to which it is emphatically scientific, abstracts from essential elements of social reality.

Social Science and Humanism

I quote from a private communication by a philosophically sophisticated sociologist who is very favorably disposed toward the scientific approach in the social sciences: "What the sociologist calls 'system,' 'role,' 'status,' 'role expectation,' 'situation,' and 'institutionalization' is experienced by the individual actor on the social scene in entirely different terms." This is not merely to say that the citizen and the social scientist mean the same things but express them in different terms. For "the social scientist qua theoretician has to follow a system of relevances entirely different from that of the actor on the social scene... His problems originate in his theoretical interest, and many elements of the social world that are scientifically relevant are irrelevant from the point of view of the actor on the social scene, and vice versa." The scientific social scientist is concerned with regularities of behavior; the citizen is concerned with good government. The relevances for the citizen are "values," "values" believed in and cherished, nay, "values" which are experienced as real qualities of real things: of man, of actions and thought, of institutions, of measures. But the scientific social scientist draws a sharp line between values and facts: he regards himself as unable to pass any value judgments.

To counteract the dangers inherent in specialization as far as these dangers can be counteracted within the social sciences, a conscious return to common-sense thinking is needed—a return to the perspective of the citizen. We must identify the whole in reference to which we should select themes of research and integrate results of research, with the over-all objectives of whole societies. By doing this, we will understand social reality as it is understood in social life by thoughtful and broad-minded men. In other words, the true matrix of social science is the Civic Art and not a general notion of science or scientific method. Social science must either be a mere handmaid of the Civic Art—in this case no great harm is done if it [418] forgets the wood for the trees—or, if it does not want to become or to remain oblivious of the noble tradition from which it sprang, if it believes that it might be able to enlighten the Civic Art, it must indeed look farther afield than the Civic Art, but it must look in the same direction as the Civic Art. Its relevances must become identical, at least at the outset, with those of the citizen or statesman; and therefore it must speak, or learn to speak, the language of the citizen and of the statesman.

From this point of view, the guiding theme of social science in this age and in this country will be democracy, or, more precisely, liberal democracy, especially in its American form. Liberal democracy will be studied with constant regard to the co-actual or co-potential alternatives and

Chapter 14

therefore especially to communism. The issue posed by communism will be faced by a conscientious, serious, and relentless critique of communism. At the same time, the dangers inherent in liberal democracy will be set forth squarely; for the friend of liberal democracy is not its flatterer. The sensitivity to these dangers will be sharpened and, if need be, awakened. From the scientistic point of view, the politically neutral—that which is common to all societies—must be looked upon as the clue to the politically relevant—that which is distinctive of the various regimes. But from the opposite point of view which I am trying to adumbrate, the emphasis is put on the politically relevant: the burning issues.

Social science cannot then rest satisfied with the over-all objectives of whole societies as they are for the most part understood in social life. Social science must clarify those objectives, ferret out their self-contradictions and halfheartednesses, and strive for knowledge of the true over-all objectives of whole societies. That is to say, the only alternative to an ever more specialized, an ever more aimless, social science is a social science ruled by the legitimate queen of the social sciences—the pursuit traditionally known by the name of ethics. Even today it is difficult, in dealing with social matters, consistently to avoid terms like "a man of character," "honesty," "loyalty," "citizenship education," etc.

This, or something like this, is, I believe, what many people have in mind when speaking of a humanistic approach, as distinguished from the scientistic approach, to social phenomena. We must still account for the term "humanism." The social scientist is a student of [419] human societies, of societies of humans. If he wishes to be loyal to his task, he must never forget that he is dealing with human things, with human beings. He must reflect on the human as human. And he must pay due attention to the fact that he himself is a human being and that social science is always a kind of self-knowledge. Social science, being the pursuit of human knowledge of human things, includes as its foundation the human knowledge of what constitutes humanity, or, rather, of what makes man complete or whole, so that he is truly human. Aristotle calls his equivalent of what now would be called social science the liberal inquiry regarding the human things, and his *Ethics* is the first, the fundamental, and the directive part of that inquiry.

But, if we understand by social science the knowledge of human things, are we not driven to the conclusion that the time-honored distinction between social science and the humanities must be abandoned? Perhaps we must follow Aristotle a step further and make a distinction between the life of society and the life of the mind, and hence assign the study of the former to social science and the study of the latter, or a certain kind of study of the latter, to the humanities.

I do not have to go into another implication of the term "humanism"—viz., the contradistinction of human studies to divinity, since our program is silent about divinity. I may limit myself to the remark that humanism may be said to imply that the moral principles are more knowable to man, or less controversial among earnest men, than theological principles.

By reflecting on what it means to be a human being, one sharpens his awareness of what is common to all human beings, if in different degrees, and of the goals toward which all human beings are directed by the fact that they are human beings. One transcends the horizon of the mere citizen—of every kind of sectionalism—and becomes a citizen of the world. Humanism as awareness of man's distinctive character as well as of man's distinctive completion, purpose, or duty issues in humaneness: in the earnest concern for both human kindness and the betterment and opening of one's mind—a blend of firm delicacy and hard-won serenity—a last and not merely last freedom from the degradation or hardening effected especially by conceit or pretense. One is tempted to say that to be inhuman is the [420] same as to be unteachable, to be unable or unwilling to listen to other human beings.

Yet, even if all were said that could be said and that cannot be said, humanism is not enough. Man, while being at least potentially a whole, is only a part of a larger whole. While forming a kind of world and even being a kind of world, man is only a little world, a microcosm. The macrocosm, the whole to which man belongs, is not human. That whole, or its origin, is either subhuman or superhuman. Man cannot be understood in his own light but only in the light of either the subhuman or the superhuman. Either man is an accidental product of a blind evolution or else the process leading to man, culminating in man, is directed toward man. Mere humanism avoids this ultimate issue. The human meaning of what we have come to call Science consists precisely in this—that the human or the higher is understood in the light of the subhuman or the lower. Mere humanism is powerless to withstand the onslaught of modern science. It is from this point that we can begin to understand again the original meaning of science, of which the contemporary meaning is only a modification: science as man's attempt to understand the whole to which he belongs. Social science, as the study of things human, cannot be based on modern science, although it may judiciously use, in a strictly subordinate fashion, both methods and results of modern science. Social science

Chapter 14

must rather be taken to contribute to the true universal science into which modern science will have to be integrated eventually.

To summarize: to treat social science in a humanistic spirit means to return from the abstractions or constructs of scientistic social science to social reality, to look at social phenomena primarily in the perspective of the citizen and the statesman, and then in the perspective of the citizen of the world, in the twofold meaning of "world": the whole human race and the all-embracing whole.

Humanism, as I have tried to present it, is in itself a moderate approach. But, looking around me, I find that it is here and now an extreme version of humanism. Some of you might think that it would be more proper on the present occasion to present the median or average opinion of present-day humanistic social scientists rather than an eccentric one. I feel this obligation, but I cannot comply with it because of the elusive character of that median opinion. I [421] shall therefore describe the extreme opposite of the view which appeals to me, or, rather, one particular expression, which is as good as any other, of that opposite extreme. Median social science humanism can be defined sufficiently for our purpose by the remark that it is located somewhere between these two extremes.

The kind of humanism to which I now turn designates itself as relativistic. It may be called a humanism for two reasons. First, it holds that the social sciences cannot be modeled on the natural sciences, because the social sciences deal with man. Second, it is animated, as it were, by nothing except openness for everything that is human. According to this view, the methods of science, of natural science, are adequate to the study of phenomena to which we have access only by observing them from without and in detachment. But the social sciences deal with phenomena whose core is indeed inaccessible to detached observation but discloses itself, at least to some extent, to the scholar who relives or re-enacts the life of the human beings whom he studies or who enters into the perspective of the actors and understands the life of the actors from their own point of view as distinguished from both his point of view and the point of view of the outside observer. Every perspective of active man is constituted by evaluation or is at any rate inseparable from it. Therefore, understanding from within means sharing in the acceptance of the values which are accepted by the societies or the individuals whom one studies, or accepting these values "histrionically" as the true values, or recognizing the position taken by the human beings under consideration as true. If one practices such understanding often and intensively enough, one realizes that perspectives or points of view cannot be criticized. All positions of this kind are equally true or untrue: true from within, untrue from without. Yet, while they cannot be criticized, they can be understood. However, I have as much right to my perspective as anyone else has to his or any society to its. And every perspective being inseparable from evaluation, I, as an acting man and not as a mere social scientist, am compelled to criticize other perspectives and the values on which they are based or which they posit. We do not end then in moral nihilism, for our belief in our values gives us strength and direction. Nor do we end in a state of perpetual war of everybody [422] against everybody, for we are permitted to "trust to reason and the council table for a peaceful coexistence."

Let us briefly examine this position, which at first glance recommends itself because of its apparent generosity and unbounded sympathy for every human position. Against a perhaps outdated version of relativism one might have argued as follows. Let us popularly define nihilism as the inability to take a stand for civilization against cannibalism. The relativist asserts that objectively civilization is not superior to cannibalism, for the case in favor of civilizaton can be matched by an equally strong or an equally weak case in favor of cannibalism.* The fact that we are opposed to cannibalism is due entirely to our historical situation. But historical situations change necessarily into other historical situations. A historical situation productive of the belief in civilization may give way to a historical situation productive of belief in cannibalism. Since the relativist holds that civilization is not intrinsically superior to cannibalism, he will placidly accept the change of civilized society into cannibal society. Yet the relativism which I am now discussing denies that our values are simply determined by our historical situation: we can transcend our historical situation and enter into entirely different perspectives. In other words, there is no reason why, say, an Englishman should not become, in the decisive respect, a Japanese. Therefore, our believing in certain values cannot be traced beyond our decision or commitment. One might even say that, to the extent to which we are still able to reflect on the relation of our values to our situation, we are still trying to shirk the responsibility for our choice. Now, if we commit ourselves to the values of civilization, our very commitment enables and compels us to take a vigorous stand against cannibalism and prevents us from placidly accepting a change of our society in the direction of cannibalism.

---

* Civilization is spelled "civilizaton" in the second occurrence in the sentence. —Eds.

Chapter 14

To stand up for one's commitment means among other things to defend it against its opponents, not only by deed but by speech as well. Speech is required especially for fortifying those who waver in their commitments to the values we cherish. The waverers are not yet decided to which cause they should commit themselves, or they do not know whether they should commit themselves to civilization or to cannibalism. In speaking to them, we cannot assume the validity of the values of civilization. And, according to the premise, there [423] is no way to convince them of the truth of those values. Hence the speech employed for buttressing the cause of civilization will be not rational discourse but mere "propaganda," a "propaganda" confronted by the equally legitimate and perhaps more effective "propaganda" in favor of cannibalism.

This notion of the human situation is said to be arrived at through the practice of sympathetic understanding. Only sympathetic understanding is said to make possible valid criticism of other points of view—a criticism which is based on nothing but our commitment and which therefore does not deny the right of our opponents to their commitments. Only sympathetic understanding, in other words, makes us truly understand the character of values and the manner in which they are legitimately adopted. But what is sympathetic understanding? Is it dependent on our own commitment, or is it independent of it? If it is independent, I am committed as an acting man, and I am uncommitted in another compartment of myself, in my capacity as a social scientist. In that latter capacity I am, so to speak, completely empty and therefore completely open to the perception and appreciation of all commitments or value systems. I go through the process of sympathetic understanding in order to reach clarity about my commitment, and this process in no way endangers my commitment, for only a part of my self is engaged in my sympathetic understanding. This means, however, that such sympathetic understanding is not serious or genuine and is, indeed, as it calls itself, "histrionic." For genuinely to understand the value system, say, of a given society, means being deeply moved and indeed gripped by the values to which the society in question is committed and to expose one's self in earnest, with a view to one's own whole life, to the claim of those values to be the true values. Genuine understanding of other commitments is then not necessarily conducive to the reassertion of one's own initial commitment. Apart from this, it follows from the inevitable distinction between serious understanding and histrionic understanding that only my own commitment, my own "depth," can possibly disclose to me the commitment, the "depth," of other human beings.

Hence my perceptivity is necessarily limited by my commitment. Universal sympathetic understanding is impossible. To speak crudely, one cannot have the cake [424] and eat it; one cannot enjoy both the advantages of universal understanding and those of existentialism.

But perhaps it is wrong to assume that all positions ultimately rest on commitments, or at any rate on commitments to specific points of view. We all remember the time when most men believed explicitly or implicitly that there is one and only one true value system of universal validity, and there are still societies and individuals who cling to this view. They too must be understood sympathetically. Would it not be harsh and even inconsistent to deprive the Bible and Plato of a privilege which is generously accorded to every savage tribe? And will sympathetic understanding of Plato not lead us to admit that absolutism is as true as relativism or that Plato was as justified in simply condemning other value positions as the relativist is in never simply condemning any value position? To this our relativist will reply that, while Plato's value system is as defensible as any other, provided it is taken to have no other support than Plato's commitment, Plato's absolutist interpretation of his value system, as well as any other absolutism, has been refuted unqualifiedly, with finality, absolutely. This means however that Plato's view as he understood it, as it reveals itself to us if we enter sympathetically into his perspective, has been refuted: it has been seen to rest on untrue theoretical premises. So-called sympathetic understanding necessarily and legitimately ends when rational criticism reveals the untruth of the position which we are attempting to understand sympathetically; and the possibility of such rational criticism is necessarily admitted by relativism, since it claims to reject absolutism on rational grounds. The example of Plato is not an isolated one. Where in fact do we find, outside certain circles of present-day Western society, any value position which does not rest on theoretical premises of one kind or another— premises which claim to be simply, absolutely, universally true, and which as such are legitimately exposed to rational criticism? I fear that the field within which relativists can practice sympathetic understanding is restricted to the community of relativists who understand each other with great sympathy because they are united by identically the same fundamental commitment, or rather by identically the same rational insight into the truth of relativism. What claims to be the final [425] triumph over provincialism reveals itself as the most amazing manifestation of provincialism.

There is a remarkable contrast between the apparent humility and the hidden arrogance of relativism. The relativist rejects the absolutism inherent in our great Western tradition—in its belief in the possibility of a rational and universal ethics or of natural right—with indignation or contempt; and he accuses that tradition of provincialism. His heart goes out to the simple preliterate people who cherish their values without raising exorbitant claims on their behalf. But these simple people do not practice histrionic or sympathetic understanding. Lacking such understanding, they do not adopt their values in the only legitimate manner, that is, as supported by nothing except their commitment. They sometimes reject Western values. Therewith they engage in invalid criticism, for valid criticism presupposes histrionic understanding. They are then provincial and narrow, as provincial and narrow as Plato and the Bible. The only people who are not provincial and narrow are the Western relativists and their Westernized followers in other cultures. They alone are right.

It almost goes without saying that relativism, if it were acted upon, would lead to complete chaos. For to say in the same breath that our sole protection against war between societies and within society is reason, and that according to reason "those individuals and societies who find it congenial to their systems of values to oppress and subjugate others" are as right as those who love peace and justice, means to appeal to reason in the very act of destroying reason.

Many humanistic social scientists are aware of the inadequacy of relativism, but they hesitate to turn to what is called "absolutism." They may be said to adhere to a qualified relativism. Whether this qualified relativism has a solid basis appears to me to be the most pressing question for social science today.

15

Letter to the *National Review* (1957)

The State of Israel

For some time I have been receiving *National Review*, and I agree with many articles appearing in the journal. There is, however, one feature of the journal which I completely fail to comprehend. It is incomprehensible to me that the authors who touch on that subject are so unqualifiedly opposed to the State of Israel.

No reasons why that stand is taken are given; mere antipathies are voiced. For I cannot call reasons such arguments as are based on gross factual error, or on complete non-comprehension of the things which matter. I am, therefore, tempted to believe that the authors in question are driven by an anti-Jewish animus; but I have learned to resist temptations. I taught at the Hebrew University in Jerusalem for the whole academic year of 1954–1955, and what I am going to say is based exclusively on what I have seen with my own eyes.

The first thing which strikes one in Israel is that the country is a Western country, which educates its many immigrants from the East in the ways of the West: Israel is the only country which as a country is an outpost of the West in the East. Furthermore, Israel is a country which is surrounded by mortal enemies of overwhelming numerical superiority, and in which a single book absolutely predominates in the instruction given in elementary schools and in high schools: the Hebrew Bible. Whatever the failings of individuals may be, the spirit of the country as a whole can justly be described in these terms: heroic austerity supported by the nearness of biblical antiquity. A conservative, I take it, is a man who believes

---

Originally published as a letter to the editor of the *National Review* (Jan. 5, 1957). —Eds.

Chapter 15

that "everything good is heritage." I know of no country today in which this belief is stronger and less lethargic than in Israel.

But the country is poor, lacks oil and many other things which fetch much money; the venture on which the country rests may well appear to be quixotic; the university and the government buildings are within easy range of Jordanian guns; the possibility of disastrous defeat or failure is obvious and always close. A conservative, I take it, is a man who despises vulgarity; but the argument which is concerned exclusively with calculations of success, and is based on blindness to the nobility of the effort, is vulgar.

I hear the argument that the country is run by labor unions. I believe that it is a gross exaggeration to say that the country is run by the labor unions. But even if it were true, a conservative, I take it, is a man who knows that the same arrangement may have very different meanings in different circumstances.

The men who are governing Israel at present came from Russia at the beginning of the century. They are much more properly described as pioneers than as labor unionists. They were the men who laid the foundations under hopelessly difficult conditions. They are justly looked up to by all non-doctrinaires as the natural aristocracy of the country, for the same reasons for which Americans look up to the Pilgrim fathers. They came from Russia, the country of Nicolai the Second and Rasputin; hence they could not have had any experience of constitutional life and of the true liberalism which is only the reverse side of constitutional democracy adorned by an exemplary judiciary.

On page 16 of the November 17 issue of the *Review*, Israel is called a racist state. The author does not say what he understands by a "racist state," nor does he offer any proof for the assertion that Israel is a racist state. Would he by any chance have in mind the fact that in the state of Israel there is no civil marriage, but only Jewish, Christian, and Muslim marriages, and therefore that mixed marriages in the non-racist sense of the term are impossible in Israel? I am not so certain that civil marriage is under all circumstances an unmitigated blessing, as to disapprove of this particular feature of the State of Israel.

Finally, I wish to say that the founder of Zionism, Herzl, was fundamentally a conservative man, guided in his Zionism by conservative considerations. The moral spine of the Jews was in danger of being broken by the so-called emancipation, which in many cases had alienated them from their heritage, and yet not given them anything more than merely formal equality; it had brought about a condition which has been called "external freedom and inner servitude"; political Zionism was the attempt to restore that inner freedom, that simple dignity, of which only people who remember their heritage and are loyal to their fate, are capable.

Political Zionism is problematic for obvious reasons. But I can never forget what it achieved as a moral force in an era of complete dissolution. It helped to stem the tide of "progressive" leveling of venerable, ancestral differences; it fulfilled a conservative function.

16

Comment on W. S. Hudson, "The Weber Thesis Reexamined" (1961)

[100] *Comment*

This meeting, I gather, is concerned with the need for reinterpretation. I am not at all certain that reinterpretation is a universal necessity, i.e., that there cannot be final or definitive interpretations especially in those areas of historical research which are the most important. But I cannot go now into this difficult theoretical subject. I must limit myself to saying that the call for reinterpretation is dangerous practically. That call tells the historian: be original! Originality is very rare and the original historians do not have to be told to be original. As for the large majority of historians, they merely get bewildered by that call. Every one of us is probably flattered by the implication that we could be original if we only tried. This implication draws our attention away from our simple and urgent duties, the duties to be careful and thorough and to think straight. It would be also a great delusion to believe that the demand for novelty has made us more receptive to novel approaches: the resistance to genuine innovations as distinguished from fads is today as great as it was in the most benighted ages.

Weber's *Protestant Ethic and the Spirit of Capitalism* revolutionized the contemporary view of the past as much as Pirenne's studies on the end of antiquity or the beginning of the Middle Ages. I for one find the work of Pirenne more solid and even more exciting than Weber's. Yet Weber's work has a much greater fascination. For it concerns directly the way in which we as modern men understand ourselves, i.e., Weber's work is more philosophic than Pirenne's.

Originally published as "Comment" (100–2) to "The Weber Thesis Reexamined," by Winthrop S. Hudson, *Church History* 30, no. 1 (Mar. 1961): 88–99. —Eds.

CHAPTER 16

The broad phenomenon with which Weber was concerned was that of the origin of modern rationalism. Like almost everyone else, Weber traced it to the coming together of Greek science on the one hand and Biblical thought on the other. Weber's peculiar contention can be stated as follows. Jakob Burckhardt had ascribed to the Renaissance the discovery of man and of the world. He thus contrasted the Renaissance and by implication modernity as a whole with medieval other-worldliness. Yet what about the this-worldliness of pagan antiquity? What is the specific difference between modern and classical Greek this-worldliness?

A classical scholar comparing directly modernity with antiquity reached the conclusion that modern life is based on a fundamental asceticism. That classical scholar was Nietzsche; he set forth that [101] thesis in the third part of his *Genealogy of Morals*, entitled "What is the Significance of Ascetic Ideals?" Weber, we may say, was the first scholar who underwent Nietzsche's influence. Trained by Nietzsche, Weber saw the profound remoteness of the capitalist spirit from all "natural instincts," even from what we may call the natural vice of avarice.

Weber traced the capitalist spirit to Calvinism. What did he understand by the capitalist spirit? Two entirely different things. (a) The limitless accumulation of capital and the profitable investment of capital is a *moral duty*. (b) The limitless accumulation of capital and the profitable investment of capital is a sacred *end in itself*. Weber never proved that the second understanding of the capitalist spirit occurs in any serious writer. As for the first view, which does occur, the question arises: on what grounds is the limitless accumulation of capital, etc., a moral duty? The authentic answer is: because it is conducive to the common good. Weber neglects this crucial point (the reference to the common good) as a purely utilitarian consideration and unimportant for his inquiry into the "irrational" source of the capitalist spirit. Because he was looking for such an "irrational" source, he was inclined to prefer definition (b). The problem of the genesis of the capitalist spirit properly stated is the problem of the emergence of this minor premise: the unlimited acquisition of capital is most conducive to the common good or to charity. The major premise which was not changed in any way by the emergence of the capitalist spirit was: it is our duty to devote ourselves to the common good or to be charitable. Weber did not succeed in tracing the minor premise to Calvinism proper; perhaps he found it in late Calvinism, i.e., in a Calvinism which had already made its peace with the world (Tawney)—with the *capitalist* world. Hence the emergence of the capitalist spirit cannot be explained

Comment on W. S. Hudson, "The Weber Thesis Reexamined"

by reference to Calvinism (Hudson 93–95). The general conclusion: one cannot trace the capitalist spirit to the Reformation.

But modernity begins not only with the Reformation, a transformation of the theological tradition, but also with the more or less contemporary and wholly independent transformation of the philosophic tradition. Weber wondered whether the origins of the capitalist spirit could not be found in the Renaissance. He answered that question in the negative because he thought that the Renaissance was the attempt to restore the spirit of classical antiquity, i.e., a spirit wholly alien to the capitalist spirit. Yet he failed to consider a fact of the utmost importance, namely, that within the Renaissance an entirely new spirit emerged, the modern secular spirit. The greatest representative of this radical change was Machiavelli and there is a straight line [102] which leads from Machiavelli to Bacon, Hobbes and other Englishmen who in various ways came to exert a powerful influence on "Puritanism." Generally speaking the Puritans were more open to the new philosophy or science both natural and moral than, e.g., Lutherans because Calvinism had broken with "pagan" philosophy (Aristotle) most radically; Puritanism was or became the natural *carrier* of a way of thinking which it had not originated in any way. By looking for the origin of the capitalist spirit in the way of thinking originated by Machiavelli one will also avoid an obvious pitfall of Weber's inquiry: Weber's study of the origin of the capitalist spirit is wholly unconcerned with the origin of the science of economics; for the science of economics is the authentic interpretation of "the capitalist spirit."

Surely, "the waning of faith" (Hudson 98) is a necessary condition for the emergence of the capitalist spirit but it is not its sufficient condition: the waning of faith is also the condition of the emergence of national socialism. The sufficient condition is the attempt at a new understanding of social reality—an understanding which is "realistic" in the sense that it conceives of the social order as based not on piety and virtue but on socially useful passions or vices.

17

"Relativism"
(1961)

[135] "Relativism" has many meanings. In order not to become confused by the "blind scholastic pedantry" that exhausts itself and its audience in the "clarification of meanings" so that it never meets the nonverbal issues, I shall work my way into our subject by examining the recent statement of a famous contemporary about "the cardinal issue," the fundamental political problem of our time. As a fundamental problem it is theoretical; it is not the problem of particular policies, but the problem of the spirit that should inform particular policies. That problem is identified by Isaiah Berlin as the problem of freedom.[1]

Berlin distinguishes two senses of freedom, a negative and a positive sense. Used in the negative sense, in which it was used by "the classical English political philosophers" or "the fathers of liberalism," "freedom" means "freedom *from*": "Some portion of human existence must remain independent of social control"; "there ought to exist a certain minimum area of personal freedom which must on no account be violated."[2] Positive freedom, on the other hand, is "freedom *for*": the freedom of the individual "to be his own master" or to participate in the social control to which he is subject.[3] This alternative regarding freedom overlaps another alternative: freedom for the empirical self or freedom for the true self. Still, negative freedom, freedom from, is more likely [136] to mean freedom for the em-

---

Originally published in *Relativism and the Study of Man*, ed. Helmut Schoeck and James W. Wiggins (Princeton, NJ: Van Nostrand, 1961), 135–57. —Eds.
1   Isaiah Berlin, *Two Concepts of Liberty* (Oxford: At the Clarendon Press, 1958), p. 51.
2   *Op. cit.*, pp. 9, 11, 47.
3   *Op. cit.*, pp. 15, 16.

Chapter 17

pirical self; whereas positive freedom, freedom for, has to a higher degree the tendency to be understood as freedom only for the true self and therefore as compatible with the most extreme coercion of the empirical selves to become some thing that their true selves allegedly desire.[4]

The freedom that Berlin cherishes is the negative freedom for "our poor, desire-ridden, passionate, empirical selves":[5] "a maximum degree of noninterference compatible with the minimum demands of social life"[6] or the "freedom to live as one prefers."[7] He seems to cherish that freedom as "an end in itself" or "an ultimate value."[8] He certainly does not believe that the older reasoning in favor of negative freedom is valid. For, contrary to the older view, negative freedom is not the "necessary condition for the growth of human genius": "Integrity, love of truth and fiery individualism grow at least as often in severely disciplined communities or under military discipline, as in more tolerant or indifferent societies"; negative freedom is a peculiarly Western ideal and even a peculiarly modern Western ideal, and even in the modern Western world it is cherished by some individuals rather than by large masses; there is no necessary connection between negative freedom and democracy.[9]

Berlin finds the true justification of negative freedom in the absurdity of the alternative. The alternative is the notion that men can be free only by participating in *the* just, *the* rational or *the* perfect society in which all just or rational ends of all members of society are harmoniously satisfied or in which everyone obeys only himself, i.e., his true self. This notion presupposes that there is a hierarchy, and therefore a fundamental harmony, of human ends. But this presupposition is "demonstrably false"; it is based on a "dogmatic and a priori certainty"; it is "not compatible with empiricism," i.e., with "any doctrine founded on knowledge derived from experience of what men are and seek"; it is the root of "the metaphysical view of politics" as opposed to the "empirical" view.[10] Experience shows us that "the ends of men are many, and not all of them in principle are compatible with each other.... The necessity of choosing between absolute [137] claims is then

---

4   *Op. cit.*, p. 19.
5   *Op. cit.*, p. 32.
6   *Op. cit.*, p. 46.
7   *Op. cit.*, p. 14 n.
8   *Op. cit.*, pp. 36, 50.
9   *Op. cit.*, pp. 13–15, 48.
10 *Op. cit.*, pp. 39 n., 54, 57 n.

an inescapable characteristic of the human condition. This gives its value to freedom... as an end in itself and not as a temporary need...."[11]

Experience, knowledge of the observable Is, seems to lead in a perfectly unobjectionable manner to knowledge of the Ought. The allegedly empirical premise would seem to be the equality of all human ends. "Mill, and liberals in general, at their most consistent... wish the frontiers between individuals and groups of men to be drawn solely with a view to preventing collisions between human purposes, all of which must be considered to be equally ultimate, uncriticizable ends in themselves. Kant and the rationalists of his type do not regard all ends as of equal value." From the context it appears that the ends that are to be regarded as equal include "the various personal aims which their individual imagination and idiosyncrasies lead men to pursue."[12]

Interference with the pursuit of ends is legitimate only to the extent to which one man's pursuit of an end collides with another man's pursuit. Yet it appears that such collisions cannot possibly be prevented: "The possibility of conflict—and of tragedy—can never be wholly eliminated from human life, either personal or social."[13] Not all collisions, but only certain kinds of collisions can and ought to be prevented by social control: "there must be *some* frontiers of freedom which nobody should ever be permitted to cross."[14] The frontiers must be of such a character as to protect a reasonably large area; it would not be sufficient to demand that every man must have the freedom to dream of the pursuit of any end he likes.

Yet the primary question concerns, not the location of the frontiers, but their status. Those frontiers must be "sacred."[15] They must be "absolute": "Genuine belief in the inviolability of a minimum extent of individual liberty entails some... absolute stand."[16] "Relativism," or the assertion that all ends are relative to the chooser and hence equal, seems to require some kind of "absolutism." Yet Berlin hesitates to go quite so far. "Different *names or natures* may be given to the rules" that determine those frontiers:

> [138] they may be called natural rights or the word of God, or Natural Law, or the demands of utility or of "the deepest interests of man"; I may

---

11 Op. cit., p. 54.
12 Op. cit., p. 38 n.
13 Op. cit., p. 54.
14 Op. cit., p. 50; italics mine.
15 Op. cit., p. 57.
16 Op. cit., p. 50.

Chapter 17

believe them to be valid *a priori*, or assert them to be *my own subjective ends, or the ends of my society or culture*. What these rules or commandments will have in common is that they are accepted so widely, and are grounded so deeply in the actual nature of men as they have developed through history, as to be, by now, an essential part of what we mean by being a normal human being. Genuine belief in the inviolability of a minimum extent of individual liberty entails *some such absolute stand*.[17]

That is to say, the demand for the sacredness of a private sphere needs a basis, an "absolute" basis, but it has no basis; any old basis, any "such absolute stand" as reference to my own subjective will or the will of my society will do. It would be short-sighted to deny that Berlin's comprehensive formula is very helpful for a political purpose—for the purpose of an anti-Communist manifesto designed to rally all anti-Communists. But we are here concerned with a theoretical problem, and in this respect we are forced to say that Berlin contradicts himself. "Freedom from" and "freedom for" are "two profoundly divergent and irreconcilable attitudes to the ends of life... each of them makes absolute claims. These claims cannot both be fully satisfied. But... the satisfaction that each of them seeks is an ultimate value which... has an equal right to be classed among the deepest interests of mankind."[18] The absolute claim for a minimum private sphere cannot be fully satisfied; it must be diluted, for the opposite claim has an equal right. Liberalism, as Berlin understands it, cannot live without an absolute basis and cannot live with an absolute basis.

Let us consider more precisely the basis of liberalism as Berlin sees it. "What these rules and commandments [*sc.* that determine the frontiers of freedom that nobody should ever be permitted to cross] will have in common is that they are accepted so widely, are grounded so deeply in the actual nature of men as they have developed through history, as to be, by now, an essential part of what we mean by being a normal human being."[19] But Berlin had told us earlier that "the domination of this ideal has been [139] the exception rather than the rule, even in the recent history of the West,"[20] i.e., that the ideal of negative freedom is not natural to man as man. Let, then, the rules in question be natural to Western man as he is now. But what about the future?

---

17 *Op. cit.*, p. 50; italics mine.
18 *Op. cit.*, pp. 51–52.
19 *Op. cit.*, p. 50.
20 *Op. cit.*, p. 13.

"Relativism"

> It may be that the ideal of freedom to live as one wishes... is only the late fruit of our declining capitalist civilization: an ideal which ... posterity will regard with... little comprehension. This may be so; but no sceptical conclusions seem to me to follow. Principles are no less sacred because their duration cannot be guaranteed.[21]

But it is also true that principles are not sacred merely in virtue of the fact that their duration cannot be guaranteed. We are still waiting to hear why Berlin's principles are regarded by him as sacred. If these principles are intrinsically valid, eternally valid, one could indeed say that it is a secondary question whether they will or will not be recognized as valid in the future and that if future generations despise the eternal verities of civilization, they will merely condemn themselves to barbarism. But can there be eternal principles on the basis of "empiricism," of the experience of men up to now? Does not the experience of the future have the same right to respect as the experience of the past and the present?

The situation would be entirely different if one could assume the possibility of a peak of experience, of an absolute moment in history, in which the fundamental condition of man is realized for the first time and in principle fully. But this would also mean that in the most important respect history, or progress, would have come to its end. Yet Berlin seems to take it for granted that in the most important respect history is unfinished or unfinishable. Hence, the ideal of negative freedom can only be "relatively valid" for him: it can be valid only for the time being. In entire accord with the spirit of our time, he quotes "an admirable writer of our time" who says: "To realize the relative validity of one's convictions and yet stand for them unflinchingly, is what distinguishes a civilized man from a barbarian."[22]

That is to say, not only are all our primary ends of relative [140] validity; even the end that suggests itself as necessary by virtue of the absolute insight into the relative validity of all our primary ends is likewise only relatively valid. On the other hand, the latter end, or the right position toward any primary end, is so absolutely valid that Berlin or his authority can build on it the absolute distinction between civilized men and barbarians. For this distinction, as set forth in the quoted passage, is obviously meant to be final and not to be subject to revision in the light of future experience.

Berlin cannot escape the necessity to which every thinking being is subject: to take a final stand, an absolute stand in accordance with what he re-

---

21 Op. cit., p. 57.
22 Op. cit., p. 57.

Chapter 17

gards as the nature of man or as the nature of the human condition or as the decisive truth and hence to assert the absolute validity of his fundamental conviction. This does not mean, of course, that his fundamental conviction is sound. One reason why I doubt that it is sound is that if his authority were right, every resolute liberal hack or thug would be a civilized man, while Plato and Kant would be barbarians.

Berlin's statement seems to me to be a characteristic document of the crisis of liberalism—of a crisis due to the fact that liberalism has abandoned its absolutist basis and is trying to become entirely relativistic. Probably the majority of our academic colleagues will say that no conclusion can be drawn against relativism from the inadequacies of Berlin's statement because these inadequacies arise from his wish to find an impossible middle ground between relativism and absolutism; if he had limited himself to saying that liberalism is merely his "own subjective end," not intrinsically superior to any other subjective end, that since the belief in liberalism is based on a value judgment, no case or no conclusive case can be made for or against liberalism, in other words, if he had not rejected the nonliberal positions as "barbarian," but had admitted that there is an indefinitely large variety of notions of civilization each of which defines barbarism in its own way, in brief, if he had remained within the confines of the positivism of our time, he would never have contradicted himself. Whether withdrawal to the citadel of that positivism or [141] of unqualified "value relativism" overcomes the crisis of liberalism or whether it merely conceals that crisis is another question.

The case for relativism has been restated recently by Arnold Brecht. He takes issue with certain arguments against relativism that I had advanced. He is not impressed by my reasoning. He deals with it chiefly under the heading of "misrepresentations." Since I know Dr. Brecht to be a polite man, I was inclined to assume that he regarded it as impolite to accuse me of mere misunderstanding: relativism is not such a deep doctrine as to be likely to be misunderstood. He blames me for having ascribed to Max Weber the view that all values are of the same rank: Weber merely asserted that "ultimate" values are "equally indemonstrable."[23] This means, however, that, as far as we know and shall ever be able to know while living on earth, or before the tribunal of human reason, the ways of life recommended by Amos

---

23 Arnold Brecht, *Political Theory* (Princeton University Press, 1959), p. 263. [See also *Leo Strauss on Political Philosophy: Responding to the Challenge of Positivism and Historicism*, ed. Catherine Zuckert (Chicago: University of Chicago Press, 2018), 99–103. Arnold Brecht was Strauss's colleague at the New School for Social Research.—Eds.]

or by Socrates are equal in value to the way of life of specialists without spirit or vision and voluptuaries without heart. And this assertion seems to me to be as absurd as the assertion that, as far as we know or shall ever be able to know, a man who is blind or mortally ill is as perfect regarding his body as a man free from all bodily defects.

Brecht blames me also for having seen "inconsistency in the fact that relativists cannot help using value judgements themselves."

> No scientific relativist would condemn words like cruelty, civilization, prostitution, or, for that matter, crime or slums, wherever they are used within a clear frame of reference as descriptive in accordance with known standards, *as long as these standards are not themselves at issue*.[24]

But, on the basis of relativism, the standards are necessarily at issue, since all value judgments are rationally questionable; the consistent relativist ought to use "value-impregnated expressions" only in quotation marks, if at all.

In the Appendix to his book, in a subsection entitled "Mis-[142]understandings,"[25] Brecht reproaches me for having asserted that, according to relativism, "civilization is not intrinsically superior to cannibalism." He says:

> Where and when has a scientific relativist ever asserted as a fact that civilization is *not* superior to cannibalism? Such apodictic negative statements would be quite contrary to the principles of Scientific Method.

I merely repeat that, according to the thesis of scientific relativism, as restated by Brecht, civilization is not, as far as we *know*, and shall ever be able to *know*, superior to cannibalism, provided that each—civilization as well as cannibalism—rests on an ultimate value of its own. This is to say nothing at all here of the fact that the use of the terms "civilizations" or "cultures" by scientific anthropology presupposes the abolition of the distinction between civilization and barbarism and therewith, in particular, the abolition of the distinction between civilization and cannibalism.

"The only question," Brecht continues, "that could be raised by some pedantic relativist or for the matter of methodological argument is, What is the scientific *evidence* for the superiority of noncannibalistic civilizations?" Since the question at issue is whether reason is completely unable to distinguish between right and wrong or noble and base, one must not be afraid of being pedantic. "How about civilizations," Brecht continues, "that

---

24 *Op. cit.*, pp. 264–265.
25 *Op. cit.*, pp. 549–550.

Chapter 17

abhor the eating of cattle or hogs?" Here Brecht seems to say that, according to scientific relativism, the eating of human beings has the same status as the eating of cattle or hogs.

> Scientific Value Relativism... is at no loss to show the superiority of noncannibalism, once "superiority" is defined... in terms other than selfish satisfaction of personal or tribal passions and with reference to humanity ... even if the term "superior" were used in a strictly selfish sense... Scientific Method would not be at the end of its resources; the long-run superiority of one pattern of [143] behavior over another can often be demonstrated even when the question is solely that of personal satisfaction.

If scientific value relativism may be able to prove the superiority of civilization to cannibalism in terms of both selfish satisfaction and unselfish satisfaction, it would indeed seem that scientific value relativism can in principle prove the superiority of civilization to cannibalism. Or is the disjunction incomplete? Must it not be incomplete if relativism is to be maintained? Is the reference to the "definition" of superiority not tantamount to a reference to such incompleteness? Is there, then, something other than satisfaction (selfish or unselfish) that is equal in rank to satisfaction before the tribunal of human reason so that one can choose dissatisfaction (pain, suffering, anguish, failure) as one's ultimate value with the same right as satisfaction? And may not dissatisfaction justify cannibalism?[26]

Brecht concludes his argument with the remark that scientific value relativism does not deny "that there may be absolutely valid, divine standards of moral value; it merely negates that this can be shown with scientific means in a serious controversy conducted in good faith." Brecht also reproaches me for having contrasted the apparent humility with the hidden arrogance of relativism. In reply to this remark he says:

> Scientific Value Relativism may indeed be too humble to offer a *scientific* decision on a question like this: whether the captain of a marooned crew ought to be condemned if he permitted his men to eat the flesh of other men killed in battle or by accident, when this was the only alternative to starving. Religious feeling and traditional education may tell us they should rather have starved, but this is no *scientific* decision.

Why did Brecht choose this example in preference to the example of men eating human flesh while they have other food in abundance? Can his sci-

---

26 Cf. also p. 430.

"Relativism"

ence legitimate the "condemnation" of what we may call frivolous cannibalism without making assumptions [144] regarding "ultimate values" which that very science must regard as questionable? Besides, I gladly admit that Brecht's version of relativism is humble, since it is based on the Kantian distinction between the knowable phenomena and the unknowable thing-in-itself.[27]

According to the positivistic interpretation of relativism which prevails in present-day social science and which Brecht very feebly qualifies,[28] reason is unable to show the superiority of unselfish gratification to selfish gratification and the absurdity of any attainable ends "which imagination and idiosyncrasies lead men to pursue." From this it follows that a bachelor without kith and kin who dedicates his whole life to the amassing of the largest possible amount of money, provided he goes about this pursuit in the most efficient manner, leads, in principle, as rational a life as the greatest benefactor of his country or of mankind. The choice among attainable ends may be made *en pleine connaissance de cause*, i.e., in full clarity about the likely consequences of the choice; it cannot in itself be rational. Reason can tell us which means are conducive to which ends; it cannot tell us which attainable ends are to be preferred to other attainable ends. Reason cannot even tell us that we ought to choose attainable ends; if someone "loves him who desires the impossible," reason may tell him that he acts irrationally, but it cannot tell him that he ought to act rationally or that acting irrationally is acting badly or basely. If rational conduct consists in choosing the right means for the right end, relativism teaches in effect that rational conduct is impossible. Relativistic social science may therefore be said to be one branch of the rational study of nonrational behavior.

But in what sense is the study rational? Social science proceeds by inductive reasoning or is concerned with prediction or with the discovery of causes. Yet what is the status of the principle of causality in social science relativism? The moderate Brecht is satisfied with the assertion that as regards causality, scientific method is grounded on common sense; he himself is inclined toward what he calls the Kantian view according to which "the human mind is so structured as to be unable to think [or as he also says "to [145] imagine"] that changes have no causes."[29] According

---

27 Cf. pp. 101, 103, 125, 158, 462 ff.
28 *Op. cit.*, pp. 124–125, 130–131.
29 *Op. cit.*, pp. 78, 81.

Chapter 17

to a more widely accepted view, the principle of causality is a mere assumption. There is no rational objection to the assumption that the universe may disappear at any moment, not only into thin air, but into absolute nothingness, and that this happening may be a vanishing, not only into nothing, but through nothing as well. What is true of the possible end of the world is true also of its beginning. Since the principle of causality is not intrinsically evident, nothing prevents us from assuming that the world has come into being out of nothing and through nothing. Not only has rationality disappeared from the behavior studied by science; the rationality of that study itself has become radically problematic. All coherence has gone. We are then entitled to say that positivistic science in general, and therefore positivistic social science in particular, is characterized by the abandonment of reason or the flight from reason. The flight from scientific reason, which has been noted with regret, is the reasonable reply to the flight of science from reason.

A Marxist writer, Georg Lukács, has written a history of nineteenth- and twentieth-century German thought under the title *Die Zerstörung der Vernunft*.[30] I believe that many of us Western social scientists must plead guilty to this accusation. For obvious reasons we must be especially interested in Lukács's critique of Max Weber's conception of social science. One may summarize that critique as follows. Weber more than any other German scholar of his generation tried to save the objectivity of social science; he believed that to do so required that social science be made "value-free" because he assumed that evaluations are transrational or irrational; but the value-free study of "facts" and their causes admittedly presupposes the selection of relevant facts; that selection is necessarily guided by reference to values; the values with reference to which the facts are to be selected must themselves be selected; and that selection, which determines in the last analysis the specific conceptual framework of the social scientist, is in principle arbitrary; hence social science is fundamentally irrational or subjectivistic.[31]

According to Lukács, an objective and evaluating social science [146] is possible provided social science does not limit itself to the study of arbitrarily selected "facts" or segments, but understands particular social phenomena in the light of the whole social situation and ultimately in the light of the

---

30 Georg Lukács, *Die Zerstörung der Vernunft* (Berlin, 1954). [Also spelled as György Lukács. An English translation is available as *The Destruction of Reason*, trans. Peter Palmer (Atlantic Highlands, NJ: Humanities Press, 1981).—Eds.]

31 Cf. pp. 484–489. [See, in Palmer's translation, 612–19.—Eds.]

"Relativism"

whole historical process. "Historical and dialectical materialism is that comprehensive view in which the progressiveness and the rationally knowable lawfulness of history are expressed in the highest form, and in fact the only comprehensive view that can give a consistent philosophic foundation to progressivism and reasonableness."[32]

Hegel's attempt to demonstrate the progressive and rational character of the historical process was based on the premise that that process is in principle completed; for if it were not completed, one could not know, for instance, whether the future stages would not lead to the self-destruction of reason. Yet, according to Marx, the historical process is not completed, not to say that it has not even begun. Besides, Marx does not admit transhistorical or natural ends with reference to which change can be diagnosed as progress or regress. It is therefore a question whether by turning from Western relativism to Marxism one escapes relativism. "Historical materialism," Lukács had said,

> can and must be applied to itself. Yet this application of materialist method to materialism does not lead to complete relativism; it does not lead to the consequence that historical materialism is not the right method. The substantive truths of Marxism are of the same quality as the truths of classical economics according to Marx's interpretation of those truths. They are truths within a certain order of society and production. As such, but only as such, they possess absolute validity. This does not exclude the emergence of societies in which other categories, other connections of truth, will be valid as a consequence of the essential structure of these societies.[33]

This would seem to mean that the substantive truths of Marxism are true until further notice; in principle we know already now that they will be replaced by different truths. Surely, the Marxist truths will be "preserved" in Hegel's sense of the term: "the 'objectivity' of the truth accessible on the lower planes is [147] not destroyed: that truth merely receives a different meaning by being integrated into a more concrete, a more comprehensive totality."[34] That is to say, Marxism will reveal itself as a one-sided truth, a half-truth. Lukács compares the truth of Marxism also to the truth of the

---

32 *Op. cit.*, p. 456. [See, in Palmer's translation, 572. —Eds.]
33 Georg Lukács, *Geschichte und Klassenbewusstsein* (Berlin, 1923), pp. 234–235. [The above appears to be Strauss's own translation. See also *History and Class Consciousness: Studies in Marxist Dialectics*, trans. Rodney Livingstone (Cambridge, MA: MIT Press, 1972), 228. —Eds.]
34 *Op. cit.*, p. 206.

Chapter 17

ideologies of the French Revolution. Marxism is as true today as those ideologies were in their time: both make or made intelligible a historical situation in such a way as to render visible for contemporaries the root of their difficulties and to show them the way out of those difficulties. But while the ideologists of the French Revolution saw clearly the rottenness of the *ancien régime* and the necessity of a revolution, they were utterly mistaken about the goodness of the new society that their revolution brought to birth.

The application to Marxism is obvious: even if Marxism were the last word regarding the ground of the rottenness of capitalist society and regarding the way in which that society can and will be destroyed, it cannot possibly be the last word regarding the new society that the revolutionary action of the proletariat brings to birth: the new society may be as rich in contradictions and oppressions as the old society, although its contradictions and oppressions will, of course, be entirely novel. For if Marxism is only the truth of our time or our society, the prospect of the classless society too is only the truth of our time and society; it may prove to be the delusion that gave the proletariat the power and the spirit to overthrow the capitalist system, whereas in fact the proletariat finds itself afterwards enslaved, no longer indeed by capital, but by an ironclad military bureaucracy.

Yet perhaps Marxism must not be applied to itself and thus made relative. Perhaps its fundamental verities are objective, scientific truths the validity of which cannot be understood in terms of their conditions or genesis. Marxism can then be regarded as a final truth of the same dignity as the theory of evolution. Yet since other truths of great importance will be discovered in the future, the "meaning" of Marxism will radically change.

But perhaps Marxism is the final truth, since it belongs to the absolute moment in history in which the realm of necessity can be surveyed in its entirety and therewith the outlines of the [148] realm of freedom can come into view for the first time. The realm of necessity coincides with the division of labor. The realm of freedom emerges with the abolition of the division of labor. Yet the original form of the division of labor is "the division of labor," not in the generation of offspring, but "in the sexual act."[35] It would seem that the realm of freedom, if brought to its perfection, will be the realm of homunculi produced in test tubes by homunculi, if it will not be, as is more likely, the earth of "the last man," of the one herd without a shepherd. For,

---

35 Karl Marx and F. Engels, *Die Deutsche Ideologie* (cited from a new edition, Berlin, 1953), p. 28. [*The German Ideology*, ed. C. J. Arthur (New York: International Publishers, 1972), 51. —Eds.]

"Relativism"

to quote Machiavelli, "as has been written by some moral philosophers, men's hands and tongue, two most noble instruments for ennobling him, would not have done their work perfectly nor would they have carried the works of men to the height to which they are seen to have been carried, if they had not been driven on by necessity": the jump from the realm of necessity into the realm of freedom will be the inglorious death of the very possibility of human excellence.

But let us return to that school which is externally the most powerful in the present-day West, to present-day positivism. That positivism is logical positivism. With some degree of truth it traces its origin to Hume. It deviates from Hume in two important respects. In the first place, deviating from Hume's teaching, it is a logical, i.e., not a psychological, teaching. The supplement added by logical positivism to the critique of reason is symbolic logic and the theory of probability; in Hume that supplement was natural belief and natural instinct. The sole or chief concern of logical positivism is the logical analysis of science. It has learned through Kant, the great critic of Hume, or through neo-Kantianism, that the question of the validity of science is radically different from the question of its psychological genesis.

The second important respect in which present-day positivism deviates from Hume is indicated by the fact that Hume was still a political philosopher. More particularly, he still taught that there are universally valid rules of justice and that those rules are not improperly called Laws of Nature. This means that "he thought and wrote before the rise of anthropology and allied [149] sciences"[36] or, more precisely stated, before "the discovery of History." Hume still viewed human things in the light of man's unchangeable nature; he did not yet conceive of man as an essentially historical being. Present-day positivism believes that it can evade the problem raised by "the discovery of History" by the same device by which it frees itself from Hume's or any other psychology: through the Kantian distinction between validity and genesis. Yet Kant was enabled to transcend psychology because he recognized an a priori; and an a priori does not have a genesis, at least not an empirical genesis. Logical positivism rejects the a priori. Hence it cannot avoid becoming involved in psychology, in the question of the empirical genesis of science out of what precedes science. One cannot stop at simply trying to answer the question, What is science? One cannot avoid raising the question, Why science? or What is the meaning of science? Since positivism denies that there is a "pure reason" or a "pure mind," it can an-

---

36 John Dewey, *Human Nature and Conduct*, Modern Library edition, p. vii.

Chapter 17

swer the question, Why science? only in terms of "the human organism." It must understand science as an activity of a certain kind of organism, as an activity fulfilling an important function in the life of that kind of organism. In brief, man is an organism that cannot live, or live well, without being able to predict, and the most efficient form of prediction is science.

This way of accounting for science has become extremely questionable. In the age of thermonuclear weapons the positive relation of science to human survival has lost all the apparent evidence that it formerly may have possessed. Furthermore, the high development of science depends on highly developed industrial societies; the predominance of such societies renders ever more difficult the survival of "underdeveloped societies." Who still dares to say that the development of those societies, i.e., their radical transformation, the destruction of their traditional way of life, is a necessary condition for those peoples' living or living well? Those peoples survived and sometimes lived happily without having an inkling of the possibility of science. While it becomes necessary to trace science to the needs of organisms of a certain kind, it is impossible to do so. For to the extent to which science could be shown to be necessary for man's living or living [150] well, one would in fact pass a rational value judgment regarding science, and we know that, according to positivism, rational value judgments are impossible.

Some positivists avoid the difficulty indicated by finding the rationale of science in democracy, without being deterred by the fact that they thus merely appeal to the dogmatic premise or the inertia of established orders and without paying attention to the complications alluded to by Berlin, or else by conceiving of science as one of the most thrilling forms of spiritual adventure, without being able to tell us what they understand by the spiritual, how it differs in their opinion from the nonspiritual, and, in particular, how it is related to the rational. Positivism grants that science depends on conditions that science itself does not produce. They are produced by the unintended coming together of various factors that may diverge as they have converged. As long as they are together, science may progress by virtue of something that looks like an innate propensity. Yet science is not autonomous; as the saying goes, thinking does not take place in a vacuum. What renders the autonomy of science questionable is not primarily the fact that science presupposes the availability of conditions external to science. If one conceives of science as a spiritual adventure, one implies that there are other forms of spiritual adventure; one cannot exclude the possibility that, just as science influences those other forms, science itself undergoes their influence. Furthermore, one must assume that the spirit changes as a consequence of its adventures, hence that the spirit may well differ from age to age, and hence that science may depend, in the direction of its interests or of its hypotheses-forming imagination, on the spirit of the age. In other words, one cannot help raising the question of the relation between scientific progress and social progress. Given the positivistic verdict regarding value judgments, positivism can no longer speak properly, or with an easy conscience, of social progress; but it continues, even if in a more or less surreptitious manner, the older tradition that believed in the natural harmony between scientific progress and social progress.

Stated generally, by virtue of the distinction between validity [151] and genesis, positivism tries to treat science as autonomous, but it is unable to do so; that distinction merely prevents it from giving due weight to the question of the human context out of which science arises and within which it exists. Positivism treats science in the way in which it would have to be treated if science were "the very highest power of man," the power by which man transcends the merely human; yet positivism cannot maintain this "Platonic" understanding of science. The question of the human context of science, which positivism fails and refuses to raise, is taken up by its most powerful present-day opponent in the West, radical historicism or, to use the better-known name, existentialism.

Existentialism came into being through the meeting, which first took place in Germany, of Kierkegaard's and Nietzsche's thought. While being related to these two illustrious names, existentialism is as nameless as positivism or idealism. But this is misleading. Existentialism, like many other movements, has a flabby periphery and a hard center. That hard core, or that thought to which alone existentialism owes its intellectual dignity, is the thought of Heidegger. In Heidegger's first great publication, the influence of Kierkegaard was indeed as powerful as that of Nietzsche. But with the increased clarity that Heidegger achieved afterward, it became clear that the root of existentialism must be sought in Nietzsche rather than in Kierkegaard: existentialism emerged by virtue of the "reception" of Kierkegaard on the part of a philosophic public that had begun to be molded by Nietzsche.

Nietzsche is *the* philosopher of relativism: the first thinker who faced the problem of relativism in its full extent and pointed to the way in which relativism can be overcome. Relativism came to Nietzsche's attention in the form of historicism—more precisely, in the form of a decayed Hegelianism. Hegel had reconciled "the discovery of History"—the alleged insight into the individual's being, in the most radical sense, the son

Chapter 17

or stepson of his time or into the dependence of a man's highest and purest thoughts on his time—with philosophy in the original meaning of the term by asserting that Hegel's time was the absolute [152] moment, the end of meaningful time: the absolute religion, Christianity, had become completely reconciled with the world; it had become completely secularized, or the *saeculum* had become completely Christian in and through the postrevolutionary State; history as meaningful change had come to its end; all theoretical and practical problems had in principle been solved; hence, the historical process was demonstrably rational.

The decayed Hegelianism with which Nietzsche was confronted preserved Hegel's "optimism" after having abandoned the ground of that "optimism," i.e., the completedness of the historical process. In fact, its "optimism" was based on the expectation of infinite future progress or on the belief in the unfinishable character of history. Under this condition, as Nietzsche saw, our own principles, including the belief in progress, will become as relative as all earlier principles had shown themselves to be; not only the thought of the past but also our own thought must be understood to depend on premises which for us are inescapable, but of which we know that they are condemned to perish. History becomes a spectacle that for the superficial is exciting and for the serious is enervating. It teaches a truth that is deadly. It shows us that culture is possible only if men are fully dedicated to principles of thought and action which they do not and cannot question, which limit their horizon and thus enable them to have a character and a style. It shows us at the same time that any principles of this kind can be questioned and even rejected.

The only way out seems to be that one turn one's back on this lesson of history, that one voluntarily choose life-giving delusion instead of deadly truth, that one fabricate a myth. But this is patently impossible for men of intellectual probity. The true solution comes to sight once one realizes the essential limitation of objective history or of objective knowledge in general. Objective history suffices for destroying the delusion of the objective validity of any principles of thought and action; it does not suffice for opening up a genuine understanding of history. The objective historian cannot grasp the substance of the past because he is a mere spectator, not dedicated or committed to substantive principles of thought and action, and this is the consequence of [153] his having realized that such principles have no objective validity. But an entirely different conclusion may and must be drawn from the realization of this objective truth. The different values respected in different epochs had no objective support, i.e.,

"Relativism"

they were human creations; they owed their being to a free human project that formed the horizon within which a culture was possible. What man did in the past unconsciously and under the delusion of submitting to what is independent of his creative act, he must now do consciously. This radically new project—the revaluation of all values—entails the rejection of all earlier values, for they have become baseless by the realization of the baseless character of their claim, by which they stand or fall, to objective validity. But precisely the realization of the origin of all such principles makes possible a new creation that presupposes this realization and is in agreement with it, yet is not deducible from it; for otherwise it would not be due to a creative act performed with intellectual probity.

It is in this way that Nietzsche may be said to have transformed the deadly truth of relativism into the most life-giving truth. To state the case with all necessary vagueness, he discovered that the life-giving comprehensive truth is subjective or transtheoretical in that it cannot be grasped detachedly and that it cannot be the same for all men or for all ages. We can do no more than allude here to the difficulties in which Nietzsche became involved in trying to overcome the difficulties that afflict his solution. I have in mind his interpretation of human creativity as a special form of the universal will to power, and the question that this interpretation entails, namely, whether he did not thus again try to find a sufficient theoretical basis for a transtheoretical teaching or message. I have in mind, in other words, his hesitation as to whether the doctrine of the will to power is his subjective project to be superseded by other such projects in the future or whether it is the final truth. We limit ourselves here to saying that the movement of Nietzsche's thought can be understood as a movement from the supremacy of history towards the supremacy of nature, a movement that bypasses the supremacy of reason throughout or tries to replace the opposition between the subjec-[154]tive and the objective (or between the conventional and the natural) by the opposition between the superficial and the profound. Existentialism is the attempt to free Nietzsche's alleged overcoming of relativism from the consequences of his relapse into metaphysics or of his recourse to nature.

Existentialism starts where positivism leaves off. Existentialism is the reaction of serious men to their own relativism. Positivism is essentially the attempt to understand science; it acts as if it knew that science is the one thing needful or at any rate man's highest possibility. It conceives of science as essentially progressive, and hence it conceives of the future of scientific development as unpredictable *in concreto*. In fact, it conceives of

Chapter 17

science as capable of infinite progress. This character of science must, however, be traced to the character of the object of science. That object is essentially accessible to reason; otherwise there could be no science. But since it reveals itself to science only in an infinite process, one can say with at least equal right that it is radically mysterious. For he who teaches, for instance, that perpetual peace is the goal of an infinite process teaches, in fact, the perpetuity of war. Existentialism is the truth of positivism, since it teaches that being is essentially or radically mysterious and that the fundamental defect of metaphysics is the assumption upon which it is based—the assumption that being is as such intelligible.

Existentialism is, however, not merely the "pessimistic" expression of the same thing of which positivism is the "optimistic" expression. Positivism asserts that the goodness of science cannot be established by science or scientific philosophy: the choice of science, of the scientific orientation, and therewith also of the scientific "picture of the world" is not a rational choice; it is as possible and as groundless as the choice of any alternative orientation. These fundamental choices are not properly interpreted by scientific psychology, for scientific psychology explains those choices on the basis of a specific fundamental choice that is not necessary, viz., the choice of the scientific orientation. The fundamental phenomenon, the only phenomenon that is not hypothetical, is the abyss of freedom: the fact that man is compelled to [155] choose groundlessly: the fundamental experience, i.e., an experience more fundamental than every science, is the experience of the objective groundlessness of all principles of thought and action, the experience of nothingness.

Man and ultimately everything must be understood in the light of this fundamental experience. The specific manner in which man and man alone is, is directly constituted by the fundamental nothingness. That manner of being is called *Existenz*. *Existenz* is articulated by the analysis of *Existenz*, which is the fundamental part of philosophy. *Existenz* is authentic or inauthentic: authentic when it faces the fundamental situation of man, inauthentic when it flees from it. The analytics of *Existenz* contains, then, an ethics, even if only a formal ethics: to the extent to which one understands *Existenz*, one realizes the general character of the truly human. The ethics is formal since it is based, not on the nature of man, on man's beingness, but on the human situation or, somewhat more precisely, on man's manner of being. Hence, it does not say that the good life is the life according to nature, according to the nature of man, but it does say, in effect, that the good life is the life according to the essential character of *Existenz*. It does not say this, however, according to Heidegger's own authoritative declaration. For if the analytics of *Existenz* contained an ethics, its cognitive status would be the same as that of Kant's transcendental analytics of subjectivity; it would be an objective teaching or it would supply final knowledge, infinite knowledge. Yet the analytics of *Existenz* is necessarily based on a specific ideal of *Existenz*, on a specific commitment; for only committed thought can understand commitment and hence *Existenz*. In other words, existentialist philosophy is subjective truth about the subjectivity of truth or finite knowledge of man's finiteness.

Yet how can finiteness be seen as finiteness if it is not seen in the light of the infinite? These and similar difficulties seem to have led Heidegger to a very thorough revision of his doctrine. One may doubt whether through that revision the fundamental relativism was overcome. I can allude here only to one point, to Heidegger's teaching regarding historical truth. The interpreter's [156] understanding of a thinker is true if it understands his thought as he understood it. According to Heidegger this is altogether impossible; it is not even a reasonable goal of understanding. Nor is it possible, in his opinion, to understand a thinker better than he understood himself; true understanding of a thinker is understanding him creatively, i.e., understanding him differently from the way in which he understood himself. This understanding necessarily implies a criticism, a fundamental criticism of the thinker in question. According to Heidegger, all thinkers prior to him have been oblivious of *Sein*, i.e., of the ground of grounds. This assertion implies, in fact, the claim that Heidegger understands the great thinkers of the past in the decisive respect better than they understood themselves.

18

Replies to Schaar and Wolin: II (1963)

[152a] The critique of my Epilogue by Professors Schaar and Wolin is distinguished by the fact that it is, as far as I know, the most acrimonious critique hitherto written of what I stand for. Critiques of this kind were to be expected. In scholarship as well as in politics there is at all times something which can be called the *status quo* and which claims to be, not indeed simply perfect, but fundamentally sound—i.e., possessing within itself the remedies for the ills from which it suffers. There is also at all times a radical dissatisfaction with the *status quo* which is felt by two different kinds of people, those who wish to disagree and those who are compelled by reason to disagree. Some of those who are satisfied with the *status quo*, happy with the achievements of which in their opinion the *status quo* can boast, the *beati possidentes*, can be expected to be annoyed by the outsiders who suspect wrongly or rightly that what claims to be wealth is in fact penury. Annoyance easily leads to ill temper and ill temper easily leads to ill-tempered actions, if not to blind, fanatical hatred and corresponding actions.

Fanaticism is precisely the vice of which I have been accused and which, it could seem, distinguishes me from those who believe in the fundamental soundness of the new political science. I have also been accused of being "disingenuous" because I made a certain remark which the critics call "ironical" immediately afterward. (p. 128) I am aware of the fact that [152b] irony is a form of dissimulation but it is generally regarded as a rather decent form of dissimulation. I am said to be guilty of disingenuousness or irony

---

Originally published in *American Political Science Review* 57, no. 1 (Mar. 1961): 152–55. This is Strauss's portion of a reply by the contributors to *Essays on the Scientific Study of Politics*, ed. Herbert J. Storing (New York: Holt, Rinehart and Winston, 1962), to a review by John Schaar and Sheldon Wolin. —Eds.

CHAPTER 18

because I called the new political science the right wing of the profession on the ground that it is the orthodoxy in the profession. The description of the present state of political science in this country which the critics give in the first two paragraphs of their article would seem to confirm that ground. I ordinarily would never speak of orthodoxy or its opposite except when speaking of religious orthodoxy or its opposite, but I remember that some of my scholarly contentions have been blamed, even in print, for being "unorthodox." This induced me to believe that in the view of my opponents there is something like orthodoxy in scholarship. I have also been accused of violating certain "obvious criteria" of "philosophical criticism." "A fair specimen of the level of argument is provided by [Strauss's] description of the new political science as 'a judicious mating of dialectical materialism and psychoanalysis to be consummated on a bed supplied by logical positivism.' (p. 312) The fact that none of the new scientists attacked in this volume would subscribe to all three positions, that there is evidence of hostility on the part of some of them towards the participants in this bedroom scene or that an honest examination of, say, Bentley's or Simon's theories, would show a logical incompatibility with one or the other of the three positions—all of this Strauss ig-[153a]nores." (p. 145) This is indeed "a fair specimen of the level of the argument" of the critics. It goes without saying that only a natural fool can ignore the incompatibility of the three positions or the fact that this incompatibility does not preclude their coexisting in more or less diluted forms in not a few people, some of whom can even be found among the new political scientists. What must be stressed is the fact that the sentence quoted by the critics is obviously not meant to be my "description of the new political science." I said: "the unprecedented political situation calls for an unprecedented political science, *perhaps* for a judicious mating of dialectical materialism and psychoanalysis to be consummated on a bed supplied by logical positivism." (p. 312) The italics are indeed not in the original. But the meaning of the sentence was clear to every reader of ordinary intelligence and fairness: one way in which the new political science might be formed is to combine dialectical materialism and psychoanalysis by claiming to transform their dogmatic and incompatible assertions into hypotheses while forgetting that claim most of the time. I am alive to the variety within the new political science: I spoke of the tension within it between "formalism" and "vulgarianism." (p. 322)

The charge of fanaticism has surprised me more than any other, for in scholarship at any rate intransigence—i.e., the habit of refusing to make concessions for the sake of peace and comity—is not fanaticism. The critics accuse me of attempting to revive the temper of an earlier age when the children of light believed that they had to defeat and to capture, if not to destroy, the children of darkness, and even of attempting to revive the practices of the Inquisition; they accuse me of accusing the new political science of "atheism, venality, conspiracy and treason." To hear them, one would think that I had charged the new political science with diabolic wickedness. Yet I said in a very visible place that "only a great fool would call the new political science diabolic." (p. 327) I criticized the new political science above all because of its lack of reflection or its narrowness. This is my reply also to the following criticism. "That charge of 'dogmatic atheism' continues to haunt the reader. From what frame of mind, what cast of thought and concern, does such a charge emerge? What is the relevance, or the propriety, of such a charge in a work which presents itself as an academic and professional discussion of academic and professional work?" (p. 128) The frame of mind is that of anti-dogmatism, and the relevance or propriety of the charge derives from the fact [153b] that academicians are supposed to free themselves from prejudices—from those of the left as well as from those of the right—as much as they can. As for the basis of my charge, the critics suspect rightly that I meant what I said when I spoke of the fact that "the new science uses sociological or psychological theories regarding religion which exclude, *without considering*, the possibility that religion rests ultimately on God's revealing Himself to man." (322; the italics are not in the original.) The critics do not deny "that the new science holds such theories regarding religion, but to establish that is not to establish the atheism of the new scientists." (p. 128) It was not I who made the transition, which is vicious in more than one sense, from "the new political science" to "the new political scientists"; for, to say nothing of other things, I have had public discussions with men of the cloth who took the side of the new political science against my criticism of it. As for the substance of my reply, the critics find it "beneath the contempt of philosophy," for science deals only with secondary causes and this limitation, essential to science, does not involve in any way a denial of "a First Cause." This distinction makes sense when the question concerns the study of eclipses of the sun or of comets, but not when it concerns the study of revealed religion, i.e., of what claims to be the human response to the immediate action of the First Cause: a study of revealed religion which is not open to the possibility mentioned cannot peacefully coexist with religion but clearly contradicts it; and if it excludes that possibility without considering it, it is in addition dogmatic. Max Weber, who had perhaps as great an influence on the new political

Chapter 18

science as Marx, Freud and logical positivism—although he was surely as little a new political scientist as Marx and Freud—took the possibility of Revelation seriously; hence his writings, even and especially those dealing with science as such, possess a depth and a claim to respect which, I believe, I have properly recognized; I venture to say that this particular open-mindedness was ultimately the reason why he was not a new political scientist. (cf. *Natural Right and History*, 73–76)

The critics are unable to see the difference between the statement which I made that "intellectual honesty is not enough" and the absurd opinion which they impute to me that "intellectual honesty represents a clever dodge." I have given the reason why in my view intellectual honesty is not enough. I am under no obligation to do anything further to enable the critics to see the difference. But when they impute to me the belief "that scholarly scruples [154a] may be suspended when combating evil," they simply calumniate. Without knowing it, they act on the belief which they impute to me. They are then excusable on the ground that they do not know what they are doing, for they claim to be standing up for "nobility of spirit and sensitivity of intellect." (p. 150)

The only criticism advanced by the critics which is substantive, not merely a repetition of criticisms made by others of some of my earlier writings, and at least apparently of some interest, concerns what I have said about common sense. "The problem crudely stated is, does science demand the repudiation of common sense?" (p. 145) I have no objection to crude statements of the problem and I admit without blushing that my own statements on this issue are crude. The crudeness is due in both cases to the fact that it is very hard to define common sense. Nevertheless we today are very frequently compelled to use the distinction between common sense and science in a commonsensical manner. The critics continue as follows: "Nowhere does Strauss indicate that many reputable writers have contended that scientific inquiries must originate in common sense...." (p. 145) The question is not so much who is or who is not a reputable writer and who is competent to judge of this, but in the first place whether the contention mentioned is characteristic of the new political science and, above all, from what point of view the contention is made: from the point of view of those who regard the transformation of all commonsense knowledge into scientific knowledge as the ideal, or from the opposite point of view. I am accused of having failed to give "a consistent definition of common sense" (p. 146); the accusation would carry greater force if the critics, who themselves take the distinction between common sense and science for granted, had supplied a definition which is not only consistent but adequate as well; they thus would have made a contribution. Their failure is due not only to the intrinsic difficulty of the task but also to a more particular reason; they believe that the statement with which Kant opens his Introduction to the *Critique of Pure Reason* deals with "common sense" because it deals with "experience." It suffices here to say that experience in Kant's sense, i.e., "knowledge of objects," comprises both commonsense knowledge and scientific knowledge. (*cf. Natural Right and History*, 79) It is simply untrue that "common sense" is ever employed by me "interchangeably with raw sense data." It is simply untrue that I "outfitted" common sense with constructs. In the passage to which the critics refer (p. 316) I explicitly speak of the [154b] empiricist understanding of common sense and not of my own, as any reader of ordinary care must have seen. I have nothing to say to people who find it illegitimate that I look for common sense among intelligent and informed citizens rather than among unintelligent and uninformed ones. To say as I did within a qualifying context that "intelligent and informed citizens distinguish soundly between important and unimportant political matters" is not to say what the critics make me say, namely, that prescientific knowledge "owns an unerring instinct for what is politically relevant or important." (p. 146) All that they say on the subject of common sense can be said only by people who regard the commonsense understanding of political things prior to scientific corroboration as cognitively worthless, i.e., agree entirely with the fundamental assertion of the new political science. As a consequence, they never for a single moment meet the sole issue to which the whole Epilogue is devoted. As might be mentioned in passing, they note with an exclamation that I have learned something from Marsilius of Padua and they suggest that the notion according to which the "world" is "a whole" is of biblical rather than of Greek origin.

What the critics say about my remarks on Aristotelian political science suffers from an almost "wilful blindness." (p. 148) Plainly, these remarks were not meant to be more than a rough sketch serving the purpose of bringing out as clearly as possible the characteristics of the new political science. They find me "at [my] most disarming" when I contend that Aristotelian political science might be superior to the new political science in regard to the understanding of the politics of the atomic age precisely because the former is not a child of the atomic age. (p. 150) To supply them with a further example of my "heavy irony," I believe indeed that Aristotelian political science is more likely to free us from certain well known delusions regarding disarmament than is the new political science.

Chapter 18

There is only one point regarding which the critics believe they agree entirely with me, and this point is indeed of great moment: they too feel an obligation toward "the best men of the coming generation." They claim that their attack on me was prompted by nothing but concern for "nobility of spirit and sensitivity of intellect," excellences which in their view are in danger if, for instance, students are "instructed in the hard doctrine that 'what is most important for political science is identical with what is most important politically' and that today 'the most important concern is the Cold War or the qualitative difference, which amounts to a [155a] conflict, between liberal democracy and communism.'" Hard doctrines may be true doctrines and, in addition, they may be in need of being taught, especially in political science departments; for where else are doctrines of this kind likely to be taught? Scholarship requires indeed detachment, but detachment is not easily won and easily preserved—scholarship requires attachment to detachment. Yet the attachment to detachment necessarily leads to attachment to the indispensable conditions of detachment and therewith also to firm rejections. In other words, the commitment to scholarship is bound to have political consequences. These consequences are not free from ambiguity since every society consists chiefly of men not committed to scholarship and there is not necessarily a harmony between the "interest" of the scholars as scholars and the "interest" of the non-scholars. The ambiguity has in our era still another source; it must be traced to a specific ambiguity of "nobility of spirit." Does "nobility of spirit" or "generosity of the spirit" call in the first place [155b] for the improvement (which presupposes the preservation in freedom from barbarian domination) of the political community to which one belongs, for its pursuit of excellence, for one's adorning the Sparta which fate has allotted to one; or does it call in the first place, as the critics seem to believe, for "compassion which cannot but sorrow for the common lot of all mankind"? By explaining their understanding of "nobility of spirit," and only by doing this, the critics touch on "the first and last questions" (p. 150) without seeing however that they have touched on a question. If I am not altogether mistaken, the alternative stated is the issue which divides the "right" at its best from the "left" at its best, and surely in this respect the critics belong to the "right." I believe them on their word when they say that they wish to be of the center, but not all issues permit of a center; there are issues which force one to face an Either-Or; more generally stated, in order to be something it is not sufficient that one wishes to be it.

19

Preface to
History of Political Philosophy
(1963)

[v] This book is intended primarily to introduce undergraduate students of political science to political philosophy. The authors and editors have done their best to take political philosophy seriously, assuming throughout that the teachings of the great political philosophers are important not only historically, as phenomena about which we must learn if we wish to understand societies of the present and the past, but also as phenomena from which we must learn if we wish to understand those societies. We believe that the questions raised by the political philosophers of the past are alive in our own society, if only in the way that questions can be alive which, in the main, are tacitly or unwittingly answered. We have written, further, in the belief that in order to understand any society, to analyze it with any depth, the analyst must himself be exposed to these enduring questions and be swayed by them.

    This book is addressed to those who for whatever reason believe that students of political science must have some understanding of the philosophic treatment of the abiding questions; to those who do not believe that political science is scientific as chemistry and physics are—subjects from which their own history is excluded. That the great majority of the profession concurs in the view that the history of political philosophy is a proper part of political science we take to be proved by the very common practice of offering courses on this subject matter.

    We tender this book to the public in full awareness that it is not a perfect historical study. It is not even a perfect textbook. It is imperfect of its kind, as we freely acknowledge, because for one thing it is not the work of

---

Originally published as the preface to the first edition of *History of Political Philosophy*, ed. Leo Strauss and Joseph Cropsey (Chicago: Rand McNally, 1963), v–vi. —Eds.

CHAPTER 19

one hand. If the hand could be found that is moved by a single mind with the necessary grasp of the literature, that hand would write, [vi] if it found time, a more coherent, more uniform book, certainly a more comprehensive book—and we will ourselves adopt it when it appears. On the other hand, it must be allowed that the reader of a collaborate work is to some extent compensated for these shortcomings by the variety of viewpoints, talents, and backgrounds that inform the parts of the volume.

We are convinced that even the most excellent textbook could serve only a limited purpose. When a student has mastered the very best secondary account of an author's teaching, he possesses an opinion of that teaching, a hearsay rather than knowledge of it. If the hearsay is accurate, then the student has right opinion; otherwise wrong opinion, but in neither case the knowledge that transcends opinion. We would be under the profoundest possible delusion if we saw nothing paradoxical in inculcating opinion about what is meant to transcend opinion. We do not believe that this textbook or any other can be more than a help or a guide to students who, while they read it, are at the same time emphatically directed to the original texts.

We have had to decide to include certain authors and subjects and to omit others. In doing so we have not meant to prejudge the issue as to what part of political philosophy is alive or deserves to be alive. Surely an argument could be made for the inclusion of Dante, Bodin, Thomas More, and Harrington, and for the exclusion of the Muslim and Jewish medievals and of Descartes, for example. The amount of space devoted to each author could also be questioned, as could our abstaining from the practice of mentioning writers' names for the sole purpose of bringing them before the student's eye. We will not bore the reader with a repetition of the anthologist's prayer for the remission of sins. Everyone knows that there cannot be a book like this without decisions and there cannot be a decision without a question as to its rightness. The most we will assert is that we believe we could defend our deeds.

We should like last to record our gratitude to the personnel of Rand McNally & Company, who have done everything possible to lighten our task. Those who ever have served as editors will know immediately the value of the publisher's cordial assistance; others could never imagine it.

L. S.
J. C.

Note: At the end of each chapter, a reading suggestion is given, divided into two parts. The part designated as A contains the works or selection that in our opinion are indispensable to the student's understanding, while the list headed B contains important additional material that can be assigned if time permits.

20

Introduction to
History of Political Philosophy
(1963)

[1] Today "political philosophy" has become almost synonymous with "ideology," not to say "myth." It surely is understood in contradistinction to "political science." The distinction between political philosophy and political science is a consequence of the fundamental distinction between philosophy and science. Even this fundamental distinction is of relatively recent origin. Traditionally, philosophy and science were not distinguished: natural science was one of the most important parts of philosophy. The great intellectual revolution of the seventeenth century which brought to light modern natural science was a revolution of a new philosophy or science against traditional (chiefly Aristotelian) philosophy or science. But the new philosophy or science was only partly successful. The most successful part of the new philosophy or science was the new natural science. By virtue of its victory, the new natural science became more and more independent of philosophy, at least apparently, and even, as it were, became an authority for philosophy. In this way the distinction between philosophy and science became generally accepted, and eventually also the distinction between political philosophy and political science as a kind of natural science of political things. Traditionally, however, political philosophy and political science were the same.

Political philosophy is not the same as political thought in general. Political thought is coeval with political life. Political philosophy, however, emerged within a particular political life, in Greece, in that past of which we have written records. According to the traditional view, the Athenian Socrates (469–399 B.C.) was the founder of political philosophy. Socrates

---

Originally published as the introduction to the first edition of *History of Political Philosophy*, ed. Leo Strauss and Joseph Cropsey (Chicago: Rand McNally, 1963), 1–6. —Eds.

CHAPTER 20

was the teacher of Plato, who in his turn was the [2] teacher of Aristotle. The political works of Plato and Aristotle are the oldest works devoted to political philosophy which have come down to us. The kind of political philosophy which was originated by Socrates is called classical political philosophy. Classical political philosophy was the predominant political philosophy until the emergence of modern political philosophy in the sixteenth and seventeenth centuries. Modern political philosophy came into being through the conscious break with the principles established by Socrates. By the same token classical political philosophy is not limited to the political teaching of Plato and Aristotle and their schools; it includes also the political teaching of the Stoics as well as the political teachings of the church fathers and the Scholastics, in so far as these teachings are not based exclusively on Divine revelation. The traditional view according to which Socrates was the founder of political philosophy is in need of some qualifications, or rather explanations; yet it is less misleading than any alternative view.

Socrates surely was not the first philosopher. This means that political philosophy was preceded by philosophy. The first philosophers are called by Aristotle "those who discourse on nature"; he distinguishes them from those "who discourse on the gods." The primary theme of philosophy, then, is "nature." What is nature? The first Greek whose work has come down to us, Homer himself, mentions "nature" only a single time; this first mention of "nature" gives us a most important hint as to what the Greek philosophers understood by "nature." In the tenth book of the *Odyssey*, Odysseus tells of what befell him on the island of the sorceress-goddess Circe. Circe had transformed many of his comrades into swine and locked them in sties. On his way to Circe's house to rescue his poor comrades, Odysseus is met by the god Hermes who wishes to preserve him. He promises Odysseus an egregious herb which will make him safe against Circe's evil arts. Hermes "drew a herb from the earth and showed me its nature. Black at the root it was, like milk its blossom; and the gods call it moly. Hard is it to dig for mortal men, but the gods can do everything." Yet the gods' ability to dig the herb with ease would be of no avail if they did not know the nature of the herb—its looks and its power—in the first place. The gods are thus omnipotent because they are, not indeed omniscient, but the knowers of the natures of the things—of natures which they have not made. "Nature" means here the character of a thing, or of a kind of thing, the way in which a thing or a kind of thing looks and acts, and the thing, or the kind of thing, is taken not to have been made by gods or men. If we were entitled to take a poetic utterance literally, we could say that the first man we know who spoke of nature was the [3] Wily Odysseus who had seen the towns of many men and had thus come to know how much the thoughts of men differ from town to town or from tribe to tribe.

It seems that the Greek word for nature (*physis*) means primarily "growth" and therefore also that into which a thing grows, the term of the growth, the character a thing has when its growth is completed, when it can do what only the fully grown thing of the kind in question can do or do well. Things like shoes or chairs do not "grow" but are "made": they are not "by nature" but "by art." On the other hand, there are things which are "by nature" without having "grown" and even without having come into being in any way. They are said to be "by nature" because they have not been made and because they are the "first things," out of which or through which all other natural things have come into being. The atoms to which the philosopher Democritus traced everything are by nature in the last sense.

Nature, however understood, is not known by nature. Nature had to be discovered. The Hebrew Bible, for example, does not have a word for nature. The equivalent in biblical Hebrew of "nature" is something like "way" or "custom." Prior to the discovery of nature, men knew that each thing or kind of thing has its "way" or its "custom"—its form of "regular behavior." There is a way or custom of fire, of dogs, of women, of madmen, of human beings: fire burns, dogs bark and wag their tails, women ovulate, madmen rave, human beings can speak. Yet there are also ways or customs of the various human tribes (Egyptians, Persians, Spartans, Moabites, Amalekites, and so on). Through the discovery of nature the radical difference between these two kinds of "ways" or "customs" came to the center of attention. The discovery of nature led to the splitting up of "way" or "custom" into "nature" (*physis*) on the one hand and "convention" or "law" (*nomos*) on the other. For instance, that human beings can speak is natural, but that this particular tribe uses this particular language is due to convention. The distinction implies that the natural is prior to the conventional. The distinction between nature and convention is fundamental for classical political philosophy and even for most of modern political philosophy, as can be seen most simply from the distinction between natural right and positive right.

Once nature was discovered and understood primarily in contradistinction to law or convention, it became possible and necessary to raise this question: Are the political things natural, and if they are, to what extent? The very question implied that the laws are not natural. But obedience to the laws was generally considered to be justice. Hence one was

CHAPTER 20

compelled to wonder whether justice is merely conventional or [4] whether there are things which are by nature just. Are even the laws merely conventional or do they have their roots in nature? Must the laws not be "according to nature," and especially according to the nature of man, if they are to be good? The laws are the foundation or the work of the political community: is the political community by nature? In the attempts to answer these questions it was presupposed that there are things which are by nature good for man as man. The precise question therefore concerns the relation of what is by nature good for man, on the one hand, to justice or right on the other. The simple alternative is this: all right is conventional or there is some natural right. Both opposed answers were given and developed prior to Socrates. For a variety of reasons it is not helpful to present here a summary of what can be known of these pre-Socratic doctrines. We shall get some notion of the conventionalist view (the view that all right is conventional) when we turn to Plato's *Republic*, which contains a summary of that view. As for the opposite view, it must suffice here to say that it was developed by Socrates and classical political philosophy in general much beyond the earlier views.

What then is meant by the assertion that Socrates was the founder of political philosophy? Socrates did not write any books. According to the most ancient reports, he turned away from the study of the divine or natural things and directed his inquiries entirely to the human things, i.e., the just things, the noble things, and the things good for man as man; he always conversed about "what is pious, what is impious, what is noble, what is base, what is just, what is unjust, what is sobriety, what is madness, what is courage, what is cowardice, what is the city, what is the statesman, what is rule over men, what is a man able to rule over men," and similar things.[1] It seems that Socrates was induced to turn away from the study of the divine or natural things by his piety. The gods do not approve of man's trying to seek out what they do not wish to reveal, especially the things in heaven and beneath the earth. A pious man will therefore investigate only the things left to men's investigation, i.e., the human things. Socrates pursued his investigations by means of conversations. This means that he started from generally held opinions. Among the generally held opinions the most authoritative ones are those sanctioned by the city and its laws—by the most solemn convention. But the generally held opinions contradict one another. It therefore becomes necessary to transcend

---

1 Xenophon, *Memorabilia* I.1.11–16.

the whole sphere of the generally held opinions, or of opinion as such, in the direction of knowledge. Since even the most authoritative opinions are only opinions, even Socrates was compelled to go the way from convention or law to nature, to ascend from law to nature. But now it appears more [5] clearly than ever before that opinion, convention, or law, contains truth, or is not arbitrary, or is in a sense natural. One may say that the law, the human law, thus proves to point to a divine or natural law as its origin. This implies, however, that the human law, precisely because it is not identical with the divine or natural law, is not unqualifiedly true or just: only natural right, justice itself, the "idea" or "form" of justice, is unqualifiedly just. Nevertheless, the human law, the law of the city, is unqualifiedly obligatory for the men subject to it provided they have the right to emigrate with their property, i.e., provided their subjection to the laws of their city was voluntary.[2]

The precise reason why Socrates became the founder of political philosophy appears when one considers the character of the questions with which he dealt in his conversations. He raised the question "What is...?" regarding everything. This question is meant to bring to light the nature of the kind of thing in question, that is, the form or the character of the thing. Socrates presupposed that knowledge of the whole is, above all, knowledge of the character, the form, the "essential" character of every part of the whole, as distinguished from knowledge of that out of which or through which the whole may have come into being. If the whole consists of essentially different parts, it is at least possible that the political things (or the human things) are essentially different from the nonpolitical things—that the political things form a class by themselves and therefore can be studied by themselves. Socrates, it seems, took the primary meaning of "nature" more seriously than any of his predecessors: he realized that "nature" is primarily "form" or "idea." If this is true, he did not simply turn away from the study of the natural things, but originated a new kind of the study of the natural things—a kind of study in which, for example, the nature or idea of justice, or natural right, and surely the nature of the human soul or man, is more important than, for example, the nature of the sun.

One cannot understand the nature of man if one does not understand the nature of human society. Socrates as well as Plato and Aristotle assumed that the most perfect form of human society is the *polis*. The *polis* is today frequently taken to be the Greek city-state. But for the classical

---

2   Plato, *Crito* 51d–e.

Chapter 20

political philosophers it was accidental that the *polis* was more common among Greeks than among non-Greeks. One would then have to say that the theme of classical political philosophy was, not the Greek city-state, but the city-state. This presupposes, however, that the city-state is one particular form of "the state." It presupposes therefore the concept of the state as comprising the city-state among other forms of the state. Yet classical political philosophy [6] lacked the concept of "the state." When people speak today of "the state," they ordinarily understand "state" in contradistinction to "society." This distinction is alien to classical political philosophy. It is not sufficient to say that *polis* (city) comprises both state and society, for the concept "city" antedates the distinction between state and society; therefore one does not understand "the city" by saying the city comprises state and society. The modern equivalent to "the city" on the level of the citizen's understanding is "the country." For when a man says, for example, that "the country is in danger," he also has not yet made a distinction between state and society. The reason why the classical political philosophers were chiefly concerned with the city was not that they were ignorant of other forms of societies in general and of political societies in particular. They knew the tribe (the nation) as well as such structures as the Persian Empire. They were chiefly concerned with the city because they preferred the city to those other forms of political society. The grounds of this preference may be said to have been these: tribes are not capable of a high civilization, and very large societies cannot be free societies. Let us remember that the authors of the *Federalist Papers* were still under a compulsion to prove that it is possible for a large society to be republican or free. Let us also remember that the authors of the *Federalist Papers* signed themselves "Publius": republicanism points back to classical antiquity and therefore also to classical political philosophy.

21

Plato
427–347 B.C.
(1963)

[33] Thirty-five dialogues and thirteen letters have come down to us as Platonic writings, not all of which are now regarded as genuine. Some scholars go so far as to doubt that any of the letters is genuine. In order not to encumber our presentation with polemics, we shall disregard the letters altogether. We must then say that Plato never speaks to us in his own name, for in his dialogues only his characters speak. Strictly, there is then no Platonic teaching; at most there is the teaching of the men who are the chief characters in his dialogues. Why Plato proceeded in this manner is not easy to say. Perhaps he was doubtful whether there can be a philosophic teaching proper. Perhaps he, too, thought like his master Socrates that philosophy is in the last analysis knowledge of ignorance. Socrates is indeed the chief character in most of the Platonic dialogues. One could say that Plato's dialogues as a whole are less the presentation of a teaching than a monument to the life of Socrates—to the core of his life: they all show how Socrates engaged in his most important work, the awakening of his fellow men and the attempting to guide them toward the good life which he himself was living. Still, Socrates is not always the chief character in Plato's dialogues; in a few he does hardly more than listen while others speak, and in one dialogue (the *Laws*) he is not even present. We mention these strange facts because they show how difficult it is to speak of Plato's teaching.

All Platonic dialogues refer more or less directly to the political question. Yet there are only three dialogues which indicate by their very titles

---

As published in *History of Political Philosophy*, ed. Leo Strauss and Joseph Cropsey, 3rd ed. (Chicago: University of Chicago Press, 1987), 33–89. —Eds.

that they are devoted to political philosophy: the *Republic*, the *Statesman*, and the *Laws*. The political teaching of Plato is accessible to us chiefly through these three works. [34]

The Republic

In the *Republic*, Socrates discusses the nature of justice with a fairly large number of people. The conversation about this general theme takes place, of course, in a particular setting: in a particular place, at a particular time, with men each of whom has his particular age, character, abilities, position in society, and appearance. While the place of the conversation is made quite clear to us, the time, i.e., the year, is not. Hence we lack certain knowledge of the political circumstances in which this conversation about the principles of politics takes place. We may assume, however, that it takes place in an era of political decay of Athens, that at any rate Socrates and the chief interlocutors (the brothers Glaukon and Adeimantos) were greatly concerned with that decay and thinking of the restoration of political health. Certain it is that Socrates makes very radical proposals of "reform" without encountering serious resistance. But there are also a few indications in the *Republic* to the effect that the longed-for reformation is not likely to succeed on the political plane or that the only possible reformation is that of the individual man.

The conversation opens with Socrates' addressing a question to the oldest man present, Kephalos, who is respectable on account of his piety as well as his wealth. Socrates' question is a model of propriety. It gives Kephalos an opportunity to speak of everything good which he possesses, to display his happiness, as it were, and it concerns the only subject about which Socrates could conceivably learn something from him: about how it feels to be very old. In the course of his answer Kephalos comes to speak of injustice and justice. He seems to imply that justice is identical with telling the truth and paying back what one has received from anyone. Socrates shows him that telling the truth and returning another man's property are not always just. At this point Kephalos' son and heir, Polemarchos, rising in defense of his father's opinion, takes the place of his father in the conversation. But the opinion which he defends is not exactly the same as his father's; if we may make use of a joke of Socrates', Polemarchos inherits only half, and perhaps even less than a half, of his father's intellectual property. Polemarchos no longer maintains that telling the truth is essential to justice. Without knowing it, he thus lays down one of the

Plato, 427–347 B.C.

principles of the *Republic*. As appears later in the work, in a well-ordered society it is necessary that one tell untruths of a certain kind to children and even to the adult subjects.[1] This example reveals the character of the discussion which occurs in the first book of the *Republic*, where Socrates refutes a number of false opinions about justice. This negative or destructive work, however, contains within itself the constructive assertions of the bulk of the *Republic*. Let us consider from this point of view the three opinions on justice discussed in the first book.

Kephalos' opinion as taken up by Polemarchos (after his father had left to perform an act of piety) is to the effect that justice consists in returning deposits. More generally stated, Kephalos holds that justice consists in returning, leaving, or giving to everyone what belongs to him. But he also holds that justice is good, i.e., salutary, not only to the giver but also to the receiver. Now it is obvious that in some cases giving to a man what belongs to him is harmful to him. Not all men make a good or wise use of what belongs to them, of their property. If we judge very strictly, we might be driven to say that very few people make a wise use of their property. If justice is to be salutary, we might be compelled to demand that everyone should own only what is "fitting" for him, what is good for him, and for as long as it is good for him. In brief, we might be compelled to demand the abolition of private property or the introduction of communism. To the extent to which there is a connection between private property and the family, we would even be compelled to demand abolition of the family or the introduction of absolute communism, i.e., of communism not only regarding property but regarding women and children as well. Above all, extremely few people will be able to determine wisely which things and which amounts of them are good for the use of each individual—or at any rate for each individual who counts; only men of exceptional wisdom are able to do this. We would then be compelled to demand that society be ruled by simply wise men, by philosophers in the strict sense, wielding absolute power. The refutation of Kephalos' view of justice thus contains the proof of the necessity of absolute communism in the sense defined, as well as of the absolute rule of the philosophers. This proof, it is hardly necessary to say, is based on the disregard of, or the abstraction from, a number of most relevant things; it is "abstract" in the extreme. If we wish to understand the *Republic*, we must find out what these disregarded things are and why they are disregarded. The *Republic* itself, carefully read, supplies the answers to these questions.

---

1   Plato *Republic* 377 ff., 389b–c, 414b–415d, 459c–d.

Chapter 21

Before going any further, we must dispose of a misunderstanding which is at present very common. The theses of the *Republic* summarized in the two preceding paragraphs clearly show that Plato, or at any rate Socrates, was not a liberal democrat. They also suffice to show that Plato was not a Communist in the sense of Marx, or a Fascist: [36] Marxist communism and fascism are incompatible with the rule of philosophers, whereas the scheme of the *Republic* stands or falls by the rule of philosophers. But let us hasten back to the *Republic*.

Whereas the first opinion on justice was only implied by Kephalos and stated by Socrates, the second opinion is stated by Polemarchos, although not without Socrates' assistance. Furthermore, Kephalos' opinion is linked in his mind with the view that injustice is bad because it is punished by the gods after death. This view forms no part of Polemarchos' opinion. He is confronted with the contradiction between the two opinions according to which justice must be salutary to the receiver and justice consists in giving to each what belongs to him. Polemarchos overcomes the contradiction by dropping the second opinion. He also modifies the first. Justice, he says, consists in helping one's friends and harming one's enemies. Justice thus understood would seem to be unqualifiedly good for the giver and for those receivers who are good to the giver. This difficulty, however, arises: If justice is taken to be giving to others what belongs to them, the only thing which the just man must know is what belongs to anyone with whom he has any dealing; this knowledge is supplied by the law, which in principle can be easily known by mere listening. But if the just man must give to his friends what is good for them, he himself must judge; he himself must be able correctly to distinguish friends from enemies; he himself must know what is good for each of his friends. Justice must include knowledge of a high order. To say the least, justice must be an art comparable to medicine, the art which knows and produces what is good for human bodies. Polemarchos is unable to identify the knowledge or the art which goes with justice or which is justice. He is therefore unable to show how justice can be salutary. The discussion points to the view that justice is the art which gives to each man what is good for his soul, i.e., that justice is identical with, or at least inseparable from, philosophy, the medicine of the soul. It points to the view that there cannot be justice among men unless the philosophers rule. But Socrates does not yet state this view. Instead he makes clear to Polemarchos that the just man will help just men rather than his "friends," and he will harm no one. He does not say that the just man will help everyone. Perhaps he means that there are human beings whom he cannot benefit. But he surely also means something more. Polemarchos' thesis may be taken to reflect a most potent opinion regarding justice—the opinion according to which justice means public-spiritedness, full dedication to one's city as a particular society which as such is potentially the enemy of other cities. Justice so understood is patriotism, and consists indeed in helping one's [37] friends, i.e., one's fellow citizens, and harming one's enemies, i.e., foreigners. Justice thus understood cannot be entirely dispensed with in any city however just, for even the most just city is a city, a particular or closed or exclusive society. Therefore Socrates himself demands later in the dialogue that the guardians of the city be by nature friendly to their own people and harsh or nasty to strangers.[2] He also demands that the citizens of the just city cease to regard all human beings as their brothers and limit the feelings and actions of fraternity to their fellow citizens alone.[3] The opinion of Polemarchos properly understood is the only one among the generally known views of justice discussed in the first book of the *Republic* which is entirely preserved in the positive or constructive part of the *Republic*. This opinion, to repeat, is to the effect that justice is full dedication to the common good; it demands that man withhold nothing of his own from his city; it demands therefore by itself—i.e., if we abstract from all other considerations—absolute communism.

The third and last opinion discussed in the first book of the *Republic* is the one maintained by Thrasymachos. He is the only speaker in the work who exhibits anger and behaves discourteously and even savagely. He is highly indignant over the result of Socrates' conversation with Polemarchos. He seems to be particularly shocked by Socrates' contention that it is not good for oneself to harm anyone or that justice is never harmful to anyone. It is most important, both for the understanding of the *Republic* and generally, that we do not behave toward Thrasymachos as Thrasymachos behaves, i.e., angrily, fanatically, or savagely. If we look then at Thrasymachos' indignation without indignation, we must admit that his violent reaction is to some extent a revolt of common sense. Since the city as city is a society which from time to time must wage war, and war is inseparable from harming innocent people,[4] the unqualified condemnation of harming

---

2   Ibid., 375b–376c.

3   Ibid., 414d–e.

4   Ibid., 471a–b.

Chapter 21

human beings would be tantamount to the condemnation of even the justest city. Apart from this, it seems to be entirely fitting that the most savage man present should maintain a most savage thesis on justice. Thrasymachos contends that justice is the advantage of the stronger. Still, this thesis proves to be only the consequence of an opinion which is not only not manifestly savage but is even highly respectable. According to that opinion, the just is the same as the lawful or legal, i.e., what the customs or laws of the city prescribe. Yet this opinion implies that there is nothing higher to which one can appeal from the man-made laws or conventions. This is the opinion now known by the name of "legal positivism," but in its origin it is not academic; it is the opinion on which all political societies tend to act. If the just is identical with the [38] legal, the source of justice is the will of the legislator. The legislator in each city is the regime—the man or body of men that rules the city: the tyrant, the common people, the men of excellence, and so on. According to Thrasymachos, each regime lays down the laws with a view to its own preservation and well-being, in a word, to its own advantage and to nothing else. From this it follows that obedience to the laws or justice is not necessarily advantageous to the ruled and may even be bad for them. And as for the rulers, justice simply does not exist: they lay down the laws with exclusive concern for their own advantage.

Let us concede for a moment that Thrasymachos' view of law and of rulers is correct. The rulers surely may make mistakes. They may command actions which are in fact disadvantageous to themselves and advantageous to the ruled. In that case the just or law-abiding subjects will in fact do what is disadvantageous to the rulers and advantageous to the subjects. When this difficulty is pointed out to him by Socrates, Thrasymachos declares after some hesitation that the rulers are not rulers if and when they make mistakes: the ruler in the strict sense is infallible, just as the artisan in the strict sense is infallible. It is this Thrasymachean notion of "the artisan in the strict sense" which Socrates uses with great felicity against Thrasymachos. For the artisan in the strict sense proves to be concerned, not with his own advantage, but with the advantage of the others whom he serves: the shoemaker makes shoes for others and only accidentally for himself; the physician prescribes things to his patients with a view to their advantage; hence if ruling is, as Thrasymachos admitted, something like an art, the ruler serves the ruled, i.e., rules for the advantage of the ruled. The artisan in the strict sense is infallible, i.e., does his job well, and he is only concerned with the well-being of others. This, however, means that art strictly understood is justice—justice in deed, and not merely in intention as law-abidingness is. "Art is justice"—this proposition reflects the Socratic assertion that virtue is knowledge. The suggestion emerging from Socrates' discussion with Thrasymachos leads to the conclusion that the just city will be an association where everyone is an artisan in the strict sense, a city of craftsmen or artificers, of men (and women) each of whom has a single job which he does well and with full dedication, i.e., without minding his own advantage and only for the good of others or for the common good. This conclusion pervades the whole teaching of the *Republic*. The city constructed there as a model is based on the principle of "one man one job." The soldiers in it are "artificers" of the freedom of the city; the philosophers in it are "artificers" of the whole common virtue; there is an "artificer" of [39] heaven; even God is presented as an artisan—as the artificer even of the eternal ideas.[5] It is because citizenship in the just city is craftsmanship of one kind or another, and the seat of craftsmanship or art is in the soul and not in the body, that the difference between the two sexes loses its importance, or the equality of the two sexes is established.[6]

Thrasymachos could have avoided his downfall if he had left matters at the common-sense view according to which rulers are of course fallible, or if he had said that all laws are framed by the rulers with a view to their apparent (and not necessarily true) advantage. Since he is not a noble man, we are entitled to suspect that he chose the alternative which proved fatal to him with a view to his own advantage. Thrasymachos was a famous teacher of rhetoric, the art of persuasion. (Hence, incidentally, he is the only man possessing an art who speaks in the *Republic*.) The art of persuasion is necessary for persuading rulers and especially ruling assemblies, at least ostensibly, of their true advantage. Even the rulers themselves need the art of persuasion in order to persuade their subjects that the laws, which are framed with exclusive regard to the benefit of the rulers, serve the benefit of the subjects. Thrasymachos' own art stands or falls by the view that prudence is of the utmost importance for ruling. The clearest expression of this view is the proposition that the ruler who makes mistakes is no longer a ruler at all.

Thrasymachos' downfall is caused not by a stringent refutation of his view of justice nor by an accidental slip on his part but by the conflict be-

---

5   *Ibid.*, 395c; 500d; 530a; 507c; 597.
6   *Ibid.*, 454c–455a; cf. 452a.

tween his depreciation of justice or his indifference to justice and the implication of his art: there is some truth in the view that art is justice. One could say—and as a matter of fact Thrasymachos himself says—that Socrates' conclusion, namely, that no ruler or other artisan ever considers his own advantage, is very simple-minded: Socrates seems to be a babe in the woods. As regards the artisans proper, they of course consider the compensation which they receive for their work. It may be true that to the extent to which the physician is concerned with what is characteristically called his honorarium, he does not exercise the art of the physician but the art of money-making; but since what is true of the physician is true of the shoemaker and any other craftsman as well, one would have to say that the only universal art, the art accompanying all arts, the art of arts, is the art of money-making; one must therefore further say that serving others or being just becomes good for the artisan only through his practicing the art of money-making, or that no one is just for the sake of justice, or that no one likes justice as such. But the most devastating argument against Socrates' reasoning is supplied by the arts which are manifestly concerned with the most ruthless and calculating exploitation of the ruled by the rulers. Such an art is the art of the shepherd—the art wisely chosen by Thrasymachos in order to destroy Socrates' argument, especially since kings and other rulers have been compared to shepherds since the oldest times. The shepherd is surely concerned with the well-being of his flock— so that the sheep will supply men with the juiciest lamb chops. As Thrasymachos puts it, the shepherds are exclusively concerned with the good of the owners and of themselves.[7] But there is obviously a difference between the owners and the shepherds: the juiciest lamb chops are for the owner and not for the shepherd, unless the shepherd is dishonest. Now, the position of Thrasymachos or of any man of his kind with regard to both rulers and ruled is precisely that of the shepherd with regard to both the owners and the sheep: Thrasymachos can securely derive benefit from the assistance which he gives to the rulers (regardless of whether they are tyrants, common people, or men of excellence) only if he is loyal to them, if he does his job for them well, if he keeps his part of the bargain, if he is just. Contrary to his assertion, he must grant that a man's justice is salutary, not only to others and especially to the rulers, but also to himself. It is partly because he has become aware of this necessity that he changes his manners so remarkably in the last part of the first book. What is true of the helpers

---

7   *Ibid.*, 343b.

of rulers is true of the rulers themselves and all other human beings (including tyrants and gangsters) who need the help of other men in their enterprises however unjust: no association can last if its members do not practice justice among themselves.[8] This, however, amounts to an admission that justice may be a mere means, if an indispensable means, for injustice—for the exploitation of outsiders. Above all, it does not dispose of the possibility that the city is a community held together by collective selfishness and nothing else, or that there is no fundamental difference between the city and a gang of robbers. These and similar difficulties explain why Socrates regards his refutation of Thrasymachos as insufficient: he says at its conclusion that he has tried to show that justice is good without having made clear what justice is.

The adequate defense or praise of justice presupposes not only knowledge of what justice is, but also an adequate attack on justice. At the beginning of the second book, Glaukon attempts to present such an attack; he claims that he restates Thrasymachos' thesis, in which he does not believe, with greater vigor than Thrasymachos had done. Glaukon also takes it for granted that the just is the same as the legal or conventional, but he attempts to show how convention emerges out of nature. By nature each man is concerned only with his own good [41] and wholly unconcerned with any other man's good to the point that he has no hesitation whatever about harming his fellows. Since everyone acts accordingly, they all bring about a situation which is unbearable for most of them; the majority, i.e., the weaklings, figure out that every one of them would be better off if they agreed among themselves as to what each of them may or may not do. What they agree upon is not stated by Glaukon, but part of it can easily be guessed: they will agree that no one may violate the life and limb, the honor, the liberty, and the property of any of the associates, i.e., the fellow citizens, and that everyone must do his best to protect his associates against outsiders. Both the abstention from such violations and the service of protection are in no way desirable in themselves but only necessary evils, yet lesser evils than universal insecurity. But what is true of the majority is not true of "the real man" who can take care of himself and who is better off if he does not submit to law or convention. Yet even the others do violence to their nature by submitting to law and justice: they submit to it only from fear of the consequences of the failure to submit, i.e., from fear of punishment of one kind or an-

---

8   *Ibid.*, 351c–352a.

CHAPTER 21

other, not voluntarily and gladly. Therefore every man would prefer injustice to justice if he could be sure of escaping detection: justice is preferable to injustice only with a view to possible detection, to one's becoming known as just to others, i.e., to good repute or other rewards. Therefore since, as Glaukon hopes, justice is choiceworthy for its own sake, he demands from Socrates a proof that the life of the just man is preferable to that of the unjust man even if the just man is thought to be unjust in the extreme and suffers all kinds of punishment or is in the depth of misery, and the unjust man is thought to be of consummate justice and receives all kinds of reward or is at the peak of happiness: the height of injustice, i.e., of the conduct according to nature, is the tacit exploitation of law or convention for one's own benefit alone, the conduct of the supremely shrewd and manly tyrant. In the discussion with Thrasymachos, the issue had become blurred by the suggestion that there is a kinship between justice and art. Glaukon makes the issue manifest by comparing the perfectly unjust man to the perfect artisan, whereas he conceives of the perfectly just man as a simple man who has no quality other than justice. With a view to the teaching of the *Republic* as a whole, one is tempted to say that Glaukon understands pure justice in the light of pure fortitude; his perfectly just man reminds one of the unknown soldier who undergoes the most painful and most humiliating death for no other purpose whatsoever except in order to die bravely and without any prospect of his noble deed ever becoming known to anyone.

[42] Glaukon's demand on Socrates is strongly supported by Adeimantos. It becomes clear from Adeimantos' speech that Glaukon's view according to which justice is choiceworthy entirely for its own sake is altogether novel, for in the traditional view justice was regarded as choiceworthy chiefly, if not exclusively, because of the divine rewards for justice and the divine punishments for injustice, and various other consequences. Adeimantos' long speech differs from Glaukon's because it brings out the fact that if justice is to be choiceworthy for its own sake, it must be easy or pleasant.[9] Glaukon's and Adeimantos' demands establish the standard by which one must judge Socrates' praise of justice; they force one to investigate whether or to what extent Socrates has proved in the *Republic* that justice is choiceworthy for its own sake or pleasant or even by itself sufficient to make a man perfectly happy in the midst of what is ordinarily believed to be the most extreme misery.

---

9   Cf. *ibid.*, 364a, c–d, 365c with 357b and 358a.

Plato, 427–347 B.C.

In order to defend the cause of justice, Socrates turns to founding, together with Glaukon and Adeimantos, a city in speech. The reason why this procedure is necessary can be stated as follows. Justice is believed to be law-abidingness or the firm will to give to everyone what belongs to him, i.e., what belongs to him according to law; yet justice is also believed to be good or salutary; but obedience to the laws or giving to everyone what belongs to him according to law is not unqualifiedly salutary since the laws may be bad; justice will be simply salutary only when the laws are good, and this requires that the regime from which the laws flow is good: justice will be fully salutary only in a good city. Socrates' procedure implies, furthermore, that he knows of no actual city which is good; this is the reason why he is compelled to found a good city. He justifies his turning to the city by the consideration that justice can be detected more easily in the city than in the human individual because the former is larger than the latter; he thus implies that there is a parallelism between the city and the human individual or, more precisely, between the city and the soul of the human individual. This means that the parallelism between the city and the human individual is based upon a certain abstraction from the human body. To the extent to which there is a parallelism between the city and the human individual or his soul, the city is at least similar to a natural being. Yet that parallelism is not complete. While the city and the individual seem equally to be able to be just, it is not certain that they can be equally happy (cf. the beginning of the fourth book). The distinction between the justice of the individual and his happiness was prepared by Glaukon's demand on Socrates that justice should be praised regardless of whether or not it has any extraneous [43] attractions. It is also prepared by the common opinion according to which justice requires complete dedication of the individual to the common good.

The founding of the good city takes place in three stages: the healthy city or the city of pigs, the purified city or the city of the armed camp, and the City of Beauty or the city ruled by philosophers.

The founding of the city is preceded by the remark that the city has its origin in human need: every human being, just or unjust, is in need of many things, and at least for this reason in need of other human beings. The healthy city satisfies properly the primary needs, the needs of the body. The proper satisfaction requires that each man exercise only one art. This means that everyone does almost all his work for others but also that the others work for him. All will exchange with one another their own products as their own products: there will be private property; by working for the

CHAPTER 21

advantage of others everyone works for his own advantage. The reason why everyone will exercise only one art is that men differ from one another by nature, i.e., different men are gifted for different arts. Since everyone will exercise that art for which he is by nature fitted, the burden will be easier on everyone. The healthy city is a happy city: it knows no poverty, no coercion or government, no war and eating of animals. It is happy in such a way that every member of it is happy: it does not need government because there is perfect harmony between everyone's service and his reward; no one encroaches on anyone else. It does not need government because everyone chooses by himself the art for which he is best fitted; there is no disharmony between natural gifts and preferences. There is also no disharmony between what is good for the individual (his choosing the art for which he is best fitted by nature) and what is good for the city: nature has so arranged things that there is no surplus of blacksmiths or deficit of shoemakers. The healthy city is happy because it is just, and it is just because it is happy; in the healthy city, justice is easy or pleasant and free from any tincture of self-sacrifice. It is just without anyone's concerning himself with its justice; it is just by nature. Nevertheless, it is found wanting. It is impossible for the same reason that anarchism in general is impossible. Anarchism would be possible if men could remain innocent, but it is of the essence of innocence that it is easily lost; men can be just only through knowledge, and men cannot acquire knowledge without effort and without antagonism. Differently stated, while the healthy city is just in a sense, it lacks virtue or excellence: such justice as it possesses is not virtue. Virtue is impossible without toil, effort, or repression of the evil in oneself. The healthy city is a city in which evil [44] is only dormant. Death is mentioned only when the transition from the healthy city to the next stage has already begun.[10] The healthy city is called a city of pigs not by Socrates but by Glaukon. Glaukon does not quite know what he says. Literally speaking, the healthy city is a city without pigs.[11]

Before the purified city can emerge or rather be established, the healthy city must have decayed. Its decay is brought about by the emancipation of the desire for unnecessary things, i.e., for things which are not necessary for the well-being or health of the body. Thus the luxurious or feverish city emerges, the city characterized by the striving for the unlimited acquisition of wealth. One can expect that in such a city the individuals will

---

10 *Ibid.*, 372d.
11 *Ibid.*, 370d–e, 373c.

no longer exercise the single art for which each is meant by nature but any art or combination of arts which is most lucrative, or that there will no longer be a strict correspondence between service and reward: hence there will be dissatisfaction and conflicts and therefore need for government which will restore justice; hence there will be need for something else which also was entirely absent from the healthy city, i.e., education at least of the rulers, and more particularly education to justice. There will certainly be need for additional territory and hence there will be war, war of aggression. Building on the principle "one man one art," Socrates demands that the army consist of men who have no art other than that of warriors. It appears that the art of the warriors or of the guardians is by far superior to the other arts. Hitherto it looked as if all arts were of equal rank and the only universal art, or the only art accompanying all arts, was the art of money-making.[12] Now we receive the first glimpse of the true order of arts. That order is hierarchic; the universal art is the highest art, the art directing all other arts, which as such cannot be practiced by the practitioners of arts other than the highest. This art of arts will prove to be philosophy. For the time being we are told only that the warrior must have a nature resembling the nature of that philosophic beast, the dog. For the warriors must be spirited and hence irascible and harsh on the one hand and gentle on the other, since they must be harsh toward strangers and gentle to their fellow citizens. They must have a disinterested liking for their fellow citizens and a disinterested dislike for foreigners. The men possessing such special natures need in addition a special education. With a view to their work they need training in the art of war. But this is not the education with which Socrates is chiefly concerned. They will be by nature the best fighters and the only ones armed and trained in arms: they will inevitably be the sole possessors of political power. Besides, the age of innocence having gone, evil is rampant in the city and therefore also [45] in the warriors. The education which the warriors more than anyone else need is therefore above all education in civic virtue. That education is "music" education, education especially through poetry and music. Not all poetry and music is apt to make men good citizens in general and good warriors or guardians in particular. Therefore the poetry and music not conducive to this moral-political end must be banished from the city. Socrates is very far from demanding that Homer and Sophocles should be replaced by the makers of edifying

---

12 *Ibid.*, 342a–b, 346c.

Chapter 21

trash; the poetry which he demands for the good city must be genuinely poetic. He demands particularly that the gods be presented as models of human excellence, i.e., of the kind of human excellence to which the guardians can and must aspire. The rulers will be taken from among the elite of the guardians. Yet the prescribed education, however excellent and effective, is not sufficient if it is not buttressed by the right kind of institutions, i.e., by absolute communism or by the completest possible abolition of privacy: everyone may enter everyone else's dwelling at will. As reward for their service to the craftsmen proper, the guardians do not receive money of any kind but only a sufficient amount of food, and, we may suppose, of the other necessities.

Let us see in what way the good city as hitherto described reveals that justice is good or even attractive for its own sake. That justice, or the observing of the just proportion between service and reward, between working for others and one's own advantage, is necessary was shown in the discussion with Thrasymachos by the example of the gang of robbers. The education of the guardians as agreed upon between Socrates and Adeimantos is not education to justice.[13] It is education to courage and moderation. The music education in particular, as distinguished from the gymnastic education, is education to moderation, and this means to love of the beautiful, i.e., of what is by nature attractive in itself. Justice in the narrow and strict sense may be said to flow from moderation or from the proper combination of moderation and courage. Socrates thus silently makes clear the difference between the gang of robbers and the good city: the essential difference consists in the fact that the armed and ruling part of the good city is animated by love of the beautiful, by the love of everything praiseworthy and graceful. The difference is not to be sought in the fact that the good city is guided in its relations to other cities, Greek or barbarian, by considerations of justice: the size of the territory of the good city is determined by that city's own moderate needs and by nothing else.[14] The difficulty appears perhaps more clearly from what Socrates says when speaking of the rulers. In addition to the other required qualities, the rulers must have the quality of caring for the city or loving the city; but a man is [46] most likely to love that whose interest he believes to be identical with his own interest or whose happiness he believes to be the condition of his own happiness. The love here mentioned is not obviously

---

13 *Ibid.*, 392a–c.
14 *Ibid.*, 423b; cf. also 398a and 422d.

disinterested in the sense that the ruler loves the city, or his serving the city, for its own sake. This may explain why Socrates demands that the rulers be honored both while they live and after their death.[15] At any rate the highest degree of caring for the city and for one another will not be forthcoming unless everyone is brought to believe in the falsehood that all fellow citizens, and only they, are brothers.[16] To say the least, the harmony between self-interest and the interest of the city, which was lost with the decay of the healthy city, has not yet been restored. No wonder then that at the beginning of the fourth book Adeimantos expresses his dissatisfaction with the condition of the soldiers in the city of the armed camp. Read within the context of the whole argument, Socrates' reply is to this effect: Only as a member of a happy city can a man be happy; only within these limits can a man, or any other part of the city, be happy; complete dedication to the happy city is justice. It remains to be seen whether complete dedication to the happy city is, or can be, happiness of the individual.

After the founding of the good city is in the main completed, Socrates and his friends turn to seeking where in it justice and injustice are, and whether the man who is to be happy must possess justice or injustice.[17] They look first for the three virtues other than justice (wisdom, courage, and moderation). In the city which is founded according to nature, wisdom resides in the rulers and in the rulers alone, for the wise men are by nature the smallest part of any city, and it would not be good for the city if they were not the only ones at its helm. In the good city, courage resides in the warrior class, for political courage, as distinguished from brutish fearlessness, arises only through education in those by nature fitted for it. Moderation on the other hand is to be found in all parts of the good city. In the present context, moderation does not mean exactly what it meant when the education of the warriors was discussed but rather the control of what is by nature worse by that which is by nature better—that control through which the whole is in harmony. In other words, moderation is the agreement of the naturally superior and inferior as to which of the two ought to rule in the city. Since controlling and being controlled differ, one must assume that the moderation of the rulers is not identical with the moderation of the ruled. While Socrates and Glaukon found the three

---

15 *Ibid.*, 414a, 465d–466c; cf. 346e ff.
16 *Ibid.*, 415b.
17 *Ibid.*, 427d.

Chapter 21

virtues mentioned in the good city with ease, it is difficult to find justice in it because, as Socrates says, justice is so obvious in it. Justice consists in everyone's doing the one thing pertaining to the city for [47] which his nature is best fitted or, simply, in everyone's minding his own business: it is by virtue of justice thus understood that the other three virtues are virtues.[18] More precisely, a city is just if each of its three parts (the money-makers, the warriors, and the rulers) does its own work and only its own work.[19] Justice is then, like moderation and unlike wisdom and courage, not a preserve of a single part but required of every part. Hence justice, like moderation, has a different character in each of the three classes. One must assume, for instance, that the justice of the wise rulers is affected by their wisdom and the justice of the money-makers is affected by their lack of wisdom, for if even the courage of the warriors is only political or civic courage, and not courage pure and simple,[20] it stands to reason that their justice too—to say nothing of the justice of the money-makers—will not be justice pure and simple. In order to discover justice pure and simple, it then becomes necessary to consider justice in the individual man. This consideration would be easiest if justice in the individual were identical with justice in the city; this would require that the individual or rather his soul consist of the same three kinds of "natures" as the city. A very provisional consideration of the soul seems to establish this requirement: the soul contains desire, spiritedness or anger,[21] and reason, just as the city consists of the money-makers, the warriors, and the rulers. Hence we may conclude that a man is just if each of these three parts of his soul does its own work and only its own work, i.e., if his soul is in a state of health. But if justice is health of the soul, and conversely injustice is disease of the soul, it is obvious that justice is good and injustice is bad, regardless of whether or not one is known to be just or unjust.[22] A man is just if the rational part in him is wise and rules,[23] and if the spirited part, being the subject and ally of the rational part, assists it in controlling the multitude of desires which almost inevitably become desires for more and

---

18 *Ibid.*, 433a–b.
19 *Ibid.*, 434c.
20 *Ibid.*, 430c; cf. *Phaedo* 82a.
21 *Republic* 441a–c.
22 *Ibid.*, 444d–445b.
23 *Ibid.*, 441e.

ever more money. This means, however, that only the man in whom wisdom rules the two other parts, i.e., only the wise man, can be truly just.[24] No wonder then that the just man eventually proves to be identical with the philosopher.[25] The money-makers and the warriors are not truly just even in the just city because their justice derives exclusively from habituation of one kind or another as distinguished from philosophy; hence in the deepest recesses of their souls they long for tyranny, i.e., for complete injustice.[26] We see then how right Socrates was when he expected to find injustice in the good city.[27] This is not to deny of course that as members of the good city the nonphilosophers will act much more justly than they would as members of inferior cities.

The justice of those who are not wise appears in a different light [48] when justice in the city is being considered, on the one hand, and justice in the soul on the other. This fact shows that the parallelism between the city and the soul is defective. This parallelism requires that, just as in the city the warriors occupy a higher rank than the money-makers, so in the soul spiritedness occupy a higher rank than desire. It is very plausible that those who uphold the city against foreign and domestic enemies and who have received a music education deserve higher respect than those who lack public responsibility as well as a music education. But it is much less plausible that spiritedness as such should deserve higher respect than desire as such. It is true that "spiritedness" includes a large variety of phenomena ranging from the most noble indignation about injustice, turpitude, and meanness down to the anger of a spoiled child who resents being deprived of anything that he desires, however bad. But the same is also true of "desire": one kind of desire is *eros*, which ranges in its healthy forms from the longing for immortality via offspring through the longing for immortality via immortal fame to the longing for immortality via participation by knowledge in the things which are unchangeable in every respect. The assertion that spiritedness is higher in rank than desire as such is then questionable. Let us never forget that while there is a philosophic *eros*, there is no philosophic spiritedness;[28] or in other words that Thrasymachos is

---

24 Cf. *ibid.*, 442c.
25 *Ibid.*, 580d–583b.
26 *Ibid.*, 619b–d.
27 *Ibid.*, 427d.
28 Cf. *ibid.*, 366c.

CHAPTER 21

much more visibly spiritedness incarnate than desire incarnate. The assertion in question is based on a deliberate abstraction from *eros*—an abstraction characteristic of the *Republic*.

This abstraction shows itself most strikingly in two facts: when Socrates mentions the fundamental needs which give rise to human society, he is silent about the need for procreation, and when he describes the tyrant, Injustice incarnate, he presents him as *Eros* incarnate.[29] In the thematic discussion of the respective rank of spiritedness and desire, he is silent about *eros*.[30] It seems that there is a tension between *eros* and the city and hence between *eros* and justice: only through the depreciation of *eros* can the city come into its own. *Eros* obeys its own laws, not the laws of the city however good; in the good city, *eros* is simply subjected to what the city requires. The good city requires that all love of one's own—all spontaneous love of one's own parents, one's own children, one's own friends and beloved—be sacrificed to the common love of the common. As far as possible, the love of one's own must be abolished except as it is love of the city as this particular city, as one's own city. As far as possible, patriotism takes the place of *eros*, and patriotism has a closer kinship to spiritedness, eagerness to fight, "waspishness," anger, and indignation than to *eros*.

While it is harmful to one's soul to jump at Plato's throat because [49] he is not a liberal democrat, it is also bad to blur the difference between Platonism and liberal democracy, for the premises "Plato is admirable" and "liberal democracy is admirable" do not legitimately lead to the conclusion that Plato was a liberal democrat. The founding of the good city started from the fact that men are by nature different, and this proved to mean that men are by nature of unequal rank. They are unequal particularly with regard to their ability to acquire virtue. The inequality which is due to nature is increased and deepened by the different kinds of education or habituation and the different ways of life (communistic or noncommunistic) which the different parts of the good city enjoy. As a result, the good city comes to resemble a caste society. A Platonic character who hears an account of the good city of the *Republic* is reminded by it of the caste system established in ancient Egypt, although it is quite clear that in Egypt the rulers were priests and not philosophers.[31] Certainly in the good city of

---

29   *Ibid.*, 573b–e, 574e–575a.
30   Cf. *ibid.*, 439d.
31   *Timaeus* 24a–b.

302

Plato, 427–347 B.C.

the *Republic*, not descent but in the first place everyone's own natural gifts determine to which class he belongs. But this leads to a difficulty. The members of the upper class, which lives communistically, are not supposed to know who their natural parents are, for they are supposed to regard all men and women belonging to the older generation as their parents. On the other hand, the gifted children of the noncommunist lower class are to be transferred to the upper class (and vice versa); since their superior gifts are not necessarily recognizable at the moment of their birth, they are likely to come to know their natural parents and even to become attached to them; this would seem to unfit them for transfer to the upper class. There are two ways in which this difficulty can be removed. The first is to extend absolute communism to the lower class; and, considering the connection between way of life and education, also to extend music education to that class.[32] According to Aristotle,[33] Socrates has left it undecided whether in the good city absolute communism is limited to the upper class or extends also to the lower class. To leave this question undecided would be in agreement with Socrates' professed low opinion of the importance of the lower class.[34] Still, there can be only little doubt that Socrates wishes to limit both communism and music education to the upper class.[35] Therefore, in order to remove the difficulty mentioned, he can hardly avoid making an individual's membership in the upper or lower class hereditary and thus violating one of the most elementary principles of justice. Apart from this, one may wonder whether a perfectly clear line between those gifted and those not gifted for the profession of warriors can be drawn, hence whether a perfectly just assignment of individuals to the upper or lower class is possible, and [50] hence whether the good city can be perfectly just.[36] But be this as it may, if communism is limited to the upper class, there will be privacy both in the money-making class and among the philosophers as philosophers, for there may very well be only a single philosopher in the city and surely never a herd: the warriors are the only class which is entirely political or public or entirely dedicated to the city; the warriors alone present therefore the clearest case of the just life in one sense of the word "just."

---

32 *Republic* 401b–c, 421e–422d, 460a, 543a.
33 *Politics* 1264a 13–17.
34 *Republic* 421a, 434a.
35 *Ibid.*, 415e, 431b–c, 456d.
36 Reconsider *ibid.*, 427d.

Chapter 21

It is necessary to understand the reason why communism is limited to the upper class or what the natural obstacle to communism is. That which is by nature private or a man's own is the body and only the body.[37] The needs or desires of the body induce men to extend the sphere of the private, of what is each man's own, as far as they can. This most powerful striving is countered by music education which brings about moderation, i.e., a most severe training of the soul of which, it seems, only a minority of men is capable. Yet this kind of education does not extirpate the natural desire of each for things or human beings of his own: the warriors will not accept absolute communism if they are not subject to the philosophers. It thus becomes clear that the striving for one's own is countered ultimately only by philosophy, by the quest for the truth which as such cannot be anyone's private possession. Whereas the private par excellence is the body, the common par excellence is the mind, the pure mind rather than the soul in general. The superiority of communism to noncommunism as taught in the *Republic* is intelligible only as a reflection of the superiority of philosophy to nonphilosophy. This clearly contradicts the result of the preceding paragraph. The contradiction can and must be resolved by the distinction between two meanings of justice. This distinction cannot become clear before one has understood the teaching of the *Republic* regarding the relation of philosophy and the city. We must therefore make a new beginning.

At the end of the fourth book, it looks as if Socrates had completed the task which Glaukon and Adeimantos had imposed on him, for he had shown that justice as health of the soul is desirable not only because of its consequences but above all for its own sake. But then, at the beginning of the fifth book, we are suddenly confronted by a new start, by the repetition of a scene which had occurred at the very beginning. Both at the very beginning and at the beginning of the fifth book (and nowhere else), Socrates' companions make a decision, nay, take a vote, and Socrates who had no share in the decision obeys it.[38] Socrates' companions behave in both cases like a city (an assembly of the citizens), if the smallest possible city.[39] But there is this decisive [51] difference between the two scenes: whereas Thrasymachos was absent from the first scene, he has become a

---

37 *Ibid.*, 464d; cf. *Laws* 739c.
38 Cf. *Republic* 449b–450a with 327b–328b.
39 Cf. *ibid.*, 369d.

member of the city in the second scene. It could seem that the foundation of the good city requires that Thrasymachos be converted into one of its citizens.

At the beginning of the fifth book Socrates' companions force him to take up the subject of communism in regard to women and children. They do not object to the proposal itself in the way in which Adeimantos had objected to the communism regarding property at the beginning of the fourth book, for even Adeimantos is no longer the same man he was at that time. They only wish to know the precise manner in which the communism regarding women and children is to be managed. Socrates replaces that question by these more incisive questions: (1) Is that communism possible? (2) Is it desirable? It appears that the communism regarding women is the consequence or presupposition of the equality of the two sexes concerning the work they must do: the city cannot afford to lose half of its adult population from its working and fighting force, and there is no essential difference between men and women regarding natural gifts for the various arts. The demand for equality of the two sexes requires a complete upheaval of custom, an upheaval which is here presented less as shocking than as laughable; the demand is justified on the ground that only the useful is fair or noble and that only what is bad, i.e., against nature, is laughable: the customary difference of conduct between the two sexes is rejected as being against nature, and the revolutionary change is meant to bring about the order according to nature.[40] For justice requires that every human being should practice the art for which he or she is fitted by nature, regardless of what custom or convention may dictate. Socrates shows first that the equality of the two sexes is possible, i.e., in agreement with the nature of the two sexes as their nature appears when viewed with regard to aptitude for the practice of the various arts, and then he shows that it is desirable. In proving this possibility, he explicitly abstracts from the difference between the two sexes in regard to procreation.[41] This means that the argument of the *Republic* as a whole, according to which the city is a community of male and female artisans, abstracts to the highest degree possible from the highest activity essential to the city which takes place "by nature" and not "by art."

Socrates then turns to the communism regarding women and children and shows that it is desirable because it will make the city more "one,"

---

40 *Ibid.*, 455d–e, 456b–c.
41 *Ibid.*, 455c–e.

Chapter 21

and hence more perfect, than a city consisting of separate families would be: the city should be as similar as possible to a single human being or to a single living body, i.e., to a natural being.[42] At [52] this point we understand somewhat better why Socrates started his discussion of justice by assuming an important parallelism between the city and the individual: he was thinking ahead of the greatest possible unity of the city. The abolition of the family does not mean of course the introduction of license or promiscuity; it means the most severe regulation of sexual intercourse from the point of view of what is useful for the city or what is required for the common good. The consideration of the useful, one might say, supersedes the consideration of the holy or sacred:[43] human males and females are to be coupled with exclusive regard to the production of the best offspring, in the spirit in which the breeders of dogs, birds, and horses proceed; the claims of *eros* are simply silenced. The new order naturally affects the customary prohibitions against incest, the most sacred rules of customary justice.[44] In the new scheme, no one will know any more his natural parents, children, brothers, and sisters, but everyone will *regard* all men of the older generation as his fathers and mothers, of his own generation as his brothers and sisters, and of the younger generation as his children.[45] This means, however, that the city constructed according to nature lives in a most important respect more according to convention than according to nature. For this reason we are disappointed to see that while Socrates takes up the question of whether communism regarding women and children is possible, he drops it immediately.[46] Since the institution under consideration is indispensable for the good city, Socrates thus leaves open the question of the possibility of the good city, i.e., of the just city, as such. And this happens to his listeners and to the readers of the *Republic* after they have made the greatest sacrifices—such as the sacrifice of *eros* as well as of the family—for the sake of the just city.

Socrates is not for long allowed to escape from his awesome duty to answer the question regarding the possibility of the just city. The manly Glaukon compels him to face that question. Perhaps we should say that

---

42 *Ibid.*, 462c–d, 464b.

43 Cf. *ibid.*, 458e.

44 Cf. *ibid.*, 461b–e.

45 *Ibid.*, 463c.

46 *Ibid.*, 466d.

by apparently escaping to the subject of war—a subject both easier in itself and more attractive to Glaukon than the communism of women and children—yet treating that subject according to the stern demands of justice and thus depriving it of much of its attractiveness, he compels Glaukon to compel him to return to the fundamental question. Be this as it may, the question to which Socrates and Glaukon return is not the same one which they left. The question which they left was whether the good city is possible in the sense that it is in agreement with human nature. The question to which they return is whether the good city is possible in the sense that it can be brought into being by the transformation of an actual city.[47] The latter ques-[53]tion might be thought to presuppose the affirmative answer to the first question, but this is not quite correct. As we learn now, our whole effort to discover what justice is (so that we would be enabled to see how it is related to happiness) was a quest for "justice itself" as a "pattern." By seeking for justice itself as a pattern we implied that the just man and the just city will not be perfectly just but will indeed approximate justice itself with particular closeness;[48] only justice itself is perfectly just.[49] This implies that not even the characteristic institutions of the just city (absolute communism, equality of the sexes, and the rule of the philosophers) are simply just. Now justice itself is not "possible" in the sense that it is capable of coming into being, because it "is" always without being capable of undergoing any change whatever. Justice is an "idea" or "form," one of many "ideas." Ideas are the only things which strictly speaking "are," i.e., are without any admixture of nonbeing, because they are beyond all becoming, and whatever is becoming is between being and nonbeing. Since the ideas are the only things which are beyond all change, they are in a sense the cause of all change and all changeable things. For example, the idea of justice is the cause for anything (human beings, cities, laws, commands, actions) becoming just. They are self-subsisting beings which subsist always. They are of utmost splendor. For instance, the idea of justice is perfectly just. But their splendor escapes the eyes of the body. The ideas are "visible" only to the eye of the mind, and the mind as mind perceives nothing but ideas. Yet, as is indicated by the facts that there are many ideas and that the mind which perceives the ideas

---

47   Ibid., 473b–c.
48   Ibid., 472b–c.
49   Ibid., 479a; cf. 538c ff.

CHAPTER 21

is radically different from the ideas themselves, there must be something higher than the ideas: "the good" or "the idea of the good" which is in a sense the cause of all ideas as well as of the mind perceiving them.[50] It is only through perception of "the good" on the part of the human beings who are by nature equipped for perceiving it that the good city can come into being and subsist for a while.

The doctrine of ideas which Socrates expounds to Glaukon is very hard to understand; to begin with it is utterly incredible, not to say that it appears to be fantastic. Hitherto we have been given to understand that justice is fundamentally a certain character of the human soul, or of the city, i.e., something which is not self-subsisting. Now we are asked to believe that it is self-subsisting, being at home as it were in an entirely different place than human beings and everything else that participates in justice.[51] No one has ever succeeded in giving a satisfactory or clear account of this doctrine of ideas. It is possible, however, to define rather precisely the central difficulty. "Idea" means primarily the looks or shape of a thing; it means then a kind or class of things [54] which are united by the fact that they all possess the same "looks," i.e., the same character and power, or the same "nature"; therewith it means the class-character or the nature of the things belonging to the class in question: the "idea" of a thing is that which we mean by trying to find out the "what" or the "nature" of a thing or a class of things (see the Introduction).* The connection between "idea" and "nature" appears in the *Republic* from the facts that "the idea of justice" is called "that which is just by nature," and that the ideas in contradistinction to the things which are not ideas or to the sensibly perceived things are said to be "in nature."[52] This does not explain, however, why the ideas are presented as "separated" from the things which are what they are by participating in an idea or, in other words, why "dogness" (the class character of dogs) should be "the true dog." It seems that two kinds of phenomena lend support to Socrates' assertion. In the first place the mathematical things as such can never be found among sensible things: no line drawn on sand or paper is a line as meant by the mathematician. Secondly and above all, what we mean by justice and kindred things is not as such, in its purity or perfection, nec-

---

50 *Ibid.*, 517c.

51 Cf. *ibid.*, 509b–510a.

*   I.e., the Introduction to *History of Political Philosophy*, included in this volume as ch. 20.—Eds.

52 *Ibid.*, 501b; 597b–d.

essarily found in human beings or societies; it rather seems that what is meant by justice transcends everything which men can ever achieve; precisely the justest men were and are the ones most aware of the shortcomings of their justice. Socrates seems to say that what is patently true of mathematical things and of the virtues is true universally: there is an idea of the bed or the table just as of the circle and of justice. Now while it is obviously reasonable to say that a perfect circle or perfect justice transcends everything which can ever be seen, it is hard to say that the perfect bed is something on which no man can ever rest. However this may be, Glaukon and Adeimantos accept this doctrine of ideas with relative ease, with greater ease than absolute communism. This paradoxical fact does not strike us with sufficient force because we somehow believe that these able young men study philosophy under Professor Socrates and have heard him expound the doctrine of ideas on innumerable occasions, if we do not believe that the *Republic* is a philosophic treatise addressed to readers familiar with more elementary (or "earlier") dialogues. Yet Plato addresses the readers of the *Republic* only through the medium of Socrates' conversation with Glaukon and the other interlocutors in the *Republic*, and Plato as the author of the *Republic* does not suggest that Glaukon—to say nothing of Adeimantos and the rest—has seriously studied the doctrine of ideas.[53] Yet while Glaukon and Adeimantos cannot be credited with a genuine understanding of the doctrine of ideas, they have heard, and in a way they know, that there are gods like *Dike* or Right,[54] and *Nike* or [55] Victory who is not this or that victory or this or that statue of Nike but a self-subsisting being which is the cause of every victory and which is of unbelievable splendor. More generally, they know that there are gods—self-subsisting beings which are the causes of everything good, which are of unbelievable splendor, and which cannot be apprehended by the senses since they never change their "form."[55] This is not to deny that there is a profound difference between the gods as understood in the "theology"[56] of the *Republic* and the ideas, or that in the *Republic* the gods are in a way replaced by the ideas. It is merely to assert that those who accept that theology and draw all conclusions from it are likely to arrive at the doctrine of ideas.

---

53 Cf. *ibid.*, 507a–c with 596a and 532c–d, contrast with *Phaedo* 65d and 74a–b.
54 *Republic* 536b; cf. 487a.
55 Cf. *ibid.*, 379a–b and 380d ff.
56 *Ibid.*, 379a.

Chapter 21

We must now return to the question of the possibility of the just city. We have learned that justice itself is not "possible" in the sense that anything which comes into being can ever be perfectly just. We learn immediately afterward that not only justice itself but also the just city is not "possible" in the sense indicated. This does not mean that the just city as meant and as sketched in the *Republic* is an idea like "justice itself," and still less that it is an "ideal": "ideal" is not a Platonic term. The just city is not a self-subsisting being like the idea of justice, located so to speak in a superheavenly place. Its status is rather like that of a painting of a perfectly beautiful human being, i.e., it is only by virtue of the painter's painting; more precisely, the just city is only "in speech": it "is" only by virtue of having been figured out with a view to justice itself or to what is by nature right on the one hand and the human all-too-human on the other. Although the just city is decidedly of lower rank than justice itself, even the just city as a pattern is not capable of coming into being as it has been blueprinted; only approximations to it can be expected in cities which are in deed and not merely in speech.[57] What this means is not clear. Does it mean that the best feasible solution will be a compromise so that we must become reconciled to a certain degree of private property (e.g., that we must permit every warrior to keep his shoes and the like as long as he lives) and a certain degree of inequality of the sexes (e.g., that certain military and administrative functions will remain the preserve of the male warriors)? There is no reason to suppose that this is what Socrates meant. In the light of the succeeding part of the conversation, the following suggestion would seem to be more plausible. The assertion according to which the just city cannot come into being as blueprinted is provisional, or prepares the assertion that the just city, while capable of coming into being, is very unlikely to come into being. At any rate, immediately after having declared that only an approximation to the good city can reasonably be expected, Socrates raises the question, [56] what feasible change in the actual cities will be the necessary and sufficient condition of their transformation into good cities? His answer is, the "coincidence" of political power and philosophy: the philosophers must rule as kings, or the kings must genuinely and adequately philosophize. As we have shown in our summary of the first book of the *Republic*, this answer is not altogether surprising. If justice is less the giving or leaving to each what the law assigns to him than the giving or leaving to each what is good for his soul, but what is good for his soul is the virtues, it follows that no one

---

[57] *Ibid.*, 472c–473a; cf. 500c–501c with 484c–d and 592b.

can be truly just who does not know "the virtues themselves," or generally the ideas, or who is not a philosopher.

By answering the question of how the good city is possible, Socrates introduces philosophy as a theme of the *Republic*. This means that in the *Republic*, philosophy is not introduced as the end of man, the end for which man should live, but as a means for realizing the just city, the city as armed camp which is characterized by absolute communism and equality of the sexes in the upper class, the class of warriors. Since the rule of philosophers is not introduced as an ingredient of the just city but only as a means for its realization, Aristotle is justified in disregarding this institution in his critical analysis of the *Republic* (*Politics* II). At any rate, Socrates succeeds in reducing the question of the possibility of the just city to the question of the possibility of the coincidence of philosophy and political power. That such a coincidence should be possible is to begin with most incredible: everyone can see that the philosophers are useless if not even harmful in politics. Socrates, who had some experiences of his own with the city of Athens— experiences to be crowned by his capital punishment—regards this accusation of the philosophers as well-founded, although in need of deeper exploration. He traces the antagonism of the cities toward the philosophers primarily to the cities: the present cities, i.e., the cities not ruled by philosophers, are like assemblies of madmen which corrupt most of those fit to become philosophers, and on which those who have succeeded against all odds in becoming philosophers rightly turn their back in disgust. But Socrates is far from absolving the philosophers altogether. Only a radical change on the part of both the cities and the philosophers can bring about that harmony between them for which they seem to be meant by nature. The change consists precisely in this: that the cities cease to be unwilling to be ruled by philosophers and the philosophers cease to be unwilling to rule the cities. This coincidence of philosophy and political power is very difficult to achieve, very improbable, but not impossible. To bring about the needed change on the part of the city, of the nonphilosophers or [57] the multitude, the right kind of persuasion is necessary and sufficient. The right kind of persuasion is supplied by the art of persuasion, the art of Thrasymachos directed by the philosopher and in the service of philosophy. No wonder then that in our context Socrates declares that he and Thrasymachos have just become friends. The multitude of the nonphilosophers is good-natured and therefore persuadable by the philosophers.[58] But if this is so, why did

---

58   *Ibid.*, 498c–502a.

CHAPTER 21

not the philosophers of old, to say nothing of Socrates himself, succeed in persuading the multitude of the supremacy of philosophy and the philosophers and thus bring about the rule of philosophers and therewith the salvation and the happiness of their cities? Strange as it may sound, in this part of the argument it appears to be easier to persuade the multitude to accept the rule of the philosophers than to persuade the philosophers to rule the multitude: the philosophers cannot be persuaded, they can only be compelled to rule the cities.[59] Only the nonphilosophers could compel the philosophers to take care of the cities. But, given the prejudice against the philosophers, this compulsion will not be forthcoming if the philosophers do not in the first place persuade the nonphilosophers to compel the philosophers to rule over them, and this persuasion will not be forthcoming, given the philosophers' unwillingness to rule. We arrive then at the conclusion that the just city is not possible because of the philosophers' unwillingness to rule.

Why are the philosophers unwilling to rule? Being dominated by the desire for knowledge as the one thing needful, or knowing that philosophy is the most pleasant and blessed possession, the philosophers have no leisure for looking down at human affairs, let alone for taking care of them.[60] The philosophers believe that while still alive they are already firmly settled, far away from their cities, in the Isles of the Blessed.[61] Hence only compulsion could induce them to take part in political life in the just city, i.e., in the city which regards the proper upbringing of the philosophers as its most important task. Having perceived the truly grand, the human things appear to the philosophers to be paltry. The very justice of the philosophers—their abstaining from wronging their fellow human beings—flows from contempt for the things for which the nonphilosophers hotly contest.[62] They know that the life not dedicated to philosophy and therefore in particular the political life is like life in a cave, so much so that the city can be identified with the Cave.[63] The cave dwellers (i.e., the non-philosophers) see only the shadows of artifacts.[64] That is to say,

---

59 *Ibid.*, 499b–c, 500d, 520a–d, 521b, 539e.
60 *Ibid.*, 485a, 501b–c, 517c.
61 *Ibid.*, 519c.
62 *Ibid.*, 486a–b.
63 *Ibid.*, 539e.
64 *Ibid.*, 514b–515c.

whatever they perceive they understand in the light of their opinions, sanctified by the fiat of legislators, regarding the just and noble things, i.e., of conventional opinions, and they do not know that these their most [58] cherished convictions possess no higher status than that of opinions. For if even the best city stands or falls by a fundamental falsehood, although a noble falsehood, it can be expected that the opinions on which the imperfect cities rest or in which they believe, will not be true. Precisely the best of the nonphilosophers, the good citizens, are passionately attached to these opinions and therefore violently opposed to philosophy,[65] which is the attempt to go beyond opinion toward knowledge: the multitude is not as persuadable by the philosophers as we sanguinely assumed in an earlier round of the argument. This is the true reason why the coincidence of philosophy and political power is, to say the least, extremely improbable: philosophy and the city tend away from one another in opposite directions.

The difficulty of overcoming the natural tension between the city and the philosophers is indicated by Socrates' turning from the question of whether the just city is "possible" in the sense of being conformable to human nature to the question of whether the just city is "possible" in the sense of being capable of being brought to light by the transformation of an actual city. The first question, understood in contradistinction to the second, points to the question whether the just city could not come into being through the settling together of men who had been wholly unassociated before. It is to this question that Socrates tacitly gives a negative answer by turning to the question of whether the just city could be brought into being by the transformation of an actual city. The good city cannot be brought to light out of human beings who have not yet undergone any human discipline, out of "primitives" or "stupid animals" or "savages" gentle or cruel; its potential members must already have acquired the rudiments of civilized life. The long process through which primitive men become civilized men cannot be the work of the founder or legislator of the good city but is presupposed by him.[66] But on the other hand, if the potential good city must be an old city, its citizens will have been thoroughly molded by their city's imperfect laws or customs, hallowed by old age, and will have become passionately attached to them. Socrates is therefore compelled to revise his original suggestion according

---

65 Ibid., 517a.
66 Cf. ibid., 376e.

Chapter 21

to which the rule of philosophers is the necessary and sufficient condition of the coming into being of the just city. Whereas he had originally suggested that the good city will come into being if the philosophers become kings, he finally suggests that the good city will come into being if, when the philosophers have become kings, they expel everyone older than ten from the city, i.e., separate the children completely from their parents and their parents' ways and bring them up in the entirely novel ways of the good city.[67] By taking over a city, [59] the philosophers make sure that their subjects will not be savages; by expelling everyone older than ten, they make sure that their subjects will not be enslaved by traditional civility. The solution is elegant. It leaves one wondering, however, how the philosophers can compel everyone older than ten to obey submissively the expulsion decree, since they cannot yet have trained a warrior class absolutely obedient to them. This is not to deny that Socrates could persuade many fine young men, and even some old ones, to believe that the multitude could be, not indeed compelled, but persuaded by the philosophers to leave their city and their children and to live in the fields so that justice will be done.

The part of the *Republic* which deals with philosophy is the most important part of the book. Accordingly, it transmits the answer to the question regarding justice to the extent to which that answer is given in the *Republic*. The explicit answer to the question of what justice is had been rather vague: justice consists in each part of the city or of the soul "doing the work for which it is by nature best fitted" or in a "kind" of doing that work; a part is just if it does its work or minds its own business "in a certain manner." The vagueness is removed if one replaces "in a certain manner" by "in the best manner" or "well": justice consists in each part doing its work well.[68] Hence the just man is the man in whom each part of the soul does its work well. Since the highest part of the soul is reason, and since this part cannot do its work well if the two other parts too do not do their work well, only the philosopher can be truly just. But the work which the philosopher does well is intrinsically attractive and in fact the most pleasant work, wholly regardless of its consequences.[69] Hence only in philosophy do justice and happiness coincide. In other words, the philosopher

---

67   *Ibid.*, 540d–541a; cf. 499b, 501a, e.

68   *Ibid.*, 433a–b and 443d; cf. Aristotle *Nicomachean Ethics* 1098a 7–12.

69   *Republic* 583a.

is the only individual who is just in the sense in which the good city is just: he is self-sufficient, truly free, or his life is as little devoted to the service of other individuals as the life of the city is devoted to the service of other cities. But the philosopher in the good city is just also in the sense that he serves his fellow men, his fellow citizens, his city, or that he obeys the law. That is to say, the philosopher is just also in the sense in which all members of the just city, and in a way all just members of any city, regardless of whether they are philosophers or nonphilosophers, are just. Yet justice in this second sense is not intrinsically attractive or choiceworthy for its own sake, but is good only with a view to its consequences, or is not noble but necessary: the philosopher serves his city, even the good city, not, as he seeks the truth, from natural inclination, from *eros*, but under compulsion.[70] It is hardly necessary to add that compulsion does not cease to be compulsion if [60] it is self-compulsion. According to a notion of justice which is more common than that suggested by Socrates' definition, justice consists in not harming others; justice thus understood proves to be in the highest case merely a concomitant of the philosopher's greatness of soul. But if justice is taken in the larger sense according to which it consists in giving to each what is good for his soul, one must distinguish between the cases in which this giving is intrinsically attractive to the giver (these will be the cases of potential philosophers) and those in which it is merely a duty or compulsory. This distinction, incidentally, underlies the difference between the voluntary conversations of Socrates (the conversations which he spontaneously seeks) and the compulsory ones (those which he cannot with propriety avoid). This clear distinction between the justice which is choiceworthy for its own sake, wholly regardless of its consequences, and identical with philosophy, and the justice which is merely necessary and identical in the highest case with the political activity of the philosopher is rendered possible by the abstraction from *eros* which is characteristic of the *Republic*. For one might well say that there is no reason why the philosopher should not engage in political activity out of that kind of love of one's own which is patriotism.[71]

By the end of the seventh book justice has come to sight fully. Socrates has in fact performed the duty laid upon him by Glaukon and Adeimantos to show that justice properly understood is choiceworthy for its own sake regardless of its consequences and therefore that justice is unqual-

---

70 *Ibid.*, 519e–520b; 540b, e.

71 Consider *Apology of Socrates* 30a.

CHAPTER 21

ifiedly preferable to injustice. Nevertheless the conversation continues, for it seems that our clear grasp of justice does not include a clear grasp of injustice but must be supplemented by a clear grasp of the wholly unjust city and the wholly unjust man: only after we have seen the wholly unjust city and the wholly unjust man with the same clarity with which we have seen the wholly just city and the wholly just man will we be able to judge whether we ought to follow Socrates' friend Thrasymachos, who chooses injustice, or Socrates himself, who chooses justice.[72] This in its turn requires that the fiction of the possibility of the just city be maintained. As a matter of fact, the *Republic* never abandons the fiction that the just city as a society of human beings, as distinguished from a society of gods or sons of gods, is possible.[73] When Socrates turns to the study of injustice, it even becomes necessary for him to reaffirm this fiction with greater force than ever before. The unjust city will be uglier and more condemnable in proportion as the just city will be more possible. But the possibility of the just city will remain doubtful if the just city was never actual. Accordingly Socrates now asserts that the just city was once actual. [61] More precisely, he makes the Muses assert it or rather imply it. The assertion that the just city was once actual is, as one might say, a mythical assertion which agrees with the mythical premise that the best is the oldest. Socrates asserts then through the mouth of the Muses that the good city was actual in the beginning, prior to the emergence of the inferior kinds of cities;[74] the inferior cities are decayed forms of the good city, soiled fragments of the pure city which was entire; hence the nearer in time a kind of inferior city is to the just city the better it is, or vice versa. It is more proper to speak of the good and inferior regimes than of the good and inferior cities (observe the transition from "cities" to "regimes" in 543d–544a). "Regime" is our translation of the Greek *politeia*. The book which we call *Republic* is in Greek entitled *Politeia*. *Politeia* is commonly translated by "constitution." The term designates the form of government understood as the form of the city, i.e., as that which gives the city its character by determining the end which the city in question pursues or what it looks up to as the highest, and simultaneously the kind of men who rule the city. For instance, oligarchy is the kind of

---

72 *Republic* 545a–b; cf. 498c–d.

73 *Laws* 739b–e.

74 Cf. *Republic* 547b.

regime in which the rich rule and therefore admiration for wealth and for the acquisition of wealth animates the city as a whole, and democracy is the kind of regime in which all free men rule and therefore freedom is the end which the city pursues. According to Socrates, there are five kinds of regime: (1) kingdom or aristocracy, the rule of the best man or the best men, that is directed toward goodness or virtue, the regime of the just city; (2) timocracy, the rule of lovers of honor or of the ambitious men which is directed toward superiority or victory; (3) oligarchy or the rule of the rich in which wealth is most highly esteemed; (4) democracy, the rule of free men in which freedom is most highly esteemed; (5) tyranny, the rule of the completely unjust man in which unqualified and unashamed injustice holds sway. The descending order of the five kinds of regime is modeled on Hesiod's descending order of the five races of men: the races of gold, of silver, of bronze, the divine race of heroes, the race of iron.[75] We see at once that the Platonic equivalent of Hesiod's divine race of heroes is democracy. We shall soon see the reason for this seemingly strange correspondence.

The *Republic* is based on the assumption that there is a strict parallelism between the city and the soul. Accordingly Socrates asserts that, just as there are five kinds of regime, so there are five kinds of characters of men, the timocratic man, for instance, corresponding to timocracy. The distinction which for a short while was popular in present-day political science between the authoritarian and the demo-[62]cratic "personalities," as corresponding to the distinction between authoritarian and democratic societies, was a dim and crude reflection of Socrates' distinction between the royal or aristocratic, the timocratic, the oligarchic, the democratic, and the tyrannical soul or man, as corresponding to the aristocratic, timocratic, oligarchic, democratic, and tyrannical regimes. In this connection it should be mentioned that in describing the regimes, Socrates does not speak of "ideologies" belonging to them; he is concerned with the character of each kind of regime and with the end which it manifestly and explicitly pursues, as well as with the political justification of the end in question in contradistinction to any transpolitical justification stemming from cosmology, theology, metaphysics, philosophy of history, myth, and the like. In his study of the inferior regimes Socrates examines in each case first the regime and then the corresponding individual or soul. He presents both the regime and the corresponding individual as coming into

---

75 Cf. *ibid.*, 546e–547a and Hesiod *Works and Days* 106 ff.

Chapter 21

being out of the preceding one. We shall consider here only his account of democracy, both because this subject is most important to citizens of a democracy and because of its intrinsic importance. Democracy arises from oligarchy, which in its turn arises from timocracy, the rule of the insufficiently musical warriors who are characterized by the supremacy of spiritedness. Oligarchy is the first regime in which desire is supreme. In oligarchy the ruling desire is that for wealth or money, or unlimited acquisitiveness. The oligarchic man is thrifty and industrious, controls all his desires other than the desire for money, lacks education, and possesses a superficial honesty derivative from the crudest self-interest. Oligarchy must give to each the unqualified right to dispose of his property as he sees fit. It thus renders inevitable the emergence of "drones," i.e., of members of the ruling class who are either burdened with debt or already bankrupt and hence disfranchised—of beggars who hanker after their squandered fortune and hope to restore their fortune and political power through a change of regime ("Catilinarian existences"). Besides, the correct oligarchs themselves, being both rich and unconcerned with virtue and honor, render themselves and especially their sons fat, spoiled, and soft. They thus become despised by the lean and tough poor. Democracy comes into being when the poor, having become aware of their superiority to the rich and perhaps being led by some drones who act as traitors to their class and possess the skills which ordinarily only members of a ruling class possess, make themselves at an opportune moment masters of the city by defeating the rich, killing and exiling a part of them, and permitting the rest to live with them in the possession of full citizen rights. Democracy itself is characterized by freedom, which includes [63] the right to say and do whatever one wishes: everyone can follow the way of life which pleases him most. Hence democracy is the regime which fosters the greatest variety: every way of life, every regime can be found in it. Hence, we must add, democracy is the only regime other than the best in which the philosopher can lead his peculiar way of life without being disturbed: it is for this reason that with some exaggeration one can compare democracy to Hesiod's age of the divine race of heroes which comes closer to the golden age than any other. Certainly in a democracy the citizen who is a philosopher is under no compulsion to participate in political life or to hold office.[76] One is thus led to wonder why Socrates did not assign to democracy the highest place among the inferior regimes, or rather the highest place simply, seeing

---

76 *Republic* 557d–e.

that the best regime is not possible. One could say that he showed his preference for democracy "by deed": by spending his whole life in democratic Athens, by fighting for her in her wars, and by dying in obedience to her laws. However this may be, he surely did not prefer democracy to all other regimes "in speech." The reason is that, being a just man, he thought of the well-being not merely of the philosophers but of the nonphilosophers as well, and he held that democracy is not designed for inducing the nonphilosophers to attempt to become as good as they possibly can, for the end of democracy is not virtue but freedom, i.e., the freedom to live either nobly or basely according to one's liking. Therefore he assigns to democracy a rank even lower than to oligarchy, since oligarchy requires some kind of restraint whereas democracy, as he presents it, abhors every kind of restraint. One could say that adapting himself to his subject matter, Socrates abandons all restraint when speaking of the regime which loathes restraint. In a democracy, he asserts, no one is compelled to rule or to be ruled if he does not like it; he can live in peace while his city is at war; capital punishment does not have the slightest consequence for the condemned man: he is not even jailed; the order of rulers and ruled is completely reversed: the father behaves as if he were a boy and the son has neither respect nor fear of the father, the teacher fears his pupils while the pupils pay no attention to the teacher, and there is complete equality of the sexes; even horses and donkeys no longer step aside when encountering human beings. Plato writes as if the Athenian democracy had not carried out Socrates' execution, and Socrates speaks as if the Athenian democracy had not engaged in an orgy of bloody persecution of guilty and innocent alike when the Hermes statues were mutilated at the beginning of the Sicilian expedition.[77] Socrates' exaggeration of the licentious mildness of democracy is matched by an almost equally strong exaggeration of the intemperance of democratic [64] man. He could indeed not avoid the latter exaggeration if he did not wish to deviate in the case of democracy from the procedure which he follows in his discussion of the inferior regimes. That procedure consists in understanding the man corresponding to an inferior regime as the son of a father corresponding to the preceding regime. Hence democratic man had to be presented as the son of an oligarchic father, as the degenerate son of a wealthy father who is concerned with nothing but making money: the democratic man is the drone, the fat, soft, and prodigal playboy, the lotus-eater who, assigning a

---

77 See Thucydides VI. 27–29 and 53–61.

Chapter 21

kind of equality to equal and unequal things, lives one day in complete surrender to his lowest desires and the next ascetically, or who, according to Karl Marx's ideal, "goes hunting in the morning, fishes in the afternoon, raises cattle in the evening, devotes himself to philosophy after dinner," i.e., does at every moment what he happens to like at that moment: the democratic man is not the lean, tough and thrifty craftsman or peasant who has a single job.[78] Socrates' deliberately exaggerated blame of democracy becomes intelligible to some extent once one considers its immediate addressee, the austere Adeimantos, who is not a friend of laughter and who had been the addressee of the austere discussion of poetry in the section on the education of the warriors: by his exaggerated blame of democracy Socrates lends words to Adeimantos' "dream" of democracy.[79] One must also not forget that the sanguine account of the multitude which was provisionally required in order to prove the harmony between the city and philosophy is in need of being redressed; the exaggerated blame of democracy reminds us with greater force than was ever before used of the disharmony between philosophy and the people.[80]

After Socrates had brought to light the entirely unjust regime and the entirely unjust man and then compared the life of the entirely unjust man with that of the perfectly just man, it became clear beyond the shadow of a doubt that justice is preferable to injustice. Nevertheless the conversation continues. Socrates suddenly returns to the question of poetry, to a question which had already been answered at great length when he discussed the education of the warriors. We must try to understand this apparently sudden return. In an explicit digression from the discussion of tyranny, Socrates had noted that the poets praise tyrants and are honored by tyrants (and also by democracy), whereas they are not honored by the three better regimes.[81] Tyranny and democracy are characterized by surrender to the sensual desires, including the most lawless ones. The tyrant is *Eros* incarnate, and the poets sing the praise of *Eros*. They pay very great attention and homage precisely to that phenomenon from which Socrates abstracts in the *Re-*[65]*public* to the best of his powers. The poets therefore foster injustice. So does Thrasymachos. But just as Socrates, in spite of

---

78 Cf. *Republic* 564c–565a and 575c.
79 Cf. *ibid.*, 563d with 389a.
80 Cf. *ibid.*, 577c–d with 428d–e and 422a, c.
81 *Ibid.*, 568a–d.

Plato, 427–347 B.C.

this, could be a friend of Thrasymachos, so there is no reason why he could not be a friend of the poets and especially of Homer. Perhaps Socrates needs the poets in order to restore, on another occasion, the dignity of *Eros*: the *Banquet*, the only Platonic dialogue in which Socrates is shown to converse with poets, is devoted entirely to *Eros*.

The foundation for the return to poetry was laid at the very beginning of the discussion of the inferior regimes and of the inferior souls. The transition from the best regime to the inferior regimes was explicitly ascribed to the Muses speaking "tragically," and the transition from the best man to the inferior men has in fact a somewhat "comical" touch:[82] poetry takes the lead when the descent from the highest theme—justice understood as philosophy—begins. The return to poetry, which is preceded by the account of the inferior regimes and the inferior souls, is followed by a discussion of "the greatest rewards for virtue," i.e., the rewards not inherent in justice or philosophy itself.[83] The return to poetry constitutes the center of that part of the *Republic* in which the conversation descends from the highest theme. This cannot be surprising, for philosophy as quest for the truth is the highest activity of man, and poetry is not concerned with the truth.

In the first discussion of poetry, which preceded by a long time the introduction of philosophy as a theme, poetry's unconcern with the truth was its chief recommendation, for at that time it was untruth that was needed.[84] The most excellent poets were expelled from the just city, not because they teach untruth, but because they teach the wrong kind of untruth. But in the meantime it has become clear that only the life of the philosophizing man in so far as he philosophizes is the just life, and that that life, so far from needing untruth, utterly rejects it.[85] The progress from the city, even the best city, to the philosopher requires, it seems, a progress from the qualified acceptance of poetry to its unqualified rejection.

In the light of philosophy, poetry reveals itself to be the imitation of imitations of the truth, i.e., of the ideas. The contemplation of the ideas is the activity of the philosopher, the imitation of the ideas is the activity of the ordinary artisan, and the imitation of the works of artisans is the

---

82 *Ibid.*, 545d–e, 549c–e.
83 *Ibid.*, 608c, 614a.
84 *Ibid.*, 377a.
85 *Ibid.*, 485c–d.

Chapter 21

activity of poets and other "imitative" artisans. To begin with, Socrates presents the order of rank in these terms: the maker of the ideas (e.g., of the idea of the bed) is the God, the maker of the imitation (of the bed which can be used) is the artisan, and the maker of the imitation of the imitation (of the painting of a bed) is the imitative artisan. Later on he restates the order of rank in these terms: [66] first the user, then the artisan, and finally the imitative artisan. The idea of the bed originates in the user who determines the "form" of the bed with a view to the end for which it is to be used. The user is then the one who possesses the highest or most authoritative knowledge: the highest knowledge is not that possessed by any artisans as such at all; the poet who stands at the opposite pole from the user does not possess any knowledge, not even right opinion.[86] In order to understand this seemingly outrageous indictment of poetry one must first identify the artisan whose work the poet imitates. The poets' themes are above all the human things referring to virtue and vice; the poets see the human things in the light of virtue, but the virtue toward which they look is an imperfect and even distorted image of virtue.[87] The artisan whom the poet imitates is the nonphilosophic legislator who is an imperfect imitator of virtue itself.[88] In particular, justice as understood by the city is necessarily the work of the legislator, for the just as understood by the city is the legal. No one expressed Socrates' suggestion more clearly than Nietzsche, who said that "the poets were always the valets of some morality...."[89] But according to the French saying, for a valet there is no hero: Are the artists and in particular the poets not aware of the secret weakness of their heroes? This is indeed the case according to Socrates. The poets bring to light, for instance, the full force of the grief which a man feels for the loss of someone dear to him—of a feeling to which a respectable man would not give adequate utterance except when he is alone, because its adequate utterance in the presence of others is not becoming and lawful: the poets bring to light that in our nature which the law forcibly restrains.[90] If this is so, if the poets are perhaps the men who understand best the nature of the passions which the law restrains, they are very far

---

86   *Ibid.*, 601c–602a.
87   *Ibid.*, 598e, 599c–e, 600e.
88   Cf. *ibid.*, 501a.
89   *The Gay Science*, No. 1.
90   *Republic* 603e–604a, 606a, c, 607a.

from being merely the servants of the legislators; they are also the men from whom the prudent legislator will learn. The genuine "quarrel between philosophy and poetry"[91] concerns, from the philosopher's point of view, not the worth of poetry as such, but the order of rank of philosophy and poetry. According to Socrates, poetry is legitimate only as ministerial to the "user" par excellence, to the king who is the philosopher, and not as autonomous. For autonomous poetry presents human life as autonomous, i.e., as not directed toward the philosophic life, and therefore it never presents the philosophic life itself except in its comical distortion; hence autonomous poetry is necessarily either tragedy or comedy since the nonphilosophic life understood as autonomous has either no way out of its fundamental difficulty or only an inept one. But ministerial poetry presents the nonphilosophic life as ministerial to the philosophic life and [67] therefore, above all, it presents the philosophic life itself.[92] The greatest example of ministerial poetry is the Platonic dialogue.

The *Republic* concludes with a discussion of the greatest rewards for justice and the greatest punishments for injustice. The discussion consists of three parts: (1) proof of the immortality of the soul; (2) the divine and human rewards and punishments for men while they are alive; (3) the rewards and punishments after death. The central part is silent about the philosophers: rewards for justice and punishments for injustice during life are needed for the nonphilosophers whose justice does not have the intrinsic attractiveness which the justice of the philosophers has. The account of the rewards and punishments after death is given in the form of a myth. The myth is not baseless, since it is based on the proof of the immortality of the souls. The soul cannot be immortal if it is composed of many things unless the composition is most perfect. But the soul as we know it from our experience lacks that perfect harmony. In order to find the truth, one would have to recover by reasoning the original or true nature of the soul.[93] This reasoning is not achieved in the *Republic*. That is to say, Socrates proves the immortality of the soul without having brought to light the nature of the soul. The situation at the end of the *Republic* corresponds precisely to the situation at the end of the first book of the *Republic* where Socrates makes clear that he has proved that justice is salutary without

---

91   Ibid., 607b.
92   Cf. *ibid.*, 604e.
93   Ibid., 611b–612a.

CHAPTER 21

knowing the "what" or nature of justice. The discussion following the first book does bring to light the nature of justice as the right order of the soul, yet how can one know the right order of the soul if one does not know the nature of the soul? Let us remember here also the fact that the parallelism between soul and city, which is the premise of the doctrine of the soul stated in the *Republic*, is evidently questionable and even untenable. The *Republic* cannot bring to light the nature of the soul because it abstracts from *eros* and from the body. If we are genuinely concerned with finding out precisely what justice is, we must take "another longer way around" in our study of the soul than the way which is taken in the *Republic*.[94] This does not mean that what we learn from the *Republic* about justice is not true or is altogether provisional. The teaching of the *Republic* regarding justice, although not complete, can yet be true in so far as the nature of justice depends decisively on the nature of the city—for even the transpolitical cannot be understood as such except if the city is understood—and the city is completely intelligible because its limits can be made perfectly manifest: to see these limits, one need not have answered the question regarding the whole; it is sufficient to have raised the question regarding the whole. The *Republic* then indeed [68] makes clear what justice is. However, as Cicero has observed, the *Republic* does not bring to light the best possible regime but rather the nature of political things—the nature of the city.[95] Socrates makes clear in the *Republic* what character the city would have to have in order to satisfy the highest needs of man. By letting us see that the city constructed in accordance with this requirement is not possible, he lets us see the essential limits, the nature, of the city.

The Statesman

The *Statesman* is preceded by the *Sophist*, which in its turn is preceded by the *Theaitetos*. The *Theaitetos* presents a conversation between Socrates and the young mathematician Theaitetos which takes place in the presence of the mature and renowned mathematician Theodoros, as well as of Theaitetos' young companion named Socrates, and which is meant to make clear what knowledge or science is. The conversation does not lead to a positive result: Socrates by himself only knows that he does not know, and Theaitetos is not like Glaukon or Adeimantos who can be assisted by

---

94 *Ibid.*, 504b, 506d.
95 Cicero *Republic* II.52.

Plato, 427–347 B.C.

Socrates (or can assist him) in bringing forth a positive teaching. On the day following Socrates' conversation with Theaitetos, Socrates again meets with Theodoros, the younger Socrates, and Theaitetos, but this time there is also present a nameless philosopher designated only as a stranger from Elea. Socrates asks the stranger whether his fellows regard the sophist, the statesman, and the philosopher as one and the same or as two or as three. It could seem that the question regarding the identity or non-identity of the sophist, the statesman, and the philosopher takes the place of the question, or is a more articulate version of the question, What is knowledge? The stranger replies that his fellows regard the sophist, the statesman or king, and the philosopher as different from one another. The fact that the philosopher is not identical with the king was recognized in the central thesis of the *Republic*, according to which the coincidence of philosophy and kingship is the condition for the salvation of cities and indeed of the human race: identical things do not have to coincide. But the *Republic* did not make sufficiently clear the cognitive status of kingship or statesmanship. From the *Republic* we can easily receive the impression that the knowledge required of the philosopher-king consists of two heterogeneous parts: the purely philosophic knowledge of the ideas which culminates in the vision of the idea of the good, on the one hand, and the merely political experience which does not have the status of knowledge at all but which enables one to find one's way in the Cave and to discern the shadows on its walls, on the other. But the indis-[69]pensable supplement to philosophic knowledge also seemed to be a kind of art or science.[96] The Eleatic stranger seems to take the second and higher view of the non-philosophic awareness peculiar to the statesman. Yet in the dialogues *Sophist* and *Statesman* he makes clear the nature of the sophist and of the statesman, i.e., the difference between the sophist and the statesman, without making clear the difference between the statesman and the philosopher. We are promised by Theodoros that the Eleatic stranger will also expound (in a sequel to the *Statesman*) what the philosopher is, but Plato does not keep his Theodoros' promise. Do we then understand what the philosopher is once we have understood what the sophist and the statesman are? Is statesmanship not, as it appeared from the *Republic*, a mere supplement to philosophy, but an ingredient of philosophy? That is to say, is statesmanship, the art or knowledge peculiar to the statesman, far from being merely the awareness necessary for finding one's way in the Cave

---

96 Cf. Plato *Republic* 484d and 539e with 501a–c.

CHAPTER 21

and far from being itself independent of the vision of the idea of the good, a condition or rather an ingredient of the vision of the idea of the good? If it were so, then "politics" would be much more important according to the *Statesman* than it is according to the *Republic*. Surely the conversation about the king or statesman takes place when Socrates is already accused of a capital crime for the commission of which he was shortly thereafter condemned and executed (see the end of the *Theaitetos*): the city seems to be much more powerfully present in the *Statesman* than in the *Republic*, where the antagonist of Socrates, Thrasymachos, only plays the city. On the other hand, however, whereas in the *Republic* Socrates founds a city, if only in speech, with the help of two brothers who are passionately concerned with justice and the city, in the *Statesman* Socrates listens silently to a nameless stranger (a man lacking political responsibility) bringing to light what the statesman is in the cool atmosphere of mathematics: the concern with finding out what the statesman is seems to be philosophic rather than political.[97] The *Statesman* seems to be much more sober than the *Republic*.

We may say that the *Statesman* is more scientific than the *Republic*. By "science" Plato understands the highest form of knowledge or rather the only kind of awareness which deserves to be called knowledge. He calls that form of knowledge "dialectics." "Dialectics" means primarily the art of conversation and then the highest form of that art, that art as practiced by Socrates, that art of conversation which is meant to bring to light the "what's" of things, or the ideas. Dialectics is then the knowledge of the ideas—a knowledge which makes no use whatever of sense experience: it moves from idea to idea until it has exhausted the whole realm of the ideas, for each idea is a part and therefore [70] points to other ideas.[98] In its completed form dialectics would descend from the highest idea, the idea ruling the realm of ideas, step by step to the lowest ideas. The movement proceeds "step by step," i.e., it follows the articulation, the natural division of the ideas. The *Statesman* as well as the *Sophist* presents an imitation of dialectics thus understood; both are meant to give an inkling of dialectics thus understood; the imitation which they present is playful. Yet the play is not mere play. If the movement from idea to idea without recourse to sense experience should be impossible, if in other words the *Republic* should be utopian not only in what it states about the city at its best but

---

97 Cf. *Statesman* 285d.
98 *Republic* 511a–d, 531a–533d, 537c.

also in what it says about philosophy or dialectics at its best, dialectics at its best, not being possible, will not be serious. The dialectics which is possible will remain dependent on experience.[99] There is a connection between this feature of the *Statesman* and the fact that the ideas as treated in the *Statesman* are classes or comprise all individuals "participating" in the idea in question and therefore do not subsist independently of the individuals or "beyond" them. However this may be, in the *Statesman* the Eleatic stranger tries to bring to light the nature of the statesman by descending from "art" or "knowledge" step by step to the art of the statesman or by dividing "art" step by step until he arrives at the art of the statesman. For a number of reasons we cannot here follow his "methodical" procedure.

Shortly after the beginning of the conversation, the Eleatic stranger makes young Socrates agree to what one may call the abolition of the distinction between the public and the private. He achieves this result in two steps. Since statesmanship or kingship is essentially a kind of knowledge, it is of no importance whether the man possessing that knowledge is clothed in the vestments of high office by virtue of having been elected, for example, or whether he lives in a private station. Second, there is no essential difference between the city and the household and hence between the statesman or king on the one hand and the householder or master (i.e., the master of slaves) on the other. Law and freedom, the characteristically political phenomena, which are inseparable from one another, are disposed of at the very beginning because statesmanship is understood as a kind of knowledge or art, or because abstraction is made from that which distinguishes the political from the arts. The Eleatic stranger abstracts here from the fact that sheer bodily force is a necessary ingredient of the rule of men over men. This abstraction is partly justified by the fact that statesmanship or kingship is a cognitive rather than a manual (or brachial) art. It is, however, not simply cognitive like arithmetic; it is an art which gives commands to human beings. But all arts which give commands [71] do so for the sake of the coming into being of something. Some of these arts give commands for the sake of the coming into being of living beings or animals, i.e., they are concerned with the breeding and nurture of animals. The kingly art is a kind of this genus of art. For the proper understanding of the kingly art it does not suffice to divide the genus "animal" into the species "brutes" and "men." This distinction is as arbitrary

---

99 Cf. *Statesman* 264c.

Chapter 21

as the distinction of the human race into Greeks and barbarians, as distinguished from the distinction into men and women; it is not a natural distinction but a distinction originating in pride.[100] The stranger's training of young Socrates in dialectics or in the art of dividing kinds or ideas or classes goes hand in hand with training in modesty or moderation. According to the stranger's division of the species of animals, man's nearest kin is even lower than it is according to Darwin's doctrine of the origin of the species. But what Darwin meant seriously and literally, the stranger means playfully.[101] Man must learn to see the lowliness of his estate in order to turn from the human to the divine, i.e., in order to be truly human.

The division of "art" leads to the result that the art of the statesman is the art concerned with the breeding and nurture of, or with the caring for, herds of the kind of animal called man. This result is manifestly insufficient, for there are many arts—e.g., medicine and matchmaking—which claim as justly to be concerned with a caring for human herds as does the political art. The error was due to the fact that the human herd was taken to be a herd of the same kind as the herds of other animals. But human herds are a very special kind of herd: the bipartition of "animal" into brutes and men originates not merely in pride. The error is removed by a myth. According to the myth now told in its fullness for the first time, there is once a time (the age of Kronos) when the god guides the whole and then a time (the age of Zeus) when the god lets the whole move by its own motion. In the age of Kronos the god ruled and took care of the animals by assigning the different species of animals to the rule and care of different gods who acted like shepherds and thus secured universal peace and affluence: there were no political societies, no private property, and no families. This does not necessarily mean that men lived happily in the age of Kronos; only if they used the then available peace and affluence for philosophizing can they be said to have lived happily. At any rate, in the present age the god does not take care of man: in the present age there is no divine providence; men must take care of themselves. Bereft of divine care, the world abounds with disorder and injustice; men must establish order and justice as well as they can, with the understanding that in this age of scarcity, communism, and hence [72] also absolute communism, is impossible. The *Statesman* may be said to bring into the open what the

---

100 *Ibid.*, 262c–263d, 266d.
101 Cf. *ibid.*, 271e, 272b–c.

Republic had left unsaid, namely, the impossibility of the best regime presented in the *Republic*.

The myth of the *Statesman* is meant to explain the error committed by the Eleatic stranger and young Socrates in the initial definition of the *Statesman*: by looking for a single art of caring for human herds they were unwittingly looking toward the age of Kronos or toward divine caring; with the disappearance of divine caring, i.e., of a caring by beings which in the eyes of everyone are superior to men, it became inevitable that every art or every man should believe itself or himself to be as much entitled to rule as every other art or every other man,[102] or that at least many arts should become competitors of the kingly art. The inevitable first consequence of the transition from the age of Kronos to the age of Zeus was the delusion that all arts and all men are equal. The mistake consisted in assuming that the kingly art is devoted to the total caring for human herds (which total caring would include the feeding and mating of the ruled) and not to a partial or limited caring. In other words, the mistake consisted in the disregard of the fact that in the case of all arts of herding other than the human art of herding human beings, the herder belongs to a different species than the members of the herd. We must then divide the whole "caring for herds" into two parts: caring for herds in which the herder belongs to the same species as the members of the herd and caring for herds in which the herder belongs to a different species than the members of the herd (human herders of brutes and divine herders of human beings). We must next divide the first of these two kinds into parts, so that we can discover which partial herding of herds in which the herder belongs to the same species as the members of the herd is the kingly art. Let us assume that the partial caring sought is "ruling cities." Ruling cities is naturally divided into ruling not willed by the ruled (ruling by sheer force) and ruling willed by the ruled; the former is tyrannical, and the latter is kingly. Here we receive the first glimpse of freedom as the specifically political theme. But at the very moment in which the stranger alludes to this difficulty, he turns away from it. He finds the whole previous procedure unsatisfactory.

The method which proves to be helpful, where the division of classes and into classes as well as the myth have failed, is the use of an example. The stranger illustrates the usefulness of examples by an example. The example is meant to illustrate man's situation in regard to knowledge—to the

---

102 *Ibid.*, 274e–275c.

CHAPTER 21

phenomenon which is the guiding theme of the trilogy *Theaitetos-Sophist-Statesman*. The example chosen is chil-[73]dren's knowledge of reading. Starting from knowledge of the letters (the "elements"), they proceed step by step to the knowledge of the shortest and easiest syllables (the combination of "elements"), and then to the knowledge of long and difficult ones. Knowledge of the whole is not possible if it is not similar to the art of reading: knowledge of the elements must be available, the elements must be fairly small in number, and not all elements must be combinable.[103] But can we say that we possess knowledge of the "elements" of the whole or that we can ever start from an absolute beginning? Did we in the *Statesman* begin from an adequate understanding of "art" or "knowledge"? Is it not true that while we necessarily long for knowledge of the whole, we are condemned to rest satisfied with partial knowledge of parts of the whole and hence never truly to transcend the sphere of opinion? Is therefore philosophy, and hence human life, not necessarily Sisyphean? Could this be the reason why the demand for freedom is not so evidently sound as many present-day lovers of freedom believe on the basis of very similar thoughts? (Perhaps this could induce one to consider Dostoyevsky's *Grand Inquisitor* in the light of Plato's *Statesman*.) After having compelled us to raise these and kindred questions, the stranger turns to his example, which is meant to throw light, not on knowledge in general or on philosophy as such, but on the kingly art. The example chosen by him is the art of weaving: he illustrates the political art by an emphatically domestic art and not by such "outgoing" arts as herding and piloting; he illustrates the most virile art by a characteristically feminine art. In order to find out what weaving is, one must divide "art," but divide it differently than they divided it at first. The analysis of the art of weaving which is made on the basis of the new division enables the stranger to elucidate art in general and the kingly art in particular before he applies explicitly the result of that analysis to the kingly art. Perhaps the most important point made in this context is the distinction between two kinds of the art of measurement: one kind which considers the greater and less in relation to one another, and another kind which considers the greater and less (now understood as excess and defect) in relation to the mean or, say, the fitting, or something similar. All arts, and especially the kingly art, make their measurements with a view to the right mean or the fitting, i.e., they are not mathematical.

---

103 Cf. *Sophist* 252d–e.

Plato, 427–347 B.C.

By explicitly applying to the kingly art the results of his analysis of the art of weaving, the stranger is enabled to make clear the relation of the kingly art to all other arts and especially to those arts which claim with some show of justice to compete with the kingly art for the [74] rule of the city. The most successful and clever competitors are those outstanding sophists who pretend to possess the kingly art, and these are the rulers of cities, i.e., the rulers lacking the kingly or statesmanly art, or practically all political rulers that were, are, and will be. Of this kind of political rule there are three sorts: the rule of one, the rule of a few, and the rule of many; but each of these three kinds is divided into two parts with a view to the difference between violence and voluntariness or between lawfulness and lawlessness; thus monarchy is distinguished from tyranny, and aristocracy from oligarchy, whereas the name of democracy is applied to the rule of the multitude regardless of whether the multitude of the poor rules over the rich with the consent of the rich and in strict obedience to the laws or with violence and more or less lawlessly. (The distinction of regimes sketched by the stranger is almost identical with the distinction developed by Aristotle in the third book of his *Politics*; but consider the difference.) None of these regimes bases its claim on the knowledge or art of the rulers, i.e., on the only claim which is unqualifiedly legitimate. It follows that the claims based on the willingness of the subjects (on consent or freedom) and on lawfulness are dubious. This judgment is defended with reference to the example of the other arts and especially of medicine. A physician is a physician whether he cures us with our will or against our will, whether he cuts us, burns us, or inflicts upon us any other pain, and whether he acts in accordance with written rules or without them; he is a physician if his ruling redounds to the benefit of our bodies. Correspondingly, the only regime which is correct or which is truly a regime is that in which the possessors of the kingly art rule, regardless of whether they rule according to laws or without laws and whether the ruled consent to their rule or not, provided their rule redounds to the benefit of the body politic; it does not make any difference whether they achieve this end by killing some or banishing them and thus reduce the bulk of the city or by bringing in citizens from abroad and thus increase its bulk.

Young Socrates, who is not shocked by what the stranger says about killing and banishing, is rather shocked by the suggestion that rule without laws (absolute rule) can be legitimate. To understand fully the response of young Socrates, one must pay attention to the fact that the stranger does not make a distinction between human laws and natural laws. The

CHAPTER 21

stranger turns the incipient indignation of young Socrates into a desire on the latter's part for discussion. Rule of law is inferior to the rule of living intelligence because laws, owing to their generality, cannot determine wisely what is right and proper in all [75] circumstances given the infinite variety of circumstances: only the wise man on the spot could correctly decide what is right and proper in the circumstances. Nevertheless laws are necessary. The few wise men cannot sit beside each of the many unwise men and tell him exactly what it is becoming for him to do. The few wise men are almost always absent from the innumerable unwise men. All laws, written or unwritten, are poor substitutes but indispensable substitutes for the individual rulings by wise men. They are crude rules of thumb which are sufficient for the large majority of cases: they treat human beings as if they were members of a herd. The freezing of crude rules of thumb into sacred, inviolable, unchangeable prescriptions which would be rejected by everyone as ridiculous if done in the sciences and the arts is a necessity in the ordering of human affairs; this necessity is the proximate cause of the ineradicable difference between the political and the suprapolitical spheres. But the main objection to laws is not that they are not susceptible of being individualized but that they are assumed to be binding on the wise man, on the man possessing the kingly art.[104] Yet even this objection is not entirely valid. As the stranger explains through images,[105] the wise man is subjected to the laws, whose justice and wisdom is inferior to his, because the unwise men cannot help distrusting the wise man, and this distrust is not entirely indefensible given the fact that they cannot understand him. They cannot believe that a wise man who would deserve to rule as a true king without laws would be willing and able to rule over them. The ultimate reason for their unbelief is the fact that no human being has that manifest superiority, in the first place regarding the body and then regarding the soul, which would induce everybody to submit to his rule without any hesitation and without any reserve.[106] The unwise men cannot help making themselves the judges of the wise man. No wonder then that the wise men are unwilling to rule over them. The unwise men must even demand of the wise man that he regard the law as simply authoritative, i.e., that he not even doubt that the established laws

---

104 *Statesman* 295b–c.
105 *Ibid.*, 297a ff.
106 *Ibid.*, 301c–e.

are perfectly just and wise; if he fails to do so, he will become guilty of corrupting the young, a capital offense; they must forbid free inquiry regarding the most important subjects. All these implications of the rule of laws must be accepted, since the only feasible alternative is the lawless rule of selfish men. The wise man must bow to the law which is inferior to him in wisdom and justice, not only in deed but in speech as well. (Here we cannot help wondering whether there are no limits to the wise man's subjection to the laws. The Platonic illustrations are these: Socrates obeyed without flinching the law which commanded him to die [76] because of his alleged corruption of the young; yet he would not have obeyed a law formally forbidding him the pursuit of philosophy. Read the *Apology of Socrates* together with the *Crito*.) The rule of law is preferable to the lawless rule of unwise men since laws, however bad, are in one way or another the outcome of some reasoning. This observation permits the ranking of the incorrect regimes, i.e., of all regimes other than the absolute rule of the true king or statesman. Law-abiding democracy is inferior to the law-abiding rule of the few (aristocracy) and to the law-abiding rule of one (monarchy), but lawless democracy is superior to the lawless rule of a few (oligarchy) and to the lawless rule of one (tyranny). "Lawless" does not mean here the complete absence of any laws or customs. It means the habitual disregard of the laws by the government and especially of those laws which are meant to restrain the power of the government: a government which can change every law or is "sovereign" is lawless. From the sequel it appears that, according to the stranger, even in the city ruled by the true king there will be laws (the true king is the true legislator), but that the true king, in contradistinction to all other rulers, may justly change the laws or act against the laws. In the absence of the true king, the stranger would probably be satisfied if the city were ruled by a code of laws framed by a wise man, one which can be changed by the unwise rulers only in extreme cases.

After the true kingly art has been separated from all other arts, it remains for the stranger to determine the peculiar work of the king. Here the example of the art of weaving takes on decisive importance. The king's work resembles a web. According to the popular view all parts of virtue are simply in harmony with one another. In fact, however, there is a tension between them. Above all, there is a tension between courage or manliness and moderation, gentleness, or concern with the seemly. This tension explains the tension and even hostility between the preponderantly manly and the preponderantly gentle human beings. The true king's

Chapter 21

task is to weave together these opposite kinds of human beings, for the people in the city who are completely unable to become either manly or moderate cannot become citizens at all. An important part of the kingly weaving together consists in intermarrying the children of preponderantly manly families and those of preponderantly gentle families. The human king must then approximate the divine shepherd by enlarging the art of ruling cities strictly understood so as to include in it the art of mating or matchmaking. The matchmaking practiced by the king is akin to the matchmaking practiced by Socrates,[107] which means that it is not identical with the latter. [77] If we were to succeed in understanding the kinship between the king's matchmaking and Socrates' matchmaking, we would have made some progress toward the understanding of the kinship between the king and the philosopher. This much can be said safely: While it is possible and even necessary to speak of "the human herd" when trying to define the king, the philosopher has nothing to do with "herds."

The *Statesman* belongs to a trilogy whose theme is knowledge. For Plato, knowledge proper or striving for knowledge proper is philosophy. Philosophy is striving for knowledge of the whole, for contemplation of the whole. The whole consists of parts; knowledge of the whole is knowledge of all parts of the whole as parts of the whole. Philosophy is the highest human activity, and man is an excellent, perhaps the most excellent, part of the whole. The whole is not a whole without man, without man's being whole or complete. But man becomes whole not without his own effort, and this effort presupposes knowledge of a particular kind: knowledge which is not contemplative or theoretical but prescriptive or commanding[108] or practical. The *Statesman* presents itself as a theoretical discussion of practical knowledge. In contradistinction to the *Statesman*, the *Republic* leads up from practical or political life to philosophy, to the theoretical life; the *Republic* presents a practical discussion of theory: it shows to men concerned with the solution of the human problem that that solution consists in the theoretical life; the knowledge which the *Republic* sets forth is prescriptive or commanding. The theoretical discussion of the highest practical knowledge (the kingly art) in the *Statesman*, merely by setting forth the character of the kingly art, takes on a commanding character: it sets forth what the ruler ought to do. While the distinction of theoretical and practical knowledge is necessary, their separation is impossible. (Consider from this point

---

107 Cf. *Theaitetos* 151b.
108 *Statesman* 260a–b.

of view the description of the theoretical life in the *Theaitetos* 173b–177c.) The kingly art is one of the arts directly concerned with making men whole or entire. The most obvious indication of every human being's incompleteness and at the same time of the manner in which it can be completed is the distinction of the human race into the two sexes: just as the union of men and women, the primary goal of *eros*, makes "man" self-sufficient for the perpetuity, not to say sempiternity, of the human species, all other kinds of incompleteness to be found in men are completed in the species, in the "idea," of man. The whole human race, and not any part of it, is self-sufficient as a part of the whole, and not as the master or conqueror of the whole. It is perhaps for this reason that the *Statesman* ends with a praise of a certain kind of matchmaking. [78]

The Laws

The *Republic* and the *Statesman* transcend the city in different but kindred ways. They show first how the city would have to transform itself if it wishes to maintain its claim to supremacy in the face of philosophy. They show then that the city is incapable of undergoing this transformation. The *Republic* shows silently that the ordinary city—i.e., the city which is not communistic and which is the association of the fathers rather than of the artisans—is the only city that is possible. The *Statesman* shows explicitly the necessity of the rule of laws. The *Republic* and the *Statesman* reveal, each in its own way, the essential limitation and therewith the essential character of the city. They thus lay the foundation for answering the question of the best political order, the best order of the city compatible with the nature of man. But they do not set forth that best possible order. This task is left for the *Laws*. We may then say that the *Laws* is the only political work proper of Plato. It is the only Platonic dialogue from which Socrates is absent. The characters of the *Laws* are old men of long political experience: a nameless Athenian stranger, the Cretan Kleinias, and the Spartan Megillos. The Athenian stranger occupies the place ordinarily occupied in the Platonic dialogues by Socrates. The conversation takes place far away from Athens, on the island of Crete, while the three old men walk from the city of Knossos to the cave of Zeus.

Our first impression is that the Athenian stranger has gone to Crete in order to discover the truth about those Greek laws which in one respect were the most renowned, for the Cretan laws were believed to have had their origin in Zeus, the highest god. The Cretan laws were akin to the

CHAPTER 21

Spartan laws, which were even more renowned than the Cretan laws and were traced to Apollo. At the suggestion of the Athenian, the three men converse about laws and regimes. The Athenian learns from the Cretan that the Cretan legislator has framed all his laws with a view to war: by nature every city is at all times in a state of undeclared war with every other city; victory in war, and hence war, is the condition for all blessings. The Athenian easily convinces the Cretan that the Cretan laws aim at the wrong end: the end is not war but peace. For if victory in war is the condition of all blessings, war is not the end: the blessings themselves belong to peace. Hence the virtue of war, courage, is the lowest part of virtue, inferior to moderation and above all to justice and wisdom. Once we have seen the natural order of the virtues, we know the highest principle of legislation, for that legislation must be concerned with virtue, with [79] the excellence of the human soul, rather than with any other goods is easily granted by the Cretan gentleman Kleinias who is assured by the Athenian that the possession of virtue is necessarily followed by the possession of health, beauty, strength, and wealth.[109] It appears that both the Spartan and the Cretan legislators, convinced as they were that the end of the city is war and not peace, provided well for the education of their subjects or fellows to courage, to self-control regarding pains and fears, by making them taste the greatest pains and fears; but they did not provide at all for education to moderation, to self-control regarding pleasures, by making them taste the greatest pleasures. In fact, if we can trust Megillos, at any rate the Spartan legislator discouraged the enjoyment of pleasure altogether.[110] The Spartan and Cretan legislators surely forbade the pleasures of drinking—pleasures freely indulged in by the Athenians. The Athenian contends that drinking, even drunkenness, properly practiced is conducive to moderation, the twin virtue of courage. In order to be properly practiced, drinking must be done in common, i.e., in a sense in public so that it can be supervised. Drinking, even drunkenness, will be salutary if the drinkers are ruled by the right kind of man. For a man to be a commander of a ship it is not sufficient that he possess the art or science of sailing; he must also be free from seasickness.[111] Art or knowledge is likewise not sufficient for ruling a banquet. Art is not sufficient for ruling any association and in particular

---

109 *Laws* 631b–d; cf. 829a–b.
110 *Ibid.*, 636e.
111 *Ibid.*, 639b–c.

the city. The banquet is a more fitting simile of the city than is the ship ("the ship of state"), for just as the banqueteers are drunk from wine, the citizens are drunk from fears, hopes, desires, and aversions and are therefore in need of being ruled by a man who is sober. Since banquets are illegal in Sparta and Crete but legal in Athens, the Athenian is compelled to justify an Athenian institution. The justification is a long speech, and long speeches were Athenian rather than Spartan and Cretan. The Athenian is then compelled to justify an Athenian institution in an Athenian manner. He is compelled to transform his non-Athenian interlocutors to some extent into Athenians. Only in this way can he correct their erroneous views about laws and therewith eventually their laws themselves. From this we understand better the character of the *Laws* as a whole. In the *Republic*[112] the Spartan and Cretan regimes were used as examples of timocracy, the kind of regime inferior only to the best regime but by far superior to democracy, i.e., the kind of regime which prevailed in Athens during most of Socrates' (and Plato's) lifetime. In the *Laws* the Athenian stranger attempts to correct timocracy, i.e., to change it into the best possible regime which is somehow in between timocracy and the best regime of the *Republic*. That [80] best possible regime will prove to be very similar to "the ancestral regime," the predemocratic regime, of Athens.

The Cretan and Spartan laws were found to be faulty because they did not permit their subjects to taste the greatest pleasures. But can drinking be said to afford the greatest pleasures, even the greatest sensual pleasures? Yet the Athenian had in mind those greatest pleasures which people can enjoy in public and to which they must be exposed in order to learn to control them. The pleasures of banquets are drinking and singing. In order to justify banquets one must therefore discuss also singing, music, and hence education as a whole:[113] the music pleasures are the greatest pleasures which people can enjoy in public and which they must learn to control by being exposed to them. The Spartan and Cretan laws suffer then from the great defect that they do not at all, or at least not sufficiently, expose their subjects to the music pleasures.[114] The reason for this is that these two societies are not towns but armed camps, a kind of herd: in Sparta and Crete even those youths who are by nature fit to be educated

---

112 *Republic* 544c.
113 *Laws* 642a.
114 Cf. *ibid.*, 673a–c.

CHAPTER 21

as individuals by private teachers are brought up merely as members of a herd. In other words, the Spartans and Cretans know only how to sing in choruses: they do not know the most beautiful song, the most noble music.[115] In the *Republic* the city of the armed camp, a greatly improved Sparta, was transcended by the City of Beauty, the city in which philosophy, the highest Muse, is duly honored. In the *Laws*, where the best possible regime is presented, this transcending does not take place. The city of the *Laws* is, however, not a city of the armed camp in any sense. Yet it has certain features in common with the city of the armed camp of the *Republic*. Just as in the *Republic*, music education proves to be education toward moderation, and such education proves to require the supervision of musicians and poets by the true statesman or legislator. Yet while in the *Republic* education to moderation proves to culminate in the love of the beautiful, in the *Laws* moderation rather takes on the colors of sense of shame or of reverence. Education is surely education to virtue, to the virtue of the citizen or to the virtue of man.[116]

The virtue of man is primarily the proper posture toward pleasures and pains or the proper control of pleasures and pains; the proper control is the control effected by right reasoning. If the result of reasoning is adopted by the city, that result becomes law; law which deserves the name is the dictate of right reasoning primarily regarding pleasures and pains. The kinship but not identity of right reasoning and good laws corresponds to the kinship but not identity of the good man and the good citizen. In order to learn to control the ordinary pleasures and pains, the citizens must be exposed from their childhood to the [81] pleasures afforded by poetry and the other imitative arts which in turn must be controlled by good or wise laws, by laws which therefore ought never to be changed; the desire for innovation so natural to poetry and the other imitative arts must be suppressed as much as possible; the means for achieving this is the consecration of the correct after it has come to light. The perfect legislator will persuade or compel the poets to teach that justice goes with pleasure and injustice with pain. The perfect legislator will demand that this manifestly salutary doctrine be taught even if it were not true.[117] This doctrine takes the place of the theology of the second book of the *Republic*. In the

---

115 *Ibid.*, 666e–667b.

116 *Ibid.*, 643c, 659d–e; 653a–b.

117 *Ibid.*, 660e–664b.

Plato, 427–347 B.C.

Republic the salutary teaching regarding the relation of justice and pleasure or happiness could not be discussed in the context of the education of the nonphilosophers because the *Republic* did not presuppose, as the *Laws* does, that the interlocutors of the chief character know what justice is.[118] The whole conversation regarding education and therewith also about the ends or principles of legislation is subsumed by the Athenian stranger under the theme "wine" and even "drunkenness" because the improvement of old laws can safely be entrusted only to well-bred old men who as such are averse to every change and who, in order to become willing to change the old laws, must undergo some rejuvenation like the one produced by the drinking of wine.

Only after having determined the end which political life is meant to serve (education and virtue), does the stranger turn to the beginning of political life or the genesis of the city in order to discover the cause of political change and in particular of the change of regimes. There have been many beginnings of political life because there have been many destructions of almost all men through floods, plagues, and similar calamities bringing with them the destruction of all arts and tools; only a few human beings survived on mountaintops or in other privileged places; it took many generations until they dared to descend to the lowlands, and during those generations the last recollection of the arts vanished. The condition out of which all cities and regimes, all arts and laws, all vice and virtue emerged is men's lack of all these things; the "out of which" something emerges is one kind of cause of the thing in question; the primary lack of what we may call civilization would seem to be the cause of all political change.[119] If man had had a perfect beginning, there would have been no cause for change, and the imperfection of his beginning is bound to have effects in all stages, however perfect, of his civilization. The stranger shows that this is the case by following the changes which human life underwent from the beginnings when men apparently were virtuous because they were, not indeed wise, but simple-minded or innocent yet in fact savage, [82] until the destruction of the original settlement of Sparta and her sister cities Messene and Argos. He only alludes with delicacy to the Spartans' despotic subjugation of the Messenians. He summarizes the result of his inquiry by enumerating the generally accepted and effective titles to rule. It is the contradiction among the titles or the claims to them which

---

118 *Republic* 392a–c.
119 *Laws* 676a, c, 678a.

CHAPTER 21

explains the change of regimes. It appears that the title to rule based on wisdom, while the highest, is only one among seven. Among the others we find the title or claim of the master to rule over his slaves, of the stronger to rule over the weaker, and of those chosen by lot to rule over those not so chosen.[120] Wisdom is not a sufficient title; a viable regime presupposes a blend of the claim based on wisdom with the claims based on the other kinds of superiority; perhaps the proper or wise blend of some of the other titles can act as a substitute for the title deriving from wisdom. The Athenian stranger does not abstract, as the Eleatic stranger does, from bodily force as a necessary ingredient of the rule of man over man. The viable regime must be mixed. The Spartan regime is mixed. But is it mixed wisely? In order to answer this question one must first see the ingredients of the right mixture in isolation. These are monarchy, of which Persia offers the outstanding example, and democracy, of which Athens offers the most outstanding example.[121] Monarchy by itself stands for the absolute rule of the wise man or of the master; democracy stands for freedom. The right mixture is that of wisdom and freedom, of wisdom and consent, of the rule of wise laws framed by a wise legislator and administered by the best members of the city and of the rule of the common people.

After the end as well as the general character of the best possible regime have been made clear, Kleinias reveals that the present conversation is of direct use to him. The Cretans plan to found a colony, and they have commissioned him together with others to take care of the project and in particular to frame laws for the colony as they see fit; they may even select foreign laws if they appear to them to be superior to the Cretan laws. The people to be settled come from Crete and from the Peloponnesos: they do not come from one and the same city. If they came from the same city, with the same language and the same laws and the same sacred rites and beliefs, they could not easily be persuaded to accept institutions different from those of their home city. On the other hand, heterogeneity of the population of a future city causes dissensions.[122] In the present case the heterogeneity seems to be sufficient to make possible considerable change for the better, i.e., the establishment of the best possible regime, and yet

---

120 *Ibid.*, 690a–d.
121 *Ibid.*, 693d.
122 *Ibid.*, 707e–708d.

not too great to prevent fusion. We have here the viable alternative to the expulsion of [83] everyone older than ten which would be required for the establishment of the best regime of the *Republic*. The traditions which the various groups of settlers bring with them will be modified rather than eradicated. Thanks to the good fortune which brought about the presence in Crete of the Athenian stranger while the sending out of the colony is in preparation, there is a fair chance that the traditions will be modified wisely. All the greater care must be taken that the new order established under the guidance of the wise man will not be changed afterward by less wise men: it ought to be exposed to change as little as possible, for any change of a wise order seems to be a change for the worse. At any rate without the chance presence of the Athenian stranger in Crete there would be no prospect of wise legislation for the new city. This makes us understand the stranger's assertion that not human beings but chance legislates: most laws are as it were dictated by calamities. Still, some room is left for the legislative art. Or, inversely, the possessor of the legislative art is helpless without good fortune, for which he can only pray. The most favorable circumstance for which the legislator would pray is that the city for which he is to frame laws be ruled by a young tyrant whose nature is in some respects the same as that of the philosopher except that he does not have to be graceful or witty, a lover of the truth, and just; his lack of justice (the fact that he is prompted by desire for his own power and glory alone) does not do harm if he is willing to listen to the wise legislator. Given this condition—given a coincidence of the greatest power with wisdom through the cooperation of the tyrant with the wise legislator—the legislator will effect the quickest and most profound change for the better in the habits of the citizens. But since the city to be founded is to undergo as little change as possible, it is perhaps more important to realize that the regime most difficult to change is oligarchy, the regime which occupies the central place in the order of regimes presented in the *Republic*.[123] Surely, the city to be founded must not be tyrannically ruled. The best regime is that in which a god or demon rules as in the age of Kronos, the golden age. The nearest imitation of divine rule is the rule of laws. But the laws in their turn depend on the man or men who can lay down and enforce the laws, i.e., the regime (monarchy, tyranny, oligarchy, aristocracy, democracy). In the case of each of these regimes a section of the city rules the rest, and therefore it rules the city with a view to a sectional interest, not

---

123 Cf. *ibid.*, 708e–712a with *Republic* 487a.

Chapter 21

to the common interest.[124] We know already the solution to this difficulty: the regime must be mixed as it was in a way in Sparta and Crete,[125] and it must adopt a code framed by a wise legislator.

The wise legislator will not limit himself to giving simple commands accompanied by sanctions, i.e., threats of punishment. This is the way for guiding slaves, not free men. He will preface the laws with preambles or preludes setting forth the reasons of the laws. Yet different kinds of reasons are needed for persuading different kinds of men, and the multiplicity of reasons may be confusing and thus endanger the simplicity of obedience. The legislator must then possess the art of saying simultaneously different things to different kinds of citizens in such a way that the legislator's speech will effect in all cases the same simple result: obedience to his laws. In acquiring this art he will be greatly helped by the poets.[126] Laws must be twofold; they must consist of the "unmixed law," the bald statement of what ought to be done or forborne "or else," i.e., the "tyrannical prescription," and the prelude to the law which gently persuades by appealing to reason.[127] The proper mixture of coercion and persuasion, of "tyranny" and "democracy,"[128] of wisdom and consent, proves everywhere to be the character of wise political arrangements.

The laws require a general prelude—an exhortation to honor the various beings which deserve honor in their proper order. Since the rule of laws is an imitation of divine rule, honor must be given first and above everything else to the gods, next to the other superhuman beings, then to the ancestors, then to one's father and mother. Everyone must also honor his soul but next to the gods. The order of rank between honoring one's soul and honoring one's parents is not made entirely clear. Honoring one's soul means acquiring the various virtues without which no one can be a good citizen. The general exhortation culminates in the proof that the virtuous life is more pleasant than the life of vice. Before the founder of the new colony can begin with the legislation proper, he must take two measures of the utmost importance. In the first place he must effect a kind of purge of the potential citizens: only the right kind of settlers must

---

124 *Laws* 713c–715b.

125 *Ibid.*, 712c–e.

126 *Ibid.*, 719b–720e.

127 *Ibid.*, 722e–723a; cf. 808d–e.

128 Cf. Aristotle *Politics* 1266a 1–3.

be admitted to the new colony. Second, the land must be distributed among those admitted to citizenship. There will then be no communism. Whatever advantages communism might have, it is not feasible if the legislator does not himself exercise tyrannical rule,[129] whereas in the present case not even the cooperation of the legislator with a tyrant is contemplated. Nevertheless, the land must remain the property of the whole city; no citizen will be the absolute owner of the land allotted to him. The land will be divided into allotments which must never be changed by selling, buying, or in any other way, and this will be achieved if every landowner must leave his entire allotment to a single son; the other sons must try to marry heiresses; to prevent the excess of the male citizen population beyond the number of the originally established allotments, re-[85]course must be had to birth control and in the extreme case to the sending out of colonies. There must not be gold and silver in the city and as little money-making as possible. It is impossible that there should be equality of property, but there ought to be an upper limit to what a citizen can own: the richest citizen must be permitted to own no more than four times what the poorest citizens own, i.e., the allotment of land including house and slaves. It is impossible to disregard the inequality of property in the distribution of political power. The citizen body will be divided into four classes according to the amount of property owned. The land assigned to each citizen must be sufficient to enable him to serve the city in war as a knight or as a hoplite. In other words, citizenship is limited to knights and hoplites. The regime seems to be what Aristotle calls a polity—a democracy limited by a considerable property qualification. But this is not correct, as appears particularly from the laws concerning membership in the Council and election to the Council. The Council is what we would call the executive part of the government; each twelfth of the Council is to govern for a month. The Council is to consist of four equally large groups, the first group being chosen from the highest property class, the second group being chosen from the second highest property class, and so on. All citizens have the same voting power, but whereas all citizens are obliged to vote for councillors from the highest property class, only the citizens of the two highest property classes are obliged to vote for councillors from the lowest property class. These arrangements are obviously meant to favor the wealthy; the regime is meant to be a mean between monarchy

---

129 *Laws* 739a–740a.

Chapter 21

and democracy[130] or, more precisely, a mean more oligarchic or aristocratic than a polity. Similar privileges are granted to the wealthy also as regards power in the Assembly and the holding of the most honorable offices. It is, however, not wealth as wealth which is favored: no craftsman or trader, however wealthy, can be a citizen. Only those can be citizens who have the leisure to devote themselves to the practice of citizen virtue.

The most conspicuous part of the legislation proper concerns impiety, which is of course treated within the context of the penal law. The fundamental impiety is atheism or the denial of the existence of gods. Since a good law will not merely punish crimes or appeal to fear but will also appeal to reason, the Athenian stranger is compelled to demonstrate the existence of gods and, since gods who do not care for men's justice, who do not reward the just and punish the unjust, are not sufficient for the city, he must demonstrate divine providence as well. The *Laws* is the only Platonic work which contains such a demonstration. It is the only Platonic work which begins with "A god." One [86] might say that it is Plato's most pious work, and that it is for this reason that he strikes therein at the root of impiety, i.e., at the opinion that there are no gods. The Athenian stranger takes up the question regarding the gods, although it was not even raised in Crete or in Sparta; it was, however, raised in Athens.[131] Kleinias strongly favors the demonstration recommended by the Athenian on the ground that it would constitute the finest and best prelude to the whole code. The Athenian cannot refute the atheists before he has stated their assertions. It appears that they assert that body is prior to soul or mind, or that soul or mind is derivative from body and, consequently, that nothing is by nature just or unjust, or that all right originates in convention. The refutation of them consists in the proof that soul is prior to body, which proof implies that there is natural right. The punishments for impiety differ according to the different kinds of impiety. It is not clear what punishment, if any, is inflicted on the atheist who is a just man; he is surely less severely punished than, for instance, the man who practices forensic rhetoric for the sake of gain. Even in cases of the other kinds of impiety, capital punishment will be extremely rare. We mention these facts because their insufficient consideration might induce ignorant people to scold Plato for his alleged lack of liberalism. We do not here describe such people as ignorant because they believe that liberalism calls for unqualified toleration of the teaching of all

---

130 Ibid., 756b–e.
131 *Ibid.*, 886; cf. 891b.

opinions however dangerous or degrading. We call them ignorant because they do not see how extraordinarily liberal Plato is according to their own standards, which cannot possibly be "absolute." The standards generally recognized in Plato's time are best illustrated by the practice of Athens, a city highly renowned for her liberality and gentleness. In Athens Socrates was punished with death because he was held not to believe in the existence of the gods worshipped by the city of Athens—of gods whose existence was known only from hearsay. In the city of the *Laws* the belief in gods is demanded only to the extent to which it is supported by demonstration; and in addition, those who are not convinced by the demonstration but are just men will not be condemned to death.

The stability of the order sketched by the Athenian stranger seems to be guaranteed as far as the stability of any political order can be: it is guaranteed by obedience on the part of the large majority of citizens to wise laws which are as unchangeable as possible, by an obedience that results chiefly from education to virtue, from the formation of character. Still, laws are only second best: no law can be as wise as the decision of a truly wise man on the spot. Provision must [87] therefore be made for, as it were, infinite progress in improving the laws in the interest of increasing improvement of the political order, as well as of counteracting the decay of the laws. Legislation must then be an unending process; at each time there must be living legislators. Laws should be changed only with the utmost caution, only in the case of universally admitted necessity. The later legislators must aim at the same commanding end as the original legislator: the excellence of the souls of the members of the city.[132] To prevent change of laws, intercourse of the citizens with foreigners must be closely supervised. No citizen shall go abroad for a private purpose. But citizens of high reputation and more than fifty years old who desire to see how other men live and especially to converse with outstanding men from whom they can learn something about the improvement of the laws are encouraged to do so.[133] Yet all these and similar measures do not suffice for the salvation of the laws and the regime; the firm foundation is still lacking. That firm foundation can only be supplied by a Nocturnal Council consisting of the most outstanding old citizens and select younger citizens of thirty years and older. The Nocturnal Council is to be for the city what the mind is for the human individual. To perform its function its members must

---

132 *Ibid.*, 769a–771a, 772a–d, 875c–d.

133 *Ibid.*, 949e ff.

CHAPTER 21

possess above everything else the most adequate knowledge possible of the single end at which all political action directly or indirectly aims. This end is virtue. Virtue is meant to be one, yet it is also many; there are four kinds of virtue, and at least two of them—wisdom and courage (or spiritedness)—are radically different from one another.[134] How then can there be a single end of the city? The Nocturnal Council cannot perform its function if it cannot answer this question, or, more generally and perhaps more precisely stated, the Nocturnal Council must include at least some men who know what the virtues themselves are or who know the ideas of the various virtues as well as what unites them, so that all together can justly be called "virtue" in the singular: is "virtue," the single end of the city, one or a whole or both or something else? They also must know, as far as is humanly possible, the truth about the gods. Solid reverence for the gods arises only from knowledge of the soul as well as of the movements of the stars. Only men who combine this knowledge with the popular or vulgar virtues can be adequate rulers of the city: one ought to hand over the city for rule to the Nocturnal Council if it comes into being. Plato brings the regime of the *Laws* around by degrees to the regime of the *Republic*.[135] Having arrived at the end of the *Laws*, we must return to the beginning of the *Republic*.

Readings

A. Plato. *Republic*.
B. Plato. *Laws*.

---

134 *Ibid.*, 963e.
135 Aristotle *Politics* 1265a 1–4.

22

Preface to
The Guide of the Perplexed
(1963)

Everyone connected with the production of this translation of Maimonides' *Guide of the Perplexed* has long felt that such a new translation was necessary. The legitimate demand that must be made of any translation is not satisfied by any of the existing modern language translations of the *Guide*. We rightly demand that a translation should remain as close as is practicable to the original, that within the limits of the possible it should give the reader an impression—both in general and in detail—resembling the impression offered by the original. In the present translation, pains have been taken to meet this demand. As far as was compatible with intelligibility, every Arabic technical term has been rendered by one and the same English term. Wherever the original is ambiguous or obscure, the translation has preserved or attempted to preserve that very ambiguity or obscurity. A special effort has been made to reproduce the artful interplay of Maimonides' Arabic text with his Hebrew and Aramaic quotations from the classic Jewish sources. Besides, considerable progress has been made, within the last generation, in the understanding of the *Guide*. These advances have, of course, been based on a close study of the original text, and as always in such cases, by virtue of these advances the existing translations prove now to be less adequate than they had appeared to be before. In other words, to the extent that earlier translators were not sufficiently sensitive to certain facets of the *Guide*, their translations failed to disclose those facets. A single example must suffice: where Maimonides speaks of "political," previous translators speak of "social"; where Maimonides says

---

Originally published as the preface to Moses Maimonides, *The Guide of the Perplexed*, trans. and ed. Shlomo Pines and Leo Strauss (Chicago: University of Chicago Press, 1963), vii–viii. N.B.: The preface was co-authored by Shlomo Pines. —Eds.

Chapter 22

"city," they translate "state"; where Maimonides speaks of "political civic actions," they speak of "social conduct." A moment's reflection shows that an entirely different perspective is provided when the political is mentioned, rather than the social.

The present translation is based on the Arabic text established by S. Munk (*Le Guide des Égarés*; 3 vols.; Paris, 1856–66) and edited with variant readings by Issachar Joel (*Dalālat al-ḥā'irīn*; Jerusalem: J. Junovitch, 5691 [1930/31]). Where the readings adopted by Munk and Joel have not been followed, this has been noted. The pagination of the Munk edition is indicated by thin vertical lines in the body of the text and by bracketed numerals in the running head. These numerals refer to those pages of the Arabic text whose beginnings are denoted by the first and last vertical lines occurring on the two facing pages. Italic type in the text has been reserved to indicate Maimonides' use of words that are clearly identifiable as being Hebrew or Aramaic. The division of the text into parts and chapters is Maimonides'. The Arabic text has no paragraphing, very little punctuation, and, of course, no capitalization; the translator is responsible for such features in this volume.

23

On the Plan of
The Guide of the Perplexed
(1965)

[775] I BELIEVE THAT it will not be amiss if I simply present the plan of the *Guide* as it has become clear to me in the course of about twenty-five years of frequently interrupted but never abandoned study. In the following scheme Roman (and Arabic) numerals at the beginning of a line indicate the sections (and subsections) of the *Guide* while the numbers given in parentheses indicate the Parts and the chapters of the book.

A. VIEWS (I 1–III 24)

A¹. VIEWS REGARDING GOD AND THE ANGELS (I 1–III 7)

I. *Biblical terms applied to God* (I 1–70)
(a) Terms suggesting the corporeality of God (and the angels) (I 1–49)
    (1) The two most important passages of the Torah which seem to suggest that God is corporeal (I 1–7)
    (2) Terms designating place, change of place, the organs of human locomotion, etc. (I 8–28)
    (3) Terms designating wrath and consuming (or taking food) which if applied to divine things refer to idolatry on the one hand and to human knowledge on the other (I 29–36)
    (4) Terms designating parts and actions of animals (I 37–49)

Originally published as "On the Plan of the Guide of the Perplexed," in the *Harry Austryn Wolfson Jubilee Volume on the Occasion of His Seventy-Fifth Birthday* (Jerusalem: American Academy for Jewish Research, 1965), 2:775–91.

This version of the beginning of "How To Begin To Study *The Guide of the Perplexed*" serves as an introduction to Pines's translation (1963) of Maimonides' *The Guide of the Perplexed*. We have reproduced the typography used in Strauss's scheme of the *Guide*, which is not found in the translation but appears in *Liberalism Ancient and Modern* (1968).—Eds.

CHAPTER 23

- (b) Terms suggesting multiplicity in God (I 50–70)
    - (5) Given that God is absolutely one and incomparable, what is the meaning of the terms applied to God in nonfigurative speech? (I 50–60)
- [776](6) The names of God and the utterances of God (I 61–67)
    - (7) The apparent multiplicity in God consequent upon His knowledge, His causality, and His governance (I 68–70)

II. *Demonstrations of the existence, unity and incorporeality of God* (I 71–II 31)

   (1) Introductory (I 71–73)
   (2) Refutation of the Kalām demonstrations (I 74–76)
   (3) The philosophic demonstrations (II 1)
   (4) Maimonides' demonstration (II 2)
   (5) The angels (II 3–12)
   (6) Creation of the world, i.e., defense of the belief in creation out of nothing against the philosophers (II 13–24)
   (7) Creation and the Law (II 25–31)

III. *Prophecy* (II 32–48)

   (1) Natural endowment and training the prerequisites of prophecy (II 32–34)
   (2) The difference between the prophecy of Moses and that of the other prophets (II 35)
   (3) The essence of prophecy (II 36–38)
   (4) The legislative prophecy (of Moses) and the Law (II 39–40)
   (5) Legal study of the prophecy of the prophets other than Moses (II 41–44)
   (6) The degrees of prophecy (II 45)
   (7) How to understand the divine and the divinely commanded actions and works as presented by the prophets (II 46–48)

IV. *The Work of the Chariot* (III 1–7)

A². VIEWS REGARDING BODILY BEINGS WHICH COME INTO BEING AND PERISH AND IN PARTICULAR REGARDING MAN (III 8–54)

V. *Providence* (III 8–24)

   (1) Statement of the problem: matter is the ground of all evils and yet matter is created by the absolutely good God (III 8–14)

On the Plan of The Guide of the Perplexed

[777] (2) The nature of the impossible or the meaning of omnipotence (III 15)
    (3) The philosophic arguments against omniscience (III 16)
    (4) The views regarding providence (III 17–18)
    (5) Jewish views on omniscience and Maimonides' discourse on this subject (III 19–21)
    (6) The book of Job as the authoritative treatment of providence (III 22–23)
    (7) The teaching of the Torah on omniscience (III 24)

B. Actions (III 25–54)

VI. *The actions commanded by God and done by God* (III 25–50)

    (1) The rationality of God's actions in general and of His legislation in particular (III 25–26)
    (2) The manifestly rational part of the commandments of the Torah (III 27–28)
    (3) The rationale of the apparently irrational part of the commandments of the Torah (III 29–33)
    (4) The inevitable limit to the rationality of the commandments of the Torah (III 34)
    (5) Division of the commandments into classes and explanation of the usefulness of each class (III 35)
    (6) Explanation of all or almost all commandments (III 36–49)
    (7) The narratives in the Torah (III 50)

VII. *Man's perfection and God's providence* (III 51–54)

    (1) True knowledge of God Himself is the prerequisite of providence (III 51–52)
    (2) True knowledge of what constitutes the human individual himself is the prerequisite of knowledge of the workings of providence (III 53–54)

The *Guide* consists then of 7 sections or of 38 subsections. Wherever feasible, each section is divided into 7 subsections; the only section which does not permit of being divided into subsections is divided into 7 chapters.

[778] The simple statement of the plan of the *Guide* suffices to show that the book is sealed with many seals. At the end of its Introduction Maimonides describes the preceding passage as follows: "It is a key permitting

CHAPTER 23

one to enter places the gates to which were locked. When those gates are opened and those places are entered, the souls will find rest therein, the eyes will be delighted, and the bodies will be eased of their toil and of their labor." The *Guide* as a whole is not merely a key to a forest but itself a forest, an enchanted forest, and hence also an enchanting forest: it is a delight for the eyes. For the tree of life is a delight for the eyes.

The enchanting character of the *Guide* does not appear immediately. At first glance the book appears merely to be strange and, in particular, to lack order and consistency. But the progress in its understanding is a progress in becoming enchanted by it. Enchanting understanding is perhaps the highest form of edification. One begins to understand the *Guide* once one sees that it is not a philosophic book—a book written by a philosopher for philosophers—but a Jewish book, a book written by a Jew for Jews. Its first premise is the old Jewish premise that being a Jew and being a philosopher are two incompatible things. Philosophers are men who try to give an account of the whole by starting from what is always accessible to man as man; Maimonides starts from the acceptance of the Torah. A Jew may make use of philosophy and Maimonides makes the most ample use of it; but as a Jew he gives his assent where as a philosopher he would suspend his assent (cf. II 16).

In accordance with this, the *Guide* is devoted to the Torah or more precisely to the true science of the Torah, of the Law. Its first purpose is to explain Biblical terms and its second purpose is to explain Biblical similes. The *Guide* is then devoted above all to Biblical exegesis, although to Biblical exegesis of a particular kind. That kind of exegesis is required because many Biblical terms and all Biblical similes have an apparent or outer and a hidden or inner meaning: the gravest errors as well as the most tormenting perplexities arise from men's understanding the Bible always according to its apparent or literal meaning. The *Guide* is then devoted [779] to "the difficulties of the Law" or to "the secrets of the Law." The most important of those secrets are the Work of the Beginning (the beginning of the Bible) and the Work of the Chariot (Ezekiel 1 and 10). The *Guide* is then devoted primarily and chiefly to the explanation of the Work of the Beginning and the Work of the Chariot.

Yet the Law whose secrets Maimonides intends to explain, forbids that they be explained in public, or to the public; they may only be explained in private and only to such individuals as possess both theoretical and political wisdom as well as the capacity of both understanding and using allusive speech; for only "the chapter headings" of the secret teaching may be transmitted even to those who belong to the natural elite. Since every explanation given in writing, at any rate in a book, is a public explanation, Maimonides seems to be compelled by his intention to transgress the Law. There were other cases in which he was under such a compulsion. The Law also forbids one to study the books of idolators on idolatry, for the first intention of the Law as a whole is to destroy every vestige of idolatry; and yet Maimonides, as he openly admits and even emphasizes, has studied all the available idolatrous books of this kind with the utmost thoroughness. Nor is this all. He goes so far as to encourage the reader of the *Guide* to study those books by himself (III 29–30, 32 and 37; *M.T.*, H. 'Abodah zara II 2 and III 2). The Law also forbids one to speculate about the date of the coming of the Messiah, yet Maimonides presents such a speculation or at least its equivalent in order to comfort his contemporaries (*Epistle to Yemen*, 62, 16 ff., and 80, 17 ff., Halkin; cf. Halkin's Introduction, pp. xii–xiii; *M.T.*, H. Melakim XII 2). Above all, the Law forbids one to seek for the reasons of the commandments, and yet Maimonides devotes almost twenty-six chapters of the *Guide* to such seeking (III 26; cf. II 25). All these irregularities have one and the same justification: Maimonides transgresses the Law "for the sake of heaven," i.e., in order to uphold or to fulfill the Law (I Introd., and III Introd.). Still, in the most important case he does not strictly speaking transgress the Law, for his written explanation of the secrets of the Law is [780] not a public but a secret explanation. The secrecy is achieved in three ways. Firstly, every word of the *Guide* is chosen with exceeding care; since very few men are able or willing to read with exceeding care, most men will fail to perceive the secret teaching. Secondly, Maimonides deliberately contradicts himself, and if a man declares both that a is b and that a is not b, he cannot be said to declare anything. Lastly, the "chapter headings" of the secret teaching are not presented in an orderly fashion but are scattered throughout the book. This permits us to understand why the plan of the *Guide* is so obscure. Maimonides succeeds in obscuring the plan immediately by failing to divide the book explicitly in sections and subsections or by dividing it explicitly only into three Parts and each Part into chapters without supplying the Parts and the chapters with headings indicating the subject matter of the Parts or of the chapters.

The plan of the *Guide* is not entirely obscure. No one can reasonably doubt for instance that II 32–48, III 1–7, and III 25–50 form sections. The plan is most obscure at the beginning and it becomes clearer as one proceeds; generally speaking it is clearer in the second half (II 13–end) than in the first half. The *Guide* is then not entirely devoted to secretly trans-

CHAPTER 23

mitting chapter headings of the secret teaching. This does not mean that the book is not in its entirety devoted to the true science of the Law. It means that the true science of the Law is partly public. This is not surprising, for the teaching of the Law itself is of necessity partly public. According to one statement, the core of the public teaching consists of the assertions that God is one, that He alone is to be worshipped, that He is incorporeal, that He is incomparable to any of His creatures and that He suffers from no defect and no passion (I 35). From other statements it would appear that the acceptance of the Law on every level of comprehension presupposes belief in God, in angels and in prophecy (III 45) or that the basic beliefs are those in God's unity and in Creation (II 13). In brief, one may say that the public teaching of the Law insofar as it refers to beliefs or to "views," can be reduced to the 13 "roots" (or dogmas) which Maimonides had put together in his *Commentary on the* [781] *Mishna*. That part of the true science of the Law which is devoted to the public teaching of the Law or which is itself public has the task of demonstrating the roots to the extent to which this is possible or of establishing the roots by means of speculation (III 51 and 54). Being speculative, that part of the true science of the Law is not exegetic; it is not necessarily in need of support by Biblical or Talmudic texts (cf. II 45 beginning). Accordingly, about 20 per cent of the chapters of the *Guide* contain no Biblical quotations and about 9 per cent of them contain no Hebrew or Aramaic expressions whatever. It is not very difficult to see (especially on the basis of III 7 end, 23 and 28) that the *Guide* as devoted to speculation on the roots of the Law or to the public teaching consists of sections II–III and V–VI as indicated in our scheme and that the sequence of these sections is rational; but one cannot understand in this manner why the book is divided into 3 Parts, or what sections I, IV, and VII and most, not to say all, subsections mean. The teaching of the *Guide* is then neither entirely public or speculative nor is it entirely secret or exegetic. For this reason the plan of the *Guide* is neither entirely obscure nor entirely clear.

Yet the *Guide* is a single whole. What then is the bond uniting its exegetic and its speculative element? One might imagine that, while speculation demonstrates the roots of the Law, exegesis proves that those roots as demonstrated by speculation are in fact taught by the Law. But in that case the *Guide* would open with chapters devoted to speculation and the opposite is manifestly true. In addition, if the exegesis dealt with the same subject matter as that speculation which demonstrates the public teaching par excellence, namely, the roots of the Law, there would be no reason why the exegesis should be secret. Maimonides does say that the Work of the Beginning is the same as natural science and the Work of the Chariot is the same as divine science (i.e., the science of the incorporeal beings or of God and the angels). This might lead one to think that the public teaching is identical with what the philosophers teach while the secret teaching makes one understand the identity of the teaching of the philosophers with the secret teaching of the Law. One can safely say that this thought [782] proves to be untenable on almost every level of one's comprehending the *Guide*: the non-identity of the teaching of the philosophers as a whole and the 13 roots of the Law as a whole is the first word and the last word of Maimonides. What he means by identifying the core of philosophy (natural science and divine science) with the highest secrets of the Law (the Work of the Beginning and the Work of the Chariot) and therewith by somehow identifying the subject matter of speculation with the subject matter of exegesis may be said to be the secret par excellence of the *Guide*.

Let us then retrace our steps. The *Guide* contains a public teaching and a secret teaching. The public teaching is addressed to every Jew including the vulgar; the secret teaching is addressed to the elite. The secret teaching is of no use to the vulgar and the elite does not need the *Guide* for being appraised of the public teaching.* To the extent to which the *Guide* is a whole, or one work, it is not addressed to the vulgar nor to the elite. To whom then is it addressed? How legitimate and important this question is appears from Maimonides' remark that the chief purpose of the *Guide* is to explain as far as possible the Work of the Beginning and the Work of the Chariot "with a view to him for whom (the book) has been composed" (III beginning). Maimonides answers our question both explicitly and implicitly. He answers it explicitly in two ways: he says on the one hand that the *Guide* is addressed to believing Jews who are perfect in their religion and in their character, have studied the sciences of the philosophers and are perplexed by the literal meaning of the Law; he says on the other hand that the book is addressed to such perfect human beings as are Law students and perplexed. He answers our question more simply by dedicating the book to his disciple Joseph and by stating that it has been composed for Joseph and his like. Joseph had come to him "from the ends of the earth" and had studied under him for a while; the

---

* This word is "apprised" in both Pines's translation of the *Guide* (vol. 1, p. xvii) and in *Liberalism Ancient and Modern* (145), though Strauss uses "appraisal" later in the paragraph; and "appraised" could make a certain kind of sense. —Eds.

CHAPTER 23

interruption of the oral instruction through Joseph's departure which "God had decreed," induced Maimonides to write the *Guide* for Joseph and his like. In the Epistle dedicatory addressed to Joseph, Maimonides extolls Joseph's virtues and indicates his limitation. Joseph had a pas-[783]sionate desire for things speculative and especially for mathematics. When he studied astronomy, mathematics and logic under Maimonides, the teacher saw that Joseph had an excellent mind and a quick grasp; he thought him therefore fit to have revealed to him allusively the secrets of the books of the prophets and he began to make such revelations. This stimulated Joseph's interest in things divine as well as in an appraisal of the Kalām; his desire for knowledge about these subjects became so great that Maimonides was compelled to warn him unceasingly to proceed in an orderly manner. It appears that Joseph was inclined to proceed impatiently or unmethodically in his study and that this defect had not been cured when he left Maimonides. The most important consequence of Joseph's defect is the fact, brought out by Maimonides' silence, that Joseph turned to divine science without having studied natural science under Maimonides or before, although natural science necessarily precedes divine science in the order of study.

The impression derived from the Epistle dedicatory is confirmed by the book itself. Maimonides frequently addresses the reader by using expressions like "know" or "you know already"; expressions of the latter kind indicate what the typical addressee knows and expressions of the former kind indicate what he does not know. One thus learns that Joseph has some knowledge of both the content and the character of divine science.* He knows for example that divine science in contradistinction to mathematics and medicine requires an extreme of rectitude and moral perfection, and in particular of humility, but he apparently does not yet know how ascetic Judaism is in matters of sex (I 34, III 52). He had learned from Maimonides' "speech" that the orthodox "views" do not last in a man if he does not confirm them by the corresponding "actions" (II 31). It goes without saying that while his knowledge of the Jewish sources is extensive it is not comparable in extent and thoroughness to Maimonides' (II 26, 33). At the beginning of the book he does not know that both according to the Jewish view and according to demonstration angels have no bodies (I 43, 49) and he certainly does not know strictly speaking [784] that God has no body (I 9). In this respect as well as in other respects his understanding

---

* "Character" is spelled "charater" in the text. —Eds.

necessarily progresses while he advances in his study of the *Guide* (cf. I 65 beginning). As for natural science, he has studied astronomy but is not aware of the conflict between the astronomical principles and the principles of natural science (II 24), because he has not studied natural science. He knows a number of things which are made clear in natural science but this does not mean that he knows them through having studied natural science (cf. I 17, 28; III 10). From the 91st chapter (II 15) it appears that while he knows Aristotle's *Topics* and Farabi's commentary on that work, he does not know the *Physics* and *On the Heaven* (cf. II 8). Nor will he acquire the science of nature as he acquires the science of God and the angels while he advances in the study of the *Guide*. For the *Guide* which is addressed to a reader not conversant with natural science, does not itself transmit natural science (II 2). The following remark occurring in the 26th chapter is particularly revealing: "It has been demonstrated that everything moved undoubtedly possesses a magnitude and is divisible; and it will be demonstrated that God possesses no magnitude and hence possesses no motion." What "has been demonstrated" has been demonstrated in the *Physics* and is simply presupposed in the *Guide*; what "will be demonstrated" belongs to divine science and not to natural science; but that which "will be demonstrated" is built on what "has been demonstrated." The student of the *Guide* acquires knowledge of divine science but not of natural science. The author of the *Guide* in contradistinction to its addressee is thoroughly versed in natural science. Still, the addressee needs some awareness of the whole in order to be able to ascend from the whole to God, for there is no way to knowledge of God except through such ascent (I 71 toward the end); he acquires that awareness through a report of some kind (I 70) which Maimonides has inserted into the *Guide*. That report is characterized by the fact that it does not contain a single mention of philosophy in general and of natural science in particular. The serious student cannot rest satisfied with that report; he must turn from that report to natural science itself which supplies the demonstration of what [785] the report merely asserts. Maimonides cannot but leave it to his reader whether he will turn to genuine speculation or whether he will be satisfied with accepting the report on the authority of Maimonides and with building on that report theological conclusions. The addressee of the *Guide* is a man regarding whom it is still undecided whether he will become a genuine man of speculation or whether he will remain a follower of authority, if of Maimonides' authority (cf. I 72 end). He stands on the point of the road where speculation branches off from acceptance of authority.

CHAPTER 23

Why did Maimonides choose an addressee of this description? What is the virtue of not being trained in natural science? We learn from the 17th chapter that natural science was treated as a secret doctrine already by the pagan philosophers "upon whom the charge of corruption would not be laid if they exposed natural science clearly:" all the more is the community of the Law—adherents obliged to treat natural science as a secret science. The reason why natural science is dangerous and is kept secret "with all kinds of artifices" is not that it undermines the Law—only the ignorant believe that (I 33), and Maimonides' whole life as well as the life of his successors refutes this suspicion. Yet it is also true that natural science has this corrupting effect on all men who are not perfect (cf. I 62). For natural science surely affects the understanding of the meaning of the Law, of the grounds on which it is to be obeyed and of the weight which is to be attached to its different parts. In a word, natural science upsets habits. By addressing a reader who is not conversant with natural science, Maimonides is compelled to proceed in a manner that does not upset habits or does so to the smallest possible degree. He acts as a moderate or conservative man.

But we must not forget that the *Guide* is written also for atypical addressees. In the first place, certain chapters of the *Guide* are explicitly said to be useful also for those who are beginners simply. Since the whole book is somehow accessible to the vulgar, it must have been written in such a way as not to be harmful to the vulgar (I Introd.; III 29). Besides, the book is also meant to be useful to such men of great intelligence as have been trained [786] fully in all philosophic sciences and as are not in the habit of bowing to any authority—in other words, to men not inferior to Maimonides in their critical faculty. Readers of this kind will be unable to bow to Maimonides' authority; he will examine all his assertions, speculative or exegetic, with all reasonable severity; and he will derive great pleasure from all chapters of the *Guide* (I Introd.; I 55, 68 end, 73, tenth premise).

How much Maimonides' choice of his typical addressee affects the plan of his book, the judicious reader will see by glancing at our scheme. It suffices to mention that no section or subsection of the *Guide* is devoted to the bodies that do not come into being and perish (cf. III 8 beginning, and I 11), i.e., to the heavenly bodies which according to Maimonides possess life and knowledge, or to "the holy bodies" to use the bold expression used by him in his *Code* (*M.T.*, H. Yesode ha-torah IV 12). In other words, no section or subsection of the *Guide* is devoted to the Work of the Beginning in the manner in which a section is devoted to the Work of the Chariot. It is more important to see that Maimonides' choice of his typical addressee is the key to the whole plan of the *Guide*, to the apparent lack of order or to the obscurity of the plan. The plan of the *Guide* appears to be obscure only as long as one does not consider for what kind of reader the book is written or as long as one seeks for an order agreeing with the essential order of subject matter. We recall the order of the sciences: logic precedes mathematics, mathematics precedes natural science, and natural science precedes divine science; and we recall that while Joseph was sufficiently trained in logic and mathematics, he is supposed to be introduced into divine science without having been trained properly in natural science. Maimonides must therefore seek for a substitute for natural science. He finds that substitute in the traditional Jewish beliefs and ultimately in the Biblical texts correctly interpreted: the immediate preparation for divine science in the *Guide* is exegetic rather than speculative. Furthermore, Maimonides wishes to proceed in a manner which changes habits to the smallest possible degree. He himself tells us which habit is in particular need of being changed. After having reported [787] the opinion of a pagan philosopher on the obstacles to speculation, he adds the remark that there exists now an obstacle which the ancient philosopher had not mentioned because it did not exist in his society: the habit of relying on revered "texts," i.e., on their literal meaning (I 31). It is for this reason that he opens his book with the explanation of Biblical terms, i.e., with showing that their true meaning is not always their literal meaning. He cures the vicious habit in question by having recourse to another habit of his addressee. The addressee was accustomed not only to accept the literally understood Biblical texts as true but also in many cases to understand Biblical texts according to traditional interpretations that differed considerably from the literal meaning. Being accustomed to listen to authoritative interpretations of Biblical texts, he is prepared to listen to Maimonides' interpretations as authoritative interpretations. The explanation of Biblical terms that is given by Maimonides authoritatively, is in the circumstances the natural substitute for natural science.

But which Biblical terms deserve primary consideration? In other words, what is the initial theme of the *Guide*? The choice of the initial theme is dictated by the right answer to the question as to which theme is the most urgent for the typical addressee and at the same time the least upsetting to him. The first theme of the *Guide* is God's incorporeality. God's incorporeality is the third of the three most fundamental truths, the preceding ones being the existence of God and His unity. The existence of

CHAPTER 23

God and His unity were admitted as unquestionable by all Jews; all Jews as Jews know that God exists and that He is one, and they know this through the Biblical revelation or the Biblical miracles. One can say that because belief in the Biblical revelation precedes speculation, and the discovery of the true meaning of revelation is the task of exegesis, exegesis precedes speculation. But as regards God's incorporeality there existed a certain confusion. The Biblical texts suggest that God is corporeal and the interpretation of these texts is not a very easy task (II 25, 31, III 28). God's incorporeality is indeed a demonstrable truth but, to say nothing of others, the addressee of the *Guide* does not come into the possession of the [788] demonstration until he has advanced into the Second Part (cf. I 1, 9, 18). The necessity to refute "corporealism" (the belief that God is corporeal) does not merely arise from the fact that corporealism is demonstrably untrue: corporealism is dangerous because it endangers the belief shared by all Jews in God's unity (I 35). On the other hand, by teaching that God is incorporeal, one does not do more than to give expression to what the Talmudic Sages believed (I 46). However, the Jewish authority who had given the most consistent and the most popularly effective expression to the belief in God's incorporeality was Onkelos the Stranger, for the primary preoccupation of his translation of the Torah into Aramaic which Joseph knew as a matter of course, was precisely to dispose of the corporealistic suggestions of the original (I 21, 27, 28, 36 end). Maimonides' innovation is then limited to his deviation from Onkelos' procedure: he does explicitly what Onkelos did implicitly; whereas Onkelos tacitly substituted non-corporealistic terms for the corporealistic terms occurring in the original, Maimonides explicitly discusses each of the terms in question by itself in an order that has no correspondence to the accidental sequence of their occurrence in the Bible. As a consequence, the discussion of corporealism in the *Guide* consists chiefly of a discussion of the various Biblical terms suggesting corporealism, and vice versa the chief subject of what Maimonides declares to be the primary purpose of the *Guide*, namely, the explanation of Biblical terms, is the explanation of Biblical terms suggesting corporealism. This is not surprising. There are no Biblical terms that suggest that God is not one whereas there are many Biblical terms that suggest that God is corporeal: the apparent difficulty created by the plural *Elohim* can be disposed of by a single sentence or by a single reference to Onkelos (I 2).

The chief reason however why it is so urgent to establish the belief in God's incorporeality is supplied by the fact that that belief is destructive

On the Plan of The Guide of the Perplexed

of idolatry. It was of course universally known that idolatry is a very grave sin, nay, that the Law has so to speak no other purpose than to destroy idolatry (I 35, III 29 end). But this evil can be completely eradicated only if everyone is brought to [789] know that God has no visible shape whatever or that He is incorporeal. Only if God is incorporeal is it absurd to make images of God and to worship such images. Only under this condition can it become manifest to everyone that the only image of God is man, living and thinking man, and that man acts as the image of God only through worshipping the invisible or hidden God alone. Not idolatry but the belief in God's corporeality is a fundamental sin. Hence, the sin of idolatry is less grave than that of believing in God's being corporeal (I 36). This being the case, it becomes indispensable that God's incorporeality be believed in by everyone regardless of whether he knows by demonstration that God is incorporeal or not; as regards the majority of men it is sufficient and necessary that they believe in this truth on the basis of authority or tradition, i.e., on a basis which the first subsections of the *Guide* are meant to supply. The teaching of God's incorporeality by means of authoritative exegesis, i.e., the most public teaching of God's incorporeality, is indispensable for destroying the last relics of paganism: the immediate source of paganism is less the ignorance of God's unity than the ignorance of His radical incorporeality (cf. I 36 with *M.T.*, H. 'Aboda zara I 1).

It is necessary that we should understand the character of the reasoning which Maimonides uses in determining the initial theme of the *Guide*. We limit ourselves to a consideration of the second point.* While the belief in Unity leads immediately to the rejection of the worship of "other gods" but not to the rejection of the worship of images of the one God, the belief in Incorporeality leads immediately only to the rejection of the worship of images or of other bodies but not to the rejection of the worship of other gods: all gods may be incorporeal. Only if the belief in God's incorporeality is based on the belief in His unity as Maimonides' argument indeed assumes, does the belief in God's incorporeality appear to be the necessary and sufficient ground for rejecting "forbidden worship" in every form, i.e., the worship of other gods as well as the worship of both natural things and artificial things. This would mean that the prohibition against idolatry in the widest sense is as much a dictate of reason as the belief in

---

* Instead of "the second point," both the *Liberalism Ancient and Modern* version (150) and Pines's translation (vol. 1, p. xxii) have "the second reason demanding the teaching of incorporeality" ("Incorporeality" in the latter version). —Eds.

Chapter 23

God's unity [790] and incorporeality. Yet Maimonides indicates that only the theoretical truths pronounced in the Decalogue (God's existence and His unity), in contradistinction to the rest of the Decalogue, are rational. This is in agreement with his denying the existence of rational commandments or prohibitions as such (II 33; cf. I 54, II 31 beginning, III 28; *Eight Chapters* VI). Given the fact that Aristotle believed in God's unity and incorporeality and yet was an idolator (I 71, III 29), Maimonides' admiration for him would be incomprehensible if the rejection of idolatry were the simple consequence of that belief. According to Maimonides, the Law agrees with Aristotle in holding that the heavenly bodies are endowed with life and intelligence and that they are superior to man in dignity; one could say that he agrees with Aristotle in implying that those holy bodies deserve more than man to be called images of God. But unlike the philosophers he does not go so far as to call those bodies "divine bodies" (II 4–6; cf. Letter to Ibn Tibbon). The true ground of the rejection of "forbidden worship" is the belief in creation out of nothing, which implies that creation is an absolutely free act of God or that God alone is the complete good that is in no way increased by creation. But creation is, according to Maimonides, not demonstrable, whereas God's unity and incorporeality are demonstrable. The reasoning underlying the determination of the initial theme of the *Guide* can then be described as follows: it conceals the difference of cognitive status between the belief in God's unity and incorporeality on the one hand and the belief in creation on the other; it is in accordance with the opinion of the Kalām. In accordance with this, Maimonides brings his disagreement with the Kalām into the open only after he has concluded his thematic discussion of God's incorporeality; in that discussion he does not even mention the Kalām.

It is necessary that we should understand as clearly as possible the situation in which Maimonides and his addressee find themselves at the beginning of the book, if not throughout the book. Maimonides knows that God is incorporeal; he knows this by a demonstration which is at least partly based on natural science. The addressee does not know that God is incorporeal; nor does [791] he learn it yet from Maimonides: he accepts the fact that God's incorporeality is demonstrated on Maimonides' authority. Both Maimonides and the addressee know that the Law is a source of knowledge of God; only the Law can establish God's incorporeality for the addressee in a manner which does not depend on Maimonides' authority. But both know that the literal meaning of the Law is not always its true meaning and that the literal meaning is certainly not the true meaning when it contradicts reason, for otherwise the Law could not be "your wisdom and your understanding in the sight of the nations" (Deuteronomy 4:6). Both know in other words that exegesis does not simply precede speculation. Yet only Maimonides knows that the corporealistic expressions of the Law are against reason and must therefore be taken as figurative. The addressee does not know and cannot know that Maimonides' figurative interpretations of those expressions are true: Maimonides does not adduce arguments based on grammar. The addressee accepts Maimonides' interpretations just as he is in the habit of accepting the Aramaic translations as correct translations or interpretations. Maimonides enters the ranks of the traditional Jewish authorities: he simply tells the addressee what to believe regarding the meaning of the Biblical terms. Maimonides introduces Reason in the guise of Authority.* He takes on the garb of authority. He tells the addressee to believe in God's incorporeality because, as he tells him, contrary to appearance, the Law does not teach corporeality, because, as he tells him, corporeality is a demonstrably wrong belief.

---

* In the *Liberalism Ancient and Modern* version, "Reason" and "Authority" are not capitalized. —Eds.

24

Review of Samuel I. Mintz, *The Hunting of Leviathan* (1965)

The Hunting of Leviathan. Seventeenth-Century Reactions to the Materialism and Moral Philosophy of Thomas Hobbes. By Samuel I. Mintz. Cambridge: Cambridge University Press, 1962. Pp. x+ 189.

[253a] The title of the book is somewhat misleading. The author deals only with hostile reactions to Hobbes's materialism and moral philosophy by Englishmen of the seventeenth century. After having surveyed Hobbes's life, his "system in retrospect," and "the contemporary setting," he discusses the seventeenth-century English reactions to Hobbes's materialism and to his moral philosophy and then summarizes his results in a conclusion. He adds an appendix containing a "Check-list of Anti-Hobbes Literature and Allusion in England, 1650–1700" and an extensive bibliography (pp. 157–83). On the proper occasion he publishes a hitherto unpublished letter to Hobbes (pp. 124–25).

The author treats his material by surveying rather than analyzing it. One could say on his behalf that most of the writings which he considers are not in need of analysis while the rest have been analyzed by other scholars.

Mintz's study leaves one with the impression that Hobbes's "substantive" influence on his contemporary countrymen was nil or, at the most, infinitesimal. He does say that, under Hobbes's influence, the arguments of his critics "assumed a Hobbist form" (p. 151) or that Hobbes compelled his critics "to combat him with his own weapons of logical exactitude and

---

Originally published as a review of *The Hunting of Leviathan: Seventeenth–Century Reactions to the Materialism and Moral Philosophy of Thomas Hobbes*, by Samuel I. Mintz, *Modern Philology* 62, no. 3 (Feb. 1965): 253–55. —Eds.

Chapter 24

severe reasoning" (p. 149). Yet "logical exactitude and severe reasoning" are not a preserve of Hobbes. In order to justify his assertion, Mintz would have to show that it was a peculiarly Hobbsian version of those intellectual virtues which molded to some extent late seventeenth-century English thought. [253b]

Hobbes was attacked in the first place on account of his materialism, materialism being regarded by all of his critics as the "main root of atheism" (p. 67). Hobbes's materialism is most vulnerable to attack since "he did not prove, or even attempt to prove, that matter alone is real" (p. 66). The argument which the more intelligent men among his critics "thought was the strongest was the one which asserted that matter in motion cannot by itself account for thought" (p. 69). The arguments used for proving this assertion were for the most part traditional (pp. 77, 85, 100–101). Mintz is silent on the question of whether Hobbes's critics saw the difference between Hobbes's materialism and traditional (say, Epicurean) materialism. Accordingly he is not concerned with the difference between the traditional arguments and the arguments peculiar to the more original among Hobbes's critics. Henry More and Joseph Glanvill, it appears, used the fact of witchcraft as an important argument for refuting materialism (pp. 86, 102–3, 109). More's doctrine according to which "all substance has dimensions" or that God himself is extended, is of a different description (pp. 88–92), but for the reason given it does not become clear whether that doctrine as peculiar to More is a response to the materialism peculiar to Hobbes.

Hobbes was attacked in the second place because of his moral teaching, especially his denial of freedom of the will and his promotion of libertinism. Bishop Bramhall's criticism of Hobbes's determinism is justly famous for its clarity and fairness as distinguished from originality (p. 113). In the words of Cudworth, he wrote "like a Scholastick divine," which implies that he regarded the will as a faculty; according to Cudworth, one refutes determinism simply by showing "that there is another substance in the world besides body." Yet "by taking the position that the will is necessarily inclined toward the good, Cudworth gave much ground to the determinists"; while "vehemently rejecting" the understanding of freedom as "indifferency," he eventually accepted "indifferency" (pp. 127–33).

The criticism of Hobbes as a promoter of [254a] libertinism emerged after the Restoration. Hobbes was made responsible for the licentiousness of the age; that criticism is worthless (pp. 135–47). The criticism of Hobbes's "egoistic psychology" was more serious; that criticism consisted of the reassertion of man's natural sociality which foreshadows Shaftesbury's "man of feeling" (p. 143). "The view that man is naturally good was most fully developed by Richard Cumberland.... In some few places Cumberland anticipated the nineteenth-century utilitarians; but he returned always to a distinctly Platonic conception of morality" (p. 145). One would like to know what were Cumberland's anticipations of utilitarianism, a distinctly anti-Platonic view, how he reconciled them with his Platonism, and, above all, whether it was not Hobbes, "admired by the Utilitarians" (p. 155), who moved Cumberland to take a few steps in the general direction of utilitarianism. The half sentence which Mintz devotes to this question (p. 154) is quite inadequate.

"The principal objection to [Hobbes]...was that he was an atheist" (pp. vii, 45). Mintz does not believe that Hobbes was an atheist. He settles the issue to his satisfaction by referring to the fact that no "overt statement" denying the existence of God occurs in Hobbes's writings and by relying mainly on what Hobbes said in his "Considerations upon the Reputation, Loyalty, Manners and Religion of Thomas Hobbes of Malmesbury" (*English Works*, ed. Molesworth, IV, 425–29). Yet, according to Mintz, "Hobbes maintained that Scripture, and not reason, is our only warrant for believing in God's existence" (p. 43), and there are serious doubts as to whether Hobbes believed in the truth of Scripture. In other words, "Cudworth referred to Hobbes as 'the Atheist'" and Cudworth "understood perfectly what Hobbes was saying" (p. 96). How inadequate Mintz's treatment of this issue is can be seen most simply from the fact that, according to him, "Hobbes thought of [God] in the Aristotelian fashion as both unmoved and uncaused" (p. 64): he fails to mention that Hobbes denies God's being unmoved (*De corpore* XXVI.1).

While disagreeing with Hobbes's seven-[254b]teenth-century critics regarding Hobbes's being an atheist, Mintz agrees with them as to Hobbes's moral teaching being "ethical relativism" (VII). His references to seventeenth-century criticisms of Hobbes's ethical relativism are scanty; those critics surely did not speak of "ethical relativism." They justly ascribed to Hobbes the doctrine that there is nothing simply and absolutely good or evil, noble or base, just or unjust. Yet in order to be exact and fair, one would have to add what Mintz fails to add, that Hobbes recognizes the existence of things which are "honorable by nature," that is, not by convention or the sovereign's fiat, to say nothing of his teaching that there is natural right and natural law. That his natural-right teaching did not meet the requirements of his contemporary critics is easily intelligible; but

CHAPTER 24

we who can view the seventeenth-century situation "in retrospect" must cease to be blind to the difference between "ethical relativism" and any form of natural right teaching. This peculiar blindness goes far to explain Mintz's over-all judgment, according to which Hobbes did not exercise any substantive influence on English seventeenth-century thought. It suffices to mention the name of Locke—a name which barely occurs in Mintz's study.

A few minor points might be mentioned here. Mintz erroneously speaks of "two treatises *Humane Nature* ... and *De Corpore Politico*, or the *Elements of Law*, both of which circulated widely in manuscript until they were combined and published in 1650" (p. 9). The true relation of the *Elements of Law* to those two treatises was cleared up by Tönnies in the preface to his edition of the *Elements of Law* in 1889. Neither in his statement on the drafts of *De corpore* (p. 9 n.) nor in his bibliography does Mintz mention Baron Cay von Brockdorff's "Die Urform der 'Computatio sive logica' des Hobbes," (*Veröffentlichungen der Hobbes-Gesellschaft*, [Kiel, 1934]). "Glanvill called this doctrine (the denial of spirit) 'Sadducism,' and saw it as the inevitable prerequisite to the denial of theism" (p. 41); Hobbes himself had said earlier (*Leviathan*, chap. viii) that "the Sadducees [did] not believe there were at all any spirits, which is [255a] very near to direct atheism"; the passage has some bearing on the question as to whether Hobbes was an atheist according to his view of atheism. Mintz asserts that Hobbes counted Cato among the classical authors who instilled their readers with democratic principles (p. 47); he does not indicate any passage where Hobbes does this. According to Mintz, Hobbes teaches that "a stable commonwealth will stamp out dissent" (p. 59); he fails to mention that Hobbes was also concerned with bringing about toleration, as Sorbière states in his preface to his French translation of De cive (1649) or that he had a bias toward the Independents (*Leviathan*, chap. xlvii). Mintz does not tell us why he believes that "Hobbes believed that any man endowed with intelligence and knowledge of the laws of reasoning can reason correctly and discover the truth; whether a man is otherwise virtuous or not is without consequence" (p. 83).

We are still in need of such a study of Hobbes's influence on English seventeenth-century thought as is based on a solid understanding of Hobbes's teaching. The author of such a study would do well if he paid proper attention to what Hobbes's seventeenth-century critics say about Hobbes's theology—natural theology on the one hand and revealed theology on the other—for it may be assumed that the present-day historian lacks the theological training and the sure grasp of theological issues which the better ones among those critics possessed as a matter of course. Furthermore, Hobbes was a European figure; he may have exercised an influence on seventeenth-century English thought by means of his continental influence. Finally, one must always keep in mind that it was not prudent at the time to acknowledge that one had learned something from Hobbes.

25

John Locke as "Authoritarian" (1967)

John Locke: Two Tracts on Government. Edited with an introduction, notes and translation by Philip Abrams. New York: Cambridge Univ. Press, 1967. 264 pp. $7.50.

[46a] This volume consists of two parts: an annotated edition of what seems to be Locke's earliest "tracts on government" (pp. 112–241), and the editor's extensive Introduction (pp. 1–111). One of the two tracts was composed in English, the other in Latin; the editor has supplied his edition of the Latin tract with an English translation. Both tracts were written shortly after the Restoration, and neither tract was ever published by Locke. The differences between the two tracts are not important (p. 113).

The "two tracts on government," as the editor calls them, are in fact disputations on the question as to "whether the civil magistrate may lawfully impose and determine the use of indifferent things in reference to religious worship." Locke answers this question in the affirmative. He takes the side of law and order against "the popular assertors of public liberty" who would only bring on "the tyranny of a religious rage" (p. 120) if the civil magistrate did not have or exercise the disputed right. Locke is all in favor of gently dealing with [46b] "the sincere and tender hearted Christians" but against allowing them "a toleration... as their right" (p. 160; cf. 185-86). He regards the people as an "untamed beast" (p. 158).

Indifferent things are things not determined by God's law. The indifferent things with which the disputations are concerned are those related to divine worship as distinguished from indifferent civil things such as

---

Originally published as "John Locke as 'Authoritarian,'" *Intercollegiate Review* 4, no. 1 (Nov.–Dec., 1967): 46–48. —Eds.

CHAPTER 25

taxes, which are on both sides admitted to be subject to determination by the civil magistrate. According to the view rejected by Locke, the civil magistrate may not determine indifferent things that concern divine worship because such determination would not be compatible with Christian liberty. Hence the most important argument adduced by the men whom Locke opposes is that "imposing things indifferent is directly contrary to Gospel precepts" (pp. 130, 142, 155, 190, 202–204). One may therefore say that the disputations belong to the province of political theology rather than to that of political philosophy.

Yet while this is true of the primary theme of the disputations, it is not unqualifiedly true of all of its implications. It suffices here to mention two of these implications or presuppositions: God's law and the origin and extent of the power of the civil magistrate.

Locke does not say much on God's law. The divine or moral law becomes known to man "either by the discoveries of reason, usually called the law of nature, or the revelation of his word" (p. 124). The question as to whether the content of the law of nature is identical with the content of the revealed law is answered negatively in the English tract, where Locke occasionally [47a] speaks of "the positive moral law of God" (p. 151), and affirmatively in the Latin tract (p. 194). This observation is not contradicted by the fact that in the English tract he occasionally speaks of "the law of God or nature" (p. 138), for he uses this expression when stating the view of his opponents. He apparently did not think it necessary to clear up the obscurity indicated.

As for the extent of the power of the civil magistrate, Locke ascribes to him "absolute, arbitrary power over all the indifferent actions of his people" (p. 123). To say the least, this sounds very different from the teaching of *Two Treatises* (II Sect. 135–37). The magistrate may "establish or alter all indifferent things as he shall judge them conducing to the good of the public," "but he alone is judge what is so and what not" (p. 150; cf. p. 126). Although the magistrate acts unjustly by commanding things forbidden by God's law, his subjects are bound to a passive obedience, i.e., may not resist his laws by force of arms (p. 192). Since "the same arbitrary power" resides in the governing assembly of a republic as in any monarch, subjects enjoy no greater freedom in a republic than under an absolute monarch (pp. 125, 201). This is quite at variance with the teaching of the *Two* [47b] *Treatises*, according to which "absolute monarchy...is indeed inconsistent with civil society" (II Sect. 90 ff.). In accordance with all this, Locke's argument in the two tracts does not depend on how one

372

decides the question as to the origin of the civil magistrate's power, viz., whether one holds that that power derives immediately from God or from the subjects (pp. 122, 128–29, 200–01)—in other words, whether the king is held to rule by divine right pure and simple or by virtue of a contract.

The two tracts would not be of interest to anyone except historians specializing in mid-seventeenth-century English theologico-political debates but for the fact that they are the work of Locke, if of the young Locke who had not yet found his own word. As the editor puts it, the author of the two tracts is an "authoritarian" rather than, as he is frequently thought to be, "the presiding genius of liberal democracy"; he surely is not "liberal" or in favor of "any... form of permissive government" (pp. 7–9, 84). Yet "authoritarian" has many meanings: most, not to say all, political philosophers who wrote prior to 1660 were "authoritarian." Hooker was "authoritarian" in one sense, Hobbes in a very different sense. In the two tracts, Locke quotes approvingly Hooker's general definition of law (p. 193) but, as the editor correctly states, he divorces that definition from its teleological context (pp. 69–70). One is not surprised to observe that Hobbes is never mentioned in the tracts. This would not by any means exclude the possibility that the tracts were influenced or inspired by Hobbes, for silence on Hobbes might have been part of the "strategy" of the young Locke as it was part of the "strategy" of the mature Locke (cf. p. 68). According to the editor, "it is essentially a Hobbesian argument that Locke deploys" (pp. 24, 69). Yet, to say nothing of his far-reaching qualifications (pp. 57, 71, 75–80), both his notion of what constitutes Hobbianism and Locke's relevant statements are too vague to enable Abrams to prove the dependence of the tracts on Hobbes.

The question regarding the Hobbianism of the young Locke may be said to be of some importance with a view to the fundamental question regarding the political phil-[48a]osophy of the mature or old Locke, to the question which would have to be stated as follows: is the natural law teaching of the mature Locke fundamentally traditional (say, Hookerian) or is it a modified version of Hobbes' natural law teaching?* Abrams admits that Locke has broken with the traditional natural law teaching but denies that he builds on the foundation laid by Hobbes (pp. 77–78). As he suggests, Locke has moved away, more or less hesitatingly, from the view according to which the law of nature is the law of reason and that it

---

* Cf. Willmoore Kendall, "John Locke Revisited," *The Intercollegiate Review*, II (January–February, 1966): 217–34. [The full citation is vol. 2, no. 4.—Eds.]

CHAPTER 25

is obligatory because it is dictated by reason, in the direction of "fideism." More precisely, while Locke never abandoned the notion that the law of nature is the law of reason or, which for him seems to be the same thing, that ethics can be made a demonstrative science, he never elaborated that ethics but asserted that the complete law of nature is available in the New Testament and only in the New Testament, i.e., only by revelation (pp. 86–90). In a word, Locke is "inconsistent" regarding the foundations of politics; "in the end he remained intellectually entangled in the tradition in which he had been educated" (p. 91). Abrams arrives at this result partly by relying on Locke's "relativistic" statements regarding "true religion," i.e., by tacitly identifying "objective moral truths" (and therefore in particular that set of moral truths which underlies the political teaching of the *Second Treatise*) with "true religion," and partly by disregarding the difference (which for Locke is crucial) between men in general and the "studiers" of the law of nature (pp. 94–95, 102, 107). Abrams could not have remained satisfied with his thesis if he had paid any attention to the fact of which he has heard and which he does not deny that "face value is something one cannot safely attribute to any work by Locke" or that the study of Locke's writings must be enlightened by understanding of the character as well as the reason of his "persistent strategy" (p. 68).

26

Liberal Education and Mass Democracy* (1967)

[73] Liberal education is education in culture or toward culture. The finished product of a liberal education is a cultured human being. "Culture" (*cultura*) means primarily agriculture: the cultivation of the soil and its products, taking care of the soil, improving the soil in accordance with its nature. "Culture" means derivatively and today chiefly the cultivation of the mind, the taking care and improving of the native faculties of the mind in accordance with the nature of the mind. Just as the soil needs cultivators of the soil, the mind needs teachers. But teachers are not as easy to come by as farmers. The teachers themselves are pupils and must be pupils. But there cannot be an infinite regress: ultimately there must be teachers who are not in turn pupils. Those teachers who are not in turn pupils are the great minds or, in order to avoid any ambiguity in a matter of such importance, the greatest minds. Such men are extremely rare. We are not likely to meet any of them in any classroom. We are not likely to meet any of them anywhere. It is a piece of good luck if there is a single one alive in one's time. For all practical purposes, pupils, of whatever degree of proficiency, have access to the teachers who are not in turn pupils, to the

---

Originally published as "Liberal Education and Mass Democracy," in *Higher Education and Modern Democracy: The Crisis of the Few and Many*, ed. Robert A. Goldwin (Chicago: Rand McNally, 1967), 73–96. —Eds.

* This essay combines major portions of two lectures given by Professor Strauss on separate occasions. "What Is Liberal Education?" a commencement address delivered to the Basic Program in Liberal Education for Adults, University of Chicago, June 6, 1959; and "Liberal Education and Responsibility," an address delivered to the Arden House Institute in Leadership Development, sponsored by the Fund for Adult Education, March, 1960. [The combined essay also redraws some of the paragraphing. —Eds.]

Chapter 26

greatest minds, only through the great books. Liberal education will then consist of studying with the proper care the great books which the greatest minds have left [74] behind—a study in which the more experienced pupils assist the less experienced pupils, including the beginners.

This is not an easy task, as would appear if we were to consider the formula which I have just mentioned. That formula requires a long commentary. Many lives have been spent and may still be spent in writing such commentaries. For instance, what is meant by the remark that the great books should be studied "with the proper care"? At present I mention only one difficulty: the greatest minds do not all tell us the same things regarding the most important themes; the community of the greatest minds is rent by discord and even by various kinds of discord. Whatever further consequences this may entail, it certainly entails the consequence that liberal education cannot be simply indoctrination. I mention yet another difficulty. "Liberal education is education in culture." In what culture? Our answer is: culture in the sense of the Western tradition. Yet Western culture is only one among many cultures. By limiting ourselves to Western culture, do we not condemn liberal education to a kind of parochialism, and is not parochialism incompatible with the liberalism, the generosity, the open-mindedness, of liberal education? Our notion of liberal education does not seem to fit an age which is aware of the fact that there is not *the* culture of *the* human mind but a variety of cultures. Obviously, "culture" if susceptible of being used in the plural is not quite the same thing as "culture" which is a *singulare tantum*, which can be used only in the singular. "Culture" is now no longer, as people say, an absolute but has become relative. It is not easy to say what culture susceptible of being used in the plural means. As a consequence of this obscurity people have suggested, explicitly or implicitly, that "culture" is any pattern of conduct common to any human group. Hence we do not hesitate to speak of the culture of suburbia or of the cultures of juvenile gangs both non-delinquent and delinquent. In other words, every human being outside of lunatic asylums is a cultured human being, for he participates in a culture. At the frontiers of research there arises the question as to whether there are not cultures also of inmates of lunatic asylums. If we contrast the present day usage of "culture" with the original meaning, it is as if someone would say that the cultivation of a garden may consist of the garden being littered with empty tin cans and [75] whiskey bottles and used papers of various descriptions thrown around the garden at random. Having arrived at this point, we realize that we have lost our way somehow. Let us then make a fresh start by raising the question: what can liberal education mean here and now?

Liberal education is literate education of a certain kind: some sort of education in letters or through letters. There is no need to make a case for literacy; every voter knows that modern democracy stands or falls by literacy. In order to understand this need we must reflect on modern democracy.

What is modern democracy? It was once said that democracy is the regime that stands or falls by virtue: a democracy is a regime in which all or most adults are men of virtue, and since virtue seems to require wisdom, a regime in which all or most adults are virtuous and wise, or the society in which all or most adults have developed their reason to a high degree, or *the* rational society. Democracy in a word is meant to be an aristocracy which has broadened into a universal aristocracy. Prior to the emergence of modern democracy some doubts were felt whether democracy thus understood is possible. As one of the two greatest minds among the theorists of democracy put it, "If there were a people consisting of gods, it would rule itself democratically. A government of such perfection is not suitable for human beings."*

This still and small voice has by now become a high-powered loudspeaker. There exists a whole science—the science which I among thousands profess to teach, political science—which so to speak has no other theme than the contrast between the original conception of democracy, or what one may call the ideal of democracy, and democracy as it is. According to an extreme view which is the predominant view in the profession, the ideal of democracy was a sheer delusion and the only thing which matters is the behavior of democracies and the behavior of men in democracies.

Modern democracy, so far from being universal aristocracy, would be mass rule were it not for the fact that the mass cannot rule but is ruled by elites, i.e., groupings of men who for whatever reason are on top or have a fair chance to arrive at the top. One of the most important virtues required for the smooth working of democracy, as far as the mass is concerned, is said to be electoral apathy, i.e., lack of public spirit; not indeed the salt of the earth but the salt of modern democracy are those citizens who read nothing except the sports page and the comic section. Democracy is then not indeed mass rule but mass culture. A mass culture is a culture which can be appropriated by the meanest capacities without

---

* Rousseau, *Social Contract* III.4. —Eds.

Chapter 26

any intellectual and moral effort whatsoever and at a very low monetary price. But even a mass culture and precisely a mass culture requires a constant supply of what are called new ideas, which are the products of what are called creative minds: even singing commercials lose their appeal if they are not varied from time to time. But democracy, even if it is only regarded as the hard shell which protects the soft mass culture, requires in the long run qualities of an entirely different kind: qualities of dedication, of concentration, of breadth and of depth.

Thus we understand most easily what liberal education means here and now. Liberal education is the counter-poison to mass culture, to the corroding effects of mass culture, to its inherent tendency to produce nothing but "specialists without spirit or vision and voluptuaries without heart."* Liberal education is the ladder by which we try to ascend from mass democracy to democracy as originally meant. Liberal education is the necessary endeavor to found an aristocracy within democratic mass society. Liberal education reminds those members of a mass democracy who have ears to hear of human greatness.

In order to understand the necessity just mentioned, one must return to the original meaning of liberal education. To begin at the beginning, the word "liberal" had, just as it has now, a political meaning: but its original political meaning is almost the opposite of its present political meaning. Originally a liberal man was a man who behaved in a manner becoming a free man as distinguished from a slave. "Liberality" referred then to slavery and presupposed it. A slave is a human being who lives for another human being, his master: he has in a sense no life of his own: he has no time for himself. The master on the other hand has all his time for himself, i.e., for the pursuits becoming him: politics and philosophy. Yet there are very many free men who are almost like slaves since they have very little time for themselves, because they have to work for their livelihood and to rest so that they can work [77] the next day. Those free men without leisure are the poor, the majority of citizens.

The truly free man who can live in [a]† manner becoming a free man is the man of leisure, the gentleman who must possess some wealth—but wealth of a certain kind: a kind of wealth the administration of which, to say nothing of its acquisition, does not take up much of his time but can

---

* Max Weber, *The Protestant Ethic and the Spirit of Capitalism*, near the end; see also Strauss's *Natural Right and History*, 42.—Eds.

† Not in original.—Eds.

be taken care of through the supervision of properly trained subordinates. The gentleman can be a gentleman farmer and not a merchant or entrepreneur, yet if he spends much of his time in the country he will not be available sufficiently for the pursuits becoming him; he must therefore live in town. His way of life will be at the mercy of those of his fellow citizens who are not gentlemen, if he and his like do not rule: the way of life of the gentlemen is not secure if they are not the unquestioned rulers of their city, if the regime of their city is not aristocratic.

One becomes a gentleman by education, by liberal education. The Greek word for education is derived from the Greek word for child: education in general, and therefore liberal education in particular, is then, to say the least, primarily not adult education. The Greek word for education is akin to the Greek word for play, and the activity of the gentlemen is emphatically earnest; in fact, the gentlemen are "the earnest ones." They are earnest because they are concerned with the most weighty matters, with the only things which deserve to be taken seriously for their own sake, with the good order of the soul and of the city.

The education of the potential gentlemen is the playful anticipation of the life of gentlemen. It consists above all in the formation of character and of taste. The fountains of that education are the poets. It is hardly necessary to say that the gentleman is in need of skills. To say nothing of reading, writing, counting, reckoning, wrestling, throwing of spears and horsemanship, he must possess the skill of administering well and nobly the affairs of his household and the affairs of his city by deed and by speech. He acquires that skill by his familiar intercourse with older or more experienced gentlemen, preferably with elder statesmen, by receiving instruction from paid teachers in the art of speaking, by reading histories and books of travel, by meditating on the works of the poets and of [78] course by taking part in political life. All this requires leisure on the part of the youths as well as on the part of their elders: it is the preserve of a certain kind of wealthy people.

This fact gives rise to the question of the justice of a society which in the best case would be governed by gentlemen ruling in their own right. Just government is government which rules in the interest of the whole society and not merely of a part. The gentlemen are therefore under an obligation to show to themselves and to others that their rule is best for everyone in the city or for the city as a whole. But justice requires that equal men be treated equally, and there is no good reason for thinking that the gentlemen are by nature superior to the vulgar. The gentlemen

CHAPTER 26

are indeed superior to the vulgar by their breeding, but the large majority of men are by nature capable of the same breeding if they are caught young, in their cradles. Only the accident of birth decides whether a given individual has a chance of becoming a gentleman or will necessarily become a villain: hence aristocracy is unjust.

The gentlemen replied as follows: the city as a whole is much too poor to enable everyone to bring up his sons so that they can become gentlemen: if you insist that the social order should correspond with tolerable strictness to the natural order, i.e., that men who are more or less equal by nature should also be equal socially or by convention, you will merely bring about a state of universal drabness. But only on the ground of a narrow conception of justice, owing its evidence to the power of the ignoble passion of envy, must one prefer a flat building which is everywhere equally drab to a structure which from a broad base of drabness rises to a narrow plateau of distinction and of grace, and which therefore gives some grace and some distinction to its very base. There must then be a few who are wealthy and well born and many who are poor and of obscure origin. Yet there seems to be no good reason why this family is elected to gentility and that family is condemned to indistinctness; that selection seems to be arbitrary, to say the least. It would indeed be foolish to deny that old wealth sometimes has its forgotten origins in crime. But it is more noble to believe, and probably also truer, that the old families are the descendants of the first settlers and from leaders in war or counsel; and it is certainly just that one be grateful.

[79] Gentlemen may rule without being rulers in their own right; they may rule on the basis of popular election. This arrangement was regarded as unsatisfactory for the following reason. It would mean that the gentlemen are strictly speaking responsible to the common people, i.e., that the higher is responsible to the lower, and this would appear to be against nature. The gentlemen regard virtue as choiceworthy for its own sake, whereas the others praise virtue as a means for acquiring wealth and honor. The gentlemen and the others disagree then as regards the end of man or the highest good; they disagree regarding first principles. Hence they cannot have genuinely common deliberations.[1] The gentlemen cannot possibly give a sufficient or intelligible account of their way of life to the others. While being responsible to themselves for the well-being of the vulgar, they cannot be responsible to the vulgar.

---

1 Cf. *Crito* 49d2–5.

Liberal Education and Mass Democracy

But even if one rests satisfied with a less exacting notion of the rule of gentlemen, the principle indicated necessarily leads one to reject democracy. Roughly speaking, democracy is the regime in which the majority of adult free males living in a city rules, but only a minority of them are educated. The principle of democracy is therefore not virtue but freedom as the right of every citizen to live as he likes. Democracy is rejected because it is as such the rule of the uneducated. One illustration must here suffice. The sophist Protagoras came to the democratic city of Athens in order to educate human beings, or teach for pay the art of administering well the affairs of one's household and of the city by deed and by speech, the political art. Since in a democracy everyone is supposed to possess the political art somehow, yet the majority, lacking equipment, cannot have acquired that art through education, Protagoras must assume that the citizens received that art through something like a divine gift, albeit a gift which becomes effective only through human punishments and rewards: the true political art, the art which enables a man not only to obey the laws but to frame laws, is acquired by education, by the highest form of education which is necessarily the preserve of those who can pay for it.

To sum up, liberal education in the original sense not only fosters civic responsibility—it is even required for the exercise of civic responsibility. By being what they are, the gentlemen are [80] meant to set the tone of society in the most direct, the least ambiguous and the most unquestionable way: by ruling it in broad daylight.

It is necessary to take a further step away from our opinions in order to understand them. The pursuits becoming the gentleman are said to be politics and philosophy. Philosophy can be understood loosely or strictly. If understood loosely, it is the same as what are now called intellectual interests. If understood strictly, it means quest for the truth about the most weighty matters or for the comprehensive truth or for the truth about the whole or for the science of the whole. When comparing politics to philosophy strictly understood, one realizes that philosophy is of higher rank than politics. Politics is the pursuit of certain ends; decent politics is the decent pursuit of decent ends. The responsible and clear distinction between ends which are decent and ends which are not is in a way presupposed by politics. It surely transcends politics. For everything which comes into being through human action, and which is therefore perishable or corruptible, presupposes incorruptible and unchangeable things—for instance, the natural order of the human soul—with a view to which we can distinguish between right and wrong actions.

Chapter 26

In the light of philosophy, liberal education takes on a new meaning: liberal education—especially education in the liberal arts—comes to sight as a preparation for philosophy. The gentleman as gentleman accepts on trust certain most weighty things which for the philosopher are the themes of investigation and of questioning. Hence the gentleman's virtue is not entirely the same as the philosopher's virtue. A sign of this difference is the fact that whereas the gentleman must be wealthy in order to do his proper work, the philosopher may be poor. Socrates lived in ten-thousandfold poverty. Once he saw many people following a horse and looking at it, and he heard some of them conversing much about it. In his surprise he approached the groom with the question whether the horse was rich. The groom looked at him as if he were not only grossly ignorant but not even sane: "How can a horse have any property?" At that Socrates understandably recovered, for he thus learned that it is lawful for a horse which is a pauper to become good provided [81] it possess a naturally good soul: it may then be lawful for Socrates to become a good man in spite of his poverty.*

Since it is not necessary for the philosopher to be wealthy, he does not need the entirely lawful arts by which one defends one's property, e.g., forensically: nor does he have to develop the habit of self-assertion in this or other respects—a habit which necessarily enters into the gentleman's virtue. Despite these differences, the gentleman's virtue is a reflection of the philosopher's virtue: one may say it is its political reflection. This is the ultimate justification of the rule of gentlemen. The rule of the gentlemen is only a reflection of the rule of the philosophers who are understood to be the men best by nature and best by education.

Given the fact that philosophy is more evidently quest for wisdom than possession of wisdom, the education of the philosopher never ceases as long as he lives; it is the adult education par excellence. For, to say nothing of other things, the highest kind of knowledge which a man may have acquired can never be simply at his disposal as other kinds of knowledge can; it is in constant need of being acquired again from the start. This leads to the following consequence. In the case of the gentleman, one can make a simple distinction between the playful education of the potential gentleman and the earnest work of the gentleman proper. In the case of the philosopher this simple distinction between the playful and the serious no longer holds, not in spite of the fact that his sole concern is with the

---

* Xenophon, *Memorabilia* IV.1.2; see also Strauss's *Xenophon's Socratic Discourse*, 160. —Eds.

weightiest matters but because of it. For this reason alone, the rule of philosophers proves to be impossible.

This leads to the difficulty that the philosophers will be ruled by the gentlemen, i.e., by their inferiors. One can solve this difficulty by assuming that the philosophers are not as such a constituent part of the city. In other words, the only teachers who are as such a constituent part of the city are the priests. The end of the city is then not the same as the end of philosophy. If the gentlemen represent the city at its best, one must say that the end of the gentleman is not the same as the end of the philosopher. What was observed regarding the gentleman in his relation to the vulgar applies even more to the philosopher in his relation to the gentlemen and *a fortiori* to all other non-philosophers: the philosopher and the [82] non-philosophers cannot have genuinely common deliberations.

There is a fundamental disproportion between philosophy and the city. In political things it is a sound rule to let sleeping dogs lie or to prefer the established to the non-established or to recognize the right of the first occupier. Philosophy stands or falls by its intransigent disregard of this rule and of anything which reminds of it. Philosophy can then live only side by side with the city. As Plato put it in the *Republic*, only in a city in which the philosophers rule, and in which they therefore owe their training in philosophy to the city, is it just that the philosopher be compelled to engage in political activity; in all other cities, i.e., in all actual cities, the philosopher does not owe his highest gift of human origin to the city and therefore is not under an obligation to do the work of the city.

In entire agreement with this, Plato suggests in his *Crito*, where he avoids the very term philosophy, that the philosopher owes indeed very much to the city and therefore he is obliged to obey at least passively even the unjust laws of the city and to die at the behest of the city. Yet he is not obliged to engage in political activity. The philosopher as philosopher is responsible to the city only to the extent that by doing his own work, by his own well being, he contributes to the well being of the city: philosophy has necessarily a humanizing or civilizing effect. The city needs philosophy but only mediately or indirectly, not to say in a diluted form. Plato has presented this state of things by comparing the city to a cave from which only a rough and steep ascent leads to the light of the sun: the city as city is more closed to philosophy than open to it.

The classics had no delusions regarding the probability of a genuine aristocracy ever becoming actual. For all practical purposes they were satisfied with a regime in which the gentlemen share power with the people

Chapter 26

in such a way that the people elect the magistrates and the council from among the gentlemen and demand an account of them at the end of their term of office. A variation of this thought is the notion of the mixed regime, in which the gentlemen form the senate and the senate occupies the key position between the popular assembly and an elected or hereditary monarch as head of the armed forces of society. There is a direct connection between the notion of the mixed regime and modern republicanism.

[83] Lest this be misunderstood, one must immediately stress the important differences between the modern doctrine and its classic original. The modern doctrine starts from the natural equality of all men and it leads therefore to the assertion that sovereignty belongs to the people; yet it understands that sovereignty in such a way as to guarantee the natural rights of each; it achieves this result by distinguishing between the sovereign and the government and by demanding that the fundamental governmental powers be separated from one another. The spring of this regime was held to be the desire of each to improve his conditions, or what came to be called his material conditions. Accordingly the commercial and industrial elite rather than the landed gentry predominated.

The fully developed doctrine required that one man have one vote, that the ballot be secret, and that the right to vote be not abridged on account of poverty, religion or race. Governmental actions on the other hand are to be open to public inspection to the highest degree possible, for government is only the representative of the people and responsible for the people. The responsibility of the people, of the electors, does not permit of legal definition and is therefore the most obvious crux of modern republicanism. In the earlier stages the solution was sought in the religious education of the people, in the education based on the Bible, of everyone to regard himself as responsible for his actions and for his thoughts to a God who would judge him, for, in the words of Locke, rational ethics proper is as much beyond the capacities of "day laborers and tradesmen, and spinsters and dairy maids" as is mathematics.

On the other hand, the same authority advises the gentlemen of England to set their sons upon Puffendorf's *Natural Right* "wherein (they) will be instructed in the natural rights of men, and the origin and foundation of society, and the duties resulting from thence."* Locke's *Some Thoughts Concerning Education* is addressed to the gentlemen rather than to "those of the meaner sort," for if the gentlemen "are by their education

---

* Samuel von Pufendorf, here called, following Locke, "Puffendorf."—Eds.

once set right, they will quickly bring all the rest into order." For, we may suppose, the gentlemen are those called upon to act as representatives of the people and they are to be prepared for this calling by a liberal education which is above all an education in "good breeding." Locke takes his models from the ancient Romans and Greeks and the [84] liberal education which he recommends consists to some extent in acquiring an easy familiarity with classical literature: "Latin I look upon as absolutely necessary to a gentleman."[2]

Several of Locke's points are brought out clearly in *The Federalist*. These writings reveal their connection with the classics simply enough by presenting themselves as the work of one Publius. This eminently sober work considers chiefly the diversity and inequality in the faculties of men which show themselves in the acquisition of property, but it is very far from being blind to the difference between business and government. According to Hamilton, the mechanics and manufacturers "know that the merchant is their natural patron and friend," their natural representative, for the merchant possesses "those acquired endowments without which, in a deliberative assembly, the greatest natural abilities are for the most part useless." Similarly, the wealthier landlords are the natural representatives of the landed interest. The natural arbiter between the landed and the moneyed interests will be "the man of the learned professions," for "the learned professions...truly form no distinct interest in society" and therefore are more likely than others to think of "the general interests of the society." It is true that in order to become a representative of the people, it sometimes suffices that one practice "with success the vicious art by which elections are too often carried," but these deplorable cases are the exception, the rule being that the representatives will be respectable landlords, merchants, and members of the learned professions. If the electorate is not depraved, there is a fair chance that it will elect as its representatives for deliberation as well as for execution those among the three groups of men "who possess most wisdom to discern, and most virtue to pursue, the common good of the society," or those who are most outstanding by "merits and talents," by "ability and virtue."[3]

Under the most favorable conditions, the men who will hold the balance of power will then be the men of the learned professions. In the best case, Hamilton's republic will be ruled by the men of [85] the learned pro-

---

2   *Some Thoughts Concerning Education*, Epistle Dedicatory, pp. 93–94, 164 and 186.

3   *The Federalist*, Nos. 10, 35, 36, 55, 57, 62 and 68.

Chapter 26

fessions. This reminds one of the rule of the philosophers. Will the men of the learned professions at least be men of liberal education? It is probable that the men of the learned professions will chiefly be lawyers.

No one ever had a greater respect for law and hence for lawyers than Edmund Burke: "God forbid I should insinuate anything derogatory to that profession, which is another priesthood, administrating the rights of sacred justice." Yet he felt compelled to describe the preponderance of lawyers in the national counsels as "mischievous." "...Law...is, in my opinion, one of the first and noblest of human sciences; a science which does more to quicken and invigorate the understanding, than all the other kinds of learning put together; but it is not apt, except in persons very happily born, to open and to liberalize the mind exactly in the same proportion." For to speak "legally and constitutionally" is not the same as to speak "prudently." "...Legislators ought to do what lawyers cannot; for they have no other rules to bind them, but the great principles of reason and equity, and the general sense of mankind."[4] The liberalization of the mind obviously requires understanding of "the great principles of reason and equity" which for Burke are the same thing as the natural law.

But it is not necessary to dwell on this particular shortcoming from which representative government might suffer. Two generations after Burke, John Stuart Mill took up the question concerning the relation of representative government and liberal education. One does not exaggerate too much by saying that he took up these two subjects in entire separation from one another. His *Inaugural Address at St. Andrews*[5] deals with liberal education as "the education of all who are not obliged by their circumstances to discontinue their scholastic studies at a very early age," not to say the education of "the favorites of nature and fortune." That speech contains a number of observations which will require our consideration and [86] reconsideration. Mill traces the "superiority" of classical literature "for purposes of education" to the fact that literature transmits to us "the wisdom of life": "In cultivating...the ancient languages as our best literary education, we are all the while laying an admirable foundation for ethical and philosophical culture." Even more admirable than "the substance" is "the form" of treatment: "It must be remembered that they had more time and that they wrote chiefly for a select class possessed of

---

4   *The Works of Edmund Burke* (Bohn Standard Library), I, 407; II, 7, 317–318; V, 295.

5   *James and John Stuart Mill on Education*, ed. by F. A. Cavenagh (Cambridge: Cambridge University Press, 1931), 151–157, by permission of the publisher.

leisure" whereas we "write in a hurry for people who read in a hurry." The classics used "the right words in the right places" or, which means the same thing, they were not "prolix."

But in *Considerations on Representative Government*,[6] Mill pointed out that liberal education has very little effect on the "miscellaneous assembly," which is the legal sovereign and which is frequently ruled by men who have no qualification for legislation except "a fluent tongue, and a faculty of getting elected by a constituency." To secure "the intellectual qualifications desirable in representatives," Mill thought, there is no other mode than proportional representation as devised by Hare and Fawcett, a scheme which in his opinion is of "perfect feasibility" and possesses "transcendent advantages."

> The natural tendency of representative government, as of modern civilization, is toward collective mediocrity: and this tendency is increased by all reductions and extensions of the franchise, their effect being to place the principal power in the hands of classes more and more below the highest level of instruction in the community.... It is an admitted fact that in the American democracy, which is constructed on this faulty model, the highly-cultivated members of the community, except such of them as are willing to sacrifice their own opinions and modes of judgment, and become the servile mouthpieces of their inferiors in knowledge, do not ever offer themselves for Congress or State legislatures, so certain is it that they would have no chance of being returned. Had a plan like Mr. Hare's by good fortune suggested itself to the enlightened and patriotic founders of the American Republic, the Federal and [87] State Assemblies would have contained many of those distinguished men, and democracy would have been spared its greatest reproach and one of its most formidable evils.

Only proportional representation which guarantees or at least does not exclude the proper representation of the best part of society in the government will transform "the falsely called democracies which now prevail, and from which the current idea of democracy is exclusively derived" into "the only true type of democracy," into democracy as originally meant. For reasons which are not all bad, Mill's remedy has come to be regarded as insufficient, not to say worthless. Perhaps it was a certain awareness of this which induced him to look for relief in another part of the body politic. From the fact that the representative assemblies are not necessarily

---

6   John Stuart Mill, *Considerations on Representative Government* (London: Routledge, undated), 93, 95, 101–102, 133–140 and 155.

Chapter 26

"a selection of the greatest political minds of the country," he drew the conclusion that for "the skilled legislation and administration" one must secure "under strict responsibility to the nation, the acquired knowledge and practiced intelligence of a specially trained and experienced few."

Mill appears to suggest that with the growth and maturity of democracy, the institutional seat of public-spirited intelligence could and should be sought in the high and middle echelons of the appointed officials. This hope presupposes that the bureaucracy can be transformed into a civil service properly so-called, the specific difference between the bureaucrat and the civil servant being that the civil servant is a liberally educated man whose liberal education affects him decisively in the performance of his duties.

Permit me to summarize the preceding argument. In the light of the original conception of modern republicanism, our present predicament appears to be caused by the decay of religious education of the people and by the decay of liberal education of the representatives of the people. By the decay of religious education I mean more than the fact that a very large part of the people no longer receive any religious education, although it is not necessary on the present occasion to think beyond that fact. The question as to whether religious education can be restored to its pristine power by the means at our disposal is beyond the scope of [88] this essay. Still, I cannot help asking these questions: Is our present concern with liberal education and our present expectation from such liberal education not due to the void created by the decay of religious education? Is such liberal education meant to perform the function formerly performed by religious education? Can liberal education perform that function?

It is certainly easier to discuss the other side of our predicament, the predicament caused by the decay of liberal education of the governors. Following Mill's suggestion, we would have to consider whether and to what extent the education of the future civil servants can and should be improved, or in other words whether the present form of their education is liberal education in a tolerably strict sense. If it is not, one would have to raise the broader question whether the present colleges and universities supply such a liberal education and whether they can be reformed. It is more modest, more pertinent and more practical to give thought to some necessary reforms of the teaching in the Departments of Political Science and perhaps also in the Law School. What I have in mind are changes less in the subjects taught than in the emphasis and in the approach: whatever broadens and deepens the understanding should be more encouraged than

Liberal Education and Mass Democracy

what in the best case cannot as such produce more than narrow and unprincipled efficiency.

No one, I trust, will misunderstand the preceding remarks and impute to me the ridiculous assertion that education has ceased to be a public or political power. One must say, however, that a new type of education or a new orientation of education has come to predominate. Just as liberal education in its original sense was supported by classical philosophy, so the new education derives its support, if not its being, from modern philosophy. According to classical philosophy, the end of the philosophers is radically different from the end or ends actually pursued by the non-philosophers. Modern philosophy comes into being when the end of philosophy is identified with the end which is capable of being actually pursued by all men. More precisely, philosophy is now asserted to be essentially subservient to the end which is capable of being actually pursued by all men.

We have suggested that the ultimate justification for the distinction between gentlemen and non-gentlemen is the distinction [89] between philosophers and non-philosophers. If this is true, it follows that by causing the purpose of the philosophers, or more generally the purpose which essentially transcends society, to collapse into the purpose of the non-philosophers, one causes the purpose of the gentlemen to collapse into the purpose of the non-gentlemen. In this respect, the modern conception of philosophy is fundamentally democratic.

The end of philosophy is now no longer what one may call disinterested contemplation of the eternal but the relief of man's estate. Philosophy thus understood could be presented with some plausibility as inspired by Biblical charity, and accordingly philosophy in the classic sense could be disparaged as pagan and as sustained by sinful pride. One may doubt whether the claim to Biblical inspiration was justified and even whether it was always raised in entire sincerity. However this may be, it is conducive to greater clarity, and at the same time in agreement with the spirit of the modern conception, to say that the moderns opposed a "realistic," earthly, not to say pedestrian conception to the "idealistic," heavenly, not to say visionary conception of the classics.

Philosophy or science was no longer an end in itself but in the service of human power, of a power to be used for making human life longer, healthier, and more abundant. The economy of scarcity, which is the tacit presupposition of all earlier social thought, was to be replaced by an economy of plenty. The radical distinction between science and manual labor was to be replaced by the smooth cooperation of the scientist and

Chapter 26

the engineer. According to the original conception, the men in control of this stupendous enterprise were the philosopher-scientists. Everything was to be done by them for the people but, as it were, nothing by the people. For the people were, to begin with, rather distrustful of the new gifts from the new sort of sorcerers, for they remembered the commandment, "thou shalt not suffer a sorcerer to live." In order to become the willing recipients of the new gifts, the people had to be enlightened. This enlightenment is the core of the new education. It is the same as the diffusion or popularization of the new science. The addressees of the popularized science were in the first stage countesses and duchesses rather than spinsters and dairy-maids, and popularized science often surpassed science proper in elegance and charm of diction.

[90] But the first step entailed all the further steps which were taken in due order. The enlightenment was destined to become universal enlightenment. It appeared that the difference of natural gifts did not have the importance which the tradition had ascribed to it; method proved to be the great equalizer of naturally unequal minds. While invention or discovery continued to remain the preserve of the few, the results could be transmitted to all. The leaders in this great enterprise did not rely entirely on the effects of formal education for weaning men away from concern with the bliss of the next world to work for happiness in this. What study did not do and perhaps could not do trade did: immensely facilitated and encouraged by the new intentions and discoveries, trade which unites all peoples, took precedence over religion which divides the peoples.

But what was to be done to moral education? The identification of the end of the gentlemen with the end of the non-gentlemen meant that the understanding of virtue as choiceworthy for its own sake gave way to an instrumental understanding of virtue: honesty is nothing but the best policy, the policy most conducive to commodious living or comfortable self-preservation. Virtue took on a narrow meaning with the final result that the word virtue fell into desuetude. There was no longer a need for a genuine conversion from the pre-moral if not immoral concern with worldly goods to the concern with the goodness of the soul, but only for the calculating transition from unenlightened to enlightened self-interest. Yet even this was not entirely necessary. It was thought that at least the majority of men will act sensibly and well if the alternative will be made unprofitable by the right kind of institution, political and economic. The devising of the right kind of institutions and their implementation came to be regarded as more important than the formation of character by liberal education.

Liberal Education and Mass Democracy

Yet let us not for one moment forget the other side of the picture. It is a demand of justice that there should be a reasonable correspondence between the social hierarchy and the natural hierarchy. The lack of such a correspondence in the old scheme was defended by the fundamental fact of scarcity. With the increasing abundance it became increasingly possible to see and to admit the element of hypocrisy which had entered into the traditional notion [91] of aristocracy; the existing aristocracies proved to be oligarchies rather than aristocracies. In other words it became increasingly easy to argue from the premise that natural inequality has very little to do with social inequality, that practically or politically speaking one may safely assume that all men are by nature equal, that all men have the same natural rights, provided one uses this rule of thumb as the major premise for reaching the conclusion that everyone should be given the same opportunity as everyone else: natural inequality has its rightful place in the use, non-use or abuse of opportunity in the race as distinguished from at the start. Thus it became possible to abolish many injustices or at least many things which had become injustices. Thus was ushered in the age of tolerance. Humanity which was formerly rather the virtue appropriate in one's dealings with one's inferiors—with the underdog—became the crowning virtue. Goodness became identical with compassion.

Originally the philosopher-scientist was thought to be in control of the progressive enterprise. Since he had no power, he had to work through the princes. The control was then in fact in the hands of the princes, if of enlightened princes. But with the progress of enlightenment, the tutelage of the princes was no longer needed. Power could be entrusted to the people. It is true that the people did not always listen to the philosopher-scientists. But apart from the fact that the same was true of princes, society came to take on such a character that it was more and more compelled to listen to the philosopher-scientist if it desired to survive. Still there remained a lag between the enlightenment coming from above and the way in which the people exercised its freedom.

One may even speak of a race: Will the people come into full possession of its freedom before it has become enlightened, and if so, what will it do with its freedom and even with the imperfect enlightenment which it will already have received? An apparent solution was found through an apparent revolt against the enlightenment and through a genuine revolt against enlightened despotism. It was said that every man has the right to political freedom, to being a member of the sovereign, by virtue of the dignity which every man has as man, the dignity of a moral being. The only thing

Chapter 26

which can be held to be unqualifiedly good is not the contemplation of the eternal, not the cultivation of the mind, [92] to say nothing of good breeding, but a good intention, and of good intentions everyone is as capable as everyone else, wholly independently of education. Accordingly, the uneducated could even appear to have an advantage over the educated: the voice of nature or of the moral law speaks in them perhaps more clearly and more decidedly than in the sophisticated who may have sophisticated away their conscience.

This belief is not the only starting point and perhaps not the best starting point, but it is for us now the most convenient starting point for understanding the assertion, which was made at that moment—the assertion that virtue is the principle of democracy and only of democracy. One conclusion from this assertion was Jacobin terror which punished not only actions and speeches but intentions as well. Another conclusion was that one must respect every man merely because he is a man, regardless of how he uses his will or his freedom, and this respect must be implemented by full political rights for everyone who is not technically criminal or insane, regardless of whether he is mature for the exercise of those rights or not. That reasoning reminds one of Locke's criticism which led him to the conclusion that one may indeed behead a tyrannical king but only with reverence for that king. It remains then at the race between the political freedom below and the enlightenment coming from above.

Hitherto I have spoken of the philosopher-scientist. That is to say, I have pretended that the original conception, the seventeenth-century conception, has retained its force. But in the meantime philosophy and science have become divorced: a philosopher need not be a scientist and a scientist need not be a philosopher. Only the title Ph.D. is left as a reminder of the past. Of the two henceforth divorced faculties of the mind, science has acquired supremacy; science is the only authority in our age of which one can say that it enjoys universal recognition. This science has no longer any essential connection with wisdom. It is a mere accident if a scientist, even a great scientist, happens to be a wise man politically or privately. Instead of the fruitful and ennobling tension between religious and liberal education, we now see the tension between the ethos of democracy and the ethos of technocracy.

During the last seventy years, it has become increasingly the [93] accepted opinion that there is no possibility of scientific and hence rational knowledge of "values," i.e., that science or reason are incompetent to distinguish between good and evil ends. It would be unfair to deny that,

Liberal Education and Mass Democracy

thanks to the survival of utilitarian habits, scientists in general and social scientists in particular still take it for granted in many cases that health, a reasonably long life and prosperity are good things and that science must find means for securing or procuring them. But these ends can no longer claim the evidence which they once possessed; they appear now to be posited by certain desires which are not "objectively" superior to the opposite desires.* Since science is then unable to justify the ends for which it seeks the means, it is in practice compelled to satisfy the ends which are sought by its customers, by the society to which the individual scientist happens to belong and hence in many cases by the mass.

We must disregard here the older traditions which fortunately still retain some of their former power, because their power is more and more corroded as time goes on. If we look then only at what is peculiar to our age or characteristic of our age, we see hardly more than the interplay of mass taste with high-grade but strictly speaking unprincipled efficiency. The technicians are, if not responsible, at any rate responsive to the demands of the mass: but a mass as mass cannot be responsible to anyone or to anything for anything. It is in this situation that we raise the question concerning liberal education and mass democracy.

In this situation the insufficiently educated are bound to have an unreasonably strong influence on education—on the determination of both the ends and the means of education. Furthermore, the very progress of science leads to an ever-increasing specialization, with the result that a man's respectability becomes dependent on his being a specialist. Scientific education is in danger of losing its value for the broadening and the deepening of the human being. The only universal science which is possible on this basis—logic or methodology—becomes itself an affair of and for technicians. The remedy for specialization is therefore sought in a new kind of universalism—a universalism which has been rendered almost inevitable by the extension of our spatial and temporal horizons. We are trying to expel the narrowness of specialization by the super-[94]ficiality of such things as general civilization courses or by what has aptly been compared to the unending cinema, as distinguished from a picture gallery, of the history of all nations in all respects: economic, scientific, artistic, religious, and political. The gigantic spectacle thus provided is in the best case exciting and entertaining; it is not instructive and educating. A hundred pages—no, ten pages of Herodotus introduces us immeasurably bet-

---

* As found in *Liberalism Ancient and Modern*, 23. —Eds.

ter into the mysterious unity of oneness and variety in human things than many volumes written in the spirit predominant in our age. Besides, human excellence or virtue can no longer be regarded as the perfection of human nature toward which man is by nature inclined or which is the goal of his eros. Since "values" are regarded as in fact conventional, the place of moral education is taken by conditioning, or more precisely, by conditioning through symbols verbal and other, or by adjustment to the society in question.

What then are the prospects for liberal education within mass democracy? What are the prospects for the liberally educated to become again a power in democracy? We are not permitted to be flatterers of democracy precisely because we are friends and allies of democracy. While we are not permitted to remain silent on the dangers to which democracy exposes itself as well as human excellence, we cannot forget the obvious fact that by giving freedom to all, democracy also gives freedom to those who care for human excellence. No one prevents us from cultivating our garden or from setting up outposts which may come to be regarded by many citizens as salutary to the republic and as deserving of giving to it its tone. Needless to say, the utmost exertion is the necessary, although by no means the sufficient, condition for success. For "men can always hope and never need to give up, in whatever fortune and in whatever travail they find themselves."* We are indeed compelled to be specialists but we can try to specialize in the most weighty matters or, to speak more simply and more nobly, in the one thing needful. As matters stand, we can expect more immediate help from the humanities rightly understood than from the sciences, from the spirit of perceptivity and delicacy than from the spirit of geometry. If I am not mistaken, this is the reason why liberal education is now becoming almost synonymous with the reading in common of the Great Books. No better beginning could have been made.

[95] We must not expect that liberal education can ever become universal education. It will always remain the obligation and the privilege of a minority. Nor can we expect that the liberally educated will become a political power in their own right. For we cannot expect that liberal education will lead all who benefit from it to understand their civic responsibility in the same way or to agree politically. Karl Marx, the father of communism, and Friedrich Nietzsche, the step-grandfather of fascism, were liberally educated on a level to which we cannot even hope to aspire.

---

*   Machiavelli, *Discourses on Livy*, II.29—Eds.

But perhaps one can say that their grandiose failures make it easier for us who have experienced those failures to understand again the old saying that wisdom cannot be separated from moderation and hence to understand that wisdom requires unhesitating loyalty to a decent constitution and even to the cause of constitutionalism. Moderation will protect us against the twin dangers of visionary expectations from politics and unmanly contempt for politics. Thus it may again become true that all liberally educated men will be politically moderate men. It is in this way that the liberally educated may again receive a hearing even in the marketplace.

No deliberation about remedies for our ills can be of any value if it is not preceded by an honest diagnosis—by a diagnosis falsified neither by unfounded hopes nor by fear of the powers that be. We must realize that we must hope almost against hope. I say this, abstracting entirely from the dangers threatening us at the hands of a barbaric and cruel, narrow-minded and cunning foreign enemy who is kept in check, if he is kept in check, only by the justified fear that what would bury us would bury him too. In thinking of remedies we may be compelled to rest satisfied with palliatives. But we must not mistake palliatives for cures.

We must remember that liberal education for adults is not merely an act of justice to those who were in their youth deprived through their poverty of an education for which they are fitted by nature. Liberal education of adults must now also compensate for the defects of an education which is liberal only in name or by courtesy. Last but not least, liberal education is concerned with the souls of men and therefore has little or no use for machines. If it becomes a machine or an industry, it becomes undistinguishable from the entertainment industry unless in respect to income and [96] publicity, to tinsel and glamor. But liberal education consists in learning to listen to still and small voices and therefore in becoming deaf to loudspeakers. Liberal education seeks light and therefore shuns the limelight.

27

A Note on Lucretius (1967)

[322] *1. The Opening (I, 1–148)*

Lucretius' work is a poetic exposition of Epicurean philosophy. The reader who opens the book for the first time and reads its opening does not know through first-hand knowledge that it is devoted to the exposition of Epicureanism. The poet leads his reader toward Epicureanism; he makes him ascend to Epicureanism. Accordingly he begins his work by appealing to sentiments which are not peculiar to Epicureans or by making statements which are not peculiarly Epicurean. The reader of the poem is in the first place its addressee, Memmius, a Roman of noble descent. The importance of his being a Roman is shown by the word which opens the poem: *Aeneadum*. He is to ascend from being a Roman to being an Epicurean.

The ascent from being a Roman to being an Epicurean requires that there be a link between Romanism and Epicureanism. Being a Roman must be more than being a member of one city among many, or being a member of any city other than Rome. The Romans, the Aeneads, are the descendants of the goddess Venus who alone guides the nature of things (21). Being a Roman means to have a kinship, denied to other men, with the guide or ruler of the whole. The goddess Venus is the joy not only of the Romans but of gods and men simply; she is the only being that guides the birth or growth not only of Romans and beings subject to Roman rule but of all living beings simply; she brings life, calm, lucidity, beauty, smiling and light everywhere, although not at all times; she arouses fond sexual

---

Originally published as "A Note on Lucretius," in *Natur und Geschichte: Karl Löwith zum 70. Geburtstag*, ed. Hermann Braun and Manfred Riedel (Stuttgart: W. Kohlhammer, 1967), 322–32. —Eds.

CHAPTER 27

love everywhere on earth; nothing glad and lovely emerges without her anywhere (1-23). Lucretius opens his poem with a praise of Venus because that goddess—and not for instance Jupiter Capitolinus—is the link between Rome and all living beings; through Venus, and only through Venus, does one ascend from Romanism to Epicureanism.

Lucretius' praise of Venus also serves the more obvious purpose of making her willing to grant him two favors. Since nothing glad and lovely emerges without her, the poet asks her to help him in writing his poem by granting abiding charm to what he will say. He tries to induce her to grant him this favor by telling her that his poem will deal with the nature of things, i.e., her mighty empire, and that it is to benefit Memmius who has [323] always been her favorite (21–28). He further asks Venus to grant peace everywhere, to all mortals; she alone can restore peace since Mars, the god of war, can be subdued only by his desire for Venus; when his desire will have been fully aroused, he will not be able to refuse her request to grant peace to the Romans; for as long as the fatherland is in the grip of war, Lucretius will lack the equanimity needed for writing his poem as perfectly as he wishes and Memmius, compelled to come to the assistance of the common weal, will lack the leisure needed for listening to the poet's verses (29–43). Only Venus can give charm to Lucretius' poem, and only Venus can restore the peace which is required for writing and enjoying that poem. This is the reason that Lucretius, although he speaks of Mars, is silent about the fact that the Romans are descendants not only of Venus but of Mars as well: Venus, not Mars, is the link between Romanism and Epicureanism.

Lucretius concludes his invocation of Venus by supporting his prayer for peace through reminding her of what she owes to herself not because she is Venus but because she is a divine being: all gods enjoy deathless life in perfect peace. By this he means in the first place that since all gods enjoy perfect peace, they all are able and willing to grant peace to men. But he also means something else: the gods enjoy perfect peace because they are self-sufficient, free from all pain and all danger, in no wise in need of men and therefore not to be swayed by men's good or bad deeds; they are altogether remote from the affairs of men (44–49). The six verses which conclude the invocation of Venus must be understood as part of their pre-Epicurean context. The poet will repeat them literally in an Epicurean context; there he introduces them by stating explicitly that the view of the gods which they convey contradicts the popular view (II, 644–45). No such statement accompanies the verses when they occur

A Note on Lucretius

first. In their pre-Epicurean context they do not exclude the possibility that the gods who do not need men in any way and cannot be swayed by any human merits and demerits, bestow blessings on some men from sheer kindness whenever it pleases them, just as Venus has always willed to bestow the greatest blessings on Memmius (26–27) and has succeeded in doing so. In asking Venus to grant abiding charm to his verses and peace to the Romans, the poet is not necessarily trying to arouse the goddess to action; he may merely wish to guide her in the action which she herself spontaneously started, the action of benefitting Memmius; he merely enlightens her as to how her entirely unsolicited wish to benefit Memmius can be fulfilled most perfectly. After all, he never suggested that Venus is omniscient; he never asked her to be his Muse or to inspire him with knowledge of the Epicurean doctrine. The six verses do cast doubt on the divinity of Mars who does not always enjoy peace and who cannot be free from all pain since he suffers from the [324] everlasting wound of sexual desire.[1] Be this as it may, we remain closer to the accepted view if we assert that the verses in question render doubtful the immediately preceding prayer to a divine being and the poet's singling out Venus as worthy of higher praise than any other deity, nay, that they render doubtful the very being of all gods as worshipped by the Romans and men in general. The verses thus understood would indicate that the invocation of Venus and especially the praise of Venus is a falsehood, if a beautiful falsehood (cf. II, 644–45). They would point toward the end of a movement which begins with the turning to Venus and to Venus alone: not all gods as worshipped by the Romans are equally remote from the true gods; Venus, the joy of the gods as worshipped by the Romans, comes closer to the true gods than any other gods worshipped by the Romans. Since Venus owes her predominance in the opening of Lucretius' poem primarily to her being the ancestress of the Romans, the movement from Venus to the true gods cannot but affect profoundly the status of Rome.

After the poet has addressed Venus in 49 verses, there remains one more thing for him to do before he can begin to expound the Epicurean doctrine: he must address Memmius. He must make it as certain as he can that Memmius will listen to the true account with a mind free from all cares and not reject it with contempt before he has grasped it. He tries to arouse Memmius' attention by indicating to him the grandeur of the poem's theme.

---

1 Cf. Hesiod, *Theogony* 11–21: Ares is not explicitly mentioned among the gods praised by the Muses. Cf. *Works and Days* 145–46.

CHAPTER 27

That theme will indeed not be Venus. The poet will "begin" to speak to Memmius about "the highest ground of heaven and the gods" and he will reveal the origins from which nature creates the things and makes them grow and into which she dissolves them again—those origins which "we" call *materies*, *genitalia corpora*, and *semina rerum*, but also, without any reference to life or sex, the first bodies since everything else that is comes from them (50–61). The nature which creates the things out of the first bodies and dissolves the things into the first bodies, cannot be herself a first body; one must pause for a moment to wonder whether the creative-destructive nature is not a god dwelling in heaven; being destructive as well as creative, he could not be Venus as celebrated in the very beginning; but the end of the passage seems to make it certain that the gods too stem from the first bodies. The first bodies cannot be expected to possess the splendor and the charm of the gods; they cannot be expected to be attractive. Why then should Memmius become concerned with those bodies? Why indeed should he not turn his back on Lucretius' poem with contempt?

In order to see why knowledge of the unattractive origins of everything including heaven and gods is most attractive one must consider how men lived before the quest for these origins started. Before that event human life was abject, crushed as it was by dreadful religion. It was a Greek who first dared to face the terror of religion and to take a stand against it. He [325] was not deterred by the dreadful tales about the gods nor by dreadful sights or sounds from on high. He was encouraged to his daring deed not only by his loathing of religion or suffering from it but also by his desire for honor, for being the first: he wished to be the first to free himself from the common bondage or imprisonment. Thanks to the power of his mind he succeeded in breaking through the walls of the world and traversing in mind the boundless whole and in bringing back to "us" knowledge of what is possible and impossible: the gods as experienced in religion are impossible. Hence "we" no longer grovel upon the earth but equal the highest (62–79).

Lucretius fears that Memmius might fear that, by acquiring the knowledge which is acquired through rising against religion and which justifies that rising, he would commit a crime. His reply is simple: religion has caused crimes more frequently than irreligion. He gives a single example: Agamemnon sadly but pitilessly sacrificed his utterly terrified virgin daughter Iphigeneia, his first-born child, in order to appease the virgin goddess Diana who would not otherwise permit the sailing of the Greek fleet against Troy (80–101). By reminding us of Diana's savage demand

A Note on Lucretius

the poet justifies once more his turning toward Venus. Apart from this, his single example would appear to be neither sufficient nor the most appropriate, for the event with which he deals occurred in the remote past, it did not occur in Rome, and there is no reason to believe that the abolition of human sacrifices was due to philosophy. Provisionally one may reply that Lucretius chooses the Greek example since it was a Greek who liberated man from religion. He thus underlines the fact that Greekness is the link between Romanism and Epicureanism, or that after having turned to Venus, the ancestress of the Romans, the Roman must turn to Greeks, to men belonging to a foreign people now enslaved by Rome, in order to become free: it was a Greek who won the greatest of all victories, a victory surpassing all Roman victories.

Whatever may be true of the crimes caused by religion, its terrors seriously endanger Memmius' happiness. Lucretius is certain that religious fear will induce Memmius to try to turn his back on the truth even after he has listened to it, for he will be exposed to the fear-inspiring inventions of seers regarding everlasting punishments after death. Even "our" Ennius, the first Roman poet who won immortal fame, speaks—not without contradicting himself—of the pale and miserable shades in Acheron and says that the shade of Homer rose to him* and began to shed bitter tears and to reveal to him the nature of things. The only way to liberate oneself from such saddening and terrifying dreams is knowledge of the nature of the soul, of its mortality, and of how it comes that "we" seem to see and hear the dead as if they were still alive; therefore man also needs knowledge of all things above [326] and below (102–35). It would seem that Memmius is threatened less by fear of the gods than by fear of what might happen to him after death; one is led to wonder whether the fear of what might happen to men after death may not be independent of the fear of gods or even precede it. By referring to Ennius, Lucretius does not supply an example of Roman crimes caused by religion, unless one were to say that spreading terrifying tales is a crime. Besides, however much Lucretius disapproves of the dangerous falsehoods propagated by Ennius, he admires that poet: well-executed fables as such, even if they serve the untruth, are praiseworthy (cf. II, 644). It is more immediately important to note that the first great Roman poet traced his knowledge of the nature of things to the first of the Greek poets: in turning to Greek wisdom Lucretius follows a most respectable Roman precedent. The opening of the

---

* Printed as "thes hade" in the original. —Eds.

CHAPTER 27

poem is not the place to speak proudly, not to say to boast, of the poet's innovation or originality (cf. I, 922–34, V, 335–337).

Lucretius is to some extent an imitator of Ennius: he will transmit the obscure findings of the Greeks to the Romans in a poem. He is aware of the difficulty of his task, a difficulty due to the poverty of his native tongue and the novelty of the matter. He is induced to undergo the labor by the worth of Memmius and the prospect of friendship with him: friendship in the true sense requires that the friends think alike about the weightiest things. The poetic presentation serves the purpose of enlightening Memmius so that he can grasp thoroughly what otherwise would remain deeply hidden (136–45).

The findings of the Greeks are obscure only for those who have not grasped them, who therefore live in darkness and are gripped by fear of what might happen to them after death. That darkness and terror cannot be dispelled by Venus or anything else resembling her or akin to her and in particular not by poetry as such but only by nature coming to sight and being penetrated (146–48).

Lucretius leads Memmius from Rome via Venus to the victorious Greek. In the remote past the Greeks defeated and destroyed Troy, protected by Venus, through religion, i.e., the sacrifice of Iphigeneia; this victory led to the founding of Rome, which defeated, but did not altogether destroy, Greece. At their peak some Greeks won, through philosophy, the most glorious victory possible.

The opening of the poem leads from Venus, the joy of gods and men, to the promise of the true joy which comes from the understanding of nature. The poem itself is meant to fulfill that promise. Let us turn at once to its ending in order to see how the promise has been fulfilled.

[327] 2. *The Ending (VI, 1138–1286)*

The last Book of the poem is the only one that begins and ends with "Athens." It almost goes without saying that no Book begins and ends with "Rome." The beginning of the last Book shows Athens' greatness and the end shows Athens' misery. Athens of outstanding fame first gave men corn, an elevated kind of life, and laws; she first gave men sweet solace of life when she brought forth the highly gifted man who by teaching wisdom and thus liberating men from anguish showed them the way to happiness. This praise of Athens must be read in the light of the beginning of the preceding Book. There Lucretius has spoken of the story that Ceres

A Note on Lucretius

taught men how to grow corn and of the fact that the god Epicurus taught men how to become wise. By correcting himself in the parallel passage the poet shows that he can, if with some difficulty, resist the temptation to deify the greatest benefactor of the human race, the most venerable among the departed.[2] He is grateful, not to any god, but in the first place to Athens and to no other city.

The last Book ends with a description of the plague which had struck Athens and which had been rendered immortal by Thucydides. This is not the ending which one would have expected, the happy ending. The poet had promised a copious speech on the gods (V, 155), a speech which would have made a happy ending. For some reason he replaced the speech on the gods, the only beings that are perfectly happy, by the description of extreme misery.

Lucretius' description of the plague differs most strikingly from its Thucydidean model in that it is completely silent about the fact that the plague occurred during a war and even owed its extremely destructive character to that war:[3] the plague was altogether a natural phenomenon, the work of nature. As a consequence the plague as presented by Lucretius is not less but more terrible than it is according to Thucydides. Since Lucretius does not present the plague in its context—in what we would call its "historical" context—since he does not present the events preceding it and following it but describes it in isolation at the end of his poem, he presents it as if it were the end of the world; he is silent on the cessation of the plague. He presents to his readers in fact a recorded experience which could give them a notion of the unrecordable end of the world. He is less explicit than Thucydides about the fact that there were many who survived the plague.[4] He dwells more than Thucydides on the fear of death which gripped those exposed to the plague—their fear of death, not of what might happen to them after death—and he is silent about their (not necessarily unsuccessful) attempts, emphasized by Thucydides, to snatch some pleasures without any regard to law before it was too late.[5] He does follow Thucydides' description of the breakdown of fear of the gods and of respect for the [328] sacred laws regarding burial. Yet this description

---

2   Cf. the *virum* in VI, 5 with the *deus ille fuit, deus* in V, 8.
3   Cf. especially 1259–63.
4   Cf. 1197–1204, 1210–11, 1226–29 with Thucydides II, 49.8 and 51.6.
5   1183, 1212; cf. 1208–12 with Thucydides II, 49.8; consider the fact that there is no passage in Lucretius which corresponds to II, 53.

Chapter 27

takes on a somewhat different meaning in the Lucretian context: one cannot say of Thucydides' work what one can say of Lucretius' work that its most important purpose is to liberate men from religion.* In order to reveal the magnitude of his enterprise, the poet returns at the end of his poem for a moment to a still more pre-Epicurean view than the one from which he had started. He says that those who, from too great a desire for life and fear of death, failed to take care of their sick, were punished afterwards with a shameful death since they themselves were neglected and left without help when they fell sick; although he does not speak of divine punishment, he suggests it. Yet he corrects himself immediately thereafter: those who from a sense of shame did take care of their sick died no less miserably than the shameless.[6] As a consequence of the misery everywhere, neither the rites thought to be of divine origin nor the gods themselves counted for much: they did not count for nothing. For while the Athenians disregarded the customs of burial which they had always observed, they did not desert the bodies of their dead kinsmen.[7] At any rate, the breakdown of religion is presented by Lucretius, as it is by Thucydides, as a sign of extreme misery: there is something worse, much worse, than religion.[8] In the Lucretian context this means that the plague which occurred in the heyday of Athenian civilization was more terrible than the sacrifice of Iphigeneia which occurred far away from Athens in the obscure past: the witnesses of Iphigeneia's slaughter were sad and terrified; they were not in a state of utter despondency; they could hope that Diana would be appeased and, to the best of their knowledge, this hope was fulfilled. And while the story of Iphigeneia's sacrifice may or may not be true, the truth of the account of the plague in Athens is vouched for by one of the most sober observers that ever was—by a man who was singularly free from religious fear. The fact that Thucydides observed and described the plague which had struck him down could seem to show that philosophy, the study of nature, is possible under the most unfavorable circumstances.

---

* A paragraph break follows in the version of the article published as "Notes on Lucretius," in *Liberalism Ancient and Modern* (New York: Basic Books, 1968), 82. —Eds.

6 Cf. 1239–46 with Thucydides II, 51.5.

7 Cf. 1278–86 (consider especially the last words of the poem) with Thucydides II, 53.4 beginning and 52.4. Cf. Epicurus' unconcern with his burial: Diogenes Laertius X, 118.

8 In his letter to Menoeceus (134) Epicurus says that there is something worse than the tale of the gods: the fate or necessity of which the *physikoi* speak.

A Note on Lucretius

Lucretius' description of the plague however, taken by itself, is far from suggesting this. It rather suggests that the mind of the philosopher stricken by the plague would lose all its powers, become filled with anguish, pain and fear, and disintegrate before he dies.[9] The plague occurred prior to Epicurus' birth, but Lucretius does not in the slightest degree suggest that Epicurus or an Epicurean would have withstood it better than anybody else.*

By contrasting directly the opening of the poem with its ending we gain the impression that the poem moves from the sweetest natural phenomenon to the saddest and ugliest or that at the beginning the poet abstracts entirely from the evils in order to accumulate them at the end. At the beginning he praises Venus, the giver of joy, charm, and peace, as the ruler of nature; [329] at the end he speaks, not even of Mars, but of the plague. Near the beginning he speaks of the sacrifice of Iphigeneia which was demanded by Diana and appeared to appease that goddess. At the end he speaks of the plague which could be thought to have been sent by Apollo but the stark terror of which is not relieved by any hope that one could appease the god who might have sent it. The poem appears to move from beautiful or comforting falsehoods to the repulsive truth. There is undoubtedly a certain falsehood implied in the isolation of the plague: the plague is as much a work of nature as procreation but not more than the latter. The plague is as much the work of nature as the golden deeds of Venus, nay, as the understanding of nature. It is doubtful whether philosophy has any remedy against the helplessness and the debasement which afflicts one if one is hit by such events as the plague. By revealing fully the nature of things, philosophy proves to be not simply a "sweet solace" (V, 21). Nevertheless, the movement from Venus to nature which is destructive as it is creative, is an ascent.

3. The Function of Lucretius' Poetry (I, 926–50 and IV, 1–25)

The movement from the untruth to the truth is not simply a movement from unrelieved darkness and terror to pure light and joy. On the contrary, the truth appears at first to be repulsive and depressing. A special effort is needed to counteract the first appearance of the truth. This special effort is beyond the power of philosophy; it is the proper work of poetry.

---

9   Cf. 1156–62, 1182–85, 1212.

*   Paragraph ends here in the reprinted article. "Notes on Lucretius," 82. —Eds.

CHAPTER 27

The poet Lucretius follows the philosopher Epicurus; he imitates him; he belongs as it were to a weaker and lower species than the teacher of the naked truth.[10] Yet precisely for this reason the poet can do something which the philosopher cannot do.

Lucretius' poetry makes bright and sweet the obscure and sad findings of the Greeks, i.e., of the philosophers.[11] The contrast between the sweetest and most exhilarating celebrated at the beginning of his poem and the saddest and most depressing described at its end—a contrast which we understand as indicative of the movement the reader must undergo—is the most striking example of the character of Lucretius' poetry.

Lucretius speaks of the character of his poetry most clearly in 25 verses which occur first immediately before his exposition of infinity and which are repeated with very minor changes at the beginning of Book IV, the Book devoted to what we may call the acts of the soul or the mind. His subject, we learn, is dark but his poem is bright. The doctrine which he sets forth seems often to be rather sad to those not initiated into it, and the multitude shrinks from it with horror. Therefore he sets it forth in a sweet poem, giving the doctrine as it were a touch of the sweet honey of the Muses. In so doing he acts like a physician who attempts to give children repulsive [330] wormwood to drink and first touches the rim of the cup with sweet honey; thus the unsuspecting children are deceived for their benefit and do not sense the bitterness of the drink which heals them.

The potential Epicurean whom Lucretius addresses may be a man of rare worth according to ordinary standards and he may have an excellent mind; in the most important respect he is to begin with quite immature. Therefore the poet must deceive him by adding something to the doctrine which he expounds, something which is alien to the doctrine and which is meant to conceal the sad, repulsive and horrible character of the doctrine. The comparison of honey and wormwood on the one hand with the poetry and the doctrine on the other does not hold in every respect: children do not necessarily learn that it was the bitter medicine which cured them whereas those readers of Lucretius' work who grasp its meaning necessarily learn that it is the doctrine which makes them sound and happy. The comparison surely holds inasmuch as in both cases the patient tastes the sweet first: thanks to the poetry what the reader tastes first is sweet. But does the reader ever taste the repulsive? Is what is primarily

---

10 III, 1–30.
11 Cf. I, 117–19, 121, 124, 136–37, 143–45.

A Note on Lucretius

repulsive if tasted by itself, noticed only after it is no longer repulsive? Will its taste eventually even be sweet? The example of Venus at the beginning and of the plague at the end would seem to show that whereas the sweet is sensed first, the repulsive or sad is sensed even at the end but in such a way that it is more bearable for the sensitive reader after he has digested the doctrine than before. Furthermore, the child may take the honeyed wormwood merely for the sake of the honey, or he may take it because he is uncomfortable; he surely is not so uncomfortable as to be willing to take the bitter potion by itself. Similarly, the potential Epicurean may be attracted to the Epicurean doctrine only because of the sweetness of Lucretius' poetry, or he may be attracted by it because he suffers from the terrors of religion; surely those terrors are not so great as to make him willing to swallow the naked truth. After all, he does not live in the age in which Agamemnon sacrificed his beloved daughter. We conclude that poetry is the link or the mediation between religion and philosophy.

How can religion be more attractive than philosophy if religion is nothing but terrifying? To answer this question, one must reconsider what the poet says at the beginning in the light of what he says later, on how men lived before the emergence of philosophy; one must consider the function of religion. Originally men lived like wild beasts, depending entirely on the spontaneous gifts of the earth, without fire and the arts as well as without laws and language, unable to conceive of a common good. They feared death because they clung to the sweet light of life, but apparently not because they feared what might happen to them after death. Nor did they fear that the sun might not rise again after it had set; the thought that sun and earth might be destructible had not occurred to them.[12] That thought occurred to them only after they had acquired language and the arts and established society and laws; then they began to doubt whether the sun will always rise and set and whether the earth will last forever: whether the world will come to an end and hence whether it did not have a beginning. There is only one protection against the fear that the walls of the world will some day crumble: the will of gods.* Religion has then the function to serve as a refuge from the fear of the end or the death of the world; it has its root in man's attachment to the world. Lucretius him-

---

12 V, 925–1010, 1087–90; cf. 601–02.

* In the foregoing (from "then they began to doubt..."), all instances of the modal "will" except the last ("will some day crumble") are found as "would" in "Notes on Lucretius," *Liberalism Ancient and Modern*, 84–85.—Eds.

Chapter 27

self wishes, not to say prays, that the day on which the huge machine of the world will fall down with a dreadful sound, will not come soon. The world to which man is attached is not the boundless whole but the visible whole—heaven and earth and what belongs to them—which is only an infinitesimal part of the boundless whole: there are infinitely many worlds both simultaneously and successively; everything to which a man can be attached—his life, his friends, his fatherland, his fame, his work—implies attachment to the world to which he belongs and which makes possible the primary objects of his attachment.[13] The recourse to the gods of religion and the fear of them is already a remedy for a more fundamental pain: the pain stemming from the divination that the lovable is not sempiternal or that the sempiternal is not lovable. Philosophy transforms the divination into a certainty. One may therefore say that philosophy is productive of the deepest pain. Man has to choose between peace of mind deriving from a pleasing delusion and peace of mind deriving from the unpleasing truth. Philosophy which, anticipating the collapse of the walls of the world, breaks through the walls of the world, abandons the attachment to the world; this abandonment is most painful. Poetry on the other hand is, like religion, rooted in that attachment but, unlike religion, it can be put into the service of detachment. Because poetry is rooted in prephilosophic attachment, because it enhances and deepens that attachment, the philosophic poet is the perfect mediator between the attachment to the world and the attachment to detachment from the world. The joy or pleasure which Lucretius' poem arouses is therefore austere, reminding of the pleasure aroused by the work of Thucydides.[14]

---

[13] V, 1211–17, 1236–40, 91–109, 114–21, 373–75, 1186–87; VI, 565–67, 597–607, 650–52, 677–79.

[14] Cf. Thucydides, I, 22.4.

28

Greek Historians*
(1968)

[656] The author starts from the premiss that "the most important aspect of the study of history is...historiography." He means by this that the most important aspect of the study of the political history of classical Greece is the critical study of Herodotus, Thucydides and Xenophon. He selected Xenophon because "the problems of the composition" of the *Hellenica*—in contradistinction apparently to the corresponding problems of Herodotus' and Thucydides' histories—would seem to have been settled: a critical study of the characteristic theories proposed as solutions to those problems would reveal the greatness of "our modern approach to the historical writing of ancient Greece," but perhaps also its limitations.

The bulk of Henry's book is devoted to such a critical study. It has led him to a "singular disappointment" (p. 191) and to the conclusion that "we are not yet ready to interpret ancient histories, like the *Hellenica*" (p. 210). There is a general and a particular cause of the failure of nineteenth and twentieth century study of Greek historical writing. The general cause is insufficient attention to the peculiarity of Greek historiography as distinguished from its modern counterpart: the ancients did not study history "for its own sake," since their approach was "esthetic" (p. 193). A moment's reflection on the historical origin of this meaning of "esthetic" would show the inadequacy of Henry's characterization of classical historiography. For the classical Greek, "history was a form of literature.... History is literature when an artist perceives the genius of an age and reveals it through

---

Originally published as "Greek Historians," *Review of Metaphysics* 21, no. 4 (June 1968): 656–66.—Eds.

* A Critical Study of W. P. Henry, *Greek Historical Writing: A Historiographical Essay Based on Xenophon's* Hellenica. (Chicago: Argonaut, Inc. 1967). [Original note.—Eds.]

the facts of history" (p. 193). This seems to be Henry's interpretation of a [657] saying of Quintilian which he renders "History has a certain affinity to poetry" (p. 191). Granting for a moment that the three classical historians perceived the spirit of the ages which they described, was their primary intention to reveal those spirits? A glance at the openings of Herodotus' and Thucydides' works would show the impropriety of this suggestion. This is to say nothing of the fact that the suggestion could not be expressed in their language. However justified Henry's criticism of nineteenth and twentieth century students of classical Greek historiography may be, he shares with them (or most of them) the prejudice that "we know today" the meaning of historiography in general and of classical historiography in particular.

The particular cause of the failure of nineteenth and twentieth century students to solve the problem of the composition of the *Hellenica* is their prejudice regarding Xenophon. They believe that Xenophon's nature is "patently simple" or that "although superficial [he] is yet sincere" or that because his manner "is candid it is uncontrived." They certainly speak about him in a "patronizing" or "condescending" way (pp. 191–192). Here Henry shows a rare awareness of an amazing defect of contemporary scholarship: the general run of present day scholars who as such have not shown particular sophistication and openmindedness, speak of Xenophon's simplemindedness or narrowmindedness as if sophistication and openmindedness were virtues that today can be acquired in the same manner in which one obtains a Ph.D. degree.

In order to show that Xenophon's manner is not "uncontrived," Henry discusses "three representative examples" (p. 193). The first is Xenophon's account of the trial of the generals who took part in the battle of the Arginusae.

> Perhaps the problem which has proved most troubling of all is that of Xenophon's treatment of Socrates in this scene. Although Xenophon does not, to be sure, neglect here to mention Socrates' firm adherence to justice, beyond this passing reference nothing is said of the actions or speech of the great philosopher throughout the whole affair. Indeed, this one remark constitutes the very sum and substance of reference to Socrates in the entire *Hellenica*—the very Socrates who was the teacher and friend of Xenophon.... So little notice is taken of Socrates here, in fact, that when Xenophon at last mentions him, he identifies him as "the son of Sophroniscus," as though the reader would not otherwise be expected to recognize which Socrates was meant (p. 194).

[658] Henry shows well that

> the development of this entire scene was obviously contrived with no other object in view than to set off the adamant refusal of the great philosopher in the face of overwhelming constraint. All objections that Xenophon in according Socrates only this one line is slighting him or that he does not recognize the meaning of his life are intolerable and can only arise from a profound misconception of the artistry of the description.... And just as Xenophon is careful not to prejudice the effect through untimely anticipation, he does not dissipate it by ponderously dwelling on the morality of Socrates' deed after it has been mentioned or try by words to increase an impression already rendered supreme (197).

According to Henry, these and similar considerations dispose of the criticisms of Xenophon based on his patronymic designation of Socrates in this passage and his complete silence in the *Hellenica* about Socrates' trial and his death (p. 199). Henry finds only one "artistic flaw" in Xenophon's account of the trial of the generals. The mention of Socrates' courageous resistance to the mob's lawless demands is immediately followed by Euryptolemus' speech in defense of the generals which is "extended, reasoned, unimpassioned" and apparently "heard out by a patient and... even sympathetic audience." This speech is presented as having taken place a few minutes after the violent eruption of the mob. Henry thinks that "this is simply impossible." "In short, art has somewhere intervened, and Xenophon has taken liberties with his matter." But is the intervention of art as such an artistic flaw? In addition, Xenophon says that Euryptolemus spoke "thereafter." "Thereafter" does not necessarily mean "immediately thereafter," as is shown by the very beginning of the *Hellenica*. Even if Euryptolemus' speech had been delivered days after Socrates' intervention, it still could have been the effect of Socrates' intervention. Above all, the immediate juxtaposition of Socrates' single sentence (in indirect speech) and Euryptolemus' long oration (in direct speech) compels us to note that Xenophon's Socrates never delivered any public speech except the speech in his own defense.

The flaw of Henry's otherwise praiseworthy interpretation of the above story is surely graver than the flaw of which he accuses Xenophon. Henry's critics could justly demand of him that he explain why Xenophon here designates Socrates with his patro-[659]nymic and why he is silent about Socrates' condemnation. Xenophon's general silence in the *Hellenica* on Socrates may have to be understood in the light of Thucydides' well known silences on Athenian "life of the mind." The questions which

Chapter 28

Henry fails to answer cannot be properly raised unless one considers the two other references to Socrates by Xenophon in his writings other than his Socratic writings (*Anabasis* III 1.4–7 and *Cyropaedia* III 1.14 and 38–40) and one interprets first Xenophon's Socratic writings. For the particular wisdom conveyed through the *Hellenica* cannot be understood except in the light of Xenophon's general understanding of wisdom, and this general understanding is identical with that of his Socrates. It is certain that the purport of the *Hellenica* does not become sufficiently clear from that work itself, as is shown by its strange opening.

Henry's two other examples deal with the question whether Xenophon's prejudices in favor of Sparta (and of Agesilaus) and against Thebes (and Epaminondas) can be used as keys to the understanding of the *Hellenica* (or its bulk). He shows that if Xenophon was simply under the spell of these prejudices, he would have ended the *Hellenica* differently (pp. 200–204). And finally he takes issue with the prejudices regarding Xenophon's prejudice. He notes in particular that the scholars who accuse him of prejudice made "no attempt to define prejudice" (p. 204). "Yet Xenophon favored Sparta and disliked Thebes—this fact is undeniable." But this fact does not prove that he was "prejudiced" toward these cities (p. 205). "This is the most important problem of Xenophon's historiography" (p. 206). The question is whether Sparta did not deserve Xenophon's admiration and Thebes did not deserve his contempt, or what to Henry seems to be the same thing, whether Xenophon's conviction regarding the two cities "was not a conviction generally shared by his contemporaries" (p. 208). Henry's answer is not satisfactory since it is not based on an explicit consideration of all passages in which Xenophon speaks in his own name of the virtues and vices of the two cities. (Cf. pp. 162–163 where he treats as equivalent a passage in which Xenophon speaks in his own name of the "aggressions" committed by Sparta and another passage in which Xenophon reports the utterance of some-[660]one else on this same subject.) Surely the faintest recollection of the Funeral Speech should have prevented him from concluding that "every Greek was philo-Laconian" (p. 210). Nevertheless, as matters stand, we must be grateful to Henry for having raised the questions which he did raise.

Henry raised these questions because of his dissatisfaction with the prevailing theories regarding the *Hellenica*, and this dissatisfaction was the result of his examination of those theories. Within that examination—the bulk of his book—there occur very few signs of his dissatisfaction with the "patronizing" or "condescending" view of Xenophon on which he speaks so strongly and so sensibly in his Epilogue. Could it be that he became dissatisfied with the "patronizing" view after he had completed the bulk of his book and that he did not think it worth his while to revise that bulk, i.e., that he wrote his book as a whole in a way resembling the way in which Xenophon is believed to have written his *Hellenica*? He is no less vocal on the "enormous deficiencies" of the first two books of the *Hellenica* than the scholars with whom he takes issue. Those two books, he says, are "a lowly and feeble production which at best hardly matches the poorest of his own efforts elsewhere" (pp. 53–54). As for the last five books, their "unity... is not great"; they suffer from "the same want of proportion that characterizes the narrative of the early books" (p. 133). In the part dominated by Agesilaus "the naiveté is contrived and the artless expression of great ideals is here wooden and stilted" (p. 156). "Xenophon was writing those parts of the *Hellenica* for those young boys he seems always to have been carrying about with him in his head" (p. 158). But how does it happen that this misplaced or spurious boyishness, while "always" present in Xenophon's head, affects only some parts of the *Hellenica*, and the *Anabasis* hardly at all? More generally stated, what is the purport of the *Hellenica* as a whole?

One of the "theories" which Henry rejects is "the thesis that in the first two books of the *Hellenica* Xenophon was intending to write the formal continuation and conclusion of Thucydides. So far from finding any conceptual relation between the two works, however, we are at a loss to discover much evidence that Xenophon was even acquainted with Thucydides' history or came under its [661] influence in any respect" (p. 49). If the thesis criticized by Henry were correct—if "Xenophon conceived his works as the completion of the history of Thucydides" (p. 53)—Thucydides' statements about his intention could be used as the key to the intention of the *Hellenica*. Accordingly, that thesis is "perhaps the most fundamental of all the assumptions made about the *Hellenica*; so basic is it, in fact, that it might appear surprising that it should be referred to as an assumption and even more surprising that the assumption should be called into question" (p. 15). And yet that thesis is the outcome of a gross fallacy—of the conclusion from the observation that the *Hellenica* "begins generally" where Thucydides' work ends, to the assertion that "Xenophon must be completing Thucydides" (p. 22, n.). How then can we discover the purport of the *Hellenica*? Henry fails to raise this question. The *Hellenica* is the only book ever written which begins with the expression "Thereafter." The absence of a normal beginning, and in particular of a proem stating the author's intention, is the beginning of the troubles that the book causes the

Chapter 28

reader. It is usually not observed that within the limits of the grammatically possible the same book also ends with "thereafter": "After the battle there was still greater disorder and confusion in Greece than before. Now let the writing be mine up to this point. As for what happened thereafter, perhaps another will care for it." If we read the first two or more pages of the book in the light of its ending, we may be inclined to think that according to Xenophon there is always confusion in the affairs of men, that what we call "history" is a sequence of states of greater or lesser confusion, and that therefore the historian can begin and end his work more or less at the points most convenient to him. "The more it changes, the more it is the same thing": At the end of the Peloponnesian war for instance, when Lysander sailed into the Piraeus, the exiles returned, and the walls of Athens were pulled down, many thought that that day was the beginning of freedom for Greece (II 2.23) but as Xenophon silently shows by the sequel, they were mistaken. "For here, I hope, begins our lasting joy," says King Edward at the end of the Third Part of King Henry the Sixth, although he is in a manner refuted by the mere presence of the future Richard III. At first glance, the view according to which "the historical process" [662] consists of confusion followed by confusion differs wholly from Thucydides' view. According to Thucydides, it seems that the historian's beginning and end is imposed on him by the beginning and the end of a grand movement or motion, such as the Peloponnesian war; the unity of Thucydides' history imitates the unity of that war. Hence the *Hellenica*, and even its first two books, cannot in any serious sense be a continuation of Thucydides' history. But this makes it all the more urgent for us to seek the conception which renders Xenophon's account of things worthy of being remembered and which gives the whole of these accounts the kind of unity that they possess. The thought suggested by the title, "Things Greek from 411 to 362," if it can be called a thought, is insufficient. Xenophon's *Banquet* is devoted to playful deeds of perfect gentlemen; for such deeds as well as serious deeds are worthy to be remembered (1.1). The *Hellenica* can be said to be devoted above all to the serious deeds of perfect gentlemen (which were performed between 411 and 362). This suggestion derives perhaps some support from the explicit excursuses occurring in the *Hellenica*, i.e., from the passages described by Xenophon himself as excursuses (for excursuses are passages which do not strictly belong to the theme of a book). The explicit excursuses occurring in the *Hellenica* (VI 1.19 and 5.1, VII 3.4 and 4.1) deal with tyrants, i.e., with such monarchic rulers as by definition are not perfect gentlemen. It almost goes without saying that one cannot lay bare Xenophon's notion of the perfect gentleman except through the study of his Socratic writings.

Finally, in trying to understand any book of Xenophon, one must always keep in mind his view that "it is noble, as well as just and pious, and more pleasant, to remember the good things rather than the bad ones" (*Anabasis* V end). Despite his sad and saddening view of "the historical process" Xenophon always tried to write nobly, justly and piously, and even pleasantly, in this sense. One surely must take this maxim into consideration in order to appreciate properly the passages which Henry disparages as "tender drivel" (p. 160).

Reflections on the purport of the *Hellenica* like those sketched in the preceding lines will induce one to contemplate a revision of the negative judgments on that book and especially on its first [663] section. For respectable reasons Xenophon could not take history as seriously as Thucydides had done. For a man whose memoirs or recollections par excellence were the private conversations of Socrates, the public speeches and deeds of the perfect gentlemen, in the common meaning of that expression, were not serious enough. Here we have the root of what one may call the levity of the *Hellenica* as contrasted with the gravity of Thucydides' work. On the basis of the *Hellenica* taken by itself one might say that Xenophon's gravity lies in his piety (cf. V 4.1). But gravity in these terms makes Thucydides none too grave. Yet the sole conversation between Xenophon and Socrates reported in the *Anabasis* would seem to show that Xenophon's posture toward piety was not altogether free of levity. Perhaps eventually one will consider the possibility that the fundamental difference between the two great historians consists in this: according to Xenophon there does not exist such a close or direct connection as Thucydides seems to suggest between the *archai* that enable one to understand "history," and the *archai* of the whole.

If one grants that the *Hellenica* is in no serious sense a completion or even a continuation of Thucydides' work, the beginning of the *Hellenica* forces one to admit that this book is a continuation of something. But of what book other than of Thucydides'? Surely Xenophon wished it to appear that he was simply continuing Thucydides; this would explain in particular why he did not take up the thread of the narrative at exactly the point at which Thucydides dropped it by accident or by design.

Scholars of the nineteenth and twentieth centuries have invested much labor in trying to show that there is a vast difference within the *Hellenica* between the section devoted to the last years of the Peloponnesian war

Chapter 28

(i.e., the section which might be regarded as a substitute for the unwritten end of Thucydides' work), and the rest of the *Hellenica*. Henry believes that he has refuted all arguments in favor of that "theory." Yet he does not discuss all of them. In particular he does not discuss the argument based on the fact that the first two books of the *Hellenica* avoid explicit references to sacrifices before battle, while such references occur frequently in the last five books. This difference belongs according to Henry to the class of "inconsequential stuff" (p. 54). Such a dismissal is [664] unjustified. The author of *Hellenica* III–VII regarded sacrifices before battle and the like as important; Thucydides and the author of *Hellenica* I–II regarded them as unimportant; the two historians regarded the question concerning the importance of sacrifices before battle as important. But this modern scholar asserts that both were wrong without even taking the trouble of refuting them, nay, of making his assertion explicit. Be this as it may, a serious study of all references occurring in *Hellenica* III–VII to sacrifices before battle and the like is indispensable. Xenophon does not in all cases refer to "such inconsequential stuff"; why did he do it in some cases and not in others?

If one reads the first two pages of the *Hellenica* just as "literature," without any scholarly intentions or pretensions, one will find them dull, uninspired, uninformative; one may even find them confused—imitating, as it were, the confusion of a war whose outcome has not yet been decided. Then suddenly the mist and darkness is pierced by a flash of lightning: Alcibiades himself appears, calls together an assembly of the Athenian warriors and says that they must fight on sea, fight on land and fight on walls, for "we have no money but the enemies have plenty of it from the king." The previous day Alcibiades had taken appropriate measures so that no news about his naval arrangements could leak out to the enemy: "whoever is caught sailing across to the opposite coast, death will be the punishment." If we stop here and go back to the beginning, we note that the name of Alcibiades is mentioned up to this point (I 1.1–15) twice as often as the name of any other individual. Xenophon thus prepares his answer to the question concerning the proximate cause (and not only the proximate cause) of Athens' final defeat: Lysander's decisive victory over the Athenians was rendered possible by the Athenian generals' contemptuous rejection of Alcibiades' advice (II 1.25–26). This subdued praise of Alcibiades, this implicit suggestion that if Alcibiades had been in command, Lysander would not have won his decisive victory, was the utmost that a man in circumstances such as the author of *Memorabilia* I 2.12–13 could do. By understanding the crucial importance of Alcibiades in the final stage of the Peloponnesian war (cf. also I 5.9), one understands other incidents narrated in the beginning of the *Hellenica* without crossing the t's and dotting the i's. [665] Examples of this are, for instance, the contrast between the Athenian generals' silly imprudence leading to the Spartan victory at Aegospotami, and Callicratidas' noble ("boyish") imprudence leading to the Athenian victory at the Arginusae, a victory followed by the Athenian *demos* murdering the victorious Athenian generals; or the contrast between the fate of those generals and even of Alcibiades and the fate of Hermocrates who was exiled (not murdered) only after he had saved Syracuse. Henry however complains about Xenophon's devoting 22 lines to "the momentous encounter" at Abydus and 36 lines to Hermocrates' "pleasant adieu" (p. 9).

One of the best sections of Henry's book is his interpretation of Xenophon's judgment on the battle of Coronea (pp. 147–154). He realizes that that judgment implies, or suggests in a subdued manner, an unfavorable judgment about the "reckless tactics" employed by Agesilaus in that battle. But it is necessary to pursue this theme much further, i.e., Xenophon's concealed and serious judgment on Agesilaus. I would not hesitate to say that Agesilaus was not a man after Xenophon's heart. How could a man with Xenophon's lack of pomposity and even gravity have unqualifiedly liked a man as absurd, as pompous, as theatrical as the Agesilaus of Xenophon's description (as distinguished from his explicit judgments)? The man after Xenophon's heart was Agesilaus' predecessor in command, Dercylidas, whom people gave the nickname "Sisyphus," a man who was once punished for his lack of discipline, who in eight days took nine cities, who did everything with the greatest deftness and minimum of fuss, and who always liked to be away from home (from Sparta). Xenophon's posture toward Agesilaus, which at first glance seems to be one of the keys to the understanding of his mind, becomes more and more a riddle the more one understands Xenophon. Agesilaus seems to have thought highly of Xenophon (Plutarch, *Agesilaus* 20.2); he, the king and the descendant of a long line of kings, may have been Xenophon's *praesidium et dulce decus*. Thus it would not be surprising if Xenophon was grateful and loyal to him. But Xenophon knew that there are duties higher than those imposed by gratitude and loyalty, that the duties imposed by gratitude and loyalty may sometimes have to be superseded by the duty to see things as they are and to communicate one's insights to those who are by nature and [666] training fit for them. The proof of this is the difference between his obtrusive and his unobtrusive judgments on Agesilaus.

29

Philosophy as a Rigorous Science and Political Philosophy (1969)

[315] As the title of the paper suggests, its main point is to indicate the contribution of the Husserlian ideal of "philosophy as a rigorous science" to political philosophy. While contemporary philosophies—positivism and existentialism—cannot entail political philosophy because of their logical structure, Husserl's ideal of philosophy as a rigorous science, with its unwillingness to compromise with its alternative, competing ideas of philosophising, can be considered as opening an avenue to political philosophy. Positivism holds that only scientific knowledge, which is independent of norms and values, is genuine knowledge, so that it rejects political philosophy, which is concerned with value judgements, as radically unscientific. Therefore, the paper does not discuss it at all. Existentialism, on the other hand, which because of its extreme historicity rejects political philosophy as radically unhistorical, is discussed through a detailed analysis of, what might be called, Heidegger's a-political philosophy of history. Heidegger's theory, which is structurally similar to those of Hegel, Marx and Nietzsche, is sketched from the perspective of the absolute moment of history, to be followed by an eschatological return of the gods.

In contradistinction, Husserl's positive contribution to political philosophy can be envisaged in the following way. Husserl's anti-psychologism and anti-Weltanschauungsphilosophie is well known. Psychologism, as a theory of knowledge, accepts nature as given, as "being-in-itself," and as such it completely overlooks the riddles inherent in the "givenness" of nature. It is, therefore, constitutionally incapable of a radical critique of

---

Originally published in "English Summaries," *Iyyun: Jerusalem Philosophical Quarterly* 20 (1969): 315–14. (Pages are numbered in dextrosinistral order.) —Eds.

Chapter 29

experience. Weltanschauungsphilosophie comes into being when the attempt is made to conceptualize life-experience of a high order. The idea of Weltanschauung differs from epoch to epoch, while the idea of philosophy as a rigorous science is supra-temporal.

The reflection on the relation of these two kinds of philosophy belongs [314] to the sphere of philosophy as a rigorous science. It comes closest to Husserl's contribution to political philosophy. He did not go on to wonder whether the single minded pursuit of philosophy as a rigorous science would not have an adverse effect on Weltanschauungsphilosophie, so as to oppress the practitioners of philosophy as a rigorous science. He seems to have taken for granted that there will always be a variety of Weltanschauungsphilosophien that peacefully coexist within one and the same society. He did not pay attention to societies that impose a single Weltanschauung on all their members, and for this reason will not tolerate philosophy as a rigorous science.

Husserl's modified position, under the impact of the events of the 1930s in Europe, was clearly stated by himself in a lecture delivered in Prague: "Those who are conservatively contented with the tradition... will fight one another, and surely the fight will take place in the sphere of political power. Already in the beginnings of philosophy persecution sets in. The men who live toward those ideas [of philosophy as a rigorous science] are outlawed. And yet: ideas are stronger than all empirical powers."

30

Machiavelli and Classical Literature (1970)

[7] My subject is not "Machiavelli and Classical Antiquity." The subject "Machiavelli and Classical *Literature*" precedes in one sense the subject "Machiavelli and Classical Antiquity"; for Machiavelli knew of classical antiquity only—or almost only—through classical literature. Second, I shall limit myself as far as possible to Machiavelli's explicit references to classical literature. From the fact that Machiavelli's sentiment on a given subject agrees with the sentiment of a classical author or of classical authors, it does not follow that Machiavelli was guided in that point by the classics; the agreement may be a coincidence. Finally, I shall concentrate on Machiavelli's two *magna opera*, the *Prince* and the *Discourses*.

But it will not be amiss if we first cast a glance at some of his other prose writings. As for the *Florentine Histories*, it is irrelevant to my present purpose whether and to what extent that work imitates ancient historians. In the *Florentine Histories* Machiavelli refers very rarely to Florentine writers. He refers still more rarely to ancient writers; he does this, strictly speaking, only when he discusses the ancient origins of Florence; in this context he mentions Pliny, Frontinus, and Tacitus. In his eulogy of Cosimo de' Medici, when he speaks of Cosimo's love of literary men and in particular of Marsilio Ficino, he mentions Plato: Ficino was "the second father of Platonic philosophy." *The Art of War* is meant [8] to bring about a renaissance—a rebirth—of the military art of the ancients, especially of the Romans. For this purpose Machiavelli uses the writings of the Roman military writers in the narrow sense (Frontinus, Vegetius) without, however, mentioning their names. This is in agreement with the fact that *The Art of*

Originally published as "Machiavelli and Classical Literature," *Review of National Literatures* 1, no. 1 (Spring, 1970): 7–25. —Eds.

CHAPTER 30

War is a dialogue between Fabrizio Colonna, an outstanding practitioner of the military art, and Cosimo, as well as some young Florentine gentlemen of great promise—a conversation that is supposed to have taken place in a garden of Cosimo's. He refers to *istoria nostra*, meaning the ancient Roman historians, but also to "*their* histories." The only ancient writers whom Machiavelli mentions in his work by name are Livy, Josephus, and Thucydides: he mentions Josephus and Thucydides once and Livy twice; in one of the two cases he even quotes Livy in Italian translation. The honor accorded to Livy, which is outstanding in the circumstances, does not surprise us: Machiavelli's *Discourses* are discourses on the first ten books of Livy.

I shall speak somewhat less briefly on *La Vita de Castruccio Castracani da Lucca*. For this graceful little work reveals Machiavelli's moral taste in a more direct or simple and more condensed manner than his great works. At the same time it reveals Machiavelli's relation to the two major trends or schools of classical moral or political thought with unusual explicitness. I cannot show this without going beyond the limits that I set for myself in this paper, but this flagrant transgression will be tacitly justified by the sequel.

Castruccio is presented by Machiavelli as the greatest man of post-classical times: he would have surpassed Philip, the father of Alexander the Great, and Scipio had he been born in antiquity. He lived forty-four years, like Philip and Scipio. He surpassed Philip and Scipio because he rose to greatness from "a low and obscure beginning and birth." He resembled the men of the first rank who either were all exposed to wild beasts or else had fathers so contemptible [9] that they made themselves sons of Jupiter or of some other god. Having been found as a baby by the sister of a priest in her garden, he was raised by her and her brother and destined for the priesthood. But as soon as he was fourteen years old, he left the ecclesiastical books and turned to arms. He found favor in the eyes of the most distinguished man of the city, a Ghibelline *condottiere*, who took him into his house and educated him as a soldier. In the shortest time Castruccio became a perfect gentleman, distinguishing himself by his prudence, his grace, and his courage. When on the point of dying his master made him the tutor of his young son and the guardian of his property, Castruccio had no choice but to make himself the ruler of his city. He won brilliant victories, rose to be the leader of the Tuscan and Lombard Ghibellines, and eventually almost became prince of Tuscany. He never married lest love of his children prevent him from showing due gratitude to the blood of his benefactor. After having described Castruccio's beginning, life, and death,

Machiavelli devotes half a page to a description of his character and thereafter more than three pages to a collection of witty remarks made by Castruccio or listened to by him. These sayings reveal to us Castruccio's mind. There are altogether thirty-four such sayings. Almost all—thirty-one—can be traced to Diogenes Laertius' *Lives of the Famous Philosophers*. Needless to say, Machiavelli does not mention Diogenes Laertius nor the philosophers whose sayings he borrows and adapts to his purpose. This silence agrees with the fact that he very rarely refers to philosophy and philosophers: in the *Prince* and the *Discourses* taken together, there occur only one reference to Aristotle and one to Plato. Of the sayings reproduced at the end of the *Castruccio*, a single one stems from Aristotle. The Aristotelian saying is surrounded on each side by two sayings of a certain Bion. Bion was a pupil of the notorious atheist Theodorus and was himself a man of many wiles, a sophist of many colors, and so shameless as to behave like [10] an atheist in the company of his fellows. The five sayings referred to are surrounded on one side by fifteen sayings of the Cyrenaic Aristippus and on the other by eleven sayings of the Cynic Diogenes. Aristippus and Diogenes *shared* an extreme contempt for convention as opposed to nature. The mind of Machiavelli's exemplary prince, as revealed by the witty remarks made by or listened to by that prince, reminds us most strongly of such undignified philosophers as Aristippus and Diogenes and hardly at all of Aristotle. These sayings reveal in an ironical manner Machiavelli's own innermost thought: they point to a thought at the center of which Aristotle is kept in bonds or overwhelmed by Bion, and of which the periphery consists of a shocking moral teaching. We could and, I believe, we should interpret this pointer as follows: Machiavelli breaks with the Great Tradition of moral and political philosophy, the tradition founded by Socrates and culminating in the work of Aristotle; he breaks with the tradition according to which there is *natural* right. Instead he opts for the classical alternative, for the view that all right is conventional. In contradistinction to Aristippus and Diogenes, Machiavelli is a *political* philosopher, a man concerned with the good society; but he understands the good society by starting from the conventionalist assumption, from the premise of extreme individualism: man is not by nature political, man is not by nature directed toward political society. Machiavelli achieves a synthesis of the two classical traditions. He achieves that synthesis by going over to a new plane from the plane on which all classical thought moved. To use what is almost his own expression, he discovered a new continent different from the only continent that was known prior to him.

CHAPTER 30

We are now prepared to consider the *Prince* to the extent to which this is possible in our present discussion. From the dedicatory Epistle we learn three things: Machiavelli's knowledge of the actions of great men stems from a long experience of modern things and a continuous reading of [11] ancient things; the *Prince* contains within the briefest compass everything Machiavelli knows; that knowledge concerns the nature of princes and the rules of princely government. Machiavelli calls the *Prince* a treatise. It is at the same time a tract for the time: it prepares the eloquent appeal, in which it culminates or with which it ends, addressed to a contemporary Italian prince to liberate Italy from the foreigners who have overrun her. Yet while the work is devoted at least at first glance to the preparation of action in contemporary Italy, it is animated and even guided by admiration for antiquity: in order to act well, the moderns must imitate the ancients. All the chapter headings are in Latin. In a sense the climax of the work is reached in Chapter 6, which is devoted to the new principalities that are acquired by one's own arms and virtue. In that chapter Machiavelli adduces the greatest examples which adumbrate the highest goal of imitation that is possible, the examples of Moses, Cyrus, Romulus, and Theseus. Despite the mention of Moses and Cyrus, the emphasis is altogether on classical antiquity. Machiavelli refers only once to the Bible, to what, as he says, is an allegory occurring in the Old Testament; but he never *quotes* the Bible. He refers once to the ancient histories, twice to the writers, once to the ancient writers, and once to the histories, meaning in all cases classical writers. He quotes four times Latin prose writers—Justinus and Tacitus each once, and Livy twice, without however mentioning their names. He once quotes Virgil explicitly, just as he once quotes explicitly from an Italian poem by Petrarch. As for Cyrus, one of the four greatest examples, he is the Cyrus described by Xenophon. The emphatic reference to Xenophon's *Education of Cyrus* occurs immediately before the most famous chapter of the *Prince*—Chapter 15—in which Machiavelli states the program of his political philosophy, a political philosophy radically opposed to the great tradition of political philosophy. He intends, he says, to write something useful, and therefore [12] he will speak of the "factual verity of the matter" as distinguished from the imagination thereof. For many have imagined republics and principalities which were never seen or known truly to exist. The reason is that those many have taken their bearings by how one ought to live; Machiavelli will take his bearings by how men do live. The polemic is primarily directed against the philosophers—that is, Plato and Aristotle—although it is probably also directed against the kingdom of God.

At any rate Machiavelli indicates here, with a lucidity and precision that have never been surpassed, the radical opposition of his political philosophy to classical political philosophy and the ground of that opposition. Yet this challenge or provocation is immediately preceded by his approval of the teaching of one of the classical philosophers, Xenophon. Xenophon is of unique importance to Machiavelli: he mentions Xenophon in the *Prince* and the *Discourses* more frequently than he does Plato, Aristotle, and Cicero taken together. Is this an accident or is it deliberate?

To answer this question, we must first understand the peculiarity of Xenophon. Machiavelli mentions, and refers approvingly to, two writings of Xenophon, the *Education of Cyrus* and the *Hiero*. In the *Education of Cyrus* Xenophon presents a dialogue between Cyrus and his father by which Cyrus is initiated into politico-military morality. Cyrus learns from his gentlemanly father to his shock—a shock which he quickly overcomes—that the common rules of justice apply only to relations among fellow citizens, or at any rate do not apply to one's relations to foreign enemies. But as Machiavelli makes clear, the lesson taught by Xenophon in the *Education of Cyrus* is broader than the one explicitly stated by Xenophon; force and fraud, but especially fraud, are indispensable not only for defeating foreign enemies but also for overcoming resistance to establishing oneself as absolute ruler within one's own community. The *Hiero* is a dialogue between a wise man and a tyrant. The tyrant is, or pretends to be, most unhappy as a consequence of his being [13] a tyrant. The wise man shows him that he would become most happy if he were to become the benefactor of his subjects. This means, in the context, that a man who has become the ruler of his city through having committed innumerable crimes of the gravest kinds can be very happy if he uses his power thus acquired for benefiting his subjects. We regard Xenophon, then, as the classical thinker who more than any other paved the way for Machiavelli. We deny therewith that the men known as sophists played that role. Not only is Machiavelli in this respect completely silent about the sophists and in particular about the dialogue between the Athenians and the Melians in Thucydides which is frequently taken as a document of sophistic thought, but according to the judgment of a most competent man—Aristotle—what is characteristic of the sophists is not the teaching that might makes right but the identification or near-identification of the political art with rhetoric. In accordance with this, Xenophon presents a pupil of Gorgias as a general quite able to command gentlemen, men who can be swayed by speech, but wholly unable to get himself obeyed by non-gen-

CHAPTER 30

tlemen; Xenophon presents himself as capable of ruling both kinds of man: Xenophon, a pupil of Socrates, can do what the pupil of Gorgias cannot do because, being a pupil of Socrates, he does not believe in the omnipotence or quasi-omnipotence of speech but knows that men can be ruled only by a mixture of persuasion and coercion, a mixture of a certain kind of speech and of the application of brachial power. It almost goes without saying that Xenophon is not a Machiavellian *avant la lettre*: Xenophon's moral universe has two poles, the one pointed to by the great political man, say, by Cyrus, and the other pointed to by Xenophon's revered master, Socrates. But there is no place for Socrates in Machiavelli's moral universe. In order to arrive at Machiavelli's thought by starting from Xenophon, one must effect a radical break with Socratic thought, one must discover a new moral continent.

The *Discourses* combines—as does the *Prince*, but in a [14] different manner, in a different key—the imitation of antiquity, the docile listening to what the ancient writers say, with a setting forth of wholly new modes and orders, with what is in fact a complete break with classical political philosophy. That the *Discourses* is meant to prepare the rebirth of the spirit of antiquity appears from its title: *Discourses on the First Decade of Livy*. That it sets forth something wholly new appears from the prooemium: the allusion to Machiavelli's being the Columbus of the moral world occurs in that prooemium. Whereas the chapter headings of the *Prince* are all in Latin, those of the *Discourses* are all in the vulgar tongue. To begin with, one can find the reconciliation of the two disparate tendencies in Machiavelli's desire to bring to light and life the institutions and the spirit of the Roman republic: those institutions and that spirit are wholly new compared with the institutions and the spirit obtaining now. This solution of the riddle of the *Discourses* is as sound and as unsound as the view that, whereas the *Prince* deals with princely government, the *Discourses* deals with republican government. These views are sound since they are based on explicit utterances of Machiavelli; they are unsound because they do not take account of other explicit utterances of Machiavelli and, above all, of what he is doing in both works.

The *Discourses* is much more difficult to understand than the Prince. A clear sign of this is that the *Prince* has a much more lucid plan and structure than the *Discourses*. The reason seems to be that in the *Discourses* Machiavelli follows two different plans: his own plan, of which there are quite a few indications, and the plan imposed on him by the sequence of the Livian stories. Closer study shows that Machiavelli's own plan (which does not become sufficiently clear from his explicit indications) and not the Livian order controls all his uses, his selection of Livian passages. Even when he seems merely to follow the Livian order, there is a Machiavellian reason for it. It is wise to assume, at least [15] to begin with, that Machiavelli's lucid and orderly mind did not forsake him when he laid down the plan of the *Discourses*. In order to discover the reason for that plan, one must among other things watch carefully his use and non-use of Livy and the various ways in which he uses him. By his use of Livy I understand primarily his explicit use of him. That explicit use consists in explicit quotations from Livy in Latin, in implicit Latin quotations, in explicit references to Livy without quotation, and in implicit but unmistakable reference to him like "*questo testo*" or "*la istoria.*" One could, of course, say that Machiavelli sometimes uses Livian material while being completely silent about its origin or even by suppressing Livian stories. But his use of Livy in this broad sense could be established in a sufficient manner only if we could read the whole work of Livy with Machiavelli's eyes, i.e., if we possessed a degree of penetration which, if we are wise, we will not claim to possess. But everyone can see easily whether Machiavelli refers or does not refer to Livy.

In order to understand the relation of Machiavelli's plan to the Livian order, one must first grasp the difference between his intention and that of Livy. Machiavelli speaks of this difference only in a very advanced part of his argument. In II, 31 ("How dangerous it is to believe exiles") he refers to an example adduced by Livy which is foreign to Livy's purpose: it is not foreign to Machiavelli's purpose. It is foreign to Livy's purpose because it is not a Roman example. Machiavelli's purpose is not simply Roman. He wishes to incite his readers to imitate the virtue of the republican Romans. *The* historian of the Roman Republic in its incorrupt state is Livy. But Livy cannot teach us that the virtues celebrated by him can be imitated by modern man. One can say, and Machiavelli himself does say, that what was possible for man once is in principle possible for man at all times. But it would be more convincing if he could show by a large variety of examples that the ancient [16] way of doing things was wise while the modern way is foolish, or that there were some modern men who did act as the ancients acted. The mere fact that Machiavelli writes as a modern for moderns implies that his intention differs from Livy's. Moreover, the general consideration referred to proves that the imitation of the ancients is physically possible, yet it does not prove that it is morally possible: the ancients were pagans, and the virtues of the pagans could be

Chapter 30

questioned as being merely resplendent vices. Machiavelli must therefore show that the virtues of the ancients were genuine virtues, and that the virtues extolled by the detractors of the ancients are not genuine; he must face and overcome a difficulty which did not exist for Livy.

We thus understand the character of the typical chapter of the *Discourses*; it deals with a Roman and a modern example. Yet by no means are all chapters typical. There are chapters which contain only ancient examples; there are chapters which contain only modern examples; there are chapters which contain only ancient examples, none of which is Roman; there are chapters which contain only ancient and Turkish examples.

A cursory reading of the *Discourses* as a whole could suggest that Machiavelli quotes a Livian statement in almost every chapter. Yet nothing would be further from the truth. Especially surprising is his procedure in the first half of the first book. In the first eleven chapters no quotation from Livy occurs; there follow four chapters containing altogether four Livy quotations, and thereafter twenty-four chapters containing no Livy quotations. There is no parallel to this thrift in the rest of the work. By understanding his procedure in the first thirty-nine chapters, we arrive at a better understanding of the meaning of his use of Livy.

The group of chapters in which Machiavelli begins to quote Livy deals with the religion of the Romans. The first chapter containing a Livy quotation contains a passionate attack on the Roman church as responsible for the irreligion [17] of the Italians and for the political weakness of Italy. The second chapter shows how the Romans—that is, the Roman nobility—used religion prudently for keeping the plebs in fear and obedience. The last chapter shows how "Roman virtue" overcame the intransigence which Rome's enemies had acquired by "virtue of religion." Just as the writers subject to the Roman caesars could not blame Caesar as the tyrant he was but instead praised Brutus, Machiavelli, being subject to the church, could not attack Christianity but extolled the religion of the pagan Romans. He uses the authority of Livy for counteracting the authority of the Bible. Livy's history is his Bible.

In the whole *Prince* and *Discourses* there occurs a single quotation from the Bible. *Discourses* I, 26 shows that a new prince in a city or country taken by him must make everything new; he must introduce new titles and new authorities and use new men; he must make the rich poor and the poor rich, as David did when he became king; *qui esurientes implevit bonis et divites dimisit inanes*, as Machiavelli quotes from the *Magnificat*. These manners of proceeding, he adds, are most cruel and inimical not only to every

Christian way of life but even to every humane one as well. The full weight of this statement is felt only by those who remember what Machiavelli says at the end of the preceding chapter; he says there that the next chapter deals with what the authors call tyranny. The term tyrant is strictly avoided in the twenty-sixth chapter, just as it is in the whole *Prince*, which happens to consist of twenty-six chapters. King David was then a tyrant. Being a tyrant, he acted as God acts according to the *Magnificat*. It is repugnant to me to spell out fully the blasphemy which Machiavelli forces his reader to think.

I have spoken of the *authority* of Livy. I use this expression here in the fullest sense: Livy's history is meant to take the place of the Bible. But the authority of Livy depends on, it presupposes, the authoritative character of ancient *Rome*. Only by establishing the authority of ancient Rome [18] can Machiavelli establish the authority of Livy. From here we understand his procedure in the first six chapters of the *Discourses*. In the first chapter, which deals with the beginnings of cities in general and of Rome in particular, he bestows high praise on ancient Egypt, a political society which flourished "in the most ancient antiquity." That praise is altogether provisional; Machiavelli retracts it tacitly but unmistakably at the beginning of the second book. That is to say, at the beginning of the first book he acts on the principle according to which the old is good and hence the oldest is best: there is no need for any further proof of the bestness of the oldest except to show that it is in fact the oldest. But this implies that the goodness of ancient Rome, which does not belong to the most ancient antiquity, is in need of proof. That proof is given in the next five chapters. The second chapter deals with the various kinds of republics and in particular with the polity of Rome. Machiavelli raises the question of whether a simple or a mixed polity is to be preferred. The mixed regime is preferred by those who in the opinion of many are wiser than the believers in simple regimes: Machiavelli follows not simply the wiser man but those who *in the opinion of many* are the wiser men; he follows authority. The argument which he presents is in fact the one given by Polybius, but Machiavelli does not mention Polybius. Following Polybius, he speaks of the mixed regimes of Sparta and of Rome. Sparta received her polity at her beginning from a single man, Lycurgus; the Roman polity emerged accidentally as a consequence of the discord between the plebs and the Senate. This seems to show that the Spartan policy was superior to the Roman. That this is the case is indeed "the opinion of many." But, Machiavelli now dares to say, those many judge inconsiderately: the grave

Chapter 30

disorders in early Rome were the first cause of Roman liberty. Furthermore, Rome is distinguished from Sparta in that in Rome the guardianship of liberty was in the hands of the plebs while in Sparta it was in the hands [19] of the nobility; the Spartan arrangement seems to be preferable, for in Sparta liberty lasted much longer than in Rome. A case can be made for both preferences. Machiavelli overcomes this embarrassment by making a distinction: the Spartan arrangement is best for a non-expansionist republic while the Roman is best for a republic which tends to become a great empire. Yet all human things are in motion and therefore the stability aimed at by Sparta is not in agreement with the nature of things and can be achieved only by lucky accident. In this way Machiavelli establishes the authority of Rome by demonstration; but in setting forth his decision he says four times *credo*. Has he then demonstrated the superiority of Rome to Sparta? Or has he merely shown that before the tribunal of unassisted reason the case for Rome is as strong as the case for Sparta, so that one is free to believe in the superiority of Rome? The fact that this discussion ends with a fourfold *credo* would seem to show that Machiavelli does not accept the superiority of Rome simply on rational grounds; in accepting the superiority of Rome he bows to authority.

In establishing the authority of Rome, Machiavelli criticizes certain critics of Rome but does not openly criticize any ancient writers in his own name. In the next section—the section which immediately precedes the section on religion, the section containing the first Livy quotations—he takes issue with the opinion "perhaps" held by "many" according to which Romulus is to be blamed for having murdered his brother Remus, that is, for having acted like Cain. He refutes that opinion by having recourse, not to any authority but to "a general rule," without however saying whether that general rule is generally accepted. When in an earlier chapter he had attacked the opinion of "many" which condemned Rome for the discord between the plebs and the Senate, he had eventually referred to the authority of Cicero. But now, when the deed to be excused is no longer the shouting in the streets and the closing of shops, as [20] it was in the earlier chapter, but murder, the murder of one's only brother, he does not betray any need for support by authority. Yet one could say that it is the authority of the divine founder of Rome which enables him to oppose to the false rule which unconditionally forbids murder the true rule which sanctions murder under certain circumstances.

A few words must be said about the second cluster of Livy quotations. Six such quotations occur in the chapter which opens the discussion of

Decemvirate. In that discussion Machiavelli treats with complete neutrality the policies required for saving liberty and those required for establishing tyranny. In order to show how a potential tyrant can be successful, he studies the actions of Appius Claudius (according to him the founder of all public and private law in Rome), who failed in his attempt to establish tyranny and whose laws retained their force despite his ruin and violent death. This neutrality, which appears elsewhere in the *Discourses* as the height of political immorality and therefore as the height of immorality simply, is a heresy comparable in enormity to the neutrality between paganism and biblical religion, a neutrality revealed in connection with the first cluster of Livy quotations. Machiavelli could not have indicated more clearly than in this manner that Livy quotations as strands of his web are ominous rather than humanistic.

Machiavelli was compelled to establish the authority of Rome because the superiority of the Roman modes and orders to all others—for example, the Spartans—is not obvious or universally admitted. In that context he had to speak of certain alleged defects of Rome which he did not deny but which were in his view vindicated by the fact that they are the price one has to pay for the best modes and orders. The status of Rome is still more enhanced by the discourses which occur in the rest of the first half of the first book. Thereafter a fundamental change makes itself felt. Rather abruptly, if circumspectly, Machiavelli begins to criticize [21] the Roman Republic even as it was in its most incorrupt period, and he goes on to do so though returning again and again to the praise of Rome. While defending the Roman institutions of dictatorship by means of "most evident reasons" against the opinion of "some writer" who had not "considered the matter well" and whose verdict "has been quite unreasonably believed," Machiavelli makes it clear that the Roman institution was not superior to a different Venetian institution which answered the same purpose equally well: the modes and orders of ancient Rome are not simply the model for the moderns. Thereafter he speaks explicitly, if with considerable euphemism, of "the defect" of the Roman agrarian law. That defect was caused in the last analysis by what, without the use of euphemism, would have to be called the avarice of the Roman nobility. It was owing to that avarice that Rome, in contrast to Sparta, did not comply with the basic rule that the public should be kept rich and all citizens be kept poor. In the context of this criticism Machiavelli refers to Livy by name for the first time since the end of the section on religion; Livy proves to be not only the celebrator of Rome but also her critic. Livy is

Chapter 30

no longer needed only for transmitting to modern man the counter-authority which enables Machiavelli to attack the established authority; from this point forward he is also needed to discredit that counter-authority. In other words, the authority is henceforth no longer the practice and policy of ancient Rome but Livy, a book; only from here on is Livy Machiavelli's Bible or his counterpart of the Bible. In the thirty-ninth chapter Machiavelli draws the decisive conclusion from his criticism of the Romans: diligent examination of things past enables one not only to foresee what will happen in every future republic if the necessary remedies used by the ancients are not applied in time but also to discover the proper remedies in case the ancients did not use or know them. Since the Roman modes and orders have been shown to be defective in more [22] than one respect, we must conclude that, according to Machiavelli, a progress beyond the ancient modes and orders is necessary or that modes and orders which are wholly new must be sought. The fundamental reason why this is necessary is this: the ancient Roman polity was the work of chance, if of chance often wisely used; the ancient Romans discovered their modes and orders in response to accidents as they arose, and they clung to them out of reverence for the ancestral. Machiavelli, however, is the first to achieve the anatomy of the Roman republic and thus to understand thoroughly the virtues and the vices of that republic. Therefore he can teach his readers how a polity similar to the Roman and better than the Roman can be deliberately constructed. What hitherto has been a lucky accident, and therefore essentially defective, can become from now on, on the new continent discovered by Machiavelli, the goal of rational desire and action. It is for this reason that the modes and orders recommended by him, even those which he took over bodily from ancient Rome, are rightly described by him as new modes and orders.

At the beginning of the second book a new dimension of the problem comes to sight. After having defended Rome against a certain opinion held by "many" and in particular by Plutarch, "a most grave writer," Machiavelli shows that it was in the last analysis the Roman Republic which destroyed freedom for many centuries in the West. Immediately thereafter he suggests a revision of his earlier verdict on the relative merits of Rome and Sparta. Rome was enabled to destroy freedom in the West—the East never knew freedom—and to make herself mistress of the world because she liberally admitted foreigners to citizenship; Sparta, though a very well-armed republic with very good laws and less tumultuous than Rome, did not achieve Roman greatness because she was fearful lest admixture of new inhabitants corrupt her ancient customs. The Roman Republic, the greatest republic or the most political community that ever [23] was, prepared the Western world for Eastern submissiveness and for the suppression of the supremacy of political or public life. The Roman Republic is on the one hand the direct opposite of the Christian Republic and on the other hand a cause of the latter and even the model for it. This is the ultimate reason why Machiavelli's judgment on Rome is ambiguous.

Machiavelli's questioning of the authority of Rome precedes and prepares his questioning of the authority of Livy. The first explicit attack on Livy occurs in the fifty-eighth chapter—that is, about twenty chapters after he had begun explicitly to criticize ancient Rome. But already in the forty-ninth chapter he grants that Livy's history may be defective in a certain point. In the same chapter, when speaking of Florence, he indicates that "true memory" of Florentine affairs is not available beyond a certain date. Could the possible defect of Livy's history be due to the fact that he did not have "true memory" of the event which he records in the passage referred to by Machiavelli? Certain it is that Livy himself speaks in that passage of the uncertainty regarding events which are remote in time. Earlier, Machiavelli had spoken of the things "which are read in the memories of ancient histories"; Livy's history, and certainly its first ten books, consist of such memories of ancient histories. But Machiavelli questions not only the simple reliability of Livian histories; he also questions Livy's selection of facts and his emphases. When he retells the story of the Decemvirate, he barely refers to the Virginia incident, which is told at such length by Livy, to say nothing of the fact that he does not mention that heinous crime when speaking of Appius Claudius' mistakes. On another occasion, when he quotes Livy's statements that the plebians had become "obedient," he makes him speak of the plebians having become "vile and weak." Machiavelli has been accused by a modern critic of completely distorting the meaning of Livy's stories and falsifying their spirit. This criticism [24] is fully justified if it is meant to imply that Machiavelli did this with full clarity about what he was doing. He consciously uses Livy for his non-Livian purposes. He deliberately transforms the Roman ruling class as it was into a ruling class as, according to him, it should have been; he makes the Roman ruling class "better" than it was; he transforms a group whose best members were men of outstanding virtue and piety into a group whose best members, being perfectly free of vulgar prejudices, were guided exclusively by Machiavellian prudence that served the insatiable desire of each for eternal glory in this world.

CHAPTER 30

Machiavelli uses Livy's work first as his counter-authority or counter-Bible; he tacitly replaces the doctrine of the Bible by the doctrine conveyed through Livy's history. Thereafter he explicitly questions the authority of Livy and thus draws our attention to what he had done tacitly in regard to the Bible. With some exaggeration one may say that he uses Livy as a *corpus vile* by means of which he can indicate how he had tacitly proceeded in regard to the *corpus nobilissimum*. This twofold use of Livy is related to the twofold character of pagan Rome which was both the enemy of the Christian church and the model for it.

Finally, Machiavelli questions authority as such or all authority. In the chapter preceding the section on religion he had said in praise of the Roman emperors from Nerva to Marcus Aurelius that the times when they ruled were the golden times when everyone could hold and defend whichever opinion he wished. Nine chapters later he says, quite casually as it might seem, that "it is good to reason about everything" whereas in the *Prince* he says that "one ought not to reason about Moses since he was a mere executor of the things which God commanded him," and that one ought not to reason about ecclesiastical principalities "for, since they are exalted and maintained by God, it would be the work of a presumptuous and temerarious man to discuss them." In this first chapter in which he takes issue with Livy (I, 58) he takes in fact issue with "all [25] writers." He says there: "I do not judge nor shall I ever judge it to be a defect to defend any opinion with reasons, provided one does not even wish to use in such defense either authority or force." He could not have stated more clearly and more gently the principle that only reason, as distinguished from authority, can command his assent. To reject authority on principle means to reject the equation of the good with the ancestral and hence of the best with the oldest; it means to derogate from the reverence for old men, the men most akin to the olden times. The first book of the *Discourses*, which almost opens with a praise of the most ancient antiquity, literally ends with a praise of the many Romans "who triumphed in their earliest youth." Machiavelli addresses his passionate and muted call to the young—to men whose prudence has not enfeebled their youthful vigor of mind, impetuosity, and audacity. Reason and youth and modernity rise up against authority, old age, and antiquity. In studying the *Discourses* we become the witnesses, and we cannot help becoming the moved witnesses, of the birth of the greatest of all youth movements: modern philosophy—a phenomenon which we know through seeing, as distinguished from reading, only in its decay, its state of deprivation, and its dotage.

Machiavelli and Classical Literature

It would be tedious if I were to read you the list of the twenty-one authors other than Livy to which Machiavelli refers in the *Discourses*. The author other than Livy to whom he refers most often is Xenophon. Next in order of frequency come Virgil, Tacitus, and Sallustius. Tacitus is the only writer an opinion of whom Machiavelli tries to "save" after having shown that it is not evidently correct. He alone receives such reverential treatment at Machiavelli's hands. We must leave it open whether this fact can be taken to mean that Machiavelli was the originator of the *Tacitismo* which in the sixteenth and seventeenth centuries played such a great role and can only with difficulty be distinguished from the Machiavellianism of the epoch.

31

A Giving of Accounts: Jacob Klein and Leo Strauss (1970)

[1a] The following giving of accounts took place at St. John's College, Annapolis, on January 30, 1970. Mr. Klein and Mr. Strauss were introduced by Dean Robert A. Goldwin:

> Mr. Klein and Mr. Strauss are going to present us tonight with two "accounts."
>
> The origin of this event is, I think, quite simple. Many of us have known them both, as our teachers, for many, many years. In a sense we can say that we know much about their teachings.
>
> But, in fact, most of us know very little of the genesis of their thought. And it occurred to us that it would be, very simply, enlightening, to hear from them their own accounts of the origin and development of their thoughts in those matters of greatest interest to us, their students....
>
> It is arranged that Mr. Klein will speak and then Mr. Strauss will speak. Then we will have questions, in our accustomed style.

Mr. Klein

This meeting has two reasons, one is accidental, the other is important. The first is the fact (and any fact is some kind of accident) that Mr. Strauss and I happen to have known each other closely, and have been friends for 50 years, and happen both to be now in Annapolis at St. John's College. The other reason, the important one, is that Mr. Strauss is not too well known in this community and that we as a real community of learners should begin to understand better why he is now a member of this com-

---

Originally published as "A Giving of Accounts" with Jacob Klein, *The College* (Annapolis, MD, and Santa Fe, NM) 22, no. 1 (Apr., 1970): 1–5. —Eds.

CHAPTER 31

munity. We thought it might be not too bad an idea, although a somewhat embarrassing one, to tell you what we have learned in our lives, what preoccupied us and what still preoccupies us. Dead Week might perhaps indeed provide the right opportunity, the *kairos*, to do that. I shall begin.

Up to my twenty-fifth year I had one great difficulty. I was a student, and so was Mr. Strauss—we studied at the same university—, and I studied all kinds of things, something called philosophy, and mathematics, and physics, and I did that quite superficially. But what preoccupied me mostly during those years was this: whatever [1b] thought I might have, and whatever interest I might have in anything, seemed to me to be located completely within me, so that I always felt that I could not really understand anything outside me, could not understand anything uttered or written by another person. I felt that I was in a kind of vicious circle, out of which I could find no escape. I wrote a dissertation, which is not worth the paper on which it was written, obtained my Ph.D. degree, and then after a short while, returned to studies.

Now, while Mr. Strauss and I were studying we had many, I should say, endless conversations about many things. His primary interests were two questions: one, the question of God; and two, the question of politics. These questions were not mine. I studied, as I said, quite superficially, Hegel, mathematics, and physics. When I resumed my studying, a certain man happened to be at the University in the little town in which I was living. This man was Martin Heidegger. Many of you have heard his name, and some of you might have read some of his works in impossible English translations. I will not talk too much about Martin Heidegger, except that I would like to say that he is the very great thinker of our time, although his moral qualities do not match his intellectual ones. When I heard him lecture, I was struck by one thing: that he was the first man who made me understand something written by another man; namely Aristotle. It broke my vicious circle. I felt that I could understand. Then I began studying seriously, for myself, seriously, not superficially.

It became clear to me that one had to distinguish the classical mode of thinking from the modern mode of thinking. Our world and our understanding, as it is today, is based on a certain change that occurred about 500 years ago, and this change pervades not only our thinking but the whole world around us. It made possible one of the greatest achievements of man, mathematical physics, and all the auxiliary disciplines connected with it. It made possible, what we call with a strange Latin word, science. This science is derived from the classical mode of thinking, but

A Giving of Accounts

this derivation is also a dilution which blinds our sight. My studies led me to conclude: we have to relearn what the ancients knew; we should still be able to persist in scientific investigations, where real progress is [2a] possible, although the science with which we are familiar is also capable of regress and of bringing about a fundamental forgetfulness of most important things. As a consequence of these studies and of this understanding, a question arose: How should people be educated?

At that time a certain political upheaval made it necessary for me to come to these United States, and to land on the St. John's campus. This great question, how to educate people, became suddenly a "practical" question. I found here a man, an extraordinary man, whose name you all know, Scott Buchanan. He was also struggling with this question, as he had been struggling all his life. Since then, as the Dean told you, I have stayed here on this campus.

Mr. Strauss, meanwhile, worked on his own, tenaciously, indefatigably, and in an exemplary way. His erudition, his zeal, his tenacity brought fruit—resplendent fruit. As so many others, I learned from him. There are indeed, I think, differences between us, although it is not quite clear to me in what they consist. And I do think that at this point it is not too important to find out what they are. Mr. Strauss might allude to them.

Mr. Strauss

I must begin with an introduction to my introduction. Some faculty members, I was told, had misgivings about this meeting. The only ones which are justified concern this question: Is it proper for people to talk about themselves in public? The general answer is: no. But there are exceptions. First, what is true of men in general is not equally true of old men. Second, and above all, people may talk about their thoughts concerning matters of public concern, and virtue is a matter of public concern. Those thoughts, it is true, are connected with our lives and I for one will have to say something about my life. But this is of interest even to me only as a starting point of considerations, of studies, which I hope are intelligible to those who do not know my starting point. Why then speak of one's life at all? Because the considerations at which I arrived are not necessarily true or correct; my life may explain my pitfalls.

The subject is the relations between Klein and me, i.e., our agreements and our differences. In my opinion we are closer to one another than to anyone else in our generation. Yet there are differences. I wish to learn

CHAPTER 31

from Klein how he sees these differences. It is possible that our disagreements have something to do with the differences of our temperaments or humors. It is more helpful and worthy, however, if I tell the tellable story of my life with special regard to how Klein affected it. I must warn you: I may commit errors of memory. Apart from this I shall not always keep to the chronological order.

I was brought up in a conservative, even orthodox Jewish home somewhere in a rural district of Germany. The "ceremonial" laws were rather strictly observed but [2b] there was very little Jewish knowledge. In the Gymnasium I became exposed to the message of German humanism. Furtively I read Schopenhauer and Nietzsche. When I was 16 and we read the *Laches* in school, I formed the plan, or the wish, to spend my life reading Plato and breeding rabbits while earning my livelihood as a rural postmaster. Without being aware of it, I had moved rather far away from my Jewish home, without any rebellion. When I was 17, I was converted to Zionism—to simple, straightforward political Zionism.

When I went to the University I tended towards the study of philosophy. For reasons of local proximity I went to the University of Marburg which had been the seat and center of the neo-Kantian school of Marburg, founded by Hermann Cohen. Cohen attracted me because he was a passionate philosopher and a Jew passionately devoted to Judaism. Cohen was at that time no longer alive and his school was in a state of disintegration. The disintegration was chiefly due to the emergence and ever increasing power of phenomenology—an approach opened up by Husserl. Husserl told me a few years later, the Marburg school begins with the roof while he begins with the foundation. But also: Cohen belonged definitely to the pre-war world. This is true also of Husserl. Most characteristic of the post-war world was the resurgence of theology: Karl Barth. (The Preface to the first edition of his commentary on the *Epistle to the Romans* is of great importance also to non-theologians: it sets forth the principles of an interpretation that is concerned exclusively with the subject matter as distinguished from historical interpretation.) Wholly independently of Barth Jewish theology was resurrected from a deep slumber by Franz Rosenzweig, a highly gifted man whom I greatly admired to the extent to which I understood him.

It was in Marburg in 1920 that I met Klein for the first time. He stood out among the philosophy students not only by his intelligence but also by his whole appearance: he was wholly non-provincial in a wholly provincial environment. I was deeply impressed by him and attracted to him. I do not know whether I acted merely in obedience to my duty or whether this was only a pretense: I approached him in order to win him over to Zionism. I failed utterly. Nevertheless, from that time on we remained in contact up to the present day.

Academic freedom meant in Germany that one could change one's university every semester and that there were no attendance requirements nor examinations in lecture courses. After having received my Ph.D. degree (a disgraceful performance) in Hamburg I went to the University of Freiburg in 1922 in order to see and hear Husserl. I did not derive great benefit from Husserl; I was probably not mature enough. My predominant interest was in theology: when I once asked Husserl about the subject, he replied, "If there is a datum 'God' we shall describe it." In his seminar on Lotze's *Logic* I read a paper in the first sentence of which the expression "sense per-[3a]ception" occurred. Husserl stopped me immediately, developed his analysis of sense perception and this took up the rest of the meeting: at the end Husserl graciously apologized. I attended regularly the lecture courses on the Social Doctrines of the Reformation and the Enlightenment by Ebbinghaus: I still remember gratefully Ebbinghaus's lively presentation of Hobbes's doctrine; Ebbinghaus shared with Hobbes a certain boyish quality. One of the unknown young men in Husserl's entourage was Heidegger. I attended his lecture course from time to time without understanding a word, but sensed that he dealt with something of the utmost importance to man as man. I understood something on one occasion: when he interpreted the beginning of the *Metaphysics*. I had never heard nor seen such a thing—such a thorough and intensive interpretation of a philosophic text. On my way home I visited Rosenzweig and said to him that compared to Heidegger, Max Weber, till then regarded by me as the incarnation of the spirit of science and scholarship, was an orphan child.

I disregard again the chronological order and explain in the most simple terms why in my opinion Heidegger won out over Husserl; he radicalized Husserl's critique of the school of Marburg and turned it against Husserl: what is primary is not the object of sense perception but the things which we handle and with which we are concerned, *pragmata*. What I could not stomach was his moral teaching, for despite his disclaimer, he had such a teaching. The key term is resoluteness without any indication as to what are the proper objects of resoluteness. There is a straight line which leads from Heidegger's resoluteness to his siding with the so-called Nazis in 1933. After that I ceased to take any interest in him for about two decades.

To return to 1922, the resurgence of theology, of what sometimes was even called orthodoxy, was in fact a profound innovation. This innovation

CHAPTER 31

had become necessary because the attack of the Enlightenment on the old orthodoxy had not been in every respect a failure. I wished to understand to what extent it was a failure and to what extent it was not. The classical statement on this subject in Hegel's *Phenomenology of the Mind* had become questionable because Hegel's whole position had been called into question by the new theology. One had to descend to a level which is, in the good and the bad sense, less sophisticated than Hegel's. The classic document of the attack on orthodoxy within Judaism, but not only within Judaism, is Spinoza's *Theological Political Treatise*.* Spinoza's *Treatise* had been subjected to a fierce criticism by Cohen—a criticism which was impressive because Cohen was entirely free from the idolatry of Spinoza as the God-intoxicated thinker but it was nevertheless inadequate. In order to form an independent judgment I began, therefore, a fresh study of the *Theological Political Treatise*. In this study I was greatly assisted by Lessing, especially his theological writings, some of them with [3b] forbidding titles. Incidentally, Lessing is also the author of the only improvised live dialogue on a philosophic subject known to me.† Lessing was always at my elbow. This meant that I learned more from him than I knew at that time. As I came to see later Lessing had said everything I had found out about the distinction between exoteric and esoteric speech and its grounds.

In 1925 Heidegger came to Marburg. Klein attended his classes regularly, and he was, naturally, deeply impressed by him. But he did not become a Heideggerian. Heidegger's work required and included what he called *Destruktion* of the tradition. (*Destruktion* is not quite so bad as destruction. It means taking down, the opposite of construction.) He intended to uproot Greek philosophy, especially Aristotle, but this presupposed the laying bare of its roots, the laying bare of it as it was in itself and not as it had come to appear in the light of the tradition and of modern philosophy. Klein was more attracted by the Aristotle brought to light and life by Heidegger than by Heidegger's own philosophy. Later Klein turned to the study of Plato in which he got hardly any help from Heidegger. Klein convinced me of two things. First, the one thing needed philosophically is in the first place a return to, a recovery of, classical philosophy; second, the way in which Plato is read, especially by professors of philosophy and by men who do philoso-

---

* *Theologico-Political Treatise.* —Eds.

† By "improvised live dialogue," Strauss means F. H. Jacobi's recounting of his conversations with Lessing in 1780. —Eds.

phy, is wholly inadequate because it does not take into account the dramatic character of the dialogues, also and especially of those of their parts which look almost like philosophic treatises. The classical scholar Friedländer had seen this to some extent, but Friedländer had no inkling of what Plato meant by philosophy. Klein and I differ somewhat in our ways of reading Plato but I have never been able to find out precisely what that difference is. Perhaps the following remarks are helpful.

The first offshoot of Klein's Platonic studies is his work on Greek logistics and the genesis of modern algebra—a work which I regard as unrivalled in the whole field of intellectual history, at least in our generation.

While Klein was engaged in this work, I continued my study of *Spinoza's Treatise* from which I had been led to Hobbes, on the one hand, and to Maimonides on the other. Maimonides was, to begin with, wholly unintelligible to me. I got the first glimmer of light when I concentrated on his prophetology and, therefore, the prophetology of the Islamic philosophers who preceded him.* One day when reading in a Latin translation Avicenna's treatise, *On the Division of the Sciences*, I came across this sentence (I quote from memory): the standard work on prophecy and revelation is Plato's *Laws*. Then I began to begin to understand Maimonides's prophetology and eventually, as I believe, the whole *Guide of the Perplexed*. Maimonides never calls himself a philosopher; he presents himself as an opponent of the philosophers. He used a kind of writing which is in the precise sense of the term, exoteric. When Klein had read [4a] the manuscript of my essay on the literary character of the *Guide of the Perplexed*, he said, "We have rediscovered exotericism." To this extent we completely agreed. But there was from the beginning this difference between us: that I attached much greater importance than Klein did and does to the tension between philosophy and the city, even the best city.

I arrived at a conclusion that I can state in the form of a syllogism: Philosophy is the attempt to replace opinion by knowledge; but opinion is the element of the city, hence philosophy is subversive, hence the philosopher must write in such a way that he will improve rather than subvert the city. In other words the virtue of the philosopher's thought is a certain kind of mania while the virtue of the philosopher's public speech is *sōphrosynē*. Philosophy is as such trans-political, trans-religious, and trans-moral but the city is and ought to be moral and religious. In the words of Thomas Aquinas only reason informed by faith knows that God must be wor-

---

* Original reads "preceeded." —Eds.

shipped, and the intellectual virtues with the exception of prudence do not presuppose moral virtue. To illustrate this point, moral man, merely moral man, the *kaloskagathos* in the common meaning of the term, is not simply closer to the philosopher than a man of the dubious morality of Alcibiades.

This view of philosophy was derived from my study of pre-modern philosophy. It implies that modern philosophy has a radically different character. In modern times the gulf between philosophy and the city was bridged, or believed to have been bridged by two innovations: 1) the ends of the philosopher and the non-philosopher are identical, because philosophy is in the service of the relief of man's estate or "science for the sake of power"; 2) philosophy can fulfill its salutary function only if its results are diffused among the non-philosophers, if popular enlightenment is possible. The high point was reached in Kant's teaching on the primacy of practical, i.e., moral reason; a teaching prepared to some extent by Rousseau: the one thing needful is a good will and of a good will all men are equally capable. If we call moralism the view that morality or moral virtue is the highest, I am doubtful if it occurs in antiquity at all.

I was confirmed in my concentration on the tension between philosophy and the *polis*, i.e., on the highest theme of political philosophy by this consideration. What distinguishes present day philosophy in its highest form, in its Heideggerian form, from classical philosophy is its historical character; it presupposes the so-called historical consciousness. It is therefore necessary to understand the partly hidden roots of that consciousness. Up to the present day when we call a man a historian without qualification (like economic historian, cultural historian, etc.) we mean a political historian. Politics and political philosophy is the matrix of the historical consciousness.

[4b] *Selection from the question period*

Question: Concerning the difference between Mr. Klein and Mr. Strauss.
Mr. Klein: I do suppose that his emphasis on the political aspect of our lives, which can never be disregarded, of course, is something I do not quite agree with. On the other hand, we do agree that if there is philosophizing, it is a completely immoderate undertaking, that cannot find, ultimately, its goal, although one has to persist in it. Now where the difference here is, is really not quite clear.
Mr. Strauss: . . . I believe that there is another way of stating the difference. Mr. Klein and I differ regarding the status of morality.

Mr. Klein: (Laughter) I am not entirely certain of that. That's all I can say. Well, I will add something to that. And that is again a question of a difference of emphasis. I think I wouldn't emphasize it so much, the morality of man, but I do think that man ought to be moral.

Mr. Strauss: Yes—sure. I did not mean that when I spoke of our difference. I think that in your scheme of things morality has a higher place than in my scheme.

Mr. Klein: I really don't think so. Why do you say that?

Mr. Strauss: Because we have frequently had quite a few conversations ... now and then, and one general formula which suggested itself to me was that you attach a higher importance to morality, as morality, than I do. Now, let me explain this. That the philosophic life, especially as Plato and Aristotle understood it, is not possible without self-control and a few other virtues almost goes without saying. If a man is habitually drunk, and so on, how can he think? But the question is, if these virtues are understood only as subservient to philosophy and for its sake, then that is no longer a moral understanding of the virtues.

Mr. Klein: That may be. (Tape break)

Mr. Strauss: ... a statement by a modern extremist, but who had a marvelous sense for Greek thought, Nietzsche—in his *Genealogy of Morals*, third treatise, "What is the Significance of Ascetic Ideals," he explains, why is a philosopher ascetic? And he makes this clear, that he is ascetic. And, he says, that is not different from the asceticism of a jockey, who in order to win a race must live very restrainedly, but that is wholly unimportant to the jockey, what is important is to win the race. If one may compare low to high things, one may say similarly of the philosopher, what counts is thinking and investigating and not morality. Of course the word morality is a "bad word" because it has so many connotations which are wholly alien to the ancients, but, I think for provisional purposes, we can accept it.

Mr. Klein: If there's something that I learned from Plato, or that I think that I learned from Plato, is to [5a] understand that nothing can be—nothing can be—that isn't in some way—and that's very difficult—good. That's why I do understand why Mr. Strauss says that the philosopher is in a certain way superior to the concern about morality, but I can not agree that the ultimate consideration of things, as far as one is capable of doing that, ever, ever, frees men of the compulsion to act rightly.

Mr. Strauss: Yes, I think that you believe that. Yes, that is what I meant.

Chapter 31

Questioner: Of what use is the city to the philosopher?
Mr. Strauss: Without cities, no philosophers. They are the conditions.
Mr. Klein: You wouldn't deny that, would you?
Questioner: But it seems to me that the city provides for the needs of the body.
Mr. Strauss: Yes, sure.
Questioner: But does it provide for the needs of the soul?
Mr. Strauss: To some extent, sure.
Questioner: Is it necessary for its existence?
Mr. Strauss: To some extent, obviously. In one way or another, even if there is no compulsory education, the city educates its citizens.
Questioner: Wouldn't the philosopher get his education from nature?
Mr. Strauss: His first education, surely not. His first [5b] education he would usually get from his father and mother, and other relatives, that is to say, from the city.

Questioner: How does it follow from the saying that everything that is, is somehow or other good, that a man should act rightly?
Mr. Klein: I would answer that very simply: He must try to be what he is. And, by the way, to be a man, a human being, is not a simple matter. The trouble with us human beings is that we are not quite complete, neither when we are born nor when we die.

32

Political Philosophy and the Crisis of Our Time (1972)

[I am naturally moved by the kind remarks made about me, but I would only like to make one brief comment. I am not as gentle as my friends would like to present me; surely my enemies would agree with me on that point. To come nearer to my subject, the two lectures which I am supposed to give tonight and tomorrow are, in fact, a single lecture, the theme of which is the crisis of our time and the crisis of political philosophy. It would have been possible to draw the line between the two lectures at very different points, and perhaps I have not drawn it in the best way. So, I ask you for your forgiveness if this lecture is fragmentary; it is meant to be incomplete. The subject is more precisely, "the crisis of our time as a consequence of the crisis of political philosophy."]

[217] The crisis of our time [,which is the point I want to develop,] has its core in the doubt of what we can call "the modern project." That modern project was successful to a considerable extent. It has created a new kind of society, a kind of society that never was before. But the inadequacy of the modern project, which has now become a matter of general knowledge and of general concern, compels us to entertain the thought that this new kind of society, our kind of society, must be animated by a spirit other than that which has animated it from the beginning. Now this modern project was originated by modern political philosophy, by the kind of political philosophy which emerged in the sixteenth and seventeenth cen-

---

Originally published in *The Post-Behavioral Era: Perspectives on Political Science*, ed. George J. Graham, Jr., and George W. Carey (New York: David McKay, 1972), 217–42; and previously as "The Crisis of Our Time" and "The Crisis of Political Philosophy" in *The Predicament of Modern Politics*, ed. Harold J. Spaeth (Detroit: University of Detroit Press, 1964), 41–54, 91–103. N.B.: Passages in square brackets are found only in the 1964 version.—Eds.

CHAPTER 32

turies. The end result of modern political philosophy is the disintegration of the very idea of political philosophy. For most political scientists today, political philosophy is not more than ideology or myth.

We have to think of the restoration of political philosophy. We have to go back to the point where the destruction of political philosophy began, to the beginnings of modern political philosophy, when modern philosophy still had to fight against the older kind of political philosophy, classical political philosophy, the political philosophy originated by Socrates and elaborated above all by Aristotle. At that time, the quarrel of the ancients and the moderns took [218] place, which is generally known only as a purely literary quarrel in France and in England, the most famous document in England being Swift's *Battle of the Books*. It was, in fact, not merely a literary quarrel. It was fundamentally a quarrel between modern philosophy, or science, and the older philosophy, or science. The quarrel was completed only with the work of Newton, which seemed to settle the issue entirely in favor of the moderns. Our task is to reawaken that quarrel, now that the modern answer has been given the opportunity to reveal its virtues and to do its worst to the old answer for more than three centuries. [In order to carry conviction, I must remain as close as possible to what is today generally accepted in the West. I cannot start from premises which today are agreed upon only by a fairly small minority. In other words, I have to argue to a considerable extent *ad hominem*. I hope this will not create a misunderstanding.]

[To avoid another kind of misunderstanding, I shall first give a sketch of tonight's lecture. The crisis of the West has been called the decline of the West, in the sense of the final decline of men. This view is not tenable, but one cannot deny that a decline, that some decline, of the West has taken place. The West has declined in power most obviously; its very survival is now threatened. This decline, however, does not constitute the crisis of the West. The crisis of the West consists in the fact that the West has become uncertain of its purpose. This purpose was the universal society, a society consisting of equal nations, each consisting of free and equal men and women, with all these nations to be fully developed as regards their power of production, thanks to science. Science to be understood as essentially in the service of human power, for the relief of man's estate. Science would bring about universal affluence. A state in which no one would have any longer any motive for encroaching on other men or on other nations. Universal affluence would lead to the universal and perfectly just society, as a perfectly happy society.]

[Many Western men have become doubtful of this project by the self-revelation of Communism as immensely powerful and as radically antagonistic to the Western notion of how this universal and just society should be established and managed. The antagonism between the West and Communism leads to the consequence that no possibility of a universal society exists in the foreseeable future. Political society remains for the foreseeable future what it always has been, particular society, society with frontiers, a closed society, concerned with self-improvement. This experience which we have had requires, however, not only a political reorientation, but also a reorientation of our thoughts regarding principles.]

[I mention here three points. First, is this particularism, or differently stated, this patriotism, not in itself better than universalism or globalism? Second, is it reasonable to expect justice and happiness as a necessary consequence of affluence? Is affluence even a necessary, although not a sufficient, condition of virtue and happiness? Is there not some truth in the notion of voluntary poverty? Is even involuntary poverty an insurmountable obstacle to virtue and happiness? And third, is the belief that science is essentially in the service of human power not a delusion, and even a degrading delusion? Now, let me begin.]

I

The assertion that we are in the grip of a crisis is hardly in need of proof. Every day's newspapers tell us of another crisis, and all these little daily crises can easily be seen to be parts, or ingredients, of the one great crisis, the crisis of our time. The core of that crisis, I submit, consists in the fact that what was originally a political philosophy has turned into an ideology. That crisis was diagnosed at the end of World War I by Spengler as a going down or decline of the West. Spengler understood by the West one culture among a small number of high cultures. But the West was for him more than one high culture among a number of them. It was for him the comprehensive culture, the only culture which had conquered the earth. Above all, it was the only culture which was open to all cultures, which did not reject the other cultures as forms of barbarism, or tolerate them condescendingly as underdeveloped. It is the only culture which has acquired full consciousness of culture as such. Whereas culture originally meant the culture of the human mind, the derivative and modern notion of culture necessarily implies that there is a variety of equally high cultures. But, precisely since the West is the culture in which culture reaches full self-consciousness, it is the final culture; the owl of Minerva begins its flight in the dusk. The decline of the West is identical with the exhaustion of the very possibility of high culture. The highest possibilities of man are exhausted. But men's highest possibilities cannot be exhausted as long as there are still high human tasks, as long as the fundamental riddles which confront man have not been solved to the extent to which they can be solved. We may, therefore, say—appealing to the [219] authority of science in our age—that Spengler's analysis and prediction is wrong. Our highest authority, natural science, considers itself susceptible of infinite progress. And this claim does not make sense, it seems, if the fundamental riddles are solved. If science is susceptible of infinite progress, there cannot be a meaningful end or completion of history. There can only be a brutal stopping of man's onward march through natural forces acting by themselves or directed by human brains and hands.

[However this may be, in one sense Spengler has proved to be right. Some decline of the West has taken place before our eyes. In 1913, the West—in fact, this country together with Great Britain and Germany—could have laid down the law for the rest of the earth without firing a shot. For at least a half century, the West controlled the whole globe with ease. Today, so far from ruling the globe, the West's very survival is endangered by the East, as it has not been since the beginning. From the *Communist Manifesto*, it would appear that the victory of Communism would be the complete victory of the West, of the synthesis which transcends the national boundaries of British industry, French revolution, and German philosophy, or with the East. We see that the victory of Communism would, indeed, mean the victory of originally Western natural science, but, at the same time, the victory of the most extreme form of Eastern despotism. However much the power of the West may have declined, however great the dangers to the West may be, that decline, that danger—nay, the defeat and the destruction of the West—would not necessarily prove that the West is in a crisis. The West could go down in honor, certain of its purpose.]

The crisis of the West consists in the West having become uncertain of its purpose. The West was once certain of its purpose, of a purpose in which all men could be united. Hence, it had a clear vision of its future as the future of mankind. We no longer have that certainty and that clarity. Some of us even despair of the future. This despair explains many forms of contemporary Western degradation. This is not meant to imply that no society can be healthy unless it is dedicated to a universal purpose, to a purpose in which all men can be united. A society may be tribal and yet healthy. But a society which was accustomed to understand itself in terms of a universal purpose cannot lose faith in that purpose without becoming

Political Philosophy and the Crisis of Our Time

completely bewildered. We find such a universal purpose expressly stated in our immediate past; for instance, in famous official declarations made during the two world wars. These declarations merely restate the purpose stated originally by the most successful form of modern political philosophy: a kind of that political philosophy which aspired to build on the foundation laid by classical political philosophy, but in opposition to the structure erected by classical political philosophy, a society superior in truth and justice to the society toward which the classics aspired.

According to that modern project, philosophy or science was no longer to be understood as essentially contemplative, but as active. It was to be in the service of the relief of man's estate, to use Bacon's beautiful phrase. It was to be cultivated for the sake of human power. It was to enable man to become the master and the owner of nature through the intellectual conquest of nature. Philosophy or science, which was originally the same thing, should make possible progress toward an ever greater prosperity. Thus, everyone would share in all the advantages of society or life, and therewith make true the full meaning of the natural right of everyone to comfortable self-preservation (Locke's phrase) and all that that right entails, and the [220] natural right of everyone to develop all his faculties fully, in concert with everyone else's doing the same. The progress toward an ever greater prosperity would thus become, or render possible, progress toward an ever greater freedom and justice. This progress would necessarily be progress toward a society embracing equally all human beings, a universal league of free and equal nations, each nation consisting of free and equal men and women. For it had come to be believed that the prosperous, free, and just society in a single country, or in a few countries, is not possible in the long run. To make the world safe for the Western democracies, one must make the whole globe democratic, each country in itself, as well as the society of nations. Good order in one country, it was thought, presupposes good order in all countries and among all countries. The movement toward the universal society, or the universal state, was thought to be guaranteed not only by the rationality, the universal validity of the goal, but also because the movement toward that goal seemed to be the movement of the large majority of men, on behalf of the large majority of men. Only those small groups of men, who hold in thrall many millions of their fellow human beings and who defend their own antiquated interests, resist that movement.

[This view of the human situation in general, and of the situation in our century in particular, retained a certain plausibility not in spite of fascism, but because of it, until Communism revealed itself even to the

CHAPTER 32

meanest capacities as Stalinism and post-Stalinism; for Trotskyism, being a flag without an army, and even without a general, was condemned or refuted by its own principle. For some time, it appeared to many teachable Westerners—to say nothing of the unteachable ones—that Communism was only a parallel movement to the Western movement; as it were, a somewhat impatient, wild, wayward twin who was bound to become mature, patient, and gentle. But, except when in mortal danger, Communism responded to fraternal greetings with contempt or, at most, with manifestly dissembled signs of friendship, and when in mortal danger it was as eager to receive Western help as it was determined to give no word of thanks in return. It was impossible for the Western movement to understand Communism as merely a new version of that external reaction against which it had been fighting for centuries. It had to admit that the Western project, which in its way had made provision against all earlier forms of evil, could not provide against the new form in speech or in deed. For some time, it seemed sufficient to say that while the Western movement agrees with Communism regarding the goal of the universal prosperous society of free and equal men and women, it disagrees with it regarding the means. For Communism, the end, the common good of the whole human race being the most sacred thing, justifies any means. Whatever contributes to the achievement of the most sacred end partakes of its sacredness and is, therefore, itself sacred. Whatever hinders the achievement of that end is devilish. The murder of Lumumba was described by a Communist as a reprehensible murder, by which he implied that there can be irreprehensible murders, I suppose like the murder of Nagy.]

[It came to be seen, then, that there is not only a difference of degree, but of kind, between the Western movement and Communism. And this difference was seen to concern morality, the choice of means. In other words, it became clearer than it had been for some time that no bloody or unbloody change of society can eradicate the evil in man. As long as there are men, there will be malice, envy, and hatred; hence, there cannot be a society which does not have to employ coercive restraints. For the same reason, it could no longer be denied that Communism will remain as long as it lasts in fact and not merely in name: the iron rule of a tyrant which is mitigated or aggravated by its fear of palace revolutions. The only restraint in which the West can put some confidence is the tyrant's fear of the West's immense military power.]

The experience of Communism has provided the Western movement with a twofold lesson: a political lesson, a lesson regarding what to expect and what to do in the foreseeable future, and a lesson regarding the principle of politics. For the foreseeable future, there cannot be a universal state, unitary or federative. Apart from the fact that there does not exist now a universal federation of nations, but only one of those nations which are called peace-loving, the federation that does exist masks the fundamental cleavage. If that federation is taken too seriously, as a milestone of man's onward march toward the perfect and, hence, universal society, one is bound to take great risks, supported by nothing but an inherited and perhaps antiquated hope, and thus endanger the very progress one endeavors to bring about. It is imaginable that in the face of the danger of thermonuclear destruction, a federation of nations, however incomplete, would outlaw wars. That is to say, wars of aggression. But this means that it acts on the assumption that all present boundaries are just, in accordance with the self-determination of nations. This assumption is a pious fraud, the fraudulence of which is more evident than its piety. In fact, the only changes of the present boun-[221]daries which are provided for are those not disagreeable to the Communists. One must also not forget the glaring disproportion between the legal equality and the factual inequality of the confederates. This factual inequality is recognized in the expression "underdeveloped nations," an expression, I have been told, coined by Stalin. The expression implies the resolve to develop them fully. That is to say, to make them either Communist or Western. And this despite the fact that the West claims to stand for cultural pluralism. Even if one could still contend that the Western purpose is as universal as the Communist, one must rest satisfied for the foreseeable future with a practical particularism. The situation resembles the one, as has often been said, which existed during those centuries when both Christianity and Islam each raised its claim, but each had to be satisfied with uneasily coexisting with its antagonist. All this amounts to saying that for the foreseeable future political society remains what it always has been: a partial or particular society whose most urgent and primary task is its self-preservation and whose highest task is its self-improvement. As for the meaning of self-improvement, we may observe that the same experience which has made the West doubtful of the viability of a world society has made it doubtful of the belief that affluence is a sufficient and even necessary condition of happiness and justice. Affluence does not cure the deepest evils.

I must say a few words about another ingredient of the modern project, and this needs a somewhat more detailed discussion. Very briefly, we can say that the modern project was distinguished from the earlier view by the fact that it implied that the improvement of society depends decisively on institutions, political or economic, as distinguished from the formation of character. An implication of this view was the simple separation—as distinguished from a distinction—of law from morality. Beyond positive law, there is a sphere of enlightenment indeed; that is to say, of a purely theoretical education as distinguished from moral education or formation of character. We may illustrate this by the example of one of the heroes of that modern project, by the example of Hobbes. Hobbes was, of course, not a simple absolutist who was charmed by Nero and such people. Hobbes wanted to have enlightened absolute sovereigns, "enlightened despots," as they came to be called. But his whole construction was of such a kind that he guaranteed only the pos-[222]sibility and necessity of despotism. The enlightened character of the despot remained a mere matter of hope.

Now this situation is repeated in a different way in the development of modern liberal democracy. Liberal democracy claims to be responsible government, a political order in which the government is responsible to the governed. The governed, of course, also have some responsibility to the government; the governed are supposed to obey the laws. But the key point is this: in order to be responsible, the government must have no secrets from the governed. "Open covenants openly arrived at"—the famous formula of President Wilson expresses this thought most clearly. Of course, liberal democracy also means limited government, the distinction between the public and the private. Not only must the private sphere be protected by the law, but it must also be understood to be impervious to the law. The laws must protect the sphere in which everyone may act and think as he pleases, in which he may be as arbitrary and prejudiced as he likes. "My home is my castle." But this is not simply true. My home is not simply my castle; it may be entered with a search warrant. The true place of secrecy is not the home but the voting booth. We can say the voting booth is the home of homes, the seat of sovereignty, the seat of secrecy. The sovereign consists of the individuals who are in no way responsible, who can in no way be held responsible: the irresponsible individual. This was not simply the original notion of liberal democracy. The original notion was that this sovereign individual was a conscientious individual, the individual limited and guided by his conscience.

It is perfectly clear that the conscientious individual creates the same difficulty as Hobbes's enlightened despot. You cannot give a legal definition of what constitutes the conscientious individual. You cannot limit voting rights to conscientious people as you can limit voting rights by property qualifications, literacy tests, and the like. Conscientiousness can only be fostered by nonlegal means, by moral education. For this no proper provision is made, and the change in this respect is well known to all[of you]. This change which has taken place and is still taking place may be called the decline of liberal democracy into permissive egalitarianism. Whereas the core of liberal democracy is the conscientious individual, the core of permissive egalitarianism is the individual with his urges. We only have to take the case of the conscientious objector; whatever you may think [223] of conscientious objectors, there is no doubt that they are people who are perfectly willing to lay down their lives for something which they regard as right. The man who wants to indulge his urges does not have the slightest intention to sacrifice his life, and hence also his urges, to the satisfaction of his urges. This is the moral decline which has taken place.

Let me illustrate this great change by another example, the concept of culture. [I have spoken at the beginning of this lecture of the concept of culture.]In its original meaning, it meant *the* culture of the human mind. By virtue of a change which took place in the nineteenth century, it became possible to speak of culture in the plural (the cultures). What has been done on a grand scale, especially by Spengler, has been repeated on a somewhat lower level, but with at least as great effect, by such anthropologists as Ruth Benedict. What, then, does culture mean today? In anthropology, and in certain parts of sociology and political science, "culture" is, of course, always used in the plural, and in such a way that you have a culture of suburbia, a culture of juvenile gangs, nondelinquent and even delinquent. And you can say, according to this recent notion of culture, there is not a single human being who is not cultured because he belongs to a culture. [At the same time, fortunately, the older notion is still maintained; when I made this remark some of you laughed, because when we speak of a cultured human being we still imply that not all human beings are cultured or possess culture.]

Looking forward to the end of the road, one can say that according to the view now prevailing in the social sciences every human being who is not an inmate of a lunatic asylum is a cultured human being. At the frontiers of research, of which we hear so much today, we find the interesting question whether the inmates of lunatic asylums also do not have a culture of their own.

Let me now return to my argument. The doubt of the modern project, which is today quite widespread, is not merely a strong but vague feeling.

Chapter 32

It has acquired the status of scientific exactitude. One may wonder whether there is a single social scientist left who would assert that the universal and prosperous society constitutes the rational solution of the human problem. For present-day social science admits and even proclaims its inability to validate any value judgments proper. The teaching originated by modern political philosophy, those heroes of the seventeenth century, in favor of the universal and prosperous society has admittedly become an ideology. That is to say, a teaching not superior in truth and justice to any other among the innumerable ideologies. Social science which studies all ideologies is itself free from all ideological biases. Through [224] this Olympian freedom it overcomes the crisis of our time. That crisis may destroy the conditions of social science; it cannot affect the validity of its findings. Social science has not always been as skeptical or as restrained as it has become during the last two generations. The change in the character of social science is not unconnected with the change in the status of the modern project. The modern project was originated by philosophers, and it was originated as something required by nature, by natural rights. The project was meant to satisfy, in the most perfect manner, the most powerful and natural needs of men. Nature was to be conquered for the sake of man, who was supposed to possess a nature, an unchangeable nature. The originators of the project took it for granted that philosophy and science are identical. After some time, it appeared that the conquest of nature requires the conquest of human nature too and, in the first place, the questioning of the unchangeability of human nature. After all, an unchangeable human nature might set absolute limits to progress. Accordingly, the natural needs of men could no longer direct the conquest of nature. The direction had to come from reason as distinguished from nature, from the rational "Ought" as distinguished from the neutral "Is." Thus, philosophy, logic, ethics, aesthetics, as the study of the "Ought" or the norms, became separated from science as the study of the "Is." While the study of the "Is," or science, succeeded ever more in increasing man's power, the ensuing discredit of reason precluded distinction between the wise, or right, and the foolish, or wrong, use of power. Science, separated from philosophy, cannot teach wisdom. There are still some people who believe that this predicament will disappear as soon as social science and psychology have caught up with physics and chemistry. This belief is wholly unreasonable. For social science and psychology, however perfected, being sciences, can only bring about a still further increase of man's power. They will enable man to manipulate men still better than ever before. They will as little teach man how to use his power over men or non-men as physics and chemistry do. The people who indulge this hope have not grasped the bearing of the distinction between facts and values, which they preach all the time. This is, indeed, the core of modern science, of modern social science as it has finally developed in the last two generations: the distinction between facts and values, with the understanding that no distinction between good or [225] bad values is rationally possible. Any end is as defensible as any other. From the point of view of reason, all values are equal. The task with which academic teachers in the social sciences are concerned is primarily to face this issue posed by the fact-value distinction. I believe that one can show that this fundamental premise of the present-day social sciences is untenable, and that one can show it on a variety of grounds. But I am now concerned with a somewhat broader issue.

When we reflect on the fact-value distinction, we see one element of it which is quite striking. The citizen does not make the fact-value distinction. He is as sure that he can reasonably distinguish between good and bad, just and unjust, as he can distinguish between true and false, or as he can judge so-called factual statements. The distinction between facts and values is alien to the citizen's understanding of political things. The distinction between facts and values becomes necessary, it seems, only when the citizen's understanding of political things is replaced by the specifically scientific understanding. The scientific understanding implies, then, a break with the pre-scientific understanding. Yet, at the same time, it remains dependent on the pre-scientific understanding. I may illustrate this by a most simple example. If someone is sent out by a sociology department to interview people, he is taught all kinds of things; he is given very detailed instructions. But one thing he is not told: address your questions to people, to human beings, and not to dogs, trees, cats, and so on. Furthermore, he is not even told how to tell human beings from dogs. This knowledge is presupposed. It is never changed, never refined, never affected by anything he learns in social science classes. This is only the most massive example of how much allegedly self-sufficient scientific knowledge presupposes of "a priori" knowledge, of pre-scientific knowledge which is not questioned for one moment in the whole process of science. Now, regardless of whether the superiority of the scientific understanding to the pre-scientific understanding can be demonstrated or not, the scientific understanding is surely secondary or derivative. Hence, social science cannot reach clarity about its doings if it does not dispose of a coherent and comprehensive understanding

CHAPTER 32

of what one may call the common sense understanding of political things which precedes all scientific understanding; in other words, if we do not primarily understand political things as they are experienced by the citizen or [226] statesman. Only if it disposes of such a coherent and comprehensive understanding of its basis or matrix can it possibly show the legitimacy and make intelligible the character of that peculiar modification of the primary understanding of political things which is the scientific understanding. This, I believe, is an evident necessity if social science or political science is to be or to become a rational enterprise. Being a modification of the primary understanding of political things, it must be understood as such a modification. We must understand the pre-scientific, the common sense understanding, the citizen's understanding of political things before we can truly understand what the modification effected by scientific understanding means.

But how can we get that understanding? How can our poor powers be sufficient for an elaboration of the pre-scientific primary citizens' understanding of political things? Fortunately for us, this terrific burden, the most basic work which can be done and must be done in order to make political science and, therefore, also the other social sciences truly sciences, rational enterprises, has been done. As in a way every one of you knows, it has been done by Aristotle in his *Politics*. That work supplies us with the classic and unforgettable analysis of the primary understanding of political phenomena.

II

This assertion is exposed to a very great variety of seemingly devastating objections. But, before presenting in the next section what this enterprise, Aristotelian political science, means, I would like to introduce a strict *ad hominem* argument in order to lead, as it were, the now preponderant part in the profession, the so-called behavioralists, if they are willing to listen to an argument, to a somewhat better understanding of what they would do if they were well advised. When you look around [yourself, not at the University of Detroit, not at other Catholic institutions, but at non-Catholic institutions], I think you can say that with very few exceptions political philosophy has disappeared. Political philosophy, the decay of political philosophy into ideology, reveals itself today most obviously in the fact that in both research and teaching political philosophy has been replaced by the history of political philosophy. Many of you have read or used the famous work by Sabine, and you only have to read the preface of

Sabine to see that what I am going to say is simply correct. Now, what does [227] this substitution of the history of political philosophy for political philosophy mean? It is, strictly speaking, absurd to replace political philosophy by the history of political philosophy. It means to replace a doctrine which claims to be true by a survey of errors, and that is exactly what Sabine, for example, does. So, political philosophy cannot be replaced by the history of political philosophy.

The discipline which takes the place of political philosophy is the one which shows the impossibility of political philosophy, and that discipline is, of course, logic. What, for the time being, is still tolerated under the name, "history of political philosophy," will find its place within a rational scheme of research and teaching in footnotes to the chapters in logic textbooks which deal with the distinction between factual judgments and value judgments. These footnotes will supply slow learners with examples of the faulty transition by which political philosophy stands or falls, from factual judgments to value judgments. They will give examples from Plato, Aristotle, Locke, Hume, or Rousseau and will show when and where these famous men committed a blunder which every ten-year-old child now knows how to avoid. Yet, it would be wrong to believe that in the new dispensation, according to the demands of logical positivism or behavioral science, the place once occupied by political philosophy is filled entirely by logic, however enlarged. A considerable part of the matter formerly treated by political philosophy is now treated by non-philosophic political science, which forms part of social science. This new political science is concerned with discovering laws of political behavior and, ultimately, universal laws of political behavior. Lest it mistake the peculiarities of the politics of the times and the places in which social science is at home for the character of all politics, it must study also the politics of other climes and other ages. The new political science thus becomes dependent upon a kind of study which belongs to the comprehensive enterprise called universal history. Now, it is controversial whether history can be modeled on the natural sciences or not, and, therefore, whether the aspiration of the new political science to become scientific in the sense of the natural sciences is sound.

At any rate, the historical studies in which the new political science must engage must become concerned not only with the workings of institutions, but with the ideologies informing these institutions as well. Within the context of these studies, the meaning of an [228] ideology is primarily the meaning in which its adherents understand it. In some cases, the ideologies

Chapter 32

are known to have been originated by outstanding men. In these cases, it becomes necessary to consider whether and how the ideology as conceived by the originator was modified by its adherents. For, precisely, if only the crude understanding of ideologies can be politically effective, it is necessary to grasp the characteristics of crude understanding. If what they call the routinization of charisma is a permitted theme, the vulgarization of thought ought to be a permitted theme also. One kind of ideology consists of the teachings of the political philosophers. These teachings may have played only a minor political role, but one cannot know this before one knows these doctrines solidly. This solid knowledge consists primarily in understanding the teachings of the political philosophers as they themselves meant them. Surely, every one of them was mistaken in believing that his teaching was a sound teaching regarding political things. Through a reliable tradition we know that this belief forms part of a rationalization, but the process of rationalization is not so thoroughly understood that it would not be worthwhile to study it in the case of the greatest minds. For all we know, there may be various kinds of rationalizations, etc. It is, then, necessary to study the political philosophies, not only as they were understood by their originators, in contradistinction to the way in which they were understood by their adherents and various kinds of their adherents, but also by their adversaries and even by detached or indifferent bystanders or historians. For indifference does not offer a sufficient guarantee against the danger that one identifies the view of the originator with a compromise between the views of his adherents and those of his adversaries. The general understanding of the political philosophies which is then absolutely necessary on the basis of behavioral political science may be said to have been rendered possible today by the shaking of all traditions; the crisis of our time may have the accidental advantage of enabling us to understand in an untraditional, a fresh manner what was hitherto understood only in a traditional, derivative manner.

[Social science, then, will not live up to its claim if it does not concern itself with the genuine understanding of the political philosophies proper, and therewith, primarily because it comes first, of classical political philosophy. As I indicated, such an understanding cannot be presumed to be available. It is sometimes asserted today that such an understanding is not even possible because all historical understanding is relative to the point of view of the historian, his country, his time. The historian cannot understand, it is said, the teaching as it was meant by its originator, but he necessarily understands it differently than its originator understood it.

Political Philosophy and the Crisis of Our Time

Ordinarily, the historian's understanding is inferior to the originator's understanding. In the best case, the understanding will be a creative transformation of the original teaching. Yet, it is hard to see how one can speak of the creative transformation of the original teaching if it is not possible to grasp the original teaching as such.]

[Be this as it may, the following point seems to be of crucial importance.] To the extent to which the social scientist succeeds in this kind of study, which is required of him by the demands of his own science, he not only enlarges the horizon of present-day social science; he even transcends the limitations of that social science. [229] For he learns to look at things in a manner which is, as it were, forbidden to the social scientist. He will have learned from his logic that his science rests on certain hypotheses, certainties, or assumptions. He learns now to suspend these assumptions because, as long as he maintains them, he has no access to his subject matter. He is thus compelled to make the assumptions of social science his theme. Far from being merely one of the innumerable themes of social science, history of political philosophy, and not logic, proves to be the pursuit concerned with the presuppositions of social science. These presuppositions prove to be modifications of the principles of modern political philosophy, which, in their turn, prove to be modifications of the principles of classical political philosophy. To the extent to which a behavioral political scientist takes his science and its requirements seriously, he is compelled to engage in such a study, in such a historical study of his own discipline, and he cannot conduct that study without questioning the dogmatic premises of his own science. Therewith, his horizon is enlarged. He must at least consider the possibility that the older political science was sounder and truer than what is regarded as political science today.

Such a return to classical political philosophy is both necessary and tentative or experimental. Not in spite, but because it is tentative, it must be carried out seriously; that is to say, without squinting at our present-day predicament. There is no danger that we can ever become oblivious of this predicament, since that predicament is the incentive to our whole concern with the classics. We cannot reasonably expect that a fresh understanding of classical political philosophy will supply us with recipes for today's use. The relative success of modern political philosophy has brought into being a kind of society wholly unknown to the classics, a kind of society in which the classical principles as stated and elaborated by the classics are not immediately applicable. Only we living today can possibly find a solution to the problems of today. An adequate understanding of the principles, as

CHAPTER 32

elaborated by the classics, may be the indispensable starting point for an adequate analysis, to be achieved by us, of present-day society in its peculiar character, and for the wise application, to be achieved by us, of these principles to our tasks.

III

[In my first lecture, I have tried to trace the crisis of our time to the crisis of political philosophy, and I suggested that a way out of the intellectual difficulties with which we are beset is a return to classical political philosophy and, in the first place, to Aristotle's *Politics*. In this lecture, I would like to discuss this return to Aristotle and the difficulties which seem to oppose it. Let me say only one more word about this crisis of political philosophy. I think it is no exaggeration to say that, generally speaking, political philosophy and even philosophy in general, has lost today its dignity and its status. Today, one can easily say that it is my philosophy to have two boiled eggs for my breakfast. What has happened to philosophy and, in particular, to political philosophy? The answer, I think, is clear.]

[There are two powers which are the recognized authorities in the Western world—in any Western country, especially in this country—which one can call positivism and historicism. Positivism is the view according to which only scientific knowledge, as defined by modern natural science, is genuine knowledge. This has the crucial implication that any assertions regarding values cannot be validated, but are mere subjective assertions. Historicism, on the other hand, is the view according to which the distinction between facts and values is ultimately not tenable because the highest principles of theoretical understanding, popularly called "categories," are inseparable from the highest principles of practice, popularly called "values," and that this "system," consisting of categories and values, is historically changeable: there is not *the* true system of categories and values. These are the two most powerful schools in the West today. Both are incompatible with political philosophy as an attempt to discover and to lay bare *the* true ends of man as man.]

[Positivism is in all respects, except one, inferior to historicism. Positivism, if it understands itself, will necessarily turn into historicism. For the basic premises of what is called science—that is to say, modern science—prove to be not evidently necessary; they are logically arbitrary, as they are admitted to be by the positivists themselves. This arbitrariness means, however, that they have been accepted in such a way that this was not merely an affair of this or that individual, but became a public factor that determined a whole period of history; it was a *historical* decision by virtue of which modern science became the power forming the modern world. Historicism, on the other hand, is more reflective than positivism because it raises a question which positivism cannot raise: *Why* science? It considers the human context out of which science stems, which positivism cannot genuinely do. Present-day positivism believes it can solve the problem simply by making a distinction between the validity of the findings of science and the genesis of science or of its findings. This distinction would make sense if science still could be understood as the perfection of the human intellect, the natural perfection of the human intellect; but no logical positivist can afford to say that. Therefore, he is forbidden to admit that the question, Why science?, must be raised, and he is surely unable to give an answer to that question. The relative merit which positivism has in this situation is that it asserts, in a very inadequate—not to say inept—manner, the notion of *the* one truth, or as it would probably prefer to call it, of objectivity. Political philosophy is an actuality in the West today only in Thomism. This creates a difficulty, however, even for the Thomists, because it gives rise to the suspicion that it is the Christian Catholic faith, and not human reason, which supports this political philosophy. Therefore, it is necessary even for the Thomists to show that the Aristotelian conception of political philosophy—Aristotle was not, after all, a Catholic Christian—has not been refuted by modern thought.]

[230] Let us look at the specific grounds on which it is claimed that Aristotle's political philosophy has been refuted. The most common reason is that modern natural science, or modern cosmology, having refuted Aristotelian cosmology (e.g., by demonstrating "evolution"), has therewith refuted the principle or the basis of Aristotelian political philosophy. Aristotle took for granted the permanence of the species, and we "know" that the species are not permanent. But even granting that evolution is an established fact, that man has come into being out of another species, man is still essentially different from non-man. The fact of essential differences—the fact that there are "forms"—has in no way been refuted by evolutionism. The starting point of Aristotle, as well as of Plato, is that the whole consists of heterogeneous beings; that there is a noetic heterogeneity of beings, this common sensible notion on which we fall back all the time, and this has in no way been refuted. I remind you of the famous seventeenth-century criticism of formal causes, a criticism, which was properly presented in its most impressive form by a comic poet, Molière, of the famous scholastic question, "Why does opium make men sleep?,"

Chapter 32

and the answer, "*Quia est in eo virtus dormitiva, cujus est natura sensus assoupire*" (Because it has a dormitive power, a sleep-making power, the nature of which consists in putting the senses to sleep). This has been a famous joke repeated in this or that form innumerably often. It amounts to saying that reference to formal causes is in no way an explanation. But the joke is not so good as it appears at first hearing: if opium did not have sleep-making power, we would not be interested in it, if the ingredients of opium did not as such have this power; when you put together the elements out of which opium consists, then this whole has a character which the elements do not have, and this character is what makes opium opium. What is true of opium is true of man, as well as of any other being. It is, then, the notion of essence, of essential difference, which distinguishes the Aristotelian and the Platonic teaching from that of the characteristically modern philosophy, and especially modern science. If there are essential differences, there can be essential differences between the common good and the private good. However far the defeat of Aristotle's cosmology may extend, it does not go to the length of having destroyed the evidence of the concept of essential differences and, therefore, of essences.

[231] The second argument, which is very common, is that Aristotle has been refuted because he was anti-democratic. I admit the fact, for I do not believe that the premises upon which some of our contemporaries seem to act—democracy is good and Aristotle is good—lead validly to the conclusion that Aristotle was a democrat. He was not a democrat. But on what grounds? Democracy meant at all times, in Greek times as well as today, the rule of all. But this is too abstract, because there is never unanimity, or hardly ever. In fact, in a democracy the majority rules. Yet, if there are stable majorities, then this stable majority will be in control in a democracy. What is that stable majority? Aristotle, in his great clarity and simplicity, said that in every *polis*, in every political society, there are two groups of people, the rich and the poor, and whatever may be the reason, the majority are the poor. Therefore, democracy is the rule of the poor. "Poor" does not mean "beggars." The poor are the people who have to earn their living, who cannot live as gentlemen. Because they are poor, they do not have the leisure for acquiring education, both sufficient theoretical and practical education, neither in maturity nor as children. They have no time for it; hence they are uneducated. And no man in his senses would say that the political community should be ruled by the uneducated. This simple argument is in no way vicious. What is our argument against it?

Aristotle took something for granted which we can no longer take for granted. He took for granted that every economy would be an economy of scarcity where the majority of men do not have leisure. We have discovered an economy of plenty and, in an economy of plenty, it is no longer true that the majority of people have to be uneducated. This is a perfectly legitimate reply to Aristotle as far as it goes. But we must see what precisely has changed. Not the principles of justice, they are the same. What has changed are the circumstances. On the very principle of justice, as Aristotle understood it, one would have to say that the argument regarding democracy as he stated it has to be modified because we have an economy of plenty. Yet this difference of circumstances is due to the modern economy, which in its turn is based on modern technology, which in its turn is based on modern science. Here we touch again on the fundamental difference between Aristotle and modern thought. A new interpretation of science, opposed to the Aristotelian interpreta-[232]tion, came to the fore in the seventeenth century in the works of Bacon, Descartes, and Hobbes. According to that new interpretation, science exists for the sake of human power and is not for the sake of understanding, as understanding, or of contemplation. As for this notion of science which is underlying the modern development, we have become doubtful whether it is as sound as it appeared for many generations. At the very latest, the explosion of the first atomic bomb made people doubtful whether the unlimited progress of science and technology is something unqualifiedly good. Not more than this is needed in order to see that Aristotle might have had a point when he denied that science is essentially in the service of the increase of human power.

Aristotle's non-democratic or anti-democratic view has apparently still another basis. This is his assumption, which he thought to be a fact, that men are by nature unequal in politically relevant respects. That they are unequal in regard to beauty would not be important, because we do not ordinarily elect officials on the ground of their being very handsome. But that there is a natural inequality regarding understanding is politically relevant. This kind of natural inequality can hardly be denied. [The only serious attempt to deny it was made by the famous Russian biologist, Lysenko, with the assistance of Stalin, but I believe this attempt has been abandoned by Khrushchev, although I do not know it.] It is, of course, recognized by modern democracy, as is shown by our speaking of equality of opportunity, which implies that differently gifted people are supposed to do very different things with the opportunity offered. Differently stated, modern democracy is representative democracy, meaning a democracy which elects the people whom it believes are above the average. Modern

CHAPTER 32

democracy as representative democracy is opposed to direct democracy.

Another objection to Aristotle—and we come somewhat closer to the key issues—is that Aristotle's whole political philosophy is narrow, or provincial. After all, he was a Greek, and the subject matter of his work is the Greek city-state, one particular form of human organization which was as important historically as any other, but which is just one among very many. This view is very common today, but it is not correct. Aristotle is not concerned with the Greek city-state. When you read the second book of the *Politics*, you see that he regarded a city like Carthage, which was a Phoenician city, as roughly equal to Sparta and definitely superior to Athens. The city-state is, then, not essentially Greek. This, however, is a minor difficulty. A more serious difficulty is this: [233] When we speak of the city-state, we imply that there is such a thing called the "state," of which there are n various forms, one of them being the city-state. This thought cannot be translated into Greek; that is, Aristotle's Greek. This concept of "state" is wholly alien to his thought. When we speak of "state" today, we ordinarily understand state in contradistinction to society. You will find it asserted in all textbooks that the Greek city—or let me now use the Greek word, "*polis*"—is not a state distinguished from a society. The *polis*, we may say, antedates the distinction of state and society. Aristotle does make a distinction between the *polis* and other associations or partnerships, but he does not bundle them all together under the title, "society," in contradistinction to the *polis*. His thought can be understood easily [by every one of you] if you only look at the right place for the modern equivalent of the concept of *polis*. That equivalent is our modern term, "the country." When you say the country is in danger, you do not make a distinction between the state and society. The country is the modern equivalent to what Aristotle understood by the city. Or look at another saying of somewhat questionable morality which still has a certain reasonableness, "my country right or wrong." You cannot possibly say, "my state right or wrong," or "my society right or wrong"; it does not sound right. "Country" is, then, truly the modern equivalent of "city." The difference is by no means unimportant. The difference indicates that the city is an urban association. The country, as the word indicates, is not necessarily urban, and this is surely due to the feudal past of modern nations. We are separated from Aristotle by a gulf which we must somehow bridge if we wish to understand him. Therefore, we must look for equivalents in our experience in order to understand, to get the experiential analogue to what Aristotle means when he speaks of the *polis*.

Let me now turn to Aristotle's own analysis of the *polis*. What is the character of the *polis*? What is the essential difference between the *polis* and all other associations? Aristotle answers: The end of the *polis* is happiness. All other associations serve a special purpose. The political society is the only association which is directed toward the complete human good, and that is called happiness. Happiness means the practice of moral virtue above everything else, the doing of noble deeds. Aristotle assumes something which is today absolutely controversial, especially in scientific circles, but which he [234] assumes is not controversial at all among reasonable people; namely, what happiness is. To develop this point fully, we would have to discuss the chapter of his *Rhetoric* where he speaks so clearly and beautifully about what happiness is. When reading that chapter, you will see that our ordinary notion of happiness is not different from the ordinary notion analyzed by Aristotle. What do we mean when calling a man happy? A man who has friends, who has good friends, who has many friends, who has children, and good children, who is healthy, reasonably wealthy, and so on. There is nothing particularly Greek about this. When we call a man happy, we mean, in the first place, that he is a contented man. But, we see from time to time people who are of a very low grade of understanding, perhaps moronic, who smile all the time. They are contented; yet no one would say that they are happy. We mean, then, by happiness a contentedness which is enviable, a reasonable contentedness. This is what all men understand by happiness, and, therefore, it is a good enough beginning for political philosophy, moral philosophy, to speak of happiness thus understood.

Yet, in modern times, surely from the seventeenth century onward, this beginning was questioned on a ground which, in present-day parlance, would be stated as follows:

Happiness is entirely subjective. What *A* understands by happiness differs from what *B* understands by happiness, and even what *A* understands by happiness is very different before he has had his dinner and after he has had his dinner. If happiness is entirely subjective, it can no longer be relevant for determining the common good. How then shall we find our bearing politically? The answer given by the founders of modern political philosophy was this: While happiness is radically subjective, the conditions of happiness are not. Whatever you may understand by happiness, in order to be happy you must be alive; second, you must be able to circulate; third, you must be able to pursue happiness as you understand happiness, and perhaps even as you understand happiness at the moment. So life, liberty, pursuit of happiness are the conditions of happiness, however you under-

Chapter 32

stand happiness. They constitute the objective conditions of happiness. They possess that objectivity, that universality, which happiness lacks. Therefore, the function of political society is not to take care that the citizens are happy, that they become doers of noble deeds, as Aristotle called it, but to [235] create the conditions of happiness, to protect them, or to use a technical term, to protect the natural rights of man; for the natural rights of man in the modern sense of the meaning are the conditions of happiness in the sense indicated. Under no circumstance may political society impose any notion of happiness upon the citizenry, for any notion of happiness would be subjective and therefore arbitrary. People will then pursue happiness; each one as he understands happiness. They all strive for happiness. This striving is partly cooperative, but also partly competitive. This striving produces something like a web. This, I believe, is what is meant primarily by society, in contradistinction to the state.

If this analysis is in principle correct, we arrive at the following conclusion: The state is superior to society because its aim or end—the securing of the conditions of happiness, however happiness may be understood—is objective, that is, the same for all. On the other hand, society is superior to the state because only as members of society, as distinguished from the state, are we concerned with the end, with happiness itself, and not with the conditions of happiness or the means of happiness. From this point of view, the public, the political, is in the service of the essentially private, of happiness, however one may understand happiness. But this fact that from one point of view the state is superior to society, from another point of view that society is superior to the state, creates a great theoretical difficulty. The solution favored by modern social thought consists in postulating another basis, distinguished from state and society, a kind of matrix for both state and society; this, I believe, is the function of the modern concept of culture or civilization as terms susceptible of being used in the plural.

I have referred to these conditions of happiness, and I have indicated that what they meant were the natural rights, the rights of man. [I would like to say a word about this subject with regard to the discussion which we had this morning.] This doctrine, which was developed in the seventeenth and eighteenth centuries, reminds us, of course, of the traditional natural law teaching, the Thomistic teaching. Outside of Catholic circles, it is rarely admitted, although it is so obvious, that there is a radical difference between the natural law teaching of the seventeenth and eighteenth century, and the medieval and classic ancient teaching. To illustrate the difference very briefly by a simple formula, the name which came into

Political Philosophy and the Crisis of Our Time

use in the eighteenth century for natural law was the rights of man, whereas the traditional name was natural law. [236] First, "law" was replaced by "rights." When people spoke of law, they always meant the duties primarily, and the rights only derivatively. When Aristotle says that what the law does not command it forbids, he gives us a notion of what law originally meant. [(I remember a modern interpreter who said that this is nonsense; the law never commands us to breathe; yet, no one can say that it forbids us to breathe. He did not make the simple reflection that by instituting military service, or perhaps by forbidding suicide, the law commands one to breathe.)] Second, "nature" is replaced by "man." In the older notion, natural law is part of a larger order, of a hierarchic order indicated by the word, "nature." In the modern view, nature has been replaced by man. Man, taken entirely by himself, is, as it were, the origin of the rights belonging to him. The term, "rights of man," is the moral equivalent to that famous beginning of modern philosophy: Descartes' *ego cogitans*, the thinking ego. In Descartes' moral work, *The Passions of the Soul*, the word "duty" never occurs; but in the key passage the word "right" occurs, which I believe is very characteristic.*

Let me return to the general reflection about the *polis*. We are frequently misled today by a kind of learning which, if kept in its place, is highly valuable. I mean what the historians and philologists tell us about the Greeks; yet this is not sufficient for understanding what men like Aristotle and Plato meant. We must make a distinction between the pre-philosophic concept of the *polis* and the philosophic concept. I am concerned here only with the philosophic concept as developed by Aristotle especially. The philosophical concept of the *polis* is that the *polis* is the natural society, the society corresponding to the nature of man, society neither too small nor too large for man's reaching his perfection. Man's natural powers, especially his powers of knowing his fellow men and caring for them, are limited. Very roughly said, a *polis* is a society which is not too large for man, for the individual's power of knowing and actively caring. The *polis* is an association in which every man can know not every other—that would be a village—but an acquaintance of every other, so that he is in a position to find out for whom he votes; that is, to whom he entrusts his life and fortune. The present discussions about metropolitan areas rediscover to some extent what Aristotle meant by the *polis* as the natural association.

But is it sufficient to say that Aristotle's political philosophy is con-

---

* *The Passions of the Soul*, art. 152, end.—Eds.

CHAPTER 32

cerned with the *polis*? You would only have to read the beginning of every book of the *Politics*, except the first, in order to see that it is not sufficient. The *polis* is only a provisional indication. The proper subject of the *Politics* is called in Greek, "*politeia*," a derivative from the word, *polis*. The ordinary English translation is [237] "constitution," which is a somewhat misleading translation because, when we speak of a constitution, we do not mean something like the constitution of an animal; we mean something like the law of the land, the fundamental law of the land. Incidentally, the historical origin of our concept of the constitution is the fundamental law. The *politeia*, as Aristotle meant it, has nothing to do with law; it is distinguished from all laws. One can render its meaning by words like the "political order" or the "political order which originates the laws including the so-called constitutional law," or perhaps more simply as the "regime." Examples are democracy, oligarchy, tyranny, etc. These phenomena[, to repeat,] originate law rather than being constituted by law. [We had a discussion today in connection with Kelsen's pure theory of law, of the basic norm, of that which is the origin of the whole legal order. According to Aristotle, that which originates the legal order is the political order, the regime.] The character of the society is formed by the regime. Since there is a variety of regimes today, as well as at all times, the question inevitably arises: Which is the preferable regime? Or to state it with the proper simplicity, which is the best regime? This is, one can say, the most important question for Aristotle. He surely is greatly concerned with discovering the order of rank of the various regimes. One cannot know the truth about any regime if one does not know how good or bad it is. For example, you do not know anything, to speak of, about democracy if you do not know its virtues and defects. This simple fact points theoretically to the thought of the regime which has no defects, the best regime, and this is indeed the highest theme for Aristotle.

Let us return to the more practical level, to the variety of regimes. This is the subject of Aristotle; not the state, as the subject of political philosophy came to be called in the nineteenth century. The state as understood in these Victorian doctrines was something politically neutral, whereas the regime as Aristotle understands it is something politically divisive. It does not have to be divisive within a given society because all may be fully satisfied with the established regime. But it is in principle divisive because there will be other regimes elsewhere, and the claims of each of these regimes to be the best necessarily clash. Aristotle's political philosophy is political not only because of its subject matter, but because Aristotle is animated by the political passion, the concern for the best regime.

There is a certain difficulty here, a grave practical and moral problem, which Aristotle indicates in a way that seems to be quite academic. He says, citizen is relative to the regime; that is, a citizen in a democracy is not necessarily a citizen in an oligarchy, etc. But if [238] citizen is relative to the regime, then surely good citizen is also relative to the regime. Here we see the great difference between the good citizen and the good man. The good man is not relative to a regime, whereas the good citizen necessarily is. This creates some difficulties for many modern readers, although if we look around us we can easily recognize present-day parallels. For example, a good Communist cannot be a good citizen in a democracy, and vice versa. The relation of the regime to what is not the regime, to "society," corresponds to the general metaphysical distinction used by Aristotle between form and matter. Metaphysical means the same as common sensible here. The regime gives to the city its form. What, then, is the matter? All kinds of things, but the most important are the people, or more simply, the inhabitants of the city considered as not affected and molded by the regime. Not the citizens as citizens, for who is and who is not a citizen is already determined by the regime. The form is higher in dignity than matter; for only the form is directly connected with the end. Therefore, the regime, and not the people on the subpolitical level, are connected with the end of civil society.

Again speaking empirically, or common sensibly, every society is characterized by the fact that it looks up to something. Even the society which is wholly materialistic looks up to materialism. Every human being is what he is by the fact that he looks up to something. Even if he does not look up to anything because he is a slave of his belly, for example, this is only a deficient mode of looking up to something. If we take a simple view of democracy, it looks up to equality, and this gives it its character. I have been told that the travelers of old China—a thousand years ago or more—when they came to a foreign country, to barbarians as they probably called them, they asked them first, "How do you greet or bow to your prince or king?" They were wiser than many present-day anthropologists, because their question was only a too-special form of the question of what do you look up to. Every society, or civilization as they say today, has its unity due to the fact that there is a certain *order* to the things which they cherish, to their values, to what they esteem. There would not be a unity if there were not one, and only one, thing which is at the top. This gives a society its character. Aristotle adds that there must be a harmony between that to

CHAPTER 32

which a society looks up and the preponderant part of a [239] society, the part of society which sets its tone; that is, the regime. This, then, is the connection between the "end" and regime, the "form," the preponderant part, which may be the majority but need not be. There were societies in which a small part of the population was the preponderant or authoritative part. There is an essential connection between the *eidos*, the form, the character of a city, and the end to which the city is dedicated. This is an empirical proposition. Here we have come to the difficulty which even very good scholars sometimes fail to solve properly[, and I would like to devote the rest of this lecture to this subject].

From his notion of the regime as *the* central and key political phenomenon, Aristotle apparently drew the conclusion that a change of regime transforms a given city into another city, and this seems to be abstruse. How can you say that Athens, when she became oligarchic, was no longer the same city as she was before that change? Aristotle's assertion seems to deny the obvious continuity of a city in spite of all changes of regime. Is it obviously not better to say that the same France which was first an absolute monarchy became thereafter a democracy, than to say that democratic France is a different country from monarchic France? Or generally stated, is it not better to say that the same substance of France takes on successively different forms, which, compared with the substance, are mere forms? Is this not the common-sensible way of saying it,* as shown by the way in which people write a history of the French constitution, or of the English constitution: the one thing, the same substance, the English constitution, undergoes these and those changes. It goes without saying that Aristotle was not blind to the continuity of the "matter," as distinguished from the discontinuity of the forms. He did not say that the sameness of a city depends exclusively on the sameness of the regime. For, in that case, there would not be, for instance, more than one democratic city. If the form alone establishes the identity, then there can be only one democratic city. He said that the sameness of the city depends above all on the sameness of the regime, but not exclusively. Nevertheless, what he says runs counter to our notions. It does not run counter to our experience.

In order to see this, we must follow his presentation more closely than is usually done. Aristotle starts from an experience. Immediately after a city has become democratic, the democrats sometimes say of a certain act,

---

* "Common-sensible" is hyphenated in this instance and on p. 475, but not at pp. 463 and 471 above. —Eds.

such as a certain contractual obligation, [240] debt, etc., that it is not an action of the city, but of the deposed oligarchs, or the deposed tyrant. The democrat, the partisan of democracy, implies that when there is no democracy there is no city which can act. It is, of course, no accident that Aristotle refers to a statement made by democrats as distinguished from oligarchs; Aristotle is always concrete. The oligarchs would not say that when there is a democracy there is no city. But they would say that the city has gone to pieces. This, however, leaves us wondering whether the city which is going to pieces can still be said simply to be. Let us say, then, that for the partisan of any regime, the city is only if it is informed by the regime which he favors. The moderate and sober people reject this extreme view and, therefore, say that the change of regime is a surface event which does not affect the being of the city at all. Those people will say that however relative the citizen may be to the regime, the good citizen is a man who serves his city well under any regime. We are very familiar with this, especially in countries where there have been changes of regime. Let us call these men the patriots, who say the fatherland is first, with the regime a strictly expediential and secondary consideration. The partisans will call the patriots turncoats, because if the regime changes the patriot changes his allegiance. Aristotle is neither a patriot in that simple sense, nor a partisan in that simple sense. He would disagree with both the partisans and the patriots. He says that a change of regime is much more radical than the patriots admit, but less radical than the partisans contend. Through a change of regime the city does not cease to be; the partisans go much too far. But the city becomes another city in a certain respect, in the most important respect. For with a change of regime, the political community becomes dedicated to an end radically different from its earlier end, and, therefore, it is the greatest and most fundamental change which a city can undergo. In making his apparently strange assertion, Aristotle thinks of the highest end to which a city can be dedicated; namely, human excellence. Is any change, he as it were asks us, which a city can undergo comparable in importance to its turning from nobility to baseness, or vice versa? We may say that his point of view is not that of the patriot, nor of the ordinary partisan, but that of the partisan of excellence. He does not say that through a change of regimes a city becomes another city in every respect. For instance, it will remain the same city with regard to obligations which the preceding regime has undertaken. [241] He fails to answer the question regarding treaty obligations not because he cannot answer it, as some people believe, but because it is not a political question strictly

CHAPTER 32

speaking, but rather, as he says, a legal question. Because he was a reasonable man, it is very easy to discern the principle which he would have followed in answering this legal question. If the deposed tyrant undertook obligations which are beneficial to the city, the city ought to honor these obligations. But if the tyrant undertook the obligations merely to feather his own nest or to pay for his bodyguard, then the city, of course, should not pay them.

In order to understand Aristotle's thesis regarding the supremacy of the regime, one has only to consider the phenomenon, which we all know, and of which we have heard so much, known by the name of loyalty. The loyalty demanded from every citizen is not mere loyalty to the bare country, to the country irrespective of the regime, but to the country *informed* by the regime, by the constitution. A fascist or Communist might claim that he undermines the Constitution of the United States out of loyalty to the United States. For, in his opinion, the Constitution is bad for the people of the United States. But his claim to be a loyal citizen will not be recognized. Someone might say that the Constitution could be changed constitutionally so that the regime would cease to be a liberal democracy and become either fascist or Communist, and that every citizen of the United States is then expected to be a loyal fascist or Communist. But no one loyal to liberal democracy, who knows what he is doing, would teach this doctrine, precisely because it is apt to undermine loyalty to liberal democracy. Only when a regime is in the state of complete decay can its transformation into another regime become publicly defensible.

We have come to distinguish between legality and legitimacy. Whatever is legal in a given society derives its ultimate legitimation from something which is the source of all law, ordinary or constitutional, from the legitimating principle—be it the sovereignty of the people, the divine right of kings, or whatever else. The legitimating principle is not simply justice, for there is a variety of principles of legitimacy. The legitimating principle is not natural law, for natural law is, as such, neutral as between democracy, aristocracy, and monarchy. The principle of legitimacy is in each case a specific notion of justice: justice democratically understood, justice oligarchically understood, justice aristocratically understood, etc. This is to [242] say, every political society derives its character from a specific public or political morality, from what it regards as publicly defensible; and this means from what the preponderant part of society, not necessarily the majority, regards as just. A given society may be characterized by extreme permissiveness, but this very permissiveness is in need of being established and defended, and it necessarily has its limits. A permissive society which permits its members every sort of non-permissiveness will soon cease to be permissive. It will vanish from the face of the earth. Not to see the city in the light of the variety of regimes means not to look at the city as a political man; that is to say, as a man concerned with a specific public morality. The variety of specific public moralities, or of regimes, necessarily gives rise to the question of the best regime, for every kind of regime claims to be the best and, therefore, forces one to face these claims, to meet them by wondering whether a given regime is best or not.

Let me conclude with a remark about a seeming self-contradiction of Aristotle regarding the highest theme of his *Politics*. He bases his thematic discussion of the best regime on the principle that the highest end of man, happiness, is the same for the individual and the city. As he makes clear, this principle would be accepted as such by everyone because it is a common sensible principle. The difficulty arises from the fact—and this arises more for Aristotle than for the ordinary citizen—that the highest end of the individual is contemplation, and not the doing of noble deeds. Aristotle seems to solve the difficulty by asserting that the city is as capable of the contemplative life as the individual. Yet it is obvious that the city is capable, at best, only of an analogue to the contemplative life. Aristotle reaches this apparent result only by an explicit abstraction appropriate to a political inquiry, strictly and narrowly conceived, from the full meaning of the best life of the individual. In such an inquiry, the transpolitical life, the superpolitical, the life of the mind in contradistinction to the political life, comes to sight only as a limit of the political. Man is more than the citizen or the city. Man transcends the city, however, only by what is best in him. This is reflected in the fact that there are examples of men of the highest excellence, whereas Aristotle has no example of cities of the highest excellence, cities informed by the best regime. Man transcends the city only by pursuing true happiness, not by pursuing happiness, however happiness may be understood.

Afterword

For a long while I had lamented that all of Strauss's English articles that were not included in his own books required quite an effort to find. With this thought in mind, I approached one of the editors of this volume about getting such a volume published. He informed me that he had been working on such a project, but had set it aside because of the difficulty of finding a publisher. For my part in reviving the project, the editors asked if I would provide an account of my own experiences in reading Strauss in the hope that this might be helpful to others.

When I first read Strauss in my teens, I was concerned with answering the challenge of moral relativism—the view that there are no rational grounds for making moral judgments—and I thought that Strauss might show me the way. Like others, I began by looking for better ways to justify my beliefs, because I was dissatisfied with the answers I currently had. I started with *Natural Right and History* and thought that in Strauss's distinction between "nature" and "convention" I had found a universal moral standard in "nature." Over time I came to see that I had imposed my own moral search upon Strauss and had failed to follow the contours of the journey Strauss was offering to take me on. I had to go from assuming that I knew where Strauss was heading to allowing Strauss's writings to guide my way. Reading Strauss was a step-by-step process in which I began with my questions and Strauss showed me how to modify my initial questions. On the basis of this modification, I was able to ask slightly different questions which reading Strauss again helped me once again modify. From the beginning and at each point of my study, Strauss could speak to me at my level of understanding. Strauss's writings do not require their own technical language. Of course, I could not understand everything, but in each reading, I could understand something which would

AFTERWORD

allow me to return and learn something more. Through this process and with the aid of teachers, I came to observe the many subtle ways Strauss guides his readers. In my initial understanding of the categories of "nature" and "convention," I had not paid sufficient attention to the "provisional...manner" (*NRH*, 82) of Strauss's presentation; he speaks of the "idea of nature" (*NRH*, 81, 82) and not just nature.

When I first began reading Strauss I assumed that he was just a scholar whose main purpose was to accurately interpret the works of others. This is an easy assumption to make, because Strauss seems to present himself in this way. In a lecture on "Existentialism," Strauss even says, "I know that I am only a scholar." Only here, in a lecture Strauss never published, and nowhere in his published writings does Strauss say this so directly of himself. However, not in any lecture nor in any published writing does Strauss call himself a philosopher. This means that the question of how Strauss understood himself, the very question that Strauss leads us to ask about the philosophers he wrote about, is an open question regarding Strauss himself. It is none the less a question we cannot avoid and eventually should not avoid asking.

In my initial readings of Strauss, I mistakenly answered this question too soon. I was too taken by my initial impressions of his writings. My error was to assume that I knew that Strauss was just a historian of philosophy whose primary task was a revision of that history as it had come to be understood by other scholars. I did not leave room in my interpretation for Strauss to also be a philosopher. Over time I came to see that Strauss was no ordinary scholar; he had his own philosophical purposes for writing and for writing in the ways that he did.

When one first looks at the contents of this collection, the first impression one gets, and not entirely incorrectly, is that these are the writings of a highly educated and modern academic. As one peruses the content one will be struck at the range and breadth of these pieces. Certainly the writings seem to span "the western tradition," but Strauss's subjects are a version of the "tradition" that is unique to Strauss. Strauss's nominees are not just the usual candidates. This already points to the idea that Strauss's scholarship is not traditional, or that Strauss's thought is not traditional. But if one steps back from the titles and looks at the contents of the pieces, one will quickly see that they are quite different from the work of any other scholar one can think of. Not to note the peculiarities of Strauss's writings is to already narrow the scope of our interpretation. Now when I read Strauss, I no longer start with feeling that I am in a familiar landscape, but I note all of the peculiar things around me. I see my first task as observing

AFTERWORD

and only later as interpreting the intentions behind the peculiarities that I note. Strauss correctly noted that the "denial of the existence of a riddle is a kind of solution of the riddle" ("An Epilogue," 211). I therefore began to note that Strauss's studies are laden with statements, discussions, and judgments that appear to go far beyond what an objective scholar would normally allow himself. Strauss's own opinions are peppered throughout. In *The City and Man*, Strauss makes a suggestion for reading Thucydides that may have some application to reading Strauss. He writes that, "After one has recovered from one's first impression, one is amazed to see how many important judgments Thucydides makes explicitly, in his own name." (145). Perhaps the most well-known preliminary judgment in Strauss's corpus is the opening sentence of *Thoughts on Machiavelli*.

Although, at least initially, he seems to present himself as a type of scholar, our working assumption should not be so rigidly maintained that it does not allow Strauss to reveal to us his own understanding of himself. In referring to Herodotus, Strauss cautions the reader in a way that could apply to our reading of Strauss:

> In attempting to answer the question regarding Herodotus' intention, one must not even assume that Herodotus was a "historian." For in making this assumption one is likely to imply that he was not a "philosopher" and thus to exclude without examination the possibility that Herodotus' intention cannot be understood without a complete revision of our "categories." ("On Collingwood's Philosophy of History," 209 above)

One of the lessons I learned from reading Strauss is the importance he places upon the question of who the intended audience or audiences of a piece of writing are. Finding this out is key to understanding what an author's intentions are, and therefore, to how he understands himself. I also learned that a careful writer often provides answers to this question within his writing. Strauss alerted me to the idea that there is not only the historical or social context within which a piece was written, but that there can also be an author's own understanding of his own context. Part of an author's context is his own account of what prompted him to write a particular piece and who his intended readers are. The goal of attempting to understand an author as he understood himself entails understanding how an author understands his context and his readers.* An author's ad-

---

* Leo Strauss, "Political Philosophy and History," in *What is Political Philosophy?* (Glencoe, IL: Free Press, 1959), 66–68.

dressees may be his contemporaries, but his audience may be people not yet born. His audience may be his contemporary friends and allies, but it could also be future allies and philosophers. Nietzsche suggested that "some are born posthumously."

With this thought in mind, I started to ask of every one of Strauss's writings; who are the intended addressees? To answer this question, I began by asking what prompted him to write a particular piece; was he asked by others to write this, or was it a freely chosen project? Then I asked whether he is writing an introduction for a wider, less specialized audience; or is he writing a fuller interpretation of one book by a particular thinker for those interested in that book or thinker. I found that very often these questions are answered in his various pieces. For each piece here, there are intended addressees. These answers helped me to understand some of the grounds for the differences between Strauss's differing presentations of himself and even differing interpretations of the same thinker. Strauss's various presentations of Hobbes may be in part due to the different audiences and purposes of Strauss's writings and in part due to developments within Strauss's own thinking about Hobbes. Sorting this all out is a formidable task, but not necessarily impossible with Strauss's guidance.

In attempting to understand how Strauss understands himself, I also started to look at how Strauss presents his intentions in different ways on different occasions. The pieces in this collection are a testament to the many intentions and the many ways in which Strauss presents his thought. One of the pieces in this collection is even entitled, "On the Intention of Rousseau." In a reply to two of his critics, Strauss laments that "they never for a single moment meet the sole issue to which the Epilogue is devoted" ("Replies to Schaar and Wolin: II," 273 above). Not only does Strauss here have a clear conscious intention he is pursuing, he even tells us that we can find it. However, Strauss is aware that an author's intentions are not always apparent. In *Thoughts on Machiavelli*, Strauss shows his awareness of the difficulties involved in discovering some author's intention by listing a variety of intentions an author can have, ranging from, "the primary, explicit, ostensible, or partial intention," all the way to "the full or true intention" (45).

Because Strauss seems to present himself as a scholar, it is easy to assume that Strauss's intention is always to objectively interpret a writer. This is an assumption that we bring to Strauss. We need to examine in each particular writing whether or not this is Strauss's full intention in that piece. This raises the possibility that Strauss may choose not to con-

AFTERWORD

vey his full understanding of a writer, if refraining from doing so serves his other particular purposes there. In any specific statement that Strauss makes about another writer, he may or may not have an incentive to understate or overstate what he writes. One can exaggerate a criticism of another thinker in order to highlight a feature of the other thinker's thought that one might want to draw attention to. For example, Nietzsche's discussion of "the problem of Socrates" may have a tenuous relation to the Socrates of the Platonic dialogues. Nietzsche may be far more concerned with using his version of Socrates to draw our attention to a problem inherent in the effects of Platonism, as opposed to giving us a presentation of Socrates that does full justice to Plato's presentation.

In "Farabi's Plato," Strauss is quite explicit that the philosopher Farabi made use of Plato for his own purposes. Of Farabi Strauss writes, "His attitude to the historical Plato is comparable to the attitude of Plato himself to the historical Socrates..." ("Fārābī's Plato," 92 above). The very titles Strauss gave to some of his works indicates Strauss's understanding that philosophers can make use of the writings of other philosophers for their own philosophical purposes. Strauss not only titled this article, "Farabi's Plato"—which Strauss uses in italics in the title but not in the essay—he called one of his books *Xenophon's Socrates*, and his book on Machiavelli, *Thoughts on Machiavelli*. Since these are Strauss's thoughts, Strauss's name is silently in the title. Even his *Studies in Platonic Political Philosophy*, which contain only a few pieces on Plato, are Strauss's Platonic studies.

This is not to imply that Strauss did not try to be accurate in many of his interpretations, such as in his books. However, in his introductions or prefaces, he might have thought that this was not the place to provide his fullest interpretation. Although trying to understand writers as they understood themselves may be Strauss's "explicit" intention some of the time, it may not be Strauss's "full or true intention" at all times. Neither am I endorsing the notion that one can discover Strauss's thought without working through his demanding and difficult studies of these writers. The road to understanding Strauss passes through detailed study of his most demanding interpretations and attentively following the signposts he inserted to guide his readers; and then comparing what Strauss writes to what his authors say in their own words. There is no short cut. My most rewarding engagements with Strauss have come from following his sequence of books from *Natural Right and History*, *Thoughts on Machiavelli*, *The City and Man*, *Socrates and Aristophanes*, through to his lengthy study of Lucretius.

AFTERWORD

Once I was aware of the possibly different purposes that Strauss has for writing about a philosopher and that the philosopher himself had for writing, significant implications opened up for understanding Strauss's own writings and Strauss's understanding of what a philosopher is. The above discussion of "Farabi's Plato" already goes some way towards revealing some aspect of Strauss's understanding of how one philosopher can write about another and Strauss's own understanding of what a philosopher is. In his introduction to *Persecution and the Art of Writing*, which makes "free use of" his article "Farabi's Plato," Strauss adds a section not found in the original article where he raises the idea of a "sociology of philosophy" that considers "the possibility that all philosophers form a class by themselves."[*] In order for philosophers to form a class there must be some characteristics that all philosophers must share regardless of their particular historical circumstances.

In leaving room for the possibility that Strauss might be a philosopher and even in the same rank as some of the philosophers he studied, this led me to also take seriously some of the implications of this thought. Among the difficulties attendant to this task is Strauss's own reticence to speak of himself as a philosopher. Writing about Plato, Strauss says, "If it is necessary to understand Plato's thought, it is necessary to understand it as Plato himself understood it, and therefore it is necessary to stop where he stopped and to look around: perhaps we shall gradually understand his reasons for stopping" (209 above). It is possible that Strauss may require of us to stop and think and inquire about where and why he stopped, and ask why he seems so reticent to speak of himself as a philosopher? Why does he make such an effort to cloak himself behind the words of others?

For Strauss to be a philosopher would seem to require that he come to some conclusions about the degree to which he agrees or disagrees with any of the philosophers he has studied. As an interpreter of other writers, Strauss's task is to understand what they thought. As a philosopher, Strauss would have to ask whether their thought is true. In his essay on Collingwood, Strauss asks these questions directly and with full awareness of how these two questions may be intertwined and connected: "The meaning of the question 'What did Plato think?' is different from the meaning of the question 'Whether that thought is true.' The former question must ultimately be answered by a reference to texts. The latter question cannot possibly be settled by reference to texts" (207 above).

---

[*] Leo Strauss, *Persecution and the Art of Writing* (Glencoe, IL: Free Press, 1952), 7–8.

AFTERWORD

Strauss goes on to say, "The historian who has no illusions about the difference of rank between himself and Plato will be very skeptical in regard to the possibility of his ever reaching adequate understanding of Plato's thought. But what is impossible for most men is not therefore intrinsically impossible" (208 above). Not only is it not impossible, it is absolutely necessary for Strauss to have done "what is impossible for most men," to answer for himself "whether that thought is true," in order for Strauss to be a philosopher, according to what Strauss here suggests.

Even if Strauss came to the conclusion that he is in complete agreement with Plato, Strauss could be a philosopher in his own right, as long as he has independently arrived at and can independently defend his agreement with Plato, i.e., without relying on Plato's authority to defend his agreement. Although Strauss's thought may have emerged from or developed out of his encounter with Plato's thought—perhaps via Farabi—once Strauss has articulated his own thought, it can be understood independently of Plato's thought. In fact, not remaining under Plato's authority would seem to be an integral part of having understood Plato's own intentions and criteria for what a philosopher is.

If to be a philosopher requires that one not bow to any authority and to rely only upon what one understands on one's own, this has implications for the relationship between Strauss's role as an interpreter of other philosophers and Strauss's own status as a philosopher. If Strauss's thought can be understood and evaluated on its own merits, independently from the thought of any other philosopher, then Strauss's standing as a philosopher is not dependent upon Strauss having correctly interpreted any other philosopher. To take Nietzsche as an example, his ranking as a philosopher is not dependent upon what he says about Socrates. What Nietzsche writes about Plato's Socrates may not accord with what Plato intended. The value of Nietzsche's thought is found in the arguments that Nietzsche makes. Nietzsche stands or falls not because of what he says about Socrates, but what he says for himself. It may turn out that Plato saw certain important issues that Nietzsche did not see, but ultimately this failure on Nietzsche's part is dependent upon the inadequacy of Nietzsche's thought and not upon his failure to interpret Plato. Ultimately a philosopher is responsible for himself and is in fact radically independent of other philosophers. He may learn a great deal from other philosophers, but in order to be a philosopher he stands alone.

This idea seems to be particularly difficult to apply to Strauss. Perhaps more than any other candidate Strauss wore the mantle of a scholar and

AFTERWORD

therefore to suggest that even if he made significant interpretive errors he could still be a philosopher does not seem quite right. Strauss seemed to devote his life to reading, teaching, and writing about other philosophers. His scholarship appears to be of his essence. Therefore, it seems to follow that if Strauss is wrong about what he says about the philosophers he devoted his life to interpreting, then this may raise questions about his status as a philosopher. However, what applies to the entire class of philosophers must also apply to Strauss if he is to be a member of that class. Like Nietzsche, Strauss could mispresent certain aspects of Plato—either intentionally, or inadvertently—and still be a philosopher.

If Strauss's full intention at times goes beyond accurately interpreting other philosophers, and he may not always reveal his full understanding in some of his interpretations, and his status as a philosopher is not dependent upon his correct interpretations of other philosophers, these possibilities make Strauss a more complex and demanding writer than I at first understood. Because I began with seeking Strauss's guidance on questions I had, I was naturally inclined to think of Strauss as an ally. I had assumed that because I thought of myself in the same camp with Strauss, he was in the same camp as me. Over time I learned that thinking of oneself as a friend to Strauss was an impediment to understanding how Strauss understood himself. I had to learn for myself that Crito, by declaring himself a friend to Socrates, may have, in his friendship, closed himself off to understanding how much Socrates differed from him. For me seeing these differences has made all the difference. It opened up the possibility of being open to Strauss.

David Yanowski

Acknowledgments

We would like to thank Susan Tarcov for her dedicated copy editing, Susan Johnson for her outstanding book design, Jenny Strauss Clay and Nathan Tarcov for their support, and John Gibbons, Katie Godfrey, and Stuart D. Warner for their advice and encouragement. Svetozar Minkov would also like to acknowledge the assistance of Heinrich Meier, Bernhardt Trout, Liam Minkov, and Kerry Thomas. The support of the Leo Strauss Foundation was essential in covering the costs of the preparation of the text, typesetting, and obtaining copyright permissions. In addition, Dr. Lenzner wishes to thank Peter Thiel for his many years of generous support. Finally, we are grateful to the journals and publishers who have granted their permission to reprint Strauss's writings in English.

Index

Abravanel, 1, 6–31
Aquinas, 2–3, 25n, 28, 87n, 88n, 96n, 104n, 107, 119, 120, 133, 178, 181, 212, 216, 443
"Aristophanean," 49
Aristotle, 1–3, 10n, 11n, 14n, 15–17, 39, 41n, 43n, 44n, 45n, 49n, 51n, 52n, 58, 61n, 63n, 75, 77, 78, 81n, 82n, 87, 93n, 98n, 100n, 101n, 104, 107, 109, 117n, 119–20, 122, 124n, 125–28, 134–35, 137n, 141, 154, 169n, 170n, 172, 180–81, 195, 197, 200, 203, 212, 214–16, 226, 234, 247, 280, 283, 303, 311, 314n, 331, 342n, 343, 346n, 357, 362, 423, 424–25, 438, 442, 445, 448, 458, 459, 462–75
Augustine, 26, 73, 94, 190
authority, 4–5, 7, 27, 30, 64, 75, 115, 175, 177–79, 203, 209, 216, 253–54, 279, 357–58, 360–61, 363, 384, 392, 428–34, 450

Averroes, 2n, 39, 75, 77, 88–89n, 96n, 104n, 107; Averroists, Averroism, 90, 105n, 107

Bacon, 119n, 137, 151, 199, 211, 247, 451, 465
Barker, Ernest, 2n, 4n
Berlin, Isaiah, 249–54, 262
Bryce, Lord, 232
Burke, Edmund, 119n, 149n, 386

Calvin, 169n; Calvinism, 246–47
Cicero, 87n, 88n, 95n, 324, 425, 430
classical mode of thinking, 438
classical political philosophy, 135, 171–73, 225–27, 241–43, 280–84, 425–26, 448, 451, 460–62; classical philosophy, 109–14, 116, 119–20, 137, 389, 444; classical philosophers, 179, 444; classical political science, 148
Cohen, Hermann, 175–76, 180–81, 184–85, 440, 442

The index includes references to Strauss's texts only. Its composition follows Strauss's own indexing principles and typography. —Eds.

Index

Collingwood, R.G., 187–210

Descartes, 92n, 98n, 119n, 137, 151, 171, 276, 465, 469
Dewey, John, 261n
Dostoyevsky, 330

Einstein, Albert, 203
exoteric, 38, 70, 77–78, 88, 91, 98–99, 128, 442–43

Fārābī, 2n, 4, 17n, 75–106, 107, 357
Federalist, The, 135, 170n, 385

Giles of Rome, 107–8
Goethe, 164n

Hegel, 109, 112, 118, 136–37, 190–91, 202, 259, 263–64, 419, 438, 442
Heidegger, 117n, 134, 263, 267, 419, 438, 441–42
Heraclitus, 122n
Herodotus, 55n, 65, 70, 189, 198, 205–6, 394, 409–10
Hesiod, 317–18, 399
historicism, 112–13, 210, 225, 263, 462
Hobbes, 94n, 111n, 119n, 134–35, 137–38n, 147, 167, 199, 201, 227, 247, 365–69, 373, 441, 443, 454, 465
Homer, 280, 297, 321, 401
Hume, 261, 459
Husik, Isaac, 175–85
Husserl, Edmund, 117n, 118, 419–20, 440–41
Hyamson, Moses, 33–40, 58n
Ibn Tufail, 88n

Isaiah, 12
Isocrates, 55n, 62n

Kant, 118, 119n, 137n, 152, 201, 251, 254, 261, 267, 273, 444
Kierkegaard, 263
Klein, Jacob, 437–46
Kraus, Paul, 2n, 77n, 99n

Justinus, 424

Leibniz, 75, 170n
Lessing, 75, 105n, 442
Livy, 205, 21, 216, 219, 422, 424, 426–35
Locke, 135, 141, 167, 227, 368, 371–74, 384–85, 392, 451, 459
Lucretius, 74, 397–408
Luther, 119, 138n

Machiavelli, 111n, 135, 147, 169n, 173, 211–19, 226–27, 247, 261, 421–35
Maimonides, 1–15, 17n, 22, 27, 29, 33–40, 75–77, 80n, 81n, 82n, 86, 89n, 90n, 91n, 92, 96n, 97, 98n, 100, 106, 107–8, 119, 176, 178, 179, 181, 182, 347–48, 349–63, 443
Marsilio Ficino, 2n, 421
Marsilius of Padua, 17n, 217, 273
Marx, Karl, 134, 259–60, 271–72, 288, 320, 394, 419
Mendelssohn, Moses, 22
Mill, John Stuart, 251, 386–88
Milton, 26n
Mohammed, 4, 169n
Montaigne, 146, 155n
Montesquieu, 20n, 101n, 148–50, 164n

INDEX

Moses, 4, 10–11, 27–28, 30–31, 169n, 350

natural right, 135, 137, 236, 282–83, 344, 367–68, 384, 423, 451
Newton, 109, 151, 203, 448
Nietzsche, 227–28, 246, 263–65, 322, 395, 419, 440, 445

Onkelos, 26, 360

Parmenides, 122
Pascal, 231–32
persecution, 69–70, 97, 159, 178, 319, 420
Plato, 2–5, 11n, 43n, 44n, 51n, 55n, 56n, 57n, 61n, 63n, 64n, 65, 66n, 67n, 68n, 69n, 70, 75–106, 109–43, 146, 166n, 169n, 171, 172, 181, 196, 200–1, 203, 207–9, 225–26, 239–40, 254, 280, 282–83, 285–346, 383, 421, 423, 424–25, 440, 442–43, 445, 459, 463, 469
Plutarch, 151n, 417, 432
Polybius, 429
problem: "fundamental political problem of our time," 249; human, 334, 456; Jewish, as a social problem, 176; of miracles, 168n; "our [modern]," 116, 125; political, 140, 166, 167, 172, 249; of relativism, 263; of society, 167
Pufendorf, Samuel von, 384n

Riedl, John O., 107–8
Rousseau, 70, 109, 135, 145–73, 227, 377, 444, 459

Sallustius, 435
Schaar, John, 269–74
Schopenhauer, 440
Seneca, 13–15, 146
Shotwell, James T., 73–74
Socrates, 46, 51, 55–57, 59n, 64, 66–67, 71, 78n, 79, 81–82, 89n, 92, 97–99, 121n, 122n, 124, 131, 139n, 146, 226, 255, 279–80, 282–83, 285–346, 382, 410–12, 415, 423, 426, 448
Spinoza, 5, 31, 135, 147n, 179, 222, 442–43
Swift, 448

Tacitus, 193, 202–3, 205, 421, 424, 435
Thucydides, 55n, 62n, 65, 70, 189, 193, 197–98, 205, 319n, 403–4, 408, 409–11, 413–16, 422, 425
Tocqueville, 232
tyranny, 63n, 114, 142, 162n, 197, 301, 317, 320, 331, 333, 341, 342, 371, 429, 431, 470

Virgil, 424, 435

Walker, Leslie J., 211–19
Weber, Max, 245–47, 254, 258, 271, 378n, 441
Wild, John, 109–43
Wolin, Sheldon, 269–74

Xenophon, 41–71, 81n, 146n, 170n, 216, 282n, 382n, 409–17, 424–26, 435

About the Editors

Steven J. Lenzner is a visiting lecturer at Ilia State University in Tbilisi.

Svetozar Y. Minkov is Professor of Philosophy and Director of the Philosophy Program at Roosevelt University in Chicago. He is president of the Leo Strauss Foundation.